W9-ABZ-373

A Life of
H. L. A. Hart

A Life of

H. L. A. Hart

THE NIGHTMARE AND
THE NOBLE DREAM

NICOLA LACEY

OXFORD
UNIVERSITY PRESS

OXFORD

UNIVERSITY PRESS

Great Clarendon Street, Oxford OX2 6DP

Oxford University Press is a department of the University of Oxford.
It furthers the University's objective of excellence in research, scholarship,
and education by publishing worldwide in

Oxford New York

Auckland Bangkok Buenos Aires Cape Town Chennai
Dar es Salaam Delhi Hong Kong Istanbul Karachi Kolkata
Kuala Lumpur Madrid Melbourne Mexico City Mumbai Nairobi
São Paulo Shanghai Taipei Tokyo Toronto

Oxford is a registered trade mark of Oxford University Press
in the UK and in certain other countries

Published in the United States
by Oxford University Press Inc., New York

First published 2004

British Library Cataloguing in Publication Data
Data available

Library of Congress Cataloging-in-Publication Data
Lacey, Nicola.
A life of H. L. A. Hart : the nightmare and the noble dream / by Nicola
Lacey.
    p. cm.
Includes bibliographical reference and index.
ISBN 0–19–927497–5 (alk. paper)
  1. Hart, H. L. A. (Herbert Lionel Adolphus), 1907– 2.   Law—
Philosophy—History—20th century. 3.   Lawyers—England—Biography. I.
Title.
K230.H3652.L33 2004
340'. 1—dc22   2004011031

5 7 9 10 8 6 4

Typeset by Newgen Imaging Systems (P) Ltd., Chennai, India
Printed in Great Britain
on acid-free paper by
Biddles Ltd., King's Lynn

For Jenifer Hart

And there goes Professor Hart striding enlightened by the years through the doorway and arcade he built (in his mind) and knows—he too saw the ruins of Yucatán once—

Allen Ginsberg, 'Sather Gate Illumination', 1955

Some discouragement, some faintness of heart at the new real future which replaces the imaginary, is not unusual, and we do not expect people to be deeply moved by what is not unusual. That element of tragedy which lies in the very fact of frequency has not yet wrought itself into the coarse emotion of mankind; and perhaps our frames could hardly bear much of it. If we had a keen vision and feeling of all ordinary human life it would be like hearing the grass grow and the squirrel's heart beat, and we should die of that roar which lies on the other side of silence. As it is, the quickest of us walk about well wadded with stupidity.

George Eliot, *Middlemarch*, 1878

The rationalism of Jews is a passion—the passion for the universal. If they have chosen this rather than something else, it is in order to fight the particularist conceptions that set them apart. Of all things in the world, reason is the most widely shared; it belongs to everybody and to nobody; it is the same to all. If reason exists, then there is no French truth or German truth, there is no Negro truth or Jewish truth. There is only one Truth, and he is best who wins it. In the face of universal and eternal laws, man himself is universal. There are no more Jews or Poles; there are men who live in Poland, others who are designated as 'of Jewish faith' on their family papers, and an agreement is always possible among them as soon as discussion bears on the universal.

Jean-Paul Sartre, *Réflexions sur la Question Juive*, 1946

Contents

CONTENTS

Part IV. AFTER THE CHAIR

Acknowledgements

I have accumulated mountainous debts of gratitude while working on this book. First and foremost, my deepest thanks go to Jenifer Hart, without whose honesty, courage, and trust this book could not have been written. This is not an authorized biography, in the sense that Jenifer Hart did not read it before publication: she did, however, give me indispensable assistance. Quite apart from her willingness to talk openly and at length to me over the last four years, and to give me access to Herbert Hart's papers and to some of her own diaries, the work which she did in gathering, organizing, and doing her own research on Herbert Hart's papers was of inestimable help to me. I should also like to express my deep thanks to Joanna Ryan, Adam Hart, and Charlie Hart, all of whom have been unfailingly helpful, open, and encouraging, and each of whom read and gave detailed and important comments on a draft. I am more grateful than I can say for the generosity of these four people.

Beyond Herbert Hart's immediate family, many of his friends, colleagues, and students gave me invaluable information in interviews: Professor Brian Barry; President Aharon Barak of the Israeli Supreme Court; Professor Vernon Bogdanor; Professor Peter Campbell; Lt.-Col. Richard Camrass VC; George Cawkwell; Professor Hugh Collins; Mrs. Barbara Dupee; Professor Ronald Dworkin; Professor Yehuda Elkana; Justice Izaak Englard; Professor Marianne Fillenz; Professor John Finnis; Professor George Fletcher; Mrs. Jean Floud; Professor Ruth Gavison; Professor Martin Golding; Professor James Griffin; Professor Peter Hacker; Sir Stuart Hampshire; Justice Dyson Heydon; Justice David Hodgson; John Hart; Lennie Hoffmann; Professor Tony Honoré; Professor Donald Horwitz; Mary Jay; Professor Harry Judge; Justice Michael Kirby; John Lucas; Professor Herbert Morris; Professor Richard Mulgan; Henry Myers; the late Professor Barry Nicholas; Professor Gerald Postema; Professor Joseph Raz; Professor Jonathan Rée; Professor Graham Richards; Professor Alan Ryan; Professor Sir Peter Strawson; Professor David Sugarman; Professor Bob Summers and Dorothy Summers; Professor Colin Tapper; Dr. John Tasioulas; Professor William Twining; Professor Jeremy Waldron; the late Bill (William Charles) Wentworth; the late Professor Sir Bernard Williams; the late Lord Wilberforce; Adrian Zuckerman. I should like to thank all of these people not only for their generosity with their time but also for their willingness to talk so frankly and, in many cases, to answer follow-up questions.

I would also like to acknowledge the kindness of a number of people who helped me in particularly important ways. Caroline Dalton gave me assistance not only with the Cox archive at New College but also in tracing a miscellany of questions about the history of Oxford University; Dr. Henry Hardy was enormously generous in providing and discussing relevant materials from the Isaiah Berlin archive, and in checking my citations with meticulous care; Professor Tony Honoré provided unstinting support and important material on jurisprudence teaching at Oxford in the 1950s; Professor Hermione Lee gave me invaluable advice about writing biography as well as much-appreciated encouragement; Professor Brian Simpson patiently answered dozens of email queries and provided me with a large amount of useful material, including many papers relating to Abraham Harari; Professor David Sugarman generously gave me access to an unpublished interview with Herbert Hart in 1988; Professor Robert Summers sent me extracts from his personal diaries containing vivid descriptions of conversations with Herbert Hart; Professor Stanley Paulson gave me important bibliographic assistance and invaluable advice about Hans Kelsen; Professor John Hall generously sent to me two letters from Ernest Gellner to Herbert Hart which he had come across in the course of his work on Gellner's biography, as well as making time for a helpful discussion; Professor Frances Olsen tracked down Herbert Hart's annotated copy of Weber's writings on law and economy in the Hebrew University Library; Miriam Schatz-Sharon of the Hebrew University Library gave me endless help in tracing the complete list of the Hart bequest through the complexities of the electronic catalogue; Dr. John Tasioulas saved me hours of labour by giving me access to his typed transcript of Herbert Hart's working notebook for *The Concept of Law*; Professor William Twining gave me his student notes taken at Herbert Hart's Oxford lectures and a mine of useful papers relating to the Bentham Committee; David Warrington and David Ferris were wonderfully helpful in setting up my visit to the Harvard Law School Archive; and the late Lord Wilberforce was exceptionally generous in sending me extracts from his diaries of the 1930s as well as annotating them with further explanatory information. I should like to record my warm thanks to all these people, as well as acknowledging formally, with gratitude, the following permissions to reproduce extracts: the Trustees of the Isaiah Berlin Literary Trust, for extracts from letters from Isaiah Berlin written up to 1946 taken from his *Flourishing: Letters 1928–1946*, ed. Henry Hardy (London: Chatto and Windus 2004) and from other as yet unpublished letters, © The Isaiah Berlin Literary Trust 2004; Susan Gellner, for extracts from the letters of Ernest Gellner held in the Library of the London School of Economics; Jenifer Hart, for material from Herbert Hart's papers and her own diary; the

Fellows of Harvard College for extracts from the letters of Lon Fuller in the Fuller archive held in the Special Collections Room, Harvard Law School; Robert Summers, for extracts from his diary; the late Richard Wilberforce for extracts from his diaries; and the Warden and Fellows of New College, Oxford for extracts from the papers of Christopher Cox (as well as a photograph); Ruth Gavison, Stephen Guest, Guenter Treitel, and Tony Honoré, for extracts from letters. I have made every effort to trace the authors of other letters from which I have quoted, and would like to apologize to anyone whom I was unable to trace. Jenifer Hart, Adam Hart, Charlie Hart, Joanna Ryan, Priscilla Austen and Ulrike Heuer kindly supplied and gave me permission to reproduce photographs, and Ian Fraser kindly allowed me to reproduce his image of New College.

I would also like to thank the following people who gave me useful information or advice in writing or in person: Professor Richard Abel; Dame Mary Arden; Mrs. Jean Austin; Sue Ashcroft-Jones; Dr. Mimi Berlin; Alice Blackford, Assistant Keeper of the Oxford University Archives; Professor Sir Tony Bottoms; Professor James Boyle; Professor E. H. Burns; Professor Peter Cane; Paul Collins; Rosamund Cummings of the University College London Archive; Professor Neil Duxbury; Professor Brendan Edgeworth; Dr. Pavlos Eleftheriadis; Professor David Estlund; Professor Marie Therès Foegen; Professor John Gardner; Natalie Gold; Professor Robert A. Gorman; Jeffrey Hackney; Professor Vinit Haksar; Professor Moshe Halbertal; Mrs. Peggy Harmer; Sjoerd van Hoorn; Michael Ignatieff; Professor Frank Jackson; Emily Jackson; Professor Ratna Kapur; Professor Sir Anthony Kenny; Professor Nan Keohane; Professor Robin Lane Fox; Santiago Legarre; Professor Laurence Lessig; Dr. Rosalyn Livshin; Jim MacAdam; Professor Geoffrey MacCormack; Professor Neil MacCormick; Adrian Marriage; Dr. Kevan Martin; Professor Yasutomo Morigiwa; Professor John Morison; Philip Morris; Professor Liam Murphy; Henry Myers; Sydney Norris; Reut Paz; Dr. Jill Peay; Dr. James Penner; Tim Rattenbury; Colin T. Reid; Professor Mario Ricciardi; Professor Simon Roberts; Professor Frederick Rosen; Professor Michael Rosen; Hamish Ross; Professor Eli Salzberger; Professor Fania Oz Salzberger; Professor Stephen Schiffer; Dr. Philip Schofield; David Sharpe; Paul Silk; Professor Jane Stapleton; Dr. Bill Stewart; Dr. Adrienne Stone; Dr. Jonathan Stone; Professor Guenter Treitel; Dr. Cornelia Vismann; David Vital; Louis Waller; Mark D. Walters; Professor Wil Waluchow; Dr. Penry Williams; Professor Sarah Worthington.

I have also had the benefit of marvellous research assistance from Zoe Guest (who helped to prepare the bibliography), Edward McCarthy (who did archival work at the Public Record Office on the Liddell diaries),

ACKNOWLEDGEMENTS

Michael Turner (who prepared the biographical information on figures referred to in the book), and Stephen Winter (who meticulously researched the Oxford University lecture lists), and of administrative assistance from Elissa Linke and the incomparable Teresa Edwards, who photocopied, re-photocopied, and dispatched serendipitous materials around the world with her inimitable style and efficiency. My warm thanks go to all these people.

I have been fortunate in having helpful feedback on drafts of the book at various stages: from audiences at the Law Program and Social and Political Theory Program at the Research School for Social Sciences at the Australian National University; at the University of Sydney Philosophy and Law Departments; at the University of Adelaide Law School; at Duke University Law School; at the University of Edinburgh; at London Metropolitan University; and at the London School of Economics Law and Philosophy departments. I am lucky to work in two very stimulating environments, and I want to record my appreciation of the interest and support which I have received from colleagues at both the London School of Economics and the Australian National University throughout my work on this project, as well as from colleagues at New York University Law School in the autumn of 2003. I also benefited a great deal from thoughtful comments on particular chapters read by Geoffrey Brennan, Nancy Cartwright, Tom Campbell, Neil Duxbury, John Finnis, Bob Goodin, Stuart Hampshire, Lewis Kornhauser, Shirley McAndrew, Victoria McGeer, Stanley Paulson, Philip Pettit, Renata Salecl, and Richard Wilberforce.

My greatest debt, however, has been to a small number of colleagues, family, and friends who read and commented on the whole of the manuscript. Hugh Collins surprised and delighted me by replacing his initial caution about the project with wholehearted enthusiasm; Ronald Dworkin gave generous feedback and advice; Elizabeth Frazer quite rightly pressed me to think more about the political implications of my interpretation of Hart's life; Stephen Guest made important comments on my handling of several issues in Hart's analytical jurisprudence; Tony Honoré gave constant encouragement and put me right on a number of important matters; Mark Lacey helped me to write my account more clearly and reminded me of some relevant events which I had forgotten; Julian Le Grand patiently read drafts at a number of stages, gave astute advice and constantly reassured me, not least by his own interest and enthusiasm, that the project was worthwhile; Gill McAndrew was my ideal 'lay' reader, and even managed to convince me that her endorsement was not entirely do with her being my mother; Ngaire Naffine improved, among other things, my prose, with her meticulous editorial eye; Joseph Raz put me right on a number of important points and gave invaluable advice; Jerry Postema and David Richards each gave me overwhelming encouragement and helped me to think through a number of issues. From their very different points of view, all these people made thoughtful and detailed comments which enormously improved the final version, somehow managing to combine intellectual and editorial criticism with exceptionally generous encouragement. I am deeply grateful to them all. My agents, Ros Edwards and Helenka Fuglewicz, have also been a fund of inspiration and support, gently but firmly pushing me to write in more accessible style than comes naturally to an academic, and giving me confidence that the effort was worthwhile.

Finally, my warmest thanks go to David Soskice for his enthusiasm for this project, for his confidence in my ability to carry it through, and for his perceptive comments on a draft. It is no exaggeration to say that this book would not have been conceived, let alone written, without his support, advice, encouragement, and companionship.

Nicola Lacey
London, December 2003

List of Illustrations

Biographer's Note on Approach and Sources

Biography is not a genre distinguished by any one methodology. But the reader of a biography is entitled to know not only the details of the biographer's sources but also something of the biographer's approach and relationship with her subject.

When I went to Oxford as a graduate student in 1979, Herbert Hart was 72. Though it was 11 years since he had retired from the Chair of Jurisprudence, he was still very much a real as well as a symbolic presence in the University. He held a fellowship at University College and regularly attended seminars, discussion groups, and university social occasions. Through a series of happy coincidences—notably my then husband's musical talents, which drew the special affection of the Harts' disabled son, Jacob—I came to know the Hart family reasonably well. We kept in touch when I moved to London to take up my first job at UCL in 1981, and resumed more regular contact when I became Law Fellow at New College in 1984. By this time I was living with an economist who was a University College colleague of Herbert's and a friend of the family's, and we formed a small part of the Harts' social circle.

The fact that I met Herbert Hart and had some relationship with him was of tremendous help in writing this book. I regard with amazement and admiration the ability of biographers who have never met their subjects to conjure them up as successfully as many do. One of my persistent frustrations in writing this book has been the dimness of my memory of conversations which would have shed further light on Herbert Hart's personality. The images which have stayed with me—of certain conversations, but above all of his presence, humour, and personal style—have been invaluable. One or two of these appear in the text, but since I personally find it irritating when biographers intrude into the narrative as visible actor rather than underlying interpreter, I have acknowledged this only in the notes. It came naturally to me, however, to write and think of Herbert Hart as 'Herbert'; and since I have tried to bring alive on the page the complicated, very human man whom so many readers of his academic work think of as the impersonal icon, H. L. A. Hart, I have decided (albeit with reservations) to retain the use of 'Herbert' in the text.

As many of my interviewees observed, Herbert Hart was a hard person to know: an intensely private man whose primary emotional contacts were often explored through discussions of the literature, music, or landscapes which he loved. I certainly could not claim to have known him in any deep sense. I was a young academic in a field which he dominated from Olympian heights, and although I plucked up the courage to have one or two informal discussions of jurisprudence with him, I was too much in awe of him to be able to relate to him directly in intellectual terms. And yet he had a mysterious capacity—again, this was noted by many people I interviewed—to communicate, indirectly, a sense of interest or concern. I felt the force of this strongly and, for this among other reasons, was very fond of him.

With Jenifer Hart, my relationship has always been warm. During one of our many discussions of Herbert, I told her that I felt I ought to be writing her life rather than his, since I found her much easier to understand. 'Well,' she replied, 'that's because I've always thought that life was too short to be discreet'. This is characteristic of her inimitable style. One of my greatest challenges was to write a biography of Herbert Hart while doing justice to Jenifer's vivid personality and substantial achievements.

It was Richard Holmes' thoughtful collection, *Footsteps*, which first alerted me to the fact that writing a biography implies living—in an attenuated but real sense—with one's subject. The lesson was reinforced when, a few days after finishing Holmes' essays, I found myself reading a passage in one of Herbert Hart's notebooks which described his impressions of the same collection. This 'living with someone' aspect of biography means that, for most biographers, it is hard to work on an unsympathetic subject. But, as in any cohabitation, a relationship can develop in unexpected ways. Since few of Herbert Hart's personal papers were in the public domain when I started work, I had little idea what I would feel about my subject by the end of the process. I was fortunate in having access to rich resources—fascinating letters and diaries, articulate and sensitive interviewees—and as a result I certainly 'know' Herbert Hart better now than I did when he died in 1992. But my greatest piece of luck has been that—leaving aside the inevitable moments of irritation or distaste which mark most human relationships—at the end of this voyage of discovery, I like him as much as when I started.

Like many legal academics of my generation, Herbert Hart's writing has been one of the primary catalysts for my own work. Since the early 1960s, it has been virtually impossible for anyone doing research in jurisprudence, political theory, or criminal justice studies to ignore Herbert Hart's contribution, and for many scholars—critics as well as admirers—he provides a key departure point. My early work was on the justification of punishment, and a large part of it was a sympathetic analysis and revision of a position originally defended by Herbert Hart. Since then, as my work has moved into fields such as feminist theory, I have come to take a more critical view of his ideas, and in particular of his vision of the distinctively philosophical boundaries of legal theory. These criticisms have shaped my interpretation of his work in this book. But they have not diminished my admiration for the clarity and vision with which he framed his ideas, nor my assessment of the decisive importance of his work to the development of legal and political theory.

When Jenifer Hart offered me the opportunity to write this biography, I had very little non-academic writing experience and no qualifications other than my knowledge of Herbert Hart and his work and a taste for biography. My approach to researching, planning, and writing was shaped by several factors. I re-read the intellectual biographies I most admired (notably Ray Monk's *Wittgenstein: The Duty of Genius* and Hermione Lee's *Virginia Woolf*) and tried to think about what made them so compelling. I also read some books which might be described as cautionary tales about biography, notably Janet Malcolm's *The Silent Woman* and—thanks to Joanna Ryan— Adam Phillips' *Darwin's Worms*. Malcolm's story sharpened my sense of both the personal dilemmas of biography and the contingency of even one's most confident interpretations. Phillips' book made me think about the impulse to make a life story neater than life itself, and to pander to the reader's desire for narrative closure and even a 'happy ending'. As a result of reading these books, I have tried to write about Herbert Hart in a way which opens up the different levels of meaning which might be given— indeed which, at different moments, he gave—to his life, without in the process being irritatingly tentative. I have also tried to end on a note which does justice to his achievements without obscuring his complexities. In these terms, the writing was a journey of 'interpretation' rather than 'discovery': though in saying this, I do not mean to imply that biography raises no questions of truth and falsehood, fact and fiction.

Several practical and ethical dilemmas arose in the course of my work. Readers will differ in their view of how satisfactorily I have resolved them. I started by familiarizing myself with the side of Herbert Hart about which I knew least, by reading his collection of diaries, notebooks, and correspondence. I then re-read his work chronologically. By this stage some clear ideas and themes were emerging, and I used these to construct an outline for the book and a set of interview questions. I then interviewed or corresponded with many of his family, friends, colleagues, and students before beginning to write the book. One dilemma had to do with the very personal nature of some of his letters and diaries. My rule of thumb was to use only the personal material which sheds light on the development of his ideas and the course of his career. But this, it turned out, was usually the case, because Herbert Hart himself moved seamlessly back and forth in his diaries between personal and professional preoccupations, and sought increasingly to draw links between the two. Though some readers may feel that I have been too generous in my use of the personal material—particularly that relating to his feelings about his sexuality and his marriage—my judgment was that it was essential to any interpretation of him as a whole person.

My most valuable source in constructing this account of Herbert Hart's life and work was the collection of papers gathered together by Jenifer Hart after his death. The collection includes a range of materials. First, there are letters: a substantial correspondence between Jenifer and Herbert Hart from the mid-1930s to the 1970s and with a range of friends, family, colleagues, and teachers throughout Herbert Hart's life. Second, there are 19 diaries and work notebooks, written at irregular intervals between 1926 and 1990. Some are travel diaries; some are intimate and highly introspective; some consist of notes about philosophy and for work in progress; one is a collection of jokes. Many blend these different styles. Dating the diaries and notebooks has often been difficult and sometimes impossible since Herbert Hart often used the same book at different times and did not always date the entries. Third, there is a small collection of Herbert Hart's academic books. On his death, the bulk of his library was left to the Hebrew University in Jerusalem, but copies of his own books and the main books dealing with his work remained with his papers. These books are heavily annotated and give an insight into his working methods. Finally, the collection includes a miscellany of family papers such as wills; a family tree; school reports; his own student essays; photographs; a box of after-dinner speeches; occasional speeches given at funerals, degree ceremonies, and so on.

This collection is as rich as it is varied, and I have drawn on it extensively. But it did confront me with some problems. Jenifer Hart, a historian by training, had done a great deal to assemble it and to date the correspondence and diaries. But the collection is not systematically organized, and I had neither the resources nor the training to put it into the sort of order which a professional archivist would have achieved before beginning work on it. I also had to contend (not always successfully) with Herbert Hart's famously Delphic handwriting, and with his habits of picking up old notebooks and annotating or adding to them, and of writing from both back and front of notebooks at different times. At several points I felt that I had been well and truly drawn into his gloriously chaotic working habits, without feeling much confidence that my efforts would bring forth the sort of crystal prose and clear structure which miraculously emerged from his own hailstorm of notes and annotations.

Interviews which I conducted with Herbert Hart's family, friends, colleagues, and students have been another invaluable resource. I have drawn liberally on the information which my interviewees so generously gave me: a complete list of interviews is given in the bibliography, and specific references are cited in the notes. I received dozens of letters and emails from Herbert Hart's friends, colleagues, and students who responded to my inquiries, answered my advertisements, or heard from other sources that I was working on this biography. These, too, have been an important source of information.

I have also been fortunate in being able to draw on the transcripts of three substantial interviews and one shorter interview given by Herbert Hart during the last decade of his life. The shorter interview was for an Israeli periodical and concerns his views on Israel; of the three longer interviews, one was for the history of Oxford University and mainly concerns his work as chair of the Committee on Student Discipline culminating in the Hart Report; one (as yet unpublished) was for an academic working on the development of legal education; one was for a Spanish legal theory journal. The last two cast some light on the development of his ideas. These interviews are listed in the bibliography.

I have of course drawn on Herbert Hart's own publications: seven monographs or collections of essays (one of them jointly authored with Tony Honoré), dozens of articles and book reviews in scholarly journals (many reprinted in the essay collections), occasional papers written for magazines such as *The Listener*, *The Economist*, *The New York Review of Books*, and several chapters of *The Hart Report* of the Committee on Student Discipline set up after the student unrest in Oxford in the late 1960s. Herbert Hart's publications appeared from the late 1940s right through to the end of his life, though the bulk of his scholarly work was published between 1957 and 1982. A virtually complete bibliography of his published writing to the mid-1980s is included in Ruth Gavison (ed.), *Issues in Contemporary Legal Philosophy: Essays in Honour of HLA Hart*, published in 1987; a further yet more complete bibliography was compiled by Stanley Paulson and published in *Ratio Juris* in 1995. My bibliography lists his most substantial publications—i.e. everything but book reviews and dictionary entries (except where specific reference is made to these in the text): I also include a few items omitted from or published after the Gavison and Paulson bibliographies.

I have also drawn on a variety of secondary literature. Of special importance were Jenifer Hart's autobiography, *Ask Me No More*, a mine of information not only about the Hart family but about the world in which she and Herbert Hart formed their relationship; Peter Hacker's *Wittgenstein's Place in Twentieth Century Analytic Philosophy* and Jonathan Rée's essay 'English Philosophy in the Fifties', which were invaluable in helping me to understand linguistic philosophy in Oxford in the 1940s and 1950s; and Miranda Carter's *Anthony Blunt: His Lives*, which helped to make the strange world of military intelligence more comprehensible. A number of other secondary sources are cited in the notes and bibliography.

There is a vast number and range of articles and books directly or indirectly concerned with Herbert Hart's contribution to legal and political philosophy, including five book-length assessments of his work. Since my purpose was to write an intellectual biography rather than an extended analysis of his scholarly legacy, I have drawn—with the useful exception of Neil MacCormick's *H. L. A. Hart*—only selectively on this literature. I have, however, discussed the mutual influence of Herbert Hart and a number of other scholars, and I have included reference to these and some other significant contributions to the jurisprudential debates launched by Herbert Hart in the bibliography. More important for my purposes were the many memoirs and obituaries of Herbert Hart, notably a memoir for the British Academy and an entry for the new Dictionary of National Biography by Tony Honoré, a memoir by Robert Summers, and the tributes published following his memorial meeting by Isaiah Berlin, Douglas Jay, Ronald Dworkin, Jean Floud, Joseph Raz, Alan Ryan, and Richard Wilberforce.

Finally, I have been lucky to be able to draw on a number of archives and private collections containing letters and other relevant materials: letters between Herbert Hart and Isaiah Berlin in the Bodleian Library, University of Oxford; information on the history of the Bentham Committee in the UCL archive: letters from Ernest Gellner to Herbert Hart in the library of the London School of Economics; letters from Herbert Hart to Christopher Cox in the archive of New College, Oxford; correspondence between Herbert Hart and Lon Fuller and other material relating to Hart's visit to Harvard in the Harvard Law School archive; extracts from the diaries of Jenifer Hart, Robert Summers, and Richard Wilberforce; the diaries of Guy Liddell, held at the Public Record Office and made public in 2003; and student notes taken at Hart's Oxford lectures by Jeffrey Hackney and William Twining.

Since my ambition was to write a book which could be read as a complete narrative, and following Herbert Hart's own example in *The Concept of Law*, I have chosen to avoid cluttering the text with endnote numbers. Readers will, however, find an account of my primary sources for each chapter, along with detailed citations and references identified by page numbers and phrases from the relevant text, in the notes at the end of the book. Readers who would like to consult the notes as they read the text may find it convenient to download the notes and bibliography from http://www.oup.co.uk/isbn/0-19-927497-5. I have also provided, following the bibliography, brief biographical details of philosophical and other figures who appear in the text and with whom not all readers may be familiar. Figures like J. L. Austin who are described fully in the text are not included in this list.

INTRODUCTION

An Outsider on the Inside

I N 1983, his seventy-sixth year, Herbert Hart was, to all external appearances, a contented, successful, emotionally and financially secure man. He was a world famous legal and political philosopher; his seventh book had just appeared; though stooped and frail as the cumulative result of arthritis and an unfortunate encounter on his beloved bicycle, he was in reasonably good health; and he enjoyed a rich social life, affectionate family relationships, and a continuing association with University College, Oxford. The impression which he gave to those who met him was entirely consistent with his objective situation: Hart's air was that of a mildly intellectually abstracted elder statesman, albeit one with an unusual gentleness and kindliness of speech and manner. With his shock of white hair and searching blue eyes whose glance held one even from behind thick lenses, he was a man with an unmistakably distinguished presence.

The gravitas and distinction of Hart's presence had a solid foundation in the remarkable achievements which he had made on his journey from his unremarkable origins as the third child of moderately well-to-do Jewish tailor parents in Yorkshire. By the time of his retirement from the Oxford Chair of Jurisprudence in 1968, he was widely regarded as having—almost single-handedly—effected a revolution in the prevailing understanding of law as a social institution. Hart was credited with having more or less reinvented the philosophy of law, reviving the English positivist and utilitarian tradition, and combining it with the insights of modern linguistic philosophy. In this field, his impact could be compared with that of, say, Wittgenstein in general philosophy. He was, quite simply, the pre-eminent English-speaking legal philosopher of the twentieth century.

He had also had a marked influence on social policy debates of the 1960s. Hart's writings on abortion, on the legalization of homosexuality and prostitution, and on capital punishment had a huge impact on informed opinion. In particular, his debate with the conservative judge Patrick Devlin about the propriety of using law to enforce conventional morality, parts of which were broadcast by the BBC, was probably *the* debate of the decade: it is still read by practically all students of law, politics, and sociology. As one contemporary campaigner put it, Hart's contribution to the debate was the nearest thing to a manifesto for the homosexual law reform movement. The issues which Hart addressed, and which his writing and broadcasting analysed for a wide audience, continue to resonate with the concerns of a wide variety of social movements. Similarly, his work on the justification of punishment continues to provide a powerful framework for assessing public policy.

These towering intellectual achievements were not, however, all that Hart had to look back on with a sense of satisfaction in 1983. By this time he had also served with distinction as Principal of Brasenose College, Oxford, overseeing its metamorphosis from an all-male environment and one of the less academically ambitious Oxford colleges towards a more intellectual and liberal institution, one of the first five colleges to admit women students. He had been a highly regarded member of the Monopolies Commission, and, looking further back, he had had a successful career at the Bar and, during the war, in military intelligence.

On a personal level, his life had also been favoured. In 1941, he married one of the most extraordinary women of her generation. From a wealthy and elite family (her father was one of the architects of the international legal order following the First World War), Jenifer Williams was a brilliant woman and an intriguing character. Strikingly attractive, with flaming golden-red hair and an uncompromisingly straightforward manner, she had been an active communist in the 1930s, and lived an experimental, Bloomsbury-inspired personal life. By the time of her marriage to Hart she was a civil servant in the Home Office, one of a handful of women to have passed the civil service exams during the previous decade. After the war she went on to become a successful academic in her own right, combining her work with managing a family of four children. This made for a complicated household, presided over by the redoubtable and utterly indispensable Nanny, but one in which a strong sense of family connection prevailed. This sustained, among other things, a remarkable sense of shared responsibility for Jenifer's and Herbert's fourth, brain-damaged, child. Even in the 1980s, with all the children in their thirties or forties, life in both their spacious (if somewhat shambolic) house in Oxford and in the idyllic Lamledra, Jenifer's family home in Cornwall, was very much an extended family affair, embracing a wide circle of friends and members of every generation.

In the midst of this apparently tranquil retirement, a problem which had rumbled through Jenifer Hart's life for many years suddenly exploded onto the public arena. In July 1983, the *Sunday Times* published an article relating to a television programme on communism to which Jenifer had contributed. The article claimed that as well as having been—as she had admitted openly for years—a member of the Communist Party for a short period in the 1930s, she had been recruited as a spy. It was suggested that, given her position in the Home Office during the 1940s, she might have passed useful information to the Russians. Furthermore, it was insinuated—both in the headline '"I was a Russian Spy" says MI5 Man's Wife', and in the text—that Herbert Hart's position in MI5 during the war might have enabled him to feed highly sensitive information to Jenifer. Given the continued interest in 'spy scandals' following the exposure of Anthony Blunt, with whom Hart had shared an office in MI5 at one point during the war, publicity and speculation about Jenifer's supposed admission seemed likely to escalate. The Harts' reaction was to issue a writ for defamation.

For any family, this would have been an unpleasant and a stressful experience. For Herbert Hart, it turned out to be devastating. After a period of intense anxiety and depression, he suffered a serious nervous breakdown. He had to be admitted to the Warneford Hospital in Oxford, where he remained until the radical step of electro-convulsive therapy finally lifted him out of the abyss. A heartbreakingly poignant letter written to his close friend Isaiah Berlin from the Warneford encapsulates all the anxieties and insecurities which, as his earlier diaries reveal, had formed the counterpoint to his successful public life: his doubts about his intellectual, practical, and emotional capacities; his sense of a yawning gap between his public status and his own sense of himself. Notwithstanding Hart's extraordinary success, his personal papers reveal that he was tormented by doubts about his own intellectual abilities, about his ability to manage his high-profile job, and about his capacity to form close relationships. Such anxieties are, perhaps, a relatively normal feature of life for most high achievers. But what is particularly intriguing about Hart's interior life is that, though he would widely be regarded as a quintessential 'insider', the fact is that he felt himself to be very much an outsider. This contrast between his public and private worlds raises fascinating questions not only about Hart's background and personality but also about the nature of his intellectual creativity and about the quality of the social world, with its various intersecting hierarchies, in which he lived. These contrasts between external success and internal perplexities, between being an insider but feeling like an outsider, constituted dynamic tensions which shaped almost all Hart's work and relationships, and they provide the themes around which this book will explore Hart's life and scholarship.

For readers not already familiar with Herbert Hart's work, it may be useful first to have a sketch of his main ideas and their importance. To understand why his work had such an extraordinary impact, one needs to know a little history. From the late eighteenth to the mid-nineteenth centuries, the utilitarian philosophers Jeremy Bentham and John Austin had developed an influential theory of law known as 'legal positivism'. Rejecting the idea that law derives its authority from God, or from some metaphysical conception of nature or reason—so-called 'natural law'—Bentham and Austin argued that law is an essentially human artefact: it is a command issued by a political superior or sovereign, to whom the populace is in a habit of obedience. In making this argument, they were taking a decisive and revolutionary step away from what had for centuries been the dominant way of thinking about law.

This promising start to the development of a conception of law appropriate to modern, secular democracies had not, however, been much developed since Austin's death. Reasons include Bentham's and Austin's rather uninviting literary styles; the fact that much of Bentham's work had never been published; and the relatively unintellectual nature of English legal education, which only found a secure place in university departments well into the twentieth century (and which remained steadfastly vocational for a yet longer period). In the decades preceding Hart's election to the Oxford Chair, such jurisprudence (legal philosophy) as was taught in Britain tended to consist in a rather dry offshoot of technical legal analysis: with painstaking (and often painful) attention to detail, writers picked apart legal concepts such as ownership, possession, or the corporation. There was no attempt either to link this analysis to any broader idea of the nature of law, or to consider how technical legal concepts assisted law to serve its various social functions. Prescriptive questions about what purposes law *ought* to pursue were left to the attention of moral and political philosophy—the latter itself a field which was relatively stagnant at this time.

Hart's work broke over the gloomy landscape of English jurisprudence like a new dawn of intellectual enlightenment. Instead of conceptual nitpicking, he provided an overall picture of law: one which spoke to his readers' common-sense understanding of legal phenomena. Hart's approach to legal philosophy was at once disarmingly simple and breathtakingly ambitious. His first single-authored book, *The Concept of Law*, claimed to provide—in the space of a mere 250 pages—a general, descriptive theory of law: an account of the actual as opposed to the ideal nature of law. In doing so, he aspired to make a contribution both to 'analytical jurisprudence' and to 'descriptive sociology'. In other words, he aimed to set out a concept of law which would illuminate all forms of law, wherever or whenever they arose. In pursuing this project, Hart returned to the insights of Austin and Bentham but, in a crucial philosophical innovation, combined their methods with those of the new linguistic philosophy represented by the work of J. L. Austin, Friedrich Waismann, and Ludwig Wittgenstein.

The nub of Hart's theory was the startlingly simple idea that law is a system of rules structurally similar to the rules of games such as chess or cricket. The rules are of different kinds, with complementary functions. Some—'primary rules'—directly govern behaviour; others—'secondary rules'—provide for the identification, interpretation, and alteration of the former. The most obvious example of primary rules would be criminal laws; examples of secondary rules range from constitutional laws to laws governing the creation of contracts, marriages, or wills.

Like his nineteenth-century counterparts, Hart insisted that law is a social, human invention: though legal rules generate genuine obligations, they are not straightforwardly moral rules. Their authority derives not from their content but from their source, which lies in a distinctively institutionalized system of social recognition. For example, a rule that we should drive on the left is authoritative not because there is any intrinsic value to driving on the left as opposed to the right. Rather, its authority derives from the fact that the rule can be identified in accordance with an agreed set of criteria for recognition, such as parliamentary enactment or judicial precedent. Precisely the same is true, moreover, of legal rules which overlap with moral standards: the legal prohibition on murder is not the same as, and derives its validity in a different way from, the moral injunction against killing.

Hart's account of how legal rules are recognized as valid and hence as generating 'real' obligations served, on the other hand, to distinguish law from a mere system of force, or 'orders backed by threats'. For, according to Hart, legal rules have not only an external but also an internal aspect: we know that a rule is in existence not only because it is regularly observed, but also because those subject to it use it as a reason or standard for behaviour, criticizing themselves or others for breaches of the rules. It was in this aspect of Hart's theory that linguistic philosophy became so important, for he built up his argument by paying close attention to linguistic practices: quoting J. L. Austin, he sought to use 'a sharpened awareness of words to sharpen our perception of the phenomena'. For example, he explored the distinction between habitual behaviour (going to the pub on Sunday lunch-time) and rule-governed behaviour (going to a place of worship as and when required by your religion); between being obliged to do something (handing over money because someone threatens to kill you if you don't) and having an obligation to do it (paying your taxes). And he pointed out that these distinctions between forced and obligatory behaviour are reflected in a whole number of features of our day-to-day language; for example in a distinction between predictive statements ('he's sure to go to the pub today') and normative statements ('she ought to go to synagogue today').

By setting out his own concept of law, Hart was doing much more than escaping the intellectual barrenness of early twentieth-century English jurisprudence or picking up the forgotten threads of connection between jurisprudence and philosophy. By moving from the early 'positivist' notion of law as a sovereign command to the notion of law as a system of rules, he also produced a theory which spoke to the social realities of law in a secular and democratic age. The concept of law as a system of rules fitted far better with the impersonal idea of authority embedded in modern democracies than did the sovereign command theory: Hart's theory of law expressed a modern understanding of the ideal of 'the rule of law and not of men'. It provided a powerful and remarkably widely applicable rationalization of the nature of legal authority in a pluralistic world. And it offered not only a descriptive account of law's social power but also an account of legal validity which purported to explain the (limited) sense in which citizens have an obligation to obey the law.

There was a further aspect of the utilitarian tradition which had been lost in twentieth-century legal philosophy and which Hart succeeded in reviving. Though arguing that law and morality were, in important ways, separate phenomena, the early positivists had also insisted on the importance of subjecting law to systematic moral and political assessment. The ambition of jurisprudence should be not only to provide a clear, descriptive concept of law but also—though as a *separate* project—to elaborate a framework for the criticism of law and for law reform. For Austin and Bentham, the framework was a utilitarian one: law, like other social arrangements, should be designed to promote the greatest happiness of the greatest number.

From the late 1950s on, Hart's work became increasingly concerned with these prescriptive questions about how law ought to be; he published influential papers which entered the debate on a number of key social and political issues. These included debates about whether those in Germany who, during the Nazi era, committed what would today be regarded as serious crimes should be punished notwithstanding that their behaviour was regarded as lawful within the Nazi regime; about whether capital punishment should be abolished; about the decriminalization of homosexuality and prostitution; about the legalization of abortion. In these works, as well as in his debate with Patrick Devlin, he successfully revived a liberalism which finds its roots in J. S. Mill's *On Liberty* and which somewhat later found expression, in revised form, in John Rawls' hugely influential *A Theory of Justice*. In *Law, Liberty and Morality*, Hart argued, against Devlin, that democratic states are not entitled to enforce moral standards for their own sake: the mere belief that, say, certain kinds of sexual activity are immoral is not enough to justify their prohibition. Moreover, he rejected Devlin's assertion that a failure to enforce conventional morality would lead to social disintegration. In certain cases protective, paternalistic legislation can be justified: a good example would be the compulsory wearing of seat-belts. But these cases are exceptional: in general, the state should respect individual freedom, intervening only to prevent or punish the commission of tangible harms. This book stands, over 40 years after its publication, as the resounding late twentieth-century statement of principled liberal social policy. Its ideas continue to echo in both political and intellectual debates about a range of social and legal issues such as criminal justice policy, euthanasia, abortion, and human rights.

Applying his philosophical and rhetorical skills to these key public issues, Hart made a decisive contribution to the emergence of a more liberal social culture in the 1960s. But his involvement in moral and political issues went hand in hand with theoretical argument, and his work on issues such as the enforcement of morality and the justification of punishment also refined and modified the philosophy of utilitarianism. His essays on rights, justice, and fairness pondered the proper weight to be attached to these moral con-siderations, as distinct from utilitarian arguments about the general social welfare, in legal or political decision-making. Working through a variety of concrete moral and political questions, he developed a distinctive, con-strained version of utilitarianism. Hart's ideas speak to issues with which courts and policy-makers struggle every day: the appropriate relationship between individual and state; the proper scope of public regulation of our private lives; the direction of criminal justice policy. He claims our interest, therefore, not only as the man who devised 'a town-planning scheme' for the 'intellectual slum of English jurisprudence', but as a man whose ideas are of continuing influence and relevance today.

Part I

NORTH AND SOUTH

CHAPTER I

Harrogate, Cheltenham, Bradford

A T the very beginning of the twentieth century, newly-weds Rose and Simeon Hart, furriers and dressmakers in the East End of London, decided to set up business in the northern spa town of Harrogate. For a relatively observant Jewish couple, this was not an obvious decision. Among the towns of the north-east of England, Leeds, which got its first synagogue in 1860, and Bradford, where a synagogue was founded in 1886, would have been more obvious choices, given their well-established Jewish communities and the fact that the Harts had cousins in both Bradford and Leeds. Harrogate's economic development had been relatively slow; full railway access to the town came only in 1862. But steady development following the arrival of the railway set up the business possibilities which Rose and Simeon saw in 1900: Harrogate had become not only a pleasant suburban retreat for those willing to travel to work in Leeds, but also an attractive stopping point for well-to-do holiday-makers from the south of England making their way to Scotland, who would frequently stay in Harrogate to take the waters and to have clothes made. A small Jewish community was already developing, its religious life centred on a number of Jewish-run boarding houses around the town, one of which provided services on High Days and Holy Days from 1895. Yet whereas in 1900 Leeds already had a Jewish population of between 20,000 and 25,000, even by 1918—the year in which a synagogue was finally established—there were only ten Jewish families in Harrogate. By 1925 this had risen to 40, of whom half worked in some form of clothing business.

That the Harts chose to move away from the much denser Jewish community of East London, and to locate themselves in this very Anglo-Saxon environment, provides us with some important clues to their own ambitions and to their attitude to their Jewish identity, and to the attitudes with which their four children—Albert, born in 1901, Reggie, in 1902, Herbert, in 1907, and Sybil, in 1915—were brought up. In early photographs, four exquisitely turned out, bright-eyed children gaze at the camera in an image which could serve as an advertisement for the advantages of a well-ordered Edwardian upbringing (and those of bespoke tailoring). The two parental favourites—Albert, the eldest son and most equable of the four children, and Herbert, his special gifts apparent from an early age—look into the camera with striking assurance. While information about the texture of their family life is scarce, it is worth setting out such information as is available and sketching a picture of the social world in which the family lived. For among these origins—individual characteristics, interpersonal family context, and broader social environment—we can find traces of many of the complex features which characterize Herbert Hart's later dispositions and career. An intense, sensitive, and highly responsible little boy who adored his mother and sister, fell in love with the Yorkshire dales before he was ten, grew up conscious of being a member of a small and somewhat socially isolated group, and developed a strong sense of himself through his passion for reading and his early successes at school, the young Herbert Hart already felt the force of the creative tensions which would make him the man he became. His sense of himself as a special or gifted person contrasted with an underlying insecurity about his social or intellectual position, realizing itself in the importance which he attached in later life to 'keeping up appearances'. His sensitivity to others and to beauty in nature and the arts, along with his aesthetic taste for the romantic, were in counterpoint with an intellectual rationalism and trenchant secularism, with a discomfort at outward displays of emotion, and with a highly developed capacity for suppressing his emotional responses. And his sense of the need—indeed entitlement—to be judged as an individual rather than as a member of a group, his hatred of discrimination, sat in productive tension with a deep sense of wanting to belong, and with a failure ever entirely to feel he had achieved this.

Both of Herbert Hart's parents came from families which had moved to England from central Europe during the course of the late eighteenth and nineteenth centuries. Herbert's mother Rose, born in 1874, was the eldest of the ten children of Samuel Samson and Fanny Rosenthal. Fanny had come to London from Poland in the early 1870s at the age of 18; Samuel moved to London a little later. The two of them set up what was to become a very successful business in women's clothing; they started in the East End, but ultimately owned a shop in fashionable Sloane Street. Their business received a Royal Warrant as costumiers to the court and had an aristocratic clientele. Rose herself received training both as a dressmaker and in broader business matters in the family firm, experience which set her in good stead for her future partnership with Simeon Hart.

Herbert's father, too, came from a family which had made its economic life in England in the clothing business, but his was a family in which there

was, on his mother's side, a significant rabbinical tradition. Simeon—
known as Sim—Hart was an imposing and somewhat austere figure
though, judging by his letters, a man of strong emotions. He was born in
1871, the son of Adelaide and Albert Hart. While Albert came to London
from East Prussia as a young man of 27 in 1851, Adelaide (née Barnett) had
been born in London in 1834, the daughter of a rabbi who had emigrated
from Krotoschin in Posen and who ultimately became chief judge of the
rabbinical court of the Great Synagogue in London. Albert and Adelaide
(who, according to family tradition, was the dominant member of the partnership) had eight children, of whom Sim was the youngest but one.

It is a mark of his continuing (though not often publicly articulated)
interest in this heritage that when the details of his ancestry were excavated
by a cousin in the late 1970s, Herbert Hart annotated them carefully, and
kept them among his personal papers. He also told his cousin in later life
that he regarded his rabbinical background as having had an effect on his
own intellectual development and success. This sense of history balanced
in Herbert, however, with an ironic, humorous but also self-protective
perspective on his forebears. When his future mother-in-law—a woman of
seamless, WASP upper-middle-class credentials—announced to him in the
late 1930s that her ancestors had been 'robber barons on the Borders',
Herbert replied: 'Mine were robber tailors in the East End'.

Within a decade of their arrival in Harrogate, Rose and Sim Hart had
established a flourishing business and a comfortable way of life. They
worked in partnership. Sim was a master tailor, furrier, and dressmaker;
Rose concentrated on dealing with clients and keeping the financial side of
the business in order. As a young boy, Herbert was observing his parents'
world with keen perception. An autobiographical fragment written in the
mid-1940s gives an intriguing glimpse of his childhood vision of Harrogate
and of the dominant place of the business in his parents' lives:

As a child, I was dimly aware of frequent visits to 'the shop' of rather grand elab-
orately upholstered women talking in high voices while they were being fitted
(very often by my father) in the fitting rooms or were being ushered out of the
door and I remember them too round the Pump Room in the overcultivated
Valley Gardens sipping their glasses of disgusting sulphur water or on hot summer afternoons lounging in deck chairs listening to the band playing selections
from Iolanthe . . . . They were the tail end of Edwardian society and the number
and elaboration of their dresses were the foundation of my family's fortune—
such as it was. The cure at Harrogate ceased to be fashionable after the 1914–18
war and this circumstance together with the growth of competition in a field
where my parents' shop had for long held almost undisputed sway started a gradual decline in the family property accelerated by my father's inability to adapt

himself to a less grand clientele. He suffered in his business as in everything else from a sort of nostalgia for the magnificent. 'Business' occupied and really dominated the lives of both of my parents.

Even as a child, Herbert's sensitivity gave him a clear view of the vulnerability which underlay the surface orderliness of the adult world, while his outsider's eye and sense of fun lent irony to his perception of Edwardian society. Apart from this fragment, we have little direct material on his childhood. But his Sheffield cousin, Teddy Isaacs, published an autobiography in the mid-1980s, and since Herbert wrote that he found Teddy's description of his early life 'evocative' and 'very like ours', this account gives us some further clues. Teddy described a household in which elaborate preparations for the Sabbath and, in particular, for the culinary and prayer-reciting rituals of festivals such as Passover were a central feature. They sat alongside the regularities of life at a (private) local primary school and the pleasures of visits to local shops and the beautiful rural environment which was easily accessible from the suburbs of even the larger northern towns of the era. Rose and Sim Hart's was a house with relatively few books but many ornaments; an 'imposing home' where the atmosphere was coloured by a 'stiff collared and starched nanny' who, given the demands of the business, not to mention the domestic customs of affluent families at the time, was a key figure in the early lives of Herbert and his siblings. They were a closely knit family, seeing much of Rose's mother and of cousins, aunts, and uncles. Herbert was particularly attached to his sister Sybil, a lively, petite girl with auburn hair and brown eyes, and shared her love of the Yorkshire dales and the Lake District. She returned his brotherly affection with something close to adoration.

Teddy remembered Rose and Sim as a kindly and generous aunt and uncle but, as the watchful Herbert was well aware, their relationship was not always an easy one. The Hart children's experience was shaped by the sometimes tense dynamics between the authoritarian Sim and the warm, indulgent Rose. In later life, Herbert recalled with distaste his father's outbursts of anger, particularly towards Rose. These memories made him resolve never to lose his temper with his own family. Their effect was such that he was able to keep his resolution with almost alarming completeness: of his four children, only one can remember him ever losing his temper. It was an apparently trivial event, an understandable moment of paternal frustration with a little girl who refused to carry her own beach clothes back from a swimming expedition. But Herbert's outburst shook her because it was, for him, exceptional.

Sim Hart was a man who was loath ever to be under an obligation. This led to a marked degree of social isolation. Someone who liked to 'rule the roost', Sim was a man of warm affections tempered by a keen—but in-constant—capacity for keeping the lid on his volatile emotions. How far this was related to a depressive strand in the family is difficult to judge, but Sim's sister Tillie suffered a nervous breakdown in the 1920s from which she never fully recovered, and Sim himself suffered nervous illnesses during the war and committed suicide in 1953. By contrast, Rose was a less complex, more unambiguously warm and accommodating person. Years later, when asked by her daughter-in-law how she had managed her anxiously awaited first meeting with Jenifer's rather snobbish mother, Rose replied that it had been perfectly easy; she knew the type because Jenifer's mother was just like one of her customers. Herbert's feeling for her is poignantly reflected in a letter which he wrote to Isaiah Berlin following Berlin's mother's death in 1974: 'I felt my mother's death [in 1953] like the roof blowing off my life even though she had taken no active part in it for years.'

Within the broader Harrogate community, the Harts were regarded with a mixture of awe and ambivalence. A Jewish Harrogate contemporary recalled that his own mother had felt intimidated by the grandeur of Sim Hart's shop and would never have dreamt of entering it. The family was regarded as isolated and somewhat stand-offish, with a sense of their own superiority. Sim Hart's continued travels north to family occasions long after his and Rose's removal to London in the late 1930s suggest that their social life was focussed on family in Leeds, Sheffield, and Bradford. But Sim did have some contact with the local Jewish community. One Harrogate contemporary, a child at the time, remembers seeing Sim's bear-like and, from the child's perspective, intimidating figure at Saturday services. He was a subscriber to the appeal for funds for the first synagogue, but had a reputation for eccentricity, and observers speculated that the material over which he invariably pored during the service in fact consisted of novels. No one remembers seeing Rose or the children, though it is certain that they would have observed High Days and Holy Days. Although the family did not use a kosher butcher, Rose's rich, generous cooking observed norms such as excluding pork and shellfish; the children were taught Hebrew and the boys had bar mitzvahs. Herbert's interest in this heritage outlasted his childhood: on a holiday in the mid-1930s, he spoke knowledgeably to his friend Richard Wilberforce of the Talmud and the system of Jewish courts.

A history of Harrogate testifies that the Harts' 'furrier and costumier' business was an 'important part of commercial life in the James Street of the 1920s and 1930s' until it closed in 1938. The book shows a photograph of the premises in an elegant late nineteenth-century row, near the railway station, to which the shop was moved in 1907, the year of Herbert's birth. The accompanying entry observes that 'it was a very up-market business which considered that its image would be improved by ripping out the beautiful ground floor colonnade . . . and treating the upper storeys with their delicate polychrome brick and stone decoration to a bland coat of white-wash. A grotesquely intrusive advertising sign was also erected'. Between the lines of this caption there is a whiff of judgment which exceeds the purely architectural.

Apart from the family's perceived sense of superiority, there was perhaps a sense of breach of the delicate, unspoken contract which governed Jewish and Gentile relations in Harrogate throughout the first half of the century. This was a contract in which the steady and well organized construction of institutions which fostered a sense of collective Jewish identity, maximized the chances of intra-community marriage and friendship, provided the basis for religious observance, and, increasingly, nurtured support for Zionism, was balanced with a self-conscious attempt to assimilate and to contribute to non-Jewish—indeed Christian—charities and activities. A comparison with Leeds is telling. The Leeds Jewish population included a high proportion of first generation immigrants from central and eastern Europe. Many of them were struggling with English as a new second or third language and working for low pay, in poor conditions, in clothing factories. A high proportion of these Jews were concentrated in the low-cost housing of the Leylands area of the city, where they were used to stone-throwing and verbal abuse from the Gentile population. Despite the existence of a more affluent Jewish population, social segregation and economic disadvantage materially shaped the development of Jewish/Gentile relations in the city.

In Harrogate, with its smaller, wealthier, and more socially homogeneous Jewish population, although complaints about prejudice or snobbery surfaced from time to time (one member of the community observed at the opening of the first dedicated synagogue in 1925 that there was a lack of friendly relations, as well as overt exclusion from a number of institutions such as golf clubs), the general emphasis was on the quiet building of a reputation for good local and national citizenship. The community being small, formal markers of progress came slowly: no Jewish person was elected to any position in local government until 1934. But the aspiration was clear: to build 'an anglicised orthodox congregation', 'a community, participating in English cultural activities, whilst wishing to maintain and uphold a separate Jewish identity'. The community's first Minister, the Rev. Eli Kahan was, accordingly, described as 'an Englishman of the Jewish persuasion'. Although Harrogate had avoided the anti-Semitic demonstrations which Leeds had seen in 1917, prompted by the (unfounded) suspicion that Jews were not making a full contribution to the war effort, this was a delicate balance, and one which may well have sat uneasily with the Harts' distinctive combination of elective social isolation and overtness about commercial success.

If their imposing shop front was a very public sign of Sim's and Rose's commercial ambitions, their decision to send Herbert to an elite boys' boarding school—a 'public' school, in English terms—was a sign of the broader ambitions which they had for their four children. The family had a keen respect for learning, which Herbert in later life attributed in part to the echoes of the rabbinical traditions of his paternal grandmother's family. Herbert and his siblings were the first generation in the family to receive a university education, and their parents' ambition for them was that they should find a firm position among the ranks of the educated, professional middle class. This ambition was largely fulfilled, with Reggie destined for an Oxford degree and a successful business career with the large shoe manufacturer Clarks, and Sybil for a degree in French Literature at University College London followed by a successful career in the Labour Relations Department of ICI. Only Albert—the cherished eldest son who had inherited his mother's warmth and with whom Herbert maintained a close relationship all his life—followed the family tradition into the clothing trade, training as a master furrier in Paris.

But Rose's and Sim's decision to send one of their children to a public school signified social as much as academic aspirations. The north-east of England boasted, after all, a number of excellent grammar schools; it was to one of these—Bradford Grammar School—that Herbert's elder brothers had already been sent. Within the family, however, there was from an early stage a shared feeling that Herbert was special. The child, like the adult who lay ahead, showed an outstanding capacity to abstract himself from whatever was going on around him: to absorb himself in books, and to retain whatever he had absorbed. This earned him a reputation for a certain kind of eccentricity: Herbert was allowed to live in his own world, one in which the normal rules did not apply quite so strictly as they did to his siblings. One later mark of this special position was his parents' relatively easy acceptance of his decision to 'marry out'. But their decision to send him, alone of their children, to a yet more elite school than Bradford was prompted above all by his parents' belief in the distinctive intellectual gifts which had made themselves apparent in Herbert's early schooling.

The Harts' aspiration to social assimilation was not, however, matched by an acceptance of religious assimilation. At this stage only two public schools in the country had separate houses for Jewish boys. It was to one of these—Cheltenham College—which Sim and Rose Hart chose, in 1918, to send their gifted son; first to the junior school, and then, in 1920, to the Jewish house of the public school itself. An all-male establishment, it was 'a very, very English—almost military—public school' in Herbert's own words.

From Herbert's point of view, the decision was, to put it mildly, not a success. Far from feeling that he had escaped from the constraints of family life or found an entrée into a new social and intellectual world, Herbert was alienated, frustrated, and miserable at Cheltenham. As long as he lived he talked vehemently of his three years there as the one genuinely unhappy period of his life. His objections to life at the school show that some of his enduring attitudes and tastes were in place by the age of 11. He found the teaching intellectually dull, and both the social and the teaching culture obsessed by the importance of athletics. He resented the school's snobbery and class-consciousness. And he objected to being labelled and—albeit by vicarious choice—segregated as a Jew, which he later likened to being 'in a kind of ghetto'. Herbert neither identified with the group of which he was compulsorily a member, nor felt any enthusiasm for belonging to the wider school culture.

What is less clear is how far he was a victim of class snobbery within the Jewish house itself, and the relative importance to him of the experience of class snobbery, of being labelled as a member of a particular ethnic/religious group (a dislike which prefigured his later anti-religious views and the centrality of individual choice to his particular brand of liberalism), and of sheer anti-Semitism. As a member of at least two minority groups at Cheltenham, and as a boy who had enjoyed a special position in his family which would have made it particularly difficult to adapt to the regimented school regime, it is not unlikely that Herbert found himself the victim of bullying. But his later reflections on his unhappiness at Cheltenham never mentioned this; nor did they mention simple homesickness. Given his warm relationships with his mother, sister, and eldest brother, it is hard to believe that he did not feel bereft. Though the failure to mention this dimension doubtless has more to do with social conventions about men of Herbert's period expressing their emotions than with his feelings at the time, his response gives us a glimpse of a boy who was already used to rationalizing his emotional responses in terms of social or intellectual criticisms rather than directly expressing his feelings. And this habit of rationalizing his feelings, along with the unhappy memory of his time at Cheltenham, echoed down the corridors of future years.

By 1921, Herbert's distress at Cheltenham was so acute that he was contemplating running away; an extreme measure for a highly responsible boy. But an unexpected resolution of his difficulties arose in the unfortunate form of a downturn in his parents' business. Economic conditions were difficult in the wake of the First World War, with holiday travel declining and the demand for luxury goods such as furs suffering a serious downturn. Sim Hart wrote sadly to Herbert to explain that he would be forced to remove him from 'this wonderful school'. For Herbert this was 'a message from heaven'. He was sent instead, following his brothers, to Bradford Grammar School, and stayed there until the end of his schooling in 1926. Yet even during his brief and unhappy time at Cheltenham, he made a mark on his teachers. On earning a scholarship to Oxford and on his graduation, he received several warm letters of congratulation from masters at the school. One of them wondered whether it would be appropriate to list Herbert's successes at Oxford as pertaining to an 'Old Cheltonian'. Herbert wrote firmly in the margin, 'No'.

Herbert's move to Bradford at last provided him with an environment in which he could realize his intellectual potential while feeling a sense of belonging and of being valued as an individual. Bradford was a boys' grammar school with high standards of education and a broad social mix of pupils. Still unsure of himself after his unhappiness at Cheltenham, Herbert at first had difficulty adjusting to this radical change of institutional culture; by a peculiarity of fate, the young Leslie Styler, a future colleague at Oxford, was delegated to take care of him in his early weeks at the school. But he quickly settled and looked back on his time at Bradford as one of the happiest of his life, and one which decisively shaped his future career. Bradford's more expansive and less tightly disciplined atmosphere allowed for walks in the beautiful countryside, for which Herbert had already developed a strong affinity, and encouraged the cultivation of his keen aesthetic sensibility. The school's staff included several distinguished teachers, and their classes gave Herbert a sense of the potential excitement of sustained intellectual exchange. Goddard, the master of classics, was interested in the ideas of the Austrian thinker Otto Spengler, whose book *The Decline of the West* advanced the thesis that civilizations went through a routine cycle of growth and decay. Goddard introduced Herbert to one of the major intellectual pleasures of philosophy, feeding his taste for the excitement of large hypotheses and generalizations while also, through the more orthodox aspects of his teaching, fostering his taste for the precise nuance of language.

Herbert became Head Boy of Bradford, and maintained a passionate gratitude to the school for the rest of his life. A letter from the Head Master, W. Edwards, on Herbert's departure in 1926 suggests, in its unaffected warmth, one of the reasons why Bradford was such a happy school. It also shows that, at the age of 18, Herbert already had the capacity to make a special impression upon those around him:

I cannot allow you to leave without telling you how much I appreciate the excellent work you have done for the school during the past year. I can sincerely say that the school never had a better Head Prefect. It has been a great relief to me to know that I had as Head of the school a boy of such loyalty and capacity whom I could always rely on. We are very proud of you and you have our affection as well as our pride. We expect great things of you. But whatever happens I hope that you will be able to look back on your schooldays with happy recollection and that you will always regard me as a warm and sincere friend and not merely as your old Head Master.

Herbert left with a distinction in four of the six subjects in his School Certificate—History, Greek, Latin, and French—and with distinctions in Greek and Latin in the Higher Certificate. He had also won a large collection of prizes in subjects ranging from Latin Verse to Political Science. A school report from 1924 is liberally smattered with the words 'excellent' and 'extraordinary': in a sole caveat—and one which Herbert might usefully have remembered in his years as an academic—the Latin teacher noted that 'The chief thing he should beware of is overwork and excessive concentration on it'. The affectionate esteem of his teachers gave Herbert a new sense of confidence. In the year before he sat his Higher School Certificate, Gilbert Murray, former classics don at New College, Oxford, had visited the school. Impressed by Herbert's prowess in translating Greek texts, Murray suggested that he sit for an open scholarship to New College. No pupils from Bradford Grammar School had been there for over half a century because it was regarded as snobbish and expensive. But Herbert, unimpressed by the 'hearty' St John's College where his brother Reggie had studied, was persuaded to try. It was a decision which he never regretted. He was successful, and went up to New College in 1926.

By now, the unhappiness and insecurity of the Cheltenham years eclipsed by the congenial framework of Bradford, Herbert was to all outward appearances a self-assured as well as an astonishingly accomplished young man. He had found satisfying outlets for his intellectual intensity, and he had discovered an aesthetic sensibility to both nature and the arts which would give him lifelong pleasure. A diary which he kept while on holiday abroad in the spring of 1926 testifies both to a return of the family fortunes and to the extraordinarily broad education which he had acquired by the time he went to University. Embarked on a marathon rail journey which took in many of the cultural highlights of Switzerland, Italy, Germany, and Belgium, he wrote with engaging freshness and amazing learning of buildings and works of art, and with an infectious and often lyrical enthusiasm for the beauty of the natural surroundings (as well as of the pleasures of comfortable hotels and good dinners). His descriptions show considerable understanding of architectural style and political history, and a confident aesthetic judgment: at Tivoli, works in the museum were 'really very fine. The Luxovisi throne is there but it did not strike me so much as the Mars (saddled with a hideous Bernini baby between its legs ...) That and the Apollo upstairs ... made the greatest impression on me'.

They also display a remarkable knowledge of foreign languages, including German, Italian, and 'semi Yiddish' (in which he conversed at the Venice Synagogue with 'Israelitica').

Already in this diary the voice of self-criticism is audible: looming large in the narrative are nearly missed trains, incompletely kept accounts, and gaps in the diary itself. In Rome, he scribbled, 'As it is obviously impossible to retrieve "in dies" what I was too lazy to record I suppose I must endeavour to put down anyhow what most impressed me'. This is the voice not just of a dutiful disposition but of a future writer in semi-self-conscious training. The sense of duty, as much as a straightforward interest in the Jewish heritage, pervades a fond postcard to his father, emphasizing the Roman sights of Jewish significance, and giving detailed accounts of the Venice synagogue and of Judaic images elsewhere in Italy. And underlying much of the text is a wry and ironic sense of humour. In one passage, memorable for its rare glimpse of Herbert's irresponsible adolescent side, he describes (how on earth did he come to be there?) a visit with a Mr. Warren and a Miss Murray to an ordination service in Rome: 'Ordination service: boring mass . . . . Eat breakfast surreptitiously—dropped a boiled egg . . .—might have been accepted as a miracle!—about 200 "ordinandi" prostrate themselves before a poor old bishop who has to continually change his clothes . . . . Name Pompiti. More Breakfast and Coffee. Then poor P. massages them with holy wax etc. and ordains them. We leave at 1—thank the lord—and head for lunch.' In this early diary, the young man thirstily absorbing high culture and natural beauty, the person who appreciates good food, comfort, and conversation, the hard-working scholar, the dutiful son, and the ironic observer are already well developed.

CHAPTER 2

An Oxford Scholar

HERBERT HART arrived at New College to take up his scholarship to read for the *Literae Humaniores* degree—a mixture of Greek, Latin, Ancient History, and Philosophy—in October 1926. A tall, slim young man with fine features and already showing the disordered dress and lack of physical coordination which became more marked with the years, he must have regarded New College with a mixture of excitement and awe. Though the all-male environment would have been familiar and even congenial to him, the self-consciously elite and predominantly public school culture had some disturbing echoes of Cheltenham. It was no accident, after all, that students were referred to as going 'up' to Oxford. Herbert's outlook on this sort of snobbishness was ambivalent. On the one hand, he disapproved of it; on the other, he wanted to belong.

Herbert was in many ways well-equipped for his entry into the social and educational hierarchy of Oxford. Though reserved in manner, he was vigorous in discussion. His extraordinary erudition and his familiarity with some of the most beautiful architectural sights of Europe gave him a conversational range and, at least on the surface, a social confidence unusual in someone of his age and background. And through his brother Reggie he already had some acquaintance with Oxford. But both the aesthetic and the intellectual environments which awaited him at New College were to shape his life in vivid and decisive ways.

With the exception of the additions of a (rather makeshift) lodge at the Holywell entrance, a library in the Holywell quad, and a graduate building just east of the city wall, New College in 1926 looked very much as it does today. To the first-time visitor, even one familiar with the streets of Oxford, New College often comes as a surprise. It sits on an unexpectedly large plot hidden away between Holywell Street and Queen's Lane, the College comprising two main groups of buildings, divided by the old city wall running through its grounds. To the south of the city wall lies the original fourteenth-century quadrangle—the 'old quad'. Constructed in cool grey-brown stone, the quad, designed in the Perpendicular style, was originally two storeys but was later extended by a third. This quadrangle embraces the soaring chapel and dining hall. A golden-stoned cloister, at once intimate and elegant, complete with beautifully carved capitols and striking gargoyles, is tucked away in the north-western corner, abutting a massive detached tower. At the eastern end, the quadrangle makes a bridge containing what was still in 1926 the College library, under which the visitor passes into the exquisitely proportioned late seventeenth- and early eighteenth-century 'garden quad'. Here two symmetrical wings, fashioned out of smooth, honey-coloured stone, which breathes a sense of warmth even on one of Oxford's many gloomy days, stretch down to a set of elegant wrought iron gates, themselves opening onto the large, verdant garden enclosed by the ancient city wall. To the north of the city wall lies the second part of the College: the 'Holywell quad' made up of the late nineteenth-century 'New Buildings'. This tall, dark grey-brown stone row is imposing and somewhat gothic in style, but it is not out of harmony, in conception, material, or scale, with the earlier buildings.

Inside the formal rooms of the College, exquisite carpets and pieces of antique furniture vie with ancient linoleum and overstuffed armchairs to define an aesthetic which, notwithstanding the inevitable ebbs and flows of taste and expenditure over the decades, could reasonably be described as the epitome of 'shabby genteel'. The overall impression—inside and out—is of great beauty, of calm, and of a certain detachment from the bustle of the world. As a future professor of Ancient History said to a young prospective colleague, weighing up the pros and cons of job offers at New College and at another college in the 1970s: 'New College is often very cold and in winter you will sometimes see water running down some of our walls. It may seem rather gloomy, but people here will always leave you alone and value your right to work steadily in your own field.' (To the touched amusement of the younger scholar, he added, 'I think it would suit you very well'.) However it struck him on first acquaintance, Herbert's special love of New College's gardens and buildings stayed with him all his life, and until his last months, he could be seen, precariously propped up by his stick, but proceeding at a slow, steady pace, walking through its grounds on his way between his home in Manor Place and his room in University College, occasionally pausing to look around him with evident appreciation.

Herbert's lasting love of New College was not simply to do with the distinctive beauty of its environment. Two other factors were uppermost in his immediate affection for the place: an extraordinary group of student peers, and an inspiring set of tutors. Though he was in a tiny minority of grammar school boys—just four of them amid the intake of about 80 under-graduates—Herbert later denied that he ever found New College to live up to its reputation for being expensive and snobbish. He was, nonetheless, taken aback by the 'awesomely destructive horseplay' which characterized the public school boy culture, bringing teams of glaziers to the college each Monday morning to replace the dozens of windows shattered during the weekend's alcoholic social excesses. And Herbert made an exception to his general approbation for a group of 'tough athletic Wykehamists'—former pupils of Winchester College—many of whom doubtless owed their places at New College more to class privilege and the legacy of Winchester's and the College's shared history than to their scholarly potential. But his long held dislike of a culture dominated by athletics did not prevent him from joining in a variety of sporting activities, and within a few weeks of his arrival, he was writing to his parents to tell them of his matches with the First Rugby XV. It is hard to tell whether this was born of real enjoyment or of a desire to fit in. In any event, right from the start, he 'adored' New College.

Among the undergraduates at the time were five members of the future (1945) Labour Government: Hugh Gaitskell (future leader of the Labour Party), Richard Crossman, Frank Pakenham (later Lord Longford), Douglas Jay, and Kenneth Younger. Though his friends ranged across scholars and commoners, and took in not only his Bradford contemporaries, most of whom were at Queen's, but also some contemporaries from his Cheltenham days, Herbert spent a large proportion of his time in the company of and in discussion with the band of self-confident Wykehamist scholars. Scholars sat at a separate table in Hall, and among them Herbert found John Sparrow, future Warden of All Souls, Richard Wilberforce, a future Law Lord, and Douglas Jay, later to hold a series of ministerial positions in post-war Labour administrations and, ultimately, to become a life peer. Each of these men were to become his lifelong friends. This was in contrast to Crossman, whom Herbert disliked—indeed he used the word 'hated'—as overbearing: someone who 'foisted his personality on one'. The antipathy was mutual: when Herbert returned to New College as a Fellow in 1945, Crossman laughed at him, 'Still worrying about the truth, I suppose?' 'I'm sure *you're* not', Herbert returned. Whether founded on affection or distrust, however, the group in which Herbert moved provided a hugely stimulating intellectual environment, one which fostered his already well-developed habit of self-teaching. This peer-based learning was enhanced by debates at institutions such as the Oxford Union and the philosophical Jowett Society. Herbert ultimately became President of the Jowett Society, and this is where he met another man with whom he was to form an important, lifelong friendship: Isaiah Berlin.

A particular bond was established between Herbert and the eccentric Douglas Jay. They were an unlikely pair. Quite apart from their very different backgrounds (Jay incidentally, alone of Herbert's contemporaries, later remembered him having a strong Yorkshire accent on his arrival at the College), their personalities could hardly have been in greater contrast. Jay was flamboyant and extrovert, though he suffered intermittent bouts of depression; Herbert was measured and, at least with those he did not know well, reserved. Jay was also famously anti-European: he disliked foreign travel and avoided leaving the shores of the British Isles unless absolutely necessary, while the cultural and linguistic heritage of Europe already held a strong attraction for Herbert. But as well as their shared brilliance and seriousness of scholarly purpose, another factor drew Herbert and Douglas Jay together at the start of their undergraduate careers. Both felt that their education so far had furnished them with more than enough Latin and Greek language and literature. In their impatience to move on to Ancient History and Philosophy, they insisted on doing their preliminary examinations in Law rather than Classics, because the Law 'Prelim' could be completed much more quickly than the classical 'Mods' course. At first, the College resisted, and threatened to take away their scholarships. But it relented, and was ultimately rewarded by both students' glittering success. Herbert graduated in 1929 with one of the top first class degrees of his year, in spite of acute jaundice which left him bedridden for almost six weeks in the term preceding his final examinations. Throughout their time at New College, he and Douglas spent much time studying together; Herbert's superior Greek and Latin supplemented Douglas's linguistic skills (although Herbert reputedly kept a private notebook of 'nuggets' of valuable information which would help him to excel in the exams).

Another important, if on the face of it unlikely, friendship was with Rhodes Scholar Bill Wentworth. Wentworth was from an influential, wealthy Australian family, and later became an MP, Minister for Aboriginal Affairs, and a lifelong campaigner on a glorious serendipity of issues ranging from (successful) advocacy of the introduction of a standard rail gauge to (less successful) opposition to globalization. In the Oxford of the late 1920s, Wentworth's confident, colourful, and already eccentric character stood in complementary contrast to Herbert's more conformist disposition: in their shared lodgings on Longwall in their final student year, Herbert judiciously turned a blind eye to Bill's frequent overnight female guests, while Bill infected the 'rather orthodox' Herbert with some of his own 'can-do' attitudes, for example teaching him to drive. Somehow, amid Herbert's almost total disagreement with what he saw as Bill's maverick political views, and Bill's view of Herbert as a 'conventional person who liked to belong', a lifelong friendship was formed, and it was one which lent Herbert an enduring presumptive fondness for Australians.

The congenial environment which New College offered Herbert was largely a product of some special intellectual relationships which spilled over into friendships. On this plane, two of his principal tutors—the philosopher Horace William Brindley (H. W. B.) Joseph and the ancient historian Christopher Cox—were of particular importance. Joseph, born in 1867 and a Fellow of New College since 1891, had been a dominant figure in both the College and Oxford philosophy for many years: he had taught (and became a close friend of) Herbert's future father-in-law. He was the son of a rector, and a Wykehamist; a deeply religious man of fixed habits who utterly devoted himself to the small community of the college. A stocky figure with silver hair, a thick white moustache, and an arresting gaze, often marked by a frown of concentration, Joseph was a man of prodigious energy and appetite for work. He was a familiar sight to generations of undergraduates, who watched in amazement as this sturdy figure ran or bicycled vigorously from one commitment to another, arriving breathlessly at lectures with his gown over his arm, or climbing ladders to clear blocked gutters in meticulous discharge of his duties as Junior Bursar. Though capable of acts of striking generosity to the few financially disadvantaged students, his stewardship of the college's property was parsimonious. On one occasion, he was seen wrestling with two large undergraduates in an attempt to rescue a tin bath from one of the not infrequent student bonfires. To the applause of the assembled company, he prevailed. The story gives a sense of the sort of tenacity which he also brought to his teaching responsibilities. His student and later colleague, Alic (A. H.) Smith, who watched this incident, recalled that: 'When later I took him a paper on logic and he seized on the first sentence which I had written, I remembered the episode and had the feeling as I clung to my sentence that it was in the same powerful grasp. It was not long before I had to let it go.' But Joseph also had a romantic side which expressed itself in his enjoyment of the countryside and his love of poetry, in particular of Wordsworth. This was fostered by his marriage to Margaret Bridges, daughter of the Poet Laureate Robert Bridges, until her premature death in 1926.

Philosophically, Joseph was a strongly committed Platonist: in Herbert's words, he 'worshipped Plato', and he pondered all his life the Platonic idea of the unity of mind and ideal of a form of life conformed to a wider Good. His philosophical interests were, however, broader than this: he was a devoted admirer of his Oxford colleague Cook Wilson ('also very clever and exuberantly pugnacious', as one colleague recalled), and the author of an influential book on logic (it was to be overtaken by the mathematical work of Bertrand Russell, with which Joseph never came to terms). A prolific writer, he also produced a swingeing critique of Marx's labour theory of value, in the hope that his analysis would dispel the embittering effects of Marx's ideas on the working classes. He was, naively, disappointed when it failed to attract much notice. Sensitivity to the reactions of his audience was not his strong point. One story has him lecturing, during a winter term near the end of his career, from the Mound in New College garden, oblivious to the inability of his damp and shivering students to concentrate on his densely packed argument.

To students and colleagues who did not share his perspective, Joseph was the epitome of intellectual rigidity who imposed his world-view and dismissed dogmatically the views of other philosophers, notably Kant. Herbert did not share this critical view of Joseph. At this stage of his life he, too, was intrigued by Platonic philosophy, and as a student he came to see things very much from Joseph's point of view. And Joseph's Socratic teaching style was highly congenial to him. Both the dialogic form of the tutorial and Joseph's focus on detail and clarity—like Herbert himself in later years, he would often interrupt a discussion to clarify even the smallest of its terms, and constantly demanded that his students explain 'what you mean'— appealed powerfully to Herbert. Ironically it was Joseph, the man who must have felt most betrayed by Herbert's later turn from Platonism and espousal of the new linguistic philosophy, who helped to inspire him with the passion for clarity, accuracy, and detail which the linguistic approach promised to satisfy. To Maurice Bowra, Joseph was a recipe for intellectual stultification; to Stuart Hampshire, he was someone who got—and taught his New College students to get—philosophy 'absolutely wrong'. To less gifted students, whom he would call back for second, third, or even fourth weekly tutorials until he had demolished every single sentence of their essays, his distinctive critical powers—his 'almost quixotic desire to seek out and destroy false argument'—were crushing. To Herbert, however (and to Jay, whose first tutorial with Joseph lasted for four hours), he was a stimulating catalyst who nurtured the shoots of philosophical interest which had already begun to grow at Bradford. As is clear from Joseph's later letters of recommendation, the admiration was mutual.

A surviving notebook of Herbert's philosophy essays from 1927 gives an interesting insight into Joseph's influence on him and a sense of some of his philosophical preoccupations while at Oxford. Two long essays on Mill's theories of causation and of mathematical reasoning, both of which attracted top, alpha marks, speak loudly of the anti-empiricist stance which Joseph favoured. In his essay on causation, having given a beautifully clear summary of Mill's notion of a cause as 'the invariable unconditional antecedent of an event', Herbert launched into a blistering attack on the idea that our experience of regularities in the world can justify our belief in uniform laws of nature or science. In a voice whose confidence he might have wondered at or even envied 20 years later (though in an argument which he would certainly have rejected) he asserted that Mill 'confuses the issues of theoretical argument and common practice', concluding that 'empiricism cannot establish the necessity of connection: its fundamental justification lies in feeling'. Mill came off worse still on mathematical reasoning. According to Herbert, he 'exhibits the confusion of mind, common to all the Nineteenth Century empiricists, between intelligible truth and the facts of experience . . .' and engages in 'characteristic sophistry'. Since 'the two spheres in which the laws of abstract science and the facts of experience are concerned are not conditioned one by the other', Mill's account of the 'part played by experience in mathematical reasoning' is 'hopelessly exaggerated'. No wonder Joseph was pleased.

But Herbert's essays on Plato and Aristotle—which, incidentally, attracted rather lower marks—show a far from unqualified endorsement of the ideas which Joseph held so dear. An essay on Plato's treatment of justice in Book One of *The Republic*, for example, suggested that the positive conception of justice which Plato wanted to advance was difficult to infer from his dialogic argument, and Herbert's essay was peppered with critical questions about Plato's conception of morality as a principle affecting not just particular actions but the conduct of life as a whole. Herbert was intrigued by the Platonic idea of the nature of reality as 'an intelligible whole or system wherein all those objects of thought which to imperfect knowledge appeared as isolated particulars . . . would, when contemplated by the fully perfected human intelligence, be seen to be participants essentially connected with each other'. He was also—significantly—fascinated by the Platonic ideas of reason as a force controlling and modifying our desires, and of desire for the good as a product of reason. But even at this stage, he was not an uncritical admirer of the Greek philosophers. Although his later legal philosophy certainly bore marks of his classical training (particularly of his familiarity with Aristotle), these early essays show a deep fascination with the empiricist tradition, and a broad familiarity with the works of Hobbes, Locke, and Hume. It would not surprise a reader of Herbert's student essays to discover that it was this terrain—indeed, the specific terrain of Mill's theory of causation—to which he would return early in his own philosophical career. And many pages of his notebook were taken up with extensive notes on Joseph's arch-enemy Kant, whose analysis of duty, obligation, and law were clearly of deep interest to Herbert. Joseph would only have been somewhat comforted by Herbert's occasional moments of frustration with Kant's written style: 'What does it mean?'

In very different style from Joseph, Christopher Cox—later to become a close friend, and destined for high office in colonial administration—also stimulated and inspired the young Herbert Hart. Cox's style, far from dialogic, was exemplary: in (sometimes wild) flows of talk, he would conjure up the context and personalities of the ancient world, giving you 'some idea of what it felt like to be Caesar, or Cicero'. Cox, born in 1899, was appointed Fellow in Ancient History in 1926, Herbert's first year at New College. With a broad smile, twinkling eyes, and aquiline features, he was attractive, highly eccentric, witty, hospitable, and capable of being hilariously funny. There was, however, a darker, depressive side to his 'life-enhancing, indeed tonic, gaiety', and he was tormented by the difficulty of bringing himself to the point of organizing his materials and writing. 'Infinitely accessible' and universally liked, Cox had a particular capacity for empathizing with his students, always treating them as his equals: 'the most callow, or the wildest of one's utterances was never dismissed out of hand but was respected as worthy of consideration'. Herbert was inspired by Cox's imagination and stimulated by his 'acute though delicate criticism. It seemed', as Herbert later wrote, 'that rather than being taught by him I was exploring the subject together with him'. One shared point with Joseph was Cox's feel for detail; though this was detail of a different genre from Joseph's emphasis on precision. In Cox's case, the intellectual sensibility was for the particularities of personality, place, time, and a grasp of their importance in the development of intellectual and social history. Something of Cox's vivid, breathless style, and his adolescent, crazy humour, is conveyed by a letter to Herbert from Nigeria where he was working as education advisor to the colonial government in the late 1940s:

The northern part of this strip of territory . . . contains a number of surprisingly named places and miniature potentates, including the elderly FON, whose 400 wives, housed in a special village, have attracted the attentions of U.N.O who are shortly sending out a commission . . . to investigate. The names on the maps include WE and WUM, and a miniature state called BUM, ruled by a chief called TUM. Yesterday I visited a school where at the end of an avenue of small Union Jacks I stood at attention while the assembled pupils greeted me with a song of the headmaster's own adapting of which the words . . . ran as follows: 'Blessed is He that Cometh [repeated three times]; Blessed is the King of England [repeated three times]; Blessed is He that cometh in the name of the King [repeated three times]'. Today I formally opened a Domestic Science Centre, sampled goods and fine linen, and planted a tree. The speech in reply included the passage 'The tree he is to plant will always remind us of Mr. Cox. It will be something shady and light. It is called the Flamboyant Tree, and it will soon burst into bright red flowers'.

It was this directness and informality which fostered the swift development of a rapport between Herbert and Cox. As early as 1927, Herbert was writing to him during the vacation in terms which exemplify the easy relations which Cox was able to form with his students (as well as Herbert's already well developed capacity for physical disorganization):

Dear Mr. Cox,

I must apologise for breaking in upon your leisure with a request savouring strongly of the term, but I wonder if you could manage to send me a list of the books you suggested as an addition to those given on the printed pamphlet. My own list which I got from you disappeared in the turmoil created by malign workmen in my rooms at college. . . . The weather up North shows every sign of continuing fluid for the rest of the vac, so that I yearn for even the sweatiest and most mosquito-ridden of Provencal days. The cold, too, appears quite Arctic to me, and crouching over the fire is a bad substitute for exposing oneself nude to Dolomite air. I hope you will let me know if you propose taking any part of the Great Route: and I will remit all pubs and Biergarten immediately; also road information if you want it.

Yours sincerely, H. L. A. Hart

In later life, Herbert saw both Cox's and Joseph's emphasis on particularities as an important corrective to the persisting taste for generalizations which his Spenglerian philosophical education at Bradford had nourished. The evident admiration each of these men felt for Herbert's abilities must have given him enormous confidence. A third tutor, the philosopher A. H. Smith, shared both this very high estimation of his gifts and the general affection for Herbert as a person. In 1929, congratulating Herbert on 'one of the best firsts of the year . . .' he wrote 'I shall miss you particularly amongst the many delightful students whom I shall be missing next year'. Smith, born in 1883 and educated at Dulwich and New College, was a tall, fine-featured, aesthetic-looking man with a keen appreciation of the visual arts and of literature. He had started his career as an influential civil servant in the Scottish Office where, for 16 years, he wrote the economic regulations required for the implementation of Westminster legislation in Scotland. In 1919, however, he took up a philosophy fellowship at New College.

Smith could hardly have been a greater contrast to Joseph. Warm, liberal, and an exceptionally shrewd judge of character, Smith, with his lively sense of humour and unusual communicative powers, provided a sympathetic counter-balance to Joseph's astringent tutorial style. 'After being pulverized by the remorseless logic of Joseph, [the students] found in [Smith's] beautiful rooms someone who would enter more sympathetically into their problems'. Smith's subtle, tentative writings on Kant, and his taste for debate with his students, provided an important intellectual contrast. While Smith did not have such a marked effect on Herbert's intellectual formation, his independent-mindedness, liberal views (though religious himself, as Dean of Divinity he refused to enforce the rule of compulsory attendance at chapel), and trenchant individualism would certainly have been congenial to Herbert. And Smith was to have a decisive effect on Herbert's later career. In 1944 he became Warden of New College, and he was keen to persuade his brilliant former pupil to return to the College as Philosophy Fellow.

Like the education which came from his peers, the influence which came from Herbert's tutors did not always take place in a formal context. To a degree which would surprise an Oxford undergraduate today, the boundaries between Senior and Junior Common Rooms were relatively blurred, at least for the students whose intelligence, social confidence, or wealth allowed them to command the extra-tutorial attention of the Fellows. While Herbert may initially have lacked the second, he was well equipped with the first, and not deficient in the third. And despite being outside the group of Wykehamist scholars who formed the favoured circle around the Warden of New College, H. A. L. Fisher, Herbert was not excluded from a taste of the broader political and social world which Fisher brought with him to the College.

H. A. L. Fisher was, by any standards, a remarkable figure. Born in 1865, his family moved in both royal and literary circles. His father, a barrister and later a judge, was private secretary to the Prince of Wales, who became the young Herbert Fisher's godfather; his mother was a daughter of one of the seven famous, gifted, and beautiful Pattle sisters, who included the photographer Julia Margaret Cameron. In his own home and that of his great aunts, some of the most influential artists, writers, and thinkers of the day— G. F. Watts, Edward Burne Jones, Matthew Arnold, Alfred Tennyson— were regular visitors, and the Fisher children stayed from time to time with the family of Leslie Stephen at St. Ives. Educated at Winchester and New College, Fisher was elected on his graduation to a Prize Fellowship in Classics, and was then offered the tutorship in Philosophy. But he turned away from what he felt to be an unduly restricted intellectual framework in favour of the study of modern history, influenced by the view of his brother-in-law, the historian F. W. Maitland, that 'No one should teach philosophy at a university unless he either thinks he has it in him to make a system of his own or is zealous to preach the system of another'. Instead, Fisher went to Paris and then to Göttingen to educate himself in European history, returning in 1889 to the Fellowship in Modern History at New College. As well as teaching across the whole range of European history and political economy—working long hours to keep himself one step ahead of his students—he began to establish a reputation as a brilliant scholar, publishing influential works on Napoleon Bonaparte, the Republican Tradition in

Europe, Medieval Empire, and a definitive History of Europe in the Cambridge Modern History series.

Beyond his academic work, Fisher maintained a strong commitment to public service and to education. In 1912, he was appointed to the Indian Public Service Commission, and took up the Vice Chancellorship of Sheffield University. In 1916, he was appointed to Lloyd George's coalition government, in which he became a cabinet member as Secretary of State for Education, and became an MP. In his ministerial role he showed outstanding political acumen and vision, particularly for someone with no previous experience of government. Bargaining hard for the resources which he believed to be necessary to the proper development of public education, and showing great resourcefulness in dealing with the many groups whose interests his reforms affected, he designed and stewarded through the parliamentary process of the Education Act of 1918. This reforming legislation improved pay and conditions for teachers, widened the curriculum, and significantly expanded access to public education, not least by raising the school leaving age. A confirmed liberal with a strong commitment to broadening access to all levels of education for the working classes and for women, his ambition was to expand secondary education from its ambit of 30,000 boys to embrace no fewer than 600,000 boys and girls. Influenced by his experience at the relatively new University of Sheffield, he also worked to secure government funding for student grants and for the universities while preserving their academic independence. He remained in government until 1922, acting as a British representative to the League of Nations and exerting some influence on Irish and Indian policy.

When, in 1925, Fisher was elected Warden of New College, he therefore —unlike his predecessors—brought to this role a broad experience of the world outside Oxford, as well as a keen perception of the parochial quality of New College in his days as a student and young Fellow. Though the religious restrictions which had confined access to New College to Anglican Wykehamists had been swept aside in the 1870s, the aura of New College as a 'little Wykehamical seminary' had persisted. This Fisher was determined to change. He was a tall, distinguished, socially accomplished, though rather mirthless figure, who combined his work as Warden with a governorship of the BBC, the Presidencies of the British Academy and the London Library, Trusteeships of the British Museum and of Rhodes House, and the Principalship of the City of London Vacation Courses for Teachers. He also founded the Oxford Preservation Trust and worked tirelessly on a number of other causes close to his liberal conscience, including the admission of women to degrees at Oxford.

This welter of demanding activities led one of the Fellows to joke in future years that 'Warden Fisher came to us from higher circles, and one sometimes had the feeling about him that he was only lent to the college'. But Fisher's influence within the four walls of New College was considerable, and the atmosphere which he created gave students like Herbert a lasting sense that New College had been a distinctively exciting place to be. Enjoying the regard which his public and scholarly reputation commanded, and which his powers as a raconteur fostered (he was famous for opening a conversation with phrases like 'As Lloyd George once said to me', and 'When I was in the Cabinet'), Fisher gathered around himself a group of what he took to be the brightest undergraduates, and saw to it that they were introduced to the influential people to whom his family and political experience had given him access. As an occasional member of this favoured group, Herbert recalled frequent walks and lively discussions with Fisher and Sunday tea parties at which he met leading figures of the day including Virginia Woolf and Lloyd George. Fisher's regard for Herbert (as well as a certain worldliness) is attested in his warm letter of congratulation in 1929: 'Though it was very difficult to believe that you would fail of the highest honours, accidents do sometimes happen and it is pleasant to have this success registered in black and white.'

In the 1920s, it was not uncommon for undergraduates who could afford it to order meals from the chef to be delivered to their rooms, and to entertain not only students but also Fellows to lunch. With the help of an allowance of £150 a year from his father to supplement his scholarship, Herbert was a member of this privileged group. One such occasion of social life across the Junior and Senior Common Room divide provides the only occasion Herbert ever encountered—or admitted to having encountered— overt anti-Semitism during his student days in Oxford. He had invited a South African Rhodes Scholar to lunch with Christopher Cox. The conversation turned to racial politics in South Africa, and the Afrikaner student (Herbert later wondered why he had invited him, and speculated that it was because of his good looks!) declared that he hated Blacks, but that he would rather sit down to lunch with a Black than with a Jew. Herbert replied that he was sitting down to lunch with a Jew. In confusion, the South African student left; he later wrote a note of apology, but their friendship was over. When Herbert recounted the story in later years, it was more with a sense of empathy for the other student's embarrassment than with any personal rancour. His description of this student as 'an innocent person' reveals the deep rationalism which led him, at least in the first instance, to attribute prejudice to ignorance rather than malice.

Given what we know of social relations in Britain generally and Oxford in particular at the time, it is implausible that Herbert should have encountered so little anti-Semitic prejudice. In the mid-1920s, there were only about 40 Jews among over 4,000 students at Oxford. By coincidence, one of them was Julius Stone: an exact contemporary of Herbert's, a fellow Yorkshireman, and also destined to become a famous legal theorist. There, however, the similarities end. Stone's family were first generation immigrants to Leeds, where his father established a reasonably successful cabinet-making business. But the family's financial and social position was markedly less privileged than that of the Harts: Stone's father never learnt to write English; the family were not well off financially and lived in the working-class Jewish Leylands district of Leeds. In this context, little value was placed on education, and Stone worked exceptionally hard in an inhospitable environment for the academic success which earned him the State and other scholarships which just made it possible for him to come to Exeter College, Oxford to study history in 1925.

The humiliations which lay in store for a student with inadequate financial resources are vividly captured in Stone's experience. On arriving at the college with his father, he was told that £25 'caution money' was required in addition to the fees. This was not a trivial amount: it represented one-seventh of the total amount which the college calculated would be necessary to cover a student's maintenance for a whole year. Father and son had to travel to London to raise the money with the help of relatives. Stone suffered embarrassment throughout his student career because he constantly had to ask his 'scout' for the cheapest food on offer; and he was excluded from a large number of societies and social occasions because he did not have the requisite money or formal clothing. It was, however, anti-Semitism as well as shortage of money and the class snobbery of Oxford which made Stone's undergraduate days so lonely and so miserable, and he resented it bitterly. (In a fascinating symptom of his own ambivalence, Stone nonetheless kept his Exeter College shield on his desk for the rest of his life.) One of only two Jewish students at Exeter, he suffered regular verbal taunts in the Junior Common Room and was enraged by the anti-Semitic tone of student publications such as Isis. A class dimension was also in issue. Even the Jewish students' society, the Adler Society, struck him as exclusive, and he preferred to put his energies into the Inter-University Jewish Federation of Great Britain and Northern Ireland—an organization which his Oxford contemporaries appear to have regarded with a supreme lack of interest.

It is not surprising that Herbert, with the strong distaste for even elective group-identification demonstrated by his reaction to the Jewish house at Cheltenham, did not participate in either of these societies. But it is interesting to speculate on the differences between his and Stone's backgrounds which underscored their experiences of Oxford. It undoubtedly had as much to do with class and wealth as with their Jewish identity. Herbert's own narrative in later life makes it clear that his experience of New College was shaped more by the fact of being a grammar school boy than by being Jewish; and that his relative wealth allowed him to make contacts and engage in activities which reduced the importance of his background in the eyes of his peers. Many of them did not even realize that he was Jewish. In the anecdote already described, the revelation of the South African student's anti-Semitism was born precisely of his ignorance that Herbert was a Jew. And in a letter written by Joseph in 1930 recommending Herbert for a research post at another college, after speaking in glowing terms of his modesty and his ability, his gift for languages, 'his merits of character and intellect—one of the intellectual leaders of the college, a friend of very various sorts of people', Joseph continued; 'I may add that I did not discover for some time the fact of his being a Jew. He hardly looks it: he doesn't parade it: he doesn't conceal it: he knows, I think, some Hebrew, and is interested in the thought of his own people. He kept in with the others of his people here; he equally easily kept in with those who were Christians'. One wonders with what ambivalence Herbert read this passage (and indeed how this letter came to be among his personal papers).

Herbert's predisposition, then, was to assimilate to the dominant culture, while also to be judged as an individual rather than as a member of a group. His educational and social background, along with his comparative wealth, allowed him to do this with ease. Money, in this context as in others, was a medium which helped people who would otherwise have been on the receiving end of overt discrimination to avoid or transcend it. But this predisposition also involved a measure of denial. Jews were specifically excluded from many Oxford clubs of the time, and it is highly unlikely that Herbert really avoided encountering any such barriers in his three years at Oxford. Stone's sensibility to, and Herbert's capacity to avoid or ignore, anti-Semitism in Oxford were shaped by their particular life experiences: Herbert's as a Jew in a well-to-do family in affluent, peaceful Harrogate; Stone's in a working-class family in Leeds, where the crucibles of economic need and inter-ethnic conflict fostered the development of a far stronger sense of group identity and solidarity. Years later when, by another quirk of fate, Stone and Herbert coincided as visiting professors at Harvard, Herbert recorded in his diary a visit to tea with Stone and his wife: 'Oh how I know that atmosphere: Leeds Jewish.' The phrase is redolent with distaste: this was a world which Herbert knew from his far more Jewish-identified Leeds cousins, and of which he wanted no part.

One other aspect of Stone's experience in Oxford highlights a further feature of the undergraduate scene of the mid-1920s: it was strikingly apolitical. In this respect Oxford appears to have been somewhat different from

Cambridge. One of the starkest political events of the decade was the General Strike of 1926. In Cambridge, the strike was supported by a substantial group of students, including members of the future Cambridge communist circle. By comparison, the response in Oxford was pale. It was not until the 1930s that any substantial degree of political consciousness infused the student body. This was an era in which the memory of the horrors of the First World War had receded, while the dangers of a second world war were not yet on the horizon: it was a time in which student hedonism could flourish. Stone, as one of a tiny number of Oxford undergraduates of the time whose early life had given him any sense of class consciousness or of the injustices of industrial capitalism unmitigated by a welfare state, was also one of the few students who supported the strike and refused to break it. Another was Hugh Gaitskell. Herbert remembered Gaitskell as the only student he knew who supported the strike—and indeed the only one of the group of future Labour politicians at New College to be a member of the Labour Club. While Jay listened avidly to radio coverage of the 1929 election in the hope of a Labour victory, he kept his political commitment to himself. When Jay said goodnight to the sombre Dr. Poole, a New College Fellow who had allowed him to listen to his radio, the latter replied: 'See you in the morning if our throats are not cut first.'

This was in contrast to the political culture which Herbert's future wife, Jenifer Williams, would encounter as an undergraduate at Somerville College only six years later. Admittedly, with a father who was an influential international lawyer, politics and public affairs had been a far more important part of her family's consciousness than of Herbert's: among her earliest memories were being taken by her parents to watch the Armistice celebrations in 1919 and to visit the First World War cemeteries in northern France. She was also acutely conscious of the widespread poverty which scarred early twentieth-century England. Nonetheless, her own account of her Oxford days, with visits to centres organized by the Women's University Settlement movement, in which students worked to help the poor, and a spreading socialist consciousness nurtured by increasing discomfort at political developments in Europe, sketches not only a different personal attitude but also a very different context from that which Herbert experienced in the late 1920s. At that time, most students were unreflectively conservative or, like Herbert, thought of themselves as liberals. But even this more reflective group was, in Herbert's memory, only dimly aware of political facts as brute as the number of unemployed.

As well as smoothing the development of his social relationships at New College, Herbert's fortunate financial position allowed him to continue to broaden his cultural horizons by travelling extensively in Europe during his vacations. His wealth was modest by many people's standards: in the letter referred to above, Joseph, in a judgment which would have outraged Stone, described Herbert's vacation travels as 'rough and cheap and adventurous', Herbert being 'a poor man'. While Herbert would have been surprised to be considered poor, his travel diaries certainly attest to the roughness, if not the cheapness, of his journeys. Often travelling with Bill Wentworth, Herbert's diaries record ambitious itineraries across France, Switzerland, Germany, Austria, Hungary, Yugoslavia, Bulgaria, Czechoslovakia, and Greece. One 'Tour en Bicyclette' in July and August 1927 took him through France, Italy, and Austria, his progress interrupted by a substantial complement of punctures and collisions as well as by large quantities of food and drink. Like the 1926 diary, this notebook evinces a palpable love of both countryside and architecture: at Chartres the 'glass [is] like embroidery' and the cathedral 'wonderful'; 'completely degenerate gothic architecture fulfilling all Ruskin's vetoed principles as to flying buttresses etc'; at Bourges 'where we constitute the object of admiration—or rather pity—of all the Bourgeois', 'soft green woods and orchards were sprinkled with poppies and purple blossoms'. Such lyrical descriptions of buildings and scenery were teamed with pretty ink sketches and with affectionate vignettes of encounters with landlords and landladies, and matched by enthusiastic details of food and wine: drink was 'plentiful' but expensive—suggesting that Herbert and his companions were treating themselves to some good wine. Nor was the energetic pursuit of cultural stimulation untempered by a little human laziness and over-indulgence: on one occasion, Herbert began a day of 'energetic sightseeing at the early hour of 12'.

In the late summer after Herbert's graduation in 1929, the bicycles were temporarily abandoned in favour of a trip by car and train reaching through central Europe to Greece. In September, Herbert wrote to Christopher Cox from Budapest:

Dear Cox,

This note I write in a bathing costume in the palatial open air swimming baths of the municipal hotel. It has artificial waves and we sink deep into . . . luxury after a stormy trip of 5 days from Calais: Tomorrow we leave . . . and hope to be in Belgrade . . . then we go to . . . [Salonika and Athens]. At least we hope so, but the roads have all been washed away. We drive or have driven so far at a terrible pace though W[entworth] is an extremely good driver and a considerable mechanic as well.

The car, however, proved less reliable than the bicycle as a mode of transport, overheating, getting stuck in mud, and needing to be baled out in various ways with humorous regularity (the baling out being provided as often by shepherds as by mechanics). In Greece, wheels were occasionally abandoned in favour of mules and horses, which turned out to be no less temperamental. Once again, an ironic commentary on the vicissitudes of weather, hotel hygiene, food, and ferry timetables sits along side a fresh, sometimes even breathless, account of temples and towns, mountains and oceans. Only occasionally, amid breakdowns, strict border controls occasioned by a kidnapping (of two members of the Turkish parliament in 1929) and other setbacks does the light voice rise in tones of anxiety. The anxious moments are often related to health, as in the case of Herbert's fear that his South African companion Hill might have caught typhoid. In this instance, though Hill turned out only to have a cold, a local epidemic provided a real basis for the worry. But these entries are a precursor of Herbert's later tendency to become preoccupied by his own health.

In southern Europe, the reserve of Herbert's English persona was thrown off. Throughout his life, photographs of holidays abroad show him particularly relaxed and animated. Notwithstanding his special feel for the English countryside, he exulted in the radiant light, balmy warmth, and vibrant public life of the South. Like Henry James—whose novels held a special place in his estimation, and whose capacity to combine acute and sympathetic observation with an exquisite detachment from his characters' stories share something with Herbert's own approach to personal relationships—he was drawn not only to the warmth and exuberance but also to a sense of the mystery and authenticity of Europe. And on these trips he continued to deepen his understanding of European culture. To a degree which was unusual for him, the aesthetic and the intellectual were in this context entwined with one another. In a later personal memoir, he wrote of Jerusalem, Istanbul, Athens, and Rome as the four cities which had made our culture what it was: without them 'life for me at any rate would be a howling wilderness'.

During both term time and these trips abroad, Herbert wrote with remarkable regularity to his parents, and these letters give fresh insight into his personality and his relationship with his family. Both the frequency and the tone of the letters reveal a close family bound together by dense family routines: Herbert's two brothers were his companions on several of his continental trips, including the one to Greece. The letters also show that—although he was sometimes a little embarrassed at doing so, or shamefaced about his liberal spending—he felt free throughout his undergraduate years to call on his parents for money: his mother seems to have spent a considerable part of her time wiring contributions of £5 or £10 to Herbert, 'Poste Restante' around Europe. In this context, Herbert was also willing to acknowledge that New College was indeed one of the most expensive in Oxford. He was, however, supplementing scholarship and allowance with quite substantial fees for writing articles, including one on Sir Walter Raleigh accepted by *The Nineteenth Century* in September 1927, for which he was paid £7.

The letters home—often referred to by Herbert as 'Megillahs', a slang Yiddish usage of an Old Testament term, the slang denoting a long, tedious, or complicated story—reflect a strong and frequently articulated consciousness of Jewish identity. On his arrival at New College, Herbert immediately wrote to tell his parents about the other Jews among the students. The letter referred to a Jewish second-year student, evidently known to his parents, who was described, in an observation which suggests a sensitivity to stereotypes of Jewish behaviour, as 'thoroughly objectionable . . . pushing himself forward into everything'. In his anxiety to assimilate, Herbert risked internalizing the very snobbery and prejudice which, at an intellectual level, he rejected so firmly. In such contrasts between Herbert Hart's feelings and his public persona lay the origins of a form of repression which was to reap many professional rewards, yet impose many personal costs, in the next two decades of his life.

CHAPTER 3

Success Snatched from Defeat: London and the Bar

BY the time of his graduation, Herbert had already planned his next step and was making preparations to qualify as a barrister. His legal aspirations had been encouraged by the fact that the family had relatives—notably a cousin of Herbert's, Louis, known as 'Boy' Hart—already in legal practice in London. His determination to practise law was formed well before he went to Oxford. He had discussed the idea with his father, who viewed with satisfaction the prospect of his gifted son embarking on precisely the sort of professional career which he had envisaged when he sent Herbert to Cheltenham.

In this period, the Bar provided nothing in the way of formal training: it was simply a matter of equipping oneself with the knowledge necessary to pass the entry examinations. But from the very beginning of his student career, Herbert had entertained an ambition to follow up his classics degree with an undergraduate degree in law based on just one further year's study. Spurred on by his brilliant success in his finals, and by the story of another student who had gained a First in a year, Herbert set out to match this achievement. He began to study with New College's Law Fellow, C. A. W. Manning, an eccentric but excellent tutor; 'a South African who believed in apartheid' but who was 'otherwise . . . very nice', as Herbert later put it. In those days, university legal education in England was still relatively limited, and despite Manning's interest in legal theory, Herbert's tutorial education amounted almost exclusively to learning the ropes of legal reasoning by immersing himself in cases. Half way through the year, he realized that he was not going to be able to get a First. So he gave up the idea of sitting law finals and opted instead for the more modest option of passing the two sets of Bar exams. The first stage of this he achieved with apparent ease: in December 1930 he wrote to Christopher Cox: 'I did the Bar exams on Thursday. They were very easy.'

His refusal to contemplate achieving anything other than first class marks gives a sense of the exceptionally high standards which Herbert set for himself. But it was also born of the fact that, despite his resolve to go to the Bar, he was far from having abandoned his academic aspirations at Oxford. His reputation as an outstanding intellect had already brought him the offer of a lectureship in philosophy at Jesus College only months after his graduation. But his sights were set higher still. In 1929 he entered the Prize Fellowship competition at All Souls, the University's only college devoted exclusively to research. Herbert's preparations for the exam were disrupted by delays on his European holiday with Wentworth, as he confided to Cox in a letter from Budapest:

The date of the All Souls is a nuisance—October 8th; it cuts off a week and we were already late in starting as Wentworth had to have his tonsils out . . . . I have scarcely had time to look at any Medieval History so I expect it will be rather a farce.

Joseph, Smith, Fisher, and Cox were nonetheless confident of his chances. Their estimation of him is vividly reflected in their testimonials. To Fisher he was a man of 'first rate ability and excellent character'; to Cox he was 'a man of outstanding ability, who is one of the two, or three, ablest Greats men among a rather unusually large number of able men whose work I have seen in the last few years . . . . A rapid and powerful mind, with admirable judgment and a wide range of learning . . . . He would have been a really strong candidate for an Oxford Fellowship in either Ancient History or Philosophy . . . a man of industry and determination, of high character, and greatly liked . . . by all who know him'. His student contemporaries were no less confident: his friend Duff Dunbar wrote that 'it would be monstrous if you were refused what you thoroughly deserve'. Refused, however, he was.

After this lack of success in 1929, when Herbert was judged as a history candidate, all of his referees hoped and expected that he would be successful the following year as a lawyer. They poured out touching letters of encouragement and support; letters which illuminate Herbert's particular impact on his tutors. As Joseph put it, 'I am very sorry you aren't keeping [John] Sparrow [another New College candidate who was elected to All Souls that year] company but . . . I have great hopes you may be successful next year. I am sure you oughtn't to be downcast, so far as the future is concerned, by this non-success'. In similar vein, Fisher assured him that 'you showed next to those who were chosen. It is much hoped that you will come in again next year as a lawyer when you will find a strong predisposition in your success'.

When, at the end of a year during which he studied hard while supporting himself by teaching English, French, and even Scripture to public schoolboys at Rugby, he was rejected a second time, the disappointment was acute. Joseph, acknowledging Herbert's characteristically self-protective stance, sympathized:

I'm very sorry you were not successful: though I know you had discounted the disappointment. But it won't alter the opinion of your friends . . . that you have every prospect of doing well at the Bar—and I hope on the Bench. I wish you'd had the help of the Fellowship; but I shan't mind so much provided you don't lose heart at all because of it.

It was Cox to whom Herbert was most explicit about his reaction to these rejections. Though blaming himself for not having given adequate advice, Cox had still not given up hope of persuading Herbert to try a third time: he wrote 'I do *blast* myself for not having known before that the A.S. lawyers really were very searching and expected a lot of law: for the obvious thing would have been for you to go in next year. (Which you cld still do)'.

But Herbert was not to be persuaded:

The morning of the day before the A.S. exam, I had decided to postpone it for a year, but at the end of my long walk over Cumnor . . . I felt so braced that I put my earlier decision down to panic, or couldn't summon up the courage to withdraw. I don't suppose it would have made an atom of difference and I should have been bored to have to carry on with the academic side of law (Roman law etc) for another year. Anyhow wild horses won't drag me to that exam again!!! Of course what I should really have done was to have spent the year on history.

Such competitions across the disciplines are inevitably unpredictable, and Herbert could have rationalized his rejection in some such terms. But references in later letters to a 'breakdown' at the time of the first failure show that he took it very hard. Years later, Herbert described to a colleague an incident which reveals just how wound up he had been about the All Souls experience. At the formal dinner to which candidates were invited, Herbert dropped a piece of cutlery, shattering a beautiful dessert plate. As he looked in horror at the fragments, he was shocked to hear someone laughing hysterically. A split second later, he realized that the laughter was coming from his own mouth.

One of Cox's testimonials implies that Herbert's parents' financial situation had once again deteriorated; financial support for the precarious early years at the Bar (the Fellowship had a stipend of £300 a year for two years, as well as providing some board and lodging) was therefore one important source of anxiety. But Herbert's keeping the warm letters of commiseration and support from his referees is testimony to the fact that it was his intellectual *amour propre* and the frustrated desire to attain a position of status within Oxford's academic hierarchy which really stung. His sense of himself was already strongly bound up with intellectual success, and Herbert's first taste of failure was bitter. In interviews later in life, though straightforward if asked about it, he rarely volunteered the fact that he had twice attempted All Souls; missing out on this ultimate mark of Oxford insider-dom remained a tender spot. The difficulty was exacerbated by the fact that some of his most valued friends—Douglas Jay, his direct competitor in 1930, Richard Wilberforce and Isaiah Berlin, both elected in 1932—were successful, and that two of the philosophers whom he most admired (and later worked with)—J. L. Austin and Stuart Hampshire—had been Prize Fellows in their time. Though Herbert's reaction to Jay's success was generous, his feelings of insecurity are palpable in his correspondence with Cox:

I'm frightfully glad about Douglas and had long previously experienced and got over any disappointment . . . . There only remains one question for you to help me to decide and that is this—do you think my performance at A.S. was sufficiently bad in law

(1) as not to warrant my being a lawyer

or/and

(2) to make it unlikely that I should obtain or be fitted to take any job Radcliffe might have to offer?

I know these queries sound like the promptings of panic and perhaps they should be discounted as such straight away (I confess they have only occurred to me in such definite shape since I obtained a book of bar exam papers to look at—I see myself getting a 3rd which tho' it doesn't matter probably as far as practice goes it might not do me much good with Radcliffe.)

A further letter five days later indicates just how badly he had taken the first rejection:

Sorry to have disturbed you by my insane mutterings. I am quite alright really—not at all like this time last year—in spite of a certain anxiety in the best of physical and psychological health.

The obligations of a Prize Fellowship being flexible, the All Souls post would have been consistent with Herbert's pursuit of his legal career. His divided feelings at the time are reflected in the fact that in 1930 Joseph, Fisher, and Cox were also writing him testimonials for a research post at Magdalen, while Cox was corresponding with him about the possibility of philosophy fellowships at Corpus Christi and Queens' Colleges. But with the All Souls disappointment behind him, Herbert ultimately decided against pursuing these other options. He headed for London and joined the Middle Temple, which awarded him a Harmsworth Scholarship. Exchanging the cloistered academic elite of Oxford for the less cloistered but certainly no less elite or male environment of the Inns of Court, Herbert prepared to throw himself into all that life as a London lawyer had to offer.

At the beginning of 1931, reading in the Temple library and 'buttering up solicitor relations', he was also meeting up again with 'a New College clique . . . Richard [Wilberforce], Duff [Dunbar] . . . and John Sparrow, of whom I'm afraid I shall never learn [not] to be mildly jealous. In his own peculiar way he reeks success as much as any wealthy profiteer tho' I mean that as a compliment and not as an insult', he told Cox. But life was not all work. The summer after his final degree exams, Herbert had learned to ride, and in 1931 he joined the Cavalry Squadron of the Territorial Army's Inns of Court Regiment so as to be able to indulge this taste in spite of his limited budget. Membership allowed him to ride each Friday evening and one Sunday a month. The decision, however, led to an accident which disrupted the start of his legal career. He was kicked by a horse, his leg was badly broken, and February 1931 saw him strung up on weights and pulleys in a military hospital in Aldershot, where he was bedridden for nearly two months. In considerable pain and frequently bored, Herbert tried to lighten his gloom and frustration by reading and listening to John Sparrow's amusing radio broadcasts. But an additional problem was that he found himself suddenly extracted from the privileged intellectual circles to which he had grown accustomed, and his ironic sketches of life in hospital for Christopher Cox reveal a somewhat dismissive attitude to his fellow-patients:

They [the other patients] writhe under their crossword puzzles as one writhed under a Joseph tutorial and the incautious speed with which I solved certain 'clues' made me suspect at once so I have ballasted myself with some impure jokes and Rugger talk . . .

The two men had now established a close friendship, each confiding to the other their intermittent struggles to overcome depression: Herbert joked to Cox that Joseph's kind letters had 'twice arrived at my most suicidal moments and induced me to lay aside the razor blade'. His recovery was slow, complicated by his contracting acute German measles and by a series of abscesses, and his stay in hospital dragged on into the early summer. As the discomfort subsided, he occupied himself by studying law, in the hope of being able at last to achieve his goal of gaining an academic qualification in law by sitting for the BCL postgraduate degree in Oxford. Once again his ambition was thwarted: his eventual discharge from hospital came only 10 days before the BCL exams, prompting him to remark to Cox that 'my efforts to get a law degree at Oxford seem doomed'. Instead, he was anticipating with some impatience a period of fussed-over convalescence at home in Harrogate. The tensions of family life were aggravated by his father's own ill health following an operation, which had made him 'more grim and dejected than I've ever known him and induced the most awful series of tempers'. By the autumn, Herbert was ready definitively to fly the nest. After returning to London for a further period of study, he sat the second set of Bar exams, and was called to the Bar in January 1932. He viewed the rite of passage from his usual ironic stance, describing it to Cox as an 'expensive and probably disastrous step', though assuring him that 'I look very striking in a wig and gown'.

Though the Bar was yet more socially exclusive and significantly less meritocratic than it is today, the early stages of practice in the 1930s were no less precarious. Herbert was fortunate in that, in spite of some early bouts of nerves over court appearances, his practice took off relatively quickly: just a few days after being called to the Bar he had already earned '2 guineas by writing an opinion on somebody's marriage settlement'. But with only a modest annual income of £150 from his father, he needed to supplement his earnings when first at the Bar. This he did by taking on occasional pieces of journalism in the form of reviews or travel writing for *John o' London's* weekly and, in 1932, by coaching fellow lawyer John Venning's classicist son for his Finals. (It was a task for which he earned £30 and a piece of advice: Venning suggested that his practice would be enhanced if he could rid himself of any vestiges of a Yorkshire accent. Herbert took the advice seriously enough to subject himself to elocution lessons.) Within a couple of years, he was able to support himself without too much difficulty. In later life, he attributed his relatively swift success to the fact that his pupillage—at 6 New Court, Lincoln's Inn—was with Wilfred Hunt, the busiest junior barrister in the chambers. Hunt was a remarkable character with an extraordinary taste for work. As Wilberforce recalled:

He would arrive at chambers at 9 a.m., work through the day, go home at 6.30, dine (modestly), sleep till 12, work from 12 till 4 a.m., sleep from 4 a.m. till 7 a.m., and the day would start again. This meant that each morning he would bring in 6–10 sets of papers with his work upon them . . . so that the pupils had to come early to study the work before it was sent out.

But early starts at Chambers were not the most extreme challenge of life as Hunt's pupil: in Herbert's experience, it not infrequently featured trips to Hunt's home to work with him between midnight and the small hours of the morning. This was a man who enjoyed teaching his pupils and who had plenty of work to pass on to younger colleagues who, like Herbert, worked casually—'devilled'—for him for a few months before taking up tenancies of their own. During Herbert's time devilling, Hunt was taken ill, so Herbert received both more and higher quality work than he could otherwise have expected. Reflecting later on his early success, he also cited the fact that his cousin, a 'go-ahead solicitor', was able to pass him work.

Herbert's Oxford and other connections would have helped in finding him his initial pupillage and perhaps in passing him a certain amount of work. But it was his reputation and skill which gained him his tenancy in such prestigious chambers. The tenancy was, Herbert immediately realized, a decisive advance. As he wrote to Cox:

[I]t is now settled that I shall stay on here which is really an enormous coup for me. My conscience is rather uneasy as to how far I've done down Richard [Wilberforce, a fellow pupil and competitor for the tenancy] but I try hard not to think about that. After all he is a person preeminently able to look after himself. Venning tells me staying here is worth a fortune.

At 6 New Court, where his colleagues included the future Court of Appeal judge Charles Eustace Harman, Herbert specialized in preparing construction summonses relating to trusts, wills, contracts, and even legislation. This was detailed, exacting work requiring meticulous precision and logic, and his education at the hands of Joseph was a superb preparation. His modesty significantly downplayed his outstanding talent for this kind of legal analysis and advocacy. Three of his Oxford contemporaries—the future House of Lords judge Richard Wilberforce, Duff Dunbar, and John Sparrow (later to be Warden of All Souls)—were also establishing careers at the Bar during this period. It is generally acknowledged that, while all were brilliant lawyers, Herbert was the most gifted of the four. In a chance encounter with a famous barrister in a Cornish hotel in the late 1940s, Stuart Hampshire was told that Herbert had been 'by far the most talented man at the Chancery Bar', and that his decision to leave was at once 'a tragic loss to the profession' and—in a word which perhaps represents an aspect of the professional ethos which Herbert later wanted to escape—'a betrayal'. An (undated) letter from a colleague or client which he kept among his papers gives a sense of his gifts as an advocate:

Before the Judgment I wish to congratulate you; I certainly was astounded at your elloquence [sic] and the very excelent [sic] way in which you made your judges take notice and listen to your submissions: the most difficult way to argue in but they liked it, one could see . . . . I cannot thank you enough for the strength and effort you supported your arguments with (especially knowing your inside feelings!) which have made me feel that we have won. What a win *for you*! . . . . P.S. Please will you collect your wine decanter [a mark of appreciation] before the bailiff gets it!

After the bruising and novel experience of failure at All Souls, this kind of admiration must have given him enormous pleasure—a pleasure which one hopes was not too much diminished by the spelling mistakes which, with typical intellectual precision, Herbert marked on the letter.

As this letter reveals, Herbert felt some ambivalence about his work at the Bar. His was a wide-ranging chancery practice, encompassing conveyancing, wills, and family settlements, and, increasingly, taxation issues—particularly about death duties—arising out of these fields. By the time his practice was disrupted by the war, it was some years since he had touched anything as basic as conveyancing, and most of his practice was high level advisory or court work. It was relentlessly demanding. The chambers were 'crammed with briefs' and, caught in a 'bloody grind', Herbert often found himself obliged to work until the early hours of the morning—a necessity which brought in its wake a crisis of domestic organization which he sketched for Cox:

Curiously, it is not the state of my correspondence or room which reflects my inability to manage things when hard worked but the state of my clothes . . . . Thousands of dirty shirts, collars, pants wait to be collected and sent to the laundry while I buy unnecessary new ones each day!

Herbert was the last person to shirk hard work, but the pressure and irregular lifestyle gradually took a toll. In 1934 he began to feel odd sensations around his heart. He consulted a doctor, who diagnosed a slight heart murmur and prescribed a more regular style of living which would help Herbert to cope with the inevitable overwork with less stress. 'The Dr. said "Get married!" but a flat's easier!', Herbert told Cox, for whom he also caricatured the ponderous legal style, describing his heart murmur as:

[A] symptom . . . which has nothing to do with the matters discussed in the next 3pp hereof but one which with the doctor's diagnosis relates to the same or dealt with on pp 5–7 hereof (that's how I speak in court).

It was not just the pomposity of legal culture which Herbert found uncongenial. Although he found the work stimulating and his colleagues pleasant, as he became more experienced, he began to feel that legal practice did not command his deep intellectual interest. Richard Wilberforce, to whom he became increasingly close during their early years at the Bar, remembered Herbert as 'loving the intellectual demands', being 'strongly competitive'; and liking 'winning and earning money'; someone who was not 'an establishment man' but who enjoyed being 'a new man'. This was almost certainly true in the years when the challenge of building up his practice was still ahead of him. By 1936, the metamorphosis from northern grammar school boy to successful London lawyer was complete: Isaiah Berlin was able to describe Herbert as 'one of our most prosperous friends' and Wilberforce remembered Herbert as:

getting work, making money, enjoying new prosperity, making his way into new circles—he was enthusiastic about the culture of public schools, especially of Winchester, and had acquired so great a knowledge of its customs, conventions, 'notions' and styles of thought that I often thought of him as an honorary Wykehamist . . .

By 1937, however, his close friend, Douglas Jay, in whose Hampstead house he had lived for some time in 1932, had the strong impression that he was not entirely comfortable with his chosen career.

Nor was the ambivalence solely intellectual. As his cases became more valuable, he found himself spending an increasing proportion of his time working for wealthy clients, the merits of whose claims did not command the conviction of his 'inside feelings'. One factor which was at play here was his quite extraordinary degree of personal honesty: though his legal skills were more than adequate to see him through a case in which he did not truly believe, he was a man who would have felt that this was at some level a betrayal of his integrity or even a form of self-violence. An equally important factor was his changing political outlook, which was moving leftwards, shaped by both his closest personal relationships and the political environment in Europe. At Douglas Jay's instigation, Herbert had begun to give occasional seminars to Labour Party groups advising on how to close the legal loopholes which allowed tax evasion. In political as in other matters, however, his feelings were marked by ambivalence, and among his letters to his left-wing future wife, Jenifer, in the late 1930s, references to 'sordidly making money' are interspersed with a very different attitude. When his friends Douglas Jay and Tommy Balogh convinced him that a majority of the Cabinet were moving towards war, he exclaimed 'This buggering war looks pretty inevitable now—I have some extraordinarily interesting cases which it will interrupt—damn it!'

Herbert's ambivalence about his work at the Bar was matched by a striking variety in his social life; a variety which he had not managed to integrate with a stable sense of himself as a person. Many of his academic colleagues were amazed when, among the memoirs produced after his death, they read Richard Wilberforce's account of Herbert's life in London in the 1930s. By this time, the two men had become close friends, meeting regularly at the theatre or ballet. Wilberforce recalled with affection Herbert's 'ability to extract amusement of high value, from low situations', and remembered that:

His great quality, which made him so specially dear to me, was intense curiosity about all varieties of life—the more special, or even comic, the better—and he was wonderfully good at getting specialists and 'characters' to talk about their niches and he to retain these and recall them for friends' delectations. He had, in addition, a first-class mind—logical and philosophical, with vast tenacity in pursuit of the truth . . . and strong convictions and values. It took some time . . . before he really accepted me with my lazier mind and often ambivalent feelings, but by 1935 we had no reserves to our friendship.

Though more work-oriented and high-minded than Wilberforce himself, Herbert had—and relished—an affluent metropolitan lifestyle. This was his first taste of life outside both family and institution, and his first encounter with a social world which included women, though in the first half of the decade his friends and acquaintances were mainly men. His social life included a generous helping of the cultural and social activities which his past tastes would have led one to predict: concerts, ballets, theatres, operas, intellectual debates, and meals at good restaurants. It also involved a wide range of reading—Baudelaire, Ivy Compton Burnett, Darwin, Balzac's 'mad pages', Trollope (whose 'superbly drawn' Mrs. Proudie 'justified or excused much boring matter', and whom he parodied exquisitely), Thackeray, Tolstoy, E. M. Forster, James Joyce, and Henry James among many others. And Herbert's life continued to include regular trips abroad, which nourished not only his taste for new sights but also his friendships.

But alongside these continuations of old patterns, Herbert's life also involved less expected diversions. These included a variety of sports—cricket, squash, and (notwithstanding the infamous Hart clumsiness, which led to a number of mishaps on the slopes) skiing—all of which had apparently escaped the opprobrium which Herbert attached to 'hearty' public school life. More surprisingly, it also included fox- and stag-hunting during weekend trips to the country to visit friends or colleagues. A letter to Jenifer in 1937 gives a flavour of these country weekends, and of the mixed feelings with which Herbert regarded them:

I have just returned from a loyal holiday with the Upper Classes. Coronation day began with a visit to the village church, where we saw a mob of Girl Guides receive the Union Jack at the Altar Steps and grasp it orgiastically as if it were (as it was) a phallic symbol. Then a visit to the Poor and then a champagne lunch, with toasts. In the afternoon village sports where I poured out lemonade—mostly on the drinkers' shoes, a wonderful speech was made to the children by the Church: 'Try to carry out the Great Work we have begun. Always remember your King'. Finally we gathered—all 500 of us—round an elm tree to listen to the King's speech. The most bizarre sight was the district nurse standing to attention—with tears in her eyes but also a cigarette in her mouth! My host was the oddest study. Apparently witless 6ft 3 and handsome, Squire and Territorial Army but a library full of books . . . . Not only read but minutely annotated. Lovely Regency House and garden in the middle of Somerset. A horse for me. Delicious food and drink. I can hardly survive.

Not to be outdone, Jenifer responded in kind:

Don't talk to me about loyalty: I had to stand up five times in my own drawing room when God Save the King was played over the wireless, though admittedly dispensation was allowed when it was virulently sung by a tremoloing soprano.

When and when is not God Save the King the genuine article? Surely an interesting point of law. But I shall never be good at dissembling: Mother said I did not look reverent enough when the old fool was taking the sacrament, and the village blacksmith said he thought I was at heart 'Republican', even after I had played ping pong in the sports and assisted a grimy child with her cream bun.

In Herbert's letter, gentle sarcasm (as well as a biting wit which sat alongside his earnest, hard-working disposition) is uppermost. But, in spite of the ironic terms in which he reported these weekends to the amused but politically disapproving Jenifer, Herbert's taste for hunting and for upper-class country weekends was a strong one, as another letter from Minehead that summer shows: 'My day's hunting must have been as painful as your operation: we galloped continuously from 11.15 to 1.35 across moors, through streams, in woods, all without a stop. I was crying with pain by the end. Then we had to "hack" back 12 and a half miles in the rain. I don't know why I think it a pleasure'. And the same summer: 'Weather uncertain but heaven. I shall not tantalize you by describing the moor. Just off to murder animals. I'd forgotten how strange I looked in hunting clothes—but rather lovely.' Herbert's solicitor cousin, Boy, kept horses at his estate near Aylesbury, and Herbert joined him from time to time for fox-hunting. Richard Wilberforce, who went stag-hunting with Herbert on Exmoor in 1936, remembers him as emerging at this time from his hard-working persona into a 'rich-ish, smart-ish sort of man, well dressed, proud of how he looked'. He was, in short, changing his class identity. Wilberforce's diary records the excitement and discomfort of the hunt, at which Herbert appears to have been remarkably at ease:

I was on a grey nag with a nasty look in her left eye . . . . The meet (of staghounds) was at Cuzzicombe Post right up on the moor . . . . My animal began to kick at others while we stood about. Eventually we were off and, after scrambling through gates and fields, out to the moor. The going was slow and . . . I began to ache . . . and then just as I thought I was dying, we stopped. And then we were off again. I was right in front, having attached myself to the right horsey looking person and we went downhill into a combe, down a nasty hard path into the stream, and there he was, in the water, dying, with the hounds on him and huntsmen with knives wading through the water by the prehistoric steps and he lifted up his head . . . and we looked and couldn't look away. Your pain for our pleasure, certainly the very extreme of both . . . . It was a fine day. Both H. and I thoroughly enjoyed it.

He was surprisingly skilful, wore a stock and had a proper whip; I only had a tie and a poor little crop. . . . Next day I had quite recovered and felt wonderfully well, not stiff at all . . . . We went a windy walk over Dunkery, H. in excellent talking spirits casting off bits of Shakespeare and Rupert Brooke.

From today's perspective, it seems strange to find this juxtaposition of pleasure in the kill and poetic sensibility in someone like Herbert. But this was a different world, and his enjoyment of hunting was as genuine as his deep, long-standing love of walking and the countryside. Yet there is in these letters a strand of discomfort about the company he was keeping which suggests that Herbert was beginning to feel that the social life which came with his success at the Bar imposed a role with which he could not entirely identify. From Minehead once again he wrote to Jenifer: 'I can't describe the horrors of staying here. They would make you actively miserable. Me they only spur to unimaginable excesses of rudeness.'

Added to these increasingly powerful social and political sources of ambivalence to life at the Bar was the fact that Herbert had never really given up his ambitions in philosophy. Throughout the 1930s he was reading philosophy regularly, and he maintained his ability to come to firm intellectual judgments even about new developments. Of A. J. Ayer's *Language, Truth and Logic*, for example, he wrote to Jenifer 'I think that if he intends to be a serious philosopher he must bitterly regret publishing this book which I think is notable only for the variety of ways in which he is able to say he is quite right . . .'. Jenifer remembers him reading H. W. B. Joseph's *Introduction to Logic* while travelling to work on the Underground in the late 1930s.

This persisting interest was not just a matter of his continuing to read philosophical works and to take an informed interest in the development of the subject. It also had to do with a sense of mission or identity. At a deep level, Herbert was always drawn to the idea of himself as a philosopher, and saw the development of ideas, when pursued to the highest level, as a distinctively valuable way of life. He communicated his persisting yen to return to philosophy to old friends in Oxford, and during his time at the Bar he received several inquiries from colleges about whether he might be interested in taking up a fellowship. In 1937, a particularly tempting inquiry seized Herbert's imagination. His former tutor A. H. Smith approached him about New College's Fellowship in Philosophy, vacated on H. W. B. Joseph's retirement. Again, it was Christopher Cox to whom Herbert turned to discuss his decision. In May he wrote several times to Cox, who was working in Khartoum. Their correspondence gives a vivid sense of the complexity of Herbert's feelings.

I think that my delay in writing to you is partly accounted for by a subconscious reluctance to think about the New College job and the agonies of decision (or indecision) connected with it. I heard from Smith about a fortnight ago . . . . My reactions to the letter were pretty definitely that although I would consider the question very carefully, I would not take the job. I was at the time feeling very pleased with my practice having won a couple of cases, London appeared peculiarly beautiful, the opera was on, and I imagined myself (or perhaps I was and am) in love.

Smith's famous powers of persuasion, however, began to work on him, and after a long conversation with Smith during a weekend in Oxford, Herbert felt differently. Significantly, he was persuaded in part by Smith's suggestion that, with his legal experience, Oxford might open doors not only to an academic career but also administrative work which might lead in time to something like a university vice chancellorship. Smith's magic, however, began to wear off the next day. Going with Smith to his mother's home in Headington, Herbert 'felt that everything including Smith was beautiful and faintly alive and that Oxford was like that and that I would become like that (faintly alive not beautiful!) too'. A philosophy seminar after dinner convinced Herbert that he would 'never have more than a dilettante interest' in the subject and that his 'interest in law at the Bar was, though weak, stronger than that'. In fact, he found his 'spirits tumbling at the sight and sound of other philosophers'. Though he felt no strong pedagogic vocation, he could teach the students competently; he also felt a 'vague moral obligation' to help the College since they so flatteringly assured him that he could do so. 'Freedom from the uncertainties and stress of the Bar' would also mean a good deal, particularly in view of his heart trouble. But he hesitated not only because of anxiety about returning to academic work after such a long gap but also because of a psychological doubt:

Though intermittently happy I feel that I should be predominantly melancholy in Oxford and the Oxford atmosphere: At the bar one just feels quasi-dead with overwork or plain bored but *not* melancholy in the insidious sapping Oxford way . . . With a flourishing secure practice in London and married I should I think be quite certainly more happy and contented than at Oxford . . . . It is really chiefly my doubts about the future and security of my practice that made me doubt about going on at the Bar rather than any positive urge for Oxford. There is just a chance that I might want to get married soon.

The pros and cons of Oxford had so many dimensions that by the end of Herbert's outpouring to Cox he had covered 15 pages—and had had more than enough of the 'bloody question' himself. He asked Cox not to '*waste time* over my silly problems' and to 'Forgive me if I've sounded conceited, pompous, or revolting but I take it you want to know what's in my mind'. In this letter, a new degree of openness had been reached in Herbert's already uniquely close relationship with Cox: in two afterthoughts, he added, 'This is the longest letter I have ever written'; and by way of further confidence about the reference to a possible marriage, 'In case it affects your attitude to this question it's Jenifer F. Williams.' Cox responded with friendly sensitivity:

The only important con in your letter, to me, is the psychological (melancholic) one. This *is* I think important, and unless you can reach a more reassured position on this head I expect you will decide against coming. *Before* you do so, I hope you will go and see Smith again and focus on this one point. He understands practically everything and has uncanny insight . . .

Cox leavened his sympathetic response to Herbert's angst with a dash of humour: responding to his doubts about exchanging the metropolitan buzz of London for the isolation of Oxford, Cox wickedly (and characteristically) added: 'And don't judge by Smith's house—I know that feeling well. After all, the tone is set there by Mrs Smith, and she *is* only faintly alive.'

Himself a lifelong bachelor, Cox continued confidently:

You would be leading a very full life and I am pretty sure you would before long be happily married. That would make the whole difference. I think you know how tremendously I want you to come (selfishly) and how certain I am of the position you would have in the college and at Oxford before moving out to wider spheres. (Incidentally the knowledge that such spheres would be open to you, as they certainly would be, should surely do much to reduce and even to annihilate the dangers of malaise.)

Both of Cox's predictions turned out to be right. As hinted in Herbert's letter, he would indeed marry Jenifer Williams; and he did not overcome his doubts about taking up the Fellowship. He wrote to Cox thanking him for his advice and telling him that, so long as his doctor assured him that he was well enough to continue at the Bar, he would not take the Oxford job:

[A]fter much agony I am against going. Not because of the apprehension of malaise though I admit that that weighs a bit but because I feel . . . in my bones that I am not meant for an academic life though it is difficult for me to say why.

In a letter written in August of that year, Smith told Herbert that he was not surprised by the decision, and announced his intention of trying to 'secure [Berlin] for a fellowship once his All Souls Fellowship expires', in spite of 'some hesitations on the score of his being rather difficult for other than first class men . . . .You know . . . ', he concluded, 'how much I should have liked to have you as a colleague, and what I thought about the value it would be to the college. But however much I regret it, I can't say that I think your decision is wrong'. Anxiety about the intellectual aspects of the Oxford job, along with Herbert's rosy prospects at the Bar, were the primary factors in the decision. And, just as he was ambivalent about the social world of his legal colleagues, Herbert had his reservations about that of Oxford. Though he enjoyed dining with Berlin at All Souls and being 'gorged with wine food talk and gossip' among lively company including Maurice Bowra, Goronwy Rees, and Rosamond Lehmann, there was something about Oxford which he found difficult. To Jenifer in 1937 he wrote: 'I loathed everybody in Oxford this weekend. They are *much* worse than Barristers.'

Herbert's reluctance to return to Oxford had to do with a feeling that, in terms of his personal development, it would be a step backwards. In London, his social life was broadening, and his thoughts of marriage show that he was at last ready to move beyond the male institutional environments—school, college, club, profession—in which he had lived most of his life. But his negative feelings about Oxford had been exacerbated by an unpleasant episode following his attempt to join an institution which epitomized that masculine, cloistered world: the Oxford and Cambridge Club. When Patrick Reilly, later a successful diplomat, nominated Herbert for membership in 1935, he was refused. Both he and Wilberforce believed this to be because he was Jewish. Wilberforce's diary gives a vivid impression of Herbert's reaction:

[Herbert] with increasing prosperity wanted to join a club and decided on the O. & C. Foolishly, as I thought, he got Reilly to propose him and Mackenzie to 2nd, very nice and estimable people but hardly the club familiars. Suddenly one day he burst into my room with a letter from R. telling him that a section of the club was violently anti-Jewish and that the committee didn't dare to go against it—recommending R. to withdraw the candidature. H. was terribly upset; he has always been sensitive about his race—he sees red when the word Nazi is mentioned—refused to travel on a German boat to Lisbon—an idea which I had; he has completely taken his place in the Wykehamist-New College set, goes everywhere; he is a man who believes, too much perhaps, in the aristocracy of the intellect. So that when he heard of this being done, and being done by that of all clubs, a university club which by its constitution sets the imprimatur of respectability on every university man, knowing too . . . how easy it is to get elected, naturally it shocks him and knocks his world from underneath him.

Despite Wilberforce's best efforts behind the scenes, the bar on Herbert's candidacy stood, and matters were made worse by the fact that it seemed likely that a judge known to Herbert, the chairman of the club, had (at the least) failed to counter the prejudice against him. Wilberforce's view was that the issue had as much to do with class and social connections as with anti-Semitism (the club already had a number of Jewish—though no women—members). But, while noting that 'we did not feel so strongly about anti-Jews before the Holocaust', he felt in retrospect that he should have been yet more 'indignant at the principle'. As for Reilly, he wrote decades later that 'I have never forgiven myself for not resigning when he was rejected. It had never occurred to me that such a thing was still possible in a civilised club.' One can only begin to imagine how this rejection affected Herbert. Certainly, it would have offended his rationalism and sense of fairness. Yet, as Wilberforce understood, these intellectual, political objections sat uncomfortably alongside the feelings prompted by other important aspects of Herbert's personality: the sensibility of his Jewish origins and his desire to fit or belong.

Added to the straightforward comparison between lawyers and academics as colleagues was the relatively fluid social world of London as compared to the more restrictive one of Oxford. Throughout the 1930s, Herbert kept in close touch with Oxford friends, in particular visiting Cox and Joseph on a regular basis and frequently dining and enjoying intellectual exchange with Berlin, Sparrow, Jay, or Wilberforce at All Souls (a regularity which may have prompted one Fellow's remark that whenever he returned to the College after a period away, the Fellows had always changed, while the guests remained the same). His group of friends in London was by no means confined to the legal world: Herbert's social circle was both broader and less conventional than that typical of barristers of the time, embracing old Oxford friends like Arnold Pilkington—'Pilks'—, Patrick Reilly, and Sheila Grant-Duff. Lunches and dinners from time to time with John Sparrow give a taste of the high-living, hard-drinking, fast-talking world which he rather enjoyed. On one occasion, Sparrow, preoccupied by a case, fell asleep and missed a rendezvous set for midnight: 'I woke . . . at 12.45, with horror. I rushed out, caught a taxi and arrived at Rules' to find it shut. These things can't be forgiven. If you could *forget* tonight it would be best. Will you, as a preliminary step, *lunch* with me tomorrow, at *one sharp*, Savoy Grill I suggest, and we will have champagne after all. I think the chances of my turning up, and punctually, are pretty strong. J.'

Richard Wilberforce had by now become not only one of Herbert's closest friends, but also his regular travel companion. Herbert continued to undertake adventurous journeys. A diary kept by Wilberforce in the 1930s records trips to France, Ireland, and a chalet in Switzerland, owned by 'Sligger' Urquhart, Dean of Balliol College, and later passed on to New College, University College, and Balliol, which was used for reading parties. The trips were characterized by intense conversations about their mutual reading (including Ivy Compton Burnett and Horace Walpole's letters) and by feats of endurance and, occasionally, hair-raising daring on their bicycles. Wilberforce, deeply attached to Herbert, paid tribute to him as—in a later annotation—'the ideal travelling companion' and wrote of him as 'my most valued friend'; 'He has such a flow of talk, all full of content which makes me feel a very empty person by comparison'. Herbert paid Wilberforce a more mixed tribute on the same trip: at Nimes, amid 'country . . . at just the right stage of ripeness . . . corn still green but miles of it broken up by olives and cypresses and poppies and lots of Roman ruins . . . ' he found 'Richard . . . an odd mixture of intelligent liberalism and narrow-mindedness in some important respects. But it is most stimulating being in this kind of way

55

with him: he throws a curious light on tiny facets of things that would otherwise escape me.' Wilberforce noted with amusement a variety of instances of Herbert's physically shambolic movements around the world, including a near-drowning episode on this same trip to Provence: 'It was all very shallow and he was walking in a nice silvery bit just before the water went over a miniature weir. Suddenly he was struggling and in a minute he was getting sucked under a ruined tower . . . . Resistance was useless and at last he disappeared. I ran round to see him come out, but he didn't . . . . How awful! But at last he emerged from a door in the tower quite unhurt. The sort of thing that could only have happened to him.' The incident had a significant impact on Herbert, who talked about it for years to come, and described it in a letter to Jenifer at the time as 'my death struggle'.

Among Herbert's wide circle of highly educated London friends, probably the most important remained Douglas Jay, who had by this time married Peggy Maxwell Garnett, with whom he was living at 42 Well Walk, just round the corner from Herbert's rented rooms in Hampstead Square, North London. Jay had become a journalist, writing for *The Economist* and later the *Daily Herald*, and specializing in economic affairs. He was closely involved with the Labour Party, and working on the question of how a non-communist, democratic socialism might be constructed in Britain. In 1937 he published his first book, which argued that the strongest case for greater social justice rested on the economist Alfred Marshall's proposition that aggregate satisfaction can be increased by the redistribution of wealth from rich to poor rather than on Marx's 'obsession with ownership and out-dated theory of value'. Jay argued that there was no reason to believe that redistribution could not be 'peacefully and democratically achieved', and that 'unemployment and cyclical depression were monetary phenomena which could be overcome by intelligent management of . . . total effective demand'. Jay called the book *The Socialist Case* 'to emphasize the extent to which Marx was a revisionist, whose dogmatism and stridency were not shared by earlier socialists such as Robert Owen'. The book also took the view that 'personal freedom was an equal value with social justice, not incompatible with it'. Jay's and Herbert's strong intellectual relationship with one another shifted seamlessly from classics across literature to politics, and in debates with Jay and other Labour-leaning friends, as with fellow members of the Savile Club, Herbert's own political views began to move towards the left.

During his student days, Herbert had already thought of himself as a liberal. But he was, by his own admission, not deeply interested in politics. The left-leaning, social democratic liberalism with which his work was later so closely identified, let alone the socialism which was such an influence on Jenifer and many others of his generation, had yet to claim his allegiance. But the world was changing fast, and Herbert was far too acute and honest a witness to be unaffected by the political situation developing in Europe in the 1930s. In the second part of the decade he got involved in helping Jewish refugees from the Nazi regime in Germany. Remarkably, he rarely spoke in later life of his feelings about Hitler's initial rise to power; nor, although he had had relatives in Berlin, did he lay particular emphasis in his condemnation of Hitler's Germany on its treatment of the Jews. But he later recalled in conversation with his children hearing 'Deutschland über Alles' chanted outside his bedroom window during a visit to German relatives in the early 1920s, and he noted with relish, in a 1938 letter to Jenifer, Maurice Bowra's view that 'the only thing to do when we win this war is to castrate all the male Germans and colonize the place with Jews', and was horrified by Chamberlain's policy of appeasement. In a personal memoir, Richard Wilberforce recalled how he and Herbert had been together when Chamberlain's return from Munich in 1938 announcing 'Peace for our time' was greeted with applause: he and Herbert had simply looked at each other 'with tears in our eyes: it was unnecessary to speak'.

But even apart from the menace of Hitler's regime in Germany, other developments combined to produce a generation of educated young men and women who felt an obligation to think about political issues and to engage in various forms of political or social activism. This was the culture which had prompted Christopher Cox to suspend his research and to undertake the advisory work on education in Africa to which he devoted himself full time from 1940 onwards. The Spanish Civil War was a radicalizing stimulus for many of this generation. Though Herbert's liberal outlook always made him uncomfortable with the more authoritarian or state-centred forms of socialism, let alone with communism, his political views, like those of many of his friends, had already moved decisively to the left by the mid 1930s. This development was accelerated by the most important relationship which Herbert formed in the latter half of the decade: that with his future wife, the beautiful, brilliant, and unconventional Jenifer Williams.

Part II

CHANGE AND CONTINUITY

CHAPTER 4

Jenifer

H ERBERT'S social life during the early 1930s centred on his enduring friendships with Douglas Jay, Isaiah Berlin, Christopher Cox, Richard Wilberforce, and John Sparrow: his relationships with colleagues, though easy and pleasant, did not run deep. His correspondence with his friends reflects affectionate, warm, and humorous relationships, as well as deep intellectual engagement. With the exception of that with Cox, it does not reveal any degree of intimacy or emotional exchange, and there is no evidence that Herbert had any significant sexual relationships during the first half of the decade. This lack of sexual relationships might be explained merely in terms of the amount of time he was devoting to his work, and the emotional reserve which characterized most of his friendships was doubtless to some degree simply a product of the prevailing culture in the 1930s. Herbert had spent most of his formative years in environments populated exclusively by men, and in spite of his fondness for his mother and sister, it was hardly surprising if he felt inhibited with women. But there was a further, more specific factor at work. In his outpouring to Cox in 1937 about his doubts about the New College job, he finally brought himself to a yet more significant confidence:

I am or have been a suppressed homosexual (I see you wince) and would become more so (I mean more homosexual and less suppressed) in Oxford.

This was probably the first time that Herbert opened up to one of his close friends about his sexual feelings and, particularly by the standards of the time, it is a remarkably intimate confidence. The fact that his apology to Cox—a broad-minded man—for burdening him with this confidence included the fear that Cox would think him 'revolting' as well as self-obsessed, and the fact that the admission about his sexuality was juxtaposed with the communication that he was contemplating marriage, suggest not only the depth of Herbert's own ambivalence about his homoerotic feelings but also his acute consciousness of social prejudices about homosexuality. But why did he associate a move to Oxford with a greater sense of homosexual orientation? Certainly, Oxford fostered a relatively openly homosexual circle around Maurice Bowra, the Warden of Wadham, and though London too provided plenty of opportunities for homosociality, Herbert perhaps felt that the less structured Oxford life presented fewer distractions or inhibitions. Whatever the truth of the matter, his admission to Cox reveals that Herbert's sense of himself as homosexual was a significant aspect of his personality, and that he felt it to be a factor in inhibiting the full development of his emotional life. At this stage, the fulcrum of Herbert's sense of security and connection still rested to a significant extent with his family in Yorkshire, with whom he corresponded regularly, and whom he visited frequently.

Herbert's relations with his siblings were mixed. He was not a fan of his second brother, Reggie. Though doubtless with an exaggeration born of embarrassment mixed with humour, he referred in a letter to Jenifer in the late 1930s to Reggie's 'quite dreadful petit bourgeois heaviness boringness awkwardness and pathological stupidity . . .'. By contrast, he was always fond of his oldest brother, Albert: indeed it was to Albert that he first confided his relationship with Jenifer. But Herbert's closest sibling relationship was with his sister, Sybil. Now a student, Sybil had been overtaken by a series of debilitating depressions, accompanied by a variety of distressing physical symptoms such as digestive upsets. As she struggled to 'master her nerves' and 'pull herself together', she poured out her feelings to Herbert in touching and sometimes painful letters. 'I feel as if I've had the most terrible strain' she wrote during one of her vacations, 'and as though I need weeks and weeks of lazing about. In the mean time I'm not doing the work I set myself to do in the vac, and I'm not on the other hand having a decent holiday. I hope you don't think I'm disgruntled in this venting my annoyance at myself, but really it is infuriating the way I always get ill at inopportune times. I can quite see why this never happens in term time; when I have a routine life and something to do I hold on, but when I get home and completely relax—then it all seems to ooze out of me, physically and mentally.'

Life at the family home at 3 Beaulieu Court in Harrogate was not always tranquil. Herbert had already had occasion to confide in Cox about his father's temper, and Sybil's letters are peppered with descriptions of family rows which she felt were a factor in her own depression: 'I think also that what brings it to a head is the amount of friction which is aroused by the process of accommodating myself to life at home.' Sybil was particularly attached to her volatile father and—notwithstanding her successful career at ICI after the war—devoted much of her life to caring for her parents at the London home to which they moved in 1938. Herbert's correspondence with her shows that by this time he had become significantly more distant from their parents. Perhaps this was what enabled him to keep using their home as a holiday retreat notwithstanding his view by this time that Jewish family ties tended to be 'neurosis-making to an extraordinary degree'. 'Air and climate pleasant here: I vegetate discreetly', he wrote to Jenifer from Harrogate in 1938.

The intimacy of Herbert's relationship with Sybil was asymmetrical: Sybil imparted confidences and Herbert took the part of supportive elder brother. This was a role which Herbert often played: his friends valued his judgment, and turned to him in times of crisis for advice or for a sympathetic ear. As early as 1931, when Herbert had only recently been his student, Christopher Cox wrote thanking him for allowing him to 'let off steam again to you and missing your train: it did me such a lot of good!' 'I can't think why the missing of my train is on your conscience. Summer evening in New College garden listening to your and the nightingale's voice is preferable to train', Herbert replied. In such encounters, the good listener typically reveals rather little of him or herself, and apart from these glimpses of what we might therefore call passive intimacy, there is little evidence of the nature of Herbert's interior life in the early 1930s. As the decade progressed, his growing intimacy with Cox provided a framework within which he could begin to explore his own feelings more openly. But the most important development in his personal life was the relationship which he began to form with Jenifer Williams in 1936.

Jenifer and Herbert met at a house party organized by the Jays at Crackington Haven in Cornwall. Scrambling across the rocks, Jenifer 'fell into conversation with another member of the party, Herbert Hart, whom I had not met before. Rock climbing was not his forte, even less than it was mine, but as we discussed Arnold Toynbee's theory of history, I became immediately aware of the tremendous power of his mind.' It is interesting that she mentions nothing about his physical appearance. Photographs of the time show a tall, striking young man with unusually fine features and a shock of thick hair. Presumably Herbert's attractive appearance was not irrelevant to Jenifer's immediate interest in him.

Jenifer Williams had graduated in history from Somerville College, Oxford the previous year. Bent on a career in the Civil Service, she was now preparing for that summer's Civil Service exam, in which she was to excel. She was placed third out of 493 candidates, the highest ranking ever achieved by a woman to that date. Her ambition to join the Civil Service itself marked her out as unusual: no woman had been successful in the exam between 1931 and 1934, and women made up fewer than five per cent of successful candidates in the ten years to 1935. But this was by no means

Jenifer's primary distinction. Even by the standards of the gifted group in which Herbert moved, Jenifer was a striking person along a whole number of dimensions. Fair-skinned, golden-red-haired, and slender, with fine cheekbones and a frank expression, she exuded vitality, determination, intensity, intelligence. This vital intensity, as much as her physical beauty, made her exceptionally attractive to men. It was an intensity which suggested a will of tremendous power, in quest of excitement as well as knowledge. What also made Jenifer fascinating were the strongly contrasting—even contradictory—elements which made up her personality: her high principles combined with an enduring taste for scandal and gossip; her intellectual and political seriousness were juxtaposed with an irreverent humour; her trenchant rationalism combined with a deep strand of impulsiveness; her sophistication was counterpoised with an occasionally startling naivety; her politics were radical, but they sat alongside an intransigence, an apparent self-confidence, a residual hauteur which were the indelible marks of her privileged and unusual childhood and adolescence.

Jenifer came from an educated, moneyed upper-middle-class background. She was the daughter of Sir John Fischer Williams and Eleanor Marjorie Hay Murray, his second wife. Sir John was a well-known international lawyer and the author of a number of books on the development of the League of Nations, of which he was a strong and influential supporter. Jenifer and her three sisters had travelled widely with their parents, spending time not only in London, Oxford, and at Lamledra (the spectacular holiday home which John and Marjorie Williams had built on a windswept headland at Gorran Haven in Cornwall), but also living and being educated for much of her childhood in Paris. In the early 1930s she spent time in Geneva, where her father was participating in the Disarmament Conference. Jenifer was wildly impatient with her mother, whom she saw as bourgeois, intrusive, and obsessed with trivia; she blamed her for creating a 'thick emotional atmosphere' which she found intensely claustrophobic. By contrast, at least as a child and teenager, she admired her father deeply. Her account of her early life suggests that she was subconsciously competing with her mother for her father's admiration. This powerful family dynamic almost certainly had a significant effect both on Jenifer's early intellectual and political development and on her later predilection for seducing intellectually powerful men.

Jenifer's early political views were decisively shaped by her father's concern with international affairs and with peace. She had grown up with a stronger social conscience than most children of her class at the time:

When we travelled, as we did every year, from Paris to Cornwall, we hired one of the many unemployed men who thronged the quay at Southampton to push our

64

large volume of luggage . . . and as we walked through the streets I was worried by the sight of groups of lean, depressed looking men standing about aimlessly. And in the 1930s I was, when motoring, constantly reminded about poverty by the sight of tramps on the roads, moving from one workhouse to the next, probably twenty-five miles away. . . . Another vivid memory is visiting some London slums in 1930. I can still visualize a woman living in a completely underground dark, damp basement, rather like a coal-hole.

Unsurprisingly, as a schoolgirl her views wavered wildly: one year she was determining to support the Labour Party, 'for why should some be rich and others suffer in poverty? It seems quite ridiculous. All men equal.'; the next she was dazzled by 'the virtues of the aristocracy' as displayed at the Eton and Harrow cricket match: 'dignified, well organized and law-abiding, so I felt it was right that they should rule until the lower classes were properly educated. The whole social scene also induced in me unusual pride in the English who alone, I thought, could behave so admirably.'

Coloured by her rebelliousness and (partial) rejection of the social values which she associated with her family, her politics gradually took a more radically pacifist and egalitarian turn. On going to university in 1932, she became involved in the Women's University Settlement Movement, devoting some free time to working with the poor. She found the efforts to provide education and material assistance 'pathetic' and the social gap unbridgeable. But her reading and conversations during her student years gradually moved her politics leftwards, and the summer of her graduation saw her working at a camp for the unemployed organized by the National Unemployed Workers Movement. Though she was initially unaware of it, the camp was run largely by members of the Communist Party. On this occasion, perhaps because of her more articulated politics, she found the communication gap easier to bridge:

I found the whole experience deeply moving, not only because of what I learnt about the lives of those less fortunate than myself. What affected me most was realizing to my astonishment that I could relate easily to working-class people. They thought I was odd of course. They teased me for saying things like 'There are three reasons for doing something, a, b, and c' . . . but they accepted me as a product of my bourgeois background and class without envy or contempt. No pressure was put on me to join the Communist Party, but by the end of my stay I was coming to feel that it was the natural thing to do.

With typical whole-heartedness, Jenifer went the whole hog and acted out her political commitment in all areas of her life, 'pooh-poohing comfort and cleanliness'; engaging in lively criticism of herself and others for all petit-bourgeois tastes; and embarking on an affair with an unemployed

65

milkman. This relationship illustrates her taste for personal experimentation and her contempt for conventional sexual mores. Equally, it was a product of her capacity to see her own ideas through. It also exemplified a certain naivety about the reactions of others, as well as a curious mix of short-sightedness and self-knowledge. As she recorded, with typically uncompromising honesty: 'I think he [her lover] supposed our relationship would be permanent, whereas I knew instinctively it could not last. Apart from the bond of Party, our interests and experiences were too divergent; the cultural gap was too wide.' At some level she knew that she could never escape that cultural identity; hence her communist activism—like Herbert's participation in upper-class house parties—must have involved a degree of semi-conscious role-playing. And in later life, though suspicious of psychoanalytic explanations of such commitments, Jenifer was able to admit that her communist affiliation was fed by her desire visibly to rebel against her own background. What presumably did not occur to her at the time was that she was replacing it with a value system just as rigid and certain of its own rectitude.

Whatever psychological factors were at play, Jenifer's decision to join the Communist Party was a serious political and intellectual one, and it was influenced by her reading and by the currency of communist sympathy among her intellectual friends. She was particularly impressed by John Middleton Murry's *The Necessity of Communism* which, while accepting the fundamentals of the Marxist analysis and critique of the injustices of industrial capitalism, argued for a humane communism unscarred by what Murry saw as the Leninist corruption of Marxist ideas, and therefore moving in a very different direction from Russian communism. Similarly, Barbara Wootton's *Plan or No Plan*, which Jenifer read in 1935, sought to combine the advantages of a planned socialist economy with the valuable features of a liberal democracy. Jenifer's utopia, therefore, was a distinctive, internationalist, liberty-respecting socialism which promised a resolution of social injustice and in particular the end of mass unemployment. Why, then, did she choose to join the Communist Party, whose approach was rigid, doctrinaire, and heavily influenced by policy in the Soviet Union?

The explanation given by the many intellectuals who joined the Party in the 1930s—including Jenifer's old Oxford friends Bernard Floud and Philip Toynbee—had essentially to do with their belief in the need to belong to an organization if they were to have any impact, combined with what they saw as the poverty of other options in the face of the disastrous collapse of Ramsay MacDonald's Labour Government. In spite of the evidence which was beginning to come out about Stalin's political repression, many on the British Left continued to see Russia as a potential force for good in the world order; party membership in Britain increased by 50 per cent between 1936 and 1939. Apart from the relatively restricted information coming out of the region—neither the extent of the mass executions nor the horror of the labour camps was clear until later—the main reason for this was the Spanish Civil War, which began just as news of the first trials emerged. Defence of the Spanish Republicans was a key issue for anyone on the Left, and it was Russia which was giving aid to the Republican movement in Spain. Hence Russia was aligned against the fascist dictatorships of Germany and Italy, which were not only aiding Franco but were also, rightly, perceived as a major threat to world peace and democracy. As the full extent of Hitler's territorial ambitions, and a clearer picture of the humanitarian outrages of his government, emerged, sympathy for Russia, and a tendency to see its internal authoritarianism as forgivable or at least corrigible in the light of its international stance, increased. As Jenifer put it in her autobiography, 'Hitler's march into Austria in March 1938 seemed more important than Bukharin's execution three days later'.

Jenifer's ambition to join the Civil Service pre-dated her joining the Communist Party; but it suited the Party's purposes very well. A friend advised her to become a secret member and to sever overt ties with the Party. Remarkably by today's standards, there were then no security checks for those taking up civil service positions, and after her spectacular performance in the entry exam, Jenifer was able, in spite of her Party membership, to take up a position in one of the most important Departments of State, the Home Office. The Russian intelligence services kept an eye on her through an anonymous contact whom she met about half a dozen times during her first year or so at the Home Office. At first this contact was an Englishman; later he was a foreigner. (It seems likely that this was 'Otto', who was to become posthumously famous as the controller of members of the Cambridge spy ring including Guy Burgess and the art historian and intelligence officer Anthony Blunt.) Her contacts never asked Jenifer if she would pass information: she was told that there were other Communists in the Civil Service but that she would not be put in touch with them at present; and she was asked what she regarded as intrusive questions about her associates and her personal life. At one point she was required to move out of an apartment into which she had moved with a friend who was a fellow Party member (the Party fearing that this might expose her affiliation). Both the contacts' concern about her private life and the elaborate—and occasionally surreal, taxi-swapping—precautions taken against being followed during their meetings suggest that there was a serious intention to recruit her as an agent. But in her early years at the Home Office she was working on aspects of criminal justice policy—children's homes, juvenile delinquency, and approved schools—which were of no interest to the Russians. This, along with her relatively recent introduction to communist sympathies and Party circles (most of the members of the Cambridge spy ring, for example, had been involved in left wing politics from the late 1920s on) may explain why she was never put under pressure to pass information.

By 1939, under the influence of the increasing evidence of Stalin's totalitarianism and the steadfastly anti-communist Labour politics of most of her closest associates, notably Herbert and Douglas and Peggy Jay—and perhaps encouraged by Britain's own stand against fascism—Jenifer's communist sympathies had waned. She never had a Party card to tear up: her association with the Party simply dissolved. Accounts of the Russian intelligence operation at this time and even into the early 1940s show that it was chaotic, under-resourced, and often obstructed by the need to pander to Stalin's latest obsessions. The Soviets failed to make contact even with some of their most active agents for extended periods, as power politics in Moscow played havoc with the provision of a stable series of spymasters in London as well as with the translation and interpretation of information in Moscow. Jenifer's unproblematic exit was probably a matter of sheer disorganization on the Soviet part. Indeed, she may simply have been forgotten.

At the time of her first meeting with Herbert in 1936, Jenifer's infatuation with communism was at its enthusiastic height. Herbert's politics were, by contrast, steadfastly liberal and social democratic. But the two shared an interest in both political history and philosophy, and a bond was quickly established between them. Significantly, the first attempt to renew their initial chance meeting came from Jenifer. Apologizing for his tardy reply to her letter referring to their meeting at Crackington Haven, Herbert told her that it was 'heavenly to be reminded of that holiday which when viewed from a lawyer's garden window seems very remote and unreal and delicious'. Already, a habit of teasing as a way of exploring their serious political differences had been established: 'I think to discharge any debt of mutual gratitude in respect of the holiday we might undertake not to shoot straight when we sight each other across the Barricades a few years hence. Or won't the Cell allow that? Ever, Herbert.'

Later in the summer Jenifer, Herbert, and two other friends went on holiday together to Yugoslavia. Herbert was by now sufficiently intrigued by Jenifer to put up with her insistence that they travel uncomfortably on the hard deck of a cargo ship. Conversely, Jenifer was sufficiently engaged by Herbert to defend her association with him to communist friends shocked by her 'non-bolshevik summer' with liberals who spent much of their time ridiculing all manifestations of Christianity—a peripheral issue from a Marxist point of view. On their return to London, they continued to correspond and to meet for dinner or to go to the ballet. Over the next year, they shared a number of further holidays and weekends with friends—including a visit by Herbert to her (absent) parents' Cornwall home at Easter 1937—and got to know each other through a regular correspondence. From a holiday with his parents on the Isle of Wight, Herbert put an ironic distance between himself and his family, while teasing Jenifer about her disapproval of bourgeois comforts:

The island is like the garden of a Victorian house in Wimbledon run wild—but not very wild. It is the worst place in the world in which to read James Joyce, as I am doing. The weather is perfect and while my parents sleep in the morning I read and while they sleep in the afternoon I walk. The comforts on the whole are not to be despised (except by you).

Herbert was, however, not above reminding Jenifer of the fruits of her privileged upbringing, even as their exchanges began to include moments of less defended communication:

I've just begun to read Baudelaire—though no doubt you lisped him in the nursery. Don't you think the line 'Eldorado banal de tous les vieux garçons' is wonderful? I shall always go there when I am old—with a few chosen friends.

In this early correspondence Jenifer and Herbert communicated with each other about their political views, testing each other's tolerance under the protective shield of humour. Another source of jokes was Jenifer's taste for colourful language—again, a symptom of her rejection of her parents' bourgeois manners: 'I feel that unless I am to lose my peculiar status in your eyes', Herbert wrote, 'this letter should open with a volley of obsceni-ties and blasphemies and be at least six pages long. Work however and sultry weather have dried me up so I can't get further than an explosive B which I present to you with all its rich potentialities.' On another weekend house party in 1937, Herbert reported that his companions' behaviour broke 'three times every minute every rubric in the Jeniferian Canon' before sign-ing himself, affectionately but ironically, 'Your Passionate Admirer'.

But their correspondence also had practical, intellectual, and aesthetic dimensions. Travel arrangements for each of their trips were discussed minutely, with Herbert conscientiously deferring to Jenifer's ascetism in matters sartorial and to her frugality in matters financial—a deferral which sat comfortably with Herbert's own persisting (and lifelong) anxiety about money. They discussed their reading, which ranged in one exchange from Wodehouse to Thackeray via nineteenth-century travel books—Wode-house being described by Herbert as 'definitely the most dangerous as propaganda on behalf of the established order'; and their letters were peppered with lyrical quotations from the poetry of Yeats, Blake, and others.

They exchanged views about history and politics: 'It does look as if Franco will only succeed now with enormous reinforcements from Germany and Italy and I suppose there is just a chance that he won't get them.' And they indulged their shared love of the English countryside; as Jenifer wrote to Herbert: 'Boscastle I regard as the acme of everything romantic and Cornish and adore it accordingly. It is unrivalled in my affections, and not only because I walked there on a beautiful evening looking at the sunset and the black cliffs in outline only with Pilks [a mutual friend] far away from the madding crowd.'

By the summer of 1937 Jenifer and Herbert had become deeply attached to one another:

Ange pleine de beauté, I hope the clock you gave Roger stopped at once. I thought viciously about you all the weekend but as I can't express my feelings otherwise than in the debauched formulae of the bourgeoisie they shan't be expressed at all. Only I love you love you love you except when I have awful feelings of panic and think you have sent me a six months notice . . . and then I hate myself rather more than usual. You *must* tell me whenever I commit a breach of covenant entitling you to re-enter. I shall always pay my rent whether lawfully demanded or not . . . (I think I prefer you as my landlord rather than licensee of my instructions.). . . . Give me some sign that the lease is still on foot—even if only a notice raising the rent, or objections to dilapidations. I must stop before I become obscene. World without end. Herbert

The legal metaphor—another familiar joke between them—is picked up in Jenifer's reply:

Lord of my love

Roger gave the clock to me—but I followed legal precedents and refused it—I will become landlord tenant slave cook whore anything you like—You were a banned subject [at her parents' home in Oxford]—so I felt miserable except when we saw Shaya [Isaiah Berlin] and I felt an undercurrent of goodwill—Tomorrow about 8.15—I can't be there before I am afraid. Guy is being very troublesome blast him.

Unlike Herbert, in 1936 Jenifer already had an active and complicated love life, and the revelation of hers and Herbert's involvement came as unpleasant news to her other main admirer at the time, the rather fragile Guy Chilver. The belief—redolent of Bloomsbury, and of the Platonic philosophy which had so influenced Herbert—that strong personal emotions could and should be under the control of reason, which characterized many of their friends' attitudes at the time, is highlighted by Guy's reaction. After a tense encounter with Jenifer and Herbert in Czechoslovakia in the summer and a tearful evening with Jenifer in London, he explained that he wasn't so much upset at having lost her to Herbert, but rather by the discovery that he was susceptible to jealousy—an emotion which he regarded as atavistic and uncivilized. He had experienced it once before, but had then comforted himself with the thought that 'its unfamiliarity made me certain that I had exorcised it almost completely'.

Within a year of their first meeting, as he confided to Cox, Herbert was already contemplating the possibility of marriage to Jenifer. What drew Jenifer, a sexually experienced, socially confident, and politically committed young woman, and Herbert, a sexually inexperienced, emotionally reserved, and considerably less political man, into a monogamous relationship so quickly? Like most highly charged relationships, theirs was an attraction of opposites and a meeting of minds—a combination which withstood some severe testing over the next 55 years. The nature of this complex equilibrium, as well as the complexion of Herbert's emotional life to this point, is vividly and often movingly revealed in their correspondence during the intense early part of their relationship.

A series of letters in the summer of 1937, when Herbert and Jenifer were already seriously committed to one another, but when neither had confided this to their families, gives a sense of the texture of their relationship at the time. It was a potent mix of intellectual connection, sexual attraction, and shared humour. During this summer, each of them had a period of ill health: Herbert needed an operation to remove his tonsils, while Jenifer had a kidney infection—a serious matter in those pre-penicillin days. Recovering quickly in hospital, eating 'rather gingerly' and intrigued by the nurses who 'are fascinating studies in body mind and sexual perversions', thoughts of Jenifer filled Herbert with 'incredible happiness; the thought of eating with you riding with you sleeping with you listening to music with you even attempting to think with you makes me shudder with joy'.

Jenifer meanwhile was more seriously ill and much less amused by the nurses:

Ange plein de santé lucky brute—Christ the infernal fools in this place. . . . Perhaps I have been put into a certified Institution for my own good. Do tell me if I have—and don't let it dawn slowly—as to telephoning, it is impossible as it is 2 floors down and I am still too incapacitated to walk further than to the lavatory—and this with great effort—Christ alive what torture this is—Do ask a selection of your nurses about chills on the kidneys. . . . There seem to be few distinguishing features except a very mild pain in the back, incontinence and then this buggering temperature. . . . I don't even seem visibly to be getting thin either, the only possible good that could come out of this hell—As to intellectual activity, when by mistake I have taken an extra dose of aspirin I have managed to toy with George Buchanan for 5 minutes or so—and in this condition at any rate I like the book a lot—Otherwise I read one line of poetry at a time, and sleep on it for 2 hours—curiously enough I find I am much more sensitive to words in this state than ordinarily. I wrote you a surrealist letter yesterday—but decided it was too shame-giving to send—. . . Love and kisses—with their real meaning and not as in one's early letters to one's parents, Jenifer

Herbert replied sympathetically:

You must be having hell my sweet: I know all there is to know about chills on kidneys. I got one myself at Cherbourg in April 1929 neglected it and was sick on Oxford station and in bed for 6 weeks with *jaundice* getting up 10 days before Greats [his final examinations] yellow as a banana. So please please be horribly careful—take every precaution however bourgeois. . . . Do anything but *don't* get jaundice the horrors of which are obscene and dangerous beyond measure. I have sent some roses and grapes to-day and hope they mitigate.

Recuperating at Lamledra, Jenifer was impatient to be with Herbert again:

Hell I do wish we were going to recuperate together—I'd give anything to lie in the sun reading at your side for a week. Whenever I read anything now I want to show it to you with, or for, some comment—even Dorothy Sayers . . .

And, notwithstanding the continued irony, the emotional tone becomes more urgent and unaffected:

Mon amour

I long for you here almost to screaming point—for although the sea is lovely in a way and the corn fields most exciting, as no doubt you found too, and there are comforts and attentions to a stultifying point, I somehow can't appreciate anything and would rather be in a back kitchen with you. . . . You are Picasso against a background of the 19th Century, Mozart compared with the previous 18C, Dante, Shakespeare, anything compared with these soulless, convention-ridden, petty, domestic, decaying Bourgeois snobs—There was never anyone who talked more or whom I wished to listen to less than my aunt: she has as all aunts no raison d'etre at all . . .

And:

Very god of very god, I had lived, or rather died, for a letter all day—and now one has come so I want to scream and tell everyone life is worth living. I feel as if I had drunk champagne—Christ how un-self sufficient one is. I am afraid you did not get mine for years—but there were no posts out for years and I sent Mariella [Jenifer's younger sister] with it specially at that. I was so thrilled when your letter came I rushed from one room to another wondering which was the nicest to read it in—and then when I did try to it had about as much effect on my brain as the last act of Figaro. . . . Christ how I decay without stimuli. I couldn't settle to anything all day: it is disgraceful. I tried The Ambassadors, but it didn't arouse my interest somehow and then Halevy's history but it's not really good. One can't go on reading indefinitely without someone to talk to—or anyway someone nice whom one wants to come into the room rather than to leave it like these fools. Father is pleasant and amiable and thinks we should give the Jews a real proper national home, big enough for them somewhere else—just as a good Liberal gesture. He also thinks the Arab *legal* case overwhelming. Mother I spend my time avoiding or annoying—I am not quite sure which is most satisfactory. Mariella complains rebelliously that the household is not stimulating, and that she would rather be at school. She tries to read during meals—when she condescends to come to them at all. There's a *monstrous* review in the Spectator of The New Republic by Christopher Hophouse—not appreciating it at all—I shall tell him to get you to read it to him and then he may see the light. . . . Yes, you and your pyjamas are a Bank Clerk's wife's dream—or rather everyone's dream—and I shall tell my nephew that I wish to feel and not hear him, except that he mimics incredibly well.

I am a vegetable unworthy of you. Please stick pins into my brain—Jenifer

By this time, Herbert and Jenifer had begun a sexual relationship. But the transition from friendship through attraction to physical intimacy had not been straightforward. In June of 1937, Herbert had taken Jenifer to Glyndebourne to hear *The Marriage of Figaro*. In the interval, while walking in the grounds, he told her that he 'could demonstrate that it would be logical' for her to marry him. She took this to be a proposal, and was so churned up by it that she was quite unable to concentrate on the last act of the opera (hence the reference to Figaro in the letter just quoted). But during a walk on the Sussex Downs the next day, Herbert withdrew the proposal, telling Jenifer that he was unsuitable for marriage. Jenifer was upset and disconcerted by this sudden revelation. Their conversation was inconclusive, but shortly afterwards Herbert felt the need to explain more fully his perplexity. His letter, which echoed the confidence which he had disclosed to Cox a month earlier, revealed the extent to which his emotional life as an adult had been blocked. He told her that a primary source of his feelings of isolation was anxiety about his sexual orientation:

Even the all-inhibiting thought that you will have to make new bets with Guy Chilver must not prevent me trying to write to you the things or some of the things you've got to know if I'm to be honest at all but which freezing self-consciousness stops me telling you when I see you.

First then—if it means anything at all—I love you or at least I do if those words describe my inability for hours and hours on end to think of anything except you; though when I say I think of you I can't tell if I mean your integrity and intelligence or your eyes and hair or my own feeling alive for the first time since I was a boy, which comes over me when I think of any of these things.

Secondly I'm useless to you at this stage as a lover. I don't mean that I am impotent physically because I'm not that in the very least. What I do mean is that I've so long suppressed the physical expression of my feelings (because I thought all my feelings were homosexual) that my whole faculty for expression has atrophied and is only gradually coming to life. Au fond I think I am both passionate and heterosexual but the effect of all the mistakes I've made or which were made for me has been to render me, on the surface and for a good many layers underneath—instinctively suspicious of my own heterosexual feelings. Yours is the only woman's body I've ever loved or from caressing [sic] I've had any physical pleasure. And I am still homosexual to this extent that I feel that if I had sat on the Downs last Sunday with some youth a tenth as beautiful as I think you in the same physical embrace I should have been thrown at once into the extremes of physical passion, whereas in fact it was only at the end that I had any difficulty in controlling myself. As for experience—none homosexual . . .

The letter is tantalizing. It illuminates the stunted nature of Herbert's emotional life and his ambivalent sexual feelings, yet does little more than hint at the sources of 'emotional atrophy' to which it refers. What were the mistakes which he had made or which had been made for him? His overconcentration on work and inability entirely to detach from his family into a fully adult emotional persona seem plausible candidates; another possibility is a habit of repression developed in his unhappy years at Cheltenham, or that he experienced some sexual bullying while there. Whatever the origins of his emotional difficulty, by his own account the most important current factor was his homoerotic orientation, along with his failure entirely to suppress—perhaps even his cultivation of—his homoerotic feelings. To the extent that the Platonic ideal of subjecting the desires to the governance of reason still resonated with Herbert—as one suspects that it did, strongly—he would have felt this to be a serious moral failing.

In the light of both his claim to Jenifer and his inhibited personality, as well as his lifelong anxiety about contravening the law, it is doubtful whether Herbert ever fully acted, physically, on these feelings. But he may well have indulged in fantasies or even flirtations with which he felt, in retrospect, uncomfortable. The latter is hinted at by the slightly hectic, distracted tone of his correspondence with John Sparrow. Sparrow was actively homosexual, as Herbert was aware: Richard Wilberforce recalled sharing many jokes with Herbert during the 1930s about Sparrow's overt displays of his sexual preferences. Ten years later in Oxford a mutual friend detected a certain teasing recognition of Herbert's homoerotic sensibilities in Sparrow's manner towards him. That he had occasionally followed his impulses to some degree is more strongly suggested by a peculiar letter found among his papers. The letter, which cannot be conclusively authenticated because

74

it is not addressed to Herbert by name, appears to be from a doorman at the Savile Club:

Dear Master . . . I can see you again on the same days next week and would be glad if you could let me know if that is O.K. for you. I haven't forgotten what you said at the *end* about not talking to anyone and being extra-cautious. Be sure you can count on me. I am a bit stuck for cash and would be glad if you could pay me in advance for next time.

This is followed by a reference to one of the 'old fogies' letting his hand fall against his as he took off his coat, and giving an extra large tip with a wink. The letter may have been a note addressed to a third party which came into Herbert's possession because he was involved as an intermediary. We can only speculate about its origins, and the reasons why Herbert—never an assiduous archivist—kept it among some of his most personal papers. Whatever the truth, the note suggests that, at the least, Herbert was no stranger to active homosexuality among his acquaintance.

Although Herbert's letter to Jenifer gave few clues to the significant 'mistakes' to which he attributed his 'emotional atrophy', one thing about it is perfectly clear: this remarkably—indeed painfully—frank revelation must have cost him an enormous effort of will. What effect must it have had on Jenifer, to whom a sexual relationship was the natural culmination of her increasing intimacy with Herbert; who was used to being sexually desired; and whose sense of her own sexual power was (and remained) a significant component of her self-esteem? In her autobiography, she recalled a straight-forward refusal to accept that Herbert's bisexual ambivalence could be a barrier to their relationship, since they enjoyed each other's company so much. But it is hard to believe that her reaction was really quite as simple as this, and a residue of doubt about the strength of his attraction to her survived, to resurface in later and more difficult periods of their relationship.

Jenifer's progressive ideas meant that she would not have been shocked by Herbert's confession of homoerotic feelings: she herself delighted in shocking others by confessing to finding both other women's and children's bodies sensually appealing. But from this time on their correspondence is marked by a persistent joking theme around bisexuality or hermaphroditic images reminiscent of Virginia Woolf's *Orlando*. These jokes do not always feel quite comfortable or light-hearted. Humour is often used to explore difficult issues. But whereas Jenifer's and Herbert's political jokes were part of a real dialogue in which they were gradually influencing one another's views, in their 'gender-bending' exchanges, there was an asymmetry. Beneath the light-hearted references, Herbert kept reinforcing the message of his own sexual ambivalence, as he tried to assimilate it with his feelings for Jenifer: 'On the way back [from hunting] I met a charming but slightly vulgar youth who asked me whether I thought him well developed for 18! Nothing however ensued upon this promising opening.' Another example is a letter from Davos in 1938, where the 'hotel was a sanatorium and still looks—and worse—still smells like one: Dark green corridors illumined by dim blue lights and the people all drab and dreary in the extreme'. Here, always physically awkward, Herbert 'can't describe the agonies' of the skiing or the patience of his companions as they wait for him, and told Jenifer that 'the people are not worth describing save this boy who is perfectly beautiful but rather too recessive polite and unexciting for my taste'.

Jenifer, by contrast, played a game, adding bisexuality to her repertoire of sexually liberated and bourgeois-shocking techniques in a way which doesn't feel quite authentic. Writing from Hampstead to Yorkshire, where Herbert was with his parents: 'I am having a grand holiday from baths but otherwise pine for your return. Don't get too great a taste for holidays apart from your devoted and passionate Master.' And from Cornwall, she made risqué jokes about her little nephew, who 'run[s] about with almost nothing on which gives me much aesthetic, though not directly sensual pleasure, unfortunately, as he is rather particular who touches him and doesn't encourage me. . . . The German girl [employed as an au pair by her sister] is going unfortunately, and I shan't be able to gaze at her beautiful figure any more or her wonderful music hall legs'. Most overtly of all, she wrote from Lamledra 'I said you had a luscious bugger boy for this weekend—and hope you have'. Really? Herbert learned to respond in kind: 'Resist the advances of all debauched beasts and/or other men and/or women till I get home.' But one suspects that this was all far more complicated for him than he wished to acknowledge, and that the deeper questions about authenticity, honesty, and openness, as well as the emotional legacy of a habit of repression, were not far from his mind. Intriguingly, it is just these issues which are explored in two verses of Oscar Wilde's *Ballad of Reading Gaol* which Herbert wrote out and apparently sent to Jenifer at about this time:

> Yet each man kills the thing he loves,
> By each let this be heard,
> Some do it with a bitter look,
> Some with a flattering word,
> The coward does it with a kiss,
> The brave man with a sword!
>
> Some kill their love when they are young,
> And some when they are old;
> Some strangle with the hands of Lust,
> Some with the hands of Gold:

The kindest use a knife, because
The dead so soon grow cold.

For Jenifer, too, there must have been a painful side to all this. On first receiving Herbert's letter, though undoubtedly frustrated by his inhibitions, she remained confident that she would be able to overcome them. In the interim, they almost certainly fanned the flames of her desire. She was, after all, a woman who liked a challenge:

Darling. . . . I cannot bear this agony of the flesh much longer. Please love me: I ask nothing else in the world.

and

My dearest Herbert, Perhaps you won't get this—or anyway won't want to. I got precisely 3 and a half hours' sleep last night and feel like blackest Hell. Do let's go away alone together: I long to. I will do anything for you except wear high heel shoes *all* the time. In devotion, Jen

But as time went on a note of desperation and even of vulnerability began to enter her letters, her desire accompanied by a real sense of attachment and the dawning realization of emotional dependence:

Ange plein de everything—it's no use just repeating that I love you for now you will think that it means nothing or anyway is a pretty unoriginal remark. But I want you and no one else in the whole wide world—I want to share and to give ad infinitum everything there is. I don't mind how dependent I am on you—so please accept a clinging limpet—I do adore I do adore—O Christ—But wilt thou accept not—the worship the heart lifts above.

And, in response to an apparently apologetic response from Herbert:

I am not quite sure what I [am] meant to hate you for. I wish I did a little more for then I might be able to think about something else, and to concentrate occasionally for a second or so, not to mention sleep. I should have thought the fascination you had for me had been only too apparent. . . . Anyway I shall try to become more boyish every day!

There is something touchingly brave about that last sentence. Jenifer's optimism, however, had not been entirely misplaced: her persistence and Herbert's strong attraction to her finally overcame his inhibitions. When their sexual relationship finally began, the experience came as an emotional *coup de foudre*:

Darling Jen. . . . I have done nothing all day long except lust and lust and lust for you. I don't want to think or read or speak to anyone but only to lie naked by your side. . . . I've felt entirely different and happy and successful and confident all day. It is exactly like being born again with all of one's faculties absolutely fresh and clear. Christ! Herbert

Soon afterwards, on a professional 'compliments and thanks' slip which he told Jenifer he sent out to 'all my prostitutes'; he wrote that 'All attempts to work have failed and my practice is ruined so you'll have to keep me—in your bed'.

And, by telegram:

DEAR JENIFER THIS IS A NIGHT TELEGRAM AND THEREFORE SUBJECT TO ALL THE INHIBITIONS OF THE POSTMASTER GENERAL NOT TO MENTION THE LAW REGARDING LIBELS OF A PARTICULAR CHARACTER STOP IN THE CIRCUMSTANCES I CAN ONLY HOPE THAT THE FRUIT THE FLOWER THE LEAVES AND THE BRANCHES AND WHATEVER ELSE I PLACED IN YOUR TWO WHITE HANDS ARE STILL UNBROKEN HERBERT

And, amid one of Herbert's rather regular health scares:

My sweet

The doctor photographed my heart today and you will receive a splendid picture of it mounted in red roses. He was puzzled by the presence of a number of blood vessels that arranged themselves so as to form the letter J whenever I took a deep breath. Apart from that and subject to seeing what the photograph is like he said there was nothing to justify leaving the Bar or not having an anaesthetic or (most important) not sleeping with you infinitum—as if anything could justify not sleeping with you for one moment. . . . I swoon with happiness . . .

The breathless, earnest tone of these initial letters—signed off with 'love passion desire', 'perpetually', 'infinitely', 'inextricably', 'incontinently'—gradually gave way to the lighter tone of the earlier correspondence. It was a lightness suffused with deep happiness: 'Our communications are bound in time to reach the sublime ineffable and be expressed by the exchange of blank sheets of paper . . .' and, parodying his parents' business patter, 'Remember any alterations will be made to the customer's pleasure and free of charge'. And from chambers: 'The Ballet was wonderful last night. Swan Lake and the Berlioz thing both pervaded with sensual images of you. In perpetuity, Herbert'.

In his new-found happiness and confidence, there is not only gratitude to Jenifer, but also evidence of Herbert's real capacity to reflect on another person's feelings: 'I shall be there at 8.50 unless I go mad before then. Did you feel like this all those times we went out together and nothing happened? If you did I can't understand your not having murdered me. Solicitors walk into my chambers and give me documents to read and look rather puzzled when

I lose the place because visions of your breasts and hair and shoulders float across the paper'. 'For the first time in my life I feel pangs of conscience:—about the way I behave to you. Tell me when I am hell as I must be often.'

Both of them felt that this would be a long-lasting relationship. But marriage was problematic. Jenifer, at 24, did not feel ready to marry: she also faced the obstacle of the Civil Service's bar on the employment of married women. She was reluctant to sacrifice the professional achievements for which she had worked with such determination. Encumbered by a commitment to neither religious nor other conventional standards, the two of them swiftly reached the conclusion that she should simply move in to Herbert's lodgings at Hampstead Square. In the late summer of 1937, Jenifer was looking forward to it rapturously:

My dearest Herbert,

I feel waves of benevolence and acute happiness floating up and through me as I think of Hampstead Square and what bliss it will be. I had thought of a list of reasons why from your point of view I should not come—but I shan't send them to you as there might *conceivably* be some you had not yet thought of. One should be practical: I read Helena Wright's book on sex. . . . I hope you admire Treasury economy in the stuff they give us to write on [tracing paper]—I told Henderson [the head of her Division] I believed in promiscuity and grew furious when he disagreed—but I don't, as I only want you—Your letter was intoxicating.

Herbert's eccentric landlady, Coucou, was initially disconcerted by Jenifer's arrival, but she soon came to the conclusion that Jenifer was a happy addition to the household, someone who might mitigate what she saw as Herbert's stressful relationship with his family. Jenifer wrote to Herbert from Hampstead in 1937, during one of his trips north to see his family, 'My angel face, I am always writing, talking to you in my imagination—and somehow I find it very difficult to implement the wonderful intentions I have. Your letter last night made me scream with laughter so much . . . that I could not possibly hold a pen still'; Jenifer went on to report that Coucou (in his reply, Herbert was careful to correct Jenifer's reference to 'Cuckoo'), had asked fondly after Herbert, opining that he looked 'wistful' when he went away: 'His family always gets him down.'

Jenifer's and Herbert's decision to move in together did not mark a change in their respective habits of spending periods of time with their families. Reading her diary in London in September 1938 while Jenifer was in Cornwall, Herbert wrote: 'It's a very good diary and much more . . . revelatory than you could have intended. But it makes me enamoured of a 17 year old edition of you—I hope not to the exclusion of the 24 year old.' At the other end of the correspondence, Jenifer 'shuddered to think of you heaping up ammunition from my diary: What a fool I was to leave it there. The more I see of these schoolgirls with their "honestly's" and mixture of self-abasement and crude self-interested laziness the more I dislike the age'. Beyond this, she replied equally fondly: 'The sea has been divine smooth flat glistening and a sort of silver blue all day. . . . There were mysterious banks of fog which drifted about and started up the fog horns which I always like. I have seldom felt so lazy or contented. I must have become infected by your equanimity somehow . . .' (She was able to reflect ruefully, however, on how lucky her sister Prue was to have a tidy husband.)

In Herbert's case, the continued sojourns with his family right into his mid-thirties were a product of habit combined with his dutiful feelings towards his parents and his sense of responsibility to and affection for his mother and sister. In Jenifer's, the explanation is more elusive—not least because her letters from Lamledra are punctuated by outbursts of extreme irritation and by constant complaints about her mother and about the prevailing household mores: 'Mariella I am in love with—and I wanted passionately last night to tell her so—but one couldn't ever—I told her about you. She was very thrilled, asked a lot about you and the legal profession. My nephew is fascinating—but the way all these people treat him drives me mad. He is made to say please and thank you the whole buggering time—and even to flatten himself against the wall when "Gran" comes along—It is insufferable. He plays the most sexual games with tins and water all the time—I can think of nothing to say to him but he looks very nice.' Her attitude to her mother ranged from the dismissive to the hostile: from the nursing home in 1937 she told Herbert that 'I've had a nauseating letter from Mother saying how miserable they were without any of us with them—and then vague comments about death, her sister having just died, with the usual yearning after some sign that there is an after life . . . '. Why, as an independent woman with an absorbing career and an important relationship, did Jenifer continue to subject herself to weeks in the company of people she found so uncongenial? The answer had to do with the strength of family conventions at the time, and probably with a certain amount of economy with the truth in the early years of her cohabitation with Herbert. But the depth of Jenifer's identification with her family, and with the privileges with which it was associated, was almost certainly deeper than she was willing to acknowledge to herself.

By the end of 1937, then, Herbert's life had taken a decisive turn. Despite his 'emotionally frozen' early adulthood, he had fallen deeply in love. It is hardly surprising that Jenifer, with her boyish, vigorous, willowy physique, her vivid personality, her striking intelligence, and her almost alarming strength of will, was the person who broke through Herbert's emotional isolation. Perhaps only someone with Jenifer's sexual experience and robust attitude to sex would have had the confidence to persist in the face of Herbert's inhibitions and doubts about his sexuality. Beyond the early physical passion, however, the issue of sex remained a complex one between them. For Herbert, the emotional closeness which sex implied was the vital (and difficult) thing; whereas for Jenifer, it was crucially important to be desired. Had sexual attraction, mutual interests, and common commitments—intellectual exchanges, a love of the English countryside and of walking, a sense of social responsibility, steadfast atheism shading into a contempt for religion—been the only things they shared, the relationship might not have lasted.

The web which bound them together was, however, more complex than this, and it had not a little to do with their respective backgrounds. For Jenifer, Herbert represented a potent mix of all that she admired in her own father. He was luminously intelligent (in this, Herbert outshone her father by a considerable degree); he was a broad-minded liberal; and, as it happened (it seems unlikely to have been irrelevant, and it made Herbert in due course a more acceptable son-in-law) he was also a New College-educated lawyer. But Herbert's Jewish trade background also meant that he represented to Jenifer something different, even something exotic. Though he had 'bourgeois' tastes, she could believe that she was not capitulating to the class system by attaching herself to him; and she could think of her attachment to Herbert as the product of all that she valued—reason, culture, intelligence—and of nothing which she rejected. For someone to whom everything had come easily—academic success, interesting friendships, a stimulating career, sexual admiration—the challenge which Herbert's emotional reserve presented was probably a further attraction. And it is not clear quite how much deep intimacy Jenifer needed or wanted: Herbert's reserve may not have worried her as it would have troubled a more emotionally vulnerable person.

Conversely, Jenifer represented to Herbert a number of things which he may not have articulated to himself, but which made him feel comfortable and successful. As his life in the earlier part of the decade shows, he was both drawn to and repelled by the privilege, self-confidence, and social ease of the upper middle classes. In Jenifer, he found a combination which he could manage. She was impeccably upper middle class, and a relationship with her gave him access to the insider culture to which, notwithstanding his protestations to the contrary, he aspired yet felt that he did not fully belong. But she came from the intelligentsia, and her radical politics removed her from the censure which Herbert might have attached to a less thoughtful and independent-minded member of her class. Her independence of mind not only appealed to his liberalism and belief in the 'aristocracy of the intellect': it probably also reassured him that she would not make emotional demands or create dependencies which he could not meet. And her recklessness and zest for life must have appealed to his more cautious temperament.

From the outside, and from the point of view of the extraordinarily rationalist perspective which, other than in moments of sexual passion, Jenifer and Herbert shared, it must have looked like a relationship made in heaven: a meeting of two gifted, attractive, and like-minded people. But in their underlying emotional lives there were cross currents. Certainly, there were strong dynamics pulling them together. But there were also differences which would make for problems in the years to come. For Herbert, his love for Jenifer brought a fundamental attachment, and along with it emotions such as jealousy which he found hard to manage and which Jenifer found difficult to understand. And the patterns formed in Herbert's early life proved more persistent than they seemed at the height of his passion in 1937. In difficult times, the pattern of withdrawal and reserve would reassert itself. For Jenifer, the habit of seeking wide admiration and stimulation would be hard to break: her need for real intimacy was relatively weak or, perhaps, her commitment to keep fighting for it was vulnerable to the intervention of other distractions. But in 1937 and for some years to come, these problems and misunderstandings were in the future, and Herbert and Jenifer enjoyed a period of profound personal happiness.

CHAPTER 5

From the Inns of Court to Military Intelligence: MI5, Marriage, and Fatherhood

I N 1939, his relationship with Jenifer firmly established and his legal practice flourishing, Herbert Hart's life, like the lives of his contemporaries, was diverted from its track by the outbreak of the Second World War. Britain's declaration of war on Germany at the beginning of September 1939 came as no surprise. Herbert had been convinced that war with Germany was inevitable since 1936, and had registered with the Voluntary Army Officers' Reserve that year. After war broke out, he was duly called up; he had an interview, which included French and German language tests, with the Military Police in Aldershot. He was told that he would be required to undertake training in December and would be sent to live under cover with a French family in order to give reports on espionage activities in France. In the event, as he told Cox:

I was slung out in the medical exam—Class III—apparently because of my heart . . . and they will only take Class I and II for the M.P. It is more maddening than I can say—I had wound up my practice and made all the preparations psychological and otherwise for going away but I suppose there is little I can do. There is a rather inferior section of the M.P. which sits about at ports and harbours which will take Class III but I don't know that I want to do that. On the other hand I can't bear the thought of going on making pots of money at the Bar through the absence of those who would be my competitors normally. Have you any suggestions? Ways into the M.P. or any of those *ministries?* Sorry to be a bore . . . but you may have heard of something.

Herbert was deeply troubled at the thought that he would be unable to contribute to what he believed was a just war. This was a normal concern, but was it also fed by memories of the prejudices about Jewish participation in the First World War which had been current in the north-east of England in his childhood? Determined to participate in some active way, he applied to join the Field Security Police, whose medical standards were lower. He regarded this prospect with his usual irony: 'Do you hear of my new job?' he wrote to Isaiah Berlin in November, 'It sounds like a music-hall turn.' Beyond the irony, he prepared earnestly; he equipped himself with some relevant accoutrements, such as warm underwear and steel rimmed glasses, and learned to ride a motorbike ('what a shame a horse won't do instead', he remarked to Cox) on which he charged 'dangerously round the streets of Hampstead'. Again he was rejected. He and Jenifer were reassured by a visit to a Harley Street specialist that the heart murmur posed no real threat to his health. But Herbert was wretched at the thought of continuing his legal practice while all his friends were contributing to the war effort.

Return to the Bar, however, he did, and carried on his practice for a few dismal but very busy months. He pondered anxiously 'the wobbling on the left' but discounted the prospect of a peace settlement, remarking to Cox that Hitler's latest pronouncements were 'poor even by his own poor standards'. On the outbreak of war he and Jenifer had moved into Douglas and Peggy Jay's house in Well Walk, Hampstead, Peggy and the Jay children (including the future diplomat and journalist, Peter) having been evacuated from London. Here they were surrounded by friends—including, a little later, Christopher Cox, now at the Colonial Office, Jenifer's old friend and fellow Home Office civil servant Francis Graham-Harrison, Patrick Reilly of the Foreign Office, and the Hungarian economist Thomas Balogh—most of whom were working in war-related public service. Though the lively company, and the fact that Douglas Jay too remained for the moment in civilian life, buoyed up Herbert's spirits, the contrast between his friends' and Jenifer's working situation and his own was painful. He asked these and other well-connected friends to look out for any opportunity which might be open to him to work in a war-related capacity.

In the summer of 1940, just such an opportunity presented itself. Jenifer, by now Private Secretary to Sir Alexander Maxwell, the Permanent Under-Secretary of State at the Home Office, was approached in June by Brigadier Jasper Harker, one of two deputies to Sir Vernon Kell, Director General of MI5. Harker asked whether she knew of anyone suitable as a recruit. She replied to Harker on 17 June, suggesting Herbert; on 29 June Herbert went to see Guy Liddell, the head of one of MI5's divisions, and on 3 July Herbert signed an Official Secrets Act declaration and was immediately put to work on highly responsible counter-espionage duties. He apparently started work before a formal recruitment check was completed: a few weeks later, Harker again came to see Jenifer to tell her that MI5 'liked Herbert and thought him very able' but wondered if he was 'all right?' Late in the day, MI5 had discovered that his home address was subject to a warrant authorizing the Post Office to intercept foreign mail directed there. The suspect turned out to be Douglas Jay, then a journalist on the *Daily Herald*, who had been reported to MI5 as having 'sinister foreign contacts'. Herbert was duly cleared and his formal appointment to MI5 confirmed. Confident of Douglas's loyalty, he was able to reassure MI5 and, ultimately, to have Douglas's file destroyed, though the imputation delayed for at least a year Douglas's recruitment by the Ministry of Labour and Supply, despite his presence on the national register of those keen to do war work. In the meantime Jenifer, her communist past not far behind her, had a nasty fright. In the course of her conversation with Harker about Herbert, the name of one of her Communist Party friends had come up, and Harker had asked her, 'You weren't a communist, were you?' 'Oh, we were all red in our youth', Jenifer replied, with a *sang froid* which belied her deep alarm.

The ramshackle procedures illustrated by Herbert's recruitment and Harker's later approach to Jenifer were typical of MI5 in the early months of the war. It was in a lamentable state. Despite some increases in staff in the years immediately before the war, it remained a small organization: in September 1939 it had 83 officers and 253 supporting staff, as compared with 35 officers and 120 others a year earlier. The organization was now utterly overwhelmed with work and was in the process of rapid expansion. By July 1940, it had grown to twice its September 1939 size, and by 1941 it had almost 900 staff.

But MI5's problems at the start of the war were not merely those of size. There was also a serious problem of quality, of both personnel and operating systems. The blacklisting of Douglas Jay is just one instance of the service's haphazard methods and poor judgment: in the absence of any systematic system of positive vetting, MI5's surveillance of the famously Anglophile and Europhobic Jay appears to have been based on nothing more substantial than his having attended, at the behest of a current woman friend, a meeting in Paris in 1936 which was addressed by the French Communist, Maurice Thorez. And yet in the same period—this was before July 1940, and the Soviet Union still had a non-aggression pact with Germany—the security services were busy recruiting men like Guy Burgess (who, though never formally employed by MI5, had run an agent for it) and Kim Philby, Communists who had already been engaged as Soviet agents. The history of Anthony Blunt's recruitment is also instructive: he received two replies to his application to join Military Intelligence in 1939, of which one rejected him (he assumed on the basis of his fellow-travelling past), while the other asked him to report to Minley Manor in Aldershot for training. After service in France in the early months of the war, Blunt was introduced to MI5 by Victor Rothschild in July 1940, and was recruited in spite of the fact that MI5 had itself questioned him about his loyalty during his training at Minley. As an MI5 officer he was later able to locate his own security file, only to discover that it consisted merely of the information that he had visited the Soviet Union and a postcard from Trinity College Cambridge fellow Maurice Dobb recommending him to the editors of the *Left Review* (Blunt assumed that further information casting doubt on his loyalty— probably in the form of a letter—had existed but never reached his file).

Until 1939, both MI5 and MI6 had been staffed largely by officers retired from public services such as the army, navy, and home and colonial police. Salaries were small, so only those with independent means or a pension were able to take up the positions. MI5 had recruited its first graduate as recently as 1936. This was Dick White, an Oxford graduate and former school-master. A cultured man with a strong interest in the arts and in writing, and the main architect of the successful Double Cross disinformation system, White would go on to become Head of MI5 and of MI6. He was followed by a trickle of well qualified, imaginative people, such as Roger Hollis, another future Director of MI5, who would form the core of the new more flexible and professional operation which began to develop in the wake of war. But the remarkable fact is that in the period before the war, Soviet Intelligence had more British graduates working for it than did MI5 and MI6 combined. Even in the initial expansion which followed the outbreak of war, the majority of new officer recruits were of the same caste as their colleagues; and many of the secretarial staff were the daughters of moneyed families—'reliable Mayfair types', as Kell described them to Jenifer—whose fathers had themselves worked in the intelligence services.

Brigadier Harker's approach to civil servants like Jenifer was a direct result of the chaos in which MI5 found itself as it struggled to manage its burgeoning and transformed workload from late 1939 onwards. On 10 June 1940, Winston Churchill forced the retirement of both the Director, Sir Vernon Kell, and his Deputy, Sir Eric Holt Wilson, replacing them provisionally with Harker (a 55-year-old former officer in the Indian police and regular soldier who had joined MI5 in 1920). To his and other officers' annoyance, as Acting Director General Harker was made to work under the supervision of political grandees Lord Swinton, Sir Joseph Ball, and Sir William Crocker. In November, still dissatisfied with the performance of MI5, Churchill asked Sir David Petrie, a former colonial police officer, to report on the organization of the service. Petrie recommended restructur-ing, and accepted appointment as Director General in March 1941, on condition that Swinton's supervision be discontinued.

But the prime movers in the shake-up which would bring men like Herbert to MI5 were Guy Liddell, head of MI5's B division, and his deputy Dick White. Liddell was an enigmatic character. A First World War hero with experience in the Special Branch, he was superficially a conventional person. But behind the bland, dapper, plump, balding (and chain-smoking) exterior lay an imaginative and independent thinker: a connoisseur of fine arts and music, and a talented cellist. Liddell could be biting in his criticism of colleagues—an illustrative description from his diary casts one of them as 'in a little water-tight compartment carrying on his work in a rather pompous and eye-washing way without any regard for war-time conditions'. He had an equally biting sense of humour—on hearing that a colleague was considering resigning because of 'jealousy on my part', he remarked 'This is certainly an interesting point of view and I am deeply intrigued to know what I am supposed to be jealous of'; while on another occasion he anticipated that an arrested suspect would find his cell 'somewhat of a change from Claridges'. But he also knew how to value his talented colleagues, and he quickly gained Herbert's affection and respect. Liddell's experience of corruption in the Special Branch—and perhaps the gradual and emotionally catastrophic breakdown of his marriage to the society heiress Calypso Baring (the couple divorced in 1943), which left him with an indelible sadness—had given him a healthy suspicion of the establishment. This in turn strengthened his determination to bring new blood into MI5. Liddell and White advocated a new recruitment strategy geared to bringing in academic high-flyers. Their plan was accepted.

As part of the new, much more broadly based intake recruited as a result of Liddell's and White's initiative—an intake which included a large number of lawyers—Herbert joined a remarkable group of colleagues. They included Cambridge graduates Victor Rothschild, who had been recruited as scientific advisor on industrial sabotage and counter-sabotage policy, and Tess Mayor, who would become Rothschild's second wife; Anthony Blunt, the distinguished art historian and (as it turned out) Soviet spy; Martin Furnival-Jones, a lawyer and a future Director General of MI5; and Hugh Astor. Initially they also included Oxford philosophers Stuart Hampshire and Gilbert Ryle and the historian Hugh Trevor Roper. These three were later moved to MI6, where they joined Cambridge graduate Kim Philby, and where Guy Burgess had been employed, briefly, in Section D, before returning to the BBC in 1940 on the section's merger with Special Operations.

The huge influx of new blood combined with the demands posed by the country's security needs created an unusual working environment. On the one hand, a culture of professionalism and of systematic organization was formed; on the other, the varied professional and personal backgrounds of the new recruits, combined with their high levels of intelligence and independent-mindedness, and with the rapid change of institutional culture, led to a relatively fluid, informal, non-hierarchical, and non-bureaucratic atmosphere very different from that of a classic civil service department of that time.

This informality fostered working relationships which also became friendships, and Herbert formed important ties with Liddell, White, Rothschild, and Mayor. Victor Rothschild and Guy Liddell were drawn together by their enjoyment of music and, a little later, the bruising experience of marital breakdown. They became close friends and shared a cottage at Tring to which many members of the group, including Herbert, retreated from time to time for weekend house parties. Liddell, Blunt, Burgess, Rothschild, and Tomàs Harris—the last originally in MI6 but later moved to MI5 to run agents in the Double Cross disinformation system—often met in the Reform Club. In the intense atmosphere of war-time London, pressure-relieving, heavy-drinking socializing was a familiar after-work activity. Though Herbert's habits were moderate when compared with the Bacchanalian standards of men like Burgess, Blunt, and other playboy characters in the security services, and though he was not a core member of the Reform Club group (in Liddell's diaries, he is referred to as 'Hart' down to late 1943, while Rothschild, White, and Philby are generally referred to by their first names) he was no stranger to the occasionally wild social life with which relatively well-to-do professionals diverted themselves in Blitz-hit London.

Herbert was assigned to B division, which was the core of MI5. It was concerned with counter-espionage, running surveillance and investigation operations which aimed to prevent espionage and identify spies within the UK. Most important of all, B Division developed and operated the highly successful 'Double Cross' system through which strategically damaging misinformation was fed back to Germany by double agents. This allowed counter-intelligence to be used as a positive rather than merely a defensive strategy. The division's methods ranged from the hair-raising to the banal via the painstakingly methodical. While the diplomatic surveillance unit developed by Blunt employed techniques such as unstitching and re-stitching diplomatic mailbags so as to examine their contents, regional officers spent much of their time gathering tiny pieces of information or following up local leads, and much of the work undertaken in London consisted of protracted and exacting analytic paperwork. Under the leadership of Liddell and White, aided by individual initiative and systematic coordination and planning, these multifarious activities added up to a division which soon came to be regarded as MI5's most important branch.

Throughout the war, Herbert's work centred on counter-espionage, but his contributions to this work took a number of forms. Initially he was in division B3B and was mainly involved in reviewing the visa or exit applications of Hungarians, Romanians, Bulgarians, and Yugoslavians. Soon afterwards, when it became clear that Hungary, Romania, and Bulgaria were likely to join the Axis powers, he was involved in the implementation of 'black and white' lists to regulate the detention of their nationals on the declaration of war.

We have little information about how Herbert coped with his sudden immersion in an entirely new working environment. His extreme discretion meant that even Jenifer knew only in the broadest terms what his work involved. But she remembered him enjoying it enormously. He was relieved to be doing important war work. He found many of his colleagues—several of whom, including Rothschild and Blunt, he had met before the war—congenial, and the un-stuffy and goal-directed atmosphere of MI5 suited him perfectly. He quickly gained Dick White's particular admiration: White 'always took Herbert's advice and followed him wherever he could'. Liddell, too, had complete confidence in Herbert: his diaries include frequent remarks such as 'Hart took the situation in hand', and—in marked contrast to his attitude to some other colleagues—not a single word of criticism. Still, it must have been a challenge for Herbert to hit the ground running in such a new field of work, especially given that at the time of his arrival MI5 was still organizationally and physically unsettled due to its rapid expansion.

In the early months, Herbert was often working and sometimes sleeping in a cell at Wormwood Scrubs. Chaos followed when Wormwood Scrubs was bombed in September 1940, causing the loss of masses of important records and necessitating a move to new premises at 58 St. James Street in Mayfair. And yet there is no trace in Herbert's correspondence of the time of any of the strain, anxiety, or soul-searching which characterized several of his subsequent changes of job. The imperative of war, the intense need to be involved, to demonstrate his loyalty and belonging, and the practical orientation of the job, with its well-defined demands, all suited him. He enjoyed the war-time camaraderie and humour, captured by a joke he liked to tell in later life about an MI5 file whose cover read, 'TOP SECRET DOCUMENTS: BURN BEFORE READING!' And amid the sometimes bizarre world of military intelligence, he always maintained a level head—even a kind of innocence: 'Everybody in the world of intelligence adored Herbert: he was the perfect intelligence officer . . . . He was absolutely accurate and reliable, but not very intuitive. He was also very sensible in a crazy world: he was perpetually amazed at what was going on. This was characteristic of him: to be amazed at ordinary human folly.'

In any event, Herbert performed well in his early role: at the beginning of 1941 he was put in charge of the more important B1B division. B1B was the steering section for B Division as a whole, and here Herbert quickly assumed a leading role in the development of counter-espionage policy. B1B received and analysed information from sources ranging from the most secret to the relatively banal and used it for counter-espionage purposes. At one end of the spectrum, its information base included the product of ISOS—intercepted radio messages sent from and received by the German Intelligence Service in the course of communications with its agents and bases outside Germany. In particular, B1B had access to the hugely important ULTRA information produced at Bletchley Park as a result of MI6 cryptographers' success in cracking the German Enigma code. But though the ISOS information was undoubtedly its most important resource, B1B also had to assimilate huge amounts of data from a range of other sources: surveillance operations; interrogations of agents or suspected agents; information from police, civilian, and military institutions across the country. B1B superintended all espionage investigations; briefed and advised the interrogators; decided, in consultation with B1A, whether a detected spy would be used as a double agent (the agents, once selected, were managed by B1A); and determined, with the Home Office and the Director of Public Prosecutions, whether a suspected spy was to be tried or simply detained.

Under Herbert's leadership, the staff of B1B amassed a treasure-trove of highly sensitive intelligence material and developed an encyclopaedic knowledge of the German intelligence attack against Britain. The real trick, however—and one for which Herbert's intellectual training, professional experience, extreme intelligence, and remarkable gift for languages equipped him superbly well—was to assimilate, interpret, and organize this information so that it could be used to maximum effect by the various different organizations to which it was relevant: B1A in running its double agents, police forces, immigration authorities, coast guards, military personnel. At a meeting of key B division staff each Wednesday, Herbert had the crucial responsibility of presenting an overview and assessment of the latest ISOS information to his colleagues. Here his lawyer's capacity to assimilate and master a brief, his ancient historian's skill in marshalling and evaluating evidence, and his philosopher's taste for precision and method all stood him in good stead. Liddell's estimation of Herbert's insight is reflected in his comment that the head of a counterpart division of MI6 'clearly has nobody to give him a general appreciation of this information in the way that Hart provides it for us'.

But in one respect, Herbert's apparently easy transition to MI5 is surprising. Among his many talents, systematic working practices were a notable exception. In his later, academic career, he lived among jumbled papers, chaotically littered studies, and repeatedly annotated, crossed out, crumpled notes. That his ways at MI5 were not entirely different is suggested by one colleague's observation that 'you could always tell when Herbert had had a file, as it had Herbert-like inkspots all over it'. His own sense of discomfort at the state of his desk is reflected in a story he told in later life of distrusting Guy Burgess and feeling he ought to cover his papers whenever Burgess came into the room. As the colleague to whom he told the story observed: 'It is hard to imagine Herbert being physically organized enough to do that!' The story is instructive: although Burgess was employed by MI6 rather than MI5, and had in any case returned to the BBC by the time Herbert joined BıB, he was apparently in the habit of wandering into MI5 relatively regularly to visit Blunt, with whom Herbert occasionally shared an office. Liddell, who had regular social contact with Burgess and Blunt, had always taken the view that left-wing sympathies were an occupational hazard of academic life and should be no barrier to employment in the intelligence services. He later protested that he too had not trusted Burgess and had urged officers not to leave papers lying around if Burgess was in the office. Herbert's repetition of this story must reflect a feeling of tension about his levels of disorganization while working in an office which he shared with two or three other officers. In the context of a mass of secret documents, his later rationale 'You don't need an orderly desk if your mind is tidy' was not entirely reassuring. Yet just as lucid, economical books and articles would emerge in later life from radically disorganized materials, so crystalline conclusions, refined hypotheses, streamlined procedures, clear instructions, and well formulated policies emerged from Herbert's awkward interactions with the mountains of paper which crossed his desk at MI5.

The reputation for reliability and acuteness which Herbert quickly established, and his capacity to inspire the trust of his colleagues not only in MI5 but also in MI6, played a crucial role in ensuring that BıB had access to the best possible information. Before his appointment, and to some extent throughout the war, the division had difficulty getting access to all the ISOS information it needed. The relationship between MI6 and MI5 was prone to produce tensions and empire-building: on occasion it produced outright animosity. For while MI5 was transforming itself into a flexible organization with a high-flying staff and a clear remit to develop policy, MI6 had maintained the military, clubby, old-boy culture of the pre-war era: it saw its main task as protecting its own agents, and its predisposition was therefore to try to keep hold of, rather than to share, its information. The tensions must have been especially acute in relation to the 'ULTRA' information from Bletchley Park's surveillance and decoding operations. So secret was the ULTRA project that even Churchill only slipped up and mentioned it two or three times during the war. At Bletchley, decoders would work in isolated booths decrypting fragments of messages. Only senior officers had access to any coherent body of information, and only the very senior saw enough to be able to grasp its meaning and assess its strategic significance. MI6 guarded this information jealously: White himself was only briefed in the spring of 1942 on the fact that the Enigma machine code had been cracked at Bletchley on Christmas Day 1941. The institutional attitude is summed up by one former MI6 officer's comment: 'MI6 owned ULTRA because MI6 owned Bletchley Park . . . . It was a pure act of favour that MI5 got anywhere near ULTRA.'

This difficult relationship between MI5 and MI6—in particular its Section V, which was in charge of all counter-espionage outside British territory, work which often overlapped with that of MI5's B Division—was a constant source of frustration and perplexity to Liddell and White, and Herbert was one of the key people they relied on to help them manage it. A fundamental problem was MI6's insistence that sharing their information would pose a security risk, and one of their key tasks was therefore to convince their MI6 counterparts that their officers were entirely trustworthy. It was a preoccupation which reached even White's subconscious, as Liddell's diary amusingly attests:

Dick has had a dream. He was walking through Trafalgar Square with Felix [Cowgill, head of MI6's Section V], when to his horrow [sic] and amazement he heard someone shouting 'ISOS! ISOS'! As he came round the corner he saw Herbert Hart selling copies at 1d. each. He expressed his regret for this incident and said he would look into the matter as soon as he got home. Felix merely replied 'Oh don't bother. I always knew that this sort of thing was going on'.

As the dream reveals, Herbert was one of the people whom it was imperative for MI6 to trust, for Liddell's and White's confidence in him led them not only to consult him regularly on how to manage the structural relationship between the two organizations but also to use him throughout the war as a key bridge to MI6. A sign of their confidence was his membership (along with each of them, as the MI5 representatives) of the Radio Security Intelligence Committee, which met fortnightly to ensure the proper coordination of work across the security services. In relation to the ULTRA material, Herbert was MI5's immediate link with MI6 and, building on Liddell's and White's negotiations to promote cooperation between the two organizations, he quickly established a more constructive and trusting working relationship with MI6 officers. It helped that, as Liddell recorded, he was '100% persona grata with Philby', and that Hugh Trevor Roper and

Herbert's future colleagues, the philosophers Gilbert Ryle and Stuart Hampshire, had by this time moved to MI6 from MI5. A high level of trust and a sense of team spirit began to develop between these four men, with Herbert at one point meeting Ryle and Hampshire once a week. This special relationship, which caused raised eyebrows in other parts of MI6, was fostered during the relatively brief period in which MI5 and MI6 were located together in Barnet. For most of the war, however, Herbert was based in St. James Street in central London, while, apart from a unit created at Ryder Street in St. James as a result of White's efforts to promote cooperation, MI6 was based at St. Albans and at Bletchley. In spite of this physical distance, and of its being 'an act of favour', the substantial access which Herbert gained to the highly sensitive ULTRA radio intercepts made a real difference to the effectiveness with which his department was able to work. Hampshire's later observation that Herbert was a 'natural cryptographer', as well as Liddell's reference to Herbert's identifying security problems with the codes used for sending messages to troops, suggest that the exchange of information and advice was not all in one direction, and that the working relationship between these small sections of MI5 and MI6 had become a close and mutually productive one.

At the end of the war, Herbert wrote a series of memoranda for the intelligence services detailing his work during the past five years, and these reports give a sense of the range of his work. It had three dimensions. The first was the assimilation, analysis, and evaluation of a vast amount of material of potential relevance to counter-espionage strategy. Second, he was responsible for the dissemination of this information, distilled into usable form, to a range of organizations in order to maximize the effectiveness of security operations. His third role was the investigation of particular cases of alleged espionage.

The assimilation aspect of his work depended on a regular flow of information, and from time to time—particularly in 1941 and 1942—Herbert knew lulls in his workload during the periods when the ULTRA information temporarily ran dry as the Germans re-set their machines and decoders struggled to crack the change of code. During these times, he and other temporarily under-employed officers often worked in a local button factory. When the information was coming in, he would be working mainly in the office, though he had regular contact with MI6, travelling occasionally to Bletchley for meetings with MI6's outside link, and also making trips to MI5 headquarters at Blenheim Palace. But the information which he had to manage was by no means restricted to ULTRA, and included data on aircraft tracks supplied by RAF Command as well as police and army reports on apprehended suspects. In a rare reference to his work in a letter to Jenifer, he estimated that he had read 1500 pages of German correspondence over 8 days. (He compensated for this by resorting in his spare time to a 'good stylist', Walter Scott: amid his heavy war work, he continued to find time not only for novels—Virginia Woolf and Henry James among others—but also for philosophical books, including the latest by Bertrand Russell.) Reports assimilating this information included memoranda on German naval espionage, on German use of Allied seamen, on operational use by the Germans of information obtained from intelligence sources, and on remnants of German organization in Belgium after the military withdrawal. In October 1942 he presented a memo to Liddell analysing the activities of the German Intelligence Service since 1939, on the basis of which a variety of conclusions were drawn about how best to focus counter-espionage policy.

The dissemination work also took a range of forms, some of which took Herbert out of London. He delivered lectures, issued reports, sets of instructions, and codes of practice, and monitored decision making on the ground so as to feed the lessons of common mistakes back into the system of advice issued by B1B to the police, coast guards, army staff, immigration officers, ship owners, and, later on, the resident US forces. The essence of the task was to assimilate the lessons to be learned from a vast amount of data, and to reduce this to a model which could then be expressed in the form of simple—sometimes hilariously so—instructions to decision makers on the ground. The sparse, clear style of many of these instructions provides an interesting foretaste of Herbert's economical written style as an academic. This work took a considerable amount of his time, for he personally delivered many of the lectures to the police and its Special Branch.

Some extracts from Herbert's 1945 memorandum give a flavour of this work and reveal its strategic importance in the preparations for Operation Overlord, in particular to the disinformation campaign carried on from early 1943 and designed to use double agents to confuse German intelligence about the location and timing of the D Day Landings in June 1944:

From early in 1941 one of the tasks performed by my section was the preparation of summaries and memoranda . . . [on] the current activities of the German Secret Services so far as this country was concerned . . . . Later I produced memoranda and summaries in a form which could be passed to the Police at lectures, and finally a good deal of lecturing to Special Branch meetings in most parts of the country, and summaries were distributed at these meetings showing the characteristic 'form' of the German agents arriving by small boat or parachute. . . . At such lectures I exhibited the types of illicit W/T [wireless/transmitter] set brought into the country by enemy agents, forged identity cards used by them, and discussed the most likely methods of catching agents of this type. In the weeks preceding OVERLORD we endeavoured to raise the general standard of efficiency in detecting agents at large who generally landed by parachute or small boat, by arranging exercises simulating as nearly as possible 'the real thing'. These exercises were held in most of the regions of Southern England and a few in the North and were not only of considerable interest to those taking part but did show what were the principal gaps during this very important period in the Security defences against this type of agent. In some cases the Police had become remarkably efficient in throwing cordons round areas where a spy was suspected, but in other respects, e.g. in detecting gross forgeries in identity cards, the level was low. The danger constituted by a spy passing as an American soldier was as we had anticipated proved by these exercises to be considerable, since in such disguise the agent generally escaped detection . . . . The main object of these lectures to Police audiences, apart from keeping their interest in security alive, was to raise their standards of discrimination and to give them some perspective or rational background to their security work, by getting them to appreciate what were likely to be dangers and what were not, and to have confidence in our approach to the security problem.

Herbert's method was to construct a model by distilling the most common features of cases detected so far. These models were designed both to direct attention to the most prevalent risks (countering, for example, the widespread misapprehension that residents, as opposed to recent entrants, posed the greatest likelihood of a security risk) and to give practical advice about identification and apprehension. Spies, for example, were classified into two main types, 'Spies illegally landed' and 'Legally landed agents'. In relation to illegally landed spies, instructions were given on their favourite landing areas, the 'time and manner of landing' ('always at night and usually low cloud, between 9pm and 3am. Several of the parachutists have been hurt on landing, e.g. strained wrists, broken ankles, or knocked themselves unconscious with gear'); 'behaviour on landing' ('immediately occupied with hiding or cutting up gear and parachute, in rabbit holes or haystacks'); their objectives ('to send reports back by W/T on aerodromes, defences, weather, civilian morale. . . . Saboteurs have arrived equipped with detonators and sabotage material with instructions to blow up factories, food dumps, interfere with communications by destroying wires, etc.'); their equipment ('W/T apparatus, disguised in suitcase, money, large sums in genuine £ notes or dollars; food, e.g. chocolate, often in Belgian wrappers or Dutch wrappers; pyramidon or aspirin tablets; large scale maps, revolver, uniform, worn over civilian clothing, uniform discarded when successful landing made'); and their documents.

Some of the most specific instructions had to do with common mistakes in forged documents:

As is now well known, the enemy has usually made a number of mistakes in completing the National Registration Identity Card, with which his agents have been provided. These errors, however, though sometimes gross and deserving attention (such as putting the street after the town, or the number after the name of the street) often escape notice on a routine challenge, and are unlikely themselves to lead to detection . . . . The Aliens Registration Certificates and Passports merit greater attention since the enemy has often failed to provide agents with the former card and to reproduce in the latter any visa or official stamp showing a legitimate entry into the country. There is also evidence that the enemy experience difficulty with our food and clothing ration books and his agents may not be supplied with these.

Under the heading of 'Detection', the instructions continue in terms redolent of Herbert's former tutor's insistent questions to his students, 'What do you mean' and 'How do you know?':

In most cases detection has been the result of a common sense question addressed to a stranger in a country district. In many cases the questions 'Where are you?' 'Where have you come from?' 'Where are you going?' have defeated a parachute agent uncertain of his whereabouts, and there is evidence that these simple questions are the most feared.

These instructions culminated in a summary for distribution to police officers likely to be called out on a search for enemy agents. The summary was organized under the headings, 'HOW A SPY MAY COME; WHERE A SPY MIGHT LAND; WHAT A SPY WILL TRY TO DO; WHAT A SPY WILL DO IMMEDIATELY ON LANDING; WHAT A SPY MAY LOOK LIKE (a youngish man . . . since landing from a parachute is a young man's job; . . . The spy will almost certainly be wearing civilian clothes, but they might have a queer cut . . .); SPIES DISGUISED AS BRITISH OR ALLIED SOLDIERS'. These were accompanied by further notes on the documents spies were likely to be carrying, how they were likely to have been recruited, their equipment, their means of communication back to Germany. These detailed instructions were updated from a data base of apprehended spies organized into tables under headings such as 'condition on landing'; 'behaviour on landing'; 'objectives'; 'when and where detected'; 'clothes'; 'place of departure'; 'place of landing'; 'time of landing'; 'method of landing', and so on.

When lecturing to army staff, Herbert's instructions included more detailed information on the structure, organization, *modus operandi*, and aims of the German Intelligence Service; but the essential structure was the same. The memos were updated regularly to take into account new information about emergent security risks such as infiltration of the Free Norwegian Forces in Britain, the penetration of Norwegian refugee organizations, and the use of French fishing vessels to attempt to land agents for espionage or sabotage purposes. These memoranda are striking for the crisp way in which they distil what must have been a vast amount of information into basic instructions communicated in an effective way for people working with very different levels of training in a variety of situations on the ground.

Much more specific were the briefings on the ISOS information given to B1B's sister department, B1A, to assist in its running of the Double Cross system. In this role, Herbert was analysing the decoded information so as to work out what sorts of disinformation might most plausibly and most damagingly be fed back to German intelligence by captured spies and others recruited as double agents. His work depended not only on a clear grasp of the decoded information and its strategic significance, but also on a broad understanding of the structure and strategy of the German intelligence services and of their relationship to German military planning more generally. Even the most painstaking and detailed of the analyses had policy implications, and policy development was a key part of Herbert's work. It stretched beyond the dissemination of information and encompassed legal policy, as the following extract from his report on forged identity cards demonstrates:

My section was concerned . . . with the best means of utilizing the existing NRIC [National Registration Identity Card] system for C/E [counter-espionage] purposes and also with the question of providing modifications in the system which might further assist us or hamper the enemy . . . . We investigated and at times advocated a number of different schemes for the improvement of the NRIC system though none of these schemes were in the event adopted. In 1941 we considered with the Registrar General changing the NRIC in certain specified areas, viz: the coastal band from Kent to Southampton, so that visitors to this area would stand out and thus attention could more easily be devoted to them. We intended to announce the fact that a change had taken place in certain areas . . . without specifying the areas or particulars of the new card, in the hope that the enemy would be left in a perplexity as to the type of card with which he should equip his agents. We abandoned the scheme, however, when it was made evident that it was difficult to attach a sanction to the obligation [on residents] . . . to exchange their cards . . . since it was realized that even if only a small percentage failed [to do so] . . . they would constitute an illusory security problem requiring investigation which might well defeat the object of this scheme by diverting or exhausting the security resources and throw an intolerable burden on the Police. . . . During 1941 and in subsequent years we pressed for an amendment of the system so as to secure that there should be a legal obligation to carry and present the card on challenge as distinct from the existing obligation merely to present the card within 48 hours at a specified Police station.

This passage could almost have been taken from Herbert's later writings in legal philosophy, and prefigures his later fascination with Benthamite utilitarianism. Yet it is a reminder, too, of the extent to which even the most liberal people have to temper their civil libertarian instincts in the context of war.

Herbert's investigative responsibilities were also heavy and took a number of forms. Between 1941 and 1944, his section was brought in only after a serious *prima facie* case had been established by section B10 or, later, by two regional officers. From May 1944, however, B1B took over preliminary enquiries as well, and quickly came to the conclusion that in most of the cases the suspicions were groundless. The majority of cases were closed, and Herbert concluded:

that a great amount of time and energy had probably been wasted in too minute an investigation of alleged espionage, since the evidence from Most Secret Sources and elsewhere available in B Division showing the true extent and character of German espionage in this country might have enabled the investigating officer to have ruled out with confidence a good number of these cases from the start.

Herbert appreciated, with the benefit of hindsight, that the infiltration of German agents had fallen well short of the organized spy ring which had been feared in the early part of the war. As he put it in another memo:

. . . the appearance on great numbers of the telegraph poles in this country of curious marks was part of the general spy scare of the summer of 1940. Reports on these marks were made at considerable expense and on analysis they proved to be almost certainly innocent. In the conditions prevailing in the summer of 1940 this analysis, absurdly elaborate as it might now appear, was probably justified, since it did provide reassuring evidence that the general apprehensions of the existence of a 5th Column in this country were ill founded.

But the problem had not merely been one of an overreaction to public alarm. As ever, there were structural reasons why so much time had been wasted:

There was . . . always a divorce, unfortunate in its consequence but due in part to the necessity for the protection of Most Secret Sources, between B1B and the sections originally responsible for these preliminary enquiries into cases of suspected espionage.

Sometimes Herbert himself was involved in investigating specific allegations against suspected agents. Though in later life he spoke seldom of his intelligence work, he did talk on several occasions about one of these investigations. Decoded messages suggested there was a spy with the code name Scott on certain shipping convoys. Herbert examined all the information and narrowed the possibilities down to certain ships which had been on trips where secrets had been divulged. An examination of the crew lists revealed no one by the name of Scott; so it was inferred that the code name might refer to a crew member of Scottish descent. Herbert had to go to Liverpool to continue the investigation. He found that there was indeed a Scottish stoker on one of the ships. The stoker's cabin was searched and a large amount of money discovered for which he could not account. The man was arrested, tried, and became one of the relatively small number of people executed for an offence under the Treachery Act 1940 during the war. In the course of the trial, Herbert, who was prosecuting, complained privately to the police that there was not enough evidence against the man. 'There will be tomorrow!' came the reply. The colleagues to whom Herbert later told this story had the impression that the experience had weighed heavily on his mind. He was particularly troubled by the use of 'strong arm' tactics to secure the conviction. Such experiences underpinned his very strong advocacy of abolition of the death penalty in his academic work. This was a world in which tactics in a seemingly insoluble espionage case included contemplation (as a last resort) of deliberately ramming the ship from which an information leak originated, with no survivors expected, and one in which Herbert's respected boss could write that 'From time to time it becomes necessary for us to liquidate a XX [double agent] who may be tied up with other agents'. For a man with Herbert's acute liberal sensibilities, this must have had its troubling side.

The extreme outcome in the case of the Scottish stoker was unusual. A more normal example would have been that of:

W. J. Hooper: Information received from a German Secret Service officer . . . Oberleutnant Hermann Giskes, referred to this man as having been in the employ of the German Secret Service in 1938 and 1939. Hooper was employed by this office since 1941 and was still employed when these allegations were made. An elaborate investigation was made by me and further evidence confirming that given by Giskes was obtained from a British renegade, A.W. Gordon Perry, and a German Abwehr (Intelligence Service) officer, Von Feldman . . . . As a result, the charges were formally established and Hooper was dismissed from the service of this office.

It is not clear whether Hooper was subsequently the object of formal charges. Not all investigations were as specific or personalized as these. In his 1945 memorandum, Herbert wrote about more strategic investigations. These included an account of his having spent, in 1941, six weeks in the Admiralty investigating the implications of captured documents which had revealed that a large number of extremely important minefields were known in detail to the Germans. Herbert wrote of 'examining German documents and the procedure adopted in the mine-laying and mine-sweeping departments of the Admiralty, and especially the distribution by the Admiralty of information relating to British minefields. As a result I was able to exclude the hypotheses that the Germans had obtained this information by means of spies or by intercepting and deciphering Admiralty signals, and to conclude with some confidence that the information had been obtained by charts of a given series lost in the ordinary course of operations'. Shipping cases made up a substantial proportion of his investigations of espionage, and his work often concerned activities outside Britain and hence the risk of boundary disputes with MI6's Section V.

Herbert made an important contribution to MI5's remarkable transformation from amateurishness and lack of direction to professionalism and effective strategic capability. In 1940, the British security service was almost totally ignorant of its German counterpart's activities. Within little more than two years, the tables had turned, with MI6's interception and analysis of German intelligence and MI5's deployment of double agents combining to give Britain not only excellent information but the capacity to feed disinformation to Germany, as in Operation Overlord. This had been achieved despite a long period of constant relocation and reorganization from mid-1940 on. By July 1941, MI5 already claimed to control most of the German espionage system in Britain through its double agents; by July 1942 it was confident that it had all German agents in Britain under its control. Crucially, the German intelligence service was unaware of the fact. Between 1941 and 1944, among the German spies detained in the UK or brought to the UK for detention, no fewer than 47 were turned into double agents. By the middle of 1943, Herbert was able to confirm that the quality of German intelligence information on Britain had deteriorated: his weekly report regaled his colleagues with the story of a long debate between Berlin and Madrid 'as to whether Chester was a port'; and in the summer of 1944 the low quality of German intelligence made this aspect of his weekly report unnecessary. Though the achievements of British Intelligence have to be balanced against the evidence that German Intelligence was a far less competent opponent than had initially been believed, the contribution of the team assembled by Liddell and White in which Herbert worked was significant.

Of equal importance in understanding the course of Herbert's life is the pleasure he took in his MI5 work. Even among a brilliant team, he was enormously valued by his colleagues. One colleague even felt that Herbert's talents were such that he had been under-utilized. The congeniality of the people he worked with and his sense of his own skill make his happiness at MI5 easy to understand even though his discretion about his work at this time leaves us with little direct evidence of how he felt about it or about how it related to the rest of his life. But having a position in public service clearly gave him a sense of security, satisfaction, and belonging which neither the Bar nor an academic position ever quite delivered to the same degree. Later in life, one of his happiest roles was as a member of the Monopolies Commission—another position which both exploited his extraordinary analytic capacities and gave him a certain quasi-public status. Yet the very secret work at MI5 served to reinforce his tendency to compartmentalize his life, and to live some of its most intense aspects in a psychological and emotional space very separate from that occupied by his closest personal relationships. And in spite of their unusual luck in managing to spend a large portion of the war together, the real intimacy which he had established with Jenifer during the late 1930s was already under pressure.

Initially, the war brought relatively few changes to Herbert's personal life. His and Jenifer's move in 1939 into the Jays' house at 42 Well Walk in Hampstead bound them yet more closely to the bohemian, intellectually lively, and politically engaged social circle in which they already moved. Their regular contacts included not only Douglas Jay, Christopher Cox, and Frances Graham-Harrison—all living at number 42—but also neighbours Hugh and Dora Gaitskell, whose household often included Gaitskell's fellow civil servant Evan Durbin, Oliver Franks, the music critic William Glock, and Clement Glock, a colourful character and chief scene-painter at Covent Garden. Jenifer's parents, who finally met Herbert in 1939, were shocked by their decision to live in a shared household. But the group of friends seem to have survived the inevitable ups and downs of cohabitation reasonably well. As Jenifer recalled:

The Hungarian economist Thomas Balogh did not last long [as a resident of 42 Well Walk] as his habits were found objectionable. He summoned the nice Czech peasant girl (Anita) who cooked for us to bring him books in the bath and was inclined to leave them floating in the water. Moreover his girlfriend's under-clothes left about in the dining room upset Christopher, as did Balogh's defeatism in the summer of 1940 and his derogatory remarks about Churchill. Nor did Tommy appreciate Christopher who, largely because he had read and taught Greats, came to symbolize for him the defects of the British Civil Service.... Patrick Reilly of the Foreign Office was a more acceptable member of our community. Oliver Franks, who lived near [and who was working with Douglas Jay in the Civil Service], sometimes spent the evening with us.

The practical difficulties of life in the war—food rationing, disrupted sleep, and, for Jenifer (though not acutely for Herbert, and certainly not for Cox, who positively enjoyed the Blitz) physical fear of air raids—drew this diverse group together. Political debates abounded at Well Walk, and contributed to Herbert's increasing leaning to the Left. At weekends, Jenifer and Herbert often fled London for the peace of Jenifer's sister

Judy's home at Newbury or the good food, wine, and lively company of Victor Rothschild's cottage at Tring, to Tommy Balolgh and his then partner Peggy Joseph's retreat at Dorchester, and to the wealthy Jewish industrialist Robert Waley-Cohen's estate on Exmoor. In doing so, they were escaping not only the tension, bombing, and claustrophobia of the city, but also the demands of accommodating a number of vivid and sometimes eccentric co-habitees. Though clearly much admired and loved by Jenifer and Herbert, Cox in particular was a challenging house-mate, with his bizarre fantasies, scatological humour, acute anxiety attacks, his taste for the Blitz (later in the war he would read a 1940 copy of the *Evening Standard* at breakfast in order to recreate the emotions which he had felt at the time), and extreme caution with money; Jenifer, and later Herbert, constantly had difficulty extracting from him money for the shared bills. The Well Walk household brought intellectual stimulation, but at the cost of a lack of privacy. From now on Herbert and Jenifer had limited opportunities for quiet intimacy.

In any event, the equilibrium of their relationship was soon to shift. By 1939 Jenifer had decided that she would like to marry Herbert, not least because she was eager to have a baby. She asked the Establishment Officer at the Home Office whether she could be given permission to marry. He told her that the marriage bar could only be waived on the recommendation of her head of department and with Treasury approval of the waiver as being in the interest of the public service. She was advised that it might be ten years before she was regarded as indispensable. (Her immediate boss, Permanent Under Secretary Sir Alexander Maxwell, suggested that she put an advert in *The Times* saying that she wished to be regarded as married though barred by the Civil Service.) Two years later, her problem was unexpectedly resolved when she was having lunch with Evelyn (later Baroness) Sharp, then working in the Treasury. Sharp remarked to Jenifer that it was a pity that women 'like us' did not ask for permission to marry, because it would be virtually impossible for the Civil Service to refuse. She undertook to make sure that the Treasury would not object if Jenifer's department made an application. Maxwell readily acceded to Jenifer's request, and the Treasury duly agreed to lift the bar. Shortly afterwards, Jenifer was promoted to Principal and moved to a post as Secretary to the Home Office Advisory Committee, which heard appeals from those detained under Defence Regulation 18.

When Herbert and Jenifer told their parents of their impending marriage, both the Harts and the Williams' were relieved that their son and daughter had decided to 'settle down'. But the first meeting between the two sets of in-laws did not take place until after the wedding, and was attended by a good deal of anxiety. When Jenifer's mother announced her intention of visiting from Cornwall, Herbert warned Jenifer: 'Do not let Sybil see quite what your mother's real reaction to my parents would be as she will a) be offended b) be incapable of keeping it to herself.' He also begged Jenifer to make sure that no anti-Semitic remarks escaped her family, warning that his parents were 'insanely anxious' to meet her mother and that his mother was 'madly excited' and would 'rampage about like a grown up Fidelity' [a small niece]. The couple were married in October 1941. Wearing yellow oilskins and riding their bicycles, they left the wedding party at Herbert's parents' West Hampstead home for a brief honeymoon in Somerset. From the Royal Oak Hotel, ever the dutiful son, Herbert wrote to his parents thanking them for the expense and trouble which had gone into the lavish party which they had laid on. He wondered what they had made of his and Jenifer's friends and provided a detailed account of the newlyweds' journey. Back in London, life at 42 Well Walk continued much as usual for the next few months. But the household, and Herbert's life, were profoundly affected by Jenifer's departure a few weeks before the arrival of their first child, Joanna, in the autumn of 1942.

In later life, Jenifer recalled that Herbert was reluctant either to marry or to become a father. Despite his strong attachment to her, he continued to feel that he was unsuited to family life. His fond letters to Jenifer written in between his weekend visits during her maternity leave at Bowling Green House, her parents' home in Oxford, show that, at least initially, he buried his doubts quite effectively. The old jokes and endearments of their early correspondence continue only slightly abated; he read books about the psychology of parenting; he tried to imagine Jenifer's experience; he anticipated that a shift from 'worshipping the mother-wife instead of desiring the mistress-wife' would be 'a stiff programme for both of us'. And though Jenifer remembered his 'deep almost neurotic antipathy towards babies and all that they involved', he took immediate pride in his baby daughter. But he was spending only weekends with Jenifer and the baby, so his exposure to the distractions of family life was, at this stage and throughout the war, minimal. Alone in London, he had no difficulty distracting himself with his absorbing work and a 'wild' social life not only in Hampstead but also at the Reform Club, the Savile Club, the Café Royal, and other fashionable locations.

Herbert and Jenifer were separated for several months, their relationship carried on through weekend visits and a correspondence which became increasingly preoccupied with domestic administrative and financial arrangements. Jenifer, determined to resume her Civil Service career, swiftly employed a nanny, the 'wise, compassionate and competent' Edith Thomas, who would more or less run the Hart household for the next 36 years. The arrangement was a quintessential product of the English class system. Though for the Hart children Nanny was the emotional anchor of the family, in the early years she hovered in a no man's land between servant and family status. She took responsibility for almost all aspects of domestic organization—shopping, cooking for the children, housework—working six and a half days a week in return for a modest salary. For some years she even slept in the nursery, which constituted her only personal space. It is hard to imagine a couple as progressive as Jenifer and Herbert contemplating such an arrangement today. Their provision for Nanny changed over time, as she gradually became the equivalent of a family member and as social attitudes shifted. But in the early days she was very much a member of staff. And one implication was that, yet again, Jenifer and Herbert had committed themselves to living under the gaze of a third party.

Jenifer returned to London, taking up again her latest position working in the Home Office Division which dealt with the police, two months after Joanna's birth. The war made it impossible to bring the baby to London, so Joanna and Nanny continued to live at Jenifer's parents' Oxford home. Herbert had looked forward to Jenifer's return as signalling a continuation of life much as it had been before Joanna's birth, assuming (with some justification) that Jenifer must be 'sick of the little angel'. A second separation was, however, not far off. Herbert was seriously disconcerted when, the following year, Jenifer suggested that they have a second child. He remonstrated with her: she hadn't told him that she would want more than one child; he feared the distractions of family life. Again, Jenifer had her way: their second child, Adam, was born in the autumn of 1944. Jenifer was once more absent from London for some time, and Herbert had relatively little time with his two children. Even when, after a period of intense pressure at work, he determined to take a holiday in 1944, there appears to have been no question of his spending the bulk of it with the family. This continuing independence helps to explain the apparent ease with which he adapted to fatherhood—but also his difficulty in adapting to family life after the war.

Admittedly, Herbert was now shouldering family responsibilities which Jenifer had formerly managed. Principal among these in 1944, when Jenifer's parents' house ceased to be available, was the extremely difficult task of finding accommodation for the children and Nanny at a safe but accessible distance from London. Though they had discussed bringing the family to London, the V bombs made it impossible; and in truth it is hard to imagine the incorporation of Nanny and two small children in the rudimentary domestic environment of Well Walk. The frustrating search for alternative accommodation—the object of an interminable set of letters between

Herbert and Jenifer—was finally resolved in 1944 when Mrs. Fisher, widow of the former Warden of New College, offered the loan of her cottage at the Devil's Punchbowl in Surrey. This proved a happy arrangement, with Mrs. Fisher herself joining the household later in the year, and Herbert and Jenifer visiting at weekends from London after Jenifer's return to work.

Herbert's and Jenifer's accommodation problems were not confined to the quest for a safe home outside London. In 1944, Peggy Jay's return to London prompted tensions at 42 Well Walk. Herbert reported to Jenifer that the house was 'like a thin crust of lava over a volcano: Already there has been a tremendous eruption, billowing clouds from below, whistling escapes of steam and stones volleying high into the air.' Many of the eruptions were precipitated by housekeeper Hilla's difficulty in coping with an influx of children, a new mistress, and an irascible Douglas Jay. This threw Herbert into tense negotiations with Jay, Cox, and Graham-Harrison, followed by protracted efforts to find alternative accommodation and furnishings. The problem was finally resolved by the removal of Hilla, Herbert, and, after her maternity leave, Jenifer to a flat owned by Peggy Jay's parents over the road at 21 Well Walk, where they set up house with Frances Graham-Harrison, his wife Carol Stewart, and—of course—Cox. By this time Herbert's life had become split into some strongly separated compartments: an intense concentration on absorbing and satisfying work; an affectionate but business-like commitment to organizing family life; and a whole-hearted engagement in a social existence not very different from that of his bachelor days.

When awaiting or recovering from the birth of a baby in Oxford or Cornwall, Jenifer was eager for news of life in London, and Herbert's letters to her in 1942 and 1944 paint an intriguing sketch of London's social world during the war. 'I have been turning turning in mazes of heat and sound— I mean a whirl of social engagements'; 'I write this in bed before embarking on one of the old literary evenings of which the strict performance of connubial duties has starved me for so long.' Solitary evenings at the Reform Club recovering from an exhausting day with the help of a bottle of claret were punctuated by frequent dinners and lunches with War Office colleagues like Liddell, White, Rothschild, Blunt, and Hampshire. Herbert also had regular social contact with Richard Wilberforce, Isaiah Berlin, John Sparrow, and, more occasionally, Guy Burgess and Arthur Koestler (whom Sparrow was at this time consulting on how to improve army morale). Meals often involved delicacies such as turtle soup and lobster and were liberally washed down with claret and followed by brandy: despite war time shortages, entertainment at the clubs and fashionable restaurants of London remained lavish. The same was true of the hospitality at the enormously wealthy Rothschild's Hertfordshire cottage. A letter written in 1944 after one such visit conjures up the wild talk of the weekend, as well as the amusing, larger than life figure of Rothschild himself:

Two letters from you greet me on my return to earth on Monday night from the Rothschild paradise . . . . The Fischer Willies [Jenifer's family] were much discussed at Tring this week-end in semi drunken—very obscene conversations. You are thought to have overpowering sex appeal by a) Tess [Mayor] b) Victor ('reeking with it') and c) Antony [sic] Blunt!!!—reported so by Tess. I could hardly believe my ears about this last and was and am *very* angry and jealous. The conversation of course under Victor's aegis rapidly degenerated into speculation about how often you wash, change your underwear . . . and all the good old topics. But you came well out if it, even though I got home my telling points about your family's fondness for regimentation in a world of scarce resources . . . . Oh the food. Enormous peaches (like 'bums' said V of course), chicken, champagne, fresh eggs, butter . . . brandy, irish whisky. A miserable wet day: but I kept the Hart flag flying by going for a long walk alone in the woods.

Was Herbert joking in his reference to jealousy and anger in relation to Blunt's comment about Jenifer? Blunt was, after all, well known to his War Office colleagues as homosexual.

In London in 1942 a more serious topic of conversation with Rothschild, Berlin, and Koestler was the fate of the Jews. Herbert's views are illuminating of his broader attitudes:

I must say (even admit) it's rather strange being 'demarried' as I consider myself. It began rather well with that dinner with Rothschild . . . . I told Peggy Jay the lines of our argument about the Jews . . . . Victor and his sister struck me as rather ignobly terrified of a British Pogrom and I wonder if there is anything else in their great anxiety to counter anti-semitism. I infuriated Koestler by saying the only problem worth bothering about was the general social problem and by saying one ought not to do anything which recognized the separateness of the Jews. His style of argumentation is a curious mixture of Marxian and literary or rather psychological reasoning and whenever I countered with a logical quibble he kept insisting that things weren't just black and white. The setting was fantastic: a private room at Claridges and floods of smoked salmon, poussins, brandy gin and all the rest. Victor is far grosser and less restrained with his sister and when not with Barbara [his first wife]. Vaguely incestuous jokes were exchanged and they seemed to eat with both hands. They got through a huge basket of cherries in a sort of race with each other.

Herbert was surrounded by interesting people. But he had mixed feelings about many of them: Koestler's politics, the vulgarity of Rothschild (described by Liddell as 'violently anti-Zionist, as far as I know Hart is too'), and Sparrow's conservatism all came in for criticism. (Sparrow's motto is described in one letter: 'There is a time for every reform when it is no longer possible to resist it': 'Filthy reactionary', Herbert commented.) Jay, Cox, and Wilberforce (who was working at the War Office and whom Herbert managed to see from time to time) remained his closest contacts. And much of his emotional energy was going into his work.

He also wrote to Jenifer of his feelings about the war. Though he felt increasingly anxious about what he should do afterwards, he yearned for its end and for a return to the 'ever-distant days of equilibrium and peace and plenty': 'Oh dear I wish the war would end: the Russians will be in Berlin in 2 months, they say'. Reflecting on a book about the First World War, he wrote: 'It is so odd reading about Liège and places where the thing is actually happening for a second time. Also it fills me with a bogus optimism to think if it failed before it may fail again. But anyhow it is hell.' Unlike many of his colleagues, he was not always optimistic about a quick conclusion, commenting in the summer of 1944: 'A SHAEF [Supreme Headquarters of the Allied Expeditionary Force] officer has just bet me that the British and U.S. troops will be in Germany before the end of the year in the form that I will pay him £1 for each month of 1944 that they are in occupation of German soil and he will pay me £2 for each month of 1945 that they are not. Safe money, I am afraid'; and in the autumn of that year, 'War news too rapid for me. I think October will see not the end but a German retreat behind the Rhine'. This cautious tone gradually gave way to a more positive and even excited one later in the year: '45 miles from Cologne seems rather good'.

Amid these professional and political concerns, worries about his own family continued to trouble Herbert from time to time. His father suffered a breakdown in 1944 and, after a period in a nursing home, required nursing care at home for some time. His despondency was a drain on the rest of the family; Herbert tried to lighten the atmosphere by visiting when he could, but he too found the atmosphere at Platts Lane lowering: 'Mother exhausted by getting up in air raids . . . Father in morbid fury. Albert in depths of pessimism.' From home in the spartan conditions of 21 Well Walk, with its leaking roof, inadequate supply of hot water, and sparse furnishings, he reported to Jenifer on the chaotic domestic arrangements which prevailed among himself, Cox, Graham-Harrison, and the latest in a war-time series of variously neurotic but consistently long suffering housekeepers. One of them, Mrs. Day, had made a good fist at taking charge of the household on Jenifer's departure: in 1942 she was reported as 'going on calmly like the great ship of state she is', and as 'revealing great qualities of leadership in her masterful administration in your absence. She keeps Cox tremendously in order . . . . He ought to get her in to work for him at his office where I am afraid he is again foundering amid file-seas of unparalleled depth. He is at Bushey with his mother this week-end.' In 1944, the occupants of number 21 were being looked after by the less imperturbable Hilla, who became increasingly strained by the bombing: 'Hilla's behaviour in an air raid as demonstrated on a miniscule [sic] scale last night is not encouraging. She waves torches madly out of uncurtained windows, says she is going (as if she could!) mad, is having a heart attack but nonetheless is strangely docile and narcotically calm the next morning. Perhaps she dopes after the all clear'; 'Aeroplanes are booming overhead and Hilla is gibbering over the ovaltine to Cox below.'

Herbert managed Cox's volatile mood changes with astonishing equanimity and no little amusement. Cox's emotional state ranged from depression ('Xtopher is back in the trough again and rather desperate') to mania: 'Xtopher has now become obsessed with the concept of a flushpan or "pan" as it has now become known: "Get into your pan". And he broke into my room last night saying "Are you in your pan? If so I'll pull the plug" Mad.' 'Xtopher . . . is in uproarious form shouting obscenities all day long "Get back to your flushpan you spot of shit" he said to me as he went into his room this morning. He won't wash or shave in our room: he professes to be disgusted by the squalor of the room and makes awful vomiting noises whenever he does come in. I think it is the sight of the double bed.' Cox's troubled attitude towards sex is also revealed by his references to Jenifer as 'the virgin bitch' and 'the mastiff bitch': 'Cox sends you his love but continually rejoices in his freedom to leave lights on, "when VB away cats will play", make noises etc'; 'Xtopher and I sat in the cellar from 9.30 to 3 or so. He was madder than ever—reviled "the mastiff bitch" in hundreds of maniacal styles, tore at his chest, snarled like a dog'; 'Cox is in insanely wild spirits—obsessed again about his breasts. He cuddles them a great deal and this morning offered to squirt milk from them into my tea. He is so fat just there that when it is shoved forward out of his pyjamas jacket it looks like the real thing. It gives him great pleasure.'

Cox's extraordinary behaviour was his way of letting off steam in the midst of his demanding work. At some level Herbert enjoyed looking after him; this was a qualified responsibility which he found less emotionally claustrophobic than the prospect of parenthood at close quarters. But there was also an element of reassurance in the juxtaposition of his own moderate emotional difficulties with Cox's evident craziness. In a moving tribute to Cox after his death in 1982, though playing Cox's eccentricities down, Herbert dwelt empathetically on his lifelong struggle with depression. He admitted that Cox's habit of demanding hours of attention, oblivious to other people's needs, could be exasperating, but remembered fondly that 'Christopher radiated not only zest and high spirits but an extraordinary kindness and sweetness of nature, and a totally unpriggish moral charm, so that . . . those to whom he gave trouble when his spirit was unquiet, found this easy to forgive and their affection for him remained undiminished'. Herbert was a key figure among these supportive friends, as Cox acknowledged in a letter of congratulation on Herbert's election to an Honorary Fellowship of New College in 1968: 'This is tremendous news and for none more than one who owes you a very, very great deal—through the ages . . . '.

The continuity of Herbert's London life did not imply that marriage and fatherhood were unimportant to him. His letters were shot through with anxiety about Jenifer: her health, whether she was eating properly, whether she was managing to keep her irritation with her mother—now referred to as 'Margarine'—at manageable levels; 'Do grasp with both hands all the eggs, cream, milk, chickens, veg and anything else which Margarine must be lusting to cram into you and don't frustrate her desire to look after you'. Occasionally Herbert sought to mediate: 'Poor old Margarine seems to be going down rather badly. Try to think of her as a wave in the rippled sea of eternity and be kind till I can take over.' But he now shared much of Jenifer's contempt for her mother; one of his filial contributions was to send 'the old thing . . . great chunks and slaps of sweet soothing gushing fudge . . . 'marvellous' 'heavenly' 'nostalgically . . . ' 'terribly kind' 'your little party' were frequent notes in a crescendo of blatant horror. Keep her quiet for a month, I hope.' (Not that Jenifer's father entirely escaped the sarcasm: 'I was sorry to have missed Joseph on Saturday and not to have been able to use on your father the careful analysis I made of his last 50 letters to The Times. It will be so out of date by the 12th December.') Herbert also attempted to downplay the levels of bombing in London so as to soothe Jenifer's worries about his safety: 'F-bombs are very little in this gorgeous weather. So don't worry. I get out at the first sign of V2 [bombing]. Probably Bletchley: might be St. Albans. The armies may however win the race.'

His letters shifted between humorous images of the children as 'the pod' or 'the beast' and tender enquiries after their well-being. They included anxious enquiries about the children's development which show that he was consulting child-rearing books—'Do read the three chapters on children's use of pictures in the fat book I have sent you. She [Joanna] should be given live beetles to watch instead of static pictures'. In another letter he gave—at a safe distance—advice on potty-training, remarking that 'The Freudian school of course say it is a manifestation of sexuality: to leave her mark on loved objects etc. etc. But I shouldn't take much notice of that'. One aspect of his feelings which was thrown into relief by fatherhood was Herbert's attitude to his Jewish identity. While Adam was given a name with Jewish associations, his second given name, Richard, had strong WASP connotations. In a letter to Jenifer, Herbert teasingly threatened her 'I divorce you if you leave this [Richard] off the register'. The name was given in part as a token of his affection for Richard Wilberforce. But an incident from his later life throws an interesting light on the choice.

In the early 1980s, Joanna gave birth to a son, Casey. In a series of letters, Herbert urged on her the importance of giving the child a 'common English name', and recalled his own discomfiture at his distinctive 'Herbert Lionel Adolphus'. So upset was he at her choice of an unusual name that for several years he simply referred to Casey as 'the child'—a practice to which Casey, with the common sense of childhood, eventually responded by referring to Herbert as 'the man'. Here again is evidence of Herbert's ambivalence between individualism and belonging. On the one hand, he was a man who, as in his argument with Koestler, resisted any measures which singled Jews out as a group. He resented being labelled as a member of a particular ethnic group, which he held to be irrelevant for most purposes and in any case his own business. On the other hand, he was a man whose consciousness of Jewish identity led him to head one letter to Jenifer '18 July 1944: Herbert's, Martin Jay's, Julius Caesar's birthday . . . Anniversary of the expulsion of Jews from U.K. (1290)', and who reacted with outraged amusement when Richard Wilberforce assumed that Adam would be christened. (Wilberforce might well have been bemused, since he was in fact asked to be Adam's godfather.) The experience of becoming a parent accentuated these complicated attitudes. In later life, Herbert appears to have managed them by keeping his parental family distinct from his life with Jenifer and the children: another form of separation which had psychological implications.

Becoming a father also raised important personal issues for Herbert and he discussed them with Jenifer. In 1944 he wrote to thank her for recommending a book by psychologist Joanna Field (pen name of Marian Milner), *A Life of One's Own*. The couple had been talking about his continued feelings of being emotionally blocked. Parenthood, and the disagreements which it had prompted, led Herbert to try once again to confront what he saw as his emotional limitations. Herbert was intrigued by Field's analysis of a 'feminine' side to personality: a side which is still, centred, and not goal-oriented. She advocated the expression of thoughts one is ashamed of—a suggestion which Herbert dutifully acted on, producing long lists which were modelled on Field's. Field also laid great emphasis on the fear of failure, and argued that we keep trying because at some level we are concerned about our identity being obliterated. Herbert could not accept her suggestion that panic and anxiety are never exactly what they seem to be and are in some sense beyond reason: he remained supremely rationalistic. But in a later letter to Jenifer, he went as far as to say that he didn't think his difficult personality and sexuality were things for which he could be blamed or held responsible. And in his diaries he tried out, painstakingly, Field's self-therapy technique of free writing:

Joanna Field amuses me. I try a bit of 'free writing' each night and the most extraordinary stuff comes out. Quite a lot of immature poetry. My only trouble I should say on rereading this verbal diarrhoea [sic] (my 'free writing', *not* this letter) is suppression of my feminine components—a considerable part of me. I must 'surrender' and 'immerse', 'develop the perceptive acceptance of the world' etc etc etc. Really though JF is quite sensible I think.

When compared with his diaries, this casual description to Jenifer seems disingenuous. For Herbert's free writing was generating some striking, often homoerotic, images and churning up some painful issues—notably his continued feeling that his sexual orientation was primarily homosexual. In 1944, a personal narrative started to appear on the left hand side of each page, and gradually took over the whole diary (typically, the arrangement was chaotic). This narrative analysed his feelings, and reported a sense of breakdown. He believed that one source of his distraction, lack of concentration, sense of unreality, and panic was the suppression of his 'female side'. At times he even found himself asking if he was 'a woman' or if active homosexuality would solve the problem (he concluded that it wouldn't).

After seven years, some of the difficult issues which had melted in the heat of Herbert's and Jenifer's early passion were now solidifying and making themselves felt in the cooler environment of their long term relationship. Herbert's sexual passivity had become painful to them both, and his attempts at self-analysis were directed not only to the more general problem of his feeling emotionally closed, but also to the specific problem of his diminishing interest in sex. Though the addresses to 'Dear Wifey' or 'Dear Wife and Mother', 'Dear Poppet', 'Dear Sweety', 'Dear little woman', like signatures such as 'your husband' and 'Daddy', are ironic, it seems clear that separation and parenthood had diluted the attraction which he felt for Jenifer as a woman. Whatever the emotional impact of the separation from Jenifer, it undoubtedly affected their ability to communicate effectively about a new topic which was making him anxious about his parental obligations and which would have further implications for family life. From the autumn of 1944 onwards, Herbert's growing uncertainty about how to shape his professional life after the war, and his contemplation of the risky step of embarking on a new career, punctuated his correspondence with Jenifer, and became a major theme in his diaries. Once again, the yearning to return to his first love, philosophy, was reasserting itself.

CHAPTER 6

Oxford from the Other Side of the Fence

I N 1944, though still heavily occupied with his responsibilities at MI5,
Herbert's thoughts were already turning to his post-war career. In the
irregular lulls in his work, and in conversation and correspondence with
friends, he began to face up to his deep distaste for the prospect of a return
to the Bar. And in his diaries, he unravelled a litany of ethical, aesthetic, and
social objections to the profession in which he had excelled throughout the
1930s: the pomposity of barristers; the distasteful social culture of the legal
profession; the lack of social utility in work the main object of which was
to save the rich money; an absence of deep intellectual stimulus. Perhaps
reflecting some discomfort about his association with 'Boy' Hart, he also
expressed a strong distaste for the importance of social contacts in obtaining
work at the Bar. In a letter to Isaiah Berlin, then working at the British
Embassy in Washington and regularly sending 'heavenly' food parcels to his
friends, Herbert referred in August to the 'vexed and vexing question of
what to do after the war if the F bombs have not settled the question for me',
and confessed that:

I view return to the Bar with disgust not to mention nausea . . . . My main objections to it are (a) the profoundly anti-social or at least a-social character of my sort
of legal work (tax evasion and the like); (b) dislike of other lawyers, judges, lawyers'
clerks, solicitors (Jewish solicitors—*o monde immonde* [o vile world]), and of the
legal mentality in all its narrow superficial and reactionary manifestations; (c) horror of the dishonesty of the legal underworld on which barristers batten like gaily
coloured fungi. I mean the company directors, the issuing houses, 'cost-making'
solicitors, dishonest deals (and dealers); (d) the likelihood that if successful the volume of my work would submerge all other intellectual interests, narrow the understanding and corrupt my life; (e) the conviction that at the end of a life as a successful
or unsuccessful barrister I shall be unable to look back on it without disgust.

Escaping in five years' time to become 'a county court judge or a legal adviser
to some public authority or government department' would, he conceded,

be preferable to the Bar: 'But I don't really like any of these things.' Notwithstanding the attractions of success and financial security—attractions to which Herbert was far from insensible—he could no longer reconcile himself to a return to his previous lifestyle and career.

The direction which his future career should take was less certain. A return to philosophy was never far from the agenda, but Herbert actively considered a range of options. The list reflects influences from both his family background and his relationship with Jenifer. He was vaguely tempted by the offer, in August 1944, of a job with the civil service rank of Assistant Secretary in the legal branch of the Allies' post-war government of Germany: 'I don't think I want to do this in the very least but it appeals to one's sense of duty, importance of winning the peace, de-nazifying Germany . . . . Can't think of anywhere more depressing than Germany . . . but I suppose I must at least examine the proposition'. Other options included some form of involvement in a public body (though, curiously, he felt himself to be an essentially apolitical creature, and some avenues of public activity were in any case blocked by Jenifer's position in the Home Office), 'work for the Jews', for a charity, or in workers' education. But none of these held the elemental attractions of philosophy, and as Herbert confronted his uncertainties through the internal dialogue set out in his diary, the reader has the impression that the outcome was virtually determined from the start.

Herbert had maintained a keen interest in philosophy, an intellectual interest fed not only by his reading but also by a number of his personal relationships including those with Berlin and Stuart Hampshire. Despite his refusal to take up the fellowship offered in 1937, A. H. Smith, now Warden of New College, still cherished the hope that Herbert would return and revive idealist philosophy, and in particular the Platonic philosophy which had been so central to Herbert's own education at the College. For the philosophical views of his former tutors Smith and Joseph were now under attack from the 'new' linguistic philosophy propounded by Gilbert Ryle and J. L. Austin, from the logical positivism of the Vienna Circle, and from the work of Ludwig Wittgenstein.

By the time of his letter to Berlin, Herbert had sounded Smith out about the possibility of a job at New College. He reported to Berlin, as he had to Jenifer, that 'my tentatively protruded finger was grasped by Smith in a way which rather now terrifies me because of my deep-seated belief that I am not adequate to a philosopher's job in spite of my continuous dalliance with the subject since leaving Oxford'. He repeatedly reassured Jenifer that he had given no firm undertaking to Smith—'I am not of course in any way committed and it may be absolutely impossible on financial grounds alone but I wish I knew my own mind better. Let me have your views (if any)'. But these reassurances were accompanied by detailed analyses of whether they could afford to take the drop in income implied by a move to academic life. He suggested ways of managing family life with him working in Oxford and her in London, arguing that they could live in Princes Risborough—convenient for both cities, and with inexpensive accommodation.

This prospect must have been unappealing to Jenifer, who relished regular contact with friends in Oxford and London, and this explains the lack of enthusiasm with which she greeted these early indications that Herbert was contemplating a move to academic life. On one occasion, a rather aggrieved Herbert wrote from London to say that Stuart Hampshire, with whom he had discussed his 'fin-de-guerre-itis' over lunch at the Escargot, had reported her as having 'ridiculed the notion of my being a don'. But Herbert continued to pour out his objections to returning to the Bar, telling her that 'philosophy is my only permanent intellectual interest and my mind like a hen returning to roost willy-nilly does return to the subject whenever I am not doing anything else'. 'Cox reports Smith as most eager to get me at New College. Oh dear—what it is to play with fire—or philosophy. Can you face Princes Risboro?' Gradually, Jenifer came round to the idea of Herbert moving to Oxford, persuaded not only that he would be an excellent academic but also (less astutely) that it would be a less stressful life and so better for his health in view of his heart murmur.

By the standards of contemporary academic life, the idea that a former undergraduate with no further academic experience should be sought out for a permanent appointment over a decade after graduation is virtually unthinkable. Even by the standards of the 1930s and 1940s, it was extraordinary, and a testimony to the regard in which Herbert had been held as a student. He was, as Stuart Hampshire put it, 'an honorary institutionally correct person'. Smith's image of Herbert as a staunch defender of the old philosophy was, however, becoming outdated. At first, Herbert was influenced by Joseph's view that the new analytical philosophy of the late 1930s was merely a crude version of some of the themes of logical positivism, drawn from Ayer's *Language, Truth and Logic* (1936), a book of which he always had a poor estimation. But gradually he came to feel that there might be something both important and subtle about the new developments. In the periods during which parts of MI5 and MI6 were housed together at Barnet or near one another in central London, Herbert had begun to debate the new philosophy with his MI6 colleagues, Stuart Hampshire and Gilbert Ryle. He found himself intrigued—even if still at this stage bemused—by its approach to the standard philosophical questions of knowledge and meaning: its abandonment of metaphysical assumptions in favour of a close analysis of linguistic usage and its lessons about the nature of the world.

Yet this very influx of new ideas, which gave a fresh dimension to Herbert's interest in the subject, was a cause of anxiety about the prospect of a return to academic work. He felt reasonably confident about teaching some of the 'applied subjects': 'Ethics, Politics, Jurisprudence and Constitutional law—a fine clutch of subjects for the children of the new world', he wrote to Jenifer. But could he, he wondered, get up to speed on the new philosophical techniques, and think of himself as an equal to men like Hampshire who had the advantage of having been professional philosophers before the war? He poured out these doubts to Berlin, and anxiously awaited his advice:

What I am tremendously doubtful about is the adequacy of my abilities and the strength of my interest in the subject. There are some parts of it, e.g. most ethical questions, most questions in the theory of knowledge, where I feel I understand anything that is now being said or written whether by Moore, Logical Positivists or anybody else and I think I will be permanently interested in them and possibly able to teach at any rate what clarity of thought and expression about such subjects demands. My greatest misgiving (amongst many) is about the whole linguistic approach to logic, meaning . . . semantics, metalanguages, object languages . . . . At present my (necessarily intermittent . . .) attempts to understand this point of view only engender panic and despair but I dimly hope that I cannot be incapable given time of understanding it. The solution or dissolution of philosophical problems in this medium is however at present incomprehensible yet terrifying to me. My main fear is that it is the fineness and accuracy of this linguistic approach which escapes my crude and conventional grasp and that it may be very difficult at 37+ to adjust one's telescope to the right focus . . . . As a result of this I have pictures of myself as a stale mumbler of the inherited doctrine, not knowing the language used by my contemporaries (much younger) and unable to learn it . . . . I am I fear a hack like Ewing [A. C. Ewing, a moral philosopher working in Cambridge] and fear of revealing the deutero-Ewing in me might just absolutely stultify me at the disagreeable age of 41, the father of 2 children (!) with no alternative occupation.

In spite of his continuing belief that there was some 'non-empirical element . . . to be taken into account in a theory of knowledge', he already contemplated focusing his energies on the new approach: 'I have during the last year dimly toyed with the idea of writing, were I ever at a University, some studies on modern empiricism, i.e. first to try to discuss what if any single thing is now meant by empiricism and then in what sense and why Russell, Moore, any logical positivists are empiricists.'

One aspect of Herbert's anxiety was the fear of giving up success and security for a new enterprise in which he might turn out to be, if not a failure, then at least only moderately successful. Alongside the fear of intellectual failure was also a fear of loss of esteem ('I have a terror of Maurice B[owra]'s disapproval', he confessed to Berlin). Herbert was, even if not in material terms, a man of serious ambition. By the consensus of his peers (and on the evidence of his lifestyle), he had been an exceptionally successful barrister—even more successful than his outstanding contemporaries Richard Wilberforce, Duff Dunbar, and John Sparrow. And he had been regarded as the ideal intelligence officer at MI5, with excellent judgment, courage, and cool-headedness in the discharge of what were sometimes unpleasant obligations. He was secure, liked, and respected. These are difficult goods to give up.

As Cox had understood in 1937, there was also a personal, psychological dimension to Herbert's doubts about becoming a philosopher. Even in the absence of the formal assessment of research output which takes place in universities today, academic life has always been an intensely individualistic, insidiously competitive, and emotionally demanding profession, requiring an odd mixture of self-confidence and self-criticism—the capacity to assimilate the criticisms of others without compromising one's sense of direction and intellectual integrity. It is often said that the adversarial tone of many academic communities flows from the lack of clear external criteria of success: perhaps more than in other walks of life, and certainly to a greater degree in the universities of the 1940s than today, success depends on fluid criteria shaping not only reputation but also—dangerously—individual self-esteem. Herbert's dialogue with himself in his increasingly searching diaries shows that he had a deep anxiety that he lacked something which he would need to survive, let alone excel, in the academic world. It was not merely a question of lack of confidence in his own intellectual qualities (though this was certainly a factor, and one which stayed with him throughout his career). It was also a question of personal strength, of capacity to maintain a sufficient belief in himself. It may also have had to do with the fact that, as Stuart Hampshire observed, though Herbert was 'highly intellectual' he was 'not an intellectual in his habits': in other words, his habits of mind were highly disciplined and his rigorous standards prevented him from entering into discussion of anything he didn't already know about—qualities which lend themselves to high standards but discourage the more speculative aspects of academic enquiry.

Like Cox, Isaiah Berlin understood this 'psychological dimension' and tried in his own gently teasing way to assuage it in his reply to Herbert's anxious letter:

How can you hesitate? the only point of the Bar I shd have thought is fame & money. If you don't mind too much about the latter you must certainly abandon it since the death of the soul it produces is automatic & inevitable. As for Maurice B.

that too is nonsense (as you in fact know well). He is today a sated power: & not a very formidable one: rather like Italy in 1900. . . . By the time I return in December or January I shall be bitterly disappointed if it—the life in Chipping Campden & all—with you & Jen commuting—won't have gone through. I didn't cable [Herbert had offered to pay for his reply] because saying 'yes yes of course accept' would have sounded hearty & silly. . . . I am sure Xtopher [Cox] supports me. love. Isaiah

Berlin also had an astute presentiment of how thoroughly Herbert would become involved in the new philosophical movement:

When you say that Ewing's is the voice you find most convincing, that is only because he repeats what we have all been taught, in slightly brushed up language. The same applies to Broad. But you won't put up with that under the strenuous attack of say Ayer & Austin, who will be back at Wadham & Magd. respectively, & will have to build a new line of defense. This you will find absorbing, believe me.

A fascinating counterpoint to Berlin's friendly encouragement emerges in a letter he wrote in December 1944 to Henry Price, Wykeham Professor of Mind and Logic at New College. Price had asked for his view of Herbert's suitability for the fellowship in general philosophy. The six-page response was a classic example of Berlin rhetoric: as one reads it, one hears his velvet tones and sees his impish, playful expression. But his carefully qualified endorsement of Herbert's abilities reflected his characteristic reluctance to threaten his own intellectual reputation by being seen to over-estimate another, and risked damning Herbert with the faint praise of favourable comparison with philosophical mediocrities. He concluded that, while Herbert would doubtless be a creditable philosopher and a reliable tutor, he would be unlikely to leave an enduring mark on the subject:

I have known Herbert Hart for the last twelve years and do not really know quite what to say. He is a man, as you say, of very first-rate ability and philosophical capacity. The main advantages seem to me to be:

(a) That he has a generally good, tough, formidable mind and a capacity for clear exposition. I still remember him as the President of the Jowett Society, when he was an undergraduate, and he was an excellent solid Cook Wilsonian then. He has not really kept up terribly much since and is very modest and self-distrustful about this himself. . . . What he is tortured by is the thought that he will never be better than Ewing and will never hold other views than Ewing. He realizes himself that this is not a very exciting state of mind to be in . . . Nevertheless, even given all this, he cannot be worse than Ewing, who, after all, is . . . in his own way, not con-temptible. . . . Now: if I am gradually to evaporate as a full-time philosopher . . . perhaps the person elected in my place in, say, two or three years' time . . . might be a really distinguished epistemologico-logical highbrow, so to speak, someone who would both lecture and write in a manner worthy of the traditions of the College, which are not, I grant you, to be far advanced, even if they are not in any way lowered, by Herbert Hart. But I do think that Hart will . . . make a very admirable teacher of the staple diet, without attaining to heights or Indian rope-tricks of any kind. I do not mean to convey that he will merely be a hack of even the highest order, although I suppose that even such persons are not to be despised . . . If Hart is willing . . . to teach these extra logical subjects and, secondly to acquire at any rate the rudiments of the Russell 'positivist' language . . . he would be, I feel sure, the best man the College can get for this purpose if it wishes to elect before the end of the War and the return of the armed forces.

(b) Hart would, of course, make an admirable colleague, College tutor, etc., being a born dean with much of the required gravitas. What I do doubt is whether he would remain at the University during the rest of his working life, and equally whether he would write anything very memorable (far be it for me to cast scorn on that myself, who has not done it either). . . . The late Mr Justice Holmes once divided good lawyers into 'razors' and 'good kitchen knives' . . . Under that classification Herbert Hart is a slender bread-knife, and any work he produces will resemble the solid pedestrian tramp of Ewing or Broad and will not provide glimpses of something new and exciting . . .

Albeit observing in the course of his characteristically prolix letter that 'the virtues outweigh the defects' and that Hart would 'provide the best obtainable tutor in philosophy', Berlin finished with the following—marvellous but not entirely reassuring—parody of the diplomatic prose by which he was surrounded in Washington:

I was more than once tempted throughout this letter to observe in answer to your query about Hart's likelihood to write a notable book that I should hesitate to advance the suggestion that circumstances might not arise under which it would not be true to conjecture that such might, indeed, prove to be the case, although I was not clear that there was any adequate reason at present for supposing that such circumstances were, in fact, necessarily likely to arise, although there was, as yet, equally no reason for ruling out such a contingency, which it would be well to bear in mind if any steps were, in fact, being contemplated to meet a situation which might conceivably develop in regard to the topic under discussion. That means 'no'.

Berlin—who admitted to having changed his view about Herbert's intellectual credentials over the next decade—can rarely have been more mistaken. In a world in which references tended to be less fulsome than they are today, this may have been a careful strategy calculated not to damage Herbert's chances by making claims about talents for which there was no professional evidence. But, as is often the case in friendships, there seems to have been an element of rivalry between the two men. As Herbert wrote to Jenifer:

No more moves in my Oxford career game save that I had already written to Shaya [as Berlin was known to his friends] to ask him to discourage me as he did it so effectually in 1937—but then his own position was involved. Nice thought.

Berlin's qualified assessment did not, in any event, deflect Warden Smith from his purpose. Smith wrote to Herbert on 10 January 1945, offering him the fellowship in philosophy, and apologizing for the delay caused by his need to get Berlin's agreement in writing:

I need not say that Berlin wholeheartedly approved: he had no hesitation or reservations whatever. Price also would welcome your appointment . . . . I cannot tell you what a relief and pleasure it would be to me personally to know that you were coming.

Herbert accepted; and Berlin greeted his decision warmly:

. . . I cannot wait before letting you know how genuinely exhilarated I am by this news . . . Of course you must identify yourself with the life of the College in the most violent and ubiquitous way at once . . . The lives of undergraduates must be open books to you; and you must not confine yourself to the better-born or better-looking either; in fact I foresee a realm of mutual persecution which is bound to yield a great deal of perverted pleasure in one way or another.

As for work, of course, I shall try to devolve all the subjects I know nothing about or hate on to you; at the moment I know nothing any more. Consequently your field is universal. But I hate Plato, Aristotle, ethics, politics (and even Kant) particularly deeply (but not a word to the W[arden] on this); consequently will you please take them at least for your province.

As the war staggered to its close, Herbert and Jenifer were therefore contemplating a further period of geographically challenged marriage— 'A pretty picture into which you could fit several sets of surrogate husbands', Herbert wrote to Jenifer. Understandably reluctant to abandon her promising career in the civil service, Jenifer was dubious about living in Oxford— as Berlin put it: 'I understand her feelings about Oxford only too well. As D. Cecil once said . . . "Bringing a wife to Oxford is like bringing her to the Gold Coast—conditions are colonial".' So the couple decided that Jenifer would be based in London with Nanny, Joanna, and Adam, while Herbert would live in New College during the week, returning to the family in London at weekends.

The plans were laid. But Herbert's uncertainties and inner dialogue continued. In May 1945, he was sent by MI5 to Germany, and the diary recorded during this trip exemplifies the way professional and personal preoccupations wove themselves together in his mind, particularly in the context of travel, when unfamiliar surroundings and the absence of domestic pressures opened up spaces for reflection and self-examination.

The precise object of Herbert's trip to Germany is obscure. It is likely that at least one purpose of his visit was to report on the state of civilian morale and to gather general intelligence, tasks for which his excellent German and astute powers of observation would have made him exceptionally suitable. His diary recorded his flight from Croydon to Frankfurt with a variety of other officials, and then his progress round the country after initial contact with SHAEF (Supreme Headquarters of the Allied Expeditionary Force) at Bad Oeynhausen, where Dick White was acting as Chief of Counter-Intelligence. In Frankfurt he had meetings with Richard Wilberforce, who was working on the revised German Criminal Procedure, and with communications experts from the War Room. His tour took him to the mountain retreat where Hitler had interviewed the Quislings (Herbert recorded his thoughts, as he lay in bed 'thinking of the previous occupant'), through Mannheim, where the scale of destruction reminded him of Pompeii, to Karlsruhe, Heidelberg, Kassel, Berlin, and finally Lübeck, via a marvellous variety of modes of transport, not excluding rickety bicycles and his own two feet.

Clearly, it was an official visit. Equally clearly, it was not a secret mission: on his return, Herbert wrote up the Berlin portion of his diary as an article for *The Economist*. His responses to the devastated landscape and its shattered, demoralized population reveal an interesting mix of feelings. He was appalled by the wreckage, shocked by the condition of the population, and struck by the fact that the Allied occupiers were at the receiving end of 'occasional hard glances, but nothing more'. The communications experts told him that the Ministry of War figures at the end of the war had wildly overestimated German military capacity: Herbert had the 'impression of a crazy gang [i.e. Hitler's government] living hand to hand—pulling off gigantic bluffs'. And yet he was intrigued by the mechanisms of survival, recording in great detail not only his visual impressions but also the ways in which the civilian population, particularly in cities like Berlin, were managing in the face of defeat, food and fuel shortages, difficulties of finding basic shelter, the absence of an organized economy or a stable currency. After noting the terrible pallor of the near-starved population, the devastated architecture, and the disgusting smell of decomposing bodies, he wrote in *The Economist*:

The best place to see the Russians and something of their unofficial relations with the Germans is the market which has sprung up under the mournful trees in the Tiergarten . . . . The market is now out of bounds for British and American troops, and has suffered occasional raids from the military police, but it is sustained by Russian patronage, though trading is more discreet than before; the Germans allow the goods they bring to market—dresses, stockings, rolls of cloth, watches—to peep out of suitcases or parcels, and no longer spread them out for display. Here is a stir, which makes the place seem, by Berlin standards, almost cheerful despite the present need which has brought clothes to the market so long before a fuel-less winter. The conventions are those of the bazaar: no private negotiations, and spectators giving advice and sensing the tone of the market . . . . Barter is not, of course, confined to the Tiergarten market . . . . In the shop windows in Charlottenburg, or mounted on notice boards, are any number of two-line advertisements, all of rigorous simplicity . . . ; 'Ich biete . . . Ich suche . . .' One has only to cross the Charlottenburger Chaussee from the Tiergarten market to be faced with Berlin's fuel problem, scarcely less urgent than the food shortage, and little easier to solve. Among the blasted trees of the Tiergarten, little parties saw branches into logs or chop logs into firewood . . . . Several women in the Bismarckstrasse were painfully dragging planks of timber, no doubt won from the ruins, though notices in the British district forbid such depredations . . . Such are the signs in the streets of the Berliners' preoccupation with food and fuel. But, drumming in their minds, is also the question: What will the winter be like? Germany was fortunate in suffering defeat at the beginning of summer, and so far warm weather has permitted many shifts and contrivances not possible in winter. But the days are shortening, and the chopping of wood in the Tiergarten sounds like a warning that the summer respite is nearly over.

A third strand in his response was a certain triumphalism: an almost cold tone strikingly at odds with his usually humane and empathetic observations on those he encountered (particularly those in unfortunate or difficult circumstances). He delighted in seeing the defeated soldiers' demoralized faces, and in evidence of the decisiveness of Germany's defeat; 'Russian ex PoW's walking past Germans—what a satisfaction'. This response was strongly tied up with his deep English identification: years later, a colleague remembered him indignantly responding to a story about ill-treatment by British troops during the war: 'But the English don't behave like that'. He noted, sardonically, that American dominance in certain sectors 'will degenerate into a US mix of inefficiency and corruption'—a judgment which was overtaken in the 1950s by his increasing admiration for many aspects of post-war America. Amid his varying reactions, the absence of any reference to the fate of the Jews is striking.

Towards the end of this intriguing journey, Herbert experienced a resurgence of anxiety about the career decision he had made. The vision of his old friend Richard Wilberforce exercising his legal and administrative skills with influence and confidence, and the realization of the huge political and social importance of managing the transition to peace in central Europe, made him wish that he had accepted the legal post in Germany which the civil service had offered the previous year. The sense of his own competence in legal and intelligence work made the prospect in front of him a frightening one. He was starting again, at the age of 38, on a career in which, applying his characteristically high standards, he doubted his own power to excel, and in which he would lag behind his contemporaries. He asked himself whether even at this stage he might write to New College to say that he had changed his mind. He began to feel that his distaste for the Bar might be over-nice: noting, after a meeting with Oppenheimer, 'his eagerness to get back and make money', he commented, 'How eccentric one's own conscience about this now seems!' Though he comforted himself with the thought that this was an experiment which he could abandon if he was not feeling settled and reasonably confident of success in two years' time, the sense of being immature—a beginner, at the cusp of change just when most men are settled in their lives—pervades his diary. He tried to work out his feelings in a fragment of autobiographical writing which reveals his deeply introspective personality:

I am 38: the War has just ended and I am on the threshold of a new career. These are three reasons for reviewing my life since they all conspire to emphasize the fact that a turning point for good or bad has been reached. I have the feeling of being in mid-stream—and of doing what is supposed to be foolish: changing horses there. Whether it is foolish or not it is certainly alarming and perhaps to look back and see what I have done so far and what sort of person I am and how I have become what I am may help me to orientate myself and to decide how to address myself to this sometimes terrifying future. In any case I have always felt the wish to do this, to pause, and before going on to assess my character powers and capabilities as life hitherto has revealed them.

The autobiography was abandoned after a few pages. But his diary makes palpable the pain, conflict, and sense of undischarged (possibly filial) obligation he was feeling: 'Unrealised stirrings of romantic boyhood spring through the adult texture of my life. The Bar and success: the true heart's yearning ambition and desire to repay.' As he gazed down on the Rhine, Belgium, and Calais on the flight home from Germany, he tried to rally his resolve: 'Out, out into the world: not to remain a middle-aged boy.' Oxford, then, was the place in which he had determined to leave what he intriguingly thought of as a form of adolescence and to forge his adult identity.

A world still composed of a majority of bachelor dons living in the semi-monastic surroundings of colleges which cloistered them from most of the concerns of everyday life does not, on the face of it, seem the most promising terrain on which to resolve an early mid-life identity crisis—especially if you are a cultured person, used to and with a taste for metropolitan life and mixed company, not to mention a wife and two small children. The Oxford University to which Herbert returned in September 1945 was indeed a cloistered, parochial, and largely masculine community. New College was not, in most ways, substantially different from the small community of scholars he had left in 1929. It was surrounded by thirty-odd other such communities, only five of which were for women; and it operated within the framework of only a fragmentary university structure. The small number of Fellows at New College (18 in all, compared with 26 in 1927 and 62 at the end of the twentieth century) further contributed to an intense and emotionally complex network of social relationships which in many respects resembled a family more than a workplace. This dynamic was accentuated by some idiosyncratic personalities and by the fact that many of them lived in College. A contemporary described New College as 'frowsty', the fellowship largely composed of a 'backlog of ghastly old boys'. For many of these men, the College simply *was* their life.

Presiding over this closely knit community was the Warden, the boyishly unassuming, winningly courteous Alic (A. H.) Smith, a bachelor whose devotion to the College was such that he was once seen dousing the stonework of the top storey of the old quadrangle with sooty water so as to blend it with the older material of the lower storeys. Smith had taken over the running of the College in 1940 on H. A. L. Fisher's sudden death in a street accident, but was not officially elected Warden until 1944. The delay was due not merely to the particular conditions of the war years but also to a certain ambivalence among his colleagues about Smith's peculiar mix of imaginative sympathy, aesthetic sensibility, and administrative Machiavellianism. His sixteen years as a powerful civil servant had given him, as one colleague noted, a taste of 'the sweets of dictatorship. These were not altogether uncongenial to him'. Tall, thin, ascetic, and tough yet with fine, intellectual features—his face was compared by Jean Cocteau to that of Erasmus—Smith combined humour, warmth, and social ease with a shrewdness and, occasionally, a ruthlessness which was described as 'inhuman', and which earned him the reputation of a 'high-minded crook' and a 'renegade bureaucrat'.

As a philosopher, Smith had his limits. On one occasion, when Herbert described to him a seminar he had just given with Austin on the distinction between the concepts of acting intentionally, recklessly, or inadvertently, he remarked that they all sounded the same to him. 'I always knew you would make a good judge, Warden', Herbert is reputed to have remarked. 'You mean a bad philosopher!' Smith replied. Whatever his potential merits as a judge, he was undoubtedly a gifted administrator: Vice Chancellor of the University in 1954 and a tireless defender of Oxford's architectural environment, Smith was a force to be reckoned with. As his former student John Sparrow put it, 'He loved a battle, and in battle he was selfless, tireless, fearless and, in a good cause, shameless'. Sparrow went on to relate a story about another college at which a vote on the governing body had resulted in the Master of that college being in a minority of one. At this, the Master remarked, 'Well, it seems we have reached a deadlock'. 'I don't think Warden Smith would have made that observation at such a juncture.' Sparrow continued; 'I think he would have regarded that as a very defeatist way of looking at the matter'.

Smith, in short, liked to get his own way—and generally did. This led to not infrequent conflicts among the Fellows of New College, not least on the issue of the College buildings, of which Smith was an energetic and innovative renovator. When it came to persuading the Fellows to buy the beautiful modern sculpture of Lazarus by Jacob Epstein which now adorns the antechapel, he prevailed. When it came to restoring the Warden's lodgings, most had to acknowledge that he had set new standards of beauty, elegance, and taste in Oxford. But when it came to replacing the eighteenth-century windows in the Founders' Library with mock Gothic windows, in an attempt to recreate the original aesthetic of the old quadrangle, Smith was humiliated. As Herbert described the incident to Berlin:

The Warden is now rampant about restoring Gothic tracery all over the College and is pressing us to remove the 18thC windows in the Wyatt room and put in copies of the founder's beastly trefoils. We had a conducted tour all over the place and were bemused by an architectural incantation which lasted well over an hour. It will be hell if he does it: a substantial proportion of us . . . want an 18C room but some fraud will be practised on us unless we're snappy.

The Fellows reluctantly agreed to one experimental window, which was overwhelmingly decided to be an aesthetic disaster. It was left in place as an ugly memorial to Smith's occasionally overweening administrative and aesthetic ambition.

The feverish and sometimes downright hysterical atmosphere among the small brotherhood over which Smith, accompanied by his lovably disobedient dog, Peter, presided is illustrated by the prevarications of Christopher Cox, who still held the fellowship in Ancient History, about his own future after the war. During the 1930s, Cox had become a key figure in the life of New College, devoting himself to the institution and its students. In 1937, he was seconded from New College to the Sudan, to be Director of Education and Principal of Gordon College. In this role, Cox displayed surprising administrative gifts: inspired by a vision of what education in the Sudan should become, he had a key influence on its development, in particular laying the foundations for the later establishment of the University of Khartoum. In 1940, a few months after his return to Oxford, he was appointed Educational Adviser to the Secretary of State for the Colonies. So began a career which would make him one of the foremost figures in the development and implementation of education policy in the colonial territories—work for which he was ultimately awarded a knighthood. From the mid 1940s on, he spent a great deal of time in Africa, which he loved, and worked with dedication to ensure that the basis for effective education and training systems was put in place during the run-up to independence.

In 1940, Cox regarded his career change as temporary, but after the war he—like Herbert, but from the opposite direction—could not decide whether he should change horses, leaving his academic position to pursue his public career on a permanent basis. It is hardly surprising that Cox should have confronted a difficult career decision because his life had taken unexpected directions as a result of a world war. Given his complex and depressive personality, nor is it surprising that this difficult decision brought Cox to the edge of a breakdown. What is surprising—indeed astonishing—is the willingness of his colleagues not only to listen to, argue about, and advise him, but also to discuss with each other the possible implications for his mental health. They agonized about whether he could sustain a normal life outside the confines of the College, ran last-minute missions to London to offer support, called conferences to decide what move to make next. In the end, a benign compromise was worked out: Cox would be elected to a supernumerary fellowship, keeping his links with the College which formed an indispensable framework for him, while pursuing his civil service career. He remained in his College rooms for the rest of his life, coming to Oxford—when not in Africa—every weekend, and contributing to the College's life through his special rapport with students. Particularly after his retirement, he devoted himself to the obsessively meticulous organization of summer reading parties at a beautiful if somewhat spartan chalet near Mont Blanc, where he presided over long walks, vigorous conversation, and pillow fights, and invariably took charge of the preparation of breakfast: 'early risers would be greeted in the rather dank outer kitchen by a figure clad in a plastic mackintosh (doubling as an apron) stirring a large pan of porridge whose mode of preparation was determined by some mosaic formula handed down many years earlier.'

His colleagues' close involvement in his career decision in 1945 reveals the degree to which Cox combined madness and magnetism. But the story also gives us a striking picture of College life, most vividly in the Fellows'—and notably in Herbert's and Warden Smith's—view of Cox as a brilliant but essentially incompetent child for whom the College had ultimate responsibility. The surviving correspondence between Herbert, Cox, and Smith about this one decision runs to over 60 pages. One wonders how many hours, days, or even weeks the oral counterpart took up.

In thinking about New College as an institution which had the capacity not only to support but also—as the other side of the coin—to infantilize its senior members, one also has to temper the account with a further, particular circumstance. Despite continuities with the 1920s and 1930s, the New College of Michaelmas Term 1945 was in one important respect a distinctive and—albeit temporarily—changed place. Instead of 80 fresh-faced 18-year-old public school and (to a much lesser extent) grammar school boys, the new Fellow in general philosophy and his colleagues were confronted by a much larger number of men in their twenties, and these war returnees swelled the total number of undergraduates in the College to 781. These were men whose education had been postponed or interrupted by a war, and whose experience of war-time service had both matured them and lent them a certain authority, particularly in relation to the Fellows who were too old or, like Herbert, not fit enough to participate in active service. The social composition of the student body had, in short, changed, and the power relations between senior and junior members had changed with it. As one 19-year-old student at the time recalled, it was 'an intimidating atmosphere': the war returnees were socially confident and highly motivated, and the smaller number of young students often felt overawed.

In managing these special circumstances, both the keen administrative skills and the particular experience of Warden Smith were of the utmost importance. He himself had arrived as a Fellow in 1919, and had shown remarkable sensitivity in dealing with many older students traumatized by their experiences in the First World War. In 1945, Smith threw himself into the task of planning the construction of temporary huts in the Holywell Quad to accommodate the extra students, and showed a remarkable ability to understand their needs:

One had been at school and formed a loyalty to that, and then one had been let loose in the Services, destroying things and behaving as if one were grown up; so that one arrived at New College suffering from an enlarged horizon and feeling that one would never contract any particular loyalties again. But the Warden saw to that . . .

The College was 'crowded to suffocation', yet the Warden knew everyone and concerned himself sympathetically and effectively with their difficulties. Smith was in his element. But it was not the easiest situation for an anxious new philosophy tutor who set himself the most exacting standards.

The cumulation of war returnees and regular admissions meant that, in his initial year, Herbert had 18 first-year students and was regularly teaching up to 20, and sometimes as many as 25 one-to-one tutorials a week; one letter recorded a working day which involved seven and a half hours of teaching. From this point on, his diaries became working notebooks: personal entries were inextricably woven with entries in which he tried to work through philosophical problems, and the narrative moved seamlessly from professional to personal contexts; from discussions of his own views of philosophical problems (discussions in which, like A. J. Ayer, he tended to refer to himself in the third person), and (first-person) reflections on the state of his mind, his marriage, and even his morals. The diaries provide an extraordinary testament to the development of his personal and professional life during this first year in Oxford. They make painful reading.

From his first tutorial, Herbert's doubts about his own capacities as a philosopher, and as a teacher, assumed almost crippling proportions. He was crushed by the tutorial workload, which spanned both general philosophy—a course focussed on the theory of knowledge, and in which linguistic philosophy was already the dominant force—and logic. He was exhausted by his efforts to do some general philosophical reading and to think through some philosophical questions about knowledge and experience for himself; and bruised by some astonishingly arrogant students. An extreme example was that of the unforgettable Browne, who seems to have grasped that Herbert was not yet entirely comfortable with the new philosophical techniques: 'Browne plainly thinks I am (a) a fool and (b) philosophically reactionary and can scarcely conceal his contempt. I try to keep cool but find it difficult to state clearly what I mean and doubt I really know what I mean.' Shortly afterwards, Browne announced in a card to Herbert that he would not be attending any more tutorials since he thought it more profitable to stay in his own room reading Russell's *Principia Mathematica*. Herbert recorded, with relief, that the Warden was 'calm about this'—another small piece of evidence of the close relations among the Fellows.

Browne was not the only student to induce a feeling of despair about his capacity to reach the standards of clarity in teaching to which he aspired and—in a phrase which recurs frequently in the diaries—'feelings of panic'. Another was Ian Little, later to become a world-famous economist and a friend of the Harts, whom Herbert was convinced took a very dim view of him as a tutor: 'He distrusts and despises my whole approach to the subject. He also hates Moore whom I gave him to read. Bad and depressing. He has obviously discussed me with Browne and is pretty contemptuous. If he drops out too, the Warden will begin to be a bit uneasy.' Even once he had developed the technique of timing the stronger students' tutorials early in the week, so that the insights and confidence gained by surviving the early tutorials would take the strain off the later ones, he found the process enervating. Geoffrey Warnock, later a famous philosopher himself, recalled that he and other students would occasionally make Herbert go pale by saying in response to one of his arguments, 'But Mr. Austin said exactly the opposite in his lectures'.

In the nature of such things, the crisis of confidence did not restrict itself to Herbert's professional life, and his diaries of the time give intriguing insights into the juxtaposition of outer confidence and inner insecurity which often characterizes people's reaction to life in elite social institutions. Herbert had a warm relationship with Warden Smith, who reluctantly reconciled himself to Herbert's turn to linguistic philosophy, and whose own experience of returning to academic life and having to get up to philosophical speed after 16 years in another profession helped him to empathize with Herbert's predicament. Herbert was also friendly with colleagues like Hampshire, Cox, and, on his return from America, Berlin. And yet Herbert appears to have felt acutely uncomfortable in the social atmosphere of New College. Given his broad experience, intellectual standing, and his happiness at the College as an undergraduate, this is surprising. The testimony of Isaiah Berlin's unhappiness on his own return to New College in 1946, and his indictment of its crusty atmosphere and the barrenness of its intellectual life, provide some clues to Herbert's unease. But his was a personal sense of insecurity rather than a feeling of dissatisfaction. Almost every lunch, dinner, or other social event recorded in his diary was attended by self-castigation at either having talked too much or not having talked enough; at having said something foolish; at having disappointed his colleagues' expectations of him; at having not had the courage to pursue an argument, or at having pursued one with too great a vehemence.

Much the same is true of Herbert's reports of seminars, at which he rarely emerged with anything better than a feeling of having avoided making a total fool of himself: Waismann's class on advanced symbolic logic, for example, 'finally extinguished my confidence'. He responded by driving himself ever harder, working after dinner each evening, reviewing his grasp of classic texts by Hume, Mill, and others while making his way through an astonishing amount of the newer philosophical literature—Russell, Whitehead, Moore, Wisdom, Urmson, Ryle, Austin, Price, Wittgenstein, and Waismann. By Christmas 1945, nostalgic for the Bar, he was beginning to feel that he would not survive beyond the two years which he had set himself as a minimum and was even contemplating an earlier escape from 'the hell of Oxford': 'How I would welcome release from this too great burden of responsibility and how fearful I am of my interest vanishing. What a nightmare at times this is.'

Most academics are familiar with feelings somewhere along the spectrum of insecurity. Herbert's, however, settled for a long time at the acute end of the scale. In a painful phrase which recurs with extraordinary regularity in the diaries, he enjoined himself to 'keep up appearances' or—equally often—castigated himself for having failed to keep them up: 'To be a fraud is bad enough, but to be an unsuccessful one is too humiliating.' His week-end or vacation trips to see the family in London complicated matters still further. While in Oxford, he felt acutely homesick. In London, he found the 'squalor' associated with life with two small children whose mother exhib-ited a healthy but perhaps exaggerated contempt for domestic luxury equally difficult to handle. One of the difficulties for him in Oxford—at least until Berlin's return—was that he felt unable to confide his feelings to anyone: his pride and sensitivity to his reputation made 'keeping up appear-ances' a priority. With friends whom he knew well outside the Oxford context, however, Herbert does seem to have shared his feelings to some extent: he told Jenifer that Tommy Balogh had told him that 'I must stop this Jewish wailing and that it was now too late to have a conscience'.

Although Jenifer was aware that he was under pressure, recording in her diary in November 1945 that she had found Herbert 'rather depressed and depressing' over the weekend, she was shocked by the depth of anxiety and despair recorded in the diaries when she read them after his death. The separations—physical and emotional—of the last three years had taken their toll, and their weekends together were often difficult, with Herbert plagued by headaches and rheumatism, and tortured by his 'present inabil-ity to cope with this subject except at the cost of excessive expenditure of mental and hence nervous energy leaving me what you find on Fridays'. At one point in 1946, Herbert's anxieties were compounded by acute feelings of 'jealousy and distance' when it became clear that Jenifer had strong feelings for another man. In a painful series of letters, he veered bet-ween apologizing for 'being horrid' at weekends and making heroic efforts to overcome his jealousy, and remonstrating with Jenifer about 'the pain you inflict on yourself and me'. 'Of course I'm burning with shame for being neurotic, brutal and all the rest . . . .[M]uch as I love you, I don't want to . . . restrict what you do as long as I know the basis is alright. And it's mad of me to doubt that and I wouldn't if I were living in London . . . . After all I'm really responsible for any difficulties that have arisen because I decided to try this Oxford arrangement'. Herbert felt caught between worlds: not yet at home in Oxford, yet not a full member of the family in London. This liminal position was one he never quite escaped.

In drawing on any person's diaries to illuminate the shape of their lives, there is always the possibility that diaries record the extremes of feeling which, spread across the broader canvas of whole days and weeks, would look less intense. Particularly when thinking about a man who had few intimate conversations with others—and about a time in which such conversations were far less normal than they would be in a similar context today—one has also to take into account the possibility that the diary forms the kind of dialogue that would now be had with a friend, a partner, or a therapist. Certainly, Herbert's failure to confide in Jenifer was significant: he was already resolving that 'I must do something about my growing isolation from Jen: in part my obsession with work in part her preoccupations . . . ' But in interpreting his diaries, it is important to balance their outpourings of self-doubt, panic, and anxiety with evidence of how others perceived him, and about how he operated in collegiate, tutorial, and domestic environments. It was not only Jenifer who was unaware of the full extent of his anxieties. His colleagues and students had no idea that he was anything other than a secure and happy man. At least one colleague realized that Herbert was finding the transition both very hard work and something of a strain, but thought that this was only to be expected. There is no evidence that he ever exhibited any signs of distress or depression in College— hence his quintessentially English project of 'keeping up appearances' seems to have been a success. Nor was it just a case of keeping up appearances. The diaries record with pleasure regular visits to and from Jenifer's family in Oxford, and moments of amused confidence, for example in marking a set of grammar school boys' scholarship essays, which Herbert saw as 'a mix of religion and argument—akin to fascism, with the Saviour being wheeled in where necessary'. His later intellectual development and the evidence of the working parts of the diaries show that he was laying some important philosophical foundations in this period, finding that 'precise analysis is—surprisingly—interesting me and clarifying things'. This, along with his developing confidence as a teacher, must have given him genuine happiness and satisfaction. But it nonetheless seems likely that the depth of introspection revealed in Herbert's diaries represents one facet of his capacity for intellectual creativity: the courage to look problems in the face and the commitment to working out every difficulty, personal or intellectual, however painful the process.

Peter Campbell, one of Herbert's students in 1946, talked of his utter amazement when, on reading Jenifer's autobiography, he learned of Herbert's anxieties. To him, Herbert had appeared the perfectly confident, articulate, and 'inspiring' tutor, always ready with an argument, whose influence as the man who 'taught me how to argue' has stayed with him throughout his life (as a successful academic in his own right). Tutorials were problem-oriented and focussed on the key questions 'What do you mean?'

and 'How do you know?' The emphasis was on precision in argument rather than marshalling evidence, with Herbert taking it 'somewhat like a lawyer—testing the consistency and coherence of statements, working towards the truth . . . and teasing out the implications of what you were saying'. These techniques would have been familiar to Herbert from both his legal and his intelligence work, and Campbell was merely one of many students—including James Joll and Geoffrey Warnock—who found Herbert an inspiring tutor who 'taught one how to think' and set them on the course of an academic career. Significantly, Campbell also confessed himself surprised to learn from Jenifer's autobiography of Herbert's Jewish ancestry. His assumption that Herbert 'had descended from generations of patrician public school boys' gives an interesting insight into both prevailing cultural presuppositions and Herbert's persona, at least as presented to his students. This disjuncture between public self and inner feeling is highlighted by Jenifer's ignorance of the depth of his depression and self-doubt. Given that their correspondence shows continuing affection and dialogue, this suggests a variety of things: a capacity for concealment and repression on Herbert's part; a lack of confidence that Jenifer could help him; a use of the diary as repository for extremes of feeling which did not characterize the whole of his life.

As the months passed, the tone of Herbert's diaries changed. The change is almost imperceptible on a continuous reading; but by late 1946 the intensity of the anxiety recorded had significantly reduced and the proportion of the text devoted to analysis of philosophical problems, reports of a sense of progress in either teaching or analysis of ideas or in contributions to seminar debates increased. In letters to Jenifer, Herbert's tutorial and administrative duties gradually became the source of light-hearted sketches rather than agonized analyses, and his wry sense of humour began to take in the comic side of College life. Berlin's return to Oxford helped; talking to him made Herbert 'think and talk better . . . so I must nerve myself to do it more'. There were still bad days on which Herbert considered returning to the Bar, but one has the impression that these remarks were more by way of a salutary self-reminder of a disliked alternative than a real consideration of abandoning his academic career. And, as the levels of insecurity and distress reduced, the diary entries become more intermittent. Significantly, the diary peters out altogether in 1947, only to be taken up again—apart from some important annotations in 1949 and 1952, and assuming that other diaries were not lost or destroyed—on his visit to Harvard in 1956. By the summer of 1948, Herbert was feeling relaxed enough to take a holiday in Florence with Jenifer, rediscovering some of the artistic sights which had inspired him 20 years before, and travelling beyond the city through the tiring means of a cattle truck.

Part of the explanation for Herbert's changing mood was his growing competence and familiarity with the routines of academic life. He had learned to manage the tutorial process with less strain and nervous exhaustion; he had got to know the College and his colleagues better; and he had begun to feel confident in their regard for him. He had also learnt to manage the split between Oxford and London (in 1947 Jenifer and the children in any case moved to Oxford); and he was beginning to feel at home with the range of philosophical issues and materials which were being debated in Oxford at the time. But, most important of all for the mental tranquillity of a man for whom professional success—in the sense of success in his own eyes quite as much as in the eyes of the world—was at the core of his identity, he had begun to get a sense of the way in which he might contribute to the debates which were forming in post-war Oxford philosophy. To understand how he came to this view, which underpinned much of his work during the 1950s, and how he gradually accumulated the self-esteem without which creative work is impossible, it is crucial to know something of the very special world in which he was working.

In the Arts and Humanities, the structure of Oxford University, beyond its colleges, was vestigial. But a hugely important part of the context in which Herbert was working was the sub-Faculty of Philosophy. In 1946, Oxford philosophy dominated philosophical scholarship in England, while British philosophy continued to dominate philosophy all over the English-speaking world. In 1952, the 50 philosophers in Oxford constituted more than a quarter of all professional philosophers in England. Little wonder, then, that these men (for they were overwhelmingly men, and the small number of women philosophers in Oxford were admitted only to something equivalent to the restricted ladies' membership available in many clubs) felt and behaved as if they ran the philosophical world. In doing so, they employed techniques and a personal style which owed not a little to the military and other official experience and authority which the leading figures—Gilbert Ryle and J. L. Austin—had enjoyed during the war.

Ryle was the dominant figure in shaping the turn to linguistic philosophy before the war, and the title of his influential *The Concept of Mind* (1949) was echoed by Herbert in his own *The Concept of Law* (1961). Ryle's institutional influence was consolidated by his appointment, as G. E. Moore's successor, to the editorship of *Mind* in 1947, a key journal in which he encouraged his Oxford colleagues to publish. This encouragement was all the more important because philosophy at the time enjoyed nothing like today's professional research culture. Undergraduate teaching was the core of the philosopher's job, and scholarly enquiry was conducted, in the vacation or at weekends, on a 'proud amateur' basis. An urbane man with a dry humour (in one seminar, he responded to the demand that he explain the assumptions on which his argument was based by echoing a well known contemporary advert for a breath-freshener: 'Assumptions are like halitosis: your best friends won't tell you, but your enemies might . . .'), Ryle stamped his authority on Oxford philosophy without personally intimidating those within his sphere. His personal style is encapsulated in the small card which he sent to a young philosopher in the mid-1950s, accepting an article for *Mind*: 'Article accepted in its entirety. Italics removed. No need to shout.'

But it was Austin, a very different personality, who became the central figure in Herbert's own philosophical development. Isaiah Berlin had strongly advised Herbert to seek him out: 'I would fish out Major Austin out of your own department and force him to talk to you—no man has greater powers of awakening the full capacity for the philosophical forces of the interior. He is argumentative in the most useful and maddening sense, but I admire him more than any other of my professional contemporaries.' Austin was, by all accounts, a formidable figure, at once magnetic and alarming. Of unremarkable stature and appearance, with a thin voice and a dry manner, he nonetheless exercised an extraordinary personal authority over the group of philosophers admitted to his coterie. Austin was phenomenally clever and very witty but a man with almost no capacity for social ease. One colleague described him as a 'sour, dour schoolmaster-type . . . a parody of an English public school boy', and even one of his most ardent admirers, Geoffrey Warnock, evoked in print the image of Austin as a 'bird of prey'. Another observer saw him as 'a sort of parody of a desiccated don . . . . His voice was flat and metallic, and seemed to be stuck on a note of disillusion. It sounds like a telephone speaking to itself'. His distance and impersonal style are exemplified by a famous story of his behaviour at a meeting of intelligence officers during the war. Bill Williams, later Warden of Rhodes House, who had been coordinating the group of officers for over a year, suggested from the chair that they might at last begin to use one another's first names. When Austin's turn came to introduce himself, he simply said 'Austin is a Christian name, too.'

A particularly important institution in the exercise of Austin's authority and in the propagation of his method and ideas was a group established in 1947 and convened in his elegant panelled rooms in Magdalen each Saturday morning. This group, of which Herbert was a founder member, was not for Professors of philosophy but rather for the tutorial Fellows—in Austin's phrase, 'the teaching hacks'. The idea was to provide some stimulus and intellectual refreshment for hard-working professional teachers; as a Professor, Ryle was excluded, and on Herbert's appointment to a Chair in 1952, he became the only professor to attend the meetings. A (presumably intended) side effect was that the teaching philosophers passed on the ideas debated on Saturday mornings to undergraduate students via that central institutional plank of Oxford's oral culture, the tutorial system. (Undergraduates still constituted the vast bulk of Oxford students, with about 300 students in Classics and the Philosophy, Politics and Economics (PPE) degree taking some philosophy courses, as compared with only about a dozen students working on doctorates or taking the B.Phil. postgraduate degree recently established by Ryle.) The Saturday morning meeting was, in short, an inspired piece of institutional design.

The *modus operandi* of these Saturday morning sessions, which fast became a crucial aspect of Herbert's working life, was that the assembled company of men (neither Iris Murdoch nor Elizabeth Anscombe was included) would discuss a short text, a presented paper, or a number of pre-agreed questions. The range of texts was catholic, including not only Aristotle but also Chomsky, Frege, and Merleau-Ponty. When, as was most common, working with a text, it was rare for the analysis to get beyond the first page or so. This was symptomatic of Austin's approach, which was to seize upon each word, in the context of what he regarded as the basic unit of analysis—the sentence in which it was used—seeking in minute detail to elicit all the shades of its meaning, the assumptions which its usage made, its relationship with other concepts. One term, the texts were abandoned in favour of a series in which each participant had to study and give an account of the rules of a particular game. Years later, Herbert remarked to a colleague that he 'probably knew more about the rules of baseball than anyone alive', this having been his allotted subject. The prevailing method of analysis is summed up in the quotation from Austin cited by Herbert in the Preface to *The Concept of Law*: 'using a sharpened awareness of words to sharpen our perception of phenomena'. It is exemplified by the following passage from one of his most famous papers:

If we are to continue to use [the] expression [doing an action] in sober philosophy, we need to ask such questions as: Is to sneeze to do an action? Or is to breathe, or to see, or to checkmate, or each one of countless others? In short, for what range of verbs, as used on what occasions, is 'doing an action' a stand-in for what they have in common, and what do those excluded severally lack?

Though Austin's writing does not capture the atmosphere which must have been generated in the intense Saturday discussions, which were enlivened by his mesmerizing oral cleverness, Peter Hacker's description gives a flavour of the finely textured yet essentially common-sensical nature of his approach:

Time was spent analysing dispositional concepts . . . for which 'disposition', 'trait', 'propensity', 'characteristic', 'habit', 'inclination', 'susceptibility', 'tendency' and so on were carefully anatomized, compared and contrasted. Apropos Wittgenstein's comparison of words to tools, the expressions 'tool', 'instrument', 'implement', 'utensil', 'appliance', 'equipment', 'apparatus', 'gear', 'kit', 'device', and 'gimmick' were examined in patient detail (were kitchen scissors, garden shears, dress-making scissors, surgeons' scissors utensils, tools or implements?) with a view to determining the most helpful analogy.

Austin's interest in language was not motivated solely by the desire to resolve philosophical questions. He found linguistic investigations of interest in their own right, and delighted in uncovering subtle, unnoticed differences in linguistic idiom. (Why 'very' allows the substitution of 'highly' in some cases ('very unusual') but not in others ('very depressed' or 'very wicked') is not a question which is likely to have interested Wittgenstein.)

At Saturday morning discussions or other seminars, Austin's manner is frequently described by those who remember the occasions—most of them, of course, junior to Austin—as 'austere' or even 'bullying' and the regime of the time as 'terrifying'. He had the capacity utterly to silence and even to shatter the confidence of anyone who failed to understand, or to play by, the prevailing rules of engagement. His obsession with precision was not confined to the seminar room. On one occasion, Austin had written to Jenifer Hart's old flame Guy Chilver, now Senior Tutor at Queen's College, to ask whether the College agreed to a student's being awarded an 'aegrotat' degree. When Chilver replied that 'the college had no objection', Austin wrote back, 'I asked you whether you agreed.' In seminars, the effect could be devastating. Any utterance would be met with a meticulous cross-examination; 'What do you mean by x? How can you know that x is true? Under what conditions would be it meaningful to say x? How is x distinct from y?' and so on. What Austin regarded as a stupid or evasive response would be dismissed as 'not philosophy', while those (numerous) philosophers not within the linguistic circle would be spoken of as 'not in touch with current trends in philosophy'—meaning, 'don't waste your time on him'. The tone was precise, sharp, and destructive: it was about winning and losing, and the culture was one of gamesmanship and king-making.

An anecdote from the 1950s illustrates Austin's personal contribution to the winners and losers culture of which, with the gradual ascendancy of Peter Strawson, he seems ultimately to have become a victim. At a seminar of the Philosophical Society, a visiting American idealist philosopher castigated the Oxford linguistic philosophers for 'chasing mice not tigers'. A graduate student of the time (later to become White's Professor of Moral Philosophy in the University), sitting behind Austin, watched as he 'uncoiled himself, snake-like, from his chair' and suggested, in his 'thin, inhuman voice', that the visiting professor might like to release a tiger and show the audience how to hunt it. With an unwise but endearing lack of caution, the visitor accepted the challenge, and duly let loose one of the most untameable philosophical tigers: the problem of free will. After five minutes of not entirely coherent analysis, he lapsed into an embarrassed silence, into which Austin hissed in a stage whisper, 'You won't catch mice that way'.

One should not infer from these stories that Austin was a completely confident, emotionally invincible man. A graduate student of the time, invited to tea with the Austins in the later 1950s, had the impression of a certain nostalgia in Austin, which he thought was 'born of an odd feeling of being so clever yet feeling there was so little in the world to be clever about'. Students and colleagues testify to his occasionally visible nervousness, most vividly seen in the fact that he sometimes dried up for several minutes at a time when lecturing. This was a man who built strong fortifications—personal and professional—to protect himself against his own vulnerabilities. In doing so, he made an extraordinary contribution to the development of post-war philosophy, opening up productive avenues of philosophical analysis though, as we shall see, closing off others.

It is not difficult to see why the appeal to ordinary language held real attractions for philosophers in the post-war era. In breaking free from the metaphysical baggage of both much classical philosophy and the continental traditions deriving from Kant among others, there was a refreshing sense that questions of relevance to the conduct of everyday life could be connected with fundamental philosophical questions and addressed in an authoritative way by philosophers. The ultimate value of analytical clarity seemed—in stark contrast to some of the more grandiose ambitions of metaphysics—to be truly within the philosopher's grasp, building on the insight that the accretions of linguistic usage reflect all the most important distinctions developed through human experience. Austin's theory of 'speech acts'—of the ways in which utterances such as 'I promise' or even 'I do' have, within certain contexts, a distinctively performative effect—showed not just, in the famous title of his collection of essays, *How To Do Things with Words*, but also how the use of words changes our social world. R. M. Hare's *The Language of Morals* (1952) carried the linguistic approach through into moral philosophy. In arguing that moral statements could be identified in terms of their distinctive logical structure which could in turn be illuminated by philosophical analysis, Hare rebutted the realist position that moral values have some 'objective' metaphysical status while avoiding the extreme logical positivist reaction which reduced moral statements to mere expressions of emotion.

In addition to the shared rejection of traditional metaphysics, the extraordinary intellectual excitement and sense of scholarly community which characterized Oxford philosophy in the 15 years after the war derived from a sense of identity constructed in opposition to a number of other streams in the history of ideas and in contemporary philosophical scholarship. Oxford's analytic, linguistic tradition was developed among men, the vast majority of whom were classicists by training. Their view of the world was shaped by the humanities rather than the sciences. In this respect, and in their outright hostility to scientific reductionism—to the claim that the scientific view of the world was exhaustive—their outlook was in sharp contrast to that of, for example, the Cambridge-based philosophy of Bertrand Russell and the early Wittgenstein. Though in many ways a diverse group, the Oxford philosophers shared an insistence on the distinctiveness of different—legal, moral, scientific—forms of knowledge. In a memorably scathing passage, Russell castigated the Oxford philosophers for their philistinism about the natural sciences, describing linguistic philosophy as an excuse for scientific ignorance cobbled together by minds impoverished by the limitations of a merely classical education: a ' "Philosophy-Without-Tears" School, so named because it makes philosophy very much easier than it has ever been before: in order to be a competent philosopher, it is only necessary to study Fowler's *Modern English Usage*'. Ryle, he wrote, 'seems to believe that a philosopher need not know anything scientific beyond what was known in the time of our ancestors when they dyed themselves with woad'. Dismissing the 'new' linguistic philosophy as 'the cult of common usage', Russell inveighed that:

The most influential school of philosophy in Britain at the present day maintains a certain linguistic doctrine to which I am unable to subscribe. The doctrine . . . consists in maintaining that the language of daily life, with words used in their ordinary meanings, suffices for philosophy, which has no need of technical terms or of changes in the signification of common terms. I find myself totally unable to accept this view. I object to it:

(1) Because it is insincere;
(2) Because it is capable of excusing ignorance of mathematics, physics, and neurology in those who have had only a classical education;
(3) Because it is advanced by some in a tone of unctuous rectitude, as if opposition to it were a sin against democracy;
(4) Because it makes philosophy trivial;
(5) Because it makes almost inevitable the perpetuation among philosophers of the muddle-headedness they have taken over from common sense.

Russell was not alone in questioning whether there was anything either new or truly intellectually subtle in the linguistic movement. Ernest Gellner, in *Words and Things*, his famous 1959 critique of the philosophical culture which he escaped in favour of a post at the LSE, sardonically described

Oxford linguistic philosophy as 'the strange love-child of Wittgenstein's messianism and Oxonian complacency'. Neither amused by Gellner's vituperative attack nor impressed by his arguments, Ryle refused to review the book in *Mind*. Bertrand Russell, claiming to be inspired by this attack on academic freedom but undoubtedly enjoying the chance to take a public swipe at Oxford philosophy, took up the cudgel on Gellner's behalf. His indignant letter of protest to *The Times* sparked off a storm of public argument between Ryle, Gellner, and a miscellany of other correspondents including philosophers, students, and even the Queen's solicitor. After 19 days, the issue was laid to rest by an editorial in *The Times*. The upshot is probably best summarized as a goalless draw.

About half the Oxford philosophers—including well-regarded scholars like J. D. Mabbott and H. E. Paton—did not endorse the linguistic approach. Some saw it as merely part of a longer tradition of concept-clarification: it was therefore part of the ground-clearing work of philosophy, work which revealed questions which cannot themselves be dealt with by linguistic methods. This judgment passes a certain test of history: among analytical philosophers today, Austin's essays, like several other works which were key to Oxford linguistic philosophy in the 1940s and 1950s, are relatively little read. But the same is not true of many works which were products or more indirect spin-offs from the Austinian circle: Peter Strawson's *Individuals* or, later, R. M. Hare's *The Language of Morals*. Nor is this the only evidence of Austin's intellectual legacy. Ironically, Austin's theory of speech acts is now being read by a new generation of philosophical iconoclasts, the postmodernists, who are again focusing on language and proclaiming, albeit from a rather different perspective, the 'death of metaphysics'. Nonetheless, the orthodox judgment on Oxford linguistic philosophy is that it never successfully escaped the 'paradox of analysis': in other words, if ordinary language indeed captures so many important distinctions and insights, how can one subject it to technical philosophical analysis without destroying the very integrity and distinctiveness of ordinary language which linguistic philosophy proclaims? It is clear, however, that what was happening in Oxford at the time generated a huge wave of excitement. This was intensified by Oxford's distinctive intellectual culture, and it is not surprising that Herbert was swept along on its tide.

The next largest philosophical grouping in the country at that time was in Cambridge, which had two professors and four lecturers in 1950. Yet though Russell's logic, Ramsey's work on mathematics, and, to some extent, Wittgenstein's *Tractatus* commanded respect, it was at first only really the moral philosopher G. E. Moore who rated with the Oxford linguistic philosophers. A widely circulated story has Austin remarking on one occasion: 'Some people like Witters but Moore is *my* man.' Hostility to the scientific Cambridge world view (as well as the cultural factors to which I shall turn in a moment) also underlay the majority of Oxford philosophers' hostility or indifference to the logical positivism of the Vienna Circle. This was the doctrine that only propositions susceptible of empirical proof could have truth value, which was propounded in the Oxford philosophers' midst by A. J. Ayer. Ayer's relationship with Austin was antagonistic. Yet as Isaiah Berlin recalled, 'although they were in a state of almost constant collision—Ayer like an irresistible missile, Austin like an immovable obstacle—the result was not a stalemate, but the most interesting, free and lively discussions of philosophy that I have ever known'.

The ambivalent attitude to the Vienna Circle, to Wittgenstein, and to continental philosophy generally among the Oxford philosophers suggests a further dimension to their genre of linguistic philosophy: its English-ness—or perhaps, non-European-ness—in cultural, stylistic, and even political terms. It is important not to overstate the Oxford philosophers' resistance to these European traditions. Ryle, who had written on Husserl, had been one of the first English philosophers to show an interest in the Vienna Circle, introducing his students to Wittgenstein's work and encouraging Ayer to go to Vienna. As for Wittgenstein, it was primarily the *Tractatus* which fell foul of Oxford's anti-scientific prejudice (although at least one doctoral student was working on that topic in Oxford from the mid-1950s). The linguistically-oriented *Philosophical Investigations* was not published until 1953, though copies of the *Blue Book* and the *Brown Book* were circulating informally in the mid-1940s, and Wittgenstein's later work formed the object of discussion at several Saturday morning sessions.

In 1947, Wittgenstein visited Oxford to address a meeting of the Jowett Society. It was an unforgettable and an uncomfortable occasion. He had declined to give a paper, preferring to respond *ex tempore* to a presentation by one of the graduate students. In what must have been a terrifying experience, Oscar Wood introduced a paper on Descartes' *Cogito*—'I think therefore I am'; Wittgenstein then took up the threads of Wood's argument, thinking aloud about whether the *Cogito* was true. His performance was vintage Wittgenstein: walking to and fro and waving his arms about wildly, his intense, tortured speech was punctuated by expostulations such as 'What I say is all rubbish'. In the audience, which included the entire Oxford philosophy department, sat Prichard, an elderly man, but still the doyen of the old-style, non-linguistic Oxford philosophy. Prichard was not going to miss this golden opportunity of making plain his views about the merits of the new philosophy. He riled Wittgenstein by interrupting repeatedly in his high, reedy voice, pointing out several misquotations from Descartes and consistently mispronouncing Wittgenstein's name. The increasingly tense atmosphere was finally shattered when Prichard jumped to his feet and accused Wittgenstein of not having answered the question. Wittgenstein replied in freezing tones: 'I think this is a very silly old man, therefore I am what?' The department instantly divided itself between those who found Wittgenstein's response unforgivably rude, and those who regarded it as a shrewd and legitimate riposte. Predictably, the division more or less corresponded with that between the pro- and anti-linguistic philosophy camps. Herbert remembered this as the occasion which revealed the full chasm between the old and new Oxford philosophy. The experience did nothing to change Wittgenstein's withering view of Oxford as 'an influenza area'.

There was no longer any doubt about which side of the Oxford chasm Herbert was standing on. His diaries of the period recorded the illumination which he found in the *Blue Book*, which he described as having helped him to let go of a crippling sense of the complexity of certain questions about knowledge, and to see his way through to a more simple and elegant analysis. Not a man known for extravagant turns of phrase, he nonetheless remarked to one of his students that when he read the *Blue Book* 'It was as if the scales fell from my eyes', while Mary Warnock remembers him 'clutching Geoffrey [Warnock] and saying, "I've been up all night! I've been up all night! I can't think of anything else"' after reading the *Philosophical Investigations*. And in later life, during a conversation with a younger colleague, he referred to the *Philosophical Investigations* as 'our bible'. Stuart Hampshire remembered that most of the Oxford philosophers recognized Wittgenstein as 'an explosion of genius in the middle of the discipline', and this is confirmed by Strawson's admiring review of the *Investigations* published in *Mind*, and by his testimony that when he first read the *Blue Book* 'I felt that I was, for the first time, seeing thought *naked* as it were'. Indeed, one of the Oxford movement's rallying cries, 'Don't look for the meaning, ask for the use', was drawn from Wittgenstein. Friedrich Waismann, at one time a collaborator of Wittgenstein's, himself held a post in Oxford from 1940 until his death in 1959, and Herbert attended his classes. In so far as it is possible to trace Wittgensteinian themes in Herbert's later work, they are mediated by Waismann's work on rules and institutions, which contributed to Herbert's own theory of the open texture of legal language.

Yet, apart from this one rather unsuccessful visit in the 1940s the Oxford group sought no contact with Wittgenstein and, as Austin's remark about 'Witters' suggests, regarded him with some suspicion. The first and most obvious reason for this was an objection to Wittgenstein's style, the elusive and sometimes playful quality of which violated the ultimate tenet of the

Oxford linguistic philosophers' faith: that of clarity. The Oxford view of ordinary language philosophy was that its virtue was precisely its common-sensical nature, its precision, and its transparency. The Oxford linguistic philosophers—including Herbert—regarded with both distrust and distaste not only Wittgenstein's elliptical and in their view needlessly difficult written style but also, later on, the guru-like persona which he cultivated and which he allowed his disciples to celebrate.

The second, and more elusive, aspect of Oxford philosophy's Englishness had to do with the Allied victory in the war. The positive manifestation of this was a resurgence of confidence that intellectual culture could deliver an English perspective distinct from the influential traditions of continental philosophy. Herbert's own attitude to the continent was a curious mixture of love for European culture and indifference to or even suspicion of European ideas. Much the same could be said of his attitude to romanticism: while he had a deep love for the romantic poets, the romantic strand in the history of ideas—Vico or Herder for example—which so intrigued his friend Berlin was close to intellectual anathema to Herbert. For some philosophers, this anti-European attitude also cashed out, negatively, in a suspicion that continental philosophy had in some sense contributed to the rise of fascism, and that there was therefore something inherently politically questionable about it.

Leaving aside specific cases such as Heidegger's engagement with Nazism, views in Oxford doubtless differed as to whether particular German philosophers, living or dead, should be held responsible for the appropriation of their ideas by fascist ideologues. But the Oxford linguistic philosophers did not subscribe to a strong version of this position. On one occasion, the issue gave rise to a striking clash between Austin and Karl Popper, who delivered a paper in which he asserted that logical positivism had contributed to the rise of fascism. It was a claim which Ayer rebutted in the strongest terms. Austin too repeatedly challenged the assertion, and Popper finally walked out of the seminar—an exit which prompted one of Austin's more brutal remarks: 'The man is a hunchback'. Their characteristic precision and reluctance to make sweeping claims prevented the Oxford philosophers from endorsing a generalization like Popper's. Yet there was a strong sense of the opportunity to make a fresh start on the English side of the channel, casting off the historical, political, and metaphysical baggage of continental traditions (the French and Italians being lumped, for these purposes, with the German traditions whose political contribution to fascism was perhaps more plausible) and constructing an indigenous, English, no-nonsense, post-war philosophy. As one philosopher, a graduate student in the early 1950s, put it, there was a feeling that much of what had gone before in philosophy was 'nonsense': 'they had won the war, got rid of the evil people, and didn't need to learn anything from earlier traditions'. Inevitably, Kant and Descartes sat alongside Aristotle and Plato in the Oxford undergraduate syllabus. But Nietzsche, Marx, Kierkegaard, and Hegel were notably absent. Only the so-called English Empiricists—Locke, Berkeley, Hobbes, Hume, and Mill (as well as, to some extent, Kant)—appear to have engaged the enthusiasm of the linguistic philosophers.

How did Herbert fit into this distinctive philosophical world, and what attractions did it hold for him? In his early years as Philosophy Fellow, he was still intending to write a book on Plato. But the linguistic philosophy movement quickly drew him in. His deep regard for—indeed awe of—Austin reflected an unlikely alliance. Herbert's personal style—though also tending to the austere and, particularly in later years, capable of intimidating those less intellectually confident than himself—was unfailingly courteous and was more humane, gentle, and overtly self-critical than Austin's. Yet Austin had the capacity to entrance even those whose personal or intellectual style differed from his own: Isaiah Berlin, a wholly different character, kept for years on his mantelpiece in All Souls a metal sign from the eponymous car makers announcing, simply 'AUSTIN'. But there is still something to be explained in the affinity between two men of such different personalities. The difference is captured by a story of a joint seminar on concepts such as intention which Austin and Herbert ran jointly in the early 1950s. At the first seminar, there was a small but respectable turnout. At the second, there were only three people in the audience. At the third, there were none. Herbert suggested that they adjourn to his rooms to have their discussion over a glass of sherry. Austin firmly declined, and the seminar, audience-less, went ahead. The story must have originated with Herbert himself, so even if it is an exaggeration, it expresses something significant about his view of Austin. It is possible that Herbert found Austin's apparent confidence and invulnerability an attractive foil to his own feelings of insecurity. It is also likely that he was drawn to the dry, commonsensical Englishness of Austin's version of linguistic philosophy—an upper class, establishment Englishness which plugged a gap in his own sense of identity, born of his searing Cheltenham experiences as a Jewish boy from a trade background. And, temperamentally, the two men shared a left-of-centre political outlook, an intellectual scrupulousness and taste for attention to detail, an attachment to the power of reasoned argument, and, perhaps most importantly, a commitment to clarity, as both an intellectual value and an aesthetic.

One can speculate with more confidence about the intellectual basis for Herbert's engagement with the linguistic philosophy school. First—and not unconnected with his need for belonging and status—the coterie around Austin and Ryle was, to put it crudely, the main show in town within the discipline in which Herbert wished to make his mark. Notwithstanding the diversity within Oxford philosophy, it was acceptance and regard among the group around Ryle, Austin, Hampshire, and Strawson which—as the course of Herbert's career over the next seven years would prove—was the ultimate mark of reputation and guarantee of success.

Secondly, common-sense, linguistic philosophy must have held some discrete attractions for a late returner to philosophy who had doubts—as his 1940s notebooks show—about his capacity to get to the bottom of the deepest questions of epistemology and logic. The flight from metaphysics, in other words, offered the seductive prospect of escape from a painful further period of apprenticeship in the arcane craft of traditional philosophy—an apprenticeship which some of Herbert's colleagues felt that he had left too soon. This was a judgment which he himself endorsed in his later work—notably in his *Essays on Bentham*. He also came to regard the illuminating power of linguistic philosophy as more limited than he had in the 1940s and 1950s. We can glimpse the fact that, right from the start, he entertained some ambivalence about his identification with the Oxford school in a correspondence which he had with Ernest Gellner in 1960, of which, unfortunately, only Gellner's letters survive. These letters make it clear that, in the wake of the row sparked off by Gellner's *Words and Things*, Herbert had written objecting to the way he had been identified with an arid approach to philosophy, and arguing that his jurisprudential work did not fit Gellner's stereotype. Replying that while having 'a very great respect indeed for the non ivory tower aspect of your work', he would 'not be inclined to give you an unqualified clearance from membership of the movement, at any rate in the past, notwithstanding your very distinguished work in jurisprudence and legal reform', Gellner astutely fixed on the cleft stick in which Herbert had put himself in by demanding such 'clearance':

Unkindly, I might add that if my book were as inaccurate about the movement as a whole as is now claimed by some, granting you special exemption would be something hardly worth having. If on the other hand it is worth having, this seems to imply that the general charges are not wholly off the mark.

Since Gellner's next letter opens by thanking Herbert for a letter in which 'you somewhat peremptorily inform me that my previous letter "will not do"', and refers to Herbert's having attested himself 'shocked' by Gellner's original letter, we can only assume that the conclusion of the correspondence was less than happy.

Despite his ambivalence about being dubbed an 'ivory tower philosopher', however, Herbert had further, strong intellectual reasons for attaching himself to the Oxford school. For, thirdly and most importantly, Austin's method gave Herbert for the first time a clear view of the distinctive contribution which he might make to philosophy. The method of painstaking, detailed analysis of linguistic usage, with its clarion call, 'look for the use, not the meaning', was premised on the idea (if not always practised on the basis) that context was all-important. As Herbert put it in later life:

His understanding and subtle analysis of language absolutely excited me . . . .[H]e was naturally interested in law and he would have made a formidable QC . . . . For example, what he was good at was characterising the very diverse uses of language that there are, and how these are not seen, and how philosophical confusion results from assimilating one kind of language to another. And then amongst these things he had the idea of what he called performative utterances. And here the law came into its own—when I say 'I hereby give you my gold pen', I'm not describing what I'm doing, I'm actually doing it . . . . And the other thing was his general interest in the diversity of rules and standards of conduct . . .

In coming to the realization that his legal background gave him an important piece of intellectual equipment, Waismann's work on context-dependent approaches to the elucidation of meaning were also an important influence on Herbert.

Austin, to his credit, realized that the intellectual traffic between New College's new Philosophy Fellow and the well-established group of linguistic philosophers was not all in one direction. He quickly recognized that Herbert had something distinctive to contribute to the development of the field, and the two began to read legal cases together, teaching from 1948 a seminar on 'Legal and Moral Responsibility' which examined the mental conditions of criminal responsibility, as well the conditions under which a person's apparently criminal conduct might be excused. In terms of Herbert's emerging intellectual identity, this was a crucial supplement to his introductory lectures (from 1947) on logic and general philosophy, and to his seminars from 1949 on Locke. Gradually, it became clear to Herbert that his years of experience as a Chancery barrister, his detailed knowledge of the subtle texture of legal reasoning, provided him with a fund of examples ripe for philosophical analysis, and by 1951/2 he was lecturing on Moral and Legal Reasoning (as well as on Legal and Political Theories in Plato). He began to realize that legal usage provided examples of conceptualization and distinction-making which could be put to use in philosophy. Here, the key example, of which he remained uncharacteristically proud throughout his life, was the concept of 'defeasibility'. Defeasibility marks a provisional fixing of meaning which can be dissolved under given circumstances. Legal rights and obligations, for example, are defeasible in this sense: if I waive your contractual obligation to me, my waiver is the condition of the dissolution of my right and your obligation. Herbert was to draw on this concept to significant effect in his jurisprudential work.

A comparison of Herbert's and Austin's essays drawing, under Herbert's influence, on legal questions (notably Austin's influential 'A Plea for Excuses') shows the intellectual benefits of Herbert's nuanced grasp of the intricacies of legal reasoning. Next to Herbert's, Austin's essays, though beautifully structured and rhetorically brilliant, look relatively simplistic in the light of a more contextualized, less abstract, analysis. The combination of legal experience and philosophical insight equipped Herbert, in short, to make an original contribution to a field which was crying out for someone with insight into the social practices within which linguistic usage develops. Herbert's legal input to seminars with Austin almost certainly contributed to the latter's development of his famous 'speech act' theory: the idea that spoken words such as 'I promise' can constitute 'performative utterances' which have direct effects in the world. Herbert's seminars on the philosophical ideas underlying the laws of Athens also reflected this developing sense of a distinct intellectual identity. As he became aware of this, his anxieties were gradually replaced by a growing sense of confidence and excitement about his philosophical future.

The genesis of Herbert's own sense of his potential contribution is illuminated by the papers he wrote during his first few years in Oxford. Throughout his career, Herbert wrote vastly more than he published: he would only release for publication work which satisfied his exceptionally high standards of rigour, insight, and clarity. Between 1945 and 1952, he published only three papers and two reviews, but the contrast between these publications provides an interesting insight into the development of his ideas and sense of his own intellectual agenda. 'A Logician's Fairytale', published in 1951, was a witty satirical analysis of the presuppositions of logic and of the pitfalls of a philosophical outlook dominated by an excessive reliance on formal logic. It was an essentially critical piece, although informed by the methods and outlook of linguistic philosophy, and close to Strawson's approach. A second paper, 'Is there Knowledge by Acquaintance?', published in the Proceedings of the Aristotelian Society in 1949, was a critical analysis of Russell's theory of knowledge, from an Austinian point of view. An influential moral philosopher described it to me as one of the 'two or three things' he would still advise a student working on the development of debates about knowledge at that time to read. It does not, however, give any strong sense of Herbert's own agenda.

By contrast, an essay on 'Law and Fact' which fed into a review published in 1951 of American legal theorist Jerome Frank's *Law and the Modern Mind* foreshadowed Herbert's later concerns. He argued that crime and other legal concepts 'straddle the world of law and fact' and demonstrate that 'special cases within systems of meaning such as law or games can illuminate general debates within philosophy'. Yet more importantly, 'The Ascription of Responsibility and Rights', published in 1948, exemplifies the intellectual cross-fertilization between law and linguistic philosophy which was to make Herbert famous over the next decade. The paper applied a radical linguistic analysis to these two concepts, arguing that they were not descriptive of anything in the world but rather made sense within practices of attribution or ascription in contexts such as legal argument: A is responsible for the murder of B; C has a right to compensation from D. Austin, among others, thought extremely highly of this paper, and its reputation in both Britain and the USA was material to Herbert's being regarded as a serious candidate for the Chair of Jurisprudence.

Herbert's own attitude to the paper is symptomatic of his more ambivalent assessment of his work. Before long, he became convinced by criticisms of its analysis, and in 1968 and 1983 declined to republish the paper in his collected essays on the basis that its argument took insufficient notice of Austin's distinction between the force and the meaning of statements—a distinction which implied that ascriptive statements could also be descriptive. He cited as one significant source of his doubts a response by Princeton philosopher George Pitcher—a persuasive response but not one which should have led Herbert to abandon the paper as decisively as he did. As one of his former research students put it, Pitcher's arguments were 'little flies making small points in a fashionable way'. More important would have been Peter Geach's frontal assault on ascriptivism in essays published from the early 1960s on (and acknowledged by Herbert in the preface to his own 1968 collection), which convinced him that ascriptivism as a broad position was unavoidably reductive: statements ascribing responsibility, on this view, collapsed into descriptive statements. But the essay remains significant for two reasons. It represents Herbert's early engagement with the implications of linguistic analysis for moral and legal philosophy. And it marks out a path which he might productively have followed: a deep absorption of Wittgensteinian ideas which could have pushed his own legal philosophy in the direction of a closer examination of the history and workings of specific social practices, such as the ascription of responsibility for crime. Though this path was followed to a significant extent in his book with Tony Honoré on causation, both *The Concept of Law* and his later essays in analytical jurisprudence mark, as we shall see, a retreat from the concrete, institution-specific analysis which is suggested by the argument of this early paper.

Herbert's growing sense of direction did not relieve him of his moments of panic and anxiety. At the annual joint meeting of the *Mind Association* and the Aristotelian Society in Bangor in 1948, J. M. Findlay—an able philosopher hostile to Herbert's position—subjected his paper to a tough critique. Herbert's reaction appears to have been quite extreme. In Gellner's second letter in 1960, he told Herbert that, 'I remember you *saying* in the discussion accompanying your paper on Acquaintance that Russell had "failed to give meaning" to the relevant expression . . . . If you do not remember uttering [this] . . . , forgive me for reminding you that your memory may be blurred owing to the fact that you completely lost your temper on that occasion, and, quite unjustly and unnecessarily, employed the word *insanity* in referring to one of your co-symposiasts'. Afterwards, Herbert was extremely upset: there was a 'painful episode' in which his Oxford colleagues had to 'rally round' to convince him that his feeling that he had failed adequately to defend his arguments did not imply that he was unfit for a philosophical career. He wrote to Jenifer:

This is to let you know that I am still alive and comparatively unharmed after a vigorous fray with Finlay [sic] last night. He is the oddest of individuals with a great strand of charlatan, playing to the gallery, and rhetoric in him, anxious at present to align himself with the reactionaries but not honestly prepared to argue on any specific issues. His denunciations of me were all considered by the progressives to be unfair or untrue and in the end he not I was done down. But Price took his part and attacked me, while Ryle took mine. So I became pawn in the game between the two professors . . . . I can't think how I let F's paper's accusations disturb me so . . .

He was, Stuart Hampshire recalled, 'like a convert to a new religion'. He could see that there was something in Findlay's argument, but could not accept that his own position could not have been better defended. His reaction was disproportionate. But it does not seem to have disturbed his psychological equilibrium for long. This was the same occasion on which he and Peter Strawson cycled back to Oxford together over three days, stopping in one seaside town, on an exceptionally hot day, for a swim in their underwear. The adamant liberalism and intellectual rigidity displayed in Herbert's reaction to Findlay was not entirely out of character. In a letter to Noel Annan in 1950, Isaiah Berlin, now back in Oxford and in frequent contact with Herbert, complained that, having read his essay on Churchill, Herbert and Hampshire had 'reproached' him 'for reactionary tendencies . . . Must we really walk in grooves so tightly controlled?'

By the beginning of the 1950s, Herbert was a well-established member of Oxford's powerful philosophical community. He was a respected participant in the Saturday morning seminars and other sessions. He had formed deep intellectual relationships not only with his old friends Berlin and Hampshire but also with Austin and Strawson (who arrived in Oxford in 1947). And he had published at least one highly regarded paper. He was no stranger to institutional politics: in 1952 he was assiduously providing Berlin with notes for a reference supporting Austin's candidature for the Chair of Moral Philosophy, while doubting his chances given the membership of the selection panel: 'I think he has a v. poor chance with this crazy gang and we shall be exceedingly lucky to get Stuart [Hampshire]. The college will rock just a little with Bullock, Stuart and me falling away simultaneously. But the Warden is delighted—he looks forward to a college in which perhaps there are only undergraduates and himself and Christopher Cox.'

Equally importantly, by dint of exceptionally hard work—his diaries show him reading and making notes late into most evenings—Herbert had acquired intellectual resources on which he would draw for the rest of his career. By the standards of the time, his published output was not unusually slight: Austin, for example, published only three articles, four symposium papers, a few reviews, and a translation of Frege during his career. Most of his work was published posthumously. But, given the short span of Herbert's career and the absence of any major published work, the fact that he was thought of as a candidate for the Chair of Jurisprudence is evidence of Austin's institutional power, the status of philosophy, and the importance in Oxford of a reputation for formidable cleverness in seminars and informal conversation.

Between 1945 and 1952, Herbert had very little contact with members of the Oxford Law Faculty. The Faculty had 22 members, the majority of whom were common lawyers working in specific fields such as contracts or trusts, with other areas of expertise including Roman law (the Regius Chair was held by Jolowicz), legal history, and comparative law (a Chair held, famously, between 1964 and 1971 by Otto Kahn Freund, with whom, significantly, Herbert appears to have had practically no intellectual contact). In England, the tradition of scholarly research and publication came later to law than to philosophy departments, and it seems likely that Herbert had a rather dim view of the intellectual calibre of the Oxford Faculty. Certainly, many of those who wrote to congratulate him on his election held such views. They variously referred to the 'terrible law faculty', with jurisprudence a 'dead-ish and sour subject'; a 'corpse' into which Herbert might inject some life, while bringing 'literacy and logic to the law school'. Legal theory, let alone legal philosophy, was a marginal occupation, though in 1952 it was represented in Oxford, by national standards, by a relatively large group of four men: Rupert Cross, later Vinerian Professor of English Law, a criminal and evidence lawyer with significant theoretical interests and who would become, along with Tony Honoré, a close colleague of Herbert's; Honoré himself, a young South African who had moved from

New College to a Law Fellowship at Queens in 1948 and who combined interests in Roman law and legal philosophy; C. K. Allen, a transitory occupant of the Jurisprudence Chair, whose book of essays on legal duties represented the kind of dry, conceptual analysis, refreshed only by a significant depth of historical scholarship, which was typical of jurisprudence of the day; and the Professor of Jurisprudence, Arthur Goodhart, an American whose work focussed on legal reasoning and the common law system of precedent. Of these four, only Cross and Honoré had philosophical interests, and only Honoré had followed these through with interdisciplinary collaboration: he and the young philosopher Tony Woozley taught a seminar on Philosophy and Legal Concepts in 1951 and 1952, the first such interdisciplinary seminar in Oxford. Herbert's view of jurisprudence at the time was that: 'It had no broad principle, no broad faith, it confronted no large question . . . . And there were no large scale inquiries into the philosophical dimensions of law or legal study. And I thought it was boring and had shut its eyes to a lot of interesting things which my legal experience and my time as a philosophy don had alerted me to.'

Most members of the Law Faculty would have expected a Law Fellow to be appointed as the successor to Goodhart as Professor of Jurisprudence at University College. Austin had other ideas. He and another man with whom Herbert had developed a close intellectual relationship, the University College philosopher (and former student of Wittgenstein) George Paul, encouraged Herbert to think of himself as a possible candidate. Quite apart from his high intellectual regard for Herbert, Austin's thinking was shaped by a belief that only a 'real' philosopher could elevate the Chair to a level of any intellectual credibility. This is strikingly reflected in his note of congratulation on Herbert's ultimate election: 'It is splendid to see the empire of philosophy annex another province in this way—not to mention the good you're going to do them'. One can imagine how members of the Law Faculty must have felt about this colonization, not to mention the triumphalism with which it was accomplished. For it was not only Austin's letter which illustrated the philosophers' sense of intellectual superiority: Magdalen Fellow Kurt Baier found it 'remarkable that lawyers can be so perceptive'; Richard Braithwaite wrote from Cambridge to celebrate Herbert's 'infiltration, or was it assault?', opining that 'Jurisprudence is quite futile unless it is treated as a branch of philosophy. But', he wondered, 'will you persuade the lawyers?'; Ryle was 'glad for the sake of the students who want to think'. Among the dozens of letters of congratulation (they included, of course, many from London friends and family, with his father, reported by Sybil to be depressed again, expecting him to fulfil the position with 'honour and dignity') there is, overall, a marked difference of tone between the philosophers and the lawyers. While the philosophers were warm and exultant, the lawyers were merely polite. Only seven Law Faculty members even bothered to write. Notable exceptions were Tony Honoré, who also wrote (anonymously) a notice for the *University Gazette* welcoming Herbert's appointment, and R.V. Heuston, who looked forward to Herbert providing a 'town planning scheme' for the 'intellectual slum of English Jurisprudence'.

Whatever their reservations about appointing a philosopher, the Faculty would have welcomed Herbert's appointment more warmly than it would have welcomed that of another possible candidate, Herbert's undergraduate contemporary, and fellow Jewish northerner, Julius Stone. Since his graduation, Stone had held a number of temporary teaching appointments in England, Australia, and New Zealand, and had written a substantial amount in the fields of international law and jurisprudence. Unlike Herbert, Stone had embraced the sociological, American approach to jurisprudence represented by the work of scholars like Roscoe Pound. Also unlike Herbert, Stone held overtly to his Jewish identity, and had strong views about the anti-Semitism and snobbery which he had encountered as an undergraduate at Exeter College and, subsequently, as a young lawyer and academic. In terms of quantity of published output, he would have stood out in Britain as a leader in the field of jurisprudence. In assessing the fact that his candidacy for the Oxford Chair was not taken seriously, a number of factors are relevant, although it is difficult to assess their relative importance. These include scepticism about the quality of his work, hostility to 'American-style', non-philosophical jurisprudence, Stone's reputation as a touchy and difficult person, and a latent anti-Semitism which would have featured more strongly in attitudes to Stone than to Herbert. This was because, though happy to acknowledge his Jewish ancestry, Herbert had cultivated what we might call an assimilated—almost protestant—English persona: as one of his closest friends put it in later life, he was 'spiritually anglicised'.

In the event, with strong support from referees, Herbert was the winner, by a slender majority, over his competitor Norman Marsh, Law Fellow and Bursar at University College. The electors included F. H. Lawson, the current holder of the Comparative Law Chair at Brasenose; Harold Hanbury, Vinerian Professor at All Souls; C. K. Allen (himself, briefly, a holder of the Chair); W. D. Ross, a philosopher from Oriel and an admirer of Herbert's paper on the ascription of responsibility; and, in the chair, Maurice Bowra, by now Vice Chancellor. While Lawson was one of Herbert's supporters, Allen, a University College colleague of Marsh, and Hanbury (though he followed the election up with a very decent letter of congratulation) were reputedly among Herbert's opponents. Hanbury's opposition was probably typical of the lawyers' resistance to the appointment of a philosopher—though he was also heard to remark that Herbert was far too untidy in personal appearance to be appointed to a Chair in the University.

The ultimate reasons for the committee's decision are impossible to reconstruct. But it is likely that the power and stature of Austin and the intellectual status of philosophy as a discipline, when combined with Herbert's high reputation and evident possession of that indefinable Oxford quality, 'cleverness', clinched the decision. Equally interesting are Herbert's own feelings about his candidacy. Though he does not appear to have been keeping a regular diary at the time, a contemporaneous annotation to his 1945 diary is referred to in one of his later diaries in terms of 'job panic'. The annotation, written on 3 April 1952, recorded:

I became Professor of Jurisprudence on 1/4 (elected on 22/3) . . . . Cold feet with prospect of inaugural and lectures ahead (October),

before moving on to introspect on his and Jenifer's relationship and his ambivalent sexual feelings. Some further insight into his thinking is provided by surviving correspondence with colleagues and friends. Four motives are apparent. The first, obviously, was the status of the post. The second was the intellectual challenge which it posed and the intellectual opportunities which it provided: it was the perfect launching pad for the revival of a genuinely philosophical jurisprudence represented in the work of the nineteenth-century philosophers Jeremy Bentham and John Austin—for whose work Herbert was already forming a strong regard—and for spreading the influence of the new linguistic philosophy. A third may have been the sense that the Chair of Jurisprudence would prove less inhibiting than the hothouse atmosphere of the undiluted linguistic philosophy group. Herbert and his close friend Isaiah Berlin each shifted their research from a strictly philosophical orientation at about this time: Herbert to jurisprudence, Berlin to intellectual history. For both of them, the move to what philosophers regarded as the periphery turned out to be a refreshing, even a liberating change. A final motivation was, characteristically, more negative. This was Herbert's feeling that he was never going to become a first rate philosopher, and that the hybrid genre of jurisprudence would be a suitable compromise. As he put it in later life, he could 'sell just a little philosophy to the lawyers'. Herbert's tragedy was that, unlike Berlin, the standards of analytic philosophy remained the benchmark against which he judged his own work—an attitude which is reflected in his diary reference to jurisprudence as 'degenerate philosophy'. At the core of his remarkable success, then, was a fractured ambition, a compromise.

Part III

THE GOLDEN AGE

CHAPTER 7

Selling Philosophy to the Lawyers: The Chair of Jurisprudence

'My dear Isaiah', Herbert wrote in the spring of 1952, 'Your postcard gave great pleasure to me and all the offence you would wish at Univ. I haven't yet joined that bright little family party but Jenifer has had a luncheon with Mrs. Goodhart and a band of Univ. ladies and I become a Fellow there on April 1. Of course I have icy feet now that I've got the chair but I suppose it would be mistaken, since I've had them so often, to treat them as serious symptoms. As for Stammler and Kelsen [two legal theorists] I cannot pretend that they've been uppermost in my thoughts . . . But I am prepared to study and digest everything—in time. I have asked for leave of absence for the Summer term partly to teach the Schools candidates at New Coll, partly (mainly) to learn the subject . . .'.

Unfortunately, no diaries survive for this period, and this letter to Berlin, along with the annotation about having cold feet already mentioned, are the only real clues to Herbert's feelings about taking up the Chair of Jurisprudence at University College. So it is difficult to say whether this latest career move engendered the kind of strain or anxiety which Herbert so often felt when on the brink of new challenges. An entry in a late notebook, however, refers to 'job panic' in 1952, and this suggests that he regarded the prospect of his translation to a high-profile position in the Law Faculty with some trepidation. But he lost no time and spared no energy in pursuing his intellectual objective of bringing law and philosophy into a productive dialogue with one another. During the summer vacation of 1952 he was trying to anticipate some of the new demands and was busy, at Lamledra, writing up a set of lectures which would nine years later be published in revised form as *The Concept of Law*. Herbert already thought of the lectures as a draft book. Both the title and the content of a paper which he published the following year, 'Philosophy of Law and Jurisprudence Britain 1945–52', give a sense of the scale of his ambition. The title implicitly marked the year of Herbert's arrival in Oxford as the beginning of an era, with the article exploring the ensuing development of a relationship between jurisprudence and linguistic philosophy. With a largely American audience in mind, Herbert mounted a spirited defence of the distinctive importance of analytical jurisprudence as compared with the Realist, sociologically-oriented legal theory current in the USA at that time. Herbert sent out another clear signal about the tradition which he sought to revive and the stamp which he hoped to put on his subject when he produced an edition of the early legal positivist John Austin's *The Province of Jurisprudence Determined* (1832) the following year. In the introduction, Herbert anticipated the central theme of *The Concept of Law* by emphasizing the place of rules in an adequate theory of law.

But it was 'Definition and Theory in Jurisprudence', Herbert's inaugural lecture as Professor of Jurisprudence, delivered in 1953, which laid out the positive and substantive agenda which he saw as defining the autonomous terrain of a jurisprudence informed by analytical philosophy. The lecture was inspired by the lengthy discussions of different varieties of rule which had taken place in Austin's Saturday morning group over the last few years. It set out Herbert's stall as a linguistic philosopher prepared both to bring the insights of philosophy to law, and to exploit his legal understanding to generate a fund of examples suitable for philosophical analysis. In the elegantly structured and closely reasoned published version, he argued that his jurisprudential predecessors, in seeking to illuminate the meaning of terms of legal art such as a 'corporation' through definition, had been both asking the wrong question and using the wrong methods to answer it. Instead, he counselled a return to Bentham's and Frege's insight that such words can only be understood in the context of sentences in which they have meaning. In the case of terms like 'corporation', standard definition *per genus et differentiam*—'an elephant is a mammal with grey hide and a trunk'—is unhelpful because what we seek is not clarification of marginal cases but rather insight into the very standard usages—'central cases'—of the terms. Herbert's argument was that the distinctive task of explanation, therefore, is to analyse the conditions under which statements including the term are true. In the case of a corporation, these conditions include a variety of legal rules and arrangements.

In constructing this argument, Herbert was laying some of the most basic foundations for *The Concept of Law*. He was also drawing on what were to remain two of his main sources of inspiration: the legal philosophy of Jeremy Bentham and modern linguistic philosophy. Though he came to view aspects of the paper's argument as mistaken because of its failure to come to terms with Austin's distinction between the meaning and the force of statements, he continued to see 'Definition and Theory' as an important contribution to jurisprudence and included it in his collected essays in 1983. At the time of its publication, the paper was received warmly on both sides of the Atlantic. At this stage, its message was still considerably more palatable to philosophers than to lawyers. But Herbert's decision to publish it in the *Law Quarterly Review*—the most prestigious English law journal of the time, and edited by his predecessor in the chair, Arthur Goodhart—appeared nonetheless to signify his determination to storm the citadel of the Law Faculty.

Herbert contemplated the walls of the citadel, however, with mixed feelings. For reasons which he sketched for Isaiah Berlin, he regarded the Law Faculty with a mixture of amused irony and marked distaste:

I am accommodating myself to the strange atmosphere of the Law Faculty. Why do they have so many parties? Hanbury seems to give a cocktail- or tea-party every day at which Danish judges of zero interest are feted. I have already attended one lecture by such a figure. Of course what is odd about the whole faculty (there are 4–5 exceptions) is that they regard themselves as a pack of failed barristers and a weak version of the Real Thing in London. It's as if the philosophers regarded themselves as merely propaideutic to the Civil Service and the Stock Exchange. Hence the odious veneration and bootlicking attitude to the judges. So I think what they most need is self-respect. Shall I give it to them? You must hold a class with me one day (Hegel?) and so help.

The 'bootlicking attitude' Herbert objected to was extreme. C. K. Allen once remarked to Tony Honoré at a dinner that it was a disgrace for an academic to criticize a judgment of the Court of Appeal (as one colleague had recently done). And under Goodhart's editorship, case notes in the *Law Quarterly Review* were famously deferential: criticisms of judicial opinions had to be packaged in mealy-mouthed phrases such as 'it is respectfully submitted that'. Herbert regarded this sort of professional culture as anti-intellectual, and although the Law Faculty included distinguished lawyers such as Tyler, Morris, Lawson, and Fifoot, he sought little contact with them. Instead, he concentrated his initial efforts close to home, focussing his attention on the '4–5 exceptions' with whom he felt some intellectual affinity.

Among his initiatives in the Law Faculty was to establish a discussion group for these philosophically-inclined lawyers. The group, which met each term-time week during his tenure of the Chair, was an immediate success, and attracted the regular participation of many of the more open-minded lawyers. Initially, Tony Honoré, Tony Woozley, then an All Souls Prize Fellow in philosophy but with an interest in law, and Rupert Cross (whose Magdalen rooms came to house the meetings) were principal among them; over time, new appointments allowed the group to expand, and it included

Patrick Fitzgerald, Tony Guest, Geoffrey Marshall, and Brian Simpson. This discussion group allowed Herbert to build up the kind of prestige and aura around legal philosophy which Austin had so successfully constructed around linguistic philosophy, and to encourage younger members of the Faculty to develop an interest in theoretical questions. But Herbert's intellectual ambitions stopped at the borderlines between legal philosophy and doctrinal legal scholarship. In later life, he admitted to having made little effort to get to know, let alone to engage intellectually with, the more influential (and still famous) lawyers such as Cheshire and Hanbury. Cheshire's book on property law he read but found dull—'I felt I knew all that from conveyancing'; C. K. Allen's work he admired for its economical written style and its historical depth and originality, but his interest was limited by the fact that Allen was not traversing 'the philosophical side of the street I was trying to walk on'. Nor did he find much to admire in the immediate history of the Chair of Jurisprudence. With the decline of the historical and comparative tradition represented by the late nineteenth- and early twentieth-century holders of the Chair—Henry Maine, Frederick Pollock, and Paul Vinogradoff—jurisprudence had been characterized by what Herbert regarded as the worst kind of dry conceptual analysis. He saw the work of his predecessor in the Chair, the American scholar Arthur Goodhart, on sources of law, precedent, and legal concepts as theoretically unsophisticated, non-philosophical, and at root merely an offshoot of standard 'black-letter' legal scholarship; in other words, as exemplary of much that he attacked in his inaugural lecture. (Goodhart returned the compliment by remarking to a visiting scholar that 'Oxford philosophy is old hat to lawyers'.) Still less was Herbert interested in what was happening in law faculties round the country. Much in the style of J. L. Austin, he saw his mission as the institution of a school of philosophical jurisprudence within the Oxford Law Faculty, and in these terms his work quickly started bearing fruit.

Beyond the weekly discussion group, another institutional means by which this mission was accomplished was through Herbert's recruitment and supervision of a number of doctoral students. Over the years they included Herbert Morris, Brian Barry, John Finnis, Vernon Bogdanor, Geoffrey MacCormack, Peter Hacker, Joseph Raz, Vinit Haksar, Ruth Gavison, Stephen Munzer, and Wil Waluchow, all of whom later became well-known academics in their own right, as well as David Hodgson, later a Justice of the Supreme Court of New South Wales. Herbert's early doctoral student, Herbert Morris, went on to a philosophy post at UCLA and later to a joint appointment with the UCLA Law School, and became one of the most distinguished North American theorists of criminal justice. His experience gives a good flavour of Herbert's style of supervision.

Morris arrived to study for his D. Phil. in 1954, having studied philosophy in the United States. He had no prior knowledge of Herbert's work. Fortuitously, his and Herbert's interests coincided: Morris was working on the philosophy of legal positivism and his thesis covered many of the issues subsequently treated in *The Concept of Law*—the nature of imperatives; rules; a critique of Kelsen and Austin. Herbert required him, like his later students, to hand in pieces of written work every fortnight or so: these he would go through with a fine toothcomb and subject to searching analysis in lengthy meetings. In supervision as in seminars, Herbert's style was critical, painstaking, and devastatingly effective in taking apart other people's views: 'the stuff of his thinking was clarity and distinctions'. Morris's feeling was that it was, intellectually, a non-reciprocal relationship: that he got everything from Herbert. Herbert was an incredibly rigorous supervisor, reading each draft several times and—after retrieving it from the almost unbelievable chaos of his somewhat gloomy rooms in University College's Victorian annex, Kybald House—returning it with several sets of detailed annotations in the margins: 'He really responded to my work and made me think with a degree of rigour and clarity I had never experienced before, even in my philosophical training: he could devastate me.'

Morris, who went on to develop interests in the psychological and emotional aspects of punishment with which he felt that Herbert was never comfortable, and who later saw a critical or negative style as common to— and a failing of—Oxford philosophy, nonetheless both admired Herbert as a person and valued the rigorous training which his supervision had provided. A sense of the prevailing style of Oxford linguistic philosophy at the time is given by Morris's account of his viva [oral examination], at which one of his examiners was J. L. Austin. Austin started with questions directed to the very first page of Morris's thesis: 'Do you mean what you say when you say . . . in the first sentence?' And so it went on. The viva lasted for three hours—'A three hour grilling', as Morris recalled. At one point in the middle Morris got irritated about being asked yet again if he meant what he had said, and stood up to Austin, raising his voice and saying 'Of course I mean it, that is why I wrote it!' Austin then 'calmed down a bit'. Morris attributed his ability to defend his thesis successfully against Austin's onslaught to Herbert's rigorous supervision: 'I remember once using the word "lubricate" in relation to the function of rules—their "lubricating" a practice, moving things along once a rule was in place. Hart said "That was an obscene word to use"! This sexual connotation of course had never occurred to me. But this was also typical of his going through things in minute detail, word by word. By the end of the thesis, I could stand by every word.'

159

On his arrival in Oxford, Morris was shy and unsure of himself: he attributed the fact that he and his supervisor never developed a very substantial relationship to this rather than to any lack of kindness on Herbert's part: 'There was the potential for a relationship which could have been of immense benefit to me, very important, but it just never worked out: it was not the right stage in my life: I couldn't exploit it, which was very sad.' But he was not alone in his perception of the arrogance of Oxford linguistic philosophy and its effects on Herbert's intellectual open-mindedness. Another story demonstrates just how much of an insider to the dominant culture Herbert had become. Vinit Haksar, who studied with Herbert in the late 1950s, found him a generous and exhilarating supervisor, but occasionally bristled at evidence of Herbert's Oxford-centred view of the world. He suspected that Herbert's view was that 'things written by people in ex colonies and at provincial universities . . . were with some honourable exceptions not worth reading'. On one occasion in about 1960 he talked to Haksar rather dismissively about Indian philosophy and asked, provocatively, if there was 'a single interesting idea' in the history of Indian philosophical thought. As Haksar recalled:

I told him that long before Hume, the Buddhists had not only commended the bundle theory of the self but, unlike Hume, they had also worked out the ethical and practical consequences of it. 'How quaint', he said. Some years later I asked him what was happening in Oxford philosophy. He said, 'We have a brilliant young philosopher called Derek Parfit. He is working on the ethical implications of the bundle theory of the self.' I don't know why but I restrained myself from reminding him of our earlier conversation.

But Herbert's occasional insider's arrogance was overshadowed by his fundamentally generous approach to supervision. Although his style with graduate students, as one would expect of the era, was a courteous kindliness tempered by social distance and a certain austerity of personal manner, several of these relationships later developed into friendships. Almost universally, Herbert's former students regarded him with an admiration which bordered—and in many cases continued to border throughout their lives—on awe. Brian Barry (himself a world-famous philosopher and a man not given to exaggerated expressions of praise) described him as 'my intellectual hero'; Vernon Bogdanor remembered him as the person who—in a phrase which recurred in several interviews—'taught me how to think'. Other words which constantly recur are 'generous', 'meticulous', and 'conscientious'. Ruth Gavison remembered the inspiration which came from 'his very own curiosity and excitement about the issues raised. He was the very opposite of pompousness. Here was this great man, the giant of legal philosophy. But he was always to the point, really addressing the arguments and the points and not the persons who were voicing them. No paternalism, no condescension.' As Joseph Raz recalled: 'Herbert was very distant . . . He seemed a bit taken aback when I argued back—the sessions were very long if you fought back—he wouldn't let you do so and lie down—there was always a vigorous exchange: very amicable but hard work!' So great was his commitment to seeing arguments through that supervisions could last for hours: on one occasion, a session which began at 2.30 was interrupted only by dinner at 7. For some students, this regular and relentless shredding was almost too much to bear: the rigour could have destructive effects. Herbert's intellectual intensity implied on occasion a certain insensitivity: in his quest for rigour and clarity he could sometimes forget the impact of his criticisms on those less acute than himself. His fundamental goodwill explains the fact that, in spite of the gruelling sessions, his students almost always stayed the course and invariably looked back on the experience with gratitude.

One other feature of Herbert's style of supervision is significant from the point of view of his qualities of intellectual leadership. Although he had a clear intellectual agenda, and despite his impatience with ideas which he thought muddled or wrong-headed, as a supervisor he was intellectually tolerant and non-directive. As one student recalled, 'He rode me on a long rein'. This was typical. Though he almost always prescribed a tough course of reading in what he saw as the philosophical classics pertaining to the student's topic, he saw his role as testing the quality of the student's ideas rather than as positively shaping the argument. As Raz recalled: 'He didn't make suggestions except for some strategic things: for example: "Do I have to read everything by Hobbes in order to say anything about him?" ("Yes!"); "Do I have to read German to understand Kelsen" ("No!").' For this reason, his students' work—unlike that of many other famous scholars' supervisees—does not fall into a dogmatically 'proto-Hartian' pattern. He always encouraged his students to pursue their own ideas, spending time for example discussing with John Finnis a Jesuit critique of empiricism which would have been deeply uncongenial to him (and which was tangential to Finnis's research), and accepting willingly Ruth Gavison's decision, after a full year's work on a subject at the core of Herbert's interests, to switch to a topic much further from them. Gavison recalls that Herbert had intuited from early in her first year that her original topic—the existence and validity of legal norms—did not 'touch her soul'. When, inspired by some lectures by political philosopher John Plamenatz, she decided to change to the topic of privacy, Herbert threw himself into what was a new area for him, reading large amounts of the relevant literature.

Herbert supervised theses dealing with a wide range of topics: constitutional theory, natural law theory, the nature of political argument, the role of interests and policies in political and moral reasoning, theories of punishment and responsibility, consequentialism in political philosophy, as well as specific topics within and modified versions of the theory of legal positivism. Among his former students and young colleagues who themselves became leading figures in jurisprudence, only Neil MacCormick (never a graduate student of Herbert's), Joseph Raz, and Wil Waluchow carried a torch for Hartian positivism—and in each of their cases the form of positivism defended was a substantially changed one. From the point of view of institution-building, of creating a vibrant intellectual tradition, this might look like a mistake. Herbert would have disagreed: as a supervisor, as in other respects, he lived as well as believed in liberalism. Despite his intellectual intensity, his professional style was relatively unencumbered by the macho dogmatism of many similarly famous academics, while the idea of occupying a guru-like persona in relation to his students would have been anathema to him. And in the longer run, his relatively 'hands-off' approach to the direction of his students' theses undoubtedly strengthened the field by allowing it to expand. There were, however, limits to this openness. The bottom line—that philosophy, and not history or the social sciences, was the foundational intellectual resource for legal theory—was never breached. From the outset, and throughout his life, Herbert not only believed that analytical jurisprudence was an autonomous intellectual terrain of distinctive importance to lawyers, but also thought that Oxford was best advised to build on its relevant intellectual strengths and traditions. These were primarily philosophical, and—to the consternation of his American counterparts—he admitted to being afflicted by the 'Oxford disease' of 'an excessive distrust' of sociology.

The intense and occasionally (though unintentionally) intimidating style which Herbert brought to supervision also characterized the graduate seminars which formed another central plank in his institutional assault on the Oxford Law Faculty. These seminars were the basis for developing Herbert's two most significant intellectual relationships with Law Faculty colleagues during his first decade as Professor. One was with Rupert Cross, initially Law Fellow at Magdalen and to become, in 1964, Vinerian Professor at All Souls. Cross was born in 1912 with cancer of the eyes, and after an operation at the age of one was left almost completely blind. This drawback he overcame with extraordinary effectiveness, with the support of a loving and happy family, a specialist education at the Worcester College for the Blind, and, later, a devoted and intellectually compatible wife. 'A marvellously efficient administrator of his intellectual resources and his energies', as Herbert put it, Cross was a man with a powerful intellect and an enormous capacity for hard work. His peaceful, almost mild expression was in striking contrast with his energetic demeanour in discussion. A warm person with a huge capacity for enjoying life, Cross attracted Herbert as much by his vigorous and sunny disposition—his 'gusto and brio'—as by their shared intellectual interests and power. Herbert developed a deep intellectual respect for Cross, as well as a personal affection. This is movingly and generously reflected in the memoir which he wrote for the British Academy on Cross's death. Herbert's description of their preparations for a joint seminar on the psychological conditions of criminal responsibility in the mid-1960s gives a strong flavour of the distinctive qualities which drew him to Cross:

No record of Cross's life would be complete without some account of his remarkable talent for combining prodigiously hard work with pleasure . . . The seminar met weekly in one term for seven or eight two-hour sessions, and preparing for it with Cross was a strenuous but most enjoyable experience. We would meet several times in the vacation before the term in which the seminar was due and we would hammer out a programme for each of the sessions. In this the main questions to be discussed in each of the sessions were carefully formulated, relevant cases and articles and chapters from books (legal and philosophical) were listed and excerpts were given from statutes and codes, and reports of working papers of such bodies as the Law Commission and the Criminal Law Revision Committee. Most of this material was selected by Cross who also organized its assembly into a dossier of about twelve pages, which was distributed to those attending the seminar . . . At each session Cross and I took turns in reading a short paper arguing in favour of some solution to the questions raised and each of us would comment on the other's paper. We pulled no punches and the resulting general discussion by the seminar was often lively . . . But our meetings in the vacation were only the first part of the preparation which Cross thought necessary. For each night before the weekly meeting he would have me to dine with him at All Souls. We would sit agreeably in the Common Room over dessert, claret, and port, which Cross found an excellent preliminary to an evening's work, and about 9 o'clock we would adjourn to his room. There, often until midnight, we would discuss the next day's session, outlining the papers we proposed to read to it and arguing in detail about the questions raised. But we also ranged farther afield into the historical, jurisprudential, and philosophical background of the issues. I learnt more from these often exhilarating discussions than I had succeeded in picking up from many books and articles. Next day, as a final act of preparation Cross would have me to an excellent tea where for an hour before the seminar began we would tie up any loose ends and make such changes as second thoughts suggested.

Seldom can seminars have been so thoroughly prepared: but Herbert's appreciation of the process had as much to do with Cross's unashamed enjoyment of mixing work and pleasure—an enjoyment which the rather ascetic Hart family culture frowned upon—as with pure intellectual satisfaction.

The result was striking, and stayed in the minds of many of those present. One contemporary remembered that, in these seminars, and later also in seminars run with criminologist Nigel Walker on criminal justice theory, Herbert 'could destroy people and didn't always realize how devastating he could be. It was marvellous to watch him dissecting things. Classes with Cross and Walker were incredibly high-powered—he was hugely well prepared: Cross was the only person who could stand up to Herbert.' So close was the two men's professional relationship that Cross would occasionally prevail on Herbert to give tutorials to his brightest undergraduates. One of them, Colin Tapper, remembers waiting nervously for his first tutorial in Herbert's monumentally untidy room at University College on a Sunday morning in 1958. Amid the papers strewn over every surface including the floor, his eye was caught by the striking image of a shoe perched precariously on the mantelpiece, where it was serving as a page marker on a copy of Russell and Whitehead's *Principia Mathematica*. A few moments later, Herbert hopped into the room on one shoe-clad foot. Herbert commented on Tapper's and his tutorial partner's essays with the same meticulousness he showed with his doctoral students (though he was bemused by the undergraduates' expectation that regular reading lists would be forthcoming). Tapper's tutorials with Herbert had an amusing sequel. After sitting his final exams, he was called in for a viva on jurisprudence. John Morris, an examiner and Tapper's second Magdalen tutor, was required to leave the room. When he returned, Tony Honoré, who had conducted the viva, said to Morris, 'He's very bright, but he's been so badly taught'.

A yet more important exchange of ideas which Herbert was enjoying in his early years as Professor of Jurisprudence was with the young Tony Honoré. Honoré, a South African, had come to Oxford as a student at New College in 1946. He moved to a teaching position at Queen's in 1948, and had already had some contact with Herbert before Herbert took up the Chair. Honoré exuded physical and intellectual vitality: his intelligence, intensity, intellectual curiosity, and enthusiasm were reflected in his sharp, inquiring, twinkling eyes and his habit—generated in part by deafness in one ear due to a war injury—of putting his head on one side and adopting a quizzical expression when listening to an argument. He and Herbert first met in a class on philosophy and legal concepts which Honoré and Tony Woozley taught in 1951/52. Herbert gave a paper on intention—'as usual, on the back of an envelope' as Honoré recalled. Herbert then invited Honoré to a paper given by Mabbott: they had a discussion afterwards, during which Herbert told Honoré, 'You are a natural philosopher'. This was a hugely important affirmation for the younger scholar. Full of nervous energy and thirsting to build up the philosophical dimension of the Law Faculty, Honoré was both flattered and encouraged by Herbert's attention. They continued to meet for casual conversations and soon discovered a common interest in the question of causation. This led to a class which they taught together in 1953 and 1954, when they began to draft a book, *Causation in the Law*. Though the book was to go through a number of revisions, and did not appear until 1959, the work on causation quickly assumed a central place in both Herbert's teaching and his research agenda. In taking a question of central interest to philosophers, and examining how it worked within legal reasoning, he was, after all, doing precisely the kind of work which had attracted him to the Chair.

This productive dialogue with Honoré, who shared Herbert's enthusiasm for linguistic philosophy but who prompted him to read cases and to become more meticulously interested in the details of legal argumentation, was undoubtedly his most important intellectual relationship of the decade. But his relationship with Honoré exemplifies another aspect of Herbert's professional conduct which contributed to the influence which he would ultimately have on the field of legal theory. This was his generosity towards younger scholars—particularly when an intellectual bond was strengthened by a current of personal affinity. Herbert was always drawn to people who shared his sense of the freshness and excitement of ideas (or indeed of a novel, a poem, a piece of music, or a stretch of countryside). During his life as an academic, many of his most important relationships took the form of an unarticulated intimacy founded on explicit intellectual connection and implicit emotional affinity. His relationship with Honoré fitted precisely into this pattern. Herbert went to lengths well beyond what was due from his professorial responsibility to smooth the path of his younger colleague's career. In 1955, for example, Honoré was ill. Herbert—though never a natural entrepreneur—raised money for him from the Rockefeller Foundation to fund a sabbatical year. This enabled Honoré to write most of the first draft of the causation book, and to spend two months researching continental theories of causation at the Max Planck Institute for Criminal Law in Freiburg.

Not all of the relationships which he developed with younger protégés were as predictable as that with Honoré. Another significant but initially less likely friendship was with Bob Summers, later a well-known American legal theorist and professor at Cornell. Herbert first met Summers in 1955 on one of his occasional forays to a 'provincial' law faculty: Southampton, where Summers was spending a year as a Fulbright Scholar. A genial and openly enthusiastic person, Summers remembers being bowled over by Herbert's interest in him. He found it hard to believe that Herbert really meant it when he suggested that Summers should look him up during his planned visit to Harvard, where Summers was to study law, the following year. In the event, the two met by chance before Summers could resolve his dilemma, and began to form a relationship which lasted the rest of Herbert's life. Herbert seems almost to have regarded Summers as a surrogate intellectual son: he later organized sabbaticals for him in Oxford and showered both him and his family with kindness. They regarded him with gratitude, affection, and something approaching reverence.

Herbert's self-absorbed manner and chaotic *modus operandi*—his notes were often little more than apparently disorganized jottings, and he was liable to mislay even these—meant that his seminar presentations were erratic in quality. But, right from the start of his career, he was a stunning performer in discussions. His advocate's experience, verbal confidence, taste for precision, speed of thinking, and courage in pursuing an argument to its limits made for intellectual fireworks. His real love was conversation in small groups—the means through which he encouraged and brought on so many younger colleagues over the next 20 years. Lecturing came less easily to him. As a professor, he had to take on some lecture courses for undergraduates. Someone with a strong sense of duty, Herbert took this institutional responsibility seriously. But his devotion to writing his undergraduate lectures on 'Definitions of Law' in the summer vacation of 1952 was born not merely of his sense of duty and need to overcome his nerves. The undergraduate lecture course also provided him with an important opportunity to convince at least a proportion of the next generation of lawyers and legal scholars that jurisprudential questions had a place at the heart of the law curriculum.

Rising to this challenge, Herbert marshalled all his skills of communication, clarity, and conciseness, and brought together in remarkably economical form most of the central ideas about legal philosophy which he had been pondering over the last seven years. His lectures provided a magisterial overview of the main figures in analytical jurisprudence—Bentham, Austin, Kelsen; of the challenge of Legal Realism posed by American scholars like John Gray and Scandinavian writers like Karl Olivecrona and Alf Ross; of the place of international law in legal theory; and of natural law theory and its basis in assumptions about human nature. They also sketched his own vision of jurisprudence as concerned with theory rather than with definition, and of law as a distinctively institutionalized system of rules whose existence, like that of a legal system, was at root a question of social fact. They summed up the main ideas and arguments which he would finally publish nine years later as *The Concept of Law*. Each week, the students were given questions to ponder. The first set gives a clear impression of Herbert's overall approach: 'What do you mean by a "question"? How can a "question" be said to be wrong? What does it mean when it is said that the questions "what is law?" and "what is a right?" are the "wrong questions to ask"?'

As a (negative) clue, students were steered towards American sociological jurist Roscoe Pound's efforts to 'define law'.

William Twining (later Quain Professor of Jurisprudence at University College London, the chair originally held by the nineteenth-century positivist John Austin) attended Herbert's lectures as a second-year law student at Brasenose in the summer term of 1954. He recalled the sense around the Law Faculty that something significant was happening, and his tutor Barry Nicholas asking him to 'go and find out what this new professor of jurisprudence was up to'. By this time, Twining himself had already been enthralled by Herbert's inaugural, '*the* Hart text', which marked his first 'intellectual engagement with law'. He remembered being 'amazed by what Hart was saying—that concepts didn't have a fixed definition or meaning. . . . It was all very fresh and striking and a real departure from the old anti-theoretical stuff on corporations and possession and so on . . . which was all based on the idea that all a lawyer needed was a few cases to work from, rather than theory or conceptual analysis'. Though later an influential figure in the development of more social science-oriented genres of legal theory, as a student Twining became a convert to the jurisprudence which Herbert was developing, and played the role of proselyte in the essays which he wrote for his initially more sceptical tutor.

Herbert's lectures did not always match their high quality substance with elegant style. Though tall and distinguished in appearance, he never really learned to control the physical awkwardness which was an offshoot of his intellectual abstraction, nor to curb the idiosyncratic mannerisms which were an occasionally distracting side effect of his concentration on ideas. Matters of presentation were, if not objects which he held in contempt, then certainly things which took a poor second place to the quality of ideas and the precision of their expression. In the early years, Herbert's lectures were held in one of the largest rooms in the lofty Victorian Examination Schools building. Twining remembers him sitting down to speak—a risky strategy in a T-shaped room with notoriously poor acoustics—with 'his head getting lower and lower and more or less meeting the table, as, as one could see under the table, he pulled at his sock'. One student of the early 1960s recalled watching Herbert sweep into the room, lean over the lectern, and 'talk thoughtfully to himself for an hour', the audience dwindling week by week—an image which resonated with that of several other former undergraduates. Yet as Twining's memory of the inaugural attests, he was capable on occasion of electrifying an audience with his intellectual vision. Lennie Hoffmann, another student of the 1950s (who went on to become Law Fellow at University College and later a successful practitioner and Law Lord) remembered Herbert's lectures as one of the two experiences of genuine intellectual excitement in his student career (the other being his discovery of Keynes' *General Theory*). These mixed stories of Herbert's lecturing performances suggest that his commitment to and energy for undergraduate lecturing was diminishing by the early 1960s, the sense of responsibility lightened by the jurisprudential teaching contributions being made by other members of the Faculty like Tony Honoré and, later, Brian Simpson. At his early lectures, however, Herbert was getting large audiences, as Honoré recalled: 'The lectures were crowded and were heard with rapt attention, though with some apprehension, as the audience saw the lecturer shuffle from distance to reading glasses, wipe them, mislay them and rediscover their whereabouts, all while expounding a complex argument.'

Herbert continued to give his general lectures 'Definitions of Law and Related Concepts' and (as he came to formulate it) 'The Concept of Law' until the end of the 1950s. But his university teaching was by no means confined to this. Other core issues in analytical jurisprudence also found their way onto his teaching agenda, with lectures on various aspects of Kelsen's theory given regularly from 1953 right through to his retirement from the Chair in 1968, and Jeremy Bentham also making (less regular) appearances in the titles of his lecture and seminar series. Normative issues—especially those bearing on criminal justice—also characterized his teaching from early on: in 1953, Herbert gave a class on 'Topics from the Report of the Royal Commission on Capital Punishment', and in 1955 he and Rupert Cross taught a seminar on 'Law and Social Justice in the Judicial Process'. He also taught analytical criminal law theory, lecturing in 1956 on 'Mind and Act in Law'—a series which dealt with the contours of human action and responsibility, and which floated many of the ideas which were later published in *Punishment and Responsibility*. A number of jointly taught seminars over the years with philosopher colleagues echoed the electric sessions he had taught with Austin, in which Herbert provided legal examples to which Austin would apply his distinctive analytic techniques. He gave regular tutorials for students reading the course on political and legal philosophy and the philosophy of history on the graduate B.Phil. degree—a supererogatory act for a Professor.

He also lectured, from 1953 through to 1966, on rights and duties, elaborating his analysis in relation to a variety of examples such as ownership and possession. In this long-running series, too, he was weaving his teaching closely together with the writing for publication which he felt equally to be a pressing (and occasionally oppressive) duty attached to the Chair. His work on rights not only encompassed the close analysis of legal concepts but also demonstrated his continued identification as a philosopher, his persisting interest in moral and political philosophy, and his belief in the relationship between analytic and normative, prescriptive strands of philosophy. In 1955, he published an essay entitled 'Are there any natural rights?' Here we see the foundations of the normative strand of Herbert's work: his interest in liberal political philosophy in general and in the distinctive role of rights and justice in political morality in particular. Herbert argued that, if there were any natural rights at all, they must rest on one basic right—the right of all individuals to be free. Within this framework, he demonstrated how different kinds of moral rights emerge: general rights, which flow from the mutual obligation of reciprocity or fair play between the citizens of a polity; and special rights, which citizens create through promises, contracts, or other social arrangements. Though this was a second paper about which Herbert later entertained doubts, and which he refused to include in his collected essays, its argument sowed seeds for future developments and anticipated later preoccupations. Its emphasis on freedom—the central tenet of his deep and enduring liberalism—looked distinctly more radical in 1955 than it would today. In this essay, Herbert was not only making a contribution to philosophy but also laying foundations for the development of the liberal social culture which his more 'applied' work advocated and which was more or less taken for granted 15 years later.

In constructing the argument for rights as deriving from a political obligation of fair play which citizens owe to one another—a distinctive version of social contract theory in which each citizen agrees to abide by the restrictions set by the polity on the basis that everyone else agrees to do the same—Herbert was thinking along lines parallel to those of John Rawls' influential essay, 'Justice as Fairness', published in 1958. The idea was further developed in Rawls' monumental *A Theory of Justice*, published in 1971, which has dominated political philosophy ever since. Rawls was a visitor to All Souls in 1965, and he and Herbert developed an important relationship which had already been initiated during Herbert's visit to the USA in 1956. It seems likely that their discussions had a significant bearing on their work: Herbert's 'Prolegomenon to the Principles of Punishment' (1959) was explicitly indebted to Rawls' 'Two Concepts of Rules' (1955); conversely, Rawls was generous in acknowledging Herbert's contributions to political philosophy. In the mid-1950s Herbert, like Rawls, had already begun to articulate how rights and justice relate to, and should modify or subvert the value of utility—the greatest happiness of the greatest number—in the framework of political morality. For both men, this turned into a lifelong preoccupation.

Herbert's Chair brought with it a variety of further institutional obligations. He discharged them with his customary meticulousness but mixed feelings. Barry Nicholas retained a vivid memory of Herbert's first experience of examining law candidates, shortly after taking up the Chair:

I remember Herbert's gentle belief, against the evidence, in the rationality of the golf blue [a student who played golf for the University] reading for a Fourth [the lowest category of Honours degree] and the intellectual excitement when at last he found someone he could argue with. . . . Like most examining boards, the four of us were ill-matched and I remember occasions when I went in fear of an eruption (I was chairman). For the oldest of us was impatient of Herbert's carefully analytical approach and he had a habit, during Herbert's vivas, of letting out what may have been deep breaths, but what sounded to me (and, I think, to Herbert) like sighs.

Nicholas's impression was that Herbert 'found the experience of examining useful in enabling him to get his bearings in the law school', but on the basis of this account one imagines that it did little to shift Herbert's intellectual reservations about his new colleagues (or theirs about him). Another aspect of Herbert's life as a professor was his fellowship at University College. Though it was unusual in those days for professors to play a large part in College affairs—a custom with which Herbert happily complied—he nonetheless had a significant impact on the College, and developed some close relationships there. Especially important were his fellow philosophers and friends: Peter Strawson, whose work Herbert particularly admired, and George Paul, a gifted linguistic philosopher and former student of Wittgenstein who now regarded himself as a prophet for Austinian philosophy and who had encouraged Herbert's candidature for the Chair. But Herbert was much more widely appreciated than this. As one Classics Fellow put it, 'I couldn't say I adored him but I came pretty close to it'. Among the characteristics which earned him this sort of admiration were his astute contributions to key strategic decisions in college meetings, his marvellous flow of conversation over lunch and dinner, his endearing scholarly abstraction (he is reported as having turned up on several occasions to dinner wearing either no tie or, more often, two ties), and an independence of mind which meant that he never baulked at being in a minority on a contested issue. One of these was the proposal, in the mid-1950s, to elect the Duke of Edinburgh to an honorary fellowship. Goodhart, the Master of the College, was beguiled by the idea. Herbert's friend George Paul thought that it would be beneficial for the Royal Family to have some contact with intellectuals. Herbert was one of only two Fellows to oppose the suggestion. He did so out of both intellectual and republican principle.

Herbert had a complicated relationship with the Master, his professorial predecessor Arthur Goodhart. (A joke around the time of Herbert's election had it that the new Professor of Jurisprudence was the Hart without the good, while another suggested that the problems of jurisprudence derived not from 'lack of heart but a lack of head'.) Goodhart was a key figure in the Oxford Law Faculty and beyond it. Editor of the influential *Law Quarterly Review* for 45 years, he was active in inviting senior judges to Oxford and in encouraging debate between academics and practitioners. He was the first Jewish head of an Oxford college. Fellow jurist and Jew though he was, Goodhart could in other respects hardly have been more different from Herbert. His scholarship was non-philosophical; he was an entrepreneurial, artful character; and he was a political conservative and a millionaire. And, though a supportive colleague to fellow Jews, he was anxious that the promotion of too many Jews to positions of influence would lead to anti-Semitism. His resulting sensitivity about Jewish appointments offended every liberal and anti-discriminatory bone in Herbert's body, and led to considerable conflict between the two men. On one occasion, when Goodhart had successfully opposed the election of the person whom both Herbert and Peter Strawson thought the best qualified candidate, on the basis that 'we don't want too many of us', Herbert was positively furious. In future years he often recounted and looked out for similar instances of what he regarded as Goodhart's indefensible attitude. In Harvard in 1956, for example, he discovered that another colleague had refused to support Julius Stone's candidature for an Oxford post on the grounds of Goodhart's attitude. Though he appreciated Goodhart's 'infinite kindness' and admired his business skills and ready wit (he is once alleged to have said in a college meeting, 'I dissent from the majority for all the reasons they have given'), Herbert saw him as an intellectual lightweight and a political reactionary. The two men nevertheless maintained an outwardly respectful relationship, and on the visit of a famous American law professor and later Supreme Court Judge to Oxford in the late 1950s, Goodhart, when asked who was 'the dean' of the Oxford Law Faculty, instantly replied, 'Professor Hart'. This comment is testimony to the towering presence which Herbert had by then established in both College and Faculty.

Within a short time, then, Herbert had built from a slender institutional base many of the foundations on which English jurisprudence would be based over the next few decades. He had also established himself as the leading figure in the field. His own assessment of his contribution was, however, typically diffident: 'The philosophers thought I was a marvellous lawyer and the lawyers thought I was a marvellous philosopher', as he later put it. His new institutional status must nonetheless have brought with it a deepened sense of self confidence, and this is reflected in the effectiveness with which he worked to pursue his professional ambitions. His institutional position, his reputation, and his growing assurance allowed him to branch out into institution-building not only at the Faculty level but also, from 1958 onwards, through his founding and editorship of the influential Clarendon Law Series published by Oxford University Press. In this series, which produced short monographs unencumbered by detailed footnotes and designed to introduce students in an interesting and thought-provoking way to various fields of law, Herbert carried forward into legal scholarship the 'anti-text book' pedagogic philosophy he was propounding so successfully in jurisprudence. Many of the early books in the series—Barry Nicholas's *Introduction to Roman Law* among others—became, like *The Concept of Law*, works which shaped the teaching of their subjects for years to come. And he was now reaching out to a broader audience with occasional visits to other universities and through regular broadcasts on BBC radio, subsequently published in *The Listener*, on topics of wide public interest such as capital punishment and criminal law reform.

But Herbert was not a man who ever found life straightforward, and as a counterpoint to his burgeoning professional success, his personal life remained a more mixed story. On the face of it, things improved decisively when Jenifer moved to Oxford in 1947, having managed to secure a post as Supervisor of Studies at the University's Institute for Adult Education—the Delegacy of Extra-Mural Studies. She and Herbert began to find opportunities to indulge once again in the foreign trips they had enjoyed together before the war, braving the inevitable post-war complications to travel to Belgium in 1947, Italy in 1948, Spain and Portugal in 1951. With remarkable energy, and perhaps finding a helpful creative outlet at a time when his academic writing was going slowly, Herbert used some of these trips to indulge his skills as an essayist, producing in particular an amusing and evocative piece on Belgium, the Belgians, their profoundly anti-German stance, and their post-war economy:

Prices are all over the place, except the prices of food sold against 'timbres'. But without 'timbres', you buy *the same thing*, including all rationed goods, only of course at a higher price—sometimes 300% higher. . . . There could surely be no better way of helping the rich and discriminating against the poor. . . . The Belgians are sceptical when you tell them there is no Black Market worth mentioning in England; in fact English virtues have become a music-hall joke.

The result of this fluid system of prices is that economic matters tend to occupy the overwhelming part of most people's thoughts. Perhaps this is why the museums show few signs of life. . . . It is true that the picture galleries in Brussels are so dark, and the pictures themselves so badly in need of cleaning . . . that one can hardly tell a Cranach from a Rubens, or a Brueghel from a Bosch; but the galleries are reasonably warm, at any rate much warmer than the street, and, if some complaints are to be believed, warmer than many private houses . . .

The cake shops are correspondingly full. It takes one's breath away to see the enormous ladies of Brussels—veritable dinosaurs—attacking with passionate intensity plates full of gigantic cakes—cloud castles of cream and sugar. They make a painful contrast with the wretched disabled youth who, with no pretence about selling one matches, simply comes round cap in hand . . .

As always, the sight of stark differences of wealth attracted Herbert's disapproval; yet the uninhibited public culture of the continent drew him:

But above all, to be out of England: to see two staid old men embracing in the street, to witness passionate scenes in cafes at all hours of the day, to hear heated quarrels, in public—about money of course; and then to be told the Belgians are slow to feel or to betray feeling, heavy and dull. For a week at any rate they are electric compared with the English. Perhaps the lights go out if one stays too long.

In Spain and Portugal in 1951, Jenifer and Herbert were (typically) travelling third class and roughing it in some less than luxurious hotels: for Jenifer, the more travel challenged personal comfort, the greater its romance. Herbert occasionally prevailed in favour of more comfortable arrangements; but the two were united in their appetite for architecture and painting, as well as for gaining some understanding of political and economic conditions from casual discussions with the local people whom they encountered. Here, Herbert was at a linguistic advantage which excited Jenifer's admiration but occasionally irritated her: she noted that Herbert was as usual tiring himself out by trying to improve his Portuguese, while a conversation in Spanish prompted her to record in her diary:

Debate re Sp. politics—English sympathy for Republicans: [the Spaniard] understood, I think, in spite of H making it sound as if the enthusiasm for the Republicans during the war had been confined to a group of emotional students at Oxford. I was irritated by this and wished once again I could speak Spanish. Felt frustrated and feeble.

The differences were not only linguistic ones. As her diary shows, Jenifer found it hard to accept that Herbert did not always share her enthusiasms or concerns. In Spain again in 1954, Jenifer recorded that 'H. dislikes [Granada] cathedral and won't look at it—which annoys me. H. perversely unmoved by danger of trees falling in gale'.

Back in Oxford, the family had installed itself in 8 New College Lane, a sunny, double-fronted, red-brick Georgian house abutting the city wall and New College cloisters and facing an exquisite medieval barn. Everyone enjoyed this beautiful environment, though Jenifer found the lack of a back garden had some disadvantages: passers-by could witness her (not always successful) efforts to keep the children under control as they played in the flag-stoned front courtyard. Domestic life proceeded smoothly thanks to the quiet competence of Nanny, who by this time must have grown used to the glorious chaos of Hart family homes. On Herbert's transfer to University College in 1952, the family had to leave New College Lane, and moved to another lovely setting which would remain their Oxford home for the rest of Herbert's life. It was a detached early twentieth-century house, owned by Merton College, and tucked away near the end of Manor Place, a quiet cul-de-sac on the edge of central Oxford. Though less elegant than New College Lane, the house was surrounded by a verdant, secluded garden, and provided lots of space for the lively, growing family.

Meanwhile, Jenifer's career was progressing, notwithstanding her playful report to Christopher Cox that she was now 'just a pathetic little house-wife'. By dint of extraordinarily hard work, leaving her office at 5pm every day and heading for an evening of research in the library, she had managed to write up her important study of the history of the British police, which was published in 1951. This opened up the opportunity of a one-year research fellowship at Nuffield College, a graduate college which specialized in the social sciences and which was at that time the only Oxford college to admit both men and women. Here Jenifer had time to engage in more detailed historical research, as well as making intellectual contacts with other Fellows such as John Plamenatz, Nigel Walker, and Michael Oakeshott. Their different political views made Jenifer and Michael Oakeshott unlikely allies, yet Jenifer fell in love with him. During this time she also did some part-time teaching on the undergraduate PPE programme for a number of colleges, and in 1952 she was elected to a fellowship in modern history, including responsibility for the politics component of the PPE degree, at St. Anne's College. Jenifer's appointment—though amply justified by her intellect and research and teaching record—illustrates that the Oxford recruitment process was hardly less unsystematic than in 1945. On hearing that she might be interested in a fellowship, her old friend the historian and journalist Elisabeth Munroe, now Treasurer of the College, recommended her to the Principal, Eleanor Plumer. After an interview with the selection committee, Jenifer had to 'run the gauntlet of the fellows' over tea in the Senior Common Room. 'One of them suddenly declared that I must be appointed because my red hair looked so good against the décor and furnishings of the room, for which incidentally she had been responsible. I knew I had made it.'

The day-to-day running of the household was now in the capable hands of the redoubtable and ever-present Nanny, assisted by a series of au pairs, many of whom became lifelong friends. Nonetheless, life in this two-career marriage was hard work. While Herbert, as always, pushed himself to the limit in pursuit of the highest professional standards, Jenifer, too, was working long hours to keep her research alive while getting up new teaching subjects and coping with tutorial loads which sometimes reached 30 hours a week. But it was not a story of unmitigated labour. During the 1950s, the Harts were regular participants at dancing parties with other academic families, and though Herbert's social life remained college-focussed, and he claimed only to go to these events to please the much more gregarious Jenifer, the evidence is that he rather enjoyed them. Work and domestic pressures were also relieved by regular family holidays with friends like George and Margaret Paul and Roger and Paula Quirk in the Lake District and at Jenifer's brother-in-law David Hubback's beautiful if spartan cottage in Snowdonia. Above all, there were the trips at Easter and during the summer vacations to the glorious views, long country walks, sea-bathing, tranquillity, and congenial company of friends at Lamledra, now shared by Jenifer and her sister Mariella.

To the Harts' many friends, colleagues, and students who participated in these house parties on the beautiful southern Cornish coast, they are an unforgettable experience which epitomizes the complex equilibrium of the Harts' family life. Lamledra, built by Jenifer's parents in the early part of the century, perches on a dramatic headland just outside Gorran Haven near Mevagissey. Isolated in its own large grounds, light and spacious, surrounded by trees, fuschia bushes, and, beyond this, an endless carpet of green stretching down towards the beach and the ocean, it is an idyll for anyone fond of swimming, walking, gardening, reading, conversation, or listening to music. But those keen on concentrating on the less physically demanding activities had to have the strength to withstand the force of Jenifer's disapproval. For although in her diaries she often reflected self-critically on her own difficulty in relaxing, the prevailing culture of the household was set by her work ethic, her strong sense of responsibility for keeping everything running, and her ascetic attitudes. This made for occasional envy of, and irritation with, Herbert. Being a mother often made it hard to concentrate on her own concerns or to enjoy a moment's solitude, Jenifer wrote in 1956:

One feels responsible for other people's happiness, and demands are made on one the whole time. . . . All these things sit more lightly on H. Of course he worries less by nature—but the great secret is to be *oblivious* of what is going on elsewhere in the house.

In Herbert, the capacity for abstracting himself from domestic affairs and settling down to enjoy an intense discussion with one of their guests was complemented by an almost complete lack of judgmentalism about how people chose to live their lives. This Jenifer could only admire:

H argues that one should only do what makes one happy and that there is virtually no other criterion—at least that others should not wish one to 'improve' oneself. Perhaps they wd. be justified in wishing this, and acting on the wish, on economic grounds—but certainly not on moral ones. The argument reflects our 2 so different backgrounds and characters. I certainly admire the absence of any feeling in him that he knows better than others how they should run their lives.

In spite of her admiration, it was not an outlook Jenifer's 'so different' character allowed her to share. One American academic visitor remembers a conversation with Herbert on the terrace being interrupted by Jenifer's expostulation 'How can you be sitting there talking about responsibility while the fuschia is growing all around you?' (This particular visitor ultimately made an ill-tempered exit after being subjected to one of Herbert's occasional sorties into culinary activity. The visitor, who was Jewish, asked what was in the risotto which Herbert had cooked for lunch: Herbert responded with a long list including, unfortunately, bacon . . .) The often elegant but generally sparse furnishings of Lamledra, the melamine crockery, and the utilitarian (though generous) approach to food—usually produced by a student hired to cook for the household—gave the first-time visitor a sense of the values which set the rhythms of the domestic economy. Further clues lay in a yellowing notice sellotaped inside one of the kitchen cupboards, instructing occupants: 'Please preserve the rational order of this cupboard.' (Particularly to visitors unfamiliar with the comfort-spurning ethic of a certain portion of the English upper middle class, a similar notice in the first floor lavatory prescribing 'Only flush when necessary' may have been more confusing.)

Particularly in later years, guests were subtly but unmistakably made to realize whether they were, in effect, Jenifer's guest or Herbert's. Herbert's guests were generally not expected to participate in activities such as kitchen-clearing, gardening, or carrying pebbles up from the beach to reinforce the supply on the terrace, though they occasionally suffered Jenifer's contempt for their cerebral sedentariness, particularly if they did not show enthusiasm—shared equally by all members of the Hart family—for bracing walks and bathing in the sea, however cold. Their social duty was to provide stimulating conversation for the assembled company and intellectual companionship for Herbert. Guests who failed overwhelmingly in their social obligations or who committed one of a small number of unforgivable sins, such as complaining about the weather or comparing the southern Cornish coastline unfavourably with the northern, were likely to end up on Jenifer's list of 'those never to be invited again'. A number of guests floated between the 'Jenifer group' and the 'Herbert group' and could on occasion find themselves caught in awkward situations, when a dispute arose about some matter lying outside the core of generally approved activities, and expressions of loyalty to one form of life or the other was required. Still, everyone enjoyed the marvellous conversation, the exquisite surroundings, and the hospitality which, for all its idiosyncracies, was both warm and generous.

Some of the tensions manifesting themselves in the social microcosm of Lamledra reveal that, beneath the surface of the Harts' domestic tranquillity and professional success lay a more complicated picture. In 1948, Herbert's and Jenifer's third child, Charles, was born. This was a cause of significant conflict. Once again, Herbert was an initially reluctant father: but on this occasion his feelings were accentuated by his belief that Jenifer had been using contraception. The especially warm and intense paternal feelings which he later developed for Charles may have been a compensation for this early upset, which he took some time to overcome.

But it is possible that Herbert's distress had also to do with a yet deeper issue, and one which he could not even acknowledge to himself. Jenifer's relationship with Michael Oakeshott—like her earlier feelings for William Glock—was part of a pattern. From the late 1940s on, Jenifer was involved in an affair with one of Herbert's closest friends, Isaiah Berlin. It is difficult to judge just how much pain his inklings about this gave Herbert. On the basis of his reaction to Jenifer's extra-marital attachment of 1945, however, one assumes that it would have been considerable. This was an important relationship for Jenifer: Stuart Hampshire recalled her extreme distress in 1955 when she discovered, through a third party, that Berlin had become engaged to Aline de Gunzbourg. What is absolutely clear is that Herbert suppressed his feelings to a startling degree: the two men's friendship continued, and Herbert's 'ignorance' of the affair survived Berlin's confession to him, on at least two occasions, that he was in love with Jenifer. His initial reply to Berlin was 'It's not possible', a remark which may have reflected Berlin's reputation as a confirmed virgin bachelor. The depth of Herbert's repression is reflected in his response to the second of these revelations, which was to say to Jenifer: 'Isaiah keeps going mad. He says *again* he's in love with you.' That Herbert had tacit knowledge of what was going on is revealed by an incident 30 years later. Aline Berlin remarked to Jenifer and Herbert that she was toying with the idea of buying the house next door to theirs so that, if she were to die before Isaiah, he could move next door to his closest friends. When she had left, Herbert remarked to Jenifer: 'What a good idea: then, if I die, you will be able to marry him at last.'

Despite her shock that Berlin had not told her of his impending marriage to another woman, Jenifer had never contemplated him as a substitute for Herbert. She did not enjoy the same degree of intellectual affinity with Berlin, nor did she think she could manage to live with him as readily as with Herbert. But Berlin did offer her what Herbert no longer could; for she appears to have conquered Berlin's own sexual reserve more decisively than she had Herbert's. Herbert's and Berlin's friendship had always been marked by a certain competitive edge, and this must have been exacerbated by Jenifer's affair. Yet in 1981, when Herbert read Neil MacCormick's description of Berlin as Herbert's 'closest friend among his philosophical colleagues', he scored out the last four words.

During this period, Herbert also had to cope with the sudden loss of both his parents. They had been living an increasingly gloomy and socially isolated life in Hampstead; his father persistently (and unnecessarily) anxious about money and seriously depressed by his declining health; his mother affected badly by her husband's depression; and his sister Sybil struggling in the teeth of her own depressive disposition—not to mention considerable professional responsibilities at ICI—to keep the household organized and reasonably content. By this stage Sim Hart was more or less housebound: a neighbour remembers seeing him on only a few occasions, one of which involved Sim's shouting irascibly at the neighbour's children to quieten down in their garden. In 1953, Sybil found Sim lying in the garden, fatally injured after a fall from an upstairs window. His death was understood in the family to have been suicide. While his brothers and sister felt that their father had lost his reason, Herbert confided to Tony Honoré that he regarded the decision as entirely rational: his father had lost interest in life. A few months later, Rose—frail, exhausted, and disoriented by Sim's death—also died. Though Herbert rarely shared his emotions with colleagues, Peter Strawson remembers his deep shock and distress at the news of his father's suicide; and Stuart Hampshire recalled Herbert's deep and helpful sympathy when, a few years later, he too lost a close relative through suicide. As for his mother's death, he felt it 'like the roof blowing off my life'. Though attached to his children, still fascinated by Jenifer, and devoted to his siblings Albert and Sybil, Herbert lived, in many ways, a work-centred and emotionally self-sufficient life. It is not surprising, then, that when the most prestigious law school in the USA invited him to visit in 1956, he was ready to contemplate a year abroad without his family.

CHAPTER 8

American Jurisprudence through English Eyes: Harvard 1956–7

IN the early September of 1956, Herbert set out from Southampton on the Queen Elizabeth, bound for New York. He was heading for the pinnacle of the American University system, Harvard, where he had been invited to spend a year visiting both Law School and Philosophy Department. The status of Harvard in American elite culture at the time far exceeded any comparable university in Britain. It is summed up by a story of a late nineteenth-century President of Harvard, who asked his secretary to place a telephone call to the then US President, Teddy Roosevelt. When the President picked up the phone, the secretary said, 'I have the President for you, Mr. Roosevelt'.

Herbert's appointment had been masterminded by Austin, who had visited the philosophy department the previous year. It was organized at the Harvard end by the philosopher Morton White, with whom Herbert was to form a warm friendship over the course of the next year, and by Lon Fuller in the Law School. Apart from a brief trip to a conference at Columbia two years before, this was Herbert's first trip to the United States. Compared with his obligations at Oxford, the year offered him a relatively relaxed schedule, and hence time to tackle the long list of writing obligations he had accumulated. Once again, he felt himself to be at a turning point, and regarded the prospect with a mixture of determination, anxiety, and introspection. The journey prompted amusing reflections on his fellow passengers at sea, nostalgic wishes that he had been able to dance (and self-castigation at his failure to have learnt) and a characteristic mishap in which he left his jacket on board ship and had to return to the docks from the city. Settling in Cambridge, Massachusetts, he turned to his diary:

Here over ten days. At the moment I feel full of great happiness in contemplating my good luck in getting what at the moment seems a God-sent opportunity.

But there have been, since leaving England, awful moments of panic, near-hysteria and needless fatigue and confusion—the last two due in great part to my fundamental inefficiency, my standing failure to *utilize* what talents or abilities I have and my lack of the *minimum* of the basic element of order, tidiness, method. . . . This costs me in the end mountains of labour, because I find myself having to rethink through questions I have pondered for years but have not reduced to ordered form. . . . All this must be controlled: and I must use this year to do it. I feel this year properly used may make the rest of life (professional and personal) good: may make the difference between comparative failure and success.

Herbert was immediately beguiled by Cambridge. He admired the colonial wooden houses and the buzz and manifest prosperity on the streets, and was vividly struck by the pace of life in an American town: 'The ranges of goods in the shops, the cars, the speed, the enormous factories, power stations, mixture of races, size of the newspapers, is extraordinarily impressive and even exhilarating. I never feel *tired* here as opposed to mentally bruised and battered by all there is to experience', he wrote to the family a few days into his visit. On his first contact with the University, he wondered at the amazing facilities of the Law School, with its 'vast buildings, august traditions, very much the ante-room of the U.S. Supreme Court', where he was given a 'grand office and carte blanche for all the wonderful facilities' including the right to borrow books from the best law library in the world. Though finding the atmosphere 'intimidating', with the vastly confident students, destined for the top of the legal profession, 'working all day and all night', and the prospect of the classes 'terrifying', Herbert found his colleagues less alarming than he had feared. A few days after his letter home, he was writing in his diary:

The Law School wonderful: the initial apprehension has worn off. Everyone—even those I ought to have expected to be hostile or contemptuous—is most friendly and apparently sincere in this. The Professors are potentates but magnanimous and it is a surprise to find references to myself (appreciative though also critical) in their case books and materials.

Herbert's initial apprehensions had not been without foundation. Harvard Law School—indeed Harvard University—presented him with an intellectual environment strikingly different from Oxford, and one which he could not reasonably have expected to be particularly welcoming. The differences ran along three main dimensions. Notwithstanding Austin's visit, linguistic philosophy was far from flavour of the month; indeed, Herbert later wrote that his seminars were like 'conducting a *battle*—so uncongenial to the local graduates is my as our mode of philosophising' (he was particularly affronted by the American view of his friend Peter Strawson, who was 'ludicrously under-rated'). And the relative intellectual status of law and philosophy was exactly the reverse of that in England, with the law school dominating the scene in terms of confidence, ability to recruit scholars and students, reputation, and wealth. In 1957, the Harvard Law School Fund, largely raised from alumni, stood at $307,620—the equivalent of nearly $2 million today; during the course of this year, in the space of a mere four weeks, the School was able to raise the $10,000 ($64,000 at today's values) needed to secure an important collection of early English law books.

But the most important difference from Herbert's point of view was that, within the self-assured law school community, the message that law and philosophy might be brought into mutually productive dialogue was regarded as a perfectly defensible but ultimately rather narrow conception of legal theory. Dean Emeritus Roscoe Pound, the presiding spirit of jurisprudence at Harvard, was now retired and in his late eighties, but 'available for consultation with interested students' in his Langdell Hall office. Pound had defended (in what Herbert regarded as terms of unnecessary length and inexcusable analytical imprecision) a sociological theory of law which focussed on the broad—dispute-resolving, administrative, organizational—functions of law in society. This conception of law as closely allied to the social sciences found its way not only into legal theory but also into the broader law curriculum, with scholars like Henry Hart and Albert Sachs exploring the nature of legal processes as enforced (as opposed to doctrinally defined). Even Lon Fuller, Carter Professor of General Jurisprudence and the person who was closest to Herbert's interests, though no fan of sociology, was bringing questions about economic imperatives and political organization into his lectures on contract law. Fuller, certainly, was interested in legal philosophy; but in this context, too, Hart could expect vigorous opposition. For Fuller was one of the most influential exponents of an anti-positivist, 'natural law' position—in other words, of the theory that law must be identified in part through appeal to moral criteria, rather than being a matter of social fact, something which may or may not have moral value. While Herbert's main complaint about the Harvard law students was their lack of precision, Fuller's was their uncritical attitude towards the substance of law and their lack of interest in ethical questions. Herbert would reasonably have felt vulnerable to being caricatured as the narrow, formalistic legal positivist. Fortunately he formed good working relationships with both Henry Hart and with Fuller, whom he reported to Jenifer as 'a nice New Englander with some quite original ideas'. As Herbert later recalled: 'He was rather testy. He couldn't keep his cool in arguments. But I liked him and he liked me. But he thought I was a radically mistaken positivist. The word positivist had a tremendously evil ring. I remember hearing somebody say, "You know he's a positivist, but he's quite a nice man"...'

A further cause of apprehension was Harvard's radically different teaching system: instruction through a series of structured questions directed to students. This potentially vicious system was vividly evoked in the famous film *The Paper Chase:* 'they bully the boys in a curious question and answer technique which they call the "case-law" method', Herbert told Jenifer. The usual stereotypes about English reserve had preceded him to Harvard. Rockefeller-funded visiting student Samuel Shuman—('wife intelligent but a little mad and so is he', Herbert reported to Jenifer) told him that before he came he was reported as cold, distant, and arrogant and that he (Shuman) was agreeably surprised! The compliment was swiftly followed by the complaint that Herbert's lectures on Natural Law 'are slight'. It is clear that Herbert had reason to wonder how he would be received.

Despite its self-confidence, the Law School had been under pressure to reform itself in the decade before Herbert's visit. After the war, a commission had been set up under the chairmanship of Supreme Court Justice and Harvard alumnus Felix Frankfurter, and the commission's report in 1947 was less than flattering. Criticism was levelled at both the structure and the substance of the syllabus. It was felt that students were put under too much pressure, with the almost exclusive use of Socratic teaching methods and the practice of putting each graduate in order of merit creating intolerable strain. And the syllabus was criticized as unduly narrow and as paying insufficient attention to interdisciplinary, comparative, and international questions. There was anxiety that other law schools which had already begun to reform their curricula would outstrip Harvard. The Law School was castigated as static and insufficiently profound, with staff suffering from a sense of inadequacy. Fuller, who moved permanently to Harvard in 1940, was an energetic advocate of educational reform. In 1953 he authored a Memorandum for the Fund of the Advancement of Education, and his long correspondence with Frankfurter after 1947 shows him to have been a prime mover in the reform of the Law School. He saw the broadly based curricula of law schools like those of the University of Wisconsin at Madison and Northwestern and Chicago Universities as exemplars of progressive reform. While pushing the reform programme, including the introduction of teacher training, the diversification of teaching methods, and the introduction of a more 'critical and empirical approach', Fuller nonetheless defended Harvard's capacity for leadership. He cited Henry Hart's Socratic teaching as a model, and advocated publishing the commission's report to initiate an internal debate about change.

The debates of the time in the *Harvard Law Record*—the weekly School magazine—have, for any legal academic, a curiously familiar ring about them, for the preoccupation with broadening the syllabus and strengthening links with other disciplines still characterizes legal education in the English-speaking world today. In the Harvard of the early 1950s, the determination of influential scholars like Fuller, Henry Hart, and Harold Berman, the existence—striking as compared with Oxford—of a coherent and autonomous faculty structure, and the possession of enormous wealth, meant that the institution was well placed to act effectively on the reform agenda. By the time of Herbert's arrival, Harvard had already changed to a considerable extent: women had been admitted in 1950, and the curriculum substantially overhauled for a second time in 1954. Though complaints about pressure on students were still a serious issue because of the intense competitiveness set up by career uncertainty, it was generally accepted that the goal was to provide a broad, liberal education.

The Law School offered what was by British standards an amazing array of courses and a rich research environment. In addition to the obvious common law subjects and a range of theoretical options, students could study Soviet law, anti-trust law, criminology, the economic theory of socialism, legal history, legal institutions, law-making processes, legislation, and several aspects of constitutional law. Research at the Law School included not only Berman's influential studies of Soviet law and economy but also the 'madly egocentric' Sheldon and Eleanor Glueck's famous work on the psychology of crime, and Roscoe Pound's arguments for an international legal order based on principles rather than rules. An Institute of Law and Social Relations had also been established. Run by a mix of lawyers and social scientists, it provided summer courses in fields such as the sociology of law and legal anthropology. The Institute's philosophy was that while legal order had certain internal structural requirements, it was also important to ask what political, economic, social, and other non-legal factors affected decision making, as well as how basic legal principles reflected the cultural postulates of a society. Despite these innovations, the curriculum was constantly under review. During 1956/57, the *Harvard Law Record* reported regularly on the latest developments at Yale, where Dean Eugene Rostow was advocating the integration of law and social studies and asserting the need for lawyers, in the new world order, to work on improving the administration of justice and methods of economic control.

The extra-curricular life of the Law School was no less varied than its curriculum. According to the *Record*, it ranged from student debates on capital punishment and nuclear weapons to fashion shows organized by the 'Faculty Wives': from lectures by influential public figures to formal dinners and balls. During Herbert's visit, Harry Truman spoke to a packed lecture theatre, reflecting thoughtfully on the role of a President, whose responsibilities he encapsulated in the phrase 'the buck stops here'. Herbert was amused by his personal ambition to walk, rather than be carried, out of the White House. Another lecturer during the course of the year was Nye Bevan, and a third Hugh Gaitskell. In spite of some hostile elements in the audience, Gaitskell's speech was regarded as making a substantial contribution to changing local perceptions of the prospect of a Labour Government in Britain. Gaitskell judged American political sentiment astutely in his comment that Kruschev 'combined the best qualities of Hitler and Goering'. Though Herbert was impressed by the extraordinary breadth of Gaitskell's knowledge and delighted by his success, he disapproved of the prevalent and exaggerated anti-communism to which Gaitskell was responding, and which was reflected in Dean Griswold's Commencement Day speech ('a mixture of June 4th at Eton and Derby Day at Epsom') to faculty and students.

Herbert's visit was very much a product of the Law School's reform movement. In his paper in support of Herbert's nomination, Fuller had written of the need to bridge the gulf between US and other English-speaking countries' legal philosophy; to bring the Law School and Philosophy Department closer; and to develop interests in important developments in semantics and logic and their application to law. The *Harvard Law Record* announced that 1956/57 was to be 'the year of jurisprudence', with no fewer than four separate courses available to second- and third-year students, taught by Lon Fuller, Herbert, and another jurisprudential visitor, Julius Stone, now Challis Professor of Jurisprudence and International Law at the University of Sydney: 'Mr Fuller's course will be based, as in the past, on his text *The Problems of Jurisprudence*. Professor Stone will deal with notions of justice and social and economic facts while Professor Hart will treat some of the more detailed facets of the subject, including theories of punishment, natural law and the elements of municipal legal systems.'

In an interview for the *Record*, Fuller elaborated: his second-year course would introduce students to 'ends of government: in examining the premises underlying the legal system, the student should gain an overview of the system's aims and its relation to the whole life of man in society'. The course covered Austin, Holmes, Gray, Maine, Bentham, J. S. Mill, Hohfeld, Aristotle on Justice, Cardozo's *The Nature of the Judicial Process*, and Pound's *Introduction to Legal Philosophy*. Fuller tried 'to relate the course to the work of practising attorney', but his overriding commitment was that 'the whole of legal philosophy should be animated by the desire to seek out those principles by which men's relations in society may be rightly and justly ordered'. This, he admitted, often met with student scepticism, many students taking the view that 'the mores can make anything right and anything wrong'. In the context of social science-oriented courses attacking students' moral dogmatism, Fuller's jurisprudence teaching was going against the grain.

But he was no enemy of the social sciences, and was also teaching a separate course on 'Freedom and Planning', drawing on figures like Polanyi, Wootton, and Hayek to explore the various possibilities for governmental management of the economy.

Stone was teaching his sociologically inspired form of legal theory, very much in the Roscoe Pound tradition, and drawing on his mammoth 900-page text *The Province and Functions of Law*. His course was extremely broad in range, covering early positivism through to contemporary pragmatism, along with more or less everything in between. By contrast, Herbert's course, in which he had 30 students, considered a number of selected issues in depth. He focussed the students' attention on a mere 40 pages of reading drawn from Gray, Austin, Bentham, Hobbes, and Kelsen. His lectures followed a similar path to those at Oxford, adapted to the American context. As well as analysing the relationship between laws, commands, and rules, he spent considerable time dissecting the American Realist project, which conceived of law in terms of predictions about judges' behaviour, and he taught sessions examining and criticizing the sociological approach. Like other teachers of jurisprudence, Herbert was not obliged to adopt the 'case-law' teaching method, though he still felt compelled in an interview with the student magazine to excuse himself from adopting a Socratic style by saying that there was no point in his doing badly what the Americans 'can do superbly well'. But he did divide his sessions into 'mini-lecturettes', pausing every 15 minutes or so to take questions from the lively and articulate students—a practice which he increasingly enjoyed, and which he resolved to take back with him to Oxford. The classes went well: 'How they *love* everything beginning with the syllable "soc-"!', but 'After the initial shock of my accent and my refusal to do sociology, and natural law, they seem to enjoy linguistics and comparisons of law with the rules of Baseball: They'll be raging positivists before we're "thru" and then there'll be a row. But the atmosphere is very stimulating: every point of view is advanced and they adore debate', he told Jenifer.

By comparison with their oral assurance and articulacy, Herbert found the students' written papers dismal in terms of both style and substance. By coincidence, Ronald Dworkin, who was to become Herbert's most challenging interlocutor, as well as his successor in the Oxford Chair, was a student at Harvard at the time; he was one of the self-appointed 'gods' editing the *Law Review*. Herbert was already aware of Dworkin's talents. In 1955, Herbert had taken a stroll around New College garden with his doctoral student Herbert Morris. Herbert was in the midst of the oppressive business of examining the undergraduate law degree. The task involved marking several hundred scripts, and its difficulty was exacerbated in Herbert's case by his prodigious levels of disorganization. (His students were frequently anxious about the fate of their essays in his famously chaotic room, and marvelled that none ever seemed to get lost: on one occasion, Herbert gestured to the piles of books and papers littering every surface of his room in University College and remarked to John Finnis: 'This [i.e. the chaos] has consumed a huge amount of my life.') Amid the hard work of marking, Herbert was excited by the performance of an American student who had scored an alpha (the highest mark) on every single one of his papers. To Morris's amazement, Herbert went on to express considerable anxiety about the implications of this student's views for the arguments of *The Concept of Law*. The student's name was Ronald Dworkin. Years later, during Dworkin's tenure of the Chair of Jurisprudence, Herbert produced his jurisprudence examination script and quoted from it in an after dinner speech. The moment of his admission to Morris marked the opening of a chapter which was at once to consolidate his institutional contribution to jurisprudence yet to prove the source of considerable intellectual and personal perplexity. But in 1957, these difficulties were in the future, and Herbert was keen to seek out the student whose papers he had so admired. Towards the end of his year at Harvard, he had dinner with Dworkin, and discussed whether he would join the Society of Fellows or go into legal practice: 'Obviously latter', Herbert observed. Though Dworkin did indeed set out on a legal career, he soon exchanged it for a post at Yale. Things would have turned out very differently in legal philosophy had Herbert's prediction proved to be right.

In the philosophy department's elegant buildings in Harvard Yard, where Herbert felt at home with the 'mainly Jewish . . . left wing intellectual' faculty, he found the students pleasant and less challenging. Here he was on familiar intellectual terrain, teaching a class on causation. Among colleagues, Herbert's main relationships were with Morton White, Marshall Cohen, and Burton Dreben, a 'gay ugly charming' mathematical philosopher who had lived with the Warnocks in Oxford. His intellectual estimation of the first two wavered: White he initially thought 'argued badly', though he thought him a 'kind of saint . . . who likes me for a) not being much cleverer than he is b) not being socially smart or proud of knowing the smart': 'nice' Cohen he judged 'careful not to commit himself on any one point—perhaps he is not as clever as he thinks or I thought'. But he both liked and enjoyed debate with all three of them. Yet there were some mutual reservations, as is illustrated by a letter from Isaiah Berlin to White in July 1957:

Herbert likes you very much indeed and I shall certainly not repeat a word. But he says exactly that about you which you say about him: about being doctrinaire etc. Yes, he is very rigid: he seems very indignant with Raphael about his attack on Strawson in *Mind*. I rather enjoyed it, without asking myself too much about how far he was being unfair.

Even though the philosophers had lower standing than the lawyers at Harvard, Herbert was discomfited to the point of having sleepless nights by his own lacklustre performance at a philosophy seminar at which he spoke on 'Knowing what you are doing'—a paper which took him back to his philosophical roots, and which, particularly in the light of Cohen's arguments, he felt he had not sufficiently thought through. By this time his own work was oriented firmly towards law. And, judging by his diaries and the regular letters he wrote to Jenifer and the children, in which he recorded his detailed impressions of the environment and its *dramatis personae*, the majority of Herbert's time was spent in the Law School.

From the beginning, Herbert was both intrigued and impressed: 'The Law School started today and I've got to know some of their formidable professors. The Jewish ones are rather interesting—all mixed up with the N. York left and politics—the paler purer Xtian ones look a little coldly at them. . . . It's so odd after philosophy being the Queen of the faculties at Oxford to find it the Cinderella here and law right up. Certainly the lawyers are far cleverer.' As with Fuller, he formed a cordial though not entirely easy relationship with Henry Hart, co-author of the influential *The Legal Process*, whom he remembered as exuding nervous energy, pacing up and down for two hours before every lecture, chain-smoking, and castigating Herbert for his mistaken positivist views. Herbert attended Paul Freund's classes on constitutional law and Stone's and Fuller's jurisprudence courses; he had friendly conversations with Roscoe Pound, whom he liked but 'got nothing out of' intellectually; and he enjoyed conversations with the genial legal historian Sam Thorne. He submitted reluctantly to the 'stiff' formal dinners given by the Dean, Erwin Griswold, whom he described as 'attractive good-hearted v. clever tough Republican . . . with tremendous vitality'; and he kept as much distance as he could manage from the regular visitor Justice Felix Frankfurter (he suspected that Judge Learned Hand's admirable essays on judicial virtues had been written with 'that chattering monkey Frankfurter's vices in mind').

Apart from Fuller, the person with whom he made the most significant intellectual contact was the criminal and constitutional lawyer, Herbert Wechsler, who was visiting from Columbia and who happened to know and admire his and Jenifer's old friend Francis Graham-Harrison. Herbert found him an 'interesting though rather gloomy character', 'dark and rather tough but alive'. Wechsler, whose marriage had recently broken down, had just turned down the top job in criminal law at Harvard because he was 'too wedded to politics friends etc in New York'. 'Like all the good criminal lawyers here', Herbert reported to Jenifer, '[he] is an active penologist much concerned with sentencing, parole boards, policy'. Wechsler had been a lawyer at Nuremberg and was now working on the influential Model Penal Code and on the reform of Massachusetts' insanity law. He and Herbert had long debates about criminal responsibility, punishment, and—most important in terms of influence on Herbert's own work—causation. Herbert had a high estimation of the 'civilised and progressive' Wechsler and, though ultimately unpersuaded, was intrigued by his rigorously utilitarian and policy-oriented approach. Over the course of the year, these regular exchanges, as well as his reading of the vast American literature on proximate cause, convinced him that his and Tony Honoré's approach would have to be modified to take more seriously the 'policy approach'—in other words, the argument that legal rules of and decisions about causation are ultimately to be explained in terms of judges' and legislators' concerns with policy issues such as law's economic impact. As a direct result of Herbert's encounter with Wechsler, the final version of *Causation in the Law* was reconstructed in terms of a debate with the policy approach.

As well as these influential private discussions, Herbert participated in the three-weekly legal philosophy discussion group held after dinner at the Signet Club. Other regular participants included White, Freund, Fuller, and Kingman Brewster. Ironically, given that it later became the central object of Ronald Dworkin's initial assault on Herbert's positivism, the theme of the group in the first semester was discretion. In his contribution, Herbert provoked a stormy debate among American lawyers unused to focussing on precise linguistic usage by setting out and analysing a number of different senses in which the term 'discretion' was used. In this session and others he was worried by the silence of the untenured professors (he suspected however that they had enjoyed watching him challenge the 'potentates'), and he developed strong views about the negative effect of the tenure track system on the confidence and creativity of younger scholars and in reinforcing the hierarchical structure of the School. Herbert also occasionally found himself drawn into other Law School activities which reflected the professional orientation of the all-graduate student body and which were much less to his taste: a good example was judging 'hugely elaborate mock trials' which combined 'all the worst sillinesses and snobberies of Oxford'.

Herbert lived at Eliot House, an elegant, ivy-clad, neo-Georgian Faculty residence on the Harvard campus, where his three spartan rooms had lovely views over the river. Once settled, he resumed the sort of lifestyle he had enjoyed during the 1930s and in the periods of Jenifer's absence from London during the war. In other words, he worked and played ferociously hard. Life was a welter of lunches, dinners, trips to the nearby towns and countryside—Salem (where he admired the fine customs house and the fan lights and mouldings of the eighteenth-century buildings), Providence,

Lexington, Concord, and Boston, which he came to appreciate more and more. Visits took in not only academics but also old friends from Oxford: in Vermont he visited a friend he had not seen for 20 years, now a vastly wealthy businessman-turned-farmer living in an exquisite eighteenth-century house 'beautifully set in a wide valley near a stream: green expanses and ravishing hills wooded all round: expensive simplicity on the inside'. Herbert was amused (and not entirely discomfited) to find himself a 'mild celebrity' in this man's eyes. Fresh from post-war rationing in Britain, he was amazed by the amount and quality of food in America, as well as by the whisky-drinking which was an integral part of practically every social occasion. And he was disarmed by the geniality of American hospitality and by the informality of many of the social events.

As always, Herbert both threw himself into social life and found it a strain: his diary is often reminiscent of his record of social occasions during his first year as a Fellow at New College, punctuated by anxieties about whether he had been too vehement, or not interesting enough, or too indiscreet. On one occasion, he worried that, under the influence of whisky, he had said too much to a dinner companion about MI5 and Guy Burgess—whose defection he described to Jenifer, in a fascinating contrast to his outraged response to Blunt's exposure in 1979, as 'interesting'. His acquaintance stretched beyond the law and philosophy communities, and he formed a lasting friendship with historian Mimi Berlin and her husband Gerry, a civil liberties lawyer with academic interests in law and psychiatry, and with literature scholar Fred Dupee and his wife Barbara, visiting from Columbia University in New York. With new acquaintances, his assessments of character were immediate, sharp, and occasionally pungent. But one person, to whom he returned constantly in his diary, troubled him. This was Julius Stone. On first acquaintance Herbert described 'My "rival" Stone' as 'genial on the surface and—I suspect—underneath'; 'the chips no longer felt on the shoulder I gather'. But this assessment wavered, as he wondered how far Stone's attitude to him was coloured by their different attitudes to their Jewish origins and by their diametrically opposed intellectual styles. Herbert felt ambivalent about Stone. He disliked his self-publicizing manner (announcements of Stone's and Hart's impending arrival at Harvard and student interviews with them in the *Record* are revealing: Stone's were long and self-aggrandizing; Herbert's were concise, diffident, and wry); shied away from his and his wife's strong association with religious Judaism and with Zionism ('she's insane about Jewish family life which I said we didn't have'); felt that his work was 'poor and cloudy and full of enormous unanalysed ideas' and spoilt by its 'enormous length'; and concluded that 'I don't ultimately trust him': 'He's odiously smooth: rather a vulture beneath the skin.' Still, he wondered if he was being fair to Stone, and felt more than a tinge of discomfort about the way Stone had been treated by English universities in general and by Oxford in particular. Despite his extensive publication record at a time when research in law schools was still at a low level, Stone had left England for New Zealand because he was unable to secure a permanent post.

The resolutions of Herbert's diary entry on arrival at Harvard had not been forgotten. He was packing in a quite extraordinary programme of work around his teaching commitments and lively social life. As he looked forward to the year, he already had no fewer than eight commitments in mind. Principal among these was the causation book with Tony Honoré, but the list also included the more distant project of writing up his Oxford lectures as an 'Introduction to Jurisprudence' for Oxford University Press and a number of immediately pressing deadlines. These were revisions for an article on which he was working with Stuart Hampshire; further work on an already drafted but in his view unsatisfactory article on legal and moral obligation for an edited collection; a reply to Bodenheimer's *University of Pennsylvania Law Review* critique of his inaugural lecture; an article on murder and capital punishment developing ideas on which he had already done a BBC broadcast (and beyond which he already anticipated a further book on 'Mind and Responsibility'); a 'reply to Shulman'; and a 'paper on the Italian legal philosophers'. During the course of the year, pressure to deliver occasional lectures around the country added two further items to the list: a paper on criminal responsibility and an essay setting out the agenda for a new version of legal positivism—the future 'Positivism and the Separation of Law and Morals'. By the end of the year, five of these projects were complete, and Herbert's ideas for the causation book had been massively affected by his engagement not only with Wechsler but with hundreds of American cases which he read in the 'basement of the Law School'.

Though never a fast writer, during this year Herbert developed or laid the foundations for the vast majority of his work over the next decade: for *Causation in the Law*; for *The Concept of Law*, and for *Punishment and Responsibility*. The stimulating American context, as he later put it, 'relaxed one's neuroses', 'Ideas started pullulating at a rather alarming rate. I thought, "Am I going mad?": I was getting so many different things inside'. Some key examples illustrate this kaleidoscope of 'different things' which was setting the pattern for the most significant part of his career. A lecture on criminal responsibility delivered at New York University and a lecture on 'Murder and the Principles of Punishment', delivered at the Harvard Club and Chicago Law School, published in journals in 1957 and 1958, became in due course Chapters 2 and 3 of *Punishment and Responsibility*. Here Herbert mapped out the liberal, restricted utilitarianism which was the hallmark of his criminal law theory. 'Analytical Jurisprudence in Mid-Century: A Reply to Professor Bodenheimer', published in 1957, shows that the main lines of argument of *The Concept of Law* were already well developed, and uses many phrases and examples which recur in the book. Here, Herbert elaborated the defence of analytical jurisprudence outlined in his inaugural lecture and his 1953 paper 'Philosophy of Law and Jurisprudence in Britain 1945–52'. Responding to Bodenheimer's critique (and, in his view, misreading) of 'Definition and Theory', Herbert defended himself against the view, common among American jurists, that positivism—the idea that law was a human artefact, its content a contingent social fact—was to be equated with formalism—the idea that judges deduce their conclusions from closed legal premises. He did so by emphasizing the 'open texture' of legal language: even from a positivist point of view, legal reasoning could never be merely deductive. In responding to the criticism that positivism neglected the importance of disciplines other than philosophy, he emphasized the distinction between theories of law and law itself: while legal practice could undoubtedly be improved by a systematic appreciation of the insights of other disciplines, legal theory, he insisted, was an autonomous intellectual approach in which philosophy was the appropriate disciplinary resource.

The tone of this paper is confident, even bullish. Yet, in defending himself against Bodenheimer's charge that his position ultimately undermined jurisprudence by redefining jurisprudential questions as ones about the usage of terms in particular legal contexts—a charge which is structurally similar to the 'paradox of analysis' critique often mounted against Austinian linguistic philosophy—Herbert sounded less than fully convinced by his own position. His argument was that students of substantive law can learn to use terms of legal art and to predict their effects without understanding their conceptual structure or normative function. But this sounded dangerously like an unstable theoretical division of labour which would carve up the teaching of law and jurisprudence between, respectively, the Realists and the philosophers. From his own point of view, this was surely to concede far too much.

Another paper showed Herbert struggling with—and troubled by—some of the deep philosophical issues which he handled with such insouciance in *The Concept of Law*, yet to which he returned, less confident that he had resolved them, in later life. In 'Legal and Moral Obligation' (1956), he demonstrated his increasing intellectual self-assurance by arguing head-on that moral philosophers could learn from a close analysis of conceptual usage in legal contexts. Taking the concept of obligation, he argued that the distinctive features of obligation in legal contexts are that they are created by words which operate in the context of rules identified by distinctive criteria of validity specifying the

191

standards which will be used as reasons for doing certain things within a particular social group. These, he argued, could shed light on the proper use of the concept of obligation in moral reasoning. His position was distinguished from American Realism by its normative as opposed to predictive view of obligation: rather than interpreting an assertion that a legal obligation exists as a prediction that a sanction will be imposed when certain behaviour occurs, his view was that obligations operate as standards and as reasons for action. Hence his view was that obligation-imposing legal rules specify, in some genuinely though not straightforwardly moral sense, what *ought* to be done. Yet his position was distinguished from that of his positivist rival Hans Kelsen by his view of the existence of any particular legal obligation as at root a matter of fact. This argument foreshadowed *The Concept of Law*. It differed from his ultimate position mainly in the place given to coercion or sanctions. Whereas in the later book he claimed that the concept of legal obligation could be understood independently of coercion, in this paper the application of coercion—albeit of various kinds—on breach of an obligation was one of the three criteria which he took as characterizing legal obligation, and as identifying the contexts in which we think it appropriate to draw on the concept of obligation, as opposed to simply what 'ought' to be done, in moral contexts. The other two criteria were reference to the accepted practice of a social group and independence of content. This latter criterion foreshadowed his much later notion of legal rules as content-independent peremptory reasons—considerations we have grounds for treating as reasons for action independent of their content. This paper is also significant because prevarications about its central thesis occupy many pages of Herbert's notebooks. Here, as in his attempts to reply to critics of his theory of legal obligation in *The Concept of Law*, he was aware of the tenuousness of the distinction between his own and Austin's or Kelsen's sanction-based position. He saw the danger that, in seeking more clearly to differentiate his own position, he would blur the boundaries between legal and moral obligation to a degree which would threaten his status as a legal positivist and move him perilously close to a natural law position.

Despite the very substantial amount which Herbert wrote during this year, he did not use every moment of his spare time to get on with writing. As usual, he was also reading widely, keeping notes in his diaries over the year on sources as diverse as Aquinas, Plato, Rawls, Bentham, and all the major figures in recent American and Scandinavian jurisprudence. Less typically, the performance-oriented American context (and perhaps the lure of earning substantial fees of up to $300 per lecture: he earned enough through occasional lectures to enable him to save most of his Harvard salary) propelled him out onto the lecture circuit in a hectic schedule which was a real challenge to someone who was not a natural performer. During the course of the year he gave lectures at the Universities of Berkeley, Seattle, Duke, North Carolina, Richmond, Chicago, Northwestern, Wisconsin, Princeton ('a demure English Shaftesbury' which 'tries to look like an English University but in fact succeeds only in looking like an English Public School'), Illinois, Champaign-Urbana, Pennsylvania, Yale, and New York and at Vassar and Swarthmore Colleges. He also made informal visits to Columbia and Cornell, where he enjoyed some 'real talk' with John Rawls—'a superior character both in character and intellect'. At many of these places he gave talks in both the Law School and the Philosophy Department. Each trip— its surroundings and its *dramatis personae*—was recorded in characteristically detailed, observant, and wry terms in his diaries and letters home. On one trip to the South he was entertained to lunch by a 'bullying Teutonic figure' before escaping to the next engagement with another colleague and his 'curious dark sad thin-lipped wife' in their 'pretty wooden house . . . in a wood', and on to another dinner at which entertainments included, to his surprised amusement, a game of charades. These private records reveal Herbert's strong impressions of the United States—impressions which he later summarized as a talk for Radio 3 on Christmas Eve of 1957.

Principal among his many positive impressions was the refreshing lack of class snobbery in America: 'Life here makes one think how very badly "public" school . . . education may in fact be operating in England. Apart from the snobberies and class divisions, perpetuations of class accents and manners being bad per se it must mean that people are recruited to jobs, in business and professions, v. often by irrelevant criteria. Great lawyers here have accents equivalent to Cockney: they just could not be great barristers at home.' (This observation was followed by a request to Jenifer for a copy of Tony Crosland's book on equality.) Herbert admired and enjoyed the energy, generosity, and enthusiasm of Americans, the significant numbers of Jewish people in academic life (this observation, frequently noted in his diaries, did not make it onto the BBC), and the sense of involvement in public affairs in the Law Schools. He was enchanted by the scale and beauty of the countryside; the richness of America's artistic collections (the National Gallery in Washington, with 'all the best Corots, Degas, Cezannes', struck him with particular force, but he was also a regular visitor to the Fogg Museum in Cambridge and the Boston Museum of Fine Arts); the grandeur and elegance of Washington; the appealing eighteenth-century architecture and sense of history in the oldest parts of Boston (visiting the 'charming calm XVIII C interior' of the Old State House, he found it 'extraordinary to think of the defiance and revolutionary resolution and speeches going on there'); the natural beauty and ethnically diverse vitality of San Francisco; the teeming streets and lively multicultural atmosphere of New York: 'somehow both touching and exciting: this mix up of races. . . . Though of course it would be hell to be poor here. . . . Yet the life and churning in the place has a poetry which Boston could not have.'

In New York just before his final departure he spent an evening watching—and being made 'to *feel* and *think*' by—Brecht's *Threepenny Opera* at a small Greenwich Village theatre, followed by dinner at a 'pansy' restaurant on Christopher Street—an experience which opened up a vista of how his own life might have been had he grown up in a similarly tolerant, diverse environment. He was intrigued by the widespread interest in psychoanalysis—'a real *faith* here!' he told Jenifer—and struck by the extremely long working hours of American professionals; 'strange this enormous burden on the top (intellectually) class when the working man's day is getting shorter and shorter'. And he was drawn by much contemporary American literature: a favourite was Salinger, whose insight into the thinking of young people Herbert particularly admired. He also developed a taste for jazz, delighting his children by bring back to Oxford an extensive collection of records then unavailable in England. He was fascinated by the strange mix of modern and old-fashioned in American life: the supermarkets, sophisticated kitchen gadgets, and general appetite for the new juxtaposed with an individualistic self-reliance, conventional domestic mores, widespread religious faith, and a pervasive moralism redolent of the Victorian age. 'I've been invited by both a Rabbi and a Catholic priest to lecture to separate meetings on how religion affects my subject. I shall refuse both, saying it does not.'

There were also, inevitably, negative impressions. Particularly on first acquaintance, Herbert found many of the cities alarming: Chicago, which reminded him of 'Dickensian London', he described as 'satanic', with its 'evil slums and broken down ill-lit houses and pubs: gaunt machinery protruding into the sky: pathetic negroes—tough-looking police and sinister prowlers all around. . . . There's a great deal of tortured, ruined country, streams, canals weaving in through the slums and skyscrapers'. He was also shocked by Chicago's annual murder rate, which was twice that of England and Wales. He was intrigued by the lack of any serious, principled difference of policy between Republican and Democratic parties; found 'grim' the lack of a public health care system; and was repelled by what he saw as the occasional vulgarity of displays of wealth. 'In his *Listener* broadcast at the end of 1957, he summarized his impressions in terms of some stable differences between English and American culture and politics. With uncharacteristically broad brush strokes, he sketched links between the landscape and culture':

If you go, say, to Vermont or Virginia, and look about you, the first impression is of how ferocious nature can be. . . . But if you look at the admirable frame houses, of which so many charming and interesting variations have been made, you are puzzled by the absence of some feature which is difficult at first to identify. . . .

It is, of course, the hedges. . . . You see at once that privacy, as an ideal, makes almost no appearance. . . . Those delightful meals taken in the open, when the meat is broiled over charcoal, often take place between houses and the lane in the full view of passers-by. . . . This extraordinary absence of privacy makes one think again about what we and they—the Americans—consider liberty to be. For us, surely, liberty is this: that there is a circle round each man, inside which he can do as he please, and it is no concern of others; this is the liberty the Englishman has inside his house and garden and behind its hedges. I think that this as an ideal makes little appeal to an enormous number of Americans; I believe you can find what the American means by liberty by looking at the Constitution of an American State. In the State of Massachusetts the Constitution provides that any member of the public may introduce a measure into the Legislature and argue for it before committees. And it seems to me that this is what an American means by liberty; the right to take part in what he would call 'the decision-making process'.

Though his own genre of liberalism always tended to the libertarian rather than to the republican end of the spectrum—to 'negative' rather than 'positive' freedom, as his friend Berlin would put it—and though his equation of American political culture with positive freedom might be questioned, Herbert was fast becoming a deep admirer of certain aspects of American democracy. In his letters home, notwithstanding his complaints about the poor overseas coverage of American newspapers, his increasingly horrified reaction to the Suez crisis (he was a vehement critic of Britain and Israel) was underpinned by the concern that it might damage what he saw as the important political alliance between Britain and America.

In his *Listener* piece, Herbert also commented on the relatively small number of women pursuing careers (particularly academic careers). His view of the, often highly educated, 'heavy' Harvard law wives was that their personalities were hidden behind a 'mask of gracious living', suffering 'from the fact that their husbands do nothing but work all day and most nights, something of the same thing as Oxford wives do from the fact that husbands sit round *talking* in men's enclosures'. He also observed the larger number of students (ironically, he thought of them as men and compared them with English 'schoolboys') receiving a university education. This, he argued, brought with it a broader but more superficial graduate education: a lesser grasp of 'detailed accuracy in writing and . . . the expression of precise nuances of thought' were disadvantages, while the enthusiasm and open-mindedness which American students brought to the 'intellectual bazaar' of the university were decisive advantages. But the single most persistent theme was Americans' tendency to 'sloppy thinking' and linguistic imprecision:

There is in America I think a wholly different attitude to precision of language, to the nuances that language can convey, and to verbal accuracy. To many Americans we appear to be fussing about the letter and often using the letter to kill the spirit. We stand on the brink, wondering about the meanings of words, while they wish to plunge in and get the drift of whole paragraphs, or some large sense of general purpose, without bothering too much about the precise meaning of what is said.

Amid the intellectual bemusement and repeated assertions of the importance of linguistic accuracy, there is a certain self-questioning. The broader, if less finely woven, intellectual canvas which Herbert witnessed in the United States was indeed making its impression on him. It would only be three years before he, too, was feeling the limits of the linguistic approach to legal theory and, though still holding to the commitment to accuracy and precision, branching out into areas of law reform and normative theorizing which he saw so vividly represented in American law schools in the late 1950s.

Intellectually, the peak of Herbert's year at Harvard came at the end of April with his one public lecture in the Law School. Returning from ten days with the family in Oxford over Christmas, he was summoned by Dean Griswold and invited to deliver the prestigious annual Oliver Wendell Holmes lecture. The invitation included a fee of $1,000—an enormous sum, equivalent to about $6,500 today. Herbert was deeply flattered (as well as delighted by the financial aspect) and accepted at once. But immediately after accepting, he suffered the deepest in a series of intellectual panics which had haunted him throughout the year. As he contemplated his long list of teaching, writing, and speaking commitments between January and April, and worried that too much pressure of work might spoil Jenifer's visit during her Easter vacation, he became increasingly anxious about whether he could deliver something of adequate quality, and prevaricated about whether he should pull out of the commitment before it was too late. After toying with a number of possible topics—sovereignty, the roots of a legal system—he settled in the end on reworking a paper he had originally delivered at the Political Studies Group the previous year, developing a frontal defence of analytical jurisprudence and of legal positivism. The lecture, as he later recalled, 'was, and was intended to be provocative'. But this very decision added to his feeling of vulnerability and exposure. He tried out versions of the lecture at no fewer than four other venues (Richmond, Swarthmore, Illinois, and Vassar) and was deeply depressed when the Vassar talk, only a fortnight before the Holmes date, went badly. As 30 April approached, Herbert spent tens of hours revising and polishing the lecture, convinced that he would be unable to hit the right tone for its expectant and intellectually diverse audience.

In the event, he could hardly have been more mistaken. Herbert managed to pull a sparkling performance out of the mysterious bag of scholarly abstraction and panicked concentration. The evening began inauspiciously with an amusing incident in which Dean Griswold had forgotten to invite him to the official dinner preceding the lecture. Finding out that he was about to stage 'Hamlet without the Prince', Griswold, 'in a terrible flap', summoned Herbert at the last minute and sat him 'next to terrible Mrs G who shouted her ghastly banalities into my deaf ears and also next to Stone who looked jealous'. But even this could not disturb Herbert's concentration. Uncharacteristically, he recognized that the lecture had gone well: 'The Holmes curiously enough was a very great success. 250 or more and I had really prepared in the end something I thought quite good, and fairly polished, and I found (by imagining myself to be alternatively Gaitskell, Geoffrey Warnock and Wilfred Green) a way of reading it as if it were not read. . . . It was the best performance I've ever done though, as you know' he wrote to Jenifer, 'that means v. little.'

In his beautifully constructed and typically densely packed lecture, 'Positivism and the Separation of Law and Morals', Herbert mapped out his agenda as the intellectual successor to the legal positivism of Jeremy Bentham and John Austin. In particular, he defended their brand of analytical jurisprudence against the charges laid by the two groups of legal theorists whom he saw as the main antagonists to his own genre of theory. He rejected the charge, current in much American Realist jurisprudence of the first half of the century, that legal positivism provides a mechanistic and formalistic vision of legal reasoning, with judges simply grinding out deductive conclusions from closed sets of premises. And, as against the claim of modern natural lawyers, he defended the positivist insistence on the lack of any necessary, conceptual connection between law and morality, and denied that this betrayed an indifference to the moral status of laws. In resounding terms, Herbert insisted on the propriety of Bentham's distinction between descriptive, 'expository' jurisprudence, and prescriptive, 'censorial' jurisprudence'. Indeed, he claimed that there are moral advantages to making a clear separation between our understanding of how to determine what the law *is* and our criticisms or vision of what it *ought to be*.

The Holmes lecture was instantly recognized as marking an important moment in the development of legal theory. Sitting in a packed auditorium in Langdell Hall, members of the audience felt the significance of the occasion as they watched Fuller's pained expression and Stone's ambivalent reaction while Herbert pushed his positivist message home. Joel Feinberg, himself to become a celebrated legal and political philosopher, remembered Fuller pacing 'back and forth at the back of the lecture hall like a hungry lion' and leaving half way through the question session. The lecture was promised to the *Harvard Law Review*. Fuller clearly felt that he deserved, as it were, a right of reply. A few days later, Herbert recorded that 'L. Fuller sweating [sic] opposite me [in the Faculty Club] announced he was going to comment . . . in HLR. I felt I ought to show signs of appreciation and apprehensiveness but I didn't'. The rest, as the saying goes, is history. Herbert's lecture and Fuller's response were duly published the next year—an exchange which Herbert rather ungenerously announced to Morton White in a letter from Oxford: 'Lon Fuller has replied at enormous length and (I think) obscurity to my Holmes Lecture. This piece of logomachy will appear in the Harvard Law Review shortly.' The two articles quickly became, and still remain, the standard scholarly reference point and teaching resource for the opposition between legal positivism and natural law theory.

The reason for this instant and lasting success is not difficult to discern. Notwithstanding Hart's caustic comment to White, both men were at their best. The sharp joinder of issue between them was thrown into relief, given poignancy, and made immediately accessible by the fact that it took place in the shadow of widespread debates about the legitimacy of the Nuremberg Trials, and centred on a vivid example. This was the case of the 'Nazi informer': a woman who, during the Third Reich, had relied on prevailing legal regulations to denounce her husband as a political dissident. After the war, the woman was charged with a criminal offence against her husband. The question was whether her legal position should be governed by the law prevailing during the Third Reich—a law now regarded as deeply unjust; or by the just law prevailing before and after the Nazi regime. In short, the case raised in direct and striking form the question whether law's validity is dependent on its credentials as just or otherwise morally acceptable. Herbert defended the view that since the woman had committed no crime under the positive law of the time, the only legally valid way of criminalizing her would be by passing a piece of retrospective legislation. Although this was, on the face of it, an unjust solution, it might nonetheless be the morally preferable thing to do: the lesser of two evils. And this solution had the distinctive advantage that it avoided blurring the distinction between 'what the law is' and 'what the law ought to be'.

At the foundation of Herbert's argument lay not so much an analytic as a substantive moral claim. It is, according to him, morally preferable, more honest, to look clearly at the variety of reasons bearing on an ethically problematic decision rather than to close off debate by dismissing certain considerations as irrelevant: arguing that something never was the law because it ought not to have been the law. There is a liberal aspect to this argument: it is up to citizens to evaluate the law, and not merely to take it that the state's announcing something as law implies that it ought to be obeyed. But there is equally a utilitarian strand to Herbert's position: an implication that things will turn out better, in terms of resistance to tyranny, if citizens understand that there are always two separate questions to be confronted: first, is this a valid rule of law? Second, should it be obeyed? Predictably, no evidence was adduced in support of the second, empirical aspect to his argument. But it had a piquancy. This was not only because it gave the lecture a moral dimension but because a famous German jurist, Gustav Radbruch, had argued influentially that the experience of the Third Reich should turn us all into natural lawyers. The positivist position, he argued, was linked to the unquestioningly compliant 'might is right' attitude widely believed to have assisted the Nazis in their rise to power.

Fuller, picking up on Radbruch's claim, argued that the Nazi law under which the woman had acted was so evil that it could not even count as a valid law. In his view, law—the process of subjecting human conduct to the governance of rules—was informed by an 'inner morality'. Unlike the theological traditions, Fuller's was not a dogmatic, substantive natural law position: rather, it was a position which built out from certain valued procedural tenets widely associated with the rule of law. These included the requirements that laws be coherent, prospective rather than retrospective, public, possible to comply with, reasonably certain in their content, and general in their application. Conformity with these procedural tenets would, over time, 'work the law pure' in a substantive sense. It was this universal 'inner morality of law' which provided the necessary connection between law and morality, and not the 'external' or substantive morality which infused the content of law in different ways in different systems. The 'inner morality' guaranteed a law worthy of 'fidelity', underpinned the existence of an obligation to obey the law, and marked the distinction between law and arbitrary power. And, Fuller claimed, Herbert's own position could not consistently deny some such connection between law and morality. For in his argument about the open texture of language, Herbert claimed that judges deal with 'penumbral' cases by reference to a 'core' of settled meaning. This, Fuller argued, suggested that legal interpretation in clear cases amounted to little more than a cataloguing procedure. Yet even in a very simple case such as a rule providing that 'no vehicles shall be allowed in the park', the idea that judges can appeal to a 'core' meaning of the single word, 'vehicle', was problematic. In deciding whether a tricycle or an army tank put in the park as a war memorial breached the rule, the core meaning of 'vehicle' in ordinary language would be next to useless in judicial interpretation: rather, judges would look to the purpose of the statute as a whole. And these questions of purpose and structure would inevitably introduce contextual and evaluative criteria in the identification of the 'core'. For Fuller, the interpretive force of these purposive criteria was closely bound up with the ideal of fidelity to law.

Ironically, this sometimes sharp debate marked the opening of a new era of friendly dialogue between the protagonists. In his assiduous replies to the dozens of letters which he received about the exchange, Fuller, though clearly delighted when assured that he had the better of the debate, told his correspondents that he had enjoyed Herbert's visit and felt that they had 'learned much from each other'. Their mutual trust was furthered by a curious incident which threatened the publication of Herbert's paper. Typically, Herbert had agonized long and soul-searchingly about the crystallization of his spoken lecture into final, publishable form, and had scrutinized every last word. To his horror, the editors of the *Law Review*—as in the case of most American law journals, they were students, and the most successful and often arrogant students at that—sent in December a set of proofs he found barely recognizable. He wrote to Fuller:

Meanwhile a spot of trouble! The L. Rev. boys had *mutilated* my article by making major excisions of what they think is irrelevant or fanciful. They have made a ghastly mess of it and of the references to Bentham and I have written to say they must not publish it under my name with these cuts which often destroy the precise nuance. I took great care and much time over what they have coolly cut out.

Could you induce them to be sensible? Such an interference with an author's draft is unthinkable here and I am astonished that so gross and insensitive a thing should be possible at Harvard.

I have told them if they will undertake to restore the listed cuts I will get down to the unwelcome task of patching it up all over again. But meanwhile I will not return the proof.

So sorry but it is important to me to get precisely what I said printed. Best of wishes. I will write anyhow on your reply.

Yours ever, Herbert Hart

It was an experience which confirmed all of Herbert's prejudices about Americans' attitude to precision. But Fuller was both sympathetic and effective in response:

Dear Herbert:

After receiving your letter I went over to the Review and found the President busily engaged in restoring your article to its original form. I am sorry for what they did, though I have to confess that this sort of thing comes close to being standard practice with articles written by American authors. Being near at hand I could save my baby from mayhem. Had I dreamed they would take such liberties with your text, I would have stood over them.

Fuller's support warmed Herbert's attitude to him, and this moment saw the inception of a friendly correspondence which they maintained until Fuller's death in 1978. Much of it centred on Herbert's objection to Fuller's central assertion: namely that law, understood as the process of subjecting human conduct to the governance of rules, was invariably informed by certain purposes. Herbert took issue with this in his review of Fuller's *The Morality of Law* in 1965, eliciting the following response from Fuller, in an exchange which is a curio of an era free of the constraints of political correctness:

I was delighted to see so sharp a joinder of issue. . . . All I can say of Miss Purpose is that the Old Girl still looks good to me. One of her enduring charms is that she is a very complex creature indeed, subject to unpredictable moods of surrender and withdrawal. I believe deeply in her without pretending that I really understand her. So the high romance of which you complain will probably continue despite your thoughtful warning that our liaison promises trouble.

This was followed by two pages of discussion of Herbert's claims in the review. The two men also exchanged references and views and cooperated on various institutional concerns, not least the effort to get jurisprudential classics and high quality modern texts published at prices affordable to students. As the reserve between them melted, Herbert and Fuller exchanged views on the first writings of Ronald Dworkin, and joked about the dangers of the linguistic approach. In 1965, sending a symposium on *The Morality of Law*, Fuller referred to Dworkin's 'new tack': 'vague and self-contradictory laws can do no harm because they are not laws at all. The absurdity of this view—reached abstractly and outside any institutional context—suggests to my prejudiced mind doubts about the whole attack on my conception of legal morality', and went on to ask Herbert's view. Later in the letter, he continued: 'In the current issue of the Journal of Legal Education there is a review by a man who has studied under both of us. At this distance in time it is a little hard for me to estimate how much damage my course did to him, but the review seems to me to reveal the truly devastating effects on a mediocre mind of too much exposure to ordinary-language philosophy.'

In retrospect, Herbert could see that his panic over the Holmes lecture—panic which troubled him intermittently throughout this unprecedentedly productive year—had been exaggerated:

Panic such as never before visited me . . . intermittently over this Holmes lecture . . . not sleeping and worrying about back-ache pains haven't helped. . . . It all went very well; I got it into satisfactory form on the morning and was calm all day. . . . Delivery seemed to impress. . . . *Why* does one panic as one did?

and:

Looking back on my various phases of panic (beginning on the QE last September) I see they were idiotic and dangerously near incapacitating. The last lap with the Holmes Lecture had bad moments—fantastic ones even: ranging from images of collapse ridicule and contempt to odd convictions that I was ill . . .

On reflection, he suspected that both panic and self-exploration helped to get him moving intellectually. But, in a courageous attempt to analyse what he saw as his failings, he was beginning to make links between his professional and his personal difficulties. Immediately after the passage about difficulties of work organization quoted at the beginning of this chapter, he wrote:

Characteristic of me to put my professional concerns in the forefront. Is it inhuman not to have thought first of personal factors—wife children home and separation from it? I have a feeling that there is a *connection* between my deficiencies as a husband and the whole sexual and emotional immaturity on the one hand and this gross incapacity for the organization and care of detail: this lack of care; this obsession with frontal attacks on major positions and inattention to slow detailed way of solving them; haste and scurry where calm and coolness are needed.

When Herbert left England in the summer of 1956, he admitted to himself that, despite the mutual tears on parting which took him aback, his relationship with Jenifer was in a mess, characterized by mutual misunderstanding and 'frozen behaviour'. Settled in Cambridge, his attitude to the separation remained ambivalent. He suffered—intermittently but acutely—'gusts of homesickness'. And as the only visitor with a working wife, so not accompanied by his family, he was occasionally defensive in the face of constant questions about why they were not with him. He peppered interviews and personal conversations with references to his children: the student magazine, for example, was told that they were disappointed he was not living in a skyscraper. He wrote home with great regularity—a letter went to Jenifer or the children at least every two or three days throughout his ten months in America; he worried about the safe arrival of his letters and packages to Oxford; and he became extremely anxious if he did not hear from the family for more than a few days. He genuinely missed their company, and was amazed, when visiting his Oxford colleague Geoffrey Warnock in Champaign Urbana, to hear him say that he 'found his children bores and wants to live apart on the other side of the green baize door like the Victorian parent'. He planned Christmas and birthday presents for the children with great care, months in advance; wrote them letters which displayed a real capacity to enter into their concerns and a capacious imagination about what would interest them about his own environment (Jo was told about the countryside; Adam about technology; Charlie about sports); and inquired solicitously of Jenifer about their educational progress and

1. Herbert as a small child

2. *From left to right*: Herbert and his two brothers, Reggie and Albert

3. *From left to right*: Reggie, Sybil, Albert, and Herbert

4. and 5. *Above left and right*: Rose and Sim Hart, Herbert's mother and father
6. *Below*: The Harts' shop in Harrogate

7. The Jewish House at Cheltenham College, 1919: Herbert is at the extreme left of the top row, and inset centre

8. New College, Oxford: the garden quad seen from the garden

(by kind permission of www.virtual-archive.co.uk <http://www.virtual-archive.co.uk>, from which the image is available as a limited edition print)

9. *Above left*: Herbert and his mother, 1927

10. *Above right*: Christopher Cox cooking porridge at the Chalet

11. *Right*: Herbert and Jenifer

12. *Left*: Fatherhood: Herbert with Joanna, 1942

13. *Below*: Herbert and Jenifer with Adam, 1946

14. J. L. Austin

15. Tony Honoré

16. Isaiah Berlin

17. 11, Manor Place, Oxford: the Hart family home from 1952

18. Herbert, Adam, Charlie, Joanna, and Nanny

19. Adam, Jacob, Joanna, and Charlie in the garden at Manor Place, early 1960s

20. Herbert reading in his room at University College, 1962

21. Climbing, *from left to right, back row*: Herbert, Paul Blaikley, Peter Strawson, Margaret Paul; *front row*: Peggy Jay, Douglas Jay

22. Herbert with Jacob, summer 1966

23. Herbert, Jacob, and Nanny, walking, Cornwall, summer 1966

24. Herbert, Joanna, Adam's first wife, Mary, with their daughter Mojo, Charlie with Jacob on his knee, Adam with Nanny standing in front of him, 1969–70

25. *Right*: Joanna, Herbert, and Charlie, seeing Charlie off to University, 1967, with Chuckaboom to the left

26. *Below, left*: Joseph Raz

27. *Below, right*: Ronald Dworkin

28. *Left*: Herbert reading on the terrace at Lamledra

29. *Below*: Walking in Cornwall: Herbert, Charlie, and friend, 1967

30. Jacob conversing with his teacher, Joy Fuller, flanked by Jean Austin (*left*) and Herbert's sister Sybil in the garden at Manor Place, 1970s

31. Herbert in Athens

32. Reality and representation: Herbert seated beneath his portrait by Derek Hill as Principal of Brasenose (1977)

33. Herbert enjoys a relaxed social occasion at Brasenose . . .

34. Herbert in his room abutting the Fellows' garden at University College, mid 1970s

35. Herbert in New College, 1976

36. Herbert, on becoming a QC, with Albert, 1984

37. Walking on wheels: Herbert, Jenifer, and Charlie, Oxford, December 1991

38. In the garden at Manor Place with Adam, July 1992

happiness at school. On the basis of his own experience of Cheltenham he initially regarded the prospect of sending Adam to a public school with extreme distaste and anticipated deferring to Jenifer's view on the question, but in the end he himself pushed the idea.

For Jenifer, too, Herbert's departure for America prompted some thinking about the state of the marriage. In her diary at Lamledra in the summer of 1956, she reflected with typically self-critical honesty:

We none of us have faced up to H's departure for the USA in a few days' time. He says v little about what he feels re leaving the children: I think he will mind leaving Charles specially. Perhaps he tries not to think about it all from that pt. of view. I don't think he minds leaving me, in the ordinary sense. Why should he? Considering what I am like. Nor do I mind his going at the moment. No doubt I shall feel lonely and miss the intellectual stimulus he provides.

Yet Herbert was still deeply bound up with Jenifer. In his diary, reactions to people and surroundings were often punctuated by reflections on what her view would have been. In their correspondence, they discussed political issues with evident mutual pleasure and exchanged Herbert's experience in America for Jenifer's work life and Oxford gossip, as well as the inevitable round of domestic and financial detail. From time to time, Herbert asked Jenifer to intervene in University matters in which he had an interest—one example being Goodhart's attempts to prevent the publication of a book by Geoffrey Marshall.

Herbert's letters were on average more cheerful and up-beat, less introspective, than his diaries. But he agonized in both, with remarkable honesty and, even by today's standards, an unusual willingness to confront psychological issues, about his capacities as a father; about his emotional failings; and about the future of his and Jenifer's marriage. At the root of all this, once again, were ambivalence about his sexuality and feelings of emotional blockage:

Thurs 14 Oct: Listening to Schubert Trio while (characteristically) writing a lecture for this afternoon! But why does one let moments like this go? When the heart begins to feel—the sensibilities exposed—not driven out or locked in by intellectual preoccupations, ambitions, coarseness, lust? At these moments affection appears what it should be, something one cannot do without and must never withhold. Music is needed to remind me of the possibility of all this. Life can't properly go on without it and the lack of it accounts for miseries in the past—my own and Jenifer's.

The deep emotional impact which music had on Herbert helped to unlock his feelings; but communicating them to Jenifer was more difficult. A trip home at Christmas, typically marred by Herbert's and Jenifer's exhaustion after their hectic teaching terms, did only a limited amount to improve matters. The turn of a new year which would bring his fiftieth birthday initiated a further strand of anxiety and introspection centred on fear of ageing and on the sense that time was slipping through his fingers:

Jan 1957 (50 this year!) Seen off at Gloucester Green . . . by Jen and children:—a wrench but in some ways exciting to come back to the fizz and stimulus of the term. Especially as Oxford was for the fortnight in some ways depressing—I felt ill and tired continually. . . . Children a great joy but the mess of J's and my relations remained and only on the last night but one (after 3 whiskies) could I talk about it. I filled her with irritation, guilt and boredom from the start; the underlying reason (or cause rather) was plain: but there's a vicious circle. One hopes it will get better; we came nearer to understanding what was wrong at least.

The ostensible problem was the couple's differing attitudes to sex, with Herbert rarely moved by a desire for sexual intimacy and Jenifer taking what she felt, in retrospect, to have been the unduly conventional view that it should be up to Herbert to initiate it. Feeling rejected, she assumed a cold and irritated manner, which inhibited Herbert further still, creating the vicious circle to which his diary refers. Both of them worked hard to overcome the problem. Herbert hoped that Jenifer's visit to America at Easter, for which he was trying to set up lectures and academic contacts which would make her trip professionally as well as personally satisfying, might improve matters. He was optimistic: after all, they would be in a more relaxed context than that prevailing in Oxford:

Meanwhile . . . a noble letter from Jen which must have cost her hell to write. She says things could be alright if we could resume: what a blow my last 10 years of declining interest in that has been. Once we've spoken as much as this we can start afresh but there are the 'perversions of my make up.' If I can get on top of the work by March—her trip here might be a good new start. But her posture of deprivation makes me feel very guilty (if one is guilty in questions of one's sexual make-up). . . . Couldn't one have taken some positive steps? Couldn't I have *not* been put off by asperities of manner? Couldn't I have stopped pursuing academic success or philosophical understanding with such exclusive passion?

Referring once again to his homoerotic leanings, he enjoined himself:

If I stop having guilt about these infantilisms then I can at least try with renewed confidence in Jen to divert my sexual energies to her. I am very elastic. What with selfishness I *really* want is to have relations with her and with men. What is bad in this (suffering for others emotional impoverishment for me) is the divorce between affections and physical pleasure. I must write some of this to Jen if only as a sign of renewed confidence.

Typically, the diary entry moved seamlessly back from this brutally honest personal self-examination to work concerns:

But must do the work in front of me and so reduce the nascent panic. No doubt the euphoria . . . or relief of self-exploration but ideas seem now to come to me.

But he replied, generously, to Jenifer:

Darling Jen,

I got your letter yesterday. It was *noble* of you to write like that and it must have been hell to write so, but I'm sure it will do a lot of good: I'm sure we can extricate ourselves from the psychological jam: and of course you mustn't ascribe it to any failure on your part. How could you, how could anyone cope better with my mixture of infantilism, pride, crudity? I don't say these to *blame* myself because this to me is the area where blame is senseless or nearly so. All that's worthwhile is learning from experience what to do for the future. I doubt if I could ever dominate in the bedroom and be passive in the drawing room: partly because with strong feminine if not masochist tastes I fall very easily into passive sexual roles and get pleasure from passivity and partly because I can't surrender all in the drawing room if you see what I mean. But most important of all is the assurance that you don't find me now repulsive: my hold on *normal* sexual activity is so precarious that phobias of all sorts throw me off balance. . . . I'm still very much as I was on that hill above Glyndebourne 20 years ago. I doubt if I *could* go to bed with any woman but you (as distinguished—alas—from almost any reasonably attractive man). I enjoy it *tremendously*—grossly too no doubt—when I do but the [illeg.] part costs something in terms of a currency of which I have too little: confidence, spontaneity of affection, union of senses and the affections. Sybil-cum-Reggie-non-Albert phenomenon. It seems mad now to have the Atlantic between us: I feel passionately I want to get back and try better but perhaps it is best so. Should we try, do you think, to have another child? I don't mean this as an amende honorable about Charles. . . . This sounds like a bargain but of course it's not—only a token of willingness to do anything to get things right. That's enough—perhaps if I go on (sitting in a cafeteria in Harvard Square with hideous Americans drinking milk round me) I shall become hysterical. But don't let the subject drop altogether out of view.

In the event, Jenifer's trip was a success:

14 April Just back from Vassar: J's trip gone well up till now: perhaps this seeming set back is not really one. . . . As usual my inhibitions go when abroad. . . . [At enjoyable dinners] I feel that J feels that I roar away and too easily exploit geniality and surface talk. But I don't really know if the irritation look of worry which did return this weekend may be due to other causes. All I can (but *must*) do is not to allow these perhaps uncontrollable dips on her part to chill me; on the contrary then if ever (how Jamesian this sounds!) I must make the biggest extension of sympathetic imagination possible. Even the marvellously

beautiful journey back through Berkshires . . . only partially diverted her. Why? Perhaps an added irritant was my poor performance at my lecture, a trial for the Holmes . . .

Once again, exemplifying precisely the over-emphasis on work of which he accused himself, the narrative went straight back to work anxieties. But in the last, less pressured weeks in Harvard following the Holmes lecture, Herbert continued to reflect on the situation and to make brave resolutions. In June, anxious about the lack of a letter from home, he wrote:

Jen's madly overworked. . . . I am gradually getting anxious to return there . . . and see the last of Charlie's—*what?*—*Babyhood?* I suppose . . . I love them all (as one sees from here) very much. J: is it peace, love, armed neutrality? What thoughts! Can one build on the good time here?

Even in this moment of professional success and personal optimism, Herbert struggled with depression. In May, he heard that Isaiah Berlin, recently appointed to the Chichele Chair of Political Theory at All Souls, had been knighted. His response was caustic. He wrote to Jenifer:

How awful about Isaiah: really horrid especially as he's starting a Chair of Political Theory. What was it said to be for? Not attacking govt. during Suez? Conversation? Solving Problem of Free Will? . . . The Queen will have to say 'Arise Sir Isaiah' v. difficult almost a tongue twister. There's much mockery here. . . . I feel it really does make him appear a bit ridiculous, and the thing about his mother is a very feeble excuse. She's had enough glory out of him already. I long to hear Oxford comments.

Berlin was well aware of Herbert's disapproval of his acceptance of the knighthood. He wrote to Morton White: 'People like the Harts . . . and others do think of me as having sold out to some vague establishment.'

Was there some special enjoyment in Herbert's forthright expression of opinions about Isaiah in his correspondence with Jenifer? During Jenifer's visit at Easter, she recorded in her diary a dinner party at which a Harvard academic criticized Isaiah as 'too literary' and insufficiently interested in political institutions. This critical view was not unusual. Early in the year, Herbert had written to her with what almost sounded like pleasure on Berlin's 'low stock' in America—the Harvard philosophers' view that he 'was au fond a snob, too pleased at moving in the top circles [and] had ceased really to think or write anything new'. And in the spring he told her that he had mixed feelings about Berlin's claims over John Plamenatz for the Chichele Chair in political theory: 'I would vote for him . . . but not with an entirely clear conscience'. (In fact he thought that George Paul would have been the obvious candidate for the job, and felt guilty that he and Paul had never got on with the jointly authored book which might have bolstered the latter's claims on a Chair.) By the following year, Herbert was reporting to White that Berlin was wearing his title 'as lightly as any cocked hat'. But he continued to regard the title as absurd and pretentious, and when offered one himself, turned it down on the basis that he disapproved of the award of public honours for work conducted in a private capacity.

Berlin's public recognition touched more than one sensitive issue for Herbert. Apart from Berlin's affair with Jenifer, there was the question of Herbert's unresolved feelings about his withdrawal from the public service in which he had felt so happy during the war. Drawing personal and professional issues together, he wondered:

Do I feel I am a good enough theoretician to justify my abstraction from practical affairs? 'social work'? At any rate I don't feel it acutely enough. Yet on a government committee I would flourish all agree but can't make the first steps. What does this show? That I only respond to competitive urges: wish to shine.

There was a hint of identification in his comment on his old friend Richard Wilberforce; 'Poor Richard W sounds plangent—has his life been always one of melancholy punctuated by successes that don't satisfy?' He wondered if he himself feared 'real intimacy with an adult . . .: omne abit in mysterium—better at least than in miseriam. What resolves? What *use* resolves?' But he was determined to break out of the cycle, and he enjoined himself to:

Think out how to exploit for good, the good new start with Jen made here during that happy five weeks; think out how to use, preserve, not coarsen the gifts and sensibilities I have—not to waste them. . . . I have touches of self-disgust occasionally when I contemplate the absence of *public* concern that distinguishes me so much from so many including Jen. Somehow I feel better *not* force myself into all that, rather deepen and make better the better sides of what I have—sympathy and understanding, devotion to children. Take off tasks from Jen which I can do quite well. And odd to be approaching 50 at this breakneck speed—or so it seems. . . . What things have been showered on me by fortune; how few, so far, the real miseries.

In view of what lay ahead, it is ironic that one of the solutions he pondered was another child—the only occasion on which he took the initiative on this important decision. Yet again, at a moment when the public, external aspect of his life was marked by success and apparent personal security, the internal aspect was much more ambivalent. Like many people, but perhaps to a greater degree, Herbert had grown used to keeping his public and private worlds firmly separated. To the world, there was the internationally-famous professor of jurisprudence, happily married with a remarkable wife and three sociable and gifted children. Internally, there was an intermittently depressed man who felt himself to be stuck in emotional adolescence, 'hurtling at breakneck speed' towards later middle age. In life as in theory, both aspects have their explanatory power. However painful, Herbert's strikingly frank and self-critical interpretations of himself were perhaps one side of the dispositional coin which produced the avalanche of intellectual creativity which marked this period of his life.

CHAPTER 9

Law in the Perspective of Philosophy: Causation in the Law, The Concept of Law

AT the end of his first term back in Oxford, Herbert wrote to his Harvard friend Morton White:

How nice to have heard from you and how shocking to reply so late. You cannot imagine, however, how strenuous the effort of resuming Oxford life has been. Unsuspected crowds of D. Phils. anxious to write on the philosophy of law beset me, and commitments to innumerable Law Reviews in the United States accounted for the rest of my term....

I am ploughing away now at our book on Causation, which has grown to mammoth size, but we hope to finish it finally in the summer. How awful a job writing a book is; how wise Austin is never to do it.

Before leaving America, Herbert had already been worried about the causation book which his reading and conversations with Wechsler had convinced him would have to be reworked. Writing on his way home in New York he described himself as—'principally impressed by need to order book round the "policy approach"—*difficult*.' And: 'If I ask what I most need to put into perspective at moment it is I suppose the book with Honoré on causation. I feel that it's too inflexible crisp and in a way remote from and unreadable by [lawyers].... I'm impressed enough by ... Wechsler to make it incumbent on me to change tone of book.'

It was not only the high workload, worries about what to lecture on in the autumn term, and the inevitable backlog of commitments which greeted his return which impeded Herbert's progress on his book with Tony Honoré. As usual, professional preoccupations were interwoven with personal ones:

Irritations: I should have anticipated and prepared for it more—English country looks ravishingly beautiful after U.S.... Garden and house all beautiful and sunny.

Adam v. handsome, Charles and Jo charming as ever. What luck I think. But have got into—almost at once—stupid little arguments with J. who has been madly over-working (30 hours plus lecturing) and term (I scarcely realise) is only one week behind. All this inhibits natural flow of feeling and we go to bed in unsympathetic moods which for me is a fatal impediment. The next few days, feeling a) mind has stopped working b) worry about redoing book on cause and confronting Honoré c) incredible drowsiness (as at Xmas) whenever I sit down. Stay in garden mostly: see nobody: toy with reading Wittgenstein's maths book. Better after one session with Honoré who takes it well.

Despite Tony Honoré's constructive attitude, Herbert's uncertainties about the causation project persisted for weeks: 'Put off for 2 years? Let down A.M.H. [Honoré]?' He also reported 'anxieties arising on a scale new to me' covering everything from Jenifer through to lost luggage via work and children, and was even contemplating pulling out of producing the written version of the successful Holmes lecture. He tried to manage his anxiety by facing the worst and comparing himself with his cousin Tilly who had lost her husband and son; by reflecting on his old friend Christopher Cox's ways of coping with depression—or 'fumes'—and by counting his blessings: 'Something more tolerable with J is building up: children really except for a few lapses remarkably happy well and handsome. Francis's [Graham Harrison] visit and suggestion I might be asked to join Royal Commission on Punishment later, flattering and interesting'.

Now really must get down to it. Second interview with Honoré who's quite of a mind for some considerable measure of redoing. There could be a super book on this subject [causation]: will ours be it? I am to tackle my existing miserable chapters and i) add philosophical preliminaries: dealing with phil. history of topic and the new method ii) introduce the issue of causation v. policy and the elimination of causation iii) say more about basis of legal responsibility iv) re-present sine qua non. A task—my god—but can be done.

Enormous difficulties in seeing now any defensible procedure for this book let alone a doctrine to expound. Can all that stuff Honoré has done really be rewritten?

Notwithstanding the agonies, Herbert was about to launch himself into a period of quite extraordinary intellectual creativity. Gradually, the clouds began to clear. Tony Honoré did not realize the depth of Herbert's doubts about the project, though he was aware that Herbert was worried by certain differences between the two of them, notably Tony Honoré's less wholehearted espousal of linguistic philosophy and more Kantian approach. At one point, Herbert suggested that they should write two separate books: on another, he cavilled at a view which Tony Honoré had expressed, describing it as 'naturrechtlich'. Honoré resisted both suggestions. Though still somewhat in awe of his older colleague, he entered energetically into debate about the reshaping of the book. He persuaded Herbert that the American materials which he had already written about and which Herbert had familiarized himself with in Harvard needed to be supplemented by European materials, and showed his usual enthusiasm even for the laborious task of rewriting the book. On Tuesday July 23, Herbert recorded:

Have after extraordinary difficulties begun very slowly to 'rewrite' my chapter. Began on Saturday with a 'sketch' of a preface in order to get my ideas clearer. Going infinitely slow and awful decisions seem to be needed at every step—sign of real inner confusion of aim?

And on 5 August he enjoined himself:

Down panic, down

Better—a bit. Preface and Chapt I of book—passable. Felt at least the way more clearly defined. . . . Of course part is that I don't *quite* know what I think and another part that this scale job demands better organising powers than mine.

In the event, the preparation of the final manuscript was to take Herbert and Tony Honoré another year. Herbert took primary responsibility for the opening, philosophical chapters of the book, and for the section on criminal law, while Tony Honoré concentrated on the sections on contract, tort, and evidence, and analysed the continental theories of causation (about which Herbert was dismissive). But both men worked over all the chapters in meticulous detail, and throughout the year met regularly each week. Honoré recalled that 'we mulled over one another's drafts until we could reach agreement on each sentence and, indeed, each word. It was an agreeable and, to me, educative collaboration. But the strenuous sessions, which might go on all day, could bring the junior partner to the point of exhaustion. In contrast the stamina, patience, and determination of the senior to get even the smallest point exactly right seemed inexhaustible, though a certain impatience with the minutiae of scholarship made him unreliable about references'. The final product, a book of nearly 500 pages, was published by Oxford University Press in 1959.

Causation in the Law is a monumental analysis of the idea of causation in criminal law, the law of torts, and the law of contract. When Ann shoots Brian who later dies after having received negligent medical treatment from Cara, has Ann, or Cara, or have both, caused Brian's death? If Eric and Freya simultaneously aim and fire a potentially fatal shot at Gareth, who later dies of his injuries, do both of them cause Gareth's death? Or is neither of them the cause, given that Gareth would have died even without either one's individual action? When a fire destroys a house, why do we tend to describe the causation in terms of the person who lit a match and poured petrol through the door rather than focussing equally on the presence of inflammable material in the house, the presence of oxygen in the air, and so on?

Following Herbert's exchange with Wechsler at Harvard, the book's argument was reconstructed in opposition to the influential school of thought which Wechsler represented and which Herbert and Tony Honoré call 'causal minimalism'. Causal minimalism claims that there is no *sui generis* concept of causation deployed in law beyond the 'factual' idea of causation as a *sine qua non*—as all the conditions but for which an event would not have happened or a consequence would not have occurred. Beyond this 'but for' sense of causation, the minimalist claims, decisions about how to attribute causal liability are based on policy considerations such as efficiency or moral considerations such as fault. For example, in the above examples we would treat both Eric and Freya as causes because both are equally at fault; we would treat Ann rather than Cara as the cause of Brian's death, unless Cara's negligence had been especially gross, because we don't want to discourage medics from intervening in emergencies.

As against this, Herbert and Tony Honoré insist that law does operate with a distinctive notion of causation richer than that of 'but for' causation. They argue, however, that most philosophical analyses of causation are inapposite to explain the legal uses of the term, because they focus on causation in the context of science, and hence seek to identify general laws of causation. This is a mistake, because no such invariant, general laws can govern the identification of causes in the essentially particularistic legal context. In law, causation is a many-faceted notion: it has to be traced not to one overarching principle but to many principles and sub-principles clustering around the centrally recognized bases for attributing causal responsibility. These central cases themselves connect with widespread, common sense understandings of causation reflected in linguistic usage. According to Herbert and Tony Honoré, voluntary human action is the centrally significant variable in the attribution of legal causal responsibility. The central case is that of action intentionally aimed towards a particular end which it produces, or done with foresight that that end will occur; secondary but important cases are those in which a person provides an opportunity for a result to be created (for example, leaving a house unlocked with the result that a burglary occurs) and in which a person incites or assists another person to produce a certain effect (for example, persuading or helping another person to kill a third person). Where, however, another voluntary human act intervenes between one human action and a consequence—particularly if that second act is 'abnormal' or unexpected; or where another abnormal event such as an 'act of god' like a storm or earthquake intervenes, the law will generally regard the causal chain as being 'broken'.

At the level of method, *Causation in the Law* represents a thoroughgoing application of the linguistic philosophical analysis to law. For Herbert's and Tony Honoré's approach is to seek to unearth the principles underlying judges' use of causal language—itself often metaphorical, as in the familiar idea of a 'chain of causation' being 'broken'—and to explore the relationship between this judicial usage and more general, common sense understandings of causation embedded in linguistic usage in particular contexts. Hence they analyse hundreds of cases, drawing out common approaches to elicit general principles, and identifying a core meaning of causation which reaches across different contexts. *Causation in the Law* presents a spirited defence of the idea that causation in law is indeed a distinctive ground for the attribution of liability, and a persuasive critique of the causal minimalist position as collapsing questions of the ground of liability (causation) into questions about its scope or extent (policy factors affecting the extent of damages or the scope of the rule), and, in doing so, as blurring what is argued to be the proper division of labour between judge and jury, between law and fact.

Causation is a taxing book to read, because the method of eliciting general principles from hundreds of cases sometimes makes it difficult to see the wood for the trees. This is least true of the early, theoretical chapters, and, perhaps for this reason, the book initially attracted more favourable notice from philosophers than from lawyers. Notable among the philosophers was P. Nowell-Smith, who described the book as 'brilliant', though voicing reservations about whether the distinction between causation and policy or fault could be sustained; while in the *Law Quarterly Review*, F. H. Newark paid the sort of insubstantial compliment which prompted Herbert's contempt for orthodox academic lawyers: a 'considerable work in both bulk and importance . . . the authors have fully sustained the Oxford tradition that the law should speak the language of the gentleman as well as that of the scholar'. *Causation in the Law* also had a warmer reception in America, where the luminary of Realist causation scholarship, Leon Green, heaped praise on it, than it did in Britain, where both Goodhart and the influential Cambridge scholar Glanville Williams gave it a lukewarm assessment. Morton White, persuaded by Herbert Wechsler to review the book for the influential *Columbia Law Review*, wrote to Herbert in September 1960:

This is just a fan note to express my great admiration for Causation in the Law. It is a splendid piece of work which I find myself in agreement with whenever my ignorance of the law does not prevent me from following the argument. . . . I hope you will not be too disappointed by your failure to get a review from a lawyer in so important a legal journal, but there may be some compensation in the fact that your philosophical views may receive more accurate exposition than a judge or a law professor might be likely to give them.

Herbert's reply reveals the extent to which he still regarded himself as a philosopher and the judgment of his philosophical peers as the true measure of his achievements:

I was delighted to get your letter and very happy that you like our book. It is wonderfully good of you to spend your time and energies reviewing it. You are of course right: the lawyers won't understand the analytical part until they are shown by someone who does. There have been 2 or 3 quite appreciative reviews here but only one by a lawyer. (It seems to sell quite well in spite of its price and length). Really I can't say how pleased we are that *you are to review it and I much prefer it* to a legal review.

Nevertheless, the book had a deep impact on legal scholarship; it was widely read and came to be cited by judges both in the UK and beyond, its success reflected in the fact that a second, expanded edition was prepared (mainly by Honoré) and published in 1985. Yet apart from this second edition, the publication of *Causation* marked the end of Herbert's productive collaboration with Tony Honoré. Though some exchange continued, with Tony Honoré giving Herbert detailed comments on the draft of *The Concept of Law*, the self-styled 'junior partner' 'felt the need to move away from Herbert's rather intense intellectual orbit' and develop his own autonomous intellectual identity. That their warm and relatively intimate relationship survived, at least in the short term, the ups and downs of co-authorship is attested by a letter written by Honoré shortly after the book's publication:

Dear Herbert,

Your gift will remind me of our rewarding collaboration. I am looking forward to 'The Golden Bowl' on holiday. It is one more proof that you are as kind as you are gifted (don't blush).

Tony

In later years, however, a certain distance grew up between the two men. Herbert, though always an admirer of Tony Honoré's intellect, had little interest in his Roman law scholarship; he was also ambivalent about *Causation*, reacting negatively when other scholars suggested to him that it was his greatest achievement. Conversely, Tony Honoré had some doubts about the quality of Herbert's subsequently published work. These doubts sometimes expressed themselves as criticism of the cavalier attitude to scholarly method prefigured in Herbert's carefree attitude to references noticed by Tony Honoré during their work on *Causation*. But a more substantial doubt was about how effectively Herbert went on to build on the foundations laid in their joint work for a productive interplay between jurisprudence and linguistic philosophy. Many philosophers regard *Causation*, with its systematic application of linguistic philosophy to a specific issue, as representing the pinnacle of the Austin school's published achievements. Sadly, its appearance marked Austin's diagnosis with cancer: he died in 1960, at the age of 48. This was a huge loss to Herbert, whose letter to White continued:

Here, for me at any rate, a good deal of the sparkle went out of the air when John Austin died. There's quite a lot of interesting movement and change but nothing to take his special place. Jean Austin has made a wonderful recovery from it all: the children are all launched in school or university careers and she is teaching philosophy herself a little this term. Luckily the money situation was not bad.

Yet Austin's death may also have been an intellectual liberation to Herbert, opening the way to an intellectual trajectory less narrowly oriented to linguistic philosophy. For *Causation* marks the limits as well as the strengths of the Austinian version of linguistic philosophy, and presents a significant example of the differences between the Oxford school and the genre of linguistic philosophy being developed in Cambridge by Ludwig Wittgenstein. The two shared a distrust of metaphysics and were agreed on the Wittgensteinian precept, 'don't look for the meaning, look to the use'. But their interpretation of this injunction differed markedly. The difference was not merely the Oxford School's stylistic preference for precision and simplicity, though this certainly contrasted sharply with Wittgenstein's elliptical, oblique approach in the *Philosophical Investigations* (which was first published in English in a translation by Elizabeth Anscombe in 1953, and had certainly come to Herbert's attention by the time he was working on *Causation*). It was also a substantive difference of understanding about how use and meaning are connected, and about the ways we can use, in Austin's words, 'a sharpened awareness of words to sharpen our perception of, though not as the final arbiter of, the phenomena'. Although this formulation was qualified—language is 'not the final arbiter'—the Oxford School's assumptions about the power of an analysis of language to contribute to our understanding of the world was significantly less cautious than the approach prevailing at Cambridge.

For neither School was the relationship between language and meaning a matter of metaphysics, or the view that words in some sense reflect fixed conceptual truths. Rather, the fluidities of usage were taken to mark important practical distinctions, and the claim was that in clarifying these, we come to a better understanding of phenomena. But Wittgenstein and the Oxford philosophers differed in their response to the 'paradox of analysis'—the fact that if language speaks for itself, it is not clear that philosophical analysis is either necessary or capable of being applied to linguistic usage without doing violence to its meaning. For philosophical analysis is itself a (distinctive) form of usage. How, then, can linguistic philosophy criticize the incoherence of the linguistic practice which it takes as its material? Herbert and Tony Honoré grappled with this problem at several points in *Causation*. One spectacular example is their departure from the general tenet of looking to usage to discern significance in their swingeing critique of lawyers' appeal to the concept of 'active force', which they castigated as 'obfuscating' rather than as a helpful way of distinguishing among 'but for' causes.

More generally, we can discern the difference between the Wittgensteinian and the Austinian approaches in Herbert's and Tony Honoré's attitude to the legal 'context' without an appreciation of which they argue that it is impossible to grasp the distinctive shape of the concept of causation in law. *Causation* is in a sense about 'causation talk' in particular contexts rather than 'causation' understood as an empirical fact or metaphysically given concept. The book's central argument is that we must focus on judicial language to elucidate discrete principles of causation which are conceptually distinct from broader patterns of attribution: causation is an autonomous condition of attribution, not to be collapsed with the policy factors (such as economic impact, distribution of loss, implications for the parties' incentives) which often restrict the ambit of attributions of responsibility. Further important sub-claims are that legal usage of causal terms is multiple, generating a 'family' of causal concepts, related to one another, rather than a single principle; that this variety of legal notions of cause is in turn related to features of the legal context, and in particular to the need to provide causal accounts of particular events (i.e. cases); and that for this reason, scientific concepts of cause, which focus on generalizations, will not be of use to lawyers. Herbert and Tony Honoré argued that moral and historical notions of cause are more like legal notions than scientific notions. Because philosophers have focussed on scientific theories, they have not contributed substantially to moral, historical, or legal understandings of causation.

These sub-claims are of particular interest in understanding the specific nature of Austinian linguistic philosophy. We can see this if we focus on the idea that the specific context in which causal statements are made makes a difference to their meaning or force. This claim itself has a variety of forms. First, causal explanation is not the same as causal attribution: the explanatory statement that a fire came about through the combination of a naked flame, combustible material, and oxygen in the air deploys a different notion of cause from the attributive statement that the person holding the match caused the fire. Secondly, the point of view from which a statement is made will affect the causal account given: a political activist might attribute a drought to governmental failure to address environmental concerns, while a meteorologist might attribute it to the weather. Thirdly, the detailed factual context will affect the causal account given: whilst we normally would not cite the presence of oxygen in the air as a causal factor in a fire, we would do so if the fire occurred in a factory where the productive process was such that oxygen had to be specifically excluded. Finally, the disciplinary context in which a causal statement is made will affect its meaning: causation in law is not the same as causation in morals, and very different from causation in science. In each of these examples, the claim that context makes a difference uses a different sense of 'context': as conceptual context (explanation rather than attribution); as the interest or point of view of speaker (e.g. 'the government caused the drought; the weather caused the drought'); as the discipline within which a causal statement is made (law, moral philosophy, history, natural science, social science, psychoanalysis); as the factual context within which a causal statement is made (oxygen in the air is not usually an abnormal factor but might be within a specialist factory). And, as Herbert and Tony Honoré sometimes note, these different contextual factors will often interact: in the disciplinary context of medicine, it will make a difference whether a doctor is making a diagnosis or prescribing a course of treatment.

But, having identified these various nuances within the central argument that context makes all the difference to the way in which causal language is used and causal concepts developed, how, and how far, do Herbert and Tony Honoré push this claim? The main description which they offer of what is distinctive about the *legal* context is the argument that it is concerned—as contrasted with science—with particulars. This is hardly a rich characterization. For a start, it does not serve to distinguish law from morality. Beyond this, Herbert and Tony Honoré simply give us a huge amount of actual linguistic data. This data is almost exclusively drawn from legal (mainly appellate) cases. The reader is given no systematic analysis of the institutional, practical, professional context in which that legal language was used: in Wittgenstein's terms, there is no exploration of the social practices or forms of life within which the causal language game is embedded. Herbert and Tony Honoré do not, for example, explore the nature of the judicial role, and despite the inclusion of UK, US, and German data, there is little discussion of how differing judicial roles or procedural systems in those countries might affect the development of legal concepts. Although Herbert to some extent filled this gap in his next book, *The Concept of Law*, and is often thought of by followers like Neil MacCormick or Joseph Raz as having had an institutional or social theory of law, his exploration of that institutional framework is relatively thin. At the end of the day, law is analysed as a body of doctrine rather than as a social practice, and 'usage' is understood as the language which makes up the doctrines.

Herbert's and Tony Honoré's Austinian approach contrasts significantly with the approach which might be drawn from Wittgenstein's *Philosophical Investigations*. For Wittgenstein circled—in the elliptical style which so alienated Austin—around a problem which Herbert himself never quite confronted. This was the precise nature of the relationship not just between language and behaviour, but more specifically between linguistic usage and the context in which it happens. In contrast with Herbert's and Tony Honoré's limited conception of context, Wittgenstein understood context to include a whole range of variables from the individual mind through to social institutions and practices—teaching, game-playing, customs, experience. What kind of a book would *Causation* have been had it been written by a legal theorist inspired by Wittgenstein rather than by Austin? We could expect it to have explored questions such as the institutional factors which restrict the extent to which judges will appeal to pragmatic or policy arguments—their sensitivity to the need to legitimate their decisions, their (system-specific) understanding of their constitutional role and so on. As an empirical matter, these institutional factors shape not only the appeal to policy in causation cases but also the development of causal concepts themselves.

The appeal to language does indeed, as Herbert and Tony Honoré saw, bring contextual factors into play. But it is far from clear that they were justified in confining their attention to language in the sense of the meaning to be elicited from usage, analysed from the page, rather than moving on to think about the way in which the contexts of usage—normative, institutional, political, and so on—shape the development of the meaning as well as the force of statements. In their Austinian zeal, Herbert and Tony Honoré reduced linguistic usage to a body of doctrine rather than seeing it as a social practice which takes place within a context the specific nature of which would merit investigation. It is interesting to speculate on what difference it would have made to Herbert's further work, and to *The Concept of Law* in particular, had he taken a broader, Wittgensteinian approach. Given Wittgenstein's emphasis on the embeddedness of language games within social practices and forms of life, it is likely that there would have been positive effects on the development of a genuinely social or institutional understanding of law. But it is also interesting to consider the reasons which prevented Herbert from pursuing this line. Certainly, an impatience with what he saw as Wittgenstein's scandalously obscure written style would have been one factor. A loyalty to—perhaps even a desire to please and win admiration from—Austin was probably another. But a third reason has a more substantial, intellectual and personal aspect. It is that, if fully pursued, the Wittgensteinian message—as Wittgenstein himself saw—undermines the pretensions of philosophy as the 'master-discipline' which illuminates our access to knowledge about the world. For once the notion of 'context' is broadened out, the inexorable conclusion is that illumination of legal practices lies not merely in an analysis of doctrinal language but in a historical and social study of the institutions and power relations within which that usage takes place. A full acceptance of Wittgenstein, in other words, would have threatened Herbert's idea of himself as a philosopher.

By the time *Causation in the Law* appeared, Herbert's work on the project which would establish his worldwide reputation as the foremost legal philosopher writing in English in the twentieth century—*The Concept of Law*—was already well advanced. He was now ready to build on the momentum created by the warm reception of the Holmes lecture and on the successful completion of *Causation*, and was determined to write up his undergraduate jurisprudence lectures as the book which he had already been planning on his arrival in Harvard in 1956. But in 1959, the year in which *Causation* appeared, two other projects seized his attention. These took him in a different direction and, in effect, marked out the course of his work over the next eight years.

In Harvard, he had already begun to deliver lectures on aspects of criminal law and criminal justice policy, notably entering into the bitter US debate about capital punishment in his lecture 'Murder and the Principles of Punishment' delivered in Chicago, and exploring the conditions of responsibility in a lecture on 'Legal Responsibility and Excuses', delivered in New York. Both lectures were published in 1958. Though criminal law had never formed part of his legal practice, the philosophical questions thrown up by this field—questions about responsibility, action, and causation—had long held his interest. And since his election to the Chair, his intellectual relationship with Rupert Cross, who argued that criminal law must always be analysed in the context of the criminal justice and penal system, had helped to broaden Herbert's interest in the field.

In 1959, Herbert was invited to become President of the philosophical Aristotelian Society; an exceptional distinction for a man holding a post in a law faculty and with his first book still in press. The invitation brought with it considerable pressure. It arrived in April, and required him to deliver his presidential address, which would be published in the prestigious *Proceedings* of the Society, a mere four months later. As ever, Herbert combined his preparation for the lecture with his teaching, giving a seminar 'Why Punish?'. And, as in the case of the Holmes lecture, he rose magnificently to the occasion, moving from his two American criminal justice essays to turn his attention to the justification of punishment more generally. In doing so, he returned to one of his most constant sources of inspiration—Bentham—but adapted Bentham's ideas in ways which resonated with John Rawls' emerging critique of utilitarianism. The work of both men would decisively shape debates about distributive justice for decades to come.

In his presidential address, 'The Prolegomenon to the Principles of Punishment', Herbert trod a middle path between retributive accounts of punishment, which hold that punishment is justified as that which the offender's behaviour deserves; and utilitarian accounts, which regard punishment as a *prima facie* evil which can only be justified by its compensating effects in terms of crime reduction, whether through deterrence of offenders or potential offenders, rehabilitation of offenders, or their incapacitation. The history of the philosophy of punishment to this point had been a long and often unedifying exchange between these two schools of thought—an exchange which could hardly be characterized as a debate, in that the opponents were speaking past each other from entirely incompatible premises. Building on Rawls' argument in his influential 'Two Concepts of Rules', published in 1955, Herbert came up with an elegant way out of the apparent impasse. He proposed a deceptively simple solution which essentially consisted in a division of conceptual labour. In formulating a theory of punishment, he argued, one needed to separate out three different questions: a question about the justifying purposes of the practice as a whole: 'why punish?'; and two questions about the distribution of punishment: 'who should be punished?', and 'how much?' He argued that the 'general justifying aim' of criminal law and punishment is the utilitarian goal of preventing crime; whereas at the point of distributing punishment—deciding who should be punished, and how much—a principle of responsibility or 'retribution in distribution' applies. In other words, the only fair terms on which we can pursue the utilitarian goals of the system at the expense of individuals is by making sure that those we punish genuinely chose to offend in the sense that they had a fair opportunity to do otherwise, and by punishing them only to a degree proportionate to their wrongdoing. This special significance to be accorded to individual agency, expressed in the choice to offend, is the ultimate hallmark of the liberalism to which Herbert was committed, and symbolizes his intellectual debts not only to Kant's famous injunction never to treat human beings merely as ends but also to the liberal tradition of Hobbes, Locke, Hume, and Mill.

It was Mill who formed the inspiration for the second important project which Herbert took on in this extraordinarily fertile year. In September 1957 the Wolfenden Committee, in its report on homosexuality and prostitution, had argued that certain areas of private morality were 'not the law's business' and that, in particular, homosexual conduct between consenting adults in private should no longer form the object of criminal prohibition. In 1959, the influential, conservative judge, Patrick Devlin, gave the Maccabean Lecture in Jurisprudence at the British Academy. He used the occasion to attack the Wolfenden Committee's general statement of principle. Social morality, Devlin argued, was a seamless web: once any part of it was weakened, the whole fabric was threatened, and with it the social order which a distinctive—in his view Christian—morality helped to bind. He argued that the punishment of certain kinds of private immorality—those such as bigamy which gave rise to widespread indignation or disgust—could be justified in the same way as the punishment of treason: as wrongs which threaten the social order as a whole.

These views were anathema to Herbert's liberal principles. The fact that they bore specifically on an issue with which he had a deep personal empathy probably spurred his determination to make a public response. In July 1959, he gave a talk, 'Immorality and Treason', on BBC radio. The talk was subsequently published in *The Listener*. Drawing on Mill's famous assertion that the only justification for invoking coercive power—particularly the state's criminalizing power—over a member of a civilized community was the prevention of harm to others, Herbert countered Devlin's claim that mere offence to conventional morality counted as a harm sufficient to justify bringing private conduct within the purview of state control. Social morality was not, he argued, a seamless web, damage to which could be equated to treason. Rather, it should be viewed as a number of parts, and the question of whether legal enforcement was compatible with liberal principles assessed in relation to each separate part. The broadcast and publication immediately attracted a large amount of attention, turning Herbert into something of a public figure. Though, unlike several colleagues including Freddie Ayer, he did not publicly associate himself with the Homosexual Law Reform Campaign—something he was to regret in later life—members of the movement remember his *Listener* article as being 'the nearest thing which we had to a manifesto'. Its arguments became the cornerstone of a wide-ranging debate about the proper limits of state power—a debate which was to gather momentum as the social changes now associated with the culture of the 1960s found their way onto the public agenda. The essay also sketched out the framework for a more elaborate development of Mill's liberalism, a project which would occupy much of Herbert's attention over the next few years.

In this period, therefore, Herbert was not only completing his major contributions to analytical jurisprudence but also laying the foundations for his distinctive contributions to political theory. The following year, he delivered another important lecture in Sheffield on 'Acts of Will and Responsibility', and received the first of what were to be many honorary doctorates. It was from the University of Stockholm, where he revelled in the lavish hospitality and elaborate rituals (including the firing of a salute of guns as his ship entered the harbour) which accompanied the award. He also took on new institutional responsibilities, becoming a Delegate to Oxford University Press in 1960. The jurisprudence book which he had been planning for several years typified his conception of the Clarendon Law Series, which he continued to edit. The book was intended to break the tradition of jurisprudential textbooks in the style of secondary commentaries which amounted, as Herbert himself put it, to 'books about books', 'designed to enable 3rd class men [sic] to get 2nds'. Helped by a period of relative stability in which he had learned to manage the responsibilities of the Chair with less strain, Herbert at last found the time and energy over the summer vacation to finish this book, writing up his undergraduate lectures as an elegant, concise monograph.

As no diary exists for this period of Herbert's life, we do not know whether the composition of *The Concept of Law* occasioned him the kind of personal anxiety and self-doubt which accompanied his work on the Holmes lecture and *Causation in the Law*. Since he had been delivering lectures on the book's main ideas since 1952, it is likely that writing the final draft was a reasonably straightforward business. But the process of working out and refining his ideas was lengthy and laborious. Herbert kept a notebook in which he sketched out his ideas for the book and pondered the various problems which arose. These 81 pages provide a fascinating insight into both his working method and the development of his ideas.

One side saying: you are blind
The other: you are seeing ghosts.
I have the dim—too dim—outline of this book in my mind. My ambition in its most grandiose form is to dispel forever the definitional will o' the wisps— the search for 'definitions' of law—by showing that all that can be done and is important to do is to characterise the *Concept* of law by identifying the main elements and organisation of elements which constitute a *standard* legal *system*. When this standard case has been established as understood without *prejudiced* description of it in terms of some single parti pris element (like 'coercion' (force) or 'justice') then, first, the doubts and indeterminacies of the non-standard case can be dealt with (international law) and secondly the relations of law with 'morals' as a means of social control can be analysed.

Very schematically the scheme (which has long been in my mind and imperfectly controlled by Mich. Term lectures) is as follows:

The Hard Core (and new to English readers) would be an illuminating survey of 'essential' features (and neglected features) of a municipal legal system.

This would . . . bring out the *multiplicity* of kinds of law: *Substantive*; Crime and Private; *Jurisdiction; Procedure; Evidence*; Constitutional (Grundnorm) and drive away the obsession with Command . . .

One novelty in the book is to be a refusal to draw topics of importance from named authors' theories but to look at *the* object

Beyond this almost completely articulated opening, the notebook consists mainly of fragments which give an intriguing glimpse of Herbert's painstaking and often tortuous working habits. The notes reveal an intense interior dialogue which was his way of developing and clarifying his philosophical ideas. The entries range from lists and fragmented notes: 'Why the core essential? How much in core?', through questions for himself: 'What, after all, does this core explain?' to exhortations: 'Cd get this clearer'.

Yesterday's question not answered: today a reversion to this old conundrum about obligation: main questions are:

A Does 'o[bligation]' involve all three or only one of the following
    I   coercion or pressure behind the rules (sanction) . . .
    II recognition of primacy of rule . . .
    III recognition of rule as giving reason for action?

B What is proper inference from fact that (logically) x's obligation is compatible with no chance of suffering sanction. . . .

and words of encouragement to himself:

It seems to get clearer—by pressing on this central theory—obligation.

From these uneven (and chaotically untidy) jottings, a fluent text emerged, its explanatory footnotes—themselves few in number—collected at the end of the volume so as not to distract the reader's attention. The aim was to present his own theory of law in an accessible student text. In fact, the book was received as an original contribution to analytical jurisprudence which moved the subject into a new era. *The Concept of Law* quickly attracted favourable reviews in many of the leading British and American law and philosophy journals, and was the object of interest in Scandinavia, Italy, Germany, Belgium, Argentina, Israel, and Japan. Herbert Morris in the *Harvard Law Review* found it 'elegantly written and brilliantly argued', 'an enormous leap ahead'. Herbert's Realist antagonist Alf Ross, writing in the *Yale Law Journal* found it 'a remarkable book. . . . Answers you have known before take on a new dimension of meaning'. In the *Journal of Philosophy*, Marcus Singer judged it to be 'an important book', likely to add 'considerable impetus to the revival of legal philosophy' and offering a 'brilliant and definitive' critique of Legal Realism. He predicted that it 'will be discussed for many years to come . . . and provide the material for innumerable doctoral dissertations'. Even the *Law*

Quarterly Review was impressed: O. Hood Phillips found it 'an original work of constructive criticism' which would 'clear the reader's head without leaving it empty'.

The Concept of Law has sold over 150,000 copies and continues to sell several thousand copies each year. It has been translated into many languages, including German, Italian, Spanish, Norwegian, Japanese, and, most recently (in 2000), Chinese. It remains, 40 years after its publication, the main point of reference for teaching analytical jurisprudence and, along with Kelsen's *The Pure Theory of Law* and *General Theory of Law and State*, the starting point for jurisprudential research in the analytic tradition. It has been read by senior judges and has had a distinctive impact on the development of judicial culture in Britain and beyond. To understand why *The Concept of Law* had such an extraordinary reception, we must take a short detour into the history of ideas.

The nineteenth-century utilitarian philosophers Jeremy Bentham and John Austin (no connection with Herbert's contemporary, J. L. Austin), developing ideas sketched earlier by Thomas Hobbes, had articulated an influential 'positivist' theory of law. Rejecting the 'natural law' idea that law derives its authority from God, or from some metaphysical conception of nature or reason, Bentham and Austin argued that law is essentially human: it is a command issued by a political superior or sovereign, to whom the populace is in a habit of obedience.

This was a promising start to the development of a conception of law suitable to modern, secular democracies. But it had not been much developed since Austin's death. Austin's and Bentham's literary styles were uninviting, and much of Bentham's work had never been published. English legal education had remained relatively unintellectual, only finding a secure place in university departments outside Oxford and Cambridge well into the twentieth century, and remaining steadfastly vocational for a yet longer period. The distinguished scholars who had worked in English law schools during the late nineteenth and early twentieth centuries— Henry Maine, F. W. Maitland, Frederick Pollock, and Paul Vinogradoff among them—deplored the dominance of the legal profession over legal scholarship. But their intellectual tastes were historical rather than philosophical. In the twentieth century, the work of the brilliant Austrian jurist Hans Kelsen, which developed a positivist 'pure' theory of law within a very different, continental philosophical tradition, was received only piecemeal in the English-speaking world. In the decades preceding Herbert's election to the Oxford Chair, the jurisprudence taught in Britain tended to consist in a rather dry offshoot of technical legal analysis: writers picked apart, with minute attention to detail, legal concepts such as ownership, possession, or the corporation. No attempt was made either to link this analysis to any broader idea of the nature of law, or to consider how technical legal concepts assisted law to serve its various social functions. Questions about what purposes law *ought* to pursue were confined to the realm of moral and political philosophy, the latter itself a relatively arid field at the time.

Herbert's approach in *The Concept of Law* was simple yet ambitious. In a mere 250 pages, he claimed to set out a general, descriptive theory of law: a theory of law as it is, and not an ideal theory of what law ought to be. This would be at once a contribution to 'analytical jurisprudence' and to 'descriptive sociology'. In other words, Herbert sought to elucidate a concept of law which would be relevant to all forms of law, wherever or whenever they arose. In pursuing this project, he returned to the insights of Austin and Bentham, Hobbes and Hume, but—in a crucial philosophical innovation—combined their methods with those of the new linguistic philosophy represented by the work of J. L. Austin, Friedrich Waismann, and—to some degree—Ludwig Wittgenstein.

The nub of Herbert's theory is the startlingly simple idea that law is a system of rules structurally similar, in both form and function, to the rules of games such as chess or cricket. The rules are of different kinds, with complementary functions. Some—'primary rules'—directly govern behaviour. But a system made up solely of primary rules would, Herbert argued, lead to a world of uncertainty, inefficiency, and stasis. Hence 'secondary rules' of recognition, adjudication, and change emerge, providing for the identification, application, and alteration of the primary rules. The most obvious example of primary rules would be criminal laws; examples of secondary rules range from constitutional laws to laws governing the creation of contracts, marriages, or wills. For Herbert, this union of primary and secondary rules was 'the key to the science of jurisprudence'.

Like his nineteenth-century counterparts, Herbert insisted that law was a social, human invention: though legal rules generate genuine obligations, they are not straightforwardly moral rules. Their authority derives not from their content but from their source, which lies in a distinctively institutionalized system of social recognition. For example, the rule that we should drive on the left is valid not because there is any intrinsic value to driving on the left as opposed to the right. Rather, it is valid because the rule can be identified in accordance with an agreed set of criteria for recognition, such as parliamentary enactment or judicial precedent. Precisely the same is true of legal rules which overlap with moral standards: the legal prohibition on murder is not the same as, and derives its validity in a different way from, the moral injunction against killing. He conceded that law is characterized by certain distinctive values—such as the principle of formal justice, or treating like cases alike—and that all legal systems, because they are geared to the survival of a social group, will contain a 'minimum content of natural law' in the form of rules governing physical integrity, property, honesty, and so on. But neither of these insights of the natural law tradition meant that valid laws are necessarily morally good.

Herbert's account of how legal rules are recognized as valid, and as generating 'real' obligations, also served to distinguish law from a mere system of force, or 'orders backed by threats'. For, he argued, legal rules have not only an external but also an internal aspect: we know that a rule is in existence not only because it is regularly observed, but also because those subject to it use it as a reason or standard for behaviour, criticizing themselves or others for breaches of the rules. It is in this aspect of Herbert's theory of law that linguistic philosophy plays a role. As in *Causation*, he builds up his argument by paying close attention to linguistic practices: quoting J. L. Austin, he announces in the Preface that he seeks to use 'a sharpened awareness of words to sharpen our perception of the phenomena'. (Significantly—and with his typically casual attitude to references—he omitted Austin's qualifier: 'though not as the final arbiter'.) For example, he explores the distinction between habitual behaviour (going to the pub on Sunday lunch time) and rule-governed behaviour (going to church on Sunday morning); between being obliged to do something (handing over money because someone threatens to kill you if you don't) and having an obligation to do it (paying your taxes).

From Herbert's working notebook, we can gain some insight into the intellectual journey which produced his lucid and economical monograph. One of the most striking features of *The Concept of Law* is its clear structure. Chapter 1 deals with jurisprudential method, setting out the case for a theory of law based on the core features of a national legal system and inveighing against the pitfalls of a purely definitional approach; Chapters 2 to 4 set out and systematically criticize the main elements of the command theory of John Austin and (though far less thoroughly) the sanction-based theory of Hans Kelsen, while marking along the way the features of these earlier, positivist accounts which need to be preserved. From these lessons, Herbert builds up in Chapters 5 and 6 his own account of law as a system of rules: a 'union of primary and secondary rules' encompassing not merely duty-imposing but also power-conferring laws. This account is then deployed to rebut the American Realist critique of positivism's allegedly over-formalistic account of judicial decision making (Chapter 7). In Chapters 8 and 9 the natural law tradition is assessed, the positivist separation of law and morality being asserted as against the naturalist position, while grains of truth inherent in that tradition are unearthed and argued to be consistent with a positivist account. Finally, mirroring Chapter 1, Chapter 10 provides a case study, using international law as a basis for illustrating how the flexible positivist theory can accommodate legal phenomena 'banished to another discipline' by the conceptual straitjacket of the early Austin's definitional approach.

The notebook illuminates how this structure emerged, but also reveals that Herbert's process of thinking out his ideas was much more a case of working from first principles, and was less derived from critique of other theories, than the final presentation of *The Concept of Law* suggests. Certainly, as the opening words of the notebook attest—and as the Holmes lecture shows—he was, right from the start, thinking of the field in terms of a dialogue between positivism and natural law theory, with American Realism interjecting occasionally from the wings. And the motivating inspiration of linguistic philosophy, with its rejection of the project of definition, occupies a similar place in the notebook to its place in the book. However, his thoughts were organized primarily around the painstaking development of what he felt was a key idea which only emerges in the fifth chapter of the book. This was the idea of rules valid by reason of their source—their institutional origin in acts of human rule-creation—as the core concept of law, with legal orders composed of a variety of such rules. The rules both compel and facilitate—vertically and horizontally, as he put it in the notebook—a range of activities; and they have an irreducibly incomplete, open character:

After all, why does it appear to *me* so important? Revelatory?—the notion of a rule binding valid by virtue of its '*source*' not content.

References to other writers in the notebook are scarce: Hans Kelsen is the only theorist who appears to preoccupy Herbert (his few companions being John Austin, Jerome Frank, Thomas Hobbes, and the Hobbes scholar Howard Warrender, of whom only the last gets more than one mention). In assessing Kelsen, it is the need to displace the centrality of sanctions in characterizing law and to diversify the concept of norms which dominates Herbert's notes. Only some way into the notebook does Herbert begin to set up the issues in a way which prefigures the book's final format, with its structurally pivotal critique of Austin and Kelsen and its deferred consideration of (and minimal concessions to) natural law:

Conviction is hardening in me that it is right to take the authoritatively identified rule (the artificial norm) and this authoritative ruling as the core of the concept of law and to bring in the crude positivism analysis with its top to bottom—fictional force or pain relation as one with understanding: and the natural law ... as a *reaction*.

This idea of natural law as a 'reaction' is proof of the extent to which Herbert thought about the structure of intellectual problems in philosophical terms: what interests him is not the history of western legal theory (in which, on the contrary, positivism was in part a reaction to natural law thinking) but the place of natural law in the conceptual map of post-war jurisprudence.

Given the debates which have grown up around *The Concept of Law*, one of the most interesting aspects of this notebook is the degree to which Herbert struggled with the concept of legal obligation. This, he quickly saw, would be the linchpin of his delicate middle way between Realism or crude positivism and natural law: the idea of law as generating genuine obligations rather than merely forcing compliance, those obligations however falling short of moral obligations.

Obligation as the differential of modern nature of law but caricatured by command. This is likely to become central idée maitresse of the book. What principles are may become clear in course of reading Warrender in this can I draw my distinction between the command habit caricature and the far more central notion of rule-like acceptance.

Identifying the issue was not, however, the same as solving it:

There is something odd, possibly something mistaken in position which I have taken v. 2 that the essence/structure of a legal system rests on acceptance of central/certain authority as binding. . . . Perhaps all I need to convey is that the obligation is strictly *obligation*. i.e.: narrower than belief in moral goodness. But? there is a muddle (in me) I suspect here.

Slowly, Herbert began to experiment with tentative formulations of a 'complex attitude' on the part of rule-followers—the idea which ultimately found expression in *The Concept of Law* as the 'critical reflective attitude' characteristic of the 'internal aspect of rules'—which might provide the clue to resolving this philosophical dilemma. Seeing that 'obligation is going to be more crucial a constituent of Chapter 3 than previous thought allowed', he began to think in terms of the citizen's accepting attitude not to the primary rules but to the secondary rules, and toyed with the idea that obligation 'entails not only accepting the obligation as one's own reason for doing the thing directed, but as *a* reason for doing it and as a reason supporting the demand that I do it'. Acceptance of law however did not amount to its moral endorsement.

Herbert was never convinced that he had satisfactorily resolved this dilemma about the restricted, but genuinely normative, notion of obligation in law: he returned frequently to the issue, trying to capture the precise sense in which law, its existence in his view a matter of social fact, generates genuine obligations to conform to its duty-imposing rules. But by moving from the notion of law as a sovereign command to the notion of law as a system of rules, he had undoubtedly produced a theory which sat more comfortably than had the command theory with impersonal, modern ideas of democratic authority. His theory of law provided a powerful and remarkably widely applicable rationalization of legal authority in a world of diverse value systems. And it neatly captured the idea of 'the rule of law and not of men'—an idea originally articulated by the Ancient Greeks but taking on a new meaning in the legitimation of democratic political arrangements in modern nation states. Herbert's theory offered both a descriptive account of law's social power and an account of legal validity which explained the restricted sense in which citizens have an obligation to obey the law.

The Concept of Law has, of course, been subject to intense scrutiny and lively criticism. Criticism has come from two very different directions. First, from the direction of the social sciences, and echoing the criticisms which can be made of *Causation in the Law* from a Wittgensteinian perspective, it has been argued that although the techniques of analytic philosophy may establish that law is simply one form of social rule, the further question of just what is distinctive about legal as opposed to other social rules can only be understood in terms of historical and social facts in which *The Concept of Law* shows little interest. From the point of view of the general social theories advanced by thinkers like Marx, Weber, and Durkheim, the book has also been criticized as naïve in failing to consider the relevance of power relations and of conflicts of interest or value to the development and stability of legal systems, and as narrow in ignoring the symbolic dimensions of law's authority. The book's claim to contribute to 'descriptive sociology' has been widely questioned, with one early reviewer, B. E. King, arguing that 'Professor Hart's great talents for linguistic analysis may . . . have a conservative effect on legal theory . . .' and that 'the point at issue is really one as to the scope of jurisprudence: whether as a social science it is to be brought under the theoretical umbrella of sociology—or whether, as mainly a study of judicial technique, it is to remain under the shadow of logic and linguistics'. Other critics have argued that the main 'data' presented—the linguistic practices out of which distinctions are drawn and put to theoretical use—are so unsystematic as to amount to, at best, a kind of Oxford Senior Common Room armchair sociology. It has also been pointed out that Herbert's argument is sometimes expressed in terms which invite confusion between analytic and historical claims. The distinction between primary and secondary rules, for example, can be taken as either a conceptual or a functional distinction: a distinction between structurally different forms of rule, or a distinction between rules with different social purposes. And the account of the emergence of secondary rules as 'curing the defects' of a system of primary rules, if taken as a historical claim, is both inaccurate and serves implicitly to represent as the acme of 'civilization' the contours of a modern Western legal order. From the perspective of the more radical of these critiques, the status of *The Concept of Law* as a work of pure description is questionable, and the very project of seeking to answer, in a general and universally applicable way, the question 'what is law?' fundamentally misconceived.

Herbert's defence against these objections was clear, if unlikely to satisfy the critics. It was simply that these sociological and historical questions were not the ones which he set himself to answer. Rather, his was essentially a philosophical project, its allusion to 'descriptive sociology' an unfortunately misleading attempt to signal his move away from the more rigidly conceptual theories of John Austin and Hans Kelsen in favour of an approach which helps us to look at the complex social phenomenon of law. King was therefore right to identify the issue as being about the scope of jurisprudence. And—in a significant contrast with *Causation*—the argument of *The Concept of Law* implied that, within the very loose constraints imposed by the so-called 'minimum content of natural law', the content of a legal system is entirely contingent, shaped by configurations of interests and other social, cultural, and political factors in its environment.

Yet there is an interesting question here about the influence of sociological thought on Herbert's work. On one occasion, John Finnis consulted one of Herbert's volumes of Max Weber and found it heavily annotated (as was the case with most of the books which Herbert read closely). Finnis later asked him on two separate occasions about Weber's influence on his account of the 'internal aspect of rules'. Herbert denied that any such influence existed, ascribing the origins of the idea instead to Peter Winch's *The Idea of a Social Science*. Finnis felt unable to respond to his denial by saying that he had seen the counter-evidence in his copy. The volume which Finnis saw, *Max Weber on Law in Economy and Society*, is now in the library of Hebrew University in Jerusalem, to which Herbert left his library of over 900 books. Herbert's annotations suggest strongly that there was a Weberian undertow in *The Concept of Law*. Weber's comments that 'Conduct . . . can be oriented on the part of actors toward their *idea* (*vorstellung*) of the existence of a *legitimate order*' and that 'Only then will an order be called "valid" if the orientation toward [its] maxims occurs, among other reasons, also because it is . . . regarded by the actor as in some way OBLIGATORY or EXEMPLARY for him' are marked with several comments and underlinings. And Weber's discussion of the variety of ways in which conduct may be orientated towards certain maxims within an order is marked 'Good, like it, likely to be useful'. Other marginal notes imply that Herbert's reading of Weber fed into his formulation of the internal aspect of rules: the notes include 'reasons for accepting . . . reasons for obeying . . . external . . . personal', and Weber's claim that 'An "EXTERNALLY" GUARANTEED ORDER may also be guaranteed "internally" ' is heavily marked. The intriguing question is just why Herbert did not acknowledge any influence from Weber when Finnis asked him. Among analytic philosophers, even the greatest thinkers in the tradition of modern social theory were regarded with some scepticism, and Herbert may have been reluctant to claim sociological credentials which were unlikely to get him much praise within the philosophical world which he inhabited. In asserting that *The Concept of Law* was an 'essay in descriptive sociology' he had, as I have already suggested, a much more straightforward claim in mind.

More troubling from Herbert's philosophical point of view than the social science criticisms were those which came from the direction of modern versions of 'natural law' theory. For example, Herbert Morris's review, though judging the distinctions between the internal and external aspects of rules to be 'of inestimable importance for legal and social theory', argued that he should have adopted a more substantial idea of what it meant to 'accept' rules. In Morris's view, acceptance was limited to cases 'where the existence of the rule would in itself be for the person a good reason for obeying it'. Later on, John Finnis argued that, ultimately, the existence of a stable legal system will depend on a core of those subject to legal rules adopting an 'internal attitude' for moral reasons, and that Hart's own 'central case' technique, combined with his view of a legal system as oriented to fostering the peaceful co-existence of its subjects, conduces to giving this moralized internal attitude a theoretical priority. Consequently—as prefigured in his notebook entries—Herbert's restricted sense of 'legal obligation', and with it his distinction between law and morality, collapses. A further object of criticism from this perspective has been Herbert's claim that when positive law 'runs out' or is ambiguous, judges simply use their discretion to decide cases according to what they think the law ought to be. This concession, it has been argued, fundamentally undermines Herbert's own claim that there is a clear distinction between law as it is and law as it ought to be. Moreover, in the hands of his successor in the Oxford Chair of Jurisprudence, Ronald Dworkin, Herbert's over-schematic account of adjudication formed the launching pad for a devastating critical onslaught on the very notion of the value-free, descriptive, general jurisprudence for which Herbert remained, all his life, a committed standard-bearer.

These and other intellectual questions about *The Concept of Law* have gradually formed themselves into both a coherent set of criticisms and a source of further jurisprudential innovation. There has also been some debate among legal theorists about the remarkable place which the volume occupies in the canon of legal theory both in and beyond the English-speaking world. Particularly in Britain, *The Concept of Law* retains its status as the 'classic' text celebrated by the contributors to the Festschrift for Herbert in 1977.

Yet sceptical voices have been raised about the conditions which fostered the growing reputation of a book which was subject to considerable criticism even in its earliest reception. Reviews had identified its under-developed account of the distinction between primary and secondary rules and its failure adequately to state the theory of legal obligation as independent of either the existence of sanctions or an overlap with morality, as well as accusing it of caricaturing Austin, Kelsen, and American Realism. As the 'socio-legal' argument that law should be studied in its social and historical context gained support, the argument was frequently heard that the *The Concept of Law* over-simplified the institutional, political, and historical foundations of law. Those sceptical of the book's intellectual value have emphasized that the major lines of criticism were already marked down in early reviews by influential figures like Jonathan Cohen and Herbert Morris, and that references to *The Concept of Law* in the leading jurisprudential commentaries used by students were initially scant and picked up only as the book's reputation grew with seemingly inexorable momentum. At their most extreme, these sceptics have attributed what they see as the intellectually puzzling success of this 'vague and parasitical little book' to factors such as the clubbish support of a powerful Oxford elite and even the personal power of Herbert Hart over the graduate students and younger colleagues whose decisions to take his book as their primary reference point undoubtedly contributed to its growing reputation.

These assertions have to be taken with a generous spoonful of salt. While reviews of *The Concept of Law* included substantial criticisms, even the most severe were quick to temper their assessment with a recognition of the book's importance. B. E. King, for example, though regretting the spin which the book would give to philosophical as opposed to sociological jurisprudence, concluded that it should be ranked 'as an outstanding contribution to legal theory'.

Inevitably, Herbert's institutional position as the Professor of Jurisprudence in Britain's most philosophically influential university, as well as his broader stature represented in honours such as his election as the President of the Aristotelian Society in 1959, his election to a Fellowship of the British Academy in 1962 and as its Vice-President in 1966 and 1967, and his election as an Honorary Bencher of the Middle Temple in 1963 would have contributed to the seriousness with which his work was received. His intellectual influence over his students cannot be doubted: liberal though he was in his direction of their work, his growing stature and reputation gave him a certain aura, and there is plenty of evidence that doctoral students and young visitors to Oxford competed jealously for his approval and attention. But the claim that he wielded this influence, either deliberately or unconsciously, to promote his own work is implausible. Even at Oxford, the heart of the alleged pro-Hart conspiracy, criticism of his work flourished, powerfully represented in a seminar run by Brian Simpson, Law Fellow at Lincoln, and his philosophy colleague Harold Cox in the mid-1960s. The book's reception by political theorists like Isaiah Berlin and John Plamenatz, who used it in their graduate seminars, was probably warmer than its reception by Herbert's Law Faculty colleagues, many of whom were quietly sceptical. And among Herbert's graduate students at the time, figures like Brian Barry, whose interests always included political economy, would hardly have been uncritical readers of *The Concept of Law* (as his subsequent work and that of other students attests).

It is also worth pondering in this context Herbert's own reaction to the book's unprecedented success, and the effect of his growing reputation on his personal and professional demeanour. As far as *The Concept of Law* is concerned, Herbert was, essentially, baffled by its reception. He was ambivalent about public praise. Recognition was important to him, but he felt uncomfortable if it was exaggerated. For example, he judged Nowell-Smith's review in the *Times Literary Supplement*, which appeared during his visit to UCLA in 1961, 'far too laudatory to be true' and worried about his American colleagues' reaction to the uncritical assessment of his work. What he had conceived as a student text was gradually being reconstructed by its reception as his *magnum opus*. On a trip to Belfast in 1967, he told William Twining that he was happy to talk about anything 'except that wretched book'. At the end of his career, he might well have agreed with the sceptics' assessment that his greatest contributions to the development of his field were his debate with Fuller, his debate with Patrick Devlin, and his sensitive interpretations of Bentham. He accepted that his claim to have produced a 'descriptive sociology', as opposed to a model which could be used by sociologists, had been misplaced. He also acknowledged publicly on many occasions the need to modify his account of legal obligation, and attempted to do so in his later work on Bentham.

The huge success of *The Concept of Law* was an intellectual inhibitor as much as a stimulus: after its publication, Herbert's return visits to the terrain of general jurisprudence were fragmentary rather than systematic, critical or interpretive rather than innovative. His intellectual vision turned instead to questions of normative political theory and social policy. When he did defend some of the central theses of *The Concept of Law* in later life, this turned out to be a frustrating and ultimately saddening experience. In late interviews, though he held to the main tenets of the book and to its attempt to reach students with a fresh, original theory of law, he was only too willing to admit that it had its flaws. Even at the pinnacle of his success, a residue of self-doubt, as well as a genuine modesty, diluted the pleasure and confidence which he gained from the book's favourable reception.

This residue of diffidence and self-doubt connected with one of Herbert's most remarkable and endearing qualities. Personally, he was almost completely unchanged—one might even say untouched—by his outstanding success. Far from being a 'front' disguising pride or ambition, Herbert's diffidence was genuine: he was surprised and pleased by the reception of his work, but continued to judge himself against the standards of philosophers like J. L. Austin, Bentham, or Mill, against whose achievements he held his own to be modest. His manner was an intriguing mixture of elements. The wavy hair now turning grey, and the lack of physical coordination partly masked by an air of scholarly *gravitas* and abstraction, Herbert certainly gave off, particularly to students, an air of distance and distinction. But the austere manner could, in a moment, be transformed by a twinkling eye and a wicked—sometimes even malicious—wit, the intellectual seriousness tempered by a keen sense of humour and interest in people. By the same token, his extreme gentleness of manner and speech could be transmuted, in the midst of discussion, to a vigorous, energetic style in which his gestures and tone of voice took on a new force. In private discussion, his face often lit up, his feelings as well as his intellect deeply engaged in any newly discovered idea or experience to be exchanged. His enthusiasm, freshness, and receptiveness to beauty, whether intellectual, natural, artistic, or literary, were undimmed by the passing years. The extraordinary impact which these distinctive qualities had on other people is exemplified by an extract from one of Antonia White's diaries of the mid-1960s, sent to Jenifer after Herbert's death by the philosopher Mary Warnock:

I enjoyed Audrey Beecham's dinner party v. much. Particularly meeting a man called Hart—professor of jurisprudence in Oxford. He talked about America and philosophy. A man I'd like to *know*. Impossible.

He radiated an aura of kindliness, even while his intellectual stature produced a kind of awe. These contrasting elements, like the reserve which could sometimes seem like remoteness, were a long-standing feature of Herbert's complex personality, and not the product of success. The diffidence related to the old doubt about his psychological suitability for intellectual work. And yet, with the benefit of hindsight, it may be seen as a key to his success: for it connected with his ability to reflect self-critically on not only his personality but also his ideas. By the standards of famous intellectuals, the extent of his desire to control his field or utter definitive statements was modest—a characteristic which perhaps also related to his sense of himself as 'not fully masculine'.

The residual diffidence also related to a further apparent contrast: that between Herbert's powerful professional persona and the much more tentative, questioning—even passive—disposition which realized itself with particular insistence in his relationship with Jenifer. As his diary, with its interweaving of the personal and the professional, reveals, despite Herbert's irritations with the course of domestic life, his strategy was essentially one of passive resistance: he retained an extraordinary ability to abstract himself from its distractions and focus on his work. His legendary absent-mindedness is evoked in an anecdote told by Robin Marsack, one of the student helpers at Manor Place in the 1970s. Dashing into the living room on his way to College, Herbert looked at her and said, 'If you see Robin, please would you ask her to . . .'! This sort of abstraction was a cause of irritation to Jenifer who, though rationalizing it as a product of Herbert's superior intellectual powers, felt the injustice of the unequal distribution of domestic responsibilities and of her large share of picking up the pieces—literally and metaphorically—in Herbert's physically and administratively chaotic personal life.

The Hart household now contained three lively teenagers, each academically gifted and with a strong personality. Herbert's involvement with its inevitably complicated routines was uneven, and the shape of his day was dictated more by the rhythms of College than of family life. But, within his emotional limits, Herbert felt a deep connection with both Jenifer and the children. Predictably, he was particularly involved in discussions about the children's education. All three were sent to a Froebel primary school, after which Joanna won a scholarship to the Oxford Girls' High School, and Charles went on to Magdalen College School. The most difficult decision concerned Adam, an independent-minded adolescent who was especially close to Jenifer. Herbert felt that the separation of boarding school—the 'very thought' of which Jenifer found 'cruel'—would be good for him. For once, Herbert's view prevailed, not least because it coincided with Adam's desire to go to boarding school. To Jenifer's regret, and surprisingly given Herbert's own unhappy experience of public school, he was sent to Bryanston, whose liberal culture—though honoured, from Adam's point of view, more in the prospectus than the regime—convinced Herbert that this would be a benign solution. As for more general interaction with his daughter and sons, though Herbert had no taste for children's games, he was an inventive story-teller who enjoyed entertaining them during long country walks, and he entered conscientiously into the children's various interests: Joanna's beloved pony and emerging plans for university (Herbert coached her carefully for her Cambridge entrance exam); Adam's passion for things electrical and mechanical; Charlie's talent for music. Though Herbert not infrequently found Adam hard to relate to, Adam has a strong memory of sitting on Herbert's lap as a small child and feeling that 'this was a very secure place to be'. And Charlie—the most reserved of the three children—had become deeply attached to Herbert. The easy quality of their relationship is well represented in a letter he wrote to Herbert at the time of the Holmes Lecture:

Dear Dad

How many people were there at your lecture, I suppose there were about 20 at the end and they were all bored but still you got your $1000. I would like to see you playing baseball. Do you know how to play yet?

We have got another girl she is Spanish . . . she is also a bit lazy she has an awfull lot of perfume she is cathalick and goes to church every Sunday.

Though work tended to come first, and while he and Jenifer felt justified in leaving the children in Nanny's care in order to enjoy walking holidays in Switzerland and trips to Spain, Italy, France, Greece, and Scandinavia, Herbert's correspondence with his children during these and professional trips reveals a closer relationship than that which would have been typical of many fathers of his class and professional standing at that time.

The children, however, were attuned to the tensions between Jenifer and Herbert, which went well beyond the intellectual arguments which were undoubtedly a binding force between them. Adam, the most questioning of the three, caused Jenifer constant anxiety with his rapid swings of mood between elation and gloom. By the time he was an early teenager, he had learned to marshal the substance of his parents' debates about political theory to astute adolescent ends, demanding of Jenifer on one occasion what legitimate basis she claimed for her authority over him. This was typical of his direct approach. At the age of eight, he had asked Jenifer 'When you divorce, will you put the interests of the children first?' But as far as Jenifer was concerned, the marriage was never under threat, and she later thought of their relationship as an efficient decision to live 'parallel lives'. In spite of the tensions, she always bore in mind the advantages of living with someone as interesting as Herbert. Yet, painfully, she also refers in her autobiography to her consciousness of the fact that no one else had ever proposed to her. Herbert, by contrast, did occasionally contemplate separation—although it seems unlikely that he ever considered it seriously. He struggled not only with the difficulty of keeping interest in a sexual relationship, but also with his distaste for Jenifer's 'asceticism' and taste for 'withering ordinary pleasures' like food: to her amused embarrassment, and in an instance which illustrates a curious failure to draw normal parental barriers, he once remarked to Joanna that 'The trouble with this marriage is that one of us doesn't like sex and the other doesn't like food'.

Yet this family structure provided a framework and a sense of continuity and belonging for which Herbert had a profound need. Twenty years into his relationship with Jenifer, and notwithstanding her affairs with other men, there were bonds of real intensity:

Things right back to sanity with Jen. . . . What a difference to the look feel and aspect of everything it makes: I hope a parallel release for her.

Herbert continued to agonize about how to recapture their old ease with each other. Towards the end of 1957 he returned again in his diary to the idea that having another child might be a solution to the intermittent distance, though he felt that 'it seems wrong to do it as a cure rather than for its own sake'. Though Herbert was not the first or the last person seriously to consider a further child as a cure for an ailing marriage, given the fact that they already had three children and that Jenifer was massively overburdened with both professional and domestic responsibilities, he must have had his doubts about the idea. But Jenifer, perhaps still reacting to the sudden end of her long affair with Berlin, had expressed a longing for another child, and Herbert felt that he could now make up for his ambivalence about the arrival of his three elder children. On holiday in Sicily in the spring of 1959, Jenifer announced to Herbert that she was pregnant:

I tell H. news at Agrigento. He doesn't seem positively pleased—but takes it fairly calmly—at any rate compared with C. [Charles]. Says he has agreed really— which is good. He then proceeds to worry about financial implications. Hopes it will be a girl because cheaper. The full responsibility of it dawns on me rather heavily after telling him—and I begin to doubt the wisdom of it all.

His first question was, 'Was it his?' I assure him it is, but make him say whose he thinks it is if not. His first guess is K. Robinson's !!! Then Walter James. [Neither of these was remotely plausible and Jenifer cannot now even recall who the latter was.] Then Stuart or Isaiah's. He wouldn't mind either of the latter. Progress.

This is evidence not only of Jenifer's attitude to the marriage but also of Herbert's underlying suspicions about her relation to Berlin: perhaps they were also at play in his joking postcard to Berlin in 1959, responding to Berlin's request for information for an obituary: 'Why is my obituary urgent? How alarming. I feel very well!'

Jenifer's and Herbert's fourth child, Jacob, was born in October 1959. It turned out to be an event with enormous ramifications not only for Jenifer and Herbert but for the whole family. Jenifer, by now 45, was pleasantly surprised by her easy pregnancy. During Jacob's birth, however, the umbilical cord was wrapped round his neck, depriving him of oxygen for a few moments. When he was delivered, the midwife would not show him to her, and she was acutely aware that something was amiss. But Jacob's health improved quickly and after a few days she was able to take him home, where he proved to be an exceptionally sunny baby. In these happier circumstances,

Jenifer more or less repressed her initial knowledge that something had gone badly wrong at the birth. In fact, Jacob's brain had been significantly damaged, and as the months and years passed, the full extent of the difficulty which he faced became all too obvious. Herbert was quicker than Jenifer to accept the full extent of Jacob's disability. When he was a few months old, and failing to show the usual signs of communication, after anxiously reading medical books, Herbert insisted that they see a paediatrician. The paediatrician confirmed that Jacob was not developing properly. Jenifer, still in denial, told the doctor that she 'supposed he would catch up'. Letters between Herbert and Jenifer during his visit to California in 1961 show that he was already aware of a significant problem which she could not acknowledge. But as the baby grew into an infant and small child, the full extent of the damage became devastatingly apparent, and Jenifer and Herbert moved frantically around medical, psychological, and educational specialists, trying to get clear advice and work out the best way of coping with Jacob's special needs. In these investigations, Herbert was the driving force, with Jenifer remaining reluctant to face up to the real scale of Jacob's disabilities.

A beautiful child with curly blond hair and features poignantly similar to Herbert's, Jacob's needs were a particular challenge because of the nature of his brain damage. He has, for example, a marked musical talent which allows him to play tunes and harmonies by ear and to transpose them into different keys on the piano; a prodigious memory; and an extraordinary, inventive verbal facility. People he dislikes are 'big black clouds'; when Jenifer is pleased with him she is 'pumped'; when she is tired, he asks if she is feeling 'crumbly'. The family's cherished Morris Minor car became, unforgettably, 'Chuckaboom' under the spell of Jacob's imagination. That these talents emerged was almost entirely due to the determination and energy with which Jenifer and Herbert approached his upbringing, for Jacob had severe behavioural problems which obstructed their expression and development. He was hyperactive and had a mania for dismantling objects such as radios, televisions, or clocks, or for emptying bookshelves and cupboards. This mania sometimes made it difficult to tell whether Manor Place, never in any case the most orderly home in Oxford, was simply untidy or had just been burgled. Conversely, he was abnormally fearful, suffering from acute anxieties which led to frequent tantrums and which could only be managed by keeping him within a very structured routine. He submitted only spasmodically and always reluctantly to the demands of hygiene and was baffled by the opprobrium attached to telling lies. As a ten-year-old, Jacob also started to have epileptic fits. All this added up to a volatile child who swung unpredictably between hyperactive, affectionate, and communicative behaviour to desperate gloom, despair, anxiety, and rage.

Jacob's arrival had a deep impact on the household at Manor Place. Adam, 15 at the time and working on his O levels, had the respite of school terms at Bryanston, while Joanna, a sixth former working towards A levels and Cambridge entrance exams, was old enough to have a certain degree of independence. Probably the greatest initial impact was on Charlie. A shy boy and still, at 11, a child himself, he had most to lose in terms of the inevitably curtailed amount of attention available from Jenifer, Herbert, and—most important of all—Nanny, who quickly bonded with and devoted herself to Jacob. Despite the clear diagnosis of the origins of Jacob's problems, which emerged during various consultations over the years, and which included an assessment of his personality problems as a form of autism, Charlie reflected wryly in later life on the fact that Jacob cracked a problem which had eluded all the ingenuity of the three elder children: how to get Jenifer's and Herbert's attention. All three of Jacob's siblings, albeit to different degrees and in different ways, believe that there was a significant social and familial dynamic to Jacob's behaviour. The fierce, possessive— even oedipal—love which he developed for Jenifer was almost certainly fed by her need in turn to be loved and needed by him.

Predictably, Jacob's presence in the family accentuated some of the tensions between Jenifer and Herbert. Apart from the evident strain of living with a disruptive and often unhappy child, and the physical and emotional impact which this must have had on the already overstretched Jenifer, the most acute source of tension was disagreement and uncertainty over the appropriate kind of medical and educational advice to seek. Even once a relatively clear diagnosis had been made, the path ahead for Jacob's education was opaque, with the local authority pronouncing him ineducable and implying that he had better simply be sent to residential care. But beneath such obvious issues there lurked a deeper source of division, which lay in the nature of Jacob's relationship to Jenifer. Though Herbert doted on Jacob as a child, Jacob's intense focus on Jenifer gradually came to be mirrored in an ambivalence towards Herbert, to whom as a teenager he often applied his negative label, 'black cloud'. Jacob, in short, became one more emotional barrier between the couple. Jacob even slept in Jenifer's room from the onset of his epileptic fits until his move to a Home Farm Trust residence at Milton Heights near Oxford in 1982.

But if Jacob's childhood put extra strains on Herbert and Jenifer as a couple, it brought out in them as individuals some extraordinary qualities which both were ready to admit might never have developed without 'the Jacob experience'. First and foremost was their dedicated and imaginative commitment to finding environments and educational opportunities which would allow Jacob to develop as fully as possible and to live as varied and happy a life as his difficulties would permit. Here they were helped by May Davidson, a sympathetic and resourceful consultant at the Warneford hospital, who persuaded an eccentric but gifted teacher who lived in a caravan on the rural edge of Oxford to set up a small 'Caravan School' to cater for Jacob and a few other disabled children. Joy Fuller, the teacher, made enormous progress, managing 'to get inside Jacob's mind and see things as he did'. As Jenifer put it:

Autism has been described as 'a feeling of being in permanent jeopardy.' Autistic children do not develop a sense of self which allows them to feel safe in the world.... They do not like being touched. They are extremely resistant to change, full of unwarranted anxieties, unable to grasp the concept of time. This leads to impatience, for since five minutes or half an hour means nothing to them, they expect things to happen at once...

Miss Fuller's technique in coping with Jacob was to give him masses of praise and to make overt statements of affection and admiration for his good qualities and abilities.... But she also talked to him about his worries, as she saw the need for him to express and formulate his problems to help him come to terms with them.... She considered it was important not to present him with anything where he might fail.... Nor should he be punished; this was not only useless but damaging. The tool used to induce more acceptable behaviour was rewards which were also given freely for any achievement. His happiness depended on feeling loved, wanted and useful. He should not see himself as a passenger, but as a contributor to life.

Herbert and Jenifer endorsed this philosophy, but one can imagine the appalling strain which it imposed on them and the rest of the family. This would have been particularly true for Jenifer. A person to whom patience did not come easily and who described herself as having 'an over-critical personality', she suddenly found herself the emotional and physical focus of Jacob's attention, constantly interrupted by him, required endlessly to repeat stories or incidents which had assumed iconic status in his febrile imagination, and to offer reassurance, not to mention to clear up after his tantrums or dismantling binges. Perhaps most difficult of all for someone with her background and temperament, she had gradually to learn that Jacob genuinely needed 'effusive expressions of praise and love'. All this she managed in a positive spirit, with remarkable energy, efficiency, and an admirable lack of self pity. No wonder that the couple's close friend Jean Floud described her as a 'reluctant saint'.

By the time Jacob had to leave Miss Fuller's Caravan School at the age of ten, he was able to read, and his behaviour and spirits were much more stable. But he was still classified by the education authority as ineducable, not least because he refused to cooperate with IQ tests. With May Davidson's help, Herbert and Jenifer battled against a wall of bureaucracy and against the wounding implication that, as academics, they were simply incapable of accepting that their son was unsuitable for education. Herbert, always the more pessimistic of the two, was beginning to feel that a residential school was inevitable: perhaps he would even have welcomed this. But Jenifer was determined to keep Jacob at home, and a solution was finally found at the Special School in Abingdon, to which Jacob travelled each day until the age of 16. Further ahead, a similar disagreement between them about Jacob's longer term future resulted, conversely, in Herbert's view prevailing. His anxieties had a productive as well as a negative side: he made financial provision through a trust fund for Jacob's future, and started pursuing options for Jacob in the event that he and Jenifer became incapable of looking after him. The Home Farm Trust provided just such a home and, notwithstanding Jenifer's regrets, Jacob finally moved to Milton Heights in 1982. He continued, however—and continued until very recently—to spend almost every other weekend at home with Jenifer. His elder sister and brothers have formed strong relationships with him, gradually assuming a wide range of responsibilities, taking him on holiday, visiting him, and having him to stay in their homes (a practice which can be very complicated: although Jacob's behaviour has stabilized, he retains a jealous dislike of babies and small children).

Beyond their particular contributions to Jacob's education and care, Herbert's and Jenifer's most impressive achievement as his parents was their remarkable flexibility and openness to his needs, irrespective of whether or not they cohered with their own value system. Probably the most spectacular example here is Jacob's conversion to Catholicism. Early on, Miss Fuller, herself a Roman Catholic, had suggested that Jacob's fears might be allayed if he could have some faith in a God who controlled the universe. Herbert and Jenifer, firm—one might even say devout—atheists though they were, readily accepted the suggestion. Miss Fuller's surmise proved to be right. A few years later, under the guidance of Karen Armstrong, one of a series of intelligent and sensitive graduates who came to live at Manor Place to help to care for him, Jacob's faith developed to the point where he wished to be baptized. Jacob was particularly attached to the Dominican church, Blackfriars, where Karen (a former nun who, ironically, was losing her faith at precisely this time) had taken him to family mass each week. Again, Jenifer and Herbert acceded readily, even fighting for Jacob's right to be baptized in the church he loved, as against the local Jesuits' claim that the Dominicans had no authority to perform the baptism. In later life, Herbert told Tony Honoré that he had come to the conclusion that, where education was concerned, even religious belief was better than a vacuum.

Given Herbert's acute capacity for anxiety, it is painful to contemplate the worries and responsibilities he was shouldering during an extraordinarily productive period in his intellectual life. While the major practical strain undoubtedly fell on Jenifer, Herbert's achievement in adapting creatively to Jacob's place in the family should not be underestimated. Aided by his well-developed capacity for drawing boundaries between his emotional and intellectual life, he maintained his professional momentum, while playing a newly active role in the family, pushing for the most complete understanding possible of Jacob's condition, and planning for his future. This was not simply a case of being well organized. When it became clear that the Home Farm Trust offered a promising long term home for Jacob, Herbert, not content with merely providing financially for Jacob's placement there, threw himself into fund-raising activities for the charity, and remained for the rest of his life one of its most devoted and effective supporters. His tolerant and empathetic understanding of Jacob's need of religion reflected his basic humanity as well as his profound liberal commitments. And, like Jenifer, his attitude to having a disabled child was unfailingly positive and free from self-pity. He was fond of Jacob; amused by him; and relaxed (his capacity for abstraction helped here) in the face of the chaos which Jacob created. Unlike Jenifer, he was not rewarded with the gift of Jacob's distinctive and touching attachment. Characteristically, he gave no inkling of the pain which this, along with the concomitant distance from Jenifer, must surely have caused him. The full ramifications of Jacob's birth, however, were still unknown in 1961, when Herbert received another prestigious invitation to visit the USA. Though guilty about the decision to 'remove himself' from the family, he accepted, and in the autumn of 1961 he set off for the social and intellectual challenges of a sabbatical in California.

CHAPTER 10

West and East, California and Israel: Law, Liberty, and Morality; Kelsen Visited; The Morality of the Criminal Law

I N early September of 1961, Herbert left Oxford for California to spend a sabbatical in the Law School and Philosophy Department at the University of California, Los Angeles (UCLA). As in 1956, he arrived in America with a strong sense of the opportunities presented by the visit, with an acute sense of the need to overcome his difficulty about 'giving my time a structure', and with the usual pre-lecturing apprehensions. Unlike in 1956, he did not take happily to his new environment. Whereas in Cambridge he had felt immediately at ease, comfortable with the East Coast way of life and attracted by its aesthetic, in 1961 he initially felt an acute distaste for California:

Scorching heat and the hard blocks of light coloured stone and glaring filling stations terribly grim unyielding and depressing even though avenues of tightly packed gracious homes with strips of green in front and trees behind compose a great deal of Westwood . . . . The whole of this part of LA seems full of aged, mostly women: Tightly permed with faces shrunk and wrinkled (due to lifting?) and painted and dressed, with scrupulous smartness, nothing out of place they look like figures from The Loved One [Evelyn Waugh's American satire] which they will shortly become poor things.

The pathos sometimes touched him:

Most pathetic on the roundabout up and down on painted horse drawn cars were only 2 old ladies. So sad: revisiting their first childhood and they looked so sad.

But Herbert's amusement at the over-preserved Los Angeles elderly was not enough to compensate for the 'ugliness and coarseness', the lack at that time of any substantial art galleries or concert halls, and the ostentatious displays of wealth which affronted him: Los Angeles was 'an inferno: terribly like Sodom and Gomorrah'; 'One has to perpetually remember', he concluded, 'not to be bluntly anti-American here'. Things improved when he moved from Westwood to a hotel near the beach in Santa Monica. Here, recovering from his first impression of parts of the coastline as 'a glaring Blackpool', he was beguiled by the beauty of the ocean and intrigued by the endless variety of people, cafés, styles of food. Over the three months, one senses Herbert's attitude to California gradually changing from distaste to curiosity:

Remarkable walk on Friday evening to Venice along sands in sunset: very beautiful. Then pub at Venice—all very strange distorted faces every conceivable race queers lesbians drug addicts . . . . Hieronymus Bosch effect as we sat round a square bar.

But his feelings for the West Coast never matched his affection for the East, and as he struggled to adapt to the heat and to an environment which revolved round the car to the extent that it was all but impossible to walk through the city, his discomfort spilled over into ambivalence about the intellectual environment, too. This led to some particularly pungent character sketches in his diary. One colleague had 'too broad, soft and gushing a mind; no stimulus, no sparks', while another 'has something—a bit coarser and bouncier than last time—Pleased with himself, perhaps with some justice'.

Herbert was met at the airport and looked after in his early weeks at UCLA by his former doctoral student, Herbert Morris. Morris remembers the familiar mix of intellectual intensity and physical chaos. On Herbert's first weekend at Santa Monica, Morris met him to take him swimming. Herbert appeared in the hotel lobby dressed in his bath robe. Swallowing his embarrassment, Morris escorted Herbert onto the beach, warning him that the waves would be too strong for him to swim in his glasses. Undeterred, Herbert plunged into the ocean bespectacled, and duly became detached from his indispensable visual aid. The glasses were the only pair which he had brought with him, and there ensued a complex set of communications with Jenifer to get another pair sent out. Another story touches on the most profound source of Herbert's dislike of this part of California. In October, Bel Air suffered a devastating fire which wiped out over 400 houses, including the homes of some UCLA academics. The fire was clearly visible from the Philosophy Department, where colleagues watched in dismay as the fire raged out of control. Amid this horror, Morris remembers being shocked by Herbert's lack of sympathy: he felt that Herbert was almost revelling in the destruction of the property of the richest inhabitants of Los Angeles. His impression is confirmed by both Herbert's diary and a letter to Jenifer: 'For once, disaster falls on the *rich* not poor (average cost of home: $70,000 stuffed with mink, jewels, antiques, etc.) Maniac town this: The houses are built in [woods] . . . the plants contain *oil* which explodes! Quite unforgettable sight.' And in his diary: 'A left-wing god would be nice.' A certain moralistic asceticism which was an offshoot of Herbert's egalitarian sympathies and which brought with it an increasing distaste for lavish displays of wealth was at the root of this episode, and of his general discomfort with the yawning gap between rich and poor in this part of America. Indeed, his feeling about what he saw as the 'grossness' of Los Angeles sometimes verged on the extreme:

Everybody on a vast scale: I hated them: felt like welcoming their destruction so rich and ugly did they appear.

Morris was assiduous in escorting Herbert around a variety of sight-seeing and social occasions: Herbert was touched by the attentions, but in the first weeks found the social life exhausting and struggled to identify people with whom he could have 'real talk'. As at Harvard, he was struck by a certain lack of rigour in American habits of discussion, and he retreated into the unappealing Oxford habit of reflecting in his diary on how clever—or how lacking in intellectual acumen—his new colleagues appeared to be: 'astringent Jenifer-like quality first rate' or 'essentially second rate: commands no firm grip . . . . Talking to him about philosophy isn't stimulating as an education. No doubt', he concluded, with a whiff of disdain, 'a mine of well ordered information about the law'. Even with those with whom one would have expected him to find common cause, he found it hard to establish an intellectual rapport. Though he found Morris personally sympathetic and felt acutely the pain which his wife's depression was obviously causing (on one visit, Herbert recorded in his diary, 'A sense (I have) of un-permanence or quasi-disaster impending there'), the old reserve between student and professor remained, reinforced by Herbert's resistance to the retributive approach to criminal responsibility, attuned to the moral emotions, which Morris was developing. Though Morris gave him his paper 'Persons and Punishment', Herbert—uncharacteristically—never commented. In the 1980s, on his last trip to LA, he surprised Morris by saying, out of the blue, that he felt guilty about him. It is likely that he was regretting both his intellectual inflexibility and his failure to talk to Morris directly about his wife's problems. Morris, who had been pained by Herbert's reserve with him, was touched and in some ways relieved by this unexpected confession so many years later.

Herbert's initial ambivalence about his new colleagues was in part a defence mechanism. In the early weeks, he worried about whether he had enough material for his lectures and classes—a worry which dissipated once he convinced himself that it would be reasonable to draw on some of his published work (a solution which he nonetheless felt to be short-changing UCLA). He also felt that some of the philosophers—they included linguistic philosophers A. and D. Kaplan and the elderly Viennese logical positivist Rudolf Carnap—were not showing much interest in him, though this impression changed as the weeks went by. As at Harvard, he was struck by the 'comparative splendour of the law school in relation to the philosophy department', but worried that 'the Law School seminar threatens to be unmanageable. Too many: too formal for a seminar: lawyers too stupid, philosophers too few and unacquainted with legal terms. But we shall see. Need to alter the seating—room with a table to sit round'.

In fact, the seminars on criminal responsibility quickly took off, generating lively discussions among the law as well as the philosophy students. In the context of this success and of philosophical discussions at evening meetings of graduate students, Herbert's attitude gradually warmed and, though he noted his colleagues' surprise at his 'brisker' debating style, the diary character sketches become more appreciative: 'acute, but understanding and able to concede points'. He was particularly impressed by Carnap, one of the intellectual inspirations for his colleague Freddie Ayer in Vienna: 'I tried a little unsuccessfully to convince him of importance of JLA [Austin] . . . . But that sort of thing didn't go over . . . . He was delightful and funny . . . . The sense of a large generosity of mind and old age happiness was very strong. Nice social atmosphere of their little wooden house in a garden—blazing wood fire . . . . Lovely unassuming lunch of chicken and mushrooms, fruit salad and ice cream. Such a change from overlavish America.' Morris took him on several occasions to Santa Barbara to hear presentations by Herbert Fingarette, who was applying psychology and psychoanalytic ideas to issues of criminal responsibility and causation. Herbert was impressed by Fingarette, with whom he had a stimulating discussion of causation, though he was amazed by Fingarette's argument that taking the unconscious into account would expand rather than contract the scope of individual responsibility and blame. Herbert also had contact with colleagues in Stanford and Berkeley, enjoying for example a discussion of a recently published paper by Lon Fuller with a group of Berkeley lawyers including the Australian torts lawyer John Fleming and sociologist of law Philip Selznick.

As always, these intellectual activities were interspersed with a catholic variety of other less taxing enjoyments. A trip to the MGM studios at Hollywood produced 'a great impression of worthlessness. Nothing to do with art'. By contrast, in San Francisco, whose colourful streets and magnificent bay immediately captured his imagination, Herbert wandered happily in Chinatown, even indulging in a consultation with a handwriting and character reading expert. He solemnly recorded her view that though he had an 'intense and immediate awareness of people', he tended to withdraw and that therefore 'people think you stand apart'. He spent a day watching the proceedings at a San Francisco court, which he found impressive: 'Everyone appears quite human—good cross-examination . . . . Some sentiment/common humanity where we lose it—thought v well of America at last for first time this trip.' He also struck up one or two personal relationships outside the professional context: 'Seen a good deal of Patrick Wilson, very nice, acute individual: a hint of sadness and loneliness. He lives in a dreary little wood hut of 2 rooms in a garden. Has wonderful records which he played me. Told him about Adam and "beat" [Adam's latest teenage interest] . . . . He at once understands and says—how marvellous— "What is there to worry about?" Not perhaps if it were here in this looser structure.' The comment reveals that Herbert was beginning to see the attractions of the relaxed social culture of the West Coast. And a further set of recordings of contemporary music, as well as volumes of the new American poetry, found their way back to Manor Place as a result of Herbert's engagement with his West Coast environment.

During these months, apart from his teaching preparation and scholarly writing, Herbert was, intriguingly, learning—or rather re-learning— Hebrew. And he was reading widely, exploring Darwin, Sartre, Bentham, Spinoza, a biography of Yeats, Genet, Day Lewis, and George Eliot. His reading prompted not only intellectual speculation but also, on occasion, introspective reveries. *Adam Bede* he found 'full of moral insight and Hegelian turns about unconscious burden of our speech and thought', while in Genet—the open Californian culture was reaching him at last—he admired and wondered at the graphic depiction of buggery and 'obscenity (if such a thing exists) of an impressive kind'. Yet more deeply, what spoke to him in the Yeats biography was emotional: 'Fascinating but the sexual background depressed me: too near home in a very different way. Yeats . . . thought probably rightly his creative activity went together with his lust and his lust (like mine) seems divorced . . . from his love. But a future of bawdy old age is terrifying . . . . What a mess.' The reading touched off a bout of depressive introspection which wavered, characteristically, between public and private concerns:

Something terrifying in the ugliness and crudity of American prosperity—the over huge portions of food, the numbed deadness of the old faces, the garishness of the streets . . . . [The book] makes me reflect on what for me the recurring moving symbols are . . . . The (English) country, boyhood—this is the age at which I am stuck subliminally. Also reading Day Lewis plangent autobiography. He says

his adolescence lasted till the 30s. Other elements in the depression—the 'news'
(Berlin) [the construction of the Berlin wall]. But I must substitute for this
some constructive program. At the moment listening to Othello on the excellent
FM wireless I have bought . . . books round me which I want to read and quiet
and comfort. Unique opportunity for something or other: But I am a bit troubled by pervasive sense of failure with Jenifer or rather with thought of what life
could be like had all that gone well. If I can get her here in December we might
start yet again—But it's getting late! Absence makes in this case the heart at least
beat again if not fonder. Her letters read as if she meant me to know she still was
emotionally moved as indeed her weeping showed, though her tears are never
direct expressions of feelings.

Plus: I must have a schedule of working hours and avoid both sense of aimless-
ness and fatigue.

Though he found letters home 'a great comfort', he worried about the
children and about getting cut off in America if the Cuban missile crisis
should lead to war: as in 1956, the 'despicable' local papers had to be supplemented by a subscription to *The Times*. An offer to visit Princeton the
following year was refused on the ground that 'I can't break off from Oxford
and family too frequently even if I bring back dollars . . .'. And amid the
intermittently introspective diary entries, ageing is a persistent preoccupation: he quoted an amusing poem by a member of the UCLA English
Department, which touched on both his sense of life passing by and his
contempt for the wealthy Los Angeles dwellers' attempts to use their money
to escape the effects of time:

> In lobby, lounge or restaurant they sink
> Deep in their chairs, regard the empty wall
> And stroke their pearls, their foxes and their mink
> As the indolence of age assaults them all.

He worried in particular about his 'diminished powers of concentration and
mind for writing'. Write, however, he must: for as well as his weekly lectures
to the philosophy students at UCLA and his seminars in the Law School,
he had a large number of other speaking engagements. These included a
trip to Eugene, Oregon. Here he survived a 'Solid dinner with lawyers in
Country Club. Dean—grave, poised and a bully probably (to his juniors) of
a fairly beneficial kind'. His host Bob Summers presented Herbert with his
criticisms of *The Concept of Law*, prompting Herbert to 'complain that he
reads my book as if he were construing a will! No doubt it ought to stand up
to that test but it won't'. His personal connection with Summers is evident:
'Very nice he is. Home to lunch with his wife. V. beautiful, sensitive and
bright—a bit sad possibly. Bob works too much and doesn't see enough of

her—so I tell him work comes second! Very bright little boys: so I thought rather sadly about Jacob.' Herbert also gave presentations at Santa Barbara, Vancouver ('heavenly place: brilliant cold autumn lovely after this perpetual Californian summer') and the University of Southern California. But by far the most significant obligations were at Stanford, where he had agreed to give the Harry Camp Lectures, and at Berkeley, where he was scheduled to undertake a public debate with Hans Kelsen.

Though *The Concept of Law* had now appeared, Herbert continued to struggle with his theory of legal obligation and to think about the precise shape of his account of rules. The debate with Kelsen offered him a direct exchange with the man who was his clearest positivist rival and whose theory, though structurally similar to Herbert's, differed from it in significant ways. Both men insisted on a clear distinction between law and morality, and subscribed to the idea that the validity of legal norms was a matter of their source or pedigree rather than their content. But while Herbert described his as a 'social fact' theory of law, the existence of law ultimately depending on empirical matters such as official compliance with a secondary rule of recognition, Kelsen distanced the empirical as much as the moral, insisting on the need for a 'pure' theory of law in which validity—the 'distinctive mode of existence of legal norms'—was generated by reference to norms higher up the chain within a closed, hierarchical system. While Herbert's theory flowed from nineteenth-century English positivism and empiricist philosophy, Kelsen's came out of a very different stable. An Austrian Jew whose career had been marked by political adversity, Kelsen had been ousted from his position as a member of the Austrian Constitutional Court in 1930 as a result of his stance in upholding the validity of remarriage for Roman Catholics. He moved to a Chair at the University of Cologne, only to be dismissed in 1933 in the wake of the first wave of anti-Semitic Nazi laws. After seven years in Geneva, he emigrated to the USA in the spring of 1940. With a poor command of spoken English, he had a difficult transition; but, with his distinguished publications and formidable intellect, he gradually made a place for himself as a successful academic in the US. Kelsen was appointed Professor of Political Science at Berkeley in 1945. His European theoretical background, however, remained with him, and it shaped his theory of law in decisive ways.

The difference which their contrasting intellectual traditions made to Herbert's *Concept of Law* and Kelsen's *Pure Theory of Law*, as well as the distinctly neo-Kantian flavour of some of Kelsen's work, is best illustrated by contrasting the two men's conceptions of the ultimate source of validation for legal rules: Herbert's 'rule of recognition' and Kelsen's 'Grundnorm' or 'Basic Norm'. For Herbert, the rule of recognition is not a valid rule of the system, because there is no higher rule from which it can derive its authority: we have to say, simply, that the rule inheres in the practices of officials. For Kelsen, whose theory was once described as 'an exercise in logic but not in life', this violated the ultimate philosophical precept that an 'ought' can never be derived from an 'is'. Since norms exist in the sphere of 'ought', they can be created (and hence validated) only by reference to other norms. Logically, therefore, an ultimate norm, rather than a factual social practice, must sit at the apex of the system. So a 'basic norm', which exists as a hypothesis, a tacit presupposition, of 'juristic consciousness', was logically necessary. The basic norm, unlike Herbert's rule of recognition, always has the same content: as Herbert put it, it postulates that the highest norms among the norms 'valid and effective' in a system—the 'historically first constitution'—ought to be obeyed. So hypothesized, it infuses the system with validity, allowing, in combination with other norms specifying the hierarchical ordering of legal sources, jurists to interpret law as a non-contradictory field of normative meaning. The effectiveness of the system was merely a necessary and not a sufficient condition for its validity. For Kelsen, the basic norm was a philosophical necessity. To Herbert, it looked like a superfluous theoretical construct: 'If a constitution specifying the various sources of law is a living reality in the sense that the courts and officials of the system actually identify the law in accordance with the criteria it provides, then the constitution is accepted and actually exists. It seems a needless reduplication to suggest that there is a further rule to the effect that the constitution (or those who "laid it down") are to be obeyed.'

But this fundamental difference should not disguise the structural similarity between Herbert's and Kelsen's theories. In each of them, the ultimate rule or norm plays a key role in identifying the rules or norms of the system and hence in identifying the system itself. And, despite Herbert's more empiricist bent, the two theories take a similarly circumscribed view of the scope of jurisprudence. Imagine, for example, a situation in which a court is confronted with a law passed by a new regime which has seized power unconstitutionally through a *coup d'état*. The Southern Rhodesian courts, faced in the 1960s with just such a case, tried to apply Kelsen's theory, asking themselves whether the 'Grundnorm' had changed. But this was a misapplication, for the implication of Kelsen's theory is that, in such a situation, the law has 'run out', and the judges are in the terrain of politics and morality. Kelsen endorsed the view that Herbert defended in his debate with Fuller: that the strength of the positivist position is its capacity clearly to specify the limits of law, rather than to pretend that there is a legal or constitutional solution to every problem. It is perfectly true that neither theory gives any guidance to judges in the transitional situation. But this was no part of either Herbert's or Kelsen's ambition in their positivist work. For in unstable situations, the identity of a legal system has to do not with philosophical logic or formal legal validity but with power relations, institutional structures, historical and cultural norms. We return, in short, to the limits of a philosophical theory of law.

The intellectual division between empiricist and metaphysical orientations which Herbert's and Kelsen's theories epitomize has long been a key feature of the field of analytic jurisprudence. This is particularly true in countries like Israel and the USA, where patterns of migration have brought both traditions with them. So the prospect of a meeting between the two giants of legal positivism gave rise to considerable intellectual excitement among American legal theorists. It turned out to be a memorable occasion. Herbert and Kelsen debated for two hours in front of a large audience, including David Daube, the Oxford Roman Lawyer, then visiting Berkeley, and Ronald Dworkin who, Herbert learnt, was now contemplating leaving legal practice to work on jurisprudence.

Arrived last Friday after early start from Santa Monica at Berkeley just in time to lunch with philosophers before a fantastic debate with Kelsen in presence of about 250 people—mainly law students and faculty and philosophers (including Daube! And Dworkin!). I thought it would be a terrible mess but it turned out not so bad. I had sent beforehand a careful letter identifying three points for discussion . . . . We more or less kept to the point . . . . K is marvellous both for 80 and as such. Short v. grave humorous. He yelled and shouted a bit, reading his replies, but there was some kind of contact. I saw him at tea in his house on the Sunday there he was v. reasonable: extraordinarily quick to pick up points. Disposed to agree about my criticisms of his talk of *validity* of the b. n. [basic norm] or of any rules which exist as actual practice. V. interested in J.L.A.'s *performatives* and wants to read what he has written.

As Herbert related to Stanley Paulson some years later, Kelsen told him:

I can well understand your interest and that of others in J. L. Austin. I, too, am interested in his work. What I cannot understand is your interest in that charlatan Wittgenstein!

Kelsen appears to have brought with him to the USA the scars of life in a Vienna marked by bitter intellectual rivalries.

Kelsen was generally regarded as having had the better of the Berkeley debate, though it was Herbert who provided the most unforgettable moment, falling backwards off his chair as Kelsen declared in stentorian tones, 'Norm is norm!' Herbert nonetheless felt that he had emerged with his reputation and dignity intact, and that his contact with Kelsen 'made me see more clearly what to say about him'. The latter's attitude to Herbert remained, however, ambivalent: he liked to say that everything which was right in *The Concept of Law* came from him, whereas everything which was wrong was Herbert's.

Herbert later wrote up his memoir of the occasion as an article for the *UCLA Law Review*, 'Kelsen Visited'. The first object of the debate had to do with the sense in which legal statements are at once factual and normative: on the one hand, they describe the legal position; on the other, they prescribe behaviour. When a lawyer says to her client, 'you ought to pay your taxes', she at once makes a factual claim (the Revenue Act, which so provides, is an existing legal enactment) and invokes a norm (the Revenue Act provides that you ought to pay your taxes). In this context, Herbert pushed the idea that there is room, in explaining the nature of law, for the possibility of a third option between factual and normative statements, and that Kelsen is perverse in denying this. This third type of statement—a 'detached' normative statement 'from a point of view'—captures the fact that the lawyer will use normative language even if she believes the tax system to be unjust: she is speaking 'as a lawyer', and while the distinctively 'legal' sense of ought which she uses is entirely meaningful, it derives its meaning from a background social fact—the existence of a legal order and of this particular rule within it. The idea of detached normative statements from a point of view presaged further developments in Herbert's own theory of legal obligation and anticipated in some respects the imaginative readings of Kelsen produced by his future student Joseph Raz.

The second focus of the debate had to do with Kelsen's claim that all legal norms take the form of a conditional direction to judges to apply sanctions on breach of the rule: 'If Smith does not pay her taxes, apply a sanction.' Here, Herbert's objection, returning to one of the central arguments of *The Concept of Law*, was that such an invariant structure is incapable of distinguishing genuinely different sorts of norms. It equates, for example, a norm whose function is to penalize behaviour with a norm whose function is only to tax behaviour: the rule about failure to pay taxes is a penal law, but the charge of taxes upon earned income is not intended to penalize earning. In the context of the debate, however, Herbert had to concede that he had not entirely managed to explain this as a difference within the structure of legal rules themselves. Though he believed that this could be done by means of differentiating distinct forms of internal attitude to rules, the account in his book had blurred the boundary between this and an argument about the external, social functions of the rules.

The final topic of the debate was Kelsen's striking claim that, notwithstanding the absolute separation of law and morality, there was no possibility of any conflict between the two: logically, it must always be possible to interpret the world as a 'non-contradictory normative field of meaning'. Here, Herbert felt himself to be on firm ground: he argued that if we think of normative statements as meaning 'I have reason to do X'—say, pay my taxes—then there is no illogicality or contradiction in saying that I have both a reason to pay my taxes and a reason not to pay my taxes. This is particularly clear where the reasons come from different systems of norms: I may have a legal reason to pay my taxes, but a moral reason not to if, for example, I believe that they will be used for immoral purposes such as the pursuit of an unjust war. To deny the possibility of such conflicts is to assume, Herbert argued, that we speak or even live only as a lawyer or only as a moralist—an argument which relates back to his idea of detached yet genuinely normative statements from specific points of view.

Intrigued by Kelsen, and stimulated by the debate, Herbert began to lecture on and continued to write about Kelsen when he returned to Oxford. This work led a few years later to another significant paper, 'Kelsen's Doctrine of the Unity of Law', which developed the themes explored in the debate. Two things are striking about the later paper. The first is Herbert's continuing commitment to keeping abreast with general developments in philosophy and applying them to jurisprudence. This is reflected in his appeal to developments in modern logic to push forward his argument about the possibility of various kinds of apparently conflicting statements co-existing without fundamental contradiction. The second striking feature is the paper's fundamental assault on the structure of Kelsen's entirely normative theory in terms of its counterintuitive implications—an assault which emphasized the importance of the empiricist aspect of his own theory. According to Kelsen, Herbert pointed out, if the UK parliament passed a Soviet Laws Validity Act incorporating Soviet into British law, this would mean that Soviet law was indeed part of British law—part of the same system. Similarly, and more realistically, Kelsen's theory implies that the law of former colonies to whom independence has been constitutionally granted are still part of British law, because they stretch back in an unbroken chain of validity to the British constitution. These odd implications, Herbert argues, can only be avoided by a more factual notion of practices of recognition by courts: Kelsen's logical normative relations of validation are neither necessary nor sufficient to explain the unity or identity of legal systems. In making this powerful argument, Herbert was sustaining the main theses of *The Concept of Law*. Yet it is hard to escape the conclusion that he was simultaneously demonstrating the need for a more culturally and institutionally grounded account of the identity of a legal system than analytical jurisprudence is capable of providing.

The debate with Kelsen behind him, Herbert confronted a yet more substantial obligation in the delivery of the three Stanford lectures, scheduled to take place after Christmas. But he was beginning to feel anxious about the family, and in the light of Jenifer's unwillingness to come to California, he decided to return to Oxford for a ten-day break at Christmas. Jenifer had, as usual, been working too hard; she had also had to handle the fact that Jacob had to undergo a minor operation ('Poor little tummy', Herbert wrote) and her own anxieties about nuclear testing. 'What on earth do you mean about the bomb?', Herbert asked, 'Scientists here say they are *delighted* at first reports of fall out—much less and less bad than anticipated . . . . What are your signs of radioactivity? . . . Forget that bomb!' He had been corresponding regularly with Joanna, who had just started her natural sciences degree at New Hall in Cambridge. 'Just a line to bolster your spirits on the threshold but I don't imagine they will need it, only I remember the first few days as intimidating and puzzling', he had written to her in October. Even in her women's college, Joanna was immediately critical of the sexual politics of the university: 'Cambridge is as reactionary, re women, as all that is it? Astonishing I wonder why?' said Herbert, with his usual rationalist's reluctance to confront prejudice. He was clearly happy at Joanna's transition to adult and university life, pleased that she had visited his old friends Victor and Tess Rothschild 'Victor is great fun don't you think—a case of *clear* obscenity and excellent employment of wealth. Tess I like v. much, her melancholy has a kind of autumnal flavour'; and he enjoyed exchanging views and gossip about Cambridge. Within a few weeks, however, Joanna had decided that sciences were not for her, and that she should transfer to philosophy. Herbert readily accepted that if her heart was not in sciences, the change was sensible. But, despite his repeated professions of reluctance to give her either advice about philosophy or his views of the Cambridge faculty, he proceeded to bombard her with both:

Yes: I agree with most of what you say about Cambridge philosophy being on the upgrade. Wisdom (who is one of the nicest of men) has done some wonderful things . . . but for years has just repeated himself . . . . Bamborough is very solemn and I should have thought a good tutor. Don't be frightened! There's nothing very formidable there but you can learn from him . . . . I'll spare you all sorts of advice I am tempted to give as to how to do philosophy except this 1) Don't plunge into the more advanced areas before the elements e.g. *DON'T* read Hampshire, Wittgenstein etc till you've done a lot of simpler things. If you do you'll find a peculiar (well known) kind of confusion and despair developing . . . . But I'll stop lecturing—till Christmas.

The letter, however, continued for two further pages, warning Joanna off various tutors: 'Snobbish and a pseudo'; 'A time-wasting vampire. Don't sit up hours with him. There is nothing to be learnt from talking to him. No doubt you have discovered most of this for yourself'. A more substantial concern, however, had to do with Joanna's temptation to leave Cambridge and move to London to live with her boyfriend, Alan Ryan, who was now setting out on an academic career in political theory, and of whom both Herbert and Jenifer had already become very fond. Herbert's visit home threatened to present him with a number of distracting family issues:

Problems with Jo, Adam and little Jacob. Jenifer too. Not sure what I shall discover.

He travelled back *via* New York, where he met up with Herbert Wechsler, and Harvard, where he visited Burton Dreben, Morton White, and John Rawls; and where Dean Griswold, pleased by his praise for the 'co-operative competition' of the Law School, offered him another visiting professorship. This was a moment of much-needed calm: Herbert exclaimed over 'Cambridge: how beautiful and civilized after LA' and reflected 'Nice morning on my own (God: how indispensable that is, for me, for happiness)'. Once he reached Oxford, George Paul, his economist wife Margaret, and Jean Austin were delighted to see him, and Herbert enjoyed his time with the children, discussing Joanna's move to philosophy and her relationship with Alan; pondering Adam's passion for beat music; appreciating Charlie's brightness at his 'less exacting phase'; and playing with Jacob ('nice to see [him] actually walking and much progress and charm. But it's absolutely clear to me he is quite abnormal. Hope I am wrong. What difficulties ahead'). Writing to thank Morton White for his hospitality in Cambridge, the preoccupations of family life and Herbert's worries about Jacob are clear: 'I've done and thought *nothing* since return. The children's upheavals though less volcanic, thank God, than they threatened are sufficiently digressing.' Thanking White for his invitation to visit Harvard again, Herbert continued that both he and Jenifer would enjoy this but 'Difficulties do rather loom'.

Herbert was, as ever, keen to try to re-establish a warmer relationship with Jenifer. Despite the fact that she was pleased with his carefully planned Christmas presents, his hopes were disappointed:

Absolute non-success with J: grating all round and very little communication. Hell. Of course allowances—overwork; strain; change of life; my deficiencies . . . but I felt and feel *angered* as not before. What to do? Can neither talk nor act to any purpose at present. Let it run or force a discussion?

This unusual expression of anger carried itself over into a worry that Nanny—the linchpin of the household and, to Jenifer's occasional irritation, one of Herbert's greatest fans—was being overworked amid the new pressures caused by Jacob's arrival. He felt, deep down, that the Christmas trip had revealed that Jenifer found his absence 'some sort of gap' and that 'I never should or could [separate]'. Yet this first moment of self-confessed anger seems to have marked a further diversion of Herbert's emotional energies away from his attempt to rebuild things with Jenifer. Instead, he increasingly channelled his affections into less challenging and complex objects. These included a close involvement in Joanna's and Alan's partnership, which offered him the combination of intellectual commun- ication and a family connection of an emotionally manageable kind. (His fondness for Alan did not, however, prevent him from being horrified when the couple decided to marry in 1962, when Joanna was just 19. He expressed his pessimistic feelings by walking round the wedding reception at New College remarking that at least he had the money to pay for a divorce.)

Back in California after a difficult journey delayed for almost twelve hours by bad weather, his attention turned to the Stanford lectures. He had already done some work on them before Christmas:

Today a lovely walk back by sea at sunset from pier. Foam—blue almost—sea— shot silk—lemon: surf rides delicious cool air. Must now get down to composing my 3 Stanford Lectures . . . . Should not be too difficult but I feel lethargic till I am forced to produce. Could be quite an amusing attack on J F Stephen, English judges and as it's got to be published worth taking some trouble.

On this occasion, the writing process seems to have been reasonably relaxed:

I wrote out fully 2 of the 3 'Camp' lectures during the first weekend after my return [from Oregon and Berkeley]—partly in sun below pier on sands and finished the third in note form.

And the occasion itself was enjoyable:

Lectures at Stanford seem very successful—large audience. Campus a pastoral rather bland affair.

Out of these favourable omens came one of Herbert's most important contributions to the political theory and social policy debates of the 1960s: *Law, Liberty and Morality*. The ostensible jumping off point for the lectures was his debate in 1959 with Patrick Devlin. But there was a deeper intellec- tual preoccupation which shaped his development of the earlier exchange, and which allowed him to revive a further aspect of the utilitarian tradi- tion which had been neglected in twentieth-century legal philosophy. This was the idea that the project of jurisprudence should be not only to provide a clear, descriptive concept of law, but also—though as a *separate* task—to elaborate a framework for the critique of law and for law reform. His positivist view asserted that law could have any content whatsoever: hence it could be used to further the welfarist and other goals of the social-democratic government of which Herbert approved and which he saw as to some extent reflected in successive post-war Labour administrations. Yet the moral and practical question of how law *should* be used—its proper limits and its desirable scope—was pressing. Herbert's work, particularly in the field of criminal justice, had become increasingly concerned with these prescriptive questions. He now turned to the elaboration of a liberalism which finds its roots in J. S. Mill's *On Liberty* and which somewhat later found expression, in revised form, in John Rawls' hugely influential *A Theory of Justice*.

In the three Stanford Lectures, Herbert argued, as against Devlin and the Victorian judge and criminal law theorist James Fitzjames Stephen, that democratic states are not entitled to enforce moral standards for their own sake. With the exception of certain special cases where paternalistic legislation can be justified, the state should respect individual freedom, intervening only to prevent or punish the commission of tangible harms. In the first lecture, Herbert delineated this central question, returning to Devlin's analogy between the enforcement of morality and the punishment of treason, which he had attacked in his *Listener* article. He then used this critical analysis to illustrate the difference between Mill's liberal position, that coercion should only be used to prevent harm to others, and Devlin's conservative stance, that a society which fails to enforce its common morality by means of law risks disintegration. In the second lecture, with his US audience in mind, he took as his focus the wide range of American offences dealing with aspects of sexual behaviour. He drew attention to the dearth of empirical evidence on how these offences are enforced, while criticizing the huge discretionary powers which their existence accorded to the police. He then launched into an assault on Devlin's argument that the historical fact that states have regularly passed legislation such as laws proscribing cruelty to animals shows that experience has held the legal enforcement of morals to be socially important.

These examples, Herbert insisted, can be explained in terms of other rationales: a utilitarian concern with animals' suffering or a paternalistic concern to protect the vulnerable. In relation to paternalistic legislation which limits individuals' freedom in the interest of their broader welfare, Herbert went on to argue that Mill's trenchantly anti-paternalistic stance could be modified without fundamental revision of the harm principle. And, he argued, this was appropriate: given changing ideas of human nature, it was no longer justifiable to judge the issue, as Mill had done, on the assumption that all citizens have 'the attitudes, knowledge and capacity for self control of a middle aged man'. It was right, for example, to allow a limited place for protective legislation not only in relation to the young or mentally incompetent but also in fields such as compulsory seatbelt laws or the regulation of drugs. He defended a form of physical paternalism, limiting people's freedom in order to prevent them harming themselves. But he maintained that this was distinct from moral paternalism or the legal enforcement of morality 'as such': so-called 'legal moralism'. He also conceded that states could be justified in prohibiting public nuisances: where, for example, a public display of obscenity causes offence, there may be a harm-based rationale for proscription. Taking a yet more controversial example, he went so far as to accept that where the religious associations of marriage are strong, bigamy might become a matter of public concern justifying criminalization. The assessment of harm, however, had to be a rigorous one, for otherwise such public nuisance legislation may amount to proscribing behaviour merely because the majority is against it. And it was always necessary to produce evidence for the harms allegedly caused by offensive behaviour, and for the positive effects of using criminal law to enforce prevailing mores. The line between a harm-based rationale and physical paternalism on the one hand and legal moralism on the other must, in short, be preserved.

In the final lecture, Herbert indicted Devlin's position that the criminal law should be used to proscribe any immorality to which the 'man on the Clapham omnibus' would react with 'intolerance, indignation and disgust': this, he argued, was an extreme form of legal moralism. In the absence of any empirical evidence that a failure to enforce morality led to social collapse, Devlin's argument amounted to the proposition that any widely held public prejudice justified criminalization, and that any change in common morality constituted, conceptually, a 'disintegration' of the social order. In Herbert's view, Devlin's argument overplayed—without adducing any empirical evidence—the power of law as a socially stabilizing and educative force. What good, he asked, can outweigh the cost in human misery of enforcing morality? Social moralities can be multiple and mutually tolerant: they do not have intrinsic worth; rather, their value is to secure happiness for individuals. A truly moral attitude is distinguished not by any particular substance but by its formal value: self-control, impartiality, reciprocity are 'universal virtues', but they can be mapped onto many different moralities. Their value cannot, however, be preserved by legal coercion: it is voluntary rather than coerced compliance which is morally valuable. There were lessons here, too, Herbert argued, for democratic theory. Mill's concern with the dangers of majoritarian democracy does not make him anti-democratic: representative democracy may be the best form of government, yet it is still subject to moral criticism; the majority should rule but this does not entail that they are always right. Devlin's argument, Herbert concluded, belonged to the 'pre-history of morality': an era which celebrated conformity through fear, the gratifying of hatred through retributive punishments, symbolic denunciation of immorality, moral conservatism. In its place, he argued, we should put a firmly Enlightenment and liberal vision of tolerance, a concern with human suffering, and a respect for human freedom, tempered only by limited paternalism.

The book which came out of the lectures, *Law, Liberty and Morality*, is written with a passionate intensity which stands out among Herbert's work. It remains, 40 years after its publication, the resounding late twentieth-century statement of principled liberal social policy, articulating a vision of a social democratic state which should use the criminal law sparingly in the interests of individual liberty. Herbert was particularly eloquent in calling attention to the misery which can be caused by the enforcement of morality: particularly in the area of sexuality, where law uses coercion to enforce standards which may conflict with people's deepest feelings, he denounced the legal enforcement of morality as a form of cruelty. The reviews of *Law, Liberty and Morality*, though largely positive, provide some telling evidence that in the first half of the supposedly permissive, 'swinging' sixties, ignorance and prejudice about homosexuality were alive and well. In the *Law Quarterly Review*, J. A. Coutts worried that the legalization of male homosexuality would open the way to 'corrupting others', while in the *Modern Law Review*, C. P. Harvey, a judge, was sympathetic to legalization, but only because of the need to reduce the risk of blackmail used by one homosexual partner on the break-up of a relationship. He also saw fit to congratulate Herbert on 'a remarkable feat' in having 'worked up such a dazzling display from such squalid material'.

Herbert's argument was not without its flaws. His impeachment of Devlin for failing to provide any empirical evidence to support his contention that the enforcement of a society's morality is necessary to preserve social stability was, it must be granted, a classic case of the pot calling the kettle black: Herbert himself provided no psychological or sociological evidence for the empirical claims which he made. A further weakness is the fact that his all-important limiting condition—the specification of what counts as harm—is not self-defining. Is, for example, depression or anxiety caused by drug-taking, or anxiety, fear, or offence occasioned by witnessing public displays of obscenity, to count as harm which justifies state coercion? Indubitably, these psychological states are unpleasant—cause disutility—for those who experience them. But if the harm principle is to act as a constraint on the overall pursuit of utility, as Herbert, like Mill, assumed, then it must have some independent specification. Without such specification, the boundary between physical and moral paternalism is fragile, and Herbert's position vulnerable to the argument that any form of offence caused by others' conduct—Devlin's 'intolerance, indignation and disgust' for example—counts as harm. Yet, beyond the persuasive call for a reasoned debate about whether something should count as harm, Herbert gave little in the way of such specification. A similar argument may be made about the distinction between public and private matters, with the bigamy example which Herbert himself used illustrating that many issues have both public and private dimensions: an impact on public standards and on private interests.

The burden of Herbert's argument was clear: a special value should be attached to human freedom. But the precise framework for a freedom-based constraint on the pursuit of utility was still forming itself in his mind. It would find clearer expression in *Punishment and Responsibility*, and would in one form or another preoccupy him for the rest of his working life. Yet in spite of its under-developed theoretical framework, the argument of *Law, Liberty and Morality* is both powerful and passionate, and the economy and eloquence with which Herbert was able to articulate a liberal position which was (and remains) vividly relevant to some of the most pressing issues of criminal law reform gave the book an instant and lasting success. Herbert's own assessment was typical: of the original *Listener* piece, he simply commented that it was 'one of my better articles'.

After his socially mixed but intellectually successful period in California, Herbert returned to Oxford at the height of his reputation, his intellectual powers, and his institutional influence. He built on the momentum, writing up the Camp Lectures and throwing himself into lectures on 'Law and Morals', and on Kelsen and Hohfeld, and into seminars on the philosophy of criminal law and punishment with Rupert Cross and, later, the criminologist Nigel Walker. His interests had decisively broadened out from analytic philosophy, and this expanded horizon was further encouraged by discussions with sociologist Jean Floud, recently arrived at Nuffield College, Oxford from the London School of Economics. Floud, alone among the sociologists he had encountered, had an intellectual style with which Herbert could identify. She was also an admirer of his work, regarding *The Concept of Law* as a 'drink of pure water' amid the obfuscations of much legal theory. But she pressed Herbert on why he had not taken more seriously the great early sociologists Max Weber and Emil Durkheim, and it was under her influence that he read Durkheim and Talcott Parsons and began to think about the implications of their thought for criminal law. But despite the insight he had gained from Weber, and his decision to commission a book on *Law in Society* for the Clarendon Law Series, Herbert's reaction to these sorts of ideas was never particularly positive. This is illustrated by his paper on 'Social Solidarity' published in 1967.

In this paper, Herbert returned to Devlin's argument that without legal enforcement of the common morality, a society risks disintegration. This time, he considered the argument from a sociological point of view, drawing an analogy between Devlin's thesis and Talcott Parsons' and Emil Durkheim's accounts of social systems' maintenance of shared values. He set out Durkheim's distinction between 'mechanical solidarity'—the underpinning of social stability by means of substantially shared values, often reflected in criminal law—and 'organic solidarity'—the underpinning of social stability by means of a complementarity of functions, often reflected in a preference for civil law regulation. While criticizing Durkheim's suggestion that a predominance of organic solidarity is a mark of civilization, he noted a strong analogy between Devlin's thesis and Durkheim's account of criminal punishment as the symbolic expression (and repression) of what is most deeply disapproved: in Durkheim's term, the *conscience collective* of a social order.

But what kind of evidence, Herbert asked, could be given for such a thesis? On the one hand, there would be comparative historical data about the decline of societies which failed to use such penal mechanisms—primitive agrarian societies or the Roman Empire, perhaps. But here the problems of systematic comparison, he suggested, are overwhelming: for example, can we assume that the conditions of stability of industrial societies are comparable with those of pre-modern social orders? On the other hand, we might look to psychological data showing that a failure to enforce core morality leads to either permissiveness which in turn leads to a general loss of individual self-control and hence indirectly to social disorder; or to moral pluralism of such a radical kind as to lead to a general weakening of the necessary minimum content of morality. In fact, he argued, neither kind of evidence exists. Read sociologically, therefore, Devlin's argument cannot be sustained. This essay is of particular interest in that it represents a radical attack not merely on Devlin's argument but on sociological method in general: Herbert suggested that sociology can never match the test of empirical rigour which it sets for itself. His view boiled down to the idea that because the social sciences can never produce evidence as compelling as the natural sciences, they are not worth pursuing. This is a convenient rationalization for staying firmly within philosophical method, which is not the sort of enterprise which concerns itself with empirical data in the first place.

Herbert was, after all, a philosopher, and he worked within a philosophical community which conceived its own boundaries narrowly. But his scepticism about the potential for a fruitful exchange between legal theory and the social sciences had to do with more than just his disciplinary background.

Philosophy was the imperial discipline at Oxford, and being a successful philosopher—even from the margins of the Law Faculty—meant being an insider. The extent to which Herbert had achieved this position—externally, if not in terms of his own feelings—is reflected in the fact that at about this time several of his University College colleagues thought of him as a potential candidate for the Mastership of the College. When asked what had prompted the thought, given that Herbert had no relevant administrative experience and was at the peak of his intellectual creativity, one of them replied, after thinking carefully: 'Well I liked him *tremendously*'. In the event, the suggestion was not pursued very far—though it was canvassed widely enough for one conservative Fellow to remark that one couldn't possibly elect as Master a man who walked across the quad with his shirt tails hanging out.

Herbert had at this time an exceptionally strong group of graduate students. They included John Finnis, Peter Hacker, and David Hodgson and would soon include Joseph Raz, with whom discussions about Kelsen and about legal obligation were to have a decisive impact on the development of Herbert's ideas. These were important professional relationships in Herbert's life. He remained, despite his institutional stature, an enthusiast; this occasionally produced startling errors of judgment, particularly about appointments to jobs. But his refreshing wholeheartedness was also, in part, what led Herbert to develop a pattern of strong personal—though indubitably platonic—relationships with a selection of the young men whom he encountered through his work. A fascinating glimpse of his Oxford life at this time is given in a diary kept by Bob Summers, who was visiting Oxford with his family in 1964–5. Characteristically, Herbert had found an unobtrusive way of offering not only help to the Summers' but also support to Jean Austin, widow of J. L. Austin, organizing for them to rent part of her house. Summers recalls finding himself in Austin's study, not substantially rearranged since the philosopher's death, still full of his books. The Summers family was invited to tea with the Harts at Manor Place—a socially uncomfortable event which was not repeated: 'Only good conversation when Harts arguing with each other over influence of Church at Oxford and when talking of US primary election campaign.' Herbert seemed tired and distracted by Jacob and the Summers' young children; Summers suspected he was concerned to get to college early for dinner. Herbert discomfited Summers, who had wondered aloud at the early hour of College dinners, by making it clear that he assumed that all civilized people knew, from reading Jane Austen, that dinner at such an hour had a long history. 'These DAMN ENGLISH INTELLECTUALS,' Summers expostulated, '. . . when H was reading Austen novels I was (at comparable age) trying to earn enough to stay in School'. But it was precisely this lack of superficial polish, combined with an affecting candour and earnestness, as well as his intelligence, which made Summers an attractive figure to Herbert.

Herbert invited Summers to dinner in University College on a regular basis. Over dinner, they discussed everything ranging from work to Oxford gossip *via* literature. After dinner, they often went on to discuss Summers' work during long sessions in which Herbert, characteristically, encouraged Summers to reduce the 'heavy encrustation of scholarship' which he saw as a general blot on American writing. Summers attended Herbert's lectures: 'Hart paces slowly—glances at notes—sometimes witty (often to his surprise and always to his delight). A rapid lecturer but clear—repeats and illustrates . . . the best [analytic jurisprudence] lectures anywhere in the world.' Herbert also arranged for Summers to attend his debate with Patrick Devlin at the Institute of Advanced Legal Studies in London in 1964: Summers recalled the elaborate politeness and respect with which the two men treated each other.

Herbert's generosity in spending time with and commenting on the work of one among many visitors to Oxford, a man who had not even been one of his graduate students, is striking. What is even more striking is the extent to which he was not only showing his own work to Summers but confiding his worries about it and sharing his views about the merits and demerits of his critics. While Summers was in Oxford, Herbert—like Summers himself—was working on a review of Fuller's new book *The Morality of Law*. Herbert described this to Summers as 'a very bad book' which 'caricatured others' views' then 'nailed them'. (When Summers replied that Fuller had stopped reading other people's publications and was no longer working hard, Herbert replied that this was understandable and 'goes with age—my own experience'.) When Herbert received Fuller's acknowledgement of his (very critical) review, he called Summers over to University College to look at the letter with him, asking his advice about whether to accede to Fuller's request to be allowed to copy the review for students. There is something attractive yet almost child-like and certainly distinctly non-professorial about this sort of exchange, which blurred the boundaries between not only friendship and collegiality but also senior and younger scholar in ways which suggest an emotional need on Herbert's part. In one of his not infrequent indulgences in Oxford gossip, he described one colleague to Summers as 'an old woman . . . married to his mother'. He also slated another colleague—his professorial predecessor, Arthur Goodhart—as having 'done a lot of good, but no good work in legal philosophy at all, and no understanding of legal philosophy or Oxford philosophy, yet lashes out'. Yet more significantly,

Herbert expressed scepticism to Summers about his old friend Isaiah Berlin's intellectual creativity. Though Berlin's brand of political theory explored through wide-ranging intellectual history was never to Herbert's more analytic taste, his willingness to talk Berlin's achievements down in this public way may have been in part a symptom of irritated personal rivalry. Most striking of all, Summers had to reassure him that he had not at all been wasting his time reviewing Fuller: 'Something seems funny . . .', Summers noted in his diary; 'He doesn't seem to have quite the air of confidence about him as of old. Don't know quite what it is . . .'

On several occasions in the early part of the year, Summers met another young visitor, the Argentinian jurisprudence scholar Genaro Carrio. Carrio also occupied a special place in Herbert's universe: Herbert described him to Summers as 'an appreciative person': 'very nice and very able' whom 'he hated to see go' back to Argentina. After his departure, Carrio wrote Herbert letters which exude gratitude and affection: 'May I tell you, without infringing a British convention, that I went to Oxford attracted by an admirable scholar and found, in addition, an admirable man?' And, in reply to a message from Herbert, Carrio wrote a letter which reveals the real bond which the two men had formed:

My short stay in Oxford was the most pleasant experience I've ever had, and you are responsible for that. I never expected such a warm reception and generous friendship, and shall never forget it. I'm also what you call 'a monad by nature' (a rather hollow one, I'm afraid), so I really enjoy the rare occasions in which I find someone whom I can call a friend without abusing this marvellous word. Thank you for giving me such an opportunity at my 'advanced age minus a few years'. Tragedy still haunts me. When my wife arrived to London, the first thing I knew from her was that . . . my eldest sister had died in a terrible automobile accident . . . . The news, which affected me deeply, stole most of the pleasure of my brief tour of the Continent. I didn't tell you anything about that in our farewell meetings not to spoil them.

I hope you are all right as well as your family. I've written you a couple of letters and am looking forward to hear some news from you. Please drop me a line.

Herbert worried about Carrio's acute personal and professional difficulties, asking Summers to write to Carrio and discussing Carrio's future with him. Though he was almost certainly unaware of it, this tendency to pick out one or two students or younger scholars for special attention fostered a competitive atmosphere among the group around him. As Summers recorded after attending one of Herbert's seminars in 1965, 'Raz seems to have caught his eye at the moment . . . . Seems [to] "get hot" on certain ones [students] from time to time'.

This was not a new pattern. In 1959, Robert Gorman, a young Fulbright scholar from Harvard, later to become Professor and Associate Dean at the University of Pennsylvania Law School, spent a year in Oxford. To his amazement, he found Herbert teaching him a weekly tutorial and paying the closest possible attention to his work: he 'interposed the gentlest comments and criticisms, and generally made me feel as though I was a worthy young scholar. He even shared a manuscript copy of the Hart and Honoré book on causation, and asked what I thought of it!' Herbert also took responsibility for making sure that Gorman, who was living outside College, was fully integrated in social life. On one occasion, Herbert gave him his ticket to an opera, which Gorman attended with Jenifer, and on another Herbert took him punting on the Cherwell (the excursion passed off without physical disaster, despite Herbert's insistence on taking charge of the punt himself). Gorman was surprised and delighted to be the object of so much attention, and credits Herbert with having shaped his future career (not least by inviting Gorman to dinner at Manor Place with Professor Charles Haar, visiting from Harvard, to discuss the possibility of his doing a doctorate in the law school). For Herbert, these sorts of encounters with clever, genial, and appreciative young men fulfilled a deep emotional need.

These almost childlike, trusting relationships are striking in a man who was in his late 50s, married, the father of four children, and at the height of his success. They suggest a certain lack of maturity, yet also an unusual and appealing openness. Isaiah Berlin—himself not immune from critical feelings about his close friend—used to observe that, for all his success and intellectual sophistication, there was something 'broken' about Herbert. In Berlin's view this had to do with his attitude to being Jewish. Unlike Berlin, Herbert never sought to identify himself with his Jewish roots. And the two men had radically different views about Israel, Berlin having strong Zionist sympathies which were entirely alien to Herbert. In 1964, however, Herbert visited Israel for the first time. This visit marked the beginning of an ambivalent yet deep involvement with Israel which lasted the rest of his life, and which illustrates that his anglicized, secular persona was not as deeply internalized as appearances suggested. The intriguing question is whether his feelings about his Jewish origins were the fundamental cause of the 'brokenness' or lack of integration, or whether it was rather that Jewishness provided a salient object onto which Herbert could project (and Berlin could rationalize) his unsettled personal identity.

The occasion for this first visit to Israel was an invitation to Herbert to deliver the Lionel Cohen lectures at the Hebrew University in Jerusalem in January 1964. Significantly, Herbert decided to use a sabbatical term to extend the two-week visit into a three-month stay. Charlie and Jenifer joined him for the first two weeks, and the family travelled from Jerusalem to Haifa, using Haifa as a base for touring Upper and Lower Galilee, then moving on to Tel Aviv and the desert, the Dead Sea, and the south. Jenifer was immediately delighted by the open, direct manner of Israelis, although somewhat taken aback that she was unable to attend one of his lectures because no women were to be there. Charlie declared that he had picked up enough interesting history and politics to fill a thousand of the general papers he would have to sit for his Oxford and Cambridge University entrance; and though Herbert never quite got over what he saw as the Israelis' rudeness, which he put down to a 'misidentification of politeness with servility', the whole family enjoyed the natural beauty and cultural richness of the trip. The trip was also the occasion of some lively family debate about local politics: Charlie, sympathetic to the Arab cause, cavilled at Jenifer's enthusiasm for the Israel project, while Herbert occupied a mediating terrain between the two, concerned to find out as much as possible about what was happening to the Palestinians, while being receptive to the Israeli vision. After Jenifer's and Charlie's return, Herbert settled to a more contemplative and complex exploration of his surroundings, recording his impressions of the country in a notebook in which, as he noted with surprise after several pages, he was writing—as if in Hebrew—from back to front.

Herbert was looked after for much of his stay by Aharon Barak, then a lecturer at the Hebrew University and later to become President (Chief Justice) of the Israeli Supreme Court. He enormously appreciated Barak's 'encyclopaedic knowledge not only of the law but of every aspect of Israeli life' and his warmth and kindness. His appreciation was heightened by the fact that his visit to the University had not been a great success. Herbert's principal responsibility was the delivery of the Lionel Cohen lectures. In these, he considered once again the relationship between criminal law and morality. In the first lecture he set out the case for reforming the law on suicide, abortion, and homosexuality along the liberal, decriminalizing lines defended in *Law, Liberty and Morality*: 'The criminal law is a clumsy instrument and we wield it largely in the dark'. In the second lecture, he turned to the topic of how criminal law should deal with those suffering from mental abnormalities, this time taking as one of his principal targets the theories of Barbara Wootton. Like Herbert, Wootton took a utilitarian view of the overall aims of the criminal justice system. Unlike Herbert, she argued that the specific goal of sentencing should be rehabilitation rather than deterrence. This orientation of the system towards reform of the offender rather than punishment meant in her view that criminal law should dispense with proof of individual responsibility, confining the trial's attention to the facts of the offence and deferring any consideration of the offender's state of mind to the much more important sentencing stage, where the focus should be how to determine the best means of treatment or rehabilitation. In Herbert's view, this violated fundamental liberal values: it was an over-paternalistic approach which failed to take individual agency seriously. It therefore prejudiced what was genuinely 'moral' about criminal law. This, he argued, is not the fact that its content necessarily reflects moral values, but that its method of judging and ascribing blame respects individual freedom and responsibility. The third lecture was on 'Contemporary British Philosophy and Jurisprudence'; it was, however, memorably advertised as 'Contemporary British Philosophy and Jewish Prudence', and accordingly attracted a large audience. Two of the lectures were subsequently published as *The Morality of the Criminal Law*, and the second found its way into Herbert's collected essays on criminal justice, *Punishment and Responsibility*.

Delivered just as he was recovering from a virus and suffering from low spirits—'Private life (so called) is such a sad sterile affair . . . . My powers or at any rate energies are waning'—Herbert was unhappy with the way the lectures went. He felt that he had over-reacted to his anxiety not to speak for too long by cutting too much material from the lectures, which were delivered to an audience which included many practitioners:

Judges found the treatment of some parts cursory. And at the little drinking party afterwards no one raved (rightly) . . ., the faithful young Dr. Barak (who was our first guide . . .) being my only assiduous attender. He assures most charmingly that the young *were* interested and only didn't ask questions because they were afraid to do so before the judges. (I see to my surprise that I am writing from back of this book as if in Hebrew).

He was pleased to discover that *Causation in the Law* was widely read in Israel, but felt that 'My books have a reputation which leaves them disappointed, I imagine, by my lectures'. Reaching beyond personal preoccupations, Herbert was also dismayed by the under-funded education system, with no free public secondary education for children outside the Kibbutz system and overcrowded universities with poorly paid staff:

Law school pretty bad: continental style professors who lecture and go home . . . no contact and no interest in pupils . . . . Young lecturers feel it wrong . . . . Enormous number of subjects superficially and mechanically taught to half time students . . .

It is a sign of the times that Herbert was shocked by student–teacher ratios of 20:1 (as compared with the now unimaginable luxury of 8:1 in England). But his criticism was not just a matter of comparative funding: it was also the lack of a culture of intellectual exchange with students. Joseph

Raz, a young scholar at the Hebrew University at the time, remembers Herbert seeming acutely uncomfortable during this visit. It is unlikely that this discomfort had entirely to do with intellectual or professional matters. More fundamentally, the trip forced him to confront what being Jewish meant to him, and how this could be reconciled with his secular liberalism. That this reconciliation was not a simple one is demonstrated by a story about one of his early social engagements at the Hebrew University. In conversation, Izhak Englard, then a young torts scholar with Kelsenian jurisprudential sympathies and later to become a Justice of the Supreme Court, asked him directly why he had not been to Israel before and what his attitude was to being Jewish. Herbert, a man who almost never lost his temper, flew into a rage, telling Englard that this was none of his business. The row was patched up, but the younger man believed that Herbert continued to feel some rancour towards him.

In the very private space of his own mind, however, Herbert was confronting precisely the question Englard had posed. He was, as one would have expected, studying the Israeli legal system, visiting the Ministry of Justice and the Supreme Court, and concluding that: 'You can . . . find here that extraordinary phenomenon, common in Israel, of the very old jostling side by side with the very new. It is indeed almost impossible to believe that some of the rules related to marriage are observed in a country which in many ways seems not merely to be of the twentieth century but of the twenty-first.' But, more significantly, he also spent a great deal of time wandering alone around the ancient sights of Jerusalem, and recorded in his diary a large number of conversations with Israelis and visitors—some of them potential settlers—whom he encountered on these solitary trips. Many of these conversations concerned the nature of the State of Israel and the place of religion within the country. In these diary reflections, there is a palpable ambivalence about not only the impact of orthodox Judaism on the developing state, but also the Jewish heritage itself. On Mount Zion, he looked at:

The view back of the old city walls; Jordan country and distant Moab mountains are wonderful . . . but the great blot is the cluster of synagogues round the (mythical) tomb of David: dark, low places—candles flickering before tablets to the dead and old men in shawls muttering and crooning over Hebrew prayers. There is a great block like the great one at Yad Vashem inscribed with the names of the concentration camps . . . . Compared to this dark impression and gloomy memorials to the recent dead, the room allegedly of the last supper . . . appeared graceful and cheerful.

Moving on to a nearby museum containing the scrolls of the law and treasures burned or mutilated by the Nazis, Herbert had a long talk with an elderly man who was working on the door and who turned out to have been a lawyer: Herbert was very taken with him, noting that his 'grave wise face' and air of 'benevolence' was 'exceptionally common here' and in contrast with 'the sharp anxious look of Jews in Europe'. 'Sweet old man: He looked as if he had seen much suffering but was quite unembittered.' At another cultural sight Herbert talked with a woman born in Sarajevo but who had moved to America and from there to Israel in 1928: she 'loved the country but was pessimistic about the people: the old idealism of 1948 was gone: they are being Americanised'. She was sceptical of Herbert's claim that, compared with England, 'the young here seemed full of social purpose'. In a hotel lobby, he had a lengthy exchange with a young American who was contemplating emigration to Israel because of his commitment to orthodox religion. 'Frightening in a way—no humour', Herbert recorded, moving on to yet another debate about whether the public establishment of religion was—as he believed but most of the people he talked to did not—dispensable and indeed undesirable for Israel. He had persuaded his sister, Sybil, to come and join the family on the trip to Galilee. Life at the hotel where they were staying turned out to involve a number of religious rituals: 'Kaddish at supper (I used dirty handkerchief for cap!) Gefilte fish served to S[ybil]'s horror.' Sybil, unlike Herbert, was not amused: she disliked Israel unambiguously and was never to return.

Towards the end of his time in Israel, Herbert spent several days staying on a Kibbutz east of Petah Tikva. Here he was fascinated by the social organization, noting in great detail in his diary the restrictions on property ownership, the system of child-rearing and elite education, the Herculean working practices, and astoundingly short holidays. He admired the effort to get a dialogue going with local Arabs and the rejection of materialism inherent in Kibbutz culture, and he was impressed by the commitment of the residents, many of whom were highly educated and had had prestigious well-paid jobs before joining the Kibbutz. But he felt some ambivalence about the closed nature of Kibbutz life, noting with amusement his hosts' comment that Oxford colleges were sorts of Kibbutzim: 'too little getting away from it!'

Until the end of his life, Herbert continued to struggle with the questions about identity and belonging which his first visit to Israel brought to the surface of his consciousness. The sensitivity which Richard Wilberforce had noted in the 1930s was, of course, touched by displays of prejudice, and Herbert in later life was more inclined to acknowledge and discuss such issues. In 1988, for example, he recounted with outrage to Bob Summers a story about David Daube, the famous Roman lawyer, being told by a senior German professor in his field that 'his hands were not fit to touch the Romans' texts'. But, as the England incident shows, it was not only rank bigotry which touched Herbert's which touched Herbert's sensitivity about Jewishness. He was torn between his liberalism and his sense of the importance of cultural heritage, between his rationalist atheism and his recognition of the importance of religion to many Israelis, and between his sense of being English and his sense of being Jewish. In an interview given to an Israeli magazine, while maintaining his opposition to Israel's being a Jewish state and support for the idea of its being 'a country to which anybody is entitled to come', he immediately went on:

At the moment a combination of historical facts and demographic realities justifies the status quo but it would be different if it were clear that the Jewish population was sinking to one tenth of the total. This might sound like sophistry to you, but in my opinion what is valuable is an inherited culture, and any sharp discarding of that is objectionable, and indeed monstrous . . . . [Culture] has no absolute priority. Where it impinges on moral judgement and denies desirable human liberties, I would subordinate the cultural aspects to the liberal principles, which are *prima facie* principles . . . . As long as the state offers reasonable support for genuine cultural features that are not Jewish, it is perfectly entitled to give preferential support to Jewish culture. Do I want to see Jewish culture established legally as being the national culture? I think I am torn between my theories and my emotions here. I am inclined to say no.

The tension between 'theories and emotions' is highly significant. The theories won out—albeit narrowly—on this point. But when it came to the question of whether Israel had been justified in rescuing only Jewish Ethiopians during the famine, it was the emotions which directed the theory:

I find it very difficult to condemn. There must be a deep-seated concern for other people who share your culture and religion. Up to a point, when this concern is weighted against other considerations, it has priority. There should be greater concern about the fate of Jews elsewhere. It's too deeply embedded in the thoughts and emotions of the people in Israel and elsewhere to deny . . . I suspect that it's too much to demand that people should disregard the ties of kith and kin absolutely—it's an ethic of fantasy that these could be put aside.

The idea of 'kith and kin' encompassing identification with an ethnic group is a view widely entertained in the communitarian social theory which has had a revival in the last 20 years. But it is not something which one would associate with Herbert's own more individualistic brand of liberalism. This interview, and Herbert's attitude to Israel more generally, provide telling clues to the degree to which his emotional and intellectual attitudes were successfully integrated. With a typically light touch, Isaiah Berlin put his finger on Herbert's contrasting responses to Israel: writing to Noel Annan in 1979, he observed that 'Herbert Hart's reactions were *very* similar to L. Woolf's: the rabbis' side curls *maddened* him. Yet he was very happy there'.

This tension between an underlying sense of Jewish identity and an intellectual commitment to its moral irrelevance was almost certainly the occasion for at least some of Herbert's personal perplexities—his 'brokenness'. His identification with his 'Jewish' and 'English' sides never seem to have been brought into a stable equilibrium. Deep in his mind, the notion of 'Jewishness' was associated with a cluster of negative and positive attributes: 'Leeds Jewish', 'Jewish wailing', 'Jewish family life', and 'Jewish religion' were to be avoided at all costs. But 'Jewish' also stood for warmth, earthiness, variety, culture, the exotic. In Santa Monica in 1961, Herbert had remarked to Herbert Morris 'How Jewish American culture is'. When asked what he meant, Herbert gestured to the huge variety of food. Despite his asceticism, there was something about Jewishness which Herbert did not want to lose, and in later life, despite his trenchantly anti-religious attitude, he regularly joined the Berlins for Seder at their home. But he was also capable of assuming a highly anglicized, patrician, almost colonial persona. In 1967, the young Joseph Raz told Herbert at the end of a supervision that he felt an obligation to return to Israel because of the outbreak of war. Herbert astounded him by saying sadly, 'It's a shame that we [i.e. Britain] don't have the influence in that region that we used to'. Yet beneath the anglicized persona, there remained a deep sense of Jewish identification which is reflected in a striking comment which Herbert made to Ronald Dworkin (and at different times to fellow Jews George Fletcher, Aharon Barak, and Joseph Raz) about the Oxford Chair of Jurisprudence. It was remarkable, Herbert said, that no English person had held the chair in recent decades. Amazed, Dworkin replied, 'But you are English'. 'No,' Herbert retorted, 'I'm Jewish'.

CHAPTER 11

Discipline, Punishment, and Responsibility

Istanbul: Marvellous town tho' deep in snow and a wind blowing from the steppes of Asia . . . . Some exquisite mosaics . . . the most wonderful food (after Israeli indifference to cooking). I see great difficulty in tearing myself away but expect to be back to 'real' life and its horrors next Sunday, Dad.

So Herbert represented his impending return from Israel in a postcard to his daughter and son-in-law. On his way home, he tarried not only in Istanbul but in another favourite city, Rome, delaying the moment when he had to take up once again the public and private responsibilities of 'real' life.

He had now reached the pinnacle of his career. With a remarkable list of achievements behind him, and still a decade away from the Oxford retirement age of 67, there was no reason to doubt that he was set for a period of flourishing intellectual creativity in which he would continue to shape the field of English jurisprudence which he already dominated. Life in Oxford was stimulating. In the mid-1960s, some of his most talented graduate students were working with him; they included Joseph Raz, Peter Hacker, David Richards (who moved after a year to work with Geoffrey Warnock), John Finnis, and Lee Irish, whose connection with the wealthy Tanner family would later enable Herbert to bring the prestigious Tanner lectures to Oxford. His spellbinding seminars with Cross were the intellectual high point of the Oxford law scene; and the legal philosophy discussion group which he had founded on taking up the Chair was now meeting twice a week in a lively group of academics and graduate students. His intellectual speed and capacity to put another person's argument with exemplary clarity and fairness even—perhaps especially—when he disagreed with it continued to make him a sparkling performer not only at his own but at colleagues' seminars. At this time he was an influential interlocutor in Brian Barry's and Jean Floud's interdisciplinary seminar on norms at Nuffield College, and in 1966 joined forces with them in a seminar on 'Sociological Evidence for Legal and Political Theories'.

Herbert formed a particularly close intellectual connection with Joseph Raz, who arrived in Oxford the year after his trip to Israel. This relationship typified Herbert's mix of professorial distance and personal concern: supervisions were exacting, with 'no personal talk for a long time; but one sensed a gentleness about him'. The gentleness bespoke a real concern: Herbert took Raz and his wife on long drives around the countryside at weekends (trips which were occasionally hair-raising due to Herbert's less than methodical driving). Another important intellectual contact was fostered by American political philosopher John Rawls' visit to All Souls in 1965. The similar tracks along which Herbert and Rawls had been working was matched by a similarity of disposition: reserved and relatively ascetic in personal style, both were at once drawn to Benthamite utilitarianism as a moral and political system of thought yet recognized the need substantially to qualify the unrestricted principle of utility: the idea that the sole end to which human action and social policy should be directed is the pursuit of the greatest happiness of the greatest number. They enjoyed long bicycle rides together in the Oxfordshire countryside, and many colleagues noticed the affinity between the two men. The affinity was not just personal and intellectual, it was political: for both men, the commitment to liberalism meant not merely an attachment to the core value of individual liberty but equally a vision of a humane, redistributive social-democratic political order in which fairness is a key concern.

Beyond Oxford, Herbert continued to shape his field through active soliciting of manuscripts for the Clarendon Series (in 1966, he signed John Finnis up to write a book on natural law, the title of which—*Natural Law and Natural Rights*—Herbert specified). He was reaching a wide academic audience with his publications. In spite of his resolution while in Israel to counter his increasing sense of fatigue by travelling less, he was making frequent trips to lecture at other universities in Britain and abroad. And he was addressing a broader audience through his lecturing and broadcasting on criminal law reform and the abolition of capital punishment.

These pleasures of status and achievement were amply matched by the further satisfaction of public recognition. An Honorary Bencher of Middle Temple in 1963 and Vice President of the British Academy in 1966 and 1967, Herbert was now also feeling the first shower in what would become a deluge of Honorary Degrees (Stockholm in 1960 was followed by Glasgow in 1965: by the end of his career he had accumulated 13, including one in Mexico, two in Israel, and three in the USA, as well as being elected Fellow of the American Academy of Arts and Sciences and the Academy of Sciences in Turin). In 1966 Harvard Law School awarded him the Ames Prize—worth the substantial sum of $1500 and incalculable prestige—for

The Concept of Law. Reflecting the still-gathering momentum of the book's reception, the prize came five years after its publication. Herbert was clearly delighted by this concrete if belated proof of his success in America: 'Ever since receiving [your letter]', he wrote to Dean Griswold, 'I have been walking on clouds.' The same year, he received the ultimate mark of the insider's arrival. In the classic indirection of the English establishment, a letter from the Prime Minister's office told him that:

I am asked by the Prime Minister to inform you, in strict confidence, that he has it in mind, on the occasion of the forthcoming list of New Year Honours, to submit your name to the Queen, with a recommendation that Her Majesty may be graciously pleased to approve the Honour of Knighthood be conferred upon you.

This, however, was an honour which Herbert's principles did not allow him to accept. The day he received the letter, he drafted his reply:

I would be most grateful if you would tell the Prime Minister how pleased I was that he should have thought of me in this connection but that I prefer to decline the honour. My reason is simply that I have always advocated and still hold the view that such honours should be given in recognition of public service as distinct from academic merit or scholarship and on this footing I do not consider myself qualified.

Despite this firmness of principle Herbert did not quite respect his assurance to the Prime Minister's office that the offer would be kept strictly confidential and—perhaps through Jenifer, who always subscribed to what she called 'the Oxford definition of a secret': something you tell to only one person at a time—the news certainly reached a few of his closest friends. Within the complex web of his friendship with Isaiah Berlin, Herbert must have felt a certain satisfaction—a sense of principled superiority—to which the refusal entitled him.

Even during this period, however, Herbert's sense of his institutional status and intellectual power was tinged with an underlying insecurity. The pressures of holding the high-profile Chair were taking their toll. Inevitably, being in such a prominent position occasionally brought with it tensions and conflicts. Herbert appears to have become less rather than more relaxed about these as his fame increased. The most spectacular of these conflicts arose in the mid-1960s. Some years before, Herbert had been one of the examiners of an Israeli student, Abraham Harari's, doctoral thesis. Harari's work was on the place of negligence in the law of torts (the law of civil wrongs leading to compensation). It included some criticisms of Herbert's and Tony Honoré's arguments in *Causation in the Law*. It was referred back for substantial revision and resubmission. When finally resubmitted, the thesis was not awarded the doctoral degree. Harari, who had in any event been reluctant to modify a thesis to which he was strongly committed, felt that the decision was unjust. He blamed it on Herbert, and attributed it to Herbert's intolerance of criticism and of views different from his own.

Harari's career was not blocked by his failure to get a doctorate. He secured a post at the University of Tasmania, and in 1962 he published a book arising from his doctoral thesis: *The Place of Negligence in the Law of Torts*. He then moved to a post at Dundee. But the sense of injustice continued to rankle, and Harari worked out his resentment in several ways. He wrote Herbert a series of increasingly accusing and hostile letters. These letters have not survived, but they must have been extreme: Herbert confided to Brian Simpson that he feared that Harari might try to kill him. Harari also began to write an essay, 'H. L. A. Hart and his *Concept of Law* (1961): An Open Letter to a Teacher of Jurisprudence'. The 'Open Letter' evolved in a number of stages: the original part was 15 pages long, but by the time Harari had finished it in 1972 it had reached 96 pages. It is made up of a coruscating and minute critique not only of Herbert's book but also of Herbert himself, interspersed with illustrative poems, biblical quotations, references to a wide range of philosophical sources from Aristotle to Wittgenstein via Hobbes, Hume, Mill, and Russell, asides to fellow teachers of jurisprudence, and quotations from reviews critical of *The Concept of Law*. Harari's letter begins:

Dear Colleague,

...

You say that you do not share my view of Hart and his work, that you think that Hart has made a 'substantial contribution to legal philosophy' and that he is a fine man. This does not surprise me. The number of people whom Hart has misled, or who because of their low ambitions and unconscious prudence espoused 'the well-endowed opinions in fashion' and became followers of Hart or trumpeters for him, is very great . . . .

A cactus in the desert remains a cactus. To regard it as a melon or a bunch of grapes is a pitiful illusion which will quickly be shattered on closer inspection (not to speak of contact).

This analogy is subject to one little qualification which arises from the difference between grapes, melons and cactuses on the one hand and legal philosophy and pretentious skull-duggery on the other. It requires but little experience and learning to distinguish between a bunch of grapes and a crop of prickly pears and to approach the latter with the requisite caution. The difference between philosophy and skull-duggery is not so easily perceived . . .

The first part of the letter was followed by an imaginary reply from a jurisprudence teacher sympathetic to Herbert's position and castigating

Harari for the immoderate terms of his open letter. This 'reply' was constructed to represent an amalgam of the substantial correspondence which Harari must by now have been receiving.

Harari's argument was that Herbert's success was due entirely to his powerful institutional position, to the intellectual poverty of contemporary English jurisprudence, to the philosophical ignorance and conservatism of lawyers, and to their taste for Herbert's comforting 'common-sense' approach. He accused Herbert—'our Oxonian oracle'—of plagiarizing, *inter alia*, John Austin and Kelsen, thinkers far more original in Harari's view than Herbert himself, while at the same time denigrating their achievements and setting them up as 'straw-men'. To Harari, *The Concept of Law* was 'arrogant', 'clumsy', 'full of defective scholarship and understanding'; 'a bad book', 'the gospel according to St. Herbert', 'a misshapen philosophical mongrel' that 'presents neither a normative nor a sociological interpretation of law' and which 'pollute[s] the jurisprudential air in the English-speaking countries'. The letter, which draws on Ernest Gellner's acid critique of Oxford philosophy, *Words and Things*, is particularly scornful of linguistic philosophy: 'how laughable and preposterous I find the suggestion that 2,500 years of Western philosophy had to await the coming of Friedrich Waismann and the Oxford school of philosophy for the insight expressed by the discovery of the open texture of empirical concepts.'

Harari's criticisms represent an extreme expression of arguments which had been put in more measured terms in a number of the reviews from which he himself quoted. The publication of these reviews undermined Harari's claim that Herbert's status had somehow protected him from proper intellectual evaluation. It would not have taken any special insight on the reader's part to recognize that there was a personal dimension to the attack:

Are my strictures harsh, dear colleague? Do you detect something 'personal' in these lines? Would you rebuke me for the use of immoderate terms? You *are* perceptive. Would that you were just a little more perceptive! It is possible to criticise or attack a man's work without by implication criticising or attacking the man? Surely it is better to be conscious of and honest about what one is doing ...

Nor would it have taken a psychiatrist to realize that there was something obsessive about Harari's critique. By page 6 of his letter, he was still labouring over page 2 of *The Concept of Law*; by page 11, he had reached page 3. Herbert, however, was seldom a person to take adversity lightly, and he agonized miserably over how to respond to Harari's missives. He enlisted Joseph Raz's help in translating passages from Hebrew and went on replying to Harari for some time. In the end, he followed friends' advice not to get further involved. What upset him was not so much any real concern about damage to his intellectual reputation as the personal nature of the attack. Harari's story is a tragic one: not only because he devoted his considerable intellectual gifts to such bitter and unconstructive ends, but also because he turned out to be suffering from a brain tumour. He died not long after the completion of the Open Letter in 1972. The Letter was never published, but remains in the possession of several recipients and has been deposited in a small number of university libraries. For Herbert, the saga had no tangible professional implications. But the personal cost to him of managing incidents such as this, and the extreme levels of anxiety which they occasioned, contributed to an increasingly urgent desire to escape the strain of holding the Chair of Jurisprudence.

On the home front, too, life continued to shower Herbert with mixed blessings. His increasing distance from Jenifer had by now issued in a period of what might be called a *détente cordiale*: revolving on difference axes, yet within a shared world of friends, family, and intellectual commitments, they were both pulled together and pushed apart by the dynamics of their relationship with their children. Liberals by temperament and belief, the widespread use of cannabis by teenagers in the 1960s presented one of the many challenges confronting them as parents. Though neither of them regarded cannabis-smoking as a particularly serious issue, Herbert's long-standing anxiety about ever being seen to be on the wrong side of the law meant that he was strongly opposed to his children having drugs at home. But parental discipline was not his strong card, and on this as on other points, his absent-mindedness led to some spectacular mishaps. In a typical moment of distraction, Herbert once opened a letter from Charlie, spending his year off between school and university in Ghana, to Adam. The letter made what Herbert found a very worrying reference to drugs. Undecided what to do about it, he left the letter in a pile of financial papers. Ten days later, he received a phone call from his bemused bank manager, to whom he had inadvertently sent the letter along with the financial papers.

As in most families, the turbulence of life with teenagers gradually resolved itself into a more tranquil pattern. While maintaining his keen interest in music, Charlie made a successful transition to undergraduate life and then to graduate study at the LSE, while Adam had graduated from Balliol College, Oxford in Philosophy, Politics and Psychology, having enjoyed regular discussions of his work with Herbert during his time as an undergraduate. Joanna's remarkable professional achievements (having moved into psychology, she was elected in 1967 the first woman fellow of King's College, Cambridge) was also a source of pleasure and pride for both Jenifer and Herbert. Herbert had also become closely involved with Jacob.

A fascinating glimpse of the Hart household at the time is given in a letter
to Joanna in the summer of 1967:

In Jenifer's absence [to a holiday in the Dolomites] the house is transformed
into a kind of zenana inhabited by women and children, apart from me, the one
male. The women include Nannie, our ex-Swedish au pair (Sidsel) with her ille-
gitimate child (Carlos), a nice undergraduate from St. Anne's and Jakie. He is
in splendid form. We had an uproarious day in London with bits of my family
at a child's fair-cum-zoo near Wimbledon, where he rode on roundabouts and
manipulated paddle boats, while jets shrieked overhead and litter blew unceas-
ingly round us. We then retired for a gigantic strawberry tea at Sybil's, but J.
was still perfectly lively and reasonable at 9pm when we returned .... Charles
descended on us the other night. He looks well though the hair is of fantastic
disorder and length. He lives in a large room in Whitechapel where he says he
studies Economics in the morning but performs with his Group ... at Midnight
three times a week at a nightclub in King St., Covent Garden to which he has
invited me. I've not yet gone but instead have been twice to the Opera ...

But Herbert and Jenifer felt the perpetual strain of making difficult decisions about Jacob's education and coping with his volatile moods and
behavioural problems. And in 1966, Adam, whose radical politics baffled yet
intrigued Herbert, announced his intention of getting married to someone
whom Herbert thought unsuitable. Herbert was yet more upset to discover
that the couple planned a joint change of name to Minrod. Adam and
Herbert had a blazing row in which Herbert called him a 'bloody fool' and
announced that he would not be attending the wedding party (which was
held at Manor Place). On the evening following the marriage, Jenifer and
Herbert had dinner at High (the Fellows') Table in University College.
Herbert asked how the occasion had gone. 'If you wanted to know, you
bloody well ought to have come', was Jenifer's reply. Herbert was painfully
aware of the strain which Jenifer was under, but often felt unable to reach
her. Leaving Oxford for a trip to New York and Rome in 1968, he was:

... seen off by Jenifer and poor appealing Jakey, happy with a box of chocolate
raisins from slot machine. Love and pity terribly strong: a gesture towards a parting
kiss for J and a sudden sight of her as an attractive girl emerging from the worried
scold. Oh dear what a mess *that* is.

Shared, if complex, friendships with Isaiah Berlin, now married to Jenifer's
former school-mate Aline de Gunzbourg, Jean Floud, Jean Austin, Francis
and Carol Graham-Harrison, Margaret Paul, and Douglas Jay were certainly a factor holding the couple together. The collapse of Douglas and
Peggy Jay's marriage in 1971 prompted an unexpected and interesting response from Jenifer. She wrote to Peggy, encouraging her to mend fences with

Douglas and urging the value of a long marriage. Herbert's response was to welcome Douglas's new and very much younger partner, Mary, with his usual tolerance and openness. Mary's immediate affection for Herbert survived a characteristic howler at their wedding in 1972, when he proposed the toast, enthusiastically but maladroitly, to 'Douglas and Peggy'.

Many of the Harts' friendships were fostered by a shared love of country holidays and, sadly, it was on one of these that tragedy had struck the colleague to whom, apart from J. L. Austin, Herbert was closest. At Easter 1962, the Harts and the Pauls went to the Lake District for one of their regular holidays in the Quirks' cottage by Coniston Water. Both George Paul and Adam, who was also a member of the party, were keen sailors. One afternoon, Herbert's and Jenifer's walk was interrupted by Adam, who had just witnessed George Paul's body being carried into the house after a sailing accident. Adam, distressed and in shock after witnessing the unsuccessful attempts to resuscitate Paul, tried nonetheless to break the news to Herbert as gently as possible. Herbert simply collapsed, his legs buckling under him. With George Paul's death, he had lost not only a close friend but also one of the two men who had encouraged and tutored his providential embrace of linguistic philosophy. In future years, Herbert and Jenifer were devoted friends to Margaret Paul and her daughters: Herbert liked to refer to Margaret, Jean Austin, and Jean Floud as '*mes trois veuves*'.

Amid the ups and downs of personal and professional life, Herbert's research continued. He was planning a further substantial publication. This time it took the form of a collection of his essays on criminal law and punishment, published over the last eight years. Several of the essays had been published in journals like the *New York Review of Books*, back issues of which were not easily available to readers. And he felt that some common themes in the essays would become more apparent if they were brought together in one volume. In *Punishment and Responsibility*, published in 1968, Herbert combined a critical and reformist approach with his analytic and linguistic focus to produce an account of the conceptual structure of criminal law, its principles of responsibility, excuse and mitigation, and an argument for the justification of punishment. His method, remarkably similar to John Rawls' idea of a 'reflective equilibrium' between our intuitions and our considered principles, was to move back and forth between actual features of criminal law systems and liberal or logical arguments, seeking the best rationalization of current arrangements, and finding resources for criticism in ideals which are immanent but not fully realized in those arrangements.

Punishment and Responsibility constitutes a remarkable testament to the confidence of a liberal outlook in the late 1960s. Herbert treated the emotive, retributive approach to punishment, which has since enjoyed such a decisive revival in criminal justice policy, as something which all sensible people would agree to be primitive and uncivilized. Although, in the form of the claim that punishment should adequately denounce wrongdoing, the retributive position is given the compliment of a brief, reasoned response, the whole thrust of the book's argument is that the rational, utilitarian approach to punishment—that punishment is in itself an evil and therefore has to be justified by reference to its countervailing good consequences such as deterrence or reform—is the position which merits attention and development. But Herbert also took very seriously the dangers of an unrestricted utilitarian approach which might justify punishing people who are not truly responsible for their crimes in the name of the greater social good. This might include, for example, 'framing' an innocent person where public feelings run high and the guilty person cannot be found, or engaging in preventive detention where it is suspected that someone is going to commit a crime. In this context, Herbert extended the spirited debate begun in his Jerusalem lectures with Baroness Wootton, whose widely discussed Hamlyn lectures had advocated abandoning the requirement of mental responsibility for crime and rather treating crime as a form of social pathology calling for the preventive and therapeutic intervention of medical and social services.

In answering both the retributivist and the radical utilitarian rehabilitationist, Herbert trod a middle path which presaged a conception towards which he reached, yet which he never quite achieved, in much of his later work: an accommodation of the relative claims of utility and of rights or justice in political morality. In the sphere of punishment, his 1959 'Prolegomenon to the Principles of Punishment', republished as the first chapter of *Punishment and Responsibility*, had come up with the hugely influential idea of a division of conceptual labour within the justification of punishment. The division was between the utilitarian, deterrent, 'general justifying aim' of criminal law and punishment as a system and the retributive or justice-based principles of responsibility and proportionality in the distribution of punishment. In the further essays in the collection, Herbert built out of this central insight accounts of how a number of more specific penal and criminal legal arrangements should be designed. The *'mens rea* principle'—the idea that everyone convicted of an offence should have been proved to be fully responsible for it in the sense of having intended or been aware of what they were doing—is an obvious offshoot of the core principle of responsibility in distribution sketched in the 'Prolegomenon'. But Herbert also argued that negligence, in the sense of inadvertence to a risk to which a reasonable person would have attended and which the defendant had the capacity to appreciate, was an adequate moral grounding for criminal conviction.

The principle of responsibility, he claimed, lay at the heart of all the familiar excuses for or mitigation of crime such as the defences of duress or provocation. In each case, the point is that there is something about the context in which the defendant exercises his or her capacities which blocks a full ascription of responsibility because the defendant's relevant capacities of understanding and/or self-control were not engaged. This relationship between certain defences and the '*mens rea* principle' he further related to the underlying yet distinct idea of voluntariness or will—a concept which he rescued deftly from a number of obfuscating interpretations such as that of the nineteenth-century positivist John Austin. These, he argued, had their roots in an outdated philosophical psychology. The essays display a vintage Herbert attention to conceptual precision, refining and elaborating core legal concepts such as intention and negligence, and distinguishing between different notions of responsibility related to ideas of capacity, causation, liability, and role. More unusually for Herbert, several of the essays—and notably the essay on capital punishment—follow through the logic of the utilitarian position, with its justifying argument for punishment as contingent on its effects, by paying close attention to empirical evidence such as criminal statistics.

Punishment and Responsibility is still regarded as one of the cornerstones of both penal philosophy and the burgeoning field of criminal law theory in Britain, Australia, Israel, and North America. Its idea of criminal responsibility as founded on human capacity and agency is the inspiration for or counterpoint to almost all serious scholarship in English in the field published over the last 35 years. And, along with *Law, Liberty and Morality*, *Punishment and Responsibility* is the part of Herbert's work which had the most significant impact on legal teaching and research beyond jurisprudence. Both books continue to feature as core texts in criminal law and criminal justice courses in many countries.

But the book's undoubted quality and lasting success cannot disguise a certain deceleration of Herbert's intellectual creativity in the second half of the 1960s. Certainly, he was deeply taken up with his intellectual life, pursuing his fascination with Kelsen in his teaching and reading; continuing to ponder the theory of rules which formed the central element of *The Concept of Law*; writing essays on Bentham's legal and political philosophy; and developing his ideas about criminal law and punishment. From the commanding heights of his scholarly achievements and institutional position, however, one would have expected him to be taking on a substantial new project. But the waning powers of concentration which had already haunted him in 1961 were making themselves felt, and this was a factor in his decision to work not on a further monograph but rather on a collection of essays.

In assessing the pace of his intellectual life, it is significant that of the nine essays in the collection, seven had been published by 1964; that the most theoretically innovative essay—the first—was published in 1959; and that of the remaining two, only one—the postscript—was substantially rewritten and expanded for the collection.

Putting the collection together, Herbert was dissatisfied with the overall coherence of the essays, but lacked the energy to rewrite them. In July 1967, he wrote to Joanna, who was visiting Harvard:

I am at the end of three weeks' terrible work correcting proofs of ten [in fact it was nine] terrible essays which I published over the last ten mis-spent years, on Punishment and Responsibility. I wish to God I had never disturbed these sleeping dogs. They are terrible, repetitive and confused. I have an assistant who checks my proofs and quotations. So far, out of hundreds of quotations and citations I have not found one accurate one. I hope you don't inherit my gift for inaccuracy to that extent. I shall never publish anything again.

This was in part a bit of light-hearted and exaggerated self-deprecation for the benefit of a daughter setting out on an academic career. But there was some reason for Herbert to feel uncomfortable about his failure to have done further work on the essays. He could have done more to draw out the broad implications for political philosophy of the argument for a restricted utilitarianism—a project of which his friend John Rawls shortly afterwards made an influential 600-page book. But in order to do so, he would have had to do some more basic thinking out of the core components of his argument. We can take an instructive example from the 'Prolegomenon'—an essay whose title itself gestures towards a further phase of theoretical development which Herbert was never to undertake.

In this essay Herbert argued that, notwithstanding the constraint which the principle of responsibility should impose on the pursuit of the general utilitarian aims of a criminal justice system, it might on occasion be justifiable to impose 'strict liability'—liability without proof of responsibility—in the overriding interests of efficiency or harm-reduction. Good examples are the relatively trivial 'regulatory' crimes such as licensing offences which carry non-stigmatizing penalties such as fines. These are justified by utilitarian gains such as the reduced costs of the criminal process and the increased ease of procuring convictions and achieving deterrence. But, Herbert argued, such arrangements are always made with a sense that a principle is being sacrificed: that a compromise is being made. His theory, however, gives us no conceptual resources which could guide the legislator or the judge as to when such a compromise *should* be made. How much of a gain in utility outweighs the risk of injustice to an individual who may be convicted without having been truly responsible for his or her act? Since the justice-based principle of responsibility in distribution and the utilitarian aim of the criminal process float in different philosophical systems, Herbert (unlike Rawls, whose theory provides a more systematic account of the relative priorities of its different normative elements) cannot give us any clues about how they should be traded off against each other.

Rhetorically, Herbert's argument suggested that the principle of responsibility provides an absolute, invariable limit on the utilitarian goals of the criminal process. This left his concessions to the need for strict liability or preventive detention functioning as exceptions which he did not truly attempt to bring within his theoretical system. The practical imperatives and institutional realities of the social world are present in *Punishment and Responsibility* to a greater degree than in any of his other books. But their relationship to the philosophy which he so elegantly developed is not entirely worked out. The tone of much of the book, as compared with the luminous prose, passionate advocacy, and easy confidence of *Law, Liberty and Morality*, seems tentative. And the revisions which Herbert did undertake are symptomatic of an intellectual quality which had originally stood him in good stead but which was gradually, in the context of his diminishing energy, becoming a handicap. This was his painstaking collection and contemplation of the most powerful challenges to his own ideas. In his early work, the meticulous effort to form a clear view of his own *vis à vis* other positions paid high scholarly interest, for it always spurred him on to the further refinement of his own ideas. But in *Punishment and Responsibility*, while references and the criticisms which they contain are minutely—almost obsessively—noted, their provocation is not really taken up. This foreshadowed his later frustrating and energy-draining preoccupation with responding to his critics.

In the grip of this sense of diminishing intellectual creativity, Herbert was turning his energies to a number of other responsibilities. In 1966, Douglas Jay, now President of the Board of Trade in Harold Wilson's Labour administration, had approached him about whether he would be interested in becoming a part-time member of the Monopolies and Mergers Commission—the body which decided whether mergers and other corporate arrangements infringed the principles of fair competition. At the time of Jay's approach, Herbert was unwell: at a conference in Bellagio, he had suffered a detached retina, and had to fly home for an operation on his eye following which he had to lie in a darkened room for some weeks. He felt unable to accept Jay's offer. Jay was contemplating an investigation of whether the prevailing organization of the professions amounted to a restrictive practice, and he thought that Herbert, with his experience of the legal profession, would be particularly well placed to contribute to such an inquiry. He therefore renewed the invitation the following year. This time, Herbert seized the opportunity to contribute to the public service which had given him such satisfaction during the war. Over the next six years, he sat as a member of 11 inquiries, including those on recommended resale prices (1967–8) and refusal to supply (1968–70), both of which are still referred to; on restrictive trade practices in professional services (1967–70); and on the proposed Glaxo mergers with Beecham and Boots (1972).

On taking up the appointment, anxious that his lack of training in economics would be a handicap, Herbert threw himself with characteristic zeal into the task of learning the rudiments of economic theory, reading widely and making notes in one of his many workbooks. While the panel was sitting, it met for about two days each fortnight in long and sometimes intellectually exhausting sessions. He was regarded as an outstandingly effective member of the Commission, applying not only his legal skills but also his general critical acumen in putting searching questions to the business people who appeared before the panel (and sometimes disconcerting them by gradually lowering his head in concentration as the complex question unfolded). He was re-appointed to the panel for a second term but resigned in 1973 because he felt that his appointment as Principal of Brasenose College would not allow him sufficient time to devote to the Commission's work. In later life, he looked back on this work with pleasure and satisfaction: 'I loved [it]; it was fascinating: [One] had a sense of really being in the works . . . . I can't imagine anything else I would have enjoyed as much as that.' Lurking in the affirmation is a slight sense of puzzlement as to why he had never been asked to chair or even to sit on one of the many committees of inquiry or Royal Commissions in fields of law reform—capital punishment, the law on obscenity and pornography—to which his expertise was more directly relevant than it was to the Monopolies Commission. Many of his friends, including Jay, would have liked to see him use his talents in such a role, and his name was included in lists of those under discussion for a life peerage in Labour Party circles. It is likely that he would have had a different attitude to a peerage, which would have involved useful work in the public service—being 'really in the works'—than to the knighthood which he was offered. But the smouldering dislike of his old adversary Richard Crossman diminished any prospects which Herbert may have had of such preferment. As Herbert reflected wryly in a late interview: 'I was all that Crossman hated: that's to say, balanced, fair, worrying about the truth.'

The University of Oxford was a beneficiary of this blocked path to public preferment, for here Herbert found a ready outlet for the taste for administration which he was now discovering. In 1967, he was asked to chair a report into the arrangements governing relations between senior and junior members in the University. The background to this inquiry was the student unrest which was sweeping spectacularly through the universities of the USA and the continent of Europe in the second half of the 1960s. Oxford, never the most political of student cultures, had seen nothing like the sit-ins and demonstrations, let alone the violence, which had split the faculties and captured the headlines in Berkeley or Paris. But its student movement was increasingly critical of the university's authoritarian and paternalistic method of managing relations with its junior members. In 1966, a committee of inquiry under Lord Franks had proposed sweeping changes to the governance structure of the University. Student affairs were dismissed in just three lines. The amending legislation necessary to implement the Franks Report was now before the Privy Council. The students therefore adopted the clever tactic of petitioning the Privy Council so as to block the progress of the University's legislation. A compromise was reached: the part of the legislation on relations with junior members would be partitioned off and subject to a further inquiry, allowing the rest of the legislation to proceed.

Although he had taken his turn in a three-year stint of running the Law Faculty Board, Herbert had had relatively little administrative experience in Oxford. He was aware of his reputation as a left-winger in the conservative circles of the University hierarchy, and he had already made his sympathies with the students clear. He was therefore 'astonished' to be asked to chair the inquiry. But the choice had an inspired logic which was later compared with Lloyd George's strategy when he warned his negotiators in Palestine that if either side stopped throwing rocks at them, they would be sacked. Herbert's left-wing credentials lent him credibility with the students, while his impeccable academic and institutional credentials gave him authority within the university establishment. He leapt at the chance to take on this new administrative role. His motivation in doing so is interesting. He was sympathetic to the students' complaints about arbitrary disciplinary power and about the resistance of many academics to reforming the syllabus; he found this kind of academic closed-mindedness 'monstrous'. Not least because of his experience as a parent, he was also interested in the student unrest as a social phenomenon. But Herbert did not think that the real grievances of American or French students had much purchase in the British context, and he viewed many of the pronouncements of the local student movement as 'nonsense'. So although he saw the need for real change in Oxford, in taking on this task, he was not motivated primarily by a sense of injustice. Rather, he later said, 'I just thought I'd enjoy doing that sort of thing'.

Filling the vacuum created by his blocked opportunities of service on a public commission, Herbert immediately set up the committee to function 'as a sort of mini Royal Commission'. He was determined to do the job thoroughly and to produce a report which would be both readable and widely read. Over the next eight months, he and his four academic colleagues spent much of their time taking written and oral evidence from students and colleagues, and they passed a further four months discussing and shaping their 150 page report. Despite the graffiti around the University—'Don't take it to Hart'—over 200 students gave evidence, encouraged by Herbert's liberal reputation and the sense that there was a real chance of reform. The most vivid cause of resentment and complaint was the role of the Proctors, two academics appointed each year to act as the guardians of student discipline. The Proctors acted as prosecutor, judge, and jury: they also had, in effect, a quasi-legislative role because of the extraordinarily broad and vague terms in which the disciplinary offences were couched. There was little recourse for students who felt that they had been treated unfairly by the Proctors. More generally, the student movement was pushing for democratization: for greater student involvement in decision making on matters directly affecting students' lives and on broader academic policy.

Even if Herbert had not carefully annotated his own copy to record that he had personally written the first two chapters and the appendix on student radicalism in Oxford (contributions which made up over half of the Report), anyone familiar with his work would easily identify the parts for which he was responsible. They are marked out by their precision and their elegant formulations of liberal principles, with solutions to all specific issues worked out through rationally defensible extensions of those articulated principles. Herbert opened the Report by reflecting on the nature of a university as a sphere for not only education but also 'free critical discussion', and on the social changes which had brought the current proposal to reduce the age of majority in Britain from 21 to 18. These changes, he argued, made many of the University's paternalistic assumptions inappropriate. The Report would respond not to the students' protests but to their rational demands. Academic matters such as staff appointments, examining, and the substance of the curriculum call, he argued, for information, transparency, consultation, and reason-giving. But, contrary to the student's demands, they do not call for representation. The analogy between a university and a political society is not a complete one: academic governance depends on experience, expertise, and authority and should therefore not be open to the full democratic process. Questions affecting students as people, on the other hand—discipline and housing for example—should be dealt with on the basis of full representative democracy.

Herbert went on to address the main cause of the students' grievance: the proctorial system. Though making some attempt to outline the perceived advantages of the current system, Herbert's own sympathies quickly become apparent. He voiced a swingeing critique of the concentration of legislative, executive, and punitive power in the hands of just two people operating, in Herbert's memorable phrase, in a 'blaze of secrecy'. There was no need, he conceded, to go as far as having full criminal procedure for matters of student discipline. But the basic principles of legality should be respected: there should be transparency about evidence; there should be the possibility of cross-examination of witnesses; there should be the right to be represented by someone of the student's choice; there should be written charges. Above all, there should be a separation of the powers currently concentrated in the Proctors' hands. His proposal was to enact a minimal basic offence: all other rules would be made by a joint committee on which senior and junior members would have equal representation.

When he agreed to chair the committee, Herbert had set out with characteristic enthusiasm to read 'almost everything I could get my hands on about student revolts everywhere'. He consulted friends in the USA and debated the issues with his friend Stuart Hampshire, a strong supporter of the students. But he found the literature which he consulted intellectually unsatisfactory, and this prompted him to write his own brief analysis of student radicalism at Oxford. Written in the beautiful tranquillity of the Villa Serbelloni in Bellagio, this Appendix to the Report was vintage Herbert optimistic rationalism, tinged with a certain conservatism about the University. It was not so much an account of the student movement but rather an analysis of the movement's political doctrines: its approach was philosophical rather than cultural or historical, and it speculated rather little about the social genesis of the movement itself. Herbert focussed on the radicals' critique of materialism, inequality, and hierarchy, along with their rejection of either the liberal-democratic or the state-socialist response to these evils. Their object, he pointed out, was not the universities as such but rather a general social revolution. On the radical view, the students' lack of experience and their short-term involvement with the University, far from being a reason for excluding them from its governance, would provide a justification for their inclusion. But Herbert was sceptical about how many students really shared this radical ideology rather than merely used the protest movement as a jumping off point for the pursuit of less fundamental complaints. This empirical analysis shaped the strategy of the Report, which was to deal decisively with the more moderate aspects of the student complaints, thus bolstering the fundamentals of the present system by giving it some liberal and democratic credentials.

The tone of the Hart Report reflects what today seems an amazing confidence in the integrity and authority of a university. But it also exemplifies

Herbert's Benthamite impatience with the claims of tradition when unsupported by rational argument. Reason and clarity were, as ever, his supreme values. In this context, the conclusion of the Appendix is of particular interest. Herbert turned, finally, to the implications for scholarship of the radical position's 'sociology of knowledge'. According to this position, academic inquiry, far from being concerned with truth, expertise, or neutral and objective knowledge, rather makes claims to knowledge which are inevitably partial, affected by interests or power. Herbert saw this stance—now a familiar position within many disciplines as a result of movements such as postmodernism, post-structuralism, and pragmatism—as utterly inimical to the ideal of liberal education bent on rational argument and the pursuit of truth. He also saw it as potentially undermining moral and political critique of issues such as the Vietnam War. In the Appendix, Herbert was fighting to preserve a world which he feared was about to change around him, and his concern about the threat of relativism framed some continuing debates with his children. Fifteen years later, the issue was a regular source of discussion between him and Adam who, as a graduate student in anthropology at Cambridge, was familiar with the phenomenological assault on positivist theories of knowledge. And two decades later, in the midst of an intellectual argument with Joanna, who had by this time left her job in Cambridge to train as a psychotherapist and who was working in feminist and psychoanalytic theory with the ideas which so discomfited Herbert, he claimed never to have understood a word of Michel Foucault, the supreme exponent of the argument that power and knowledge are inextricably linked. And yet the Appendix shows that he was quick to understand the full implications of the radical position. Despite his left-wing sympathies, these were implications which held no more attraction for him than had Marxism in the 1930s.

The Hart Report was a model of clarity and accessibility and a skilful political compromise. After vigorous debate in the University's rarely convened parliament, Congregation, practically all of the Report's recommendations were adopted. The Lloyd George strategy had worked: the Committee had had to bear all relevant interests in mind, and the opponents at both extremes of the debate continued to throw rocks. There was a great deal of hostility from the right, with traditionalists like Herbert's former student and philosophical admirer John Lucas appalled at what they saw as capitulation to student demands. Even the more moderate conservatives were critical of the Report's tone, which was thought to be insufficiently respectful to the Proctors. On the left, Stuart Hampshire wrote a critical review in *The Listener* condemning the Report as 'bourgeois' and castigating the committee for not going much further down the road to full student incorporation in the democratic self-governance of the University. Herbert later recalled an exchange with his colleague Brian Simpson, recently a Proctor, who described the Report as a 'dog's dinner': their mutual regard was not enhanced when Herbert, being unfamiliar with the expression, asked him to explain what he meant by it. In Simpson's view, the Report was hypocritical: the Proctors had not in fact expelled a student in living memory, whereas the Colleges regularly suspended or even expelled students without observing any vestige of fair procedure. The authors of the Report were therefore taking, in relation to the University, a moral high ground which they failed to occupy in their college positions. In retrospect, characteristically self-critical, Herbert felt that Hampshire had had the best of the argument. Interviewed about the history of the University in 1988, Herbert said that the Report should indeed have gone further, and that the arguments for excluding student representatives from Faculty committees and the General Board had not ultimately been convincing. Essentially, he felt that he had failed fully to endorse the implications of his own principles. His self-criticism represents the credo according to which he typically assessed his own behaviour: 'I ought', he said, 'to have been more liberal.'

Herbert's involvement in the administrative work of the Monopolies Commission and the Oxford inquiry gave him satisfaction and a sense of purpose during a period in which he was anxiously contemplating his academic future. Though not due to retire from the Chair of Jurisprudence until 1974, he was gradually coming to the conclusion that it was time to resign. When he finally announced his decision, during the work of the inquiry in 1968, most of his colleagues were baffled. This was not surprising. The genesis of Herbert's decision lay in the complex and intense interior world which he displayed to other people only rarely and interstitially. His admission to Joanna of his feelings about *Punishment and Responsibility* was one instance. Another was his remark to Joseph Raz, during one of their weekend excursions to the country, that he felt that he had said everything he had to say and was perplexed about what to work on next. Accustomed to Herbert's typical reserve, Raz found this confession troubling and embarrassing: he made no response, and Herbert did not repeat the confidence. But after 16 years of virtually unbroken public success and recognition, Herbert was exhausted. This was not simply to do with the demands of his job which were, by today's standards, relatively light. Rather, it had to do with the strain of maintaining his outward assurance and composure while struggling internally with self-doubt. Trapped in the spotlight of his fame, he was finding the pressure constantly to come up with new ideas unbearable. Increasingly, he was overtaken by panics like the ones he had experienced over Abraham Harari and while correcting the proofs of

Punishment and Responsibility. The role of the great man was one he played with distinction, but it would never come naturally to him.

The prospect of early retirement, however, presented him with a number of substantial problems. Not least, there was a financial problem. Herbert had not worked in academic life long enough to earn anything like a full pension, and even with Jenifer's salary and the not inconsiderable royalties from his publications, the family would not have enough money to sustain a household which still needed the services of Nanny and of student carers to help with Jacob. Herbert also worried about providing for Jacob's and Nanny's futures. Even leaving aside these financial concerns, it was inconceivable that Herbert, with his strong sense of duty and intellectual mission, should simply give up work. A partial solution to the first problem and an attractive resolution of the second was, however, within his grasp. As he felt his thirst for developing his own ideas diminishing, he was already finding an intellectually and emotionally satisfying alternative in his work on Jeremy Bentham. If he had said everything he himself wanted to say, what could be a more useful contribution to his field or a more appropriate use of his intellectual gifts than the effort to bring to light and open to contemporary interpretation the work of a scholar whose reputation was lower than Herbert felt his writing merited and whose ideas had so often been the source of his own inspiration?

Having identified this project, the only problem was to find an institutional framework within which he could pursue it. This, too, was easily resolved. Herbert applied for and was awarded a grant from the Nuffield Foundation to work on the systematic publication of Bentham's writings and the philosophical analysis of his ideas. University College, only too eager to maintain its links with one of its most distinguished Fellows, readily agreed to appoint Herbert to a Research Fellowship which would allow him to keep his College rooms and membership of the Senior Common Room. Though his salary and institutional status would be reduced, these he regarded as prices well worth paying for the psychological space and intellectual freedom which escape from the Chair and research on Bentham seemed to promise.

But there was one other problem created by his resignation from the Chair, and it was one which Herbert was less obviously in a position to address. This was the question of succession. Having built up the prestige not only of jurisprudence as a domain but also of the Oxford Chair as its throne, Herbert was anxious that his work would be continued by someone with real energy and intellectual acumen. He was also determined that his successor would continue the tradition of genuinely philosophical jurisprudence which he had revived. The clear rule being that professors and other academics should not be directly involved in the appointment of their successors, one might have expected Herbert to nurse these ambitions privately, and to restrict his interventions to writing references and giving informal advice. There was, moreover, an obviously suitable successor within Oxford: Herbert's friend and co-author Tony Honoré. This makes it all the more surprising that Herbert's involvement in the appointment of his successor was, to put it mildly, proactive. Feeling, perhaps, that Honoré's broader academic interests might dilute his concentration on legal philosophy, Herbert made a bold and decisive intervention in the search for a new professor, and one which was to put a new distance between him and Honoré. He wrote to Ronald Dworkin, whose examination papers he had marked 12 years before, and who was now lecturing at Yale Law School, to ask if he would be interested.

Dworkin, who had at this stage published relatively little, and who had no idea that Herbert had been following his career, was amazed at this informal approach. Herbert had, however, been pondering his work intently. In his article, 'Is Law a System of Rules?' published in 1967, Dworkin had built on the insights sketched in the examination paper which had so impressed Herbert, mounting a frontal assault on Herbert's argument that law is composed exclusively of social rules whose existence and validity depend on their source or pedigree. On a trip to visit the New York office of Oxford University Press in April 1968, Herbert arranged to meet Dworkin and his wife for lunch. In New York, he had a number of commitments: work on a paper on Kelsen and a meeting with philosophers Marshall Cohen and Joel Feinberg, with whom he had been corresponding about their shared interest in criminal responsibility. He was also preoccupied by OUP's failure to take the international reach of its work sufficiently seriously. But these concerns were engulfed by his preoccupation with getting to grips with Dworkin's ideas. His diary entries recorded just before the trip give a painful impression of the anxieties which he was hoping to escape by vacating the Chair:

Make this—last journey to America as Oxford Professor of Jurisprudence— a rounded and calm effort: not harsh dogmatic but an offer of co-operation and discovery .... Not to spoil one thing by worry about another. Mood very impatient e.g. agitation last evening on Oxford train on reading so late Dworkin on me on Model of Rules: a sort of intellectual panic set in. No way to approach things: Criticism to be more calmly embraced as part of a joint philosophical effort ...

And in New York, as the meeting with the Dworkins approached, Herbert constantly found himself returning to Dworkin's article:

[Meeting at OUP] took till 4—then back to find Ronnie Dworkin's reply difficult and I haven't yet got to the bottom of it. But I must put my paper in order first .... To dine with Feinberg. Before that thought I must read again RD's piece on Rules .... *Must get this ridiculous Kelsen paper under control.* So now (9a.m.) try. 11/2 [hours] *calm* work ... and then a break ... redigesting of his paper before meeting Dworkins at 1. But what a fuss—for Prof of Jurisprudence at Oxford aet. 60 after 16 years in the Chair—perhaps the agony has a function?

At the 'delightful gay lunch', both Herbert's paper on Kelsen and the possibility of Dworkin's putting in for the Oxford Chair were discussed. The informal approach was followed a little later by an official inquiry from the University, and in June of 1969 Dworkin and his wife, Betsy, visited Oxford. Betsy Dworkin was unimpressed, and Dworkin told Herbert that he would refuse the job. In September, a letter offering it to him nonetheless arrived. Betsy Dworkin was persuaded that it might be wise to accept the formal offer, but Dworkin, regularly in touch with Herbert about the course of the negotiations, told him that he felt he should put the University on notice that he would be unlikely to stay in Oxford long. 'There is no one to be put on notice: there is no such performative utterance!' Herbert replied, encouraging him to accept. Dworkin accepted the post, persuaded not least by the prospect of regular intellectual exchange with the man whom he regarded as the pre-eminent legal philosopher of the twentieth century and in counterpoint to whose work he was already developing his own theory of law. The following summer, just before moving to Oxford, the Dworkins invited Herbert to join them on holiday in a beautiful house on a large estate in Draguignan. Here, the conversation hardly touched on jurisprudence: instead, it revolved around literature, often discussed amid marvellous country walks and sumptuous dinners (with Herbert intoxicated by the former and oblivious to the latter). The Dworkins were amazed by the depth of his reading and beguiled by his dazzling talk, often in fluent French: they were struck in particular by his acute feel for Henry James. They felt that a friendship was being formed, and looked forward to developing it in Oxford.

Though Herbert was not a member of the formal appointment panel, his decisive influence on the appointment of his successor is clear. He even went so far as to ring at least one of the electors on several occasions pressing Dworkin's claims (the elector, not himself a legal theorist, having not heard of Ronald Dworkin, asked, 'Do you mean the one [a philosopher of the same name] from Southampton?'). From the appointing panel's perspective, it is understandable that the informal imprimatur of a man who had been an unqualified success in the job, and who was so well placed to assess the quality of potential candidates, would have been persuasive. What is more interesting is Herbert's own impulse to stretch the conventions as far, or perhaps further, than they could go, and to leave his mark on the Chair even after he had vacated it.

Far from what a critic like Harari would have expected, Herbert had not chosen a successor who was cast entirely in his own image. In seeking to secure Dworkin's appointment, Herbert was, certainly, ensuring that the main disciplinary inspiration for legal theory in Oxford would continue to be philosophy, and that the normative legal theory emanating from the Chair would have impeccably liberal credentials. But Dworkin's philosophy was not the Oxford linguistic philosophy which had inspired Herbert, and Dworkin's liberalism was flavoured with the deep engagement with issues of constitutional politics which had so impressed Herbert at Harvard in 1957 yet which never became one of his own central preoccupations. Herbert was painfully aware that Dworkin was already promising—or threatening—to become his most influential critic. In his diary, he soothed himself, in a striking analogy, with the idea that Dworkin might produce '*Philosophical Investigations to my Tractatus*'. But by recruiting the man whom he saw as the most gifted legal philosopher qualified for the Chair, Herbert put the overall discipline before his own reputation. For in securing the part of his legacy which pertained to the orientation and quality of his field, he was adding the prestige of the Oxford Chair to what he saw as the most vigorous critique of his personal contribution.

Part IV

AFTER THE CHAIR

CHAPTER 12

Old Turks and Young Fogeys: Bentham and Brasenose

ALTHOUGH Herbert's decision to take early retirement from the Oxford Chair in 1968 was born of a loss of intellectual confidence and the feeling that he had no further original contribution to make, this turning point was far from marking the end of his intellectual work. His decision to devote himself to the further analysis and editing of the works of Bentham had a long genesis. In 1965, he had written to Isaiah Berlin, who was then visiting Princeton:

[I]t is plain that my fantasy about pursuing Benthamite studies at All Souls is not a practical one under present circumstances. I talked to John [Sparrow, then Warden of All Souls] about it, but I was not disappointed because I never thought there was much reality in the plan.

All Souls was destined once again to elude him. Not so Bentham. As Sydney Smith had observed nearly 150 years earlier, Jeremy Bentham needed a middle-man:

Neither gods, men nor booksellers can doubt the necessity of a middle-man between Mr. Bentham and the public. Mr. Bentham is long: Mr. Bentham is occasionally involved and obscure; Mr. Bentham invents new and alarming expressions; Mr. Bentham loves division and sub-division, and he loves method itself more than its consequences. Those only therefore who know his originality, his knowledge, his vigour and his boldness, will recur to the works themselves. The great mass of readers will not purchase improvement at so dear a rate but will choose rather to become acquainted with Mr. Bentham through the medium of the reviews—after that eminent philosopher has been washed, trimmed, shaved and forced into clean linen.

But what, wondered many of Herbert's admirers, drew the most successful English-speaking legal philosopher to resign his Chair in favour of devoting himself to becoming an intellectual valet?

At one level, the source of Herbert's fascination with Bentham is obvious: ever since his inaugural lecture, his published works had demonstrated his regard for Bentham as a profound source of insight. Bentham's 'extraordinary combination of a fly's eye for detail, with an eagle's eye for illuminating generalizations applicable across wide areas of social life' resonated with Herbert's longest standing intellectual disposition, and he admired Bentham's astonishing range, which 'includes topics as diverse as poor relief, Christianity and the Church of England, model prisons, birth control, grammar, logic, usury, and much of economics' as well as slavery, cruelty to animals, and a panoply of law reform topics, especially in criminal law and the law of evidence. The fact that much of Bentham's work—notably the work which anticipated John Austin's command theory of law—had remained unpublished or published only in unsatisfactory or incomplete form, gave Herbert a clear scholarly rationale for this new direction. There was something deeply appealing to Herbert in the man whose 'eagle's eye view' articulated the sweeping principle of utility:

Nature has placed mankind under the governance of two sovereign masters, *pain* and *pleasure*. It is for them alone to point out what we ought to do, as well as to determine what we shall do. On the one hand the standard of right and wrong, on the other the chain of causes and effects, are fastened to their throne. . . . The *principle of utility* recognizes this subjection, and assumes it for the foundation of that system, the object of which is to rear the fabric of felicity by the hands of reason and of law. . . . By the principle of utility is meant that principle which approves or disapproves of every action whatsoever, according to the tendency which it appears to have to augment or diminish the happiness of the party whose interest is in question. . . . I say of every action whatsoever; and therefore not only of every action of a private individual, but of every measure of government. . . . An action . . . may be said to be conformable to the principle of utility . . . when the tendency it has to augment the happiness of the community is greater than any it has to diminish it.

Yet more appealing to Herbert, this was equally a man whose 'fly's eye view' could interest him not only in the details of prison architecture but even in prisoners' bedding:

Beds stuffed with straw: one side covered with the cheapest linen of hempen cloth for summer: the other with coarse woollen cloth for winter. Stretching the under sheet on hooks pins or buttons will save the quantity usually added for tucking in. In cold weather that the woollen may be in contact with the body the sheet might be omitted. . . . Straw, the more frequently changed the better particularly in warm months. To the extent of the quantity wanted for littering cattle, the change will cost nothing, and beyond that quantity the expense will only be the difference between the value of the straw as straw and the value of it as manure.

Bentham's complex vision is exemplified by the Panopticon prison—an ingenious structure in which each prisoner could be seen at any moment without being aware of the fact, which inspired the design of several actual prisons and which became the metaphor used by Michel Foucault for the totalitarian aspects of modern governmental technology. This must have given Herbert's liberal temperament pause for thought. Yet he was as far from Marx's view of Bentham as 'the arch philistine . . . that insipid, pedantic, leather-tongued oracle of the ordinary bourgeois intelligence of the nineteenth century' as it was possible to be.

There were also a number of psychological factors at play in both Herbert's decision to concentrate on the editing and interpretation of another scholar's work, and his specific choice of Bentham. In the first place, this new role allowed him to sidestep the increasing pressure to speak in his own voice in answer to the rapidly multiplying commentators on his own work. At the same time, the proximity between Bentham's and Herbert's views meant that commentaries on Bentham afforded Herbert the opportunity of oblique revision and refinement of his own ideas. Secondly, his genuine, if exaggerated, feelings of diffidence and discomfort about his own success were assuaged by the devotion of his energies to a scholar whom he felt to be both a more original thinker and to have been inadequately recognized. Thirdly, he felt at some level a personal affinity with and affection for the eccentric and deeply obsessive Bentham. Colleagues remember the pleasure which Herbert took in recounting stories of Bentham's monumental peculiarities, and this amusement is reflected in the introduction to Herbert's essays on his idiosyncratic forebear. His amusement at Bentham's eccentricity is invariably tinged with real empathy, as is witnessed by the way in which he was able to write of Bentham's sadness at his increasing distance from the man with whom Herbert told Morton White that Bentham had been 'in love', and in whose name he later uttered some of his most influential views on the American Declaration of Independence. This was John Lind:

the son of an impoverished Anglican clergyman whose affairs had been looked after by Bentham's father. . . . As some very vivid and moving letters testify, Bentham formed with Lind a most intimate friendship. Indeed, on Bentham's side it was a passionate one, so that when the friendship cooled after a quarrel, Bentham could write sadly to Lind, 'there was a time when I doubted whether, so long as you were alive, I could live without you. It became necessary for me to try: I have tried and I have succeeded.'

Herbert admired Bentham's egalitarian instincts and his trenchant rationalism and anti-traditionalism—'Why speak of learning from the wisdom of our ancestors rather than their folly?'; he identified with Bentham's vulnerability and sense of remaining an outsider to the early Victorian Establishment of which he was the most vehement critic; and he found Bentham's obsessions endearing.

Having secured the Nuffield Foundation research grant to continue his fellowship at University College and to support his 'Benthamite' endeavour, Herbert threw himself into the task, both intellectually and institutionally. Bentham's papers—like his skeleton and clothing—were in the possession of University College London [UCL], the first entirely non-denominational university in England. Bentham had been involved in the College's pre-development, and his follower John Austin had been the first (not entirely successful) holder of its Chair of Jurisprudence. Bentham's directions in relation to his body, which he left to his medical friend Southwood Smith, were observed minutely by the College: his head rested for some time in a box above the entrance to the Council Chamber, while the skeleton, clothed in a wax effigy and the dead man's own clothing—an 'auto-icon'—sits in a glass case at the end of the College's South Cloister, where it probably causes more perplexity to tourists than it serves Bentham's intended, utilitarian function of showing that even dead bodies could be put to use and of puncturing 'primitive horror' about dissection, which 'originates in ignorance'.

The College's treatment of Bentham's papers had, however, been more haphazard. After Bentham's death, John Bowring, his executor, had prepared an unsatisfactory edition of Bentham's works before depositing the manuscripts at UCL. There they languished for some time, the mania for detail and classification satirized by Sydney Smith making Bentham a challenge for scholars and a dubious prospect for commercially minded publishers. But the problem went deeper than this. For in his utilitarian concern to avoid waste, Bentham tended to write not only horizontally along each sheet of paper, but then vertically as well. Though devoted editors like Charles Everett had made some progress towards systematic publication, the quality of organization, attribution, and presentation of what had been published by the late 1960s still left much to be desired. At UCL, a Bentham Manuscripts Committee had been set up in 1932, the centenary of Bentham's death, with a lecture by C. K. Ogden the jumping off point for a major fund-raising effort. But once again, the efforts lapsed, and it was not until 1959, when a new Bentham Committee was established, that things began to move forward. Freddie Ayer, at that time Grote Professor of Mind and Logic at UCL, had shamed the Provost (the head of UCL) into taking action by suggesting that if the College was not going to do anything with the papers, it might as well sell them to the highest (American) bidder. The new Committee duly began to plan a systematic edition. In 1961 the historian and future general editor J. H. Burns arrived and, with the support of the energetic Ayer and Lionel Robbins, the plans began to take shape. By the late 1960s the Bentham Project, as it came to be known, had secured some funds for research assistance in organizing and preserving the archive. But much remained to be done.

Herbert, who had already had substantial contact with the Project, now had time to become more fully involved. After his resignation from the Oxford Chair, he joined the Project's organizing committee, later becoming its Chair and one of its principal fund-raisers: he remained an active member of the committee until poor health forced him to take a more passive, advisory role in 1991. In the intervening 23 years, he was an indefatigable supporter, pursuing funds not only in Britain from bodies like the British Academy, but also from the German Marshall fund, and from a variety of charitable foundations in the US. Equally important, he negotiated with Oxford University Press a systematic publication plan when problems arose with the current, University of London's Athlone press in the mid-1970s. Herbert's work on the Bentham Committee was recognized by UCL in the award of an Honorary Fellowship in 1987.

Within two years of Herbert's resignation from the Chair, the first fruits of this new involvement became apparent. In 1970, a new edition of Bentham's major work of moral, political, and normative legal philosophy, *An Introduction to the Principles of Morals and Legislation*, was produced by Herbert and Jimmy Burns. Prefaced by a brief introduction, Bentham's most economical and persuasive statement of the philosophical system of utilitarianism, the principle that all human action should be devoted to the pursuit of the happiness of the community as a whole—or 'the greatest happiness of the greatest number', a phrase which has become the best known label for utilitarianism although one the appropriateness of which Bentham himself equivocated over—now became available in an elegant and accessible edition. The same year, Herbert produced an edition of Bentham's major contribution to analytical jurisprudence, *Of Laws in General*. This was of particular importance, for the work had remained unpublished for over 150 years until produced by Charles Everett under the different title *The Limits of Jurisprudence Defined* in 1945. Apart from the poor presentation, incompleteness, and inaccessibility of that edition, Herbert was able to draw on evidence available from the Bentham archive to produce a more accurate text and to shed light on its relationship with Bentham's other work, as well as restoring to the work the title which Bentham himself had chosen for it. Although he had research assistance in preparing this edition, the detailed labour which Herbert himself had to undertake should not be discounted: the man whose attitude to close textual scholarship Tony Honoré had sometimes found irritatingly casual now found himself poring over near-indecipherable manuscripts with an enormous, page-sized magnifying glass. As well as working in this editorial capacity, Herbert was pushing forward his project of pressing close readings of the newly available Bentham texts into the service of contemporary analytical jurisprudence. Between his resignation from the Chair of

Jurisprudence and becoming Principal of Brasenose College in 1973, he produced important critical papers on *Of Laws in General* (1971) and on Bentham's account of legal powers (1972), his conception of legal rights (1973), and his advocacy of the need to demystify legal language (1973) (the last a topic on which he delivered the Modern Law Review Chorley lecture at the London School of Economics in 1972). These papers he conceived as laying the foundations for a major book or even multi-volume work on Bentham.

These contributions to Bentham scholarship would almost certainly have been more than enough to satisfy the Nuffield Foundation which was now paying his salary. But Herbert's efforts did not rest here. In 1969, he was also working on a paper on the late nineteenth-century German jurist Jhering's contribution to jurisprudence—a paper for which he had to do a substantial amount of reading in German, given that many of Jhering's publications had never been translated. He also continued to think about issues of law reform, and at this time he was particularly concerned with the topic of abortion. The partial legalization of abortion in England and Wales, of which he had been a powerful advocate, had been effected by the Abortion Act 1967, and Herbert was now keen to trace the consequences of the legislation. He worked with David Soskice, a young economics colleague at University College, to trace the statistical evidence which might illuminate declining recourse to dangerous 'back-street' abortions and hence bolster the utilitarian case for maintaining and indeed extending legal access to abortion. The challenge to come up with the clearest and most convincing case for abortion was sharpened by his forthcoming lecture tour of New Zealand and Australia, where he had agreed to speak on the topic to a variety of audiences, including some conservative religious and medical groups. Freed from the institutional responsibilities of the Chair of Jurisprudence, Herbert was able to extend his trip to New Zealand and Australia to indulge in some of the adventurous cultural tourism of which he had been fond all his life. In March 1971, he and Jenifer travelled to Teheran and Isapahan, from where they went on to India, visiting Delhi, Jaipur, and Agra, and then to Hong Kong. From Hong Kong, Jenifer travelled home via Tokyo and Moscow, while Herbert continued to New Zealand, where he spent several weeks; to Fiji and Western Samoa; to Australia; to Japan, where he had OUP business; and finally to Nepal, from which he travelled back to England in June. The detailed diary which he recorded during the trip is unusually free from introspection or the anxieties of professional obligation: it also illustrates that, at 64, Herbert had lost none of his youthful enthusiasm for new places, new people, new experiences.

As usual, his reactions were decisive. Teheran, though he enjoyed the artistic riches in the near-empty museums, he detested: 'city of horror . . . rubble with modern giant buildings stuck in . . . feels like the worst features of middle ages and of mechanised XXth Century combined'. But in Isapahan, unlike Jenifer who found the formalized repetition 'stiff', he found the soaring domes and tiled motifs 'extraordinarily grand' and admired (perhaps with a touch of envy) the 'great air of tranquillity and abstraction from life' within the mosques: 'Question of "beauty" or comparison with W. art rather absurd. Totally different form of impact on eyes and suggestion of tactile impression.' He lamented the 'tiny resources to stave off decay' and was deeply moved by the plight of the students who offered their services as guides and who showed 'touching eagerness to learn at least English . . .'. They 'left a deep, agreeable yet sad, impression on me'. Herbert recorded in detail what he had learnt from these students: one took him and Jenifer to visit his remote village; another 'about 20 not a student but worked in a firm printing designs on cloth had a face like a gentle version of Omar Sharif: great charm smiling eyes regular features: wonderful white teeth. Worked 6 days a week printing cloth (8–9 hours a day) and then night school including learning English. Father dead: mother employed . . . making carpets two brothers at school and sister: he supported them. No complaint: delighted to walk and talk. . . . Helped me to buy oranges, warned me about taxi system. . . . Shook hands warmly and went off. Conscious of poverty, restrictions of life, but marvellous dignity and charm'.

In India, where he and Jenifer were guests of the family of Vinit Haksar, one of Herbert's former doctoral students, he was overwhelmed by the teeming streets and the contrast between the beauty of the ancient architecture and the poverty and urban squalor. As ever, he gathered as much information about social issues (average wages, employment rates, birth control practices) as he could from everyone he met, commenting wryly on the awkwardness of some of the social events, while opening himself utterly to the aesthetic experiences:

Taj: lovely light ivory-looking miracle of symmetry: delicate flower decoration: delicious garden: nothing wedding-cake like as feared. Extraordinary detail as well as noble proportions: a poetic structure!

Sweet little boys [begging on a bus heading back from Agra to Delhi]: bright-eyed, merry, but what a future . . .

and in Delhi:

What a slum this whole place is—terrifying heart-rending grief-making. Negligence of education perhaps the worst British contribution to all this.

After the contrasts of India, the more orderly bustle of Hong Kong was soothing, and the aesthetics enticingly easy to locate within an existing frame of reference: 'glittering lights all over heights and waterfront—like

San Francisco only better.' By Easter, after a brief stop-over with his old New College friend Bill Wentworth in Australia, Herbert had already been in the main object of his journey, New Zealand, for two weeks, and he contemplated the reception of his lectures as he sketched a dramatic view of Mount Cook in his diary. He enjoyed the scenery, the large airy houses, and the hospitality of Erich Geiringer, a well known doctor and psycho-analyst and former lover of Jenifer's sister Mariella:

Still a polymath, great vitality and critical powers and has become *the* anti-establishment figure in NZ . . .

His wife, 22 years younger than Erich, Herbert thought 'in some ways his victim—though obviously deep attachment. E. has a kind of recklessness'.

New Zealand's social culture intrigued Herbert. On the one hand, he was repelled by the smugness, insularity, boring food, and social conservatism which he encountered in many of its cities, and which he satirized with unusual vehemence (and more than a touch of upper middle class English snobbery) in letters home to his children:

The place has its charms: it's an Anglo-Saxon Switzerland both physically and socially: no real poor; bottom is Middle Class (i.e. lower MC.) with of course attendant horrors of philistinism, narrowness and religion—but of course won-derful to see no Asia-type or even UK-type poverty, slums or socially deferring classes. (Natural beauty is overwhelming). Bus drivers, farm workers all speak to you man to man, shake hands. Marvellously beautiful country also fantastic fertility; millions of lambs grazing: heavenly trees now in autumn colours (though most are v. exotic evergreens). S. Island where I now am lyrical Alps and Glaciers. . . . Lectures quite fun: Abortion is a big issue here; and torrents of questions and objections to legalization from powerful Catholic doctor group. Society is horribly narrow minded, crude, ungainly, philistine, unimagi-native, pathetically nostalgic for England of about 50 years ago and afraid of change. Food, except in private houses, is execrable. . . . Typical conversation at my dinner table (you are allotted a seat, if alone, with others), 'India over-crowded? Send them a lot of pooves' (i.e. queers). 'Ha Ha.'. But the universities on the whole are surprisingly liberal; proportionately a lot of hippies who are *not* persecuted and even the squarest of professors say how much for the good the old dogmatic mechanical teaching has been transformed by student demands. . . . Maoris here look rather frayed and sad: not ill-treated but obvi-ously their Polynesian life gets mangled in this kind of economy. Seem physi-cally vulnerable (TB incidence high—rather like Red Indians left in USA).

On the other hand, he was beguiled by much of the countryside, by Auckland—'such a beautiful place—gardens, trees, subtropical air'; and by the beauty of the early Maori wood carvings which he saw at its museum. It helped that, despite some conservative medico-legal audiences to whom his liberal plea for abortion rights must have been politically indigestible to say the least, he felt that the lectures were on the whole going down well. Though at one 'stiff establishment legal-medical meeting' he endured 'a rain of questions from hostile Catholic doctors—some of unbelievable stupidity', at several of his venues he 'felt I was both contributing something and learning something'. At least in relation to the former, he was not mistaken. Stephen Guest, then a student at the University of Otago in Dunedin and later to become a professor of jurisprudence at UCL, wrote to Jenifer after Herbert's death: 'Herbert converted me to jurisprudence by his lecture in Dunedin . . . on abortion: I had never heard anything like it—the clarity, the conviction, the straight-speaking'. Guest was part of a younger generation in New Zealand to whom Herbert's ideas were a refreshing and even inspiring change, and whose place in New Zealand society contributed to the fact that Herbert found it less seamlessly conservative than he had anticipated. In particular, pondering how his own children would have fitted into this social world, he was impressed by the widespread tolerance of the 'hippie youth culture' with its 'long hair and fur coats' in this 'superficially hearty society'. As he left the country, he reflected on the 'Adam-like' hippies as 'a vivifying force' in this 'otherwise smug . . . narrow community', acknowledging that New Zealand had been 'very different from what I thought to find—crew cut—tough—rugby-playing brutalities'.

Before moving on to further lectures in Australia, Herbert spent a few days travelling round Fiji and Western Samoa, where he visited schools and education projects and gave a number of talks on disciplinary systems in education, drawing on his work for the Hart Report. Here he was captivated by the vivid natural beauty, and the grace and energy of the local people: his diary is thick with lyrical descriptions: 'incredibly green opalescent coral reefs, fjords and then just sea . . .'; lists of tropical plants; descriptions of local dress—'amazingly beautiful coloured shirts, flowers behind ears'—and found himself getting caught up in the relaxed, uninhibited open-air lifestyle. On one school visit, 'rhythm so wonderful as beaten out on drums and hand clapping that I find myself more or less able to move fingers and even feet with it. Taken in charge by rather wild marvellous girl . . . felt slap on back to delight and roar of laughter'. But, ever the astute observer of tension or sadness, his diary is also peppered with moving little character sketches of the local officials, many of whom felt themselves to be isolated and alienated: 'Thin sad man—all the struggles of alcoholic in his face. Wonder how she came to marry him. Pity? Or good looks before his decay?'

Back in Australia with the Wentworths—Bill at this stage just hanging on to his post as Minister for Social Services—Herbert was again attuned to a strand of 'something sad underlying Bill's brio' and jotted down an affectionate if wry vignette of life in the affluent Australian political classes: 'Baked in heavenly sunshine in surf on beach . . . in Newport. Garage men, shopkeepers call him Bill . . . Barbara . . . (blue hair!) . . . many of the traits of Conservative English lady but without the coldness. . . . Hates cooking and said so. . . . Sadness behind the young-old gaiety (death of their daughter?). . . . Walk round edge of Pitt Water. . . . Heavenly view of Hawkesbury. . . . Boats all over water. Out to lunch at Eleanora Country Club (No Jewish members: "They do rather take over"—Barbara).' A sense of the special impact which Herbert had on people is given by Barbara Wentworth's letter to Jenifer after his death, in which she remembered him as 'of all the people . . . who stayed with us at Newport during the 28 years we lived there . . . by far the most fascinating, and so marvellously unaware of the fact'. At the Wentworths' Herbert encountered once again his old rival and juristic contemporary Julius Stone, now emeritus professor at Sydney University: 'thinner, nicer, less egoistic', was Herbert's terse summary. A successful presentation of the abortion lecture at Melbourne University and a quick visit to the capital Canberra, concluded Herbert's only trip to Australia.

But his travels were not over, and he now set off for several days in Japan, visiting the Japanese office of OUP and making a long trip to Kyoto enjoying the guidance and 'extreme solicitude' of a young OUP employee, Inoue. The formal gardens with their 'charming delicate stone bridges on little walkways', the lacquered interiors, and richly decorated royal palaces captured his aesthetic imagination; the 'impression of docile industry' impressed him; the national politics, with its concern to distance Japanese policy from American influence interested him; the elegant cross-legged kimono-wearing dinners fascinated him; and Inoue's kindness awed him. But he soon began to feel concerned to the point of embarrassment about how to reciprocate and how to communicate sufficiently clearly his appreciation at moments when Inoue— 'poor nice man'—appeared to think 'that he has made some "mistake" in conduct of my trip'; 'Felt guilty about imposing my Western taste on him . . . Poor man wearing himself out for me.' The elaborate hierarchy of Japanese social relations, in which Inoue appears to have been nominated as more or less Herbert's attendant during the trip, left him deeply uncomfortable, and though he was intrigued by the very differentness of Japan, with its male-oriented social life, geisha parties, formality, and attention to aesthetic detail, he did not feel at ease there. Tokyo's 'scruffy grey warehouse-looking buildings' in particular he found unappealing: a joke found its way into the margin of his diary: 'First prize: one week in Tokyo. Second prize: Two weeks in Tokyo'. As he left, he summed it up: 'In a way glad to leave Japan. Some of it horrid . . . though individuals very attractive. Rather an itch to get home now'.

Homebound he indeed was, but via Nepal, where he had looked forward to the stunning mountain scenery. But he had failed to anticipate the heat, the itch to get home, and the risk of food-poisoning. Tired by months of travelling, he nonetheless had the energy to record in detail the landscape with its 'grass-green hills and dramatic valleys' and the striking image of a Nepalese funeral, with burning funeral pyre, saffron-dressed elderly widow, moving cries: 'Very simple and beautiful in its own way'. But the last three months had furnished so many striking and beautiful images, and Herbert was ready to return to the familiar rhythms of life at home.

I have already mentioned that this long—110 page—1971 diary is striking for its lack of introspection. There are, however, two significant exceptions. While in New Zealand, at a moment of anxiety before lecturing, Herbert enjoined himself to have more 'confidence in my own powers', to 'do something in my subject every day', and 'to keep the activity going'. The diminishing energy and confidence which had led him to resign from the Chair, albeit temporarily held at bay by the irresistible momentum of a lecture tour, were still troubling him. Similarly, his new professional situation had done nothing to remove the perplexities of family life, and as he flew home, he began to reflect on these once again: 'Problems . . . no doubt . . . Jen Jakey Nanny not to speak of job doubt—Bentham—Monop. C'ee . . . find I have written nothing on "subjective side" here. Must preserve Geiringer-type calm and perspective amongst all my tangles: select what is worth doing . . .'

In an old mantra, he enjoined himself to 'coolness and leisurely exhilarated contemplation of things'. But his worries about the emotional climate of Manor Place were not without foundation. In his absence, various tensions had arisen, and Nanny, now suffering from arthritis, was uncertain of her future role in the household. As Charlie, writing to Herbert in New Zealand, bitingly put it, Nanny was suffering from

. . . the Hart family norm of intra-family hostility (QV love!). . . . The parameters are rather unchangeable (e.g. Mama) . . .

In a letter to Joanna, Adam, and Charlie, Herbert confessed:

some guilt about this rather heavenly abstraction from what are I fear horrors at 11 M.P [Manor Place] . . . Poor Nanny: Erich very keen that a Swedish injection . . . should be tried instead of operation. . . . Why not send her to Stockholm if it is done there? Do what you can to sustain her belief in being wanted which is, I agree, at the centre of the problem.

And to Joanna:

Sad about Nanny: I agree entirely that this is the emotional situation and we must just do what we can to make her feel wanted and contributing (as of course, even on the lowest criteria, she does tremendously). There is of course a problem about Jakey's emancipation—to the extent that this is a reality—but I would have thought that a shift to a more *Grandmotherly* part was possible if handled properly and if it is necessary. I agree too that it is hell that Ma has the feelings or lack of feelings she does (mixed in with guilt of course).

The worries about Nanny and about Jacob's future, exacerbated by Jenifer's continuing reluctance to accept that a long-term solution would have to be found in terms of residential care for Jacob, represent no more than the sorts of problems thrown up by any family the size and complexity of the Harts'. But underlying these worries remained the subtext of Herbert's stalled relationship with Jenifer and, as a diary written in the summer of 1970 records, the tension between the couple had now been revived by a recurrence of Herbert's career doubts. The episode was astonishingly acute. Settled into his new, less taxing institutional life, and with three major pieces of work appearing during the year, Herbert plummeted headlong into a severe depression precipitated by a casual inquiry about whether he would be interested in becoming the head of a college. In 1970, Wadham College consulted Herbert about the candidature of his old friend Stuart Hampshire for their Wardenship. During the course of the conversation, one of the Fellows asked whether Herbert himself might be interested. Taken aback, and feeling the question to be inappropriate in the context of a discussion of Hampshire, Herbert said that he was not. Jenifer was dismayed, and told Herbert that she would very much have liked him to pursue the idea. His instinctively negative reaction seems unlikely to have been prompted only by his feelings of loyalty to Hampshire: his attitude to headships of colleges had never been entirely positive, and he had also discouraged preliminary approaches from Pembroke and Trinity. His book of jokes, collected for after-dinner speeches, included several inscriptions of H. A. L. Fisher's response when approached about whether he would be interested in becoming Warden of New College: 'It may yet come to that.' And five years earlier, Herbert had written to Isaiah Berlin, who was contemplating becoming the founding head of Wolfson, a new graduate college:

As for your own possible future at Iffley, here again Jenifer and I are rather divided. She thinks that both the cause of graduates and of non-dons would be immensely advanced by your taking on this to me repellent sounding job. She only begs you to put aside the illusion that Jessup is quite nice. I on the other hand feel that the place is almost certain to be a rather empty façade for a long time, and that both the business of collecting money . . . and the poring over of building plans . . . are not remotely the proper exercise of your talents, although you could do both exceedingly well. . . . I was roundly ticked off by my Master, when on the subject being raised at dinner, I said I thought your talents could be better employed; he obviously felt that the whole utility and status of Heads of Houses were slighted by my observations . . .

Given that the Master of University College, Lord Redcliffe Maude, was a man so notorious for his imperturbable politeness that it was said that 'with him, one has to learn to take the smooth with the smooth', one assumes that Herbert's comments had been rather acid. Yet, shortly after uttering his decisive and instinctive refusal to Wadham, Herbert began to feel overwhelmed by regrets which he found himself unable to exorcise by his usual method of analysing the pros and cons in his diary. He began to question his assumption that being a Head of House was not for him and that Jacob's existence— which, in a painful but significant phrase, he refers to as 'the Jane Eyre element'—made it out of the question. Why he wondered, had he not at least asked advice or looked into the details: it would, after all, have enabled him to:

escape 1) this constant torment I have to produce scholarly work to justify my Nuffield Fellowship 2) the need to grind over my rather tired insights about jurisprudence 3) the need to defend myself against critics (eg Dw[orkin] and/or F[innis]) of my published works. The dawning conviction that I would have enjoyed, once started, the cooperative administrative work, the opportunities for J as hostess etc, the social obligations, speeches etc and of course the status and sense of belonging to and being a working part of a great ongoing concern (University as well as College) as compared with the relatively solitary and unstructured life of work on and about Bentham. Worse—the sense of my [illegible] to J: who *did* say 'I would like Wadham—we are in a *rut* now' though she was just curtly negative when I asked if she would give up her fellowship.

In increasingly distressed entries—'All this has been overwhelming at times'—he accuses himself of rigidity of posture perhaps 'connected with non-existent relationship with J and my solitary emotional life' and once again resolves to improve the marriage: 'to attempt again to make our relationship *human*.' He tries to soothe himself by listing the advantages he could have in the next four years which the Wadham job would have made impossible; 'Bentham work with Burns; contemplation; contacts with Wasserstrom, Raz, Lyons' and more contact with all the children—'the children especially Jakey are some kind of altar on which to lay my love—a thing I have not done much of in recent years except in Jakey's case'. Anticipating (and dreading) his trip to New Zealand, he recognizes how important the familiarity of family routines are to him. But he cannot rid himself of the 'sense of having pushed myself aside out of contact with ongoing business of life', and this connects with his feelings of failure towards Jenifer:

I feel that I have done her a great injury and though I can't make a dramatic change of attitude . . . and would get nothing out of a 'confession' to her I must . . . take small steps . . . I've told her (in a letter) about my regrets: will say more if given a chance. . . . Engage, engage . . . and make it, make it up with J—let pride and stiffness go—tormenting regrets.

There is a strong suggestion here of Herbert's consciousness that, whatever Jenifer's failings—her acerbity, her impatience, her affairs with other men—he himself had contributed to her unhappiness and had failed to give her the sort of warmth and support which she might have expected. He cannot have been unaware of the pressures her demanding job and anxieties about Jacob brought with them, and he must have wondered whether he really valued her properly. At St. Anne's, her personal concern for her students, as well as her acuity as a tutor, were legendary: both this and her concern for Jacob and commitment to the family show that, beneath her ascetic exterior, she was someone who had strong supportive capacities. Nan Keohane, an American student of Jenifer's in the early 1960s who went on to become a well known political scientist and ultimately the President of Duke University, recalls Jenifer as the person who saw her through her degree, giving her—alone of the St. Anne's Fellows—unwavering intellectual and personal support when, at the end of her first year, she married. Jenifer even arranged for the engagement party to be held at Manor Place. This story is typical. Herbert must have felt guilty not only about his inability to make Jenifer feel wanted sexually but also that it was invariably Jenifer who, at a practical level, sorted out the inevitable complexities of family life—whether dealing with Jacob's tantrums, recruiting cooks and helpers, or sorting out crises with children and grandchildren. He was also well aware of Jenifer's intelligence: yet his sense of the fact that her own career lay in the shadow of both his success and of her large share of family responsibilities often seems to have realized itself in an impatience or dismissiveness towards her which was a denial of his knowledge. This underlying guilt towards Jenifer heightened his feelings about having ignored her wishes in relation to Wadham; he must also have realized that his expectation that she would give up her fellowship to become an unpaid Warden's consort was both unrealistic and unworthy of his generally progressive views. In their different ways, both Jenifer and Herbert were people capable of feeling and showing real love and concern for others. But, in spite of the complementary values, tastes, and interests holding them together, they found it difficult to do so for each other.

As always, Herbert's feelings of personal failure jumble themselves up in his diary into a complex web of interlinking preoccupations: financial worries about being jobless at the end of the Nuffield grant, injunctions to organize his work better—'I must I think *structure* the Bentham work more', and the need to 'take it all more lightly'; 'don't reply to the critics e.g. Dw[orkin] and

Fi[nnis] unless I feel like doing so.' This is a clear instance of Herbert consciously using his diary as a form of self-therapy: 'I write this to lay out and so I hope control the wave of panic—the most acute I've felt—that seized me in the early hours of the morning in bed which I have had to try to still with a pill.' But the combination of occasional tranquillizers and diary analysis was not working, and in the end Herbert consulted a doctor, who surprised him with his sympathetic recognition of a 'regret obsession', which he diagnosed as a manifestation of an underlying chronic anxiety condition which might be hard to eliminate. The doctor also reassured Herbert that he might well have been right in thinking that moving Jacob from Manor Place to the Wadham lodgings would be unduly disruptive, and he prescribed a course of librium. By the time of his departure for New Zealand six months later, Herbert's anxieties were under control.

What explains this headlong plunge into depression, and Herbert's inability to come to terms with the apparently perfectly sensible decision to decline the offer of yet more of the institutional responsibilities which he felt himself to be escaping when he resigned the Chair of Jurisprudence? The episode suggests that the project of devoting himself to Bentham studies was indeed a 'fantasy': not in the sense of being unrealistic at a practical level, but in the deeper sense that it promised an illusory escape from anxieties which, far from originating in everyday work pressures, were in fact alleviated by the containing structures of institutionalized professional life. With many of these removed, Herbert—in an extreme version of an experience which many academics have on sabbatical leave and which other people often feel when first on holiday after a period of intense work— found himself confronting, unmediated, his own fragile psychology and the brutal imperative of individual creativity.

The very limited impact which Herbert's huge professional success had had on this fragility is illustrated by another incident which occurred shortly after the Wadham episode. Bikhu Parekh, a young political theorist, published a collection of extracts from Bentham's work in political philosophy. In the footnotes of the collection, he also published a list of corrections to textual errors made in Herbert's edition of *Of Laws in General*, noting in the Preface that '[s]ince Professor Hart's work is widely used by Bentham scholars, I have indicated in appropriate places where our readings differ'. The footnotes recorded several dozen differences, the majority trivial ('every' rather than 'any', 'but' rather than 'yet' for example); in most of them, Herbert's reading accorded with the earlier, Everett edition. Recent work by Philip Schofield and Frederick Rosen on a revised edition has revealed not only further textual errors but also that whoever did the detailed work on the last two chapters did not have a proper grasp of Bentham's working methods, leading to some serious structural problems. Parekh's scholarly zeal was generally regarded in the Bentham Committee as somewhat tactless, the upshot an embarrassing but not disastrous episode. But Herbert's reaction verged on the hysterical. Since the errors were born of his lack of taste for detailed editorial work and consequent over-reliance on research assistance, he had reason to feel ashamed of the lack of self-knowledge which had led him into work to which he was not obviously suited. Parekh's list implied that he had been lazy in following Everett on a number of points rather than doing the meticulous research himself, or that he had not supervised his assistants adequately. Herbert was distressed to what his colleagues thought was an extraordinary degree. He offered to resign from the Committee, and even talked to one colleague of suicide, so deeply did he feel the shame of this public exposure. The episode gave yet greater momentum to his desire to escape the pressures of a purely research-oriented life.

As Herbert circles repeatedly around the 'Wadham question' in his 1970 diary, the impression is of a psychological state not unlike mourning. The pills—and the absorbing professional and cultural activities of the New Zealand trip—distracted him for a while. But the diary makes one feel that it was almost certain that, when the next opportunity for institutional diversion presented itself, Herbert, notwithstanding his careful utilitarian rationalizations of the decision not to pursue the Wadham job, would grasp the chance with both hands. 'How odd', he reflected, 'that university admin-istration which I once shrank from should now appear a *boon*'. And in fact, shortly after his return from New Zealand, Herbert was approached by Hertford College, who were planning to elect a new Principal. Jenifer, convinced that he would make an excellent Head of House, and herself eager for this mark of a successful Oxford partnership, was keen for him to pursue this position in the University establishment. Herbert went to a meeting and talked to the Fellows who, as he later recalled:

[S]eemed satisfied, but I made it plain that I wouldn't live in college, partly (but only partly) because my youngest boy happened to be mentally handi-capped, and it wasn't very suitable. But anyhow I had a beautiful house . . . which was ideal, with garden and the President's [sic] Lodgings were far less suit-able for me and my family. . . . [T]hey wrote to me and said 'yes, it's perfectly alright'. And then a week later they said that 'oh dear, we find that we shall have to alter the statutes, because the statutes say "only in cases of emergency may the Principal live outside" '. And then they let it be known that they couldn't be sure of a sufficient majority about this. This is what they told me. And so I said 'look here, I'm going to relieve you of anxieties. I'm not going to have myself creating dissension amongst your governing body. I'm withdrawing'.

There the episode might have ended: a dismal but not unfamiliar tale of vestigial survivals of an earlier era in Oxford College statutes, aggravated by contemporary conservatism. In the event, however, this was not quite the full story. As Herbert recalled:

Years later I was placed next to [Harold] Macmillan at a college feast, and I said 'Do you enjoy your functions as Visitor of a college, as well as Chancellor [of Oxford University]?' (He was Visitor at Hertford). He said, 'Oh yes, I do, but there was one very disturbing episode. They wanted to appoint a man, a very good man I was told, a lawyer, to be Principal, and he was a Jew, and they hadn't recognized this, or hadn't realized there was any difficulty about this. And I looked up the statutes and I paid for counsel's opinion myself, and it turned out that it was a bar. I mean, it was positively dreadful in the 1970s that a college in Oxford had to turn down a perfectly reputable man because he was a Jew, and I cast about and then luckily the man had said that he wouldn't be able to live in college. And I looked into the statutes, and got counsel's opinion for the second time, and found that this business that they might allow the Principal to live out in the case of emergency would not cover this case. And so they were able to say that the reason why they couldn't appoint him was because of this.' . . . I thought to myself, as I sat next to him—we got on rather well . . . —'Shall I tell you?' But I thought it would be *too* painful. Isaiah said I was absolutely wrong, should have said it, and that he could take anything. But I didn't.

This story illustrates that Herbert's attitude to crude displays of prejudice had changed very little during the 60-odd years since his encounter with the South African who 'would rather sit down to lunch with a black than a Jew': his dominant feeling was vicarious embarrassment (although he told the story in later life with no little amusement). In fact, Macmillan—a famous opponent of any form of anti-Semitism—was embroidering the facts. Hertford's statutes did not contain any bar on Jewish appointments. There was, however, a complex history to the decision not to change the statutes so as to enable Herbert to be appointed, and it was not unconnected with religious affiliation. In 1871, the University Test Act abolished the restriction of the Oxford and Cambridge fellowship to single men who were practising members of the Church of England. At that date, Hertford was still Magdalen Hall, but its Principal, Dr. Michell, was keen to secure the funds which could sustain its establishment as a full College of the University. In 1874, he received what must have appeared a gift from heaven. It took the form of a letter from Thomas Charles Baring, who was offering substantial funds in return for the right to name the first appointed Fellows. Baring undertook not to name anyone who had not taken 'at least one first class', but specified that they would be single members of the Church of England. Because this restriction was manifestly contrary to the spirit of the

University Test Act, his offer had already been declined by Brasenose. Magdalen Hall's pending change of status, however, gave an opportunity for this controversial issue to be fudged: Baring's money was accepted, and the Bill providing for Hertford's creation passed into legislation in 1874, notwithstanding some opposition from the Prime Minister, Gladstone and the Home Secretary, Sir William Harcourt. The Act made no mention of the Baring restriction, which appears only to have been applied to the first intake of Fellows.

Hertford's statutes provided, therefore, no religious barrier to Herbert's appointment. But in his interview with the Fellows, he had declared his lack of religious affiliation and had said that he would be willing to attend chapel services on special occasions only. This prompted the chaplain and two other Fellows to write to Macmillan raising objections to the College's choice, and it was this letter which Macmillan probably interpreted as motivated by anti-Semitism. Whether there was any truth in this more limited surmise it is impossible to establish, although Barry Nicholas was taken aback when, shortly after Herbert's election as Principal of Brasenose, a Hertford colleague greeted him in the street by saying; 'I gather you have elected Hirsch [a German-Jewish version of the name "Hart"] as Principal'— a remark which Nicholas took to be anti-Semitic. It does, however, seem likely that the objections to Herbert's lack of religious affiliation may have had some impact in splitting the Governing Body on the issue of waiving the residence requirement. After all, if having a disabled child for whom the Lodgings are unsuitable accommodation does not justify modifying the requirement—particularly in circumstances where the candidate's own home is, as Herbert's was, less than ten minutes' walk from the College—one wonders what would. Certainly, there were those among the Fellows who felt that Herbert had been badly treated. A letter from one of them to Herbert at the time of his withdrawal in October 1971 is eloquent in its reserve:

I want to thank you for remaining our candidate for so long. The discussion and the vote in the Governing Body showed how much the College needs you . . .

while another, who wrote to express his regret at Herbert's treatment, received 'a characteristically generous and urbane reply'.

It is a nice irony that the next approach which Herbert received was from Brasenose, the college which had turned down the Baring money because of the religious conditions attached to it. In fact, the irony was a double one: for while this principled stance would certainly have earned Herbert's respect had he been aware of it, in other ways Brasenose was an unlikely destination for someone of Herbert's personal and intellectual disposition. The college had lost the early nineteenth-century intellectual status which George Eliot's fictional scholar, Edward Casaubon, had held in anxious awe, and had instead become the natural home of upper class sportsmen:

My whole transition to Brasenose was really rather astonishing. I thought of myself as the last kind of person for a college like that . . . in my undergraduate days we used to discuss whether Brasenose *was* a college or an athletic association.

As one joke put it, Brasenose 'toiled at games and played at books'. Though the College's culture had changed somewhat since the 1920s, it was still in the early 1970s seen as a conservative, sports-oriented, and unintellectual environment: as one colleague congratulating Herbert on his election teased, 'So glad to hear you've joined the hearties at long last'. But the College was at a turning point, with the recent decision to become one of the first small group of men's colleges to admit women representing a significant change, albeit one the ultimate impact of which was still unclear. One Brasenose Fellow, also writing to congratulate Herbert, summed it up:

Though it has its fair share of individual and corporate myths, which can at times be inconvenient, BNC is in my experience a healthy and equable society, as well as friendly and hospitable. But it has, in my opinion, lost something of the sense of direction which it enjoyed, in very different ways, under the guidance of Principals Stallybrass and Last . . . The policy of co-residence, just adopted, may be seen as something of a gamble to mend course.

The incumbent of the Principalship at the time, Noel Hall, was a smooth-mannered, genial former diplomat who plied the students with pink gin and stories of the war and who did little to counter Brasenose's cosy and unchallenging atmosphere. So the choice of, as one Fellow put it, 'an academic icon' to succeed him as head of the College was far from obvious. But though there was a significant group of Fellows—many of them scientists—who saw no need for change, the process of choosing Herbert, quietly master-minded by the ever-resourceful Barry Nicholas (soon to become Professor of Comparative Law and later himself Principal of the College), appears to have been a relatively smooth affair. Herbert was elected in June 1972 by an overwhelming majority, and took up his position in the autumn of 1973. His arrival therefore coincided with that of another 'civilising influence': the first intake of women students. Letters of congratulation to Herbert in the summer of 1972 show that even some of his closest friends (including Jean Floud, then herself Principal of Newnham College Cambridge) had been unaware of his ambition to become the head of a college: these people greeted the decision with surprise, though also with the pleasure in another's pleasure that is the mark of true friendship. Philosophy colleagues crowed at the appointment of another philosopher as Head of House: 'the Lit. Hum. conspiracy theory of Oxford social history is correct'; 'what a philosophical triangle [along with Stuart Hampshire at Wadham and Geoffrey Warnock, elected at Hertford after Herbert's withdrawal] is now formed in that quarter of Oxford!' Other heads of colleges applauded the added 'dignity' which Herbert would bring to the role, though his friend Stuart Hampshire combined this accolade with a small foretaste of some of the less appealing aspects of the job he was about to take on:

I am very pleased that Heads of Colleges will be, by such a wide margin, a better lot next year, and that the uncertain profession (or status) will have more *dignity*—much more. I hope that you will enjoy Brasenose. My impression is that they are not old and pompous, which are about the worst things in Colleges, I think. I have the impression that they do not begin sentences with words like, 'Well, bursar, . . .' That always makes me want to be back among the urban blights in the US.

Herbert must have taken particular pleasure in fond letters from former students praising his 'unique capacity for intellectual excitement plus personal concern'; and in the warm welcome from Otto Kahn Freund, Professor of Comparative Law at Brasenose ('If I say I am delighted I am making the biggest understatement I have ever been guilty of'); the pleasure was probably mixed with amusement at the retiring chaplain, his former fellow classicist at Bradford Grammar School, Leslie Styler's rather self-congratulatory greeting:

Little did I think on the day that Lewis brought you into Robertson's 4th classical classroom that 51 years later I should take part in electing you to the Principalship of Brasenose.

Yet more interesting are the letters which throw light on the Oxford establishment and on Herbert's curious position within it. He had recently been elected to the 1792 Club—an elite group of Heads of Colleges, Vice Chancellors, former Vice Chancellors and the like. The group evidently felt they were according Herbert an enormous honour in including a mere ex-Professor among their number. As John Sparrow wrote:

Congratulations! All your friends rejoice, and Brasenose must (or at least ought to) be delighted—and I hope you're pleased yourself. John. What a sound instinct the Brethren had in choosing you! Now you will feel *really* at home at the Club.

While Sparrow's letter is distinguished by a whiff of irony, it is not clear that the same can be said of a note from another college head:

Dear Brother—I was very happy to see you elected at BNC. If for no other reason, it adds increased *dignity* to the Club.

In fact, Herbert was already finding the Club's dinners unbearably tedious, and Brasenose, ironically, provided him with a gracious exit. He waited until it was his turn to host the dinner, put on an elegant spread, and then resigned from the Club. Perhaps the 'status or position' of being head of a college allowed him to look clear-sightedly at this more trivial mark of belonging.

But the most perceptive letter which Herbert received at this time was from his old friend and tutor, Christopher Cox, now retired from the Civil Service and living full time in New College. Time had done nothing to diminish the soaring flow of Cox's prose, and he looked back to Herbert's physical jerkiness as an intellectually enthusiastic undergraduate and wondered how this would affect his gravitas as Principal:

It is splendid that they should have seated you in the throne once warmed by Last and Sonners. They are very lucky indeed—if only you could have kept yourself in pickle another year or 2 for New College. . . . You will of course, as I should have told them if they'd referred to me, fall off the throne from time to time, but not from intoxication or ineptitude, only from the convulsive physical accompaniments to cerebral leaps—how well the coal scuttle and I remember them: 'stimulated and stimulating' my confidential reports used to read. As for Lady C [Jenifer], or the VB as for some reason you used to call her in my company, she will be a chatelaine and a half—and I hope she'll go on master-minding St Anne's as well. Seriously, I hope it wasn't a difficult decision and you're pleased.

There is an implicit question in that last sentence. But Herbert *was* pleased, and he does not seem to have hesitated. When he took up the beautiful Elizabethan apartments overlooking Radcliffe Square which came with the job the following year, however, he had a baptism of fire.

When I got there there was trouble. The scouts complained that they were having too much work to do, too many dinners in Hall to be responsible for . . . serving, and they went on strike, and . . . so we switched over to a cafeteria thing for a short time . . . and then it simmered down. But I thought, 'My God, what have I let myself in for. I've become a hotel manager, which is the last . . . jack of all trades that I wanted to head for.'

He fast came to the conclusion that Stuart Hampshire's assessment of 'old and pompous' as the major Oxford problem was wide of the mark: Herbert famously coined the phrase 'old turks and young fogeys' to sum up the Brasenose fellowship, and it is clear where his sympathies lay. As his affectionate regard for Bentham illustrates, he always had a taste for old turks. There were, however, young turks as well, and some of them—law fellow Peter Birks as Tutor for Admissions and Herbert's former doctoral student Vernon Bogdanor, the Politics Fellow—became important allies in Herbert's modernizing project at Brasenose. This took a number of forms. The prospectus was re-written so as to encourage state school applicants; Herbert irritated the colleague who was producing it by requiring him to remove long references to the College's heraldry, which he dismissed as 'a frightfully nobby hobby' which would put off applicants from ordinary backgrounds. The traditional dinners for successful sporting teams were now accompanied by special dinners for scholars, in an attempt to re-order the cultural hierarchy somewhat in favour of the academic. A new events committee was created to expand the range and heighten the profile of cultural occasions: each term-time Sunday evening Herbert would host, with legendary urbanity, lectures by public figures—politicians, writers like William Golding and John Mortimer, famous academics like Kahn Freund, artists including Howard Hodgkin—whom he thought should interest the students. A visiting arts fellowship was created. Herbert also used his connections with the hugely wealthy Mormon Tanner family, to one of whom he had acted as kindly and revered supervisor in the mid-1960s, to bring funding for a set of distinguished Tanner lectures to the College. Though a small core of right-wing fellows retained a deep suspicion of and even antagonism to Herbert and occasionally scored telling victories, he usually managed to run the College as he saw fit. He was assisted by what some of his allies regarded as an astonishing lack of awareness of the depth of some of the antagonisms. Rarely troubled by such feelings of local partisanship and hostility himself, Herbert was strikingly—and touchingly—insensitive to it in others. As one Brasenose colleague put it, 'Herbert had no sense of original sin in people'.

Herbert's astonishing intellectual speed made him a sometimes formidable and often witty chair of meetings. The shade of J. L. Austin walked with him into the Brasenose Governing Body: if an unsuspecting colleague asked him 'Do you mean that . . .?' he would reply firmly, 'No: if I had meant that, I would have said it'. On one occasion when a building firm who had done some rather unsuccessful roofing for the College was soliciting suggestions for an advertising motto, he said without a moment's hesitation, 'It's obvious: "*Après moi le déluge*" '. But his democratic instincts, which dictated that everyone's voice should be heard, sometimes led to very lengthy discussions. This might have led to dissension, but in putting his stamp on the College, and in gaining authority even among the fogeys, Herbert had the advantage of his considerable intellectual aura, as well as what was in some senses a remarkable piece of luck: the Hulme Trust.

Very shortly after his arrival, as he tried to learn about his new environment (he was the first Principal to have been neither a student nor a Fellow of the College), Herbert realized that Brasenose was not benefiting as it should from a principal source of its income. The Hulme Trust originated in an early nineteenth-century foundation set up to look after Lancastrian would-be lawyers and parsons at Brasenose who were in need of support for their professional training. During the course of the century, a surplus had built up and a substantial part of the fund was diverted to local interests in Manchester. In 1907 there had been a new settlement, with part of what was now a large surplus given to Brasenose and used to buy the college's High Street buildings and to finish its new quadrangle, as well as supporting further scholarships and university taxes. But in the period after 1907, the fund was once again mismanaged; Brasenose had no representation on its governing board, and gradually more and more of its proceeds were being misapplied to local purposes. At the time of Herbert's election, Brasenose had already instructed London solicitors to try to renegotiate the scheme under which the Trust was operating, but little real progress had been made.

   This was a field to which Herbert's experience as a practising lawyer was of direct relevance. He immediately saw that the Charity Commissioners' scheme of 1881 was 'prolix and needlessly elaborate', leading to both friction between College and trustees and misunderstanding of the true purposes of the Trust. With Barry Nicholas's help, he swiftly devoted himself to renegotiating the scheme, to the enormous advantage of the college. He dismissed the London solicitors, prepared several cases for the courts, drafted endless memoranda and versions of a revised scheme, and travelled, often with Nicholas, for whom his affection and respect were rapidly growing, to Manchester for long meetings with the trustees and to London for meetings with barristers. On one such occasion Nicholas remembered Herbert being greeted with touching warmth by his former Clerk. Relatively quickly, a new scheme which was vastly more satisfactory to the College was agreed.

   The authority which this remarkable piece of legal, diplomatic, and administrative adroitness lent him helped to secure Herbert's status as one of the very few college heads who managed this notoriously tricky position to almost universal approbation. As compared with his contribution to the college's financial security, and with his reputation for prodigiously hard work (which included meticulous preparation not only for college and Hulme Trust meetings but also for welcome speeches to students, after-dinner talks, and so on), his peculiarities as Principal were mere peccadilloes. They did, however, occasionally cause raised eyebrows. His egalitarian asceticism led him to be genuinely shocked by the amount and quality of food and wine served at college dinners, and he quickly let it be known—to the irritation of several fellows and the consternation of the wine steward—that he disapproved of these 'Lucullan feasts'. On one occasion, he announced that he would not attend the Christmas dinner unless the usual number of courses was reduced (to the relief of most of the Fellows, the Lucullan tradition generally prevailed). His intellectualism and asceticism sometimes coloured his relationship with the undergraduates. Among them, Herbert connected most readily with those who were clever and academically motivated. As Principal, he taught tutorials in jurisprudence from time to time. With the exception of his occasional tutorials for Rupert Cross's most gifted students, it was his first experience of teaching law undergraduates and his first undergraduate teaching for 20 years, and he was dismayed by this lesson in most students' lack of philosophical sophistication.

The students were generally fond of 'Herbie', their absent-minded professorial Principal. But Herbert's attempts to reach the less intellectually motivated students, some of whom found him austere, could be hit and miss. Many enjoyed the Sunday evening lectures and his willingness to address undergraduate societies (on one occasion, interestingly, he addressed the Jewish Society on the theme 'On being a Jew at Oxford'). But his and Jenifer's discos were regarded by some students as embarrassing, while even some of the more liberal Fellows frowned at the bright yellow lino which Jenifer (who, as Cox had predicted, was enjoying her role as 'chatelaine' and combining it energetically and effectively with her post at St. Anne's) had introduced into one of the Elizabethan rooms of the Principal's Lodgings. Herbert also retained a vestigial dislike of the tough, hard-drinking, rugby-playing public school type. Although colleagues joked that his liberalism meant that, when an undergraduate was in academic or other difficulty, he was inclined to regard *both* coming from a public school *and* coming from a less privileged background as mitigating social disadvantages, they also remember him going pale with rage when on one occasion a drunken undergraduate threw an empty bottle from the quad through the Senior Common Room window. One colleague remembers this episode as a striking exception to his usual scrupulous fairness: he was inclined to expel the offending student—a Wykehamist—from the College.

Though invariably kindly, Herbert was not always sensitive or imaginative in his social interactions. Visiting clergy bored him, and were invariably left with colleagues; if conversation at dinner was interesting, he would allow it to continue even though this kept the staff at work longer; and at the annual staff Christmas party, which took the form of a disco at a local hotel, he was visibly uncomfortable and commented to his scout—to the latter's consternation—'It's like a scene out of Breughel'. It would be wrong, however, to give the impression that he connected only with those with whom he shared intellectual, cultural, or political affinities. While, certainly, he was a hugely important intellectual influence on like-minded students and colleagues—there can be few college principals who read and comment on the entire manuscript of one of their Fellows' books, as Herbert later did for the young law Fellow Hugh Collins—he also made connections with less likely allies. Striking among these was his close relationship with Graham Richards, a young chemistry Fellow of generally conservative views, whose company he hugely enjoyed and to whom he spoke with unusual openness (and a little exaggeration) of his work during the war. Like most of the younger men with whom Herbert formed a special attachment over the years, Richards was warm, genial, open, and steadfastly heterosexual. So different were his and Herbert's positions on the College's political spectrum that many colleagues did not even notice their friendship, and were surprised to be told of it. But Herbert's more acute observers, including Jenifer, were well aware of it.

Herbert's sense of the respect and indeed affection of his Brasenose colleagues, along with the sense of carrying out to a high standard a set of professional obligations which had a certain public dimension, gave him substantial satisfaction and relief from the acute anxieties which had troubled him in 1970. He was happy in the Principalship, though whether he ever conceived the sort of affection for Brasenose which he had for New College is doubtful: one entry among his book of notes for speeches at college occasions asks 'If colleges are like countries, New College = England: Brasenose, where?'. Though he regretted that the duties at Brasenose meant that he had to resign from his yet more public responsibilities at the Monopolies Commission, the institutional framework turned out, like MI5, to suit him extremely well. But, unlike many people attracted to elite administrative jobs in conservative institutions, and despite Herbert's natural air of authority and even gravitas, his job at Brasenose changed him not one iota: he remained the almost innocent, often unguarded enthusiast which he had always been. His dress and manner remained shambolic (he loved to tell, against himself, stories of the upshot of his physical clumsiness, including the descent into the bathwater of a speech carefully prepared to welcome the Bishop of Durham to Brasenose); holidays still centred on family and friends at Lamledra and in Wales and with the Berlins in Italy; his appetite for the countryside and mountain walking was undimmed (friends remember their alarm at his wobbly ascent of the difficult Pig Track on Snowdon in 1976); and his fund-raising activities and organization of concerts at Ditchley Park for the Home Farm Trust continued undiminished.

His unusual, simple, unaffected quality, and the response which it evoked in other people, is captured by an incident which took place on his way back from a holiday in Italy with the Berlins in the summer of 1976. After stopping off to visit the beautiful walled city of Lucca, Herbert rejoined the train to Pisa. Having settled himself in a carriage, he heard an announcement asking passengers in that carriage to move to another carriage further forward. He moved; the train set off; and he suddenly realized that he had left his briefcase, which contained his money, passport, and plane ticket, in the original carriage, which was still sitting on the platform at Lucca. As he described the incident in a letter to Aline Berlin:

The effect on me was to make me lose control (I say it in shame though it proved my salvation). I shouted out in Italian 'Dio mio, ho perdotto tutto: passporto, biglietti, denario!' or some such words. This *electrified* the whole carriage; and then an absolutely charming middle aged couple came up, speaking English, and said the chances were good that the discarded carriage would have been cleared by railway officials who would have found the briefcase and handed it in. So they advised me to return to Lucca on reaching Pisa. When I said 'But I have no money on me for a ticket', they *gave* me 1000 Lire! Wasn't it an extraordinary act of kindness?

After various further acts of Italian kindness and efficiency, Herbert was indeed reunited with his briefcase, just in time to catch his plane (though he almost missed it trying to return the 1000 lire and, failing this, to find a charity to which to donate it). His reflection on the incident is typical:

Had I not lost my head and shrieked out in Italian, I would not have got off at the little station and might not have recovered the case in time. So this rather shaming *reaction* had survival value!

Just as Brasenose did nothing to alter Herbert's personal habits and manner, it left his intellectual appetites unchanged. Once he had the job reasonably well under control, and in particular once the time-consuming negotiations over the Hulme Trust were concluded, he felt the call of his academic work returning, and during his last two years as Principal he was finding the time and self-confidence to do some fresh work, as well as continuing his relationship with the Bentham Project and lecturing on Bentham both in the UK and the USA. He gave lectures in New York and Chicago in 1976, and in New Orleans and at Columbia University in 1978 during a trip on which he was also soliciting American funds for the Bentham Project. In 1977 he and Burns produced a further contribution to the systematic edition of Bentham's works: *A Comment on the Commentaries* and *A Fragment on Government*, including a substantial introduction.

The same year, marking his 70th birthday, Herbert was moved by the presentation of a powerful volume celebrating his work, edited by two of his former doctoral students, Peter Hacker and Joseph Raz, and including contributions from the most eminent legal philosophers in and beyond Oxford, ranging across every aspect of his analytic and normative work. He also continued to involve himself to some extent in Law Faculty business. Earlier in the decade he had given his support—after an initial reluctance overcome by vigorous discussions with Jean Floud—to the foundation of a centre for socio-legal studies, and in 1972 he had given a seminar with Ronald Dworkin and Stuart Hampshire on John Rawls' *Theory of Justice*. Though this marked the end of his formal University teaching contribution, he continued to attend the legal and moral philosophy discussion group which he had founded as Professor and which had been continued by his successor, Ronald Dworkin, in Tony Honoré's rooms in All Souls. Here he sat, uncharacteristically quiet, as he heard Dworkin's critique of his own position unfold. The vast majority of the group being inclined to take his side in the developing debate with Dworkin, Herbert contented himself with making 'mild punctuating remarks' in a reasonably friendly but 'not tremendously warm' manner. He was similarly attentive, and somewhat more communicative, in a presentation by John Mackie on 'The Third Theory of Law' (i.e. Dworkin) in 1978. His editorial work for Oxford University Press continued. But juggling all these different commitments must have been a strain, and the initial excitement of the Brasenose job had worn off as the challenge which it presented was conquered. When the Governing Body offered to renew his Principalship for two further years in 1977, he said that he would accept only one, and he retired from his position in 1978.

By this time, the influential lawyer, former adviser to Harold Wilson and Labour peer Arnold Goodman had become head of University College. Goodman, encouraged by Herbert's many admirers at the college, and in particular by the classicist George Cawkwell, raised money from the Thorne Trust to offer Herbert a Research Fellowship, and provided him with an attractive room abutting the secluded Fellows' Garden. So began a cordial, if unlikely, relationship between the two men. Goodman was everything which Herbert might have been but had chosen not to be: a successful lawyer, politically involved, an immensely wealthy bon viveur, and self-consciously (though not religiously) Jewish. He was also massively entrepreneurial, and a man whose cunning and chutzpah were legendary. When the timid Vice Master of University College had met with Goodman at the House of Lords to find out if he might be interested in being a candidate for the Mastership, he had uttered only half a sentence when Goodman interrupted, exclaiming, 'No need to go on my dear boy: I know what you're going to say: I accept!'— with which he produced a chilled bottle of champagne. The hapless Vice Master returned to Oxford to confess to his colleagues, who saw no option but to ratify Goodman's extraordinary *fait-accompli*. While this kind of manoeuvring, along with Goodman's general reputation as a wheeler and dealer, would have been distasteful to Herbert, the two men shared a deep love of the arts, and Herbert warmed to Goodman's kindness over the years. He returned gratefully to the College where he had held the Chair whose stature his anointed successor was furthering, and where he still had many friends.

Installed once again in University College, Herbert threw himself into all the local activities. He became an enthusiastic member of Cawkwell's dining society for graduates in law, politics, philosophy, and economics, 'The Bentham': 'Marvellous,' said Herbert, 'maximising pleasure'. On these and comparable occasions he showed his customary charm and informality. One new graduate student remembers freezing with anxiety as, seated next to Herbert, she witnessed with horror the arrival of the worst possible dish to eat with any measure of dignity in polite company: trout with almonds. Focussing firmly on her plate, she was amazed and delighted to hear Herbert, entirely relaxed, continuing to chat away about topics of mutual interest amid an ever-increasing circumference of scattered almonds and trout bones: legal theory was skated over lightly in favour of the more absorbing topics of Jane Austen novels and classical music. When Herbert found that her husband played at a Cornish music festival which he and Jenifer attended, he immediately said, 'Oh but you must come and visit us at Lamledra' (an invitation which he and Jenifer promptly followed up after the dinner).

He was, in short, happy to have descended from 'the throne of Last and Sonners', and ready to take up again with both hands the reins of his intellectual work. But at 71, with four successful careers and a substantial body of published work behind him, it is perhaps not surprising that Herbert could not find the energy to produce the major work on Bentham which he had envisaged. Instead, he opted once again for the alternative of further editorial work and a collection of essays. In 1982, he and Burns published with Methuen a further imprint of their edition of the *Introduction to the Principles of Morals and Legislation*. For this edition, Herbert produced a new and substantial introduction to the text. Beyond this, while five of the essays which he chose for his own collection of essays on Bentham were substantially unchanged versions of works published between 1964 and 1976, the introduction and four further chapters were more materially reworked versions of papers published between 1962 and 1980 (the last a fine essay on Bentham and Mill on natural rights written for the *New York Review of Books*); and a final essay, on 'Commands and Authoritative Reasons', was written specifically for the collection. Taken together, these essays constitute, even by Herbert's high standards, a substantial contribution not only to Bentham scholarship but to legal and political theory and to intellectual history.

The *Essays on Bentham*, published in 1982, took up the key conceptual counters of Bentham's theory—his concepts of rights, powers, and obligations, his critique of natural rights, his distinctive theory of definition, his ideas on the individuation of laws, and his development of a logic of the will underlying the force of law. Herbert not only asserted Bentham's place as the founder of modern, analytical jurisprudence, but also argued that his ideas about definition and about the need for a logic of will as distinct from an Aristotelian logic of understanding anticipated by well over a century ideas developed by Frege, Russell, and Wittgenstein. While Herbert rejected central aspects of Bentham's theory—notably his account of law as based on commands of the sovereign—the force of his admiration for Bentham makes itself felt throughout the book. Herbert admired his rationalism, his commitment to intellectual clarity, his hostility to emotional argument, and his impatience with the mystificatory aspects—technical language, archaic dress—of established social practices such as law.

Though the ostensible purpose of the essays is the revision, defence, and clarification of Bentham's work, Herbert also used the essays as a vehicle in which to advance and refine many of his own claims, and in particular those of *The Concept of Law*. Responding to his former student Joseph Raz's critical analysis of his ideas, Herbert refined his own concept of legal obligation and authority in terms of law as providing peremptory, content-independent reasons for action. He also indulged in a swingeing critique of the legal theory of his successor in the Oxford Chair, Ronald Dworkin, in a confident style which contrasts starkly with his uncertainty in dialogue with Dworkin from the mid-1980s onwards. The different treatment of these two writers shows Herbert at this stage implicitly marking out Raz, rather than Dworkin, as his true intellectual successor. Herbert's research during the 1970s had not concerned itself solely with Bentham, and he was also planning a further collection of *Essays in Jurisprudence and Philosophy*, published in 1983. The two books have, respectively, blue and brown covers which it has been suggested were intended to echo Wittgenstein's blue and brown books. Yet, as one reviewer noticed, Herbert's approach to philosophy was fundamentally different from that of Wittgenstein: while the latter's later work was devoted to arguing that the task of philosophy was simply one of clarification or elucidation, Herbert continued to see it in more ambitious terms: as having the capacity to answer problems. The essays were greeted as 'a major commentary on developments in legal philosophy', written by 'an acute critic, a courageous and fair-minded controversialist, a writer of considerable literary skill'. Like the *Essays on Bentham*, the essays in the 'brown book' bring together work published over a long period of time—from the inaugural lecture of 1953 to his final original paper, an essay on the House of Lords' recent decisions on the law of criminal attempts, written for his friend Rupert Cross's memorial volume and originally published in 1981. It is a testament to Herbert's continuing intellectual power that participants in the seminar to which the original version of this last paper was delivered recall the complete inability of the audience to come up with any convincing criticisms of it: it was so thoroughly worked out, every argument so neatly tied up, that the audience was in the end reduced to virtual silence.

This was not the only relatively recent essay in the 1983 collection. Both Herbert's continuing interest in developments in legal and political philosophy and his enormous reputation made it inevitable that he would take up debate with his critics and that he would be asked to write reviews and critical pieces on important works in his field. During the 1970s, these factors had drawn him into printed debate not only with Ronald Dworkin but also with the influential political philosophers John Rawls and Robert Nozick. Three essays collected under the rubric 'Liberty, Utility and Rights' within the collection give the sense not only of a scholar of hugely powerful intellect but also of someone who had a flawless command of the rapidly developing field of liberal political theory. In his later work, Rawls attested that he still had not resolved to his own satisfaction his response to Herbert's critique of the priority to which his *A Theory of Justice* accorded the principle of liberty (a critique which Herbert had first presented to a mesmerized audience at his seminar with Dworkin and Hampshire in 1972). As compared with some of the essays in *Punishment and Responsibility*, the tone in these essays of the mid-1970s is assured and decisive; it is as if Herbert's primary focus on the work of other scholars relieved him of a sense of pressure to speak in his own voice and enabled him, paradoxically, to do just that. The essays testify to the richness of his intellectual resources—linguistic philosophy, philosophical logic, classical philosophy, the liberal tradition, twentieth-century American and Scandinavian legal theory, as well as history and, to some extent, the classics of modern sociology such as Durkheim, Weber, and Parsons; they reveal him as a fair-minded, acute, and magisterial commentator on the unfolding theoretical scene. However, they also give the impression of a writer who no longer has the force, conviction, or energy to push his critical arguments through to the full articulation of a distinctive position. Of particular interest in this context is Herbert's assessment of Mill's revision of Bentham in his partially developed attempt to delineate concepts of rights and of justice or fairness as values whose force is, if not independent of, at least distinct from that of utility. This is a preoccupation which is also at work in Herbert's sympathetic engagement with John Rawls and in his critique of Nozick and of Dworkin in the aptly entitled 'Between Utility and Rights'. It is, however, never entirely worked through, and Herbert's vision of an accommodation of utility and rights in a pluralistic political philosophy remained at the level of critique rather than positive elaboration.

On the publication of his 'blue and brown books', Herbert's major contributions to legal and political philosophy were complete. With the lifetime tenure of a pleasant room and congenial fellowship at University College, all seemed set for an enjoyable and productive semi-retirement. In 1982, he and Jenifer had resolved one of their most worrying personal preoccupations: Jacob was moved happily and permanently to Home Farm Trust accommodation at Milton Heights, near enough to allow him to come home most weekends. Nanny, too, had made a happy transition. Herbert had supported her decision to leave the household on her retirement and often visited her in her council flat in Headington. He also paid her rent and gave her a capital sum to ensure that she was comfortable financially. Though his health had become more frail as a result of arthritis and, later, a cycling accident in Cornwall, he was well enough still to enjoy country walks, to ride his bicycle around Oxford and Lamledra, and to travel to Italy, Cornwall, and other favourite spots. He was cautiously developing relationships with those of his grandchildren who were sufficiently near to make this possible. Among his and Jenifer's children, Joanna was now a psychotherapist; Adam had moved on from his graduate degree at Cambridge to take up a position at the Tavistock Institute of Human Relations, doing research on young people in care, pending starting doctoral studies at Sussex; and Charlie was a bass player in a successful R'n'B band: all lived in London, and all remained much in touch with their parents. Herbert also continued to see his sister Sybil and brother Albert on a regular basis; and his relationship with Jenifer had settled into a more contented, if parallel, pattern. His mind was still alive not only to intellectual activities but to music, books, poetry, nature. A further conference celebrating his work was planned by his former student Ruth Gavison at the Hebrew University in 1984. The emotional storms of the past seemed to be over, and the future set for the plain sailing of continuity and contentment.

CHAPTER 13

The Nightmare and the Noble Dream

H ERBERT's move back to University College in 1978 set him once again in the immediate environment of his successor, Ronald Dworkin. In his nine years in the Oxford Chair, Dworkin had established a phenomenal reputation. A collection of his essays, *Taking Rights Seriously*, had been published in 1977 to huge attention and critical acclaim, and he was a regular and astute commentator on legal and social issues in more general publications such as the *New York Review of Books*. As a lecturer and in seminars, his astonishing speed and appetite for debate, as well as his facility for coming up with vivid examples to illustrate his arguments, made him a mesmerizing performer. His undergraduate lectures and graduate seminars—often held jointly with philosophers or economists—were drawing large numbers, and he was attracting talented graduate students to Oxford. A slight but powerfully energetic figure whose informal, flamboyant, North American persona and well cut suits marked him out from most of his still formal and tweed-clad professorial colleagues, Dworkin's vigorous and iconoclastic style is evoked by a response he was fond of making to students who had the assurance to question his decisive assertions by venturing, tentatively, 'But isn't that just your opinion?' 'Why does everyone here say "In my opinion" all the time—is it a kind of English cough?', Dworkin would ask with a smile of mock-bewilderment; 'Of *course* it's my opinion; why else would I assert it?'

Herbert had, of course, continued to encounter Dworkin in a range of seminars and discussion groups. But the friendship and close intellectual exchange which both men had looked forward to in the summer of 1969 had never really developed. Apart from the successful joint seminar on Rawls with Stuart Hampshire in 1972, Herbert had declined Dworkin's suggestion that they might teach together. And during Herbert's years at Brasenose a certain distance had grown up between the two. This seems to have had to do with Herbert's perception of Dworkin's attitude to first, Oxford and second, himself.

Despite his seemingly boundless confidence and effortless success, Dworkin's transition to Oxford had not been without its difficulties. It was more than just a matter of the Oxford Law Faculty not being exactly Dworkin's natural intellectual or cultural home. His wife, Betsy—an elegant, vivid, and powerful figure in her own right, and accustomed to playing a leading role in the active social life at Yale—found Oxford's social culture cold, dry, and unappealing. A sense of how her new environment must have struck her after the lively and privileged East Coast life she was used to is given by an amusing tale of her mother's first visit to the couple in Oxford: she took one look at the interior of their large but somewhat spartan house in central Oxford, asked Dworkin what on earth he thought he was doing bringing her daughter to such a place, and ordered a taxi back to London. Betsy Dworkin's dislike of Oxford came to a head during one of the Law Faculty's rather stilted social events during which another Professor came up to her and said, superciliously, 'I don't usually talk to Faculty wives, but I'll make an exception in your case'. 'Don't bother!' was her emphatic reply. Herself an academic, she decided to solve the problem by finding a job in London: the family decamped, and Dworkin came to Oxford each week to do his teaching and carry out his other professorial duties.

Twenty years later, this had become a relatively common way of approaching life as an Oxford academic. But in the 1970s, it was still frowned upon, and Dworkin felt a certain reserve developing among some of his more traditional colleagues, who interpreted the move to London as a mark of his contempt for Oxford. There was also the fact that Herbert was, at more than one level, a hard act to follow. The combination of his intellectual stature, his wit, and his modest, fresh, innocent personal style marked him out in the intense Oxford environment as a figure for whom others could feel not only affection and admiration but something near to reverence, even a form of hero-worship. Douglas Millen, the redoubtable long-serving Head Porter of University College, used to like to say to anyone he could get to listen that Professor Hart, whom he (like many others) regarded as the quintessential Oxford gentleman, had forgotten more than Professor Dworkin would ever know. Though trivial in themselves, the currency of such stories must have contributed subtly to Dworkin's sense that, notwithstanding his academic reputation and large contribution to the University's intellectual life, he was not entirely accepted at Oxford. The feeling intensified when, in the mid-1980s, he negotiated to hold his position on a part-time basis, spending half of each year teaching at New York University. Dworkin, hearing that Jenifer Hart had expressed scathing views of this arrangement, attributed Herbert's growing reserve with him to his identification with Jenifer's and other people's criticisms.

Herbert did indeed regret Dworkin's decision to split his time between the USA and Oxford. But he cannot have been really surprised by it. After all, Dworkin had warned him right from the start that he would be unlikely to stay at Oxford in the long term, and by this time there was already a significant 'brain-drain' from British to American Universities prompted by low morale and relatively poor salaries in Britain as the Thatcher Government's cuts in public spending began to bite. Certainly, Herbert's own dutiful conscientiousness as Professor of Jurisprudence made him a critical observer of his successor. But it is unlikely that Herbert's increasing *froideur* towards Dworkin was simply a matter of the latter's conduct in the Oxford Chair. Equally, it had to do with Herbert's complicated attitude towards Dworkin's scholarship, and in particular towards Dworkin's treatment of his own work.

From his very earliest encounters with Dworkin's ideas, Herbert had recognized that they presented a formidable challenge to his own position. This recognition, along with his general feeling of pressure to reply to his critics, virtually ensured that his relationship with Dworkin would be a complex one. The tricky equilibrium would have been considerably more stable if the early warmth between the two men had flourished. As it was, Herbert's sensitivity to Dworkin's criticisms was fuelled by a sense that there was something wilful or even lacking in honesty about Dworkin's reading of his work. And, despite his own outstanding talent for intellectual debate, Herbert found the experience of debating ideas with Dworkin increasingly frustrating—a frustration which would have been accentuated by the contrast between Herbert's meticulous style in discussion and Dworkin's more free-wheeling approach. Both men, with their extraordinary intellectual speed and range, were spellbinding speakers, but Herbert's unshakeable commitment to clarity and precision, forged in the J. L. Austin school of linguistic philosophy, could hardly have been more different from Dworkin's ostensibly bolder, more sweeping approach. Herbert's ambivalence towards his successor may have been further exacerbated not only by a social discomfort with Dworkin's personal style and frank enjoyment of his affluent lifestyle but also—though Herbert would certainly have hated to think this—by an unacknowledged sense that Dworkin owed him a certain level of gratitude or recognition as the predecessor who had pressed his claims to the Chair. Though these matters of social vulnerability and professional insecurity are surprising in such established and successful figures, without such factors it is hard to make sense of the chasm which was opening up between two men who should have been united by so many important shared intellectual and political commitments: a fixed belief in the importance of philosophical jurisprudence and a fierce attachment to liberal values principal among them.

In his early essays, Dworkin had mounted both a substantive and a methodological attack on Herbert's approach to jurisprudence. The right way to proceed, he argued, was not to ask the general question, 'what is law?', but rather to elucidate the nature of law by considering how judges decide what the law is in hard cases. He suggested that, far from being bound only by rules identified and validated in terms of their sources or pedigree, as claimed by Herbert's account of the rule of recognition, judges also did—and should—regard themselves as bound by broader legal principles such as the principle that 'no man may profit from his own wrong' or the standard of 'good faith' in contracts. These principles differed from rules in two ways. First, they were not identified in terms of their pedigree, but rather in terms of two different dimensions: their degree of 'fit' with institutional history, and their support within institutional, background (social), or even the judge's view of critical morality. So, second, principles, unlike rules, did not apply in an 'all or nothing' way to cases. Rather, they had a dimension of weight or force which the judge was engaged in balancing in any complex case. This in turn meant that principles had both a factual and an irreducibly evaluative dimension, and that legal reasoning was a close relation of moral reasoning.

In a hard case, the judge's duty—summed up in the metaphor of the all-powerful judge 'Hercules', whom Dworkin had playfully (and in many people's view, disrespectfully) contrasted with a less ambitious judicial colleague, 'Herbert'—was to draw on the available principles to come up with the solution which fitted within the overall account or 'theory' which best justified the content of the legal system to date. Far from being merely a supplement to legal rules, principles expressing individual rights were, Dworkin argued, the fundamental counters of a legal order, ultimately determining not only the outcome of cases but the importance to be attached to formally articulated legal rules. Herbert's 'union of primary and secondary rules' amounted, therefore, not to the 'key to the science of jurisprudence' but rather to little more than 'rules of thumb' useful to unimaginative 'black letter' lawyers.

In elaborating his theory of adjudication, Dworkin drew an analogy with literature. Imagine, he suggested, a 'chain novel' in which someone is asked to write the final chapter of an unfinished work of fiction. Far from having an unconstrained choice about how to complete the narrative, such a decision-maker would be constrained by all sorts of factors: the characters' development so far, the novelist's depiction of the social world and so on. It would be implausible both for the writer of the chain novel and for the judge merely to claim—as Herbert claimed was the situation of judges in cases where the law was ambiguous or incomplete—that they had discretion to decide as they saw fit. Just as the writer of the last chapters of an unfinished *Middlemarch* would be precluded from depicting a selfish, morally indifferent Dorothea Brooke eloping with Tertius Lydgate, so it would be impossible for a judge in a difficult contract case to rewrite the history of the common law by ignoring the requirement for an offer to have been accepted for a contract to exist. Dworkin's theory, moreover, had both a factual and an evaluative aspect. Empirically, he argued that judges simply *do* regard themselves as bound by principles, and reason not as if they are making the law up in difficult cases but rather as if they are bound to find what the law already is. Politically, he claimed that this was constitutionally appropriate: to argue, with Herbert, that judges have broad discretion is to allot them a role as quasi-legislators, a role for which they have no democratic mandate.

In spite of his deep distaste for replying to critics, and his fear of the panic which it sometimes engendered, by the time that his grasp of the Brasenose job was giving him time to get back to some writing, Herbert was quick to come to a public view of Dworkin's emerging ideas. In 'The Nightmare and the Noble Dream', a lecture published in the *Georgia Law Review* in 1977 (and later reproduced in the *Essays in Jurisprudence and Philosophy*), Herbert sketched a bold map of the American twentieth-century jurisprudential scene. American legal theory was, he argued, focussed on adjudication because it was organized around the need to justify the power of judges to strike down democratically validated legislation on constitutional grounds. American legal theorists have reacted to this distinctive constitutional situation, he suggested, in one of two ways: the 'nightmare' of total indeterminacy and unconstrained judicial discretion and the 'noble dream' of complete legal determinacy. The 'nightmare', represented by the Realist jurisprudence of the early part of the twentieth century—Holmes, Frank, Llewellyn, and Gray (and later, in Herbert's view, by the 'critical legal studies' of scholars like Roberto Unger and Duncan Kennedy)—indulges in scepticism about whether judges are bound by law at all in either complex constitutional cases or more generally. This sceptical conclusion, which Herbert associated with the philosophical pragmatism of Dewey and with Veblen's economics, was tempered by a plea for a more scientific approach to policy making in courts: if judges do indeed make law, it is important at least to ensure that they do so effectively. But, Herbert argued, echoing the view defended in *The Concept of Law*, the Realist position is a gross overreaction which blinds itself to the genuinely normative, action-guiding nature of law.

By contrast, the American 'noble dream' is particularistic and holistic: it finds reasons constraining judges' discretion *within* the resources of particular legal systems, and it sees law as consisting in more than merely rules, asserting that even when appearances are to the contrary, judges are in fact finding and declaring rather than making law. Pound's vision of general principles informing the law along with Llewellyn's account of the 'grand style' in adjudication are two examples. Another—curiously omitted in Herbert's essay and little acknowledged in Dworkin's work—is Lon Fuller's account of the 'inner morality of law'. But the principal and the most extreme example is Dworkin's view of law as a seamless web of principles which, according to an article published in 1977, dictate 'one right answer' waiting to be found by judges in virtually every case in a reasonably sophisticated legal order. Herbert resoundingly predicted that the one right answer thesis would be found implausible by lawyers, and that philosophers would remain unconvinced by the argument that any coherent debate about, for example, which Shakespeare comedy is the funniest assumes the existence of a right answer. But in Dworkin's rejection of judges' utilitarian, policy-based reasoning and normative espousal of individual rights as the basis for principled adjudication Herbert saw the promise of a hugely important project: the delineation of a theory of rights or justice as separate from utility. Even so, he judged that the currency of the law and economics movement led by Richard Posner was testimony to the fact that utilitarianism was unlikely soon to be eradicated from normative US legal thought.

In this essay, there is no inkling of any uncertainty let alone lack of confidence in Herbert's assessment of Dworkin's work: the tone is assured and magisterial. Much the same can be said of Herbert's swipes at Dworkin in the *Essays on Bentham*, although here the tone is subtly modulated by a further element akin to impatience. In the essay on legal duty and obligation, Herbert focussed on the implications of Dworkin's theory for the position of judge Hercules within a wicked legal system. Imagine, Herbert suggested, Hercules confronted with a decision which forces him to choose between an answer which best fits with the history of the relevant legal institutions and that which best fits with the political morality to which he himself subscribes. Dworkin, Herbert argued:

agrees that in such systems no set of principles which we can find morally acceptable would fit the explicit law. In such cases, a judge's moral duty may be to lie and conceal what the law is because the least odious of the principles which will fit the system may yet be too odious to be enforced. None the less, Dworkin accepts that under the explicit rules of such wicked systems, legal rights and duties arise as *prima facie* moral rights and duties though they may conflict dramatically with the true objective background morality which may require the judge to lie, in which case the *prima facie* moral right which is also a legal right would be overridden in conflict with the requirements of background morality.

In my view these conclusions surrender the idea that legal rights and duties are a species of moral right or duties, or reduces the idea to utter triviality with no bite against the positivist or anyone else; for on this view, the justifying principles allegedly embedded in the law which generate the alleged moral component of legal right and legal duty impose no restraints at all.

This formulation of Dworkin's theory, Herbert concluded, 'seems indistinguishable from legal positivism'. He then went on to consider Dworkin's further argument that the moral force of such legal principles as do fit with a wicked legal system is to be explained in terms of considerations of fairness deriving from the moral duty to treat like cases alike. This he dismissed decisively:

This last-ditch defence designed to show a minimal moral component in all legal rights and duties even in a wicked legal system, seems to me hopeless,

going on to contrast Dworkin's theory unfavourably with Joseph Raz's in his view subtler account of the continuity in meaning between rights and duties in legal and moral contexts.

Herbert's complicated attitude to Dworkin surfaced in his relationship with his final doctoral student, Wil Waluchow. Waluchow, who arrived in Oxford in 1977, was working on the defence of legal positivism against Dworkin's critique. It was a topic which his original supervisor, R. M. Hare, found so boring that after a year he pronounced himself unable to read Waluchow's work. Devastated, Waluchow returned to his College to find a note from Herbert, to whom Hare had sent his work, saying that he found it fascinating and inviting Waluchow to dinner. From this point on, Herbert showered Waluchow with all the kindness and intellectual attention which Hare had so spectacularly withheld. On one occasion, knowing that Waluchow had just returned from Canada after a sudden bereavement, he even cycled five miles to Waluchow's home for a supervision to save him from having to come into College. Herbert discussed with Waluchow his own plans for an essay responding to some of the criticisms mounted against the principal contentions of *The Concept of Law*. And as Waluchow's work developed, Herbert began to use him as a go-between with Dworkin. After reading one of his chapters, Herbert said, 'We must see what Ronnie thinks of all this'. Dworkin agreed to read Waluchow's work, commenting on about 90 pages of text. As Waluchow tells the story:

Of course he disagreed with almost everything I had to say, but he was both gracious and extremely helpful. In the course of our discussions, Professor Dworkin asked me: 'What does Herbert think of all this?' My reply: 'He seemed to agree with the line of argument'. Professor Dworkin's response was to shake his head and mutter something inaudible. The following day I heard from Professor Hart. He wanted to know, 'What did Ronnie have to say?'. I told him and he chuckled.

Until his graduation in 1980, Waluchow continued to occupy this position as intermediary between Herbert and Ronald Dworkin, both of whom apparently preferred to communicate through him rather than directly. When Waluchow defended his doctoral thesis in front of his examiners, Neil MacCormick and John Mackie—both of them sympathetic to positivism—Herbert was yet more nervous than his student. At a congratulatory lunch afterwards, he confided, 'You're the last. I can no longer take the pressure of having a young scholar's career in my hands'.

Notwithstanding the assertive tone of his published criticisms of Dworkin's theory, Herbert was already beginning to feel doubts about how to formulate a more general response. The anxiety about replying to critics which had underpinned his depression a decade earlier was now reasserting itself. *The Concept of Law* was almost 20 years old: a second imprint, including a bibliography of selected critical writings, had been published in 1972. He now envisaged a second edition which would include two appendices: the second, an expanded bibliography of critical writings; the first, an essay answering critics. In 1980, writing from Cornwall to Joanna just after the birth of her son, Herbert told her:

I purport here to work at my beastly 'Reply to my critics' to go into my book's next imprint, and have got badly stuck, not knowing what I think and unable to work out some puzzles.

As he contemplated the task, foremost in his mind was the old question of how to modify his theory of legal obligation:

At first just going through the book listing the points which I see to be wrong, doubtful or know to be attacked, seemed a tolerably *pleasant* occupation, but on reaching topic of *obligation* and turning aside from book to read the critics whose criticisms I had really not read (Patricia White and Baier) I see I am in deep trouble with sense that a really large set of errors chiefly (not alas exclusively) about morals will have to be confessed and task seems immense.

Among these errors, Herbert felt that the principal were his 'mistaken view that moral obligation is an affair of social rules' and his identification of obligation in terms of the three criteria of social pressure supporting the standard, the call for sacrifice in demands for obedience, and the perceived importance of the standard. These, he now saw, did not account for all cases of even legal obligation, a particular problem being the obligations created by statutory as opposed to customary rules. He worried, furthermore, that any revisions he might make would either render it impossible to differentiate his own position from the earlier positivist account of obligation as equivalent to the demands of a gunman, or else from the fully moral account of obligation espoused by natural lawyers. As his natural law colleague

John Finnis described the dilemma, 'Everywhere he looked out there was dark or dangerous territory'. The solution, he was beginning to think, was to be found in the idea that those using the language of legal obligation are speaking from a special point of view: a point of view which is at once genuinely normative yet normatively restricted in that it is detached from complete moral endorsement: 'I see I will have to make great use of the Raz/Mackie argument about speaking from a point of view or from within a specific institution.' He was quick to see, however, that this would necessitate a more cautious restatement of his claim about the lack of any conceptual connection between law and morality. And even with these intellectual glimmers, the task seemed daunting:

Quite panic-generating! But remember there is time and a *larger framework may present itself into which these revisions fit and mistakes calmly confronted*: Stand back!

And the next day:

So pick up task (struggle with my *soul* (a) to do this large task at all (b) to be able to be honest about errors without *wrecking* the book....*Courage and calm both needed! (fantastic at 72!)*

Last night kept awake for a time by panic thought about this! Why not cool: what does it matter to confess errors even as large as this at my age? (Life of errors: why have I had success?)

As was usual with Herbert, the anxieties, broken nights, chaotic notebooks, and intimidating list of 'PLAIN ERRORS AND DIFFICULTIES TO BE MET' gradually generated steadily accumulating insights, as he worked his way exhaustively (and exhaustingly) through and took detailed notes on a huge number of critical articles, most of them by American authors. 'Illuminating talks' with Joseph Raz contributed to this progress, and he began to feel his 'spirits rising' and even to envisage 'an Indian summer of work for publication'. He was getting a firmer grasp of the central problem of legal obligation and of how to manage the tensions in his view of law's normative, ought-creating character: 'reasons for accepting rules as guides or standards may vary over the full range of oughts (morals, concern for others, self interest) yet when I characterize 'normative language' I speak of it being used to refer to *justified* demands'. The tension could be resolved, he thought, by delineating a 'thin notion of acceptance' as 'commitment in advance to a course of conduct', while the 'special character of judges' duty under the rule of recognition' could be explicated in terms of a role-based duty generating a 'legal reason for obeying an Act of Parliament'. Further criticisms would also have to be addressed. These included analysis of his less than clear account of the relationship of the distinctions between duty-imposing and power-conferring and between primary and secondary rules, along with his conflation of laws' distinctive conceptual, normative structure (imposing duties and creating powers) with their varying social functions (proscribing conduct, creating facilities, resolving disputes and so on); of his treatment of judicial discretion; and of his account of the conceptual separation of law and morality. He also felt that his claim to have provided a descriptive sociology, as opposed to the 'normative concepts required for a descriptive sociology', had been misplaced. But all this could be dealt with, he believed, so as to leave intact 'the original structure and positivist character' of *The Concept of Law*, with its view of 'law as a complex structure of social fact the moral value of which is an entirely contingent matter'.

At this stage Dworkin, whose questioning of the need for a purely descriptive jurisprudence he saw as 'at best reckless, misguided', appeared to Herbert the 'least of my worries'. Certainly, he was already envisaging a special section on Dworkin in the Appendix and was tracing carefully—and sometimes with bemusement—what he saw as significant 'shifts of key' between the earlier and later chapters of *Taking Rights Seriously* towards a greater concentration on the moral credentials of legal principles at the expense of the more positivism-friendly theme of their 'fit' with legal institutions. But Herbert still saw Dworkin as, essentially, a legal positivist, and one whose account of the nature of legal reasoning, with its 'myth' of Hercules, was subject to decisive empirical objection. Herbert now envisaged a refinement of his arguments in *The Concept of Law* which would answer Dworkin without affecting the overall structure of its thesis. More could be said of the role of principles, and their relationship to the rule of recognition explained; a more detailed account of legal reasoning could displace Dworkin's critique of his view of the breadth of judges' discretion; and an answer would have to be found to Dworkin's telling objection that Herbert's account of morality as a system of social rules only works for conventional morality and not for critical (even if convergent) morality. Stephen Guest, who was present at a seminar which Herbert gave at University College London in 1981, remembers him 'producing an extraordinarily clear-headed criticism of Ronnie Dworkin's thesis from the back of a cheque-book: he said he had jotted it down on the train'. Had nothing happened radically to change either Dworkin's position or Herbert's ability to concentrate on his view of it, it seems virtually certain that he would have published a crisp and effective response by the mid-1980s. In the event, however, events conspired fundamentally to change both of these variables between 1983 and 1986.

From 1981 to 1983, Herbert continued to make detailed notes in preparation for the new essay, but his time was also taken up with his work on Bentham and with the preparation of his two collections of essays. Once this was done, another intellectual project occupied much of his attention: his commitment to producing a response to the papers to be delivered at the 1984 conference in his honour to be held at the Hebrew University in Jerusalem, where many of his most astute critics, including Dworkin, would be assembled. But as he was beginning to contemplate this task, a much more radical source of distraction presented itself.

In 1962 and again in 1966, in an era of public anxiety about spying, Jenifer had been interviewed by MI5, whom she told of her meetings in 1937 with a foreign communist 'contact' whom she later realized was hoping to recruit her as a Soviet agent. She explained the basis of her communist sympathies, and made it clear that she had never been asked for information by the KGB and that in any event she had by 1939 at the latest severed her connections with the Communist Party and lost her sympathy with the communist cause. The 1966 interview, at which one of the interviewers was 'spycatcher' Peter Wright, was long and unpleasant, and subsequent events gave her some reason to think that the interviewers had not been entirely satisfied with her account. In 1981, a book by Chapman Pincher had implied, though without naming Jenifer, that she had been an active Soviet agent, and the following year she had considered legal action in relation to an article published in *The Observer*, which contained several inaccuracies. The exposure of Anthony Blunt in 1979 as a KGB agent and his subsequent vilification in the media had given unprecedented publicity to the issue of communist infiltration of government institutions, and the following year, Nigel West (pen name of the Conservative politician Rupert Allason) had published a book about MI5 which had not only implied that a Civil Service discussion group of which Jenifer was a member had been engaged in illicit activities but also mentioned Herbert's name, referring to his position in MI5. Colleagues remember Herbert's acute shock and indignation at learning of Blunt's treachery: they also remember his anxiety about the subsequent insinuations about Jenifer.

In the summer of 1982, Jenifer was approached by Christopher Andrew, a fellow of Corpus Christi College. Andrew asked if she would be willing to appear in a TV programme on intelligence in the 1930s. He told her that he was concerned to make a serious historical documentary, and believed that she could help to set in proper historical context the communist sympathies of many intellectuals in the 1930s. Jenifer, feeling that this would be an important contribution, and hoping that her participation would give her an opportunity to answer Pincher's and others' allegations, agreed to do the interview, and spoke frankly to Andrew about the basis for her own commitment to communist ideals, as well as about the circumstances which gradually eroded that commitment. The interview was scheduled for broadcast on 27 July 1983. Its airing was preceded by a number of BBC press releases which gave a misleading and rather sensational view of Jenifer's contribution. These press releases gave rise to a number of newspaper articles alleging that she had been recruited by the KGB while working in the Home Office. Unfortunately, Jenifer herself aggravated the scandal in a maladroit attempt to set the record straight. As the press releases appeared, she had been rung by Simon Freeman, a journalist and former lodger of hers and Herbert's at Manor Place. Freeman gave her to understand that he would like to write a piece defending her. She spoke frankly but incautiously to him about her position in the 1930s. Unknown to Jenifer, Freeman was taping the conversation, and he drew on it to construct, with Barry Penrose, the most damaging of all the items published at the time. It appeared in the *Sunday Times* on 17 July under the headline ' "I was a Russian Spy" says MI5 man's wife'. The article included several references to Herbert, noting that he had worked at MI5 alongside Blunt, implying that he might have known of Jenifer's 'spying' activities, and insinuating that he might have been involved himself.

Herbert's and Jenifer's reaction was decisive. They consulted Lord Goodman, who immediately issued a statement denying the truth of the claims and who put them in touch with a leading libel lawyer, Peter Carter Ruck. Carter Ruck took statements from them and prepared the case that they had been defamed by the *Sunday Times*; writs were issued, and a full retraction and apology was demanded. As these events unfolded, however, Herbert's psychological equilibrium began to waver.

At first, he was shaken but tried to take a philosophical view. Writing from Cornwall in August to thank Isaiah and Aline Berlin, with whom he had just enjoyed another Italian holiday, Herbert reported that:

Since I got back the Times and Sunday Times have been keeping up the Russian 'spy' stories and heralding two books to appear later in the year. One is by the man who produced Jenifer's ill-fated television talk and the other by the horrid Chapman Pincher. Both promise 'startling' revelations. I thought Stuart [Hampshire]'s hit back about the 'hypocritical and slimy McCarthyism of the press' was excellent and was glad to see it taken up in a very good article in the Guardian against spy-pornography.

He went on calmly to news of his holiday reading (Dickens' *Our Mutual Friend*—'a mad book and dubiously worth the great labour of getting through ... but there are certainly several riveting things in the book')—and an idea for one of the games of wit or ingenuity which he was famous for inventing. The game consisted in a thought experiment in which the Harts' and the Berlins' guests wake up to find themselves with the other family, and involved wry comparisons of the comportment of their respective guests:

Our lot are a very mixed bag viz Carol and Francis G[raham]-H[arrison], Alan and Kate Ryan [Herbert and Jenifer had maintained a close relationship with Alan since his and Joanna's separation], A. Zuckerman and his current girl Miss Taverne, our old Nanny, two student helpers, J Raz and son, our Joanna, Adam and Jacob; the daughter in law of Flora Solomons (a white Russian who is said to have denounced Jenifer) and various quarter Russian children. Somehow I think our lot would have a better time with you than your lot with us! Jenifer's patience with e.g. Lady Avon [Anthony Eden's widow and a frequent companion of Arnold Goodman] would give out sooner (and more explosively) than Aline's with Adam. But the topic might provide another game don't you think?

A few weeks later, however, his mood had darkened:

Do you remember the long letter I wrote to you ... after my Pisa train mishap? 'Dio mio', I shouted out in that train, 'ho perduto tutto!'. Well, here is another occasion for shouting 'Dio mio etc'; but I don't this time see a happy ending. I've just read your excellent letter to Jenifer but I am not so much responding to that as giving vent to a strong wish to be able to think through with you our rather daunting perplexities when you return to Oxford in Sept; and meanwhile say how I see them. (I won't go into the past save to say (1) Oddly, my first thought when the storm burst was 'Thank god my parents are dead'. *Isn't* it odd?: they have been dead 30 years (2) I found no temptation to reproach Jenifer while privately marvelling at her combination of intelligence, honesty, naiveté, pedantic attention to insignificant detail and blindness to essential things.)

Arnold G[oodman] has been marvellous: his letter silenced all comment and since we have actually issued writs there *can* be no comment till the case is tried (if it is) which will be 10–12 months hence. But he cannot act as our solicitor (he is director of the Times) and has transferred us to the best libel lawyers. Initially they thought we had a very strong case but while still encouraging are a bit cooler. *Rightly* cooler, I think, because though the broadcast taken by itself would appear harmless to anyone who understood the atmosphere of the 1930's, a 1983 *jury* (and the case *would* be a jury case) may not draw distinctions between C[ommunist].P[arty].G.B. of 1936 and the Soviets of 1983. Anyhow Jenifer was trapped into a (tape recorded!) conversation with one of the journalists in which she said 'I mean one felt one wasn't a narrow patriot: I never felt much loyalty to my country, but don't say that'!!! Of course she meant she was anti-war, internationalist (not 'pro-Russian') but the paper cites her words as their reason for saying that whatever the inaccuracies of the headlines the article *as a whole* was not libellous. They have offered to pay our costs to date and publish a statement that she never passed information but leaving standing the statement that she admitted she was a 'Russian spy'. We turned this offer down and meanwhile I am pursuing the action ... It may be that they will offer some real apology and withdrawal and even damages but I doubt it. So my real dilemma is this choice of evils:

(A) A full scale libel action which will be a *cause célèbre* to the delight of the press in which details of our private lives will be paraded (living together 2 and a half years before marrying in 1941; I being recommended to MI5 by Jen when asked if she knew anyone suitable in 1940; my not telling MI5 that Jen had communist contacts down to 1938.) (Of course I thought it was all childish nonsense and was anyhow over and done with in 1938). Jen will be a bad witness having to explain away silly phrases she used and under tough cross-examination, might say silly things and almost certainly alienate a jury. The costs of losing such an action could be £70,000–£80,000 (which I could find alright without damaging Jacob's provision). Anyhow imagine the strain!

(B) If we abandon action for libel what will the 'world' think? No doubt the papers will make as much as they can of the 'Harts withdraw'; though possibly after the lapse of a year and the relatively harmless TV broadcast this may not be so exciting. But if they do what happens to my public 'persona' such as it is? Do I cease to appear in public e.g. at fundraising events for Jacob's Home Farm Trust (Patrons are royals (Pr. Anne.))? British Academy? What about American connections. Israel? Rothschild Foundation? . . .

So you see the weighing of evils is not easy and perhaps one has become a bit hysterical in imagining the worst. Our lawyers (excellent people) say 'see how things develop'. Richard Wilberforce (two very kind letters) was glad we had issued writs but hoped we would not have to fight (he stressed the lack of understanding now of the 1930s). Some family pressure not to drag Jen or oneself through the ordeal of a trial etc but just live on the good opinion of those whose opinion we value (meaning our friends). My *instinct* is to choose (A) above so that even if unsuccessful I can be seen to deny on oath any dishonourable inference or innuendo. But that may be just too much 'instinct'.

Herbert's extreme sensitivity about his public 'persona' and his initial inclination to pursue the action are telling. But, back in Oxford on 6 September, with the *Sunday Times* offering a limited compromise involving payment of the legal costs to date and the substitution for the word 'spy' of something more acceptable to Jenifer, Herbert wrote again to the Berlins, thanking them for their telephoned advice, sounding more measured and confessing that:

I have great difficulty in forcing myself to attend to the bloody case; but obviously we shall have to press on in the hope of getting a substantial retraction though I agree entirely with your view about actually fighting the case.

Herbert's Boston friend, Gerry Rubin, whom he consulted about the case, found him 'uncertain, confused, angry and fearful'; Rubin advised Herbert, 'Nobody ever wins a defamation suit'. With friends counselling a settlement, press photographers ambushing the family outside Manor Place, and the mounting strain of all the publicity, a compromise was reached, and on 18 September the *Sunday Times* published a brief and, in Herbert's and Jenifer's view, wholly inadequate apology. Jenifer remained outraged and defiant: Isaiah Berlin told her that she should have known better and compared her to Bishop Wilberforce, who had earned the nickname 'Soapy Sam' because although he was always in hot water his hands were always clean. For Herbert, the initial response was one of relief. Yet the worry about the impact of the scandal continued to haunt him and, still in the grip of his frustrated instinct publicly to deny the allegations against him on oath, he was unable to let go of his obsessive concern about them.

In the weeks which followed the settlement, several friends and colleagues noticed that Herbert was in a state of acute anxiety. He was repeatedly articulating worries not merely about the stalled libel action but about his tax affairs. Visiting Douglas and Mary Jay, he talked manically the whole weekend about the *Sunday Times* article, repeating, 'Everyone will think I was a spy: you don't think it do you?', and refusing to be calmed by their assurances both that nothing was further from their minds and that the matter would soon pass out of public notice. Then, during a long walk, he began to talk obsessively about the fact that he feared that he had filed incorrect information on his tax return. The Jays tried to reassure him, but they were deeply troubled by his distress and by what seemed to them the irrational degree of his anxiety. Adrian Zuckerman (who had moved from Israel to a Law Fellowship at University College in 1972 and who had become a close friend of the Harts) also remembers him repeatedly coming in to lunch in College in a state of 'obsessive anxiety' about his tax affairs. The first time that it happened, Zuckerman asked him all about it, said that it didn't sound too serious, and suggested that he ring up the Inland Revenue and sort it out if he was worried. He seemed reassured, but then came in again in just the same state the next day. It became increasingly difficult to manage conversations with him, as his anxieties deepened and started to include the belief that there would be a wave of anti-Semitism in England which would somehow 'blow everything up and lead to Israel being destroyed'. Zuckerman felt that the tax obsession as well as this irrationally extreme worry about sudden anti-Semitism revealed that Herbert's deepest anxieties had to do with unresolved feelings about his Jewish identity and unease about social attitudes to Jews: his surmise was that the tax anxiety connected to a stereotype of Jews as being not quite straightforward about money.

Into this toxic mix of real and imagined causes for anxiety there now dropped yet another problem. One of the remarkable, and positive, things about the 'spy scandal' had been the fact that Jenifer and Herbert had managed to maintain a unified stance. One can only imagine Jenifer's complicated feelings about the episode. A gifted person in her own right, after 40 years of working in Herbert's shadow, she was now in the limelight, but in a disagreeable way, and causing huge anxiety to Herbert and other family and friends. Yet Herbert had avoided any recriminations over her lack of caution in dealing with the press, and she in turn had been willing to be swayed by his ultimately circumspect approach to the litigation. But this concordat was about to be shattered by a conflict generated by another of Jenifer's impulsive actions inspired by her political views and implacable sense of right and wrong. In the autumn of 1983, Princess Anne, the patron of the Home Farm Trust, was due to visit Milton Heights, the home in which Jacob now lived. To Jenifer's intense irritation, the home was catapulted into a frenzy of redecoration, re-carpeting, and general beautification in preparation for the visit. This Jenifer regarded as both a waste of money and a piece of window-dressing of which Princess Anne, if she had any sense, would have disapproved. She wrote to the Princess, signing herself merely as 'a concerned parent', to ask her whether she was aware of the misguided policy and whether she approved of it. Princess Anne's private secretary forwarded the letter to the Headquarters of the Home Farm Trust, and the Trust in turn informed Herbert of the embarrassing matter. Suspecting that Jenifer might have had some hand in it, he confronted her. In what she soon came to regard as a yet greater mistake than sending the letter anonymously in the first place, she initially denied that she had been its author, but the truth soon had to be confessed.

Jenifer was already alarmed about Herbert's mental state; in the wake of his discovery about her letter, she had sleepless nights as she struggled with her own feelings of shame and with his reaction, which was extreme. Understandably, he was furious with Jenifer, both for writing the letter anonymously and for lying about it; and he was mortified by the embarrassment she had caused the Trust. But this fundamentally trivial episode also seems to have sparked off deep feelings of anxiety and vulnerability, of being a perpetual outsider to the English establishment to which he was, despite his trenchant liberalism, so firmly attached. This connected with the similarly based psychological fall-out of the spy scandal. Herbert began to experience yet more extreme anxiety and paranoia: he believed that Jacob would be required to leave Milton Heights. The mania surrendered only to bouts of almost catatonic depression, the external circumstances probably aggravated by the underlying family predisposition to depressive illness, particularly in old age, which had also manifested itself in his father and sister. In late October, he was admitted to the Warneford psychiatric hospital in Oxford. On 26 November 1983, feeling scarcely any better, he wrote sadly to Berlin:

Dear Isaiah,

Can you find someone instead of me—Stuart would of course be perfectly capable—to grade the Rothschild Fellowship candidates for interview as well as attend the interviews? I have been in this hospital under heavy sedation on anti-depressant drugs for nearly four weeks and seem to have lost all power of decision and judgment and dare not take on the task even if I can concentrate on anything except my own mental state and inability to fit with the regime here. Everything required of one (e.g. laying up and now serving up for meals) is in theory voluntary—operated on a rota which the patients construct every day. There is moral but no actual coercive pressure to do the chores; but I make a fearful totally feeble mess of it and I stand out as totally inept and despised by the general run of patients who are used to this sort of thing. I only get by by being helped out by staff who have other jobs. I cannot, in fact, take on the simplest task such as the chairing of meetings of patients which take place every day except Sat. and Sunday. Of course behind all this are many problems of practical life (some v difficult ones concerned with my sister [who was also seriously depressed] and Jacob's trust) and the ordeal of facing the Jerusalem conference. They are proposing ECT as a way of shattering what they call my 'depression' and I have virtually consented to it being administered next week (But the immediate thing is warning you about the grading for interviews) or they can get coercive powers to administer it. I did start when I first came in here on an ineffectual hunger-strike in a mood of depression when I first came in here but gave it up when they said they could drip-feed me and would have to do so if I persisted.

I fear I will have created great trouble.

Yours, Herbert

The letter's repetitions and moments of disjuncture, as well as its formal ending (almost all of Herbert's other letters to Isaiah are signed, 'Love, Herbert') indicate his seriously disordered emotional state.

Herbert also described his feelings of distress at his ineptitude in the Warneford to Mary and Douglas Jay when he visited them later in the year: he had, he said, particularly hated the group therapy, in which he felt inadequate in his unwillingness and inability to open up his most private feelings to public scrutiny. But, like his agonized diary outpourings over the years, his painful letter to Berlin captured only one part of his experience, the distance of writing allowing him to express feelings which were harder to articulate face to face. With friends such as Jean Floud and Marianne Fillenz, he put on a brave front, happily accepting the informal style of the hospital staff, welcoming visits, and not seeming particularly depressed. His mood was, however, volatile: Joseph Raz, who also visited, found him in a state of clinical depression: the visit was so painful that he is unable to recall very much about it.

344

Yet to Jean Floud Herbert even expressed pride in having served breakfast to other patients—the very subject of his outburst to Berlin.

Fillenz had the distinct impression that Herbert was in some ways relieved to be away from the intense pressures of home for a few weeks and to be entirely looked after—an account which would explain his difficulty with the self-governing aspects of the hospital regime. She and Floud also remembered his warm relations with staff and other patients—a memory which is confirmed by several affectionate letters to Jenifer after his death, in which one fellow patient said that Herbert was the person who had made his time in the Warneford tolerable. Adam, too, remembered him taking pleasure in his allotted task of ordering and cataloguing the hospital's record collection—remarkable in view of Herbert's general lack of orderliness. It is unlikely, however, that Herbert would have consented to ECT (electroconvulsive therapy) had he not been experiencing extreme and persistent distress. In the event, he did recover relatively quickly after its administration, and he later told colleagues—to one of whom he remarked that he had been 'living with madmen'—that he attributed his recovery to ECT. He returned home in mid-December, calm and more cheerful but still weak.

As Herbert slowly took up his normal life once again, the spectre of the Jerusalem conference the following March began to reassert itself. He scaled down the commitment to reply to the other participants, promising only to make impromptu responses as they occurred to him, and deferring the construction of a full commentary until after the conference. Even so, he was nervous about the event. Joseph Raz had two of the most anxious days of his life wondering if Herbert would crack up; in private he was still very fragile, although, typically, he seemed perfectly alright in public. Raz's own feelings about the conference were ambivalent, and this in turn gave rise to a further complication for both him and Herbert. Since the 1967 war, Raz, a critic of Israel's policy on the Palestinian issue, had refused to set foot in eastern Jerusalem or the other occupied territories unless invited to do so by a Palestinian, and travelled to Israel only with reservations. He was now reluctant to go to a publicly funded conference during the occupation, a gesture which he equated with travelling to a government-funded event in apartheid South Africa. On the other hand, he felt that he owed it to Herbert to attend. He squared his political conscience with his sense of personal obligation by deciding to organize a seminar in the free time scheduled into the Jerusalem event at the Palestinian university, Bir Zeit.

The philosophers at Bir Zeit, struggling in a financially and even physically embattled environment—the week of the conference, Bir Zeit's academics were banned from holding meetings on the campus—were delighted at the prospect of hosting a conference with such distinguished international participants, and gladly agreed to set up a one day seminar on a human rights theme. In accordance with his principle of lending political support to the Palestinian University through a gesture of intellectual engagement, Raz insisted that the topic be approached from a philosophical perspective. He then approached the other non-Israeli participants, but did not tell the Israeli organizers of the Jerusalem conference, whom he felt would have been put in an awkward position had they been invited. His approach came late in the day, and some participants decided not to take part. But several, including John Finnis, David Lyons, Neil MacCormick, and Gerald Postema, agreed to go. Bir Zeit put on a touchingly warm welcome, with a flower-laden seminar table and a glorious dinner at an Arab restaurant in the evening, and the academics engaged enthusiastically in both collective and one-to-one debate.

For Raz, a key question about this venture was whether Herbert—himself a critic of the occupation and signatory to at least one public letter of protest—would agree to come to Bir Zeit. He agonized; he wavered; but in the end he decided not to join the seminar. Raz was deeply disappointed, but was naturally reluctant to try to persuade him. He remained uncertain about whether Herbert refused because of the fear of offending his hosts or because he did not want to lend his imprimatur to the event. It is also possible that in his still fragile condition, Herbert felt that yet another public appearance would be an intolerable strain. But given his lifelong sensitivity about belonging and being accepted, which manifested itself in a marked reluctance to cause offence, it is likely Herbert's fear of upsetting his hosts, who were annoyed by Raz's initiative, was uppermost in his mind.

In Jerusalem, in spite of the frisson caused by the side trip to Bir Zeit, the main conference was a success, with Herbert, as usual, finding the resources to appear calm and intellectually in command when in public situations. The long-anticipated confrontation with Dworkin was muted: Gavison responded orally at his public lecture, while Herbert later produced a written response. He spoke formally only at the conference reception, thanking the speakers for their tributes and apologizing for being such a bad correspondent. In private conversation, he seemed preoccupied with his personal life, talking to Gavison about his relations with his brother and sister and, particularly, his children, of whom he spoke with pride mixed with some regrets about how they had been brought up. Herbert also found time to enjoy visits to some of his favourite parts of Jerusalem. John Finnis, Herbert's former student, and Law Fellow at University College since 1966, remembers him suggesting that they take the long walk up the Mount of Olives by the Garden of Gethsemane on a stunningly beautiful day. Wandering down into the valley, up the hill, by a church and along newly laid walkways, they finally reached a bench with views overlooking The Temple Mount and the old city of Jerusalem, and there they sat companionably and ate their sandwich lunch. Finnis remembers this as the only personal conversation in their 30-year relationship: Herbert alluded to the fact that they were seeing Jerusalem through very different eyes. After some casual observations on architecture and so on, there was a silence, and Finnis, a devout Catholic, believed that each was reflecting on the entirely different significance that the city laid out before them had for each of them.

It was only after Herbert's death that Finnis became aware of the full extent of his antipathy to religion. The pains which Herbert had taken to disguise his strong views from a student and colleague with whom he had very regular contact must have been considerable: after all, the last chapter of Finnis's book, *Natural Law and Natural Rights*, which Herbert commissioned for the Clarendon Law Series, is entitled 'Nature, Reason, God'. Herbert, Finnis recalled, thought for a long time 'about the fact of that chapter', and ultimately suggested that it be placed as an Appendix to the book. Although Herbert worried that the chapter, which presents a theological basis for the book's argument, might undermine the book as a work of philosophy, he made little comment, leaving the final decision on its position to Finnis. This, like his avoidance of the topic of religion in encounters with Finnis, was typical of both his liberalism and his concern not to cause offence.

Back in England, friends and colleagues were working to make it clear to Herbert that the 'spy scandal' had not affected their regard or respect for him. Later in 1984, he received a further accolade from the legal profession, and one which may well have been motivated by the kindly aim of making some unambiguous public statement of belief in Herbert's complete exoneration: he was appointed an Honorary QC. This honour he gladly accepted, even enjoying his trip to the ceremony in London, which he attended dressed in the elaborate traditional robes, and in the company of his much-loved brother, Albert. A photograph of him in his ceremonial robes as QC was sent later that year to Isaiah Berlin on his seventieth birthday: intriguingly, in the light of their complex relationship, it was inscribed with the caption, 'I judge you well'.

Work, too, continued. Herbert and Tony Honoré had agreed to produce a second edition of *Causation in the Law*, which duly appeared in 1985. In the wake of Herbert's breakdown, Tony Honoré had undertaken virtually all of the work for the new edition, though Herbert had contributed to drafting a few pages which appear at the end of the introduction—pages the importance of which Honoré acknowledges with characteristic generosity. But the need to produce a written contribution to the published collection of papers for the Jerusalem conference which was to be edited by the conference organizer, Ruth Gavison, as well as the old project of an appendix for *The Concept of*

Law, now presented themselves as unavoidable obligations, and ones in which Herbert could not rely on the support of a co-author. After a sticky start, but spurred on by the resolution to make a fresh attempt based on a greater willingness to concede errors and to let go of the pressure to find an answer to every critical point, he found himself able to engage productively with several of the Jerusalem papers, particularly those by David Lyons and Gerald Postema. In September of 1984, he introduced his latest notebook thoughts in a striking way:

Sunday Sept 2/84 Romance (born again?)

Conviction that I must reverse the extreme aspect of my legal theory particularly over rigid separation doctrine. Partly this decision has been generated in me by grappling with Postema contribution.... Intricate but in many ways excellent and suggestive. Partly it is the rising to the surface of a concession to critics I have long felt uneasy about *not* making. Main thing is that without this I felt *blocked* in writing replies both to the Conference papers which I am supposed to do and also the much deferred general reply promised as an appendix to the C of L. I feel some sort of *liberation* at the prospect of acknowledging the need to modify and withdraw. But there are of course many 'rocks and shoals' to be steered through in this new course to the extent that I felt I didn't really understand the often complex points made (e.g. by Postema).... To see therefore if this new (born again) resolution will ease my path and start things flowing rather than (as I have felt to my despair recently) silting up in a dry river bed.

Sept 3: Today: continue with Postema. But now (born again) with flexible openness to possibility that he is right and I am to fit in concessions to what I think best in him. But steady—no *wholesale* jettisoning of my whole 'position'. It looks as if the central concession is admission that law claims moral basis for conformity.

A relatively full reply to Postema emerged from these resolutions. But Herbert's formulations of the concessions which he had enjoined himself to make were, in his notes for the reply, strikingly focussed on their implications for his further response to Ronald Dworkin, whose critique of Herbert's positivism was increasingly directed to the descriptive nature of his theory:

NB that even if *moral force is part of meaning of propositions of law* theory of law that asserts this can still be itself descriptive.... Descriptive theory must include this *fact* (i.e. that most officials and many subjects take internal attitude and hence use rules as guides for actions and evaluation) *but does not therefore cease to be descriptive*.... Does Dw rejection of descriptive theory make simple mistake of treating a theory *that states that* propositions of law are guides as itself not a description but an evaluation ... A large and pervasive error—in Dw—to think that just because m[oral] beliefs are 'constitutent of legal institutions' and not (as I argue) merely contingent accompaniments—Does not follow that th[eory] of law cannot be wholly descr[iptive].

Though he must have been worried about this unusual difficulty in grasping critics' points, Herbert was making real progress in clarifying his ideas through his reply to Postema, asserting for example that 'judges' committed and detached statements of law have same content and truth conditions and are distinguished only by their expressive functions and the practical dispositions they manifest'. But even as he constructed his response to Postema, it was really Dworkin with whom Herbert was preoccupied.

In 1983, Herbert had more or less crystallized his response to Dworkin's critique of *The Concept of Law*. But by the time he had recovered from his breakdown and returned to the vexed question of the appendix, Dworkin's views had moved on. The publication of his substantial monograph, *Law's Empire*, in 1986 marked a significant change of direction, as well as an 'upping of the ante' in his poker contest with Herbert. Declining to give an account of the relationship between this and his earlier work, Dworkin now presented his readers with a sweeping vision of law as an interpretive practice structured around values of reciprocity and fairness which enable the universal right to equal respect and concern to be met, and the ideal of 'law as integrity' to be achieved. His new position was both more and less ambitious than his earlier one. It was less ambitious in the sense that it was, explicitly, applicable only to certain kinds of systems—i.e. those whose moral and political commitments were capable of underpinning the structure of principles necessary to the pursuit of 'law as integrity' (a term which has distinct echoes of Fuller's notion of a 'morality of aspiration' capable of underpinning 'fidelity to law'). In Dworkin's revised view, only these systems counted as genuinely 'legal' systems. The new book was more ambitious, however, in the level of detail to which it elaborated both its underlying political philosophy and its account of different aspects of legal reasoning (statutory, common law, constitutional). It also presented a commanding vision and critique of the entire field of legal philosophy, organized around a welter of newly coined or adapted classifications: 'semantic theories'; 'hard and soft positivism'; 'internal and external scepticism'; 'conventionalism', and 'pragmatism', to mention only a few.

Herbert was quick to understand that his projected analysis of Dworkin's earlier work would not be adequate as a response to *Law's Empire*. In particular, his empirical critique of the early account of Hercules' adjudicative practices was now beside the point:

Dw no longer has to face factual ... q[uestion] since his new q is whether judges' legal practice can be seen in a better light if it is *assumed* they are works of applying Dw's test ...

Herbert had, however, extreme difficulty in coming to a view of Dworkin's overall arguments in *Law's Empire* clear enough either to satisfy himself or to form the basis for a general response. Once again, he tried to make a fresh start on the appendix, which he now conceived as an essay on 'The Concept of Law Reconsidered'. But from now on his notes became a painful, repetitious collection of thoughts circling round Dworkin's new thesis, and a mass of annotations to his notebooks of the early 1980s. He tried a number of approaches. First, he attempted to make sense of Dworkin's kaleidoscopic range of new distinctions and of his own place within them. But should he concentrate on a rebuttal of Dworkin's caricature of positivism as suffering from 'the semantic sting' (i.e. as making the mistake of viewing legal theory as an answer to a question about the meaning of the word, 'law'); or should he train his attention on Dworkin's charge that his version of positivism was an unsatisfactory form of 'conventionalism', incapable of explaining the nature of legal argumentation in controversial cases? He tried to address these questions by resorting to the technique of exceptionally close readings of Dworkin's text: but he found that this usually successful method, to which he was deeply intellectually committed, was hard to apply to Dworkin's fluid and sometimes elusive analytic style.

Herbert then tried to get to grips with Dworkin by stepping back from the details of his argument and trying to understand its philosophical basis. With remarkable energy, he threw himself into close readings of philosophers such as Simon Blackburn, Donald Davidson, Susan Hurley, Sabina Lovibond, John MacDowell, and Bernard Williams. But even with a fresh view of contemporary debates in moral philosophy, Herbert had difficulty in making sense of Dworkin's approach to questions such as the nature of truth claims and the status of morality.

Finally, Herbert resorted to another trusted technique: working out the consequences of Dworkin's position for concrete issues such as the status of wicked legal systems and the position of judges within them. Yet again, insights were slow to come: it was difficult to apply Dworkin's theory to concrete cases when the theory itself was slipping through his fingers. He struggled to see why it was not enough for Dworkin to accept merely that legal propositions entailed a 'claim of belief in morality' (as opposed to actual moral legitimacy), a point which he was ready to concede, along with the idea that law 'involves institutions . . . being acknowledged to have right (moral) to "bind" subjects'. He laboured to understand how the dimensions of 'fit' and 'morality' related to each other in this yet more holistic statement of Dworkin's theory. But, despite months and months of intensive work, and hundreds of pages of notes, things were not becoming any clearer to him. In a fascinating and poignant marginal note, he scribbled, 'Look for despair over job changes etc—15/1/45 17/2/45 2/4/52', an entry which reveals that he used the paths through depression tracked in his earlier diaries as emotional resources in later moments of anxiety.

In the end, Herbert focussed his attention on an argument which is superficially attractive but ultimately not entirely satisfactory. This was the thought that his own and Dworkin's projects were fundamentally different, and might even be understood as complementary to one another. 'New approach', he wrote in late 1985: 'reply to Dworkin by making case for a *general descriptive JP*'. *The Concept of Law*, he repeatedly asserted, is '*NOT* a branch of justificatory moral or political theory': while *Law's Empire* advances an ideal vision and a legitimating argument for a certain conception of law, it neither engages in, nor undermines the validity of, the project of producing a general, universally applicable, and fundamentally descriptive theory of law such as Herbert himself had sought to provide. He thought that this descriptive project could survive what he now recognized to be a further complication: that the 'description . . . will involve *selection* of some elements for a cluster and the selection will be *evaluative* (not morally) in sense of answerable to some criteria of *importance* (Raz [though in fact this point is made more forcefully by Finnis]) and among these will be "relevance to moral judgment". So though description and evaluation are different they are in such ways connected. . . . This is parallel though different from Aristotle's real definition and "real essence" where the elements in the definition are seen as *necessarily combined . . .*'. Since disputes about what elements could satisfy the implicit criterion used to select the 'central case' would inevitably make such descriptive analysis controversial, these controversies, he recognized, would have to be accommodated as 'pivotal rather than borderline' cases.

With the move towards an essay defending a division of labour between his and Dworkin's theory—the one descriptive and the other justificatory—Herbert escaped one element of his dilemma: he avoided the need to synthesize and comment on every aspect of Dworkin's theory, and was able instead to organize his thoughts more firmly around a defence and elaboration of his own views. But in doing so, he faced the difficulty that Dworkin himself roundly denied the possibility of compatibility, and continued to insist that his theory contradicted some central tenets of *The Concept of Law*. Herbert risked, therefore, giving the impression that he was simply failing to respond to Dworkin's challenge. Moreover, in focussing his argument on the representation of his own theory as entirely descriptive, he was turning his back on an insight which had been powerfully defended in his own early work—though one which had rather dropped out of sight in his later writings. This was the argument, put with particular force in the Holmes lecture, that there was a strong *moral* case for espousing the inclusive, positivist concept of law according to which even morally unappealing standards may count as fully valid legal rules. In 1957, his argument had been that the clarity gained by a differentiation of legal and moral standards had both intrinsic moral and intellectual merit and political advantages. It was honest to be clear-sighted about the different considerations at play for citizens confronted with evil laws: first, are they legally valid; second, should they be obeyed? And this clear-sightedness would be more likely to foster the reflective approach to legal obedience which properly underlies liberal citizenship and a robust attitude to tyranny. Why had these persuasive arguments disappeared from later statements of his position? One can only speculate; but it seems likely that he recognized that they were claims the ultimate proof of which depended on further moral argument or empirical data. And in constructing his legal philosophy Herbert was, as all the evidence shows, reluctant to involve himself in the investigation of such wide-ranging questions. As Ronald Dworkin would later put it in one of his many assaults on positivism's limited scope, 'positivists are drawn to their conception of law not for its inherent appeal, but because it allows them to treat legal philosophy as an autonomous, analytic, and self-contained discipline'.

Earlier, I described Ronald Dworkin's contest with Herbert in terms of a poker game in which the stakes were constantly being raised. But the poker metaphor, with its implication of each side hiding their strategy from the other, is in some ways a more apposite description of Herbert's side of the encounter than of Dworkin's. For the remarkable fact is that, despite their frequent contacts at University College and their regular encounters in seminars and at conferences such as the Jerusalem event, Dworkin was for several years unaware of the fact that Herbert was working on a reply to his critique of legal positivism. Finally, he learnt about it from Isaiah Berlin, with whom Herbert was discussing the reply regularly and who mischievously told Dworkin, 'I agree with him you know!' Once others too had confirmed that Herbert was working on a response to his work, Dworkin asked him if he would like to discuss it. Herbert responded in a cool and discouraging way. Perhaps he felt that Dworkin had not paid him the reciprocal compliment of discussing his criticisms of *The Concept of Law* before trying them out on others; perhaps he had simply had enough of intellectual encounters in which he felt that the parameters kept changing. Dworkin, baffled and somewhat hurt, let the matter drop.

Just as his intellectual exchange with Dworkin in person had ossified, Herbert's work on his reply, despite over ten years of work, remained unfinished at his death. At Ruth Gavison's prompting, he had had some of his notes typed up in the late 1980s: these centred on his reply to Dworkin. But even these fell short of the standards of elegance, clarity, and comprehensiveness to which Herbert always aspired. Dutiful to the last, he could not bring himself to give up the effort, but his energy was running out. After his death,

Gavison, deeply fond of Herbert and one of his most eloquent admirers, wrote to Jenifer:

Since I teach Herbert's stuff a lot, on different levels, it is especially hard not to continue the dialogue I keep having with him on these questions of legal philosophy which have intrigued us. I take it that not much was done with the epilogue to *The Concept of Law*? I have the sense that this is the way he wanted it: He did not feel he was up to it. I hope, at least, he managed to read all the novels he liked.

Part of the 'epilogue' did, however, find its way into the public domain. In preparing the second edition of *The Concept of Law*, Joseph Raz and Penelope Bulloch, with the help of a young legal theorist, Timothy Endicott, put together as complete a version of the response to Dworkin as could be constructed from Herbert's notes. The second edition appeared in 1994, two years after Herbert's death, with the new material as a 'Postscript'. Like *The Concept of Law* itself, the 'Postscript' has generated a large amount of scholarly attention, including a volume of 12 essays devoted exclusively to its analysis by leading legal theorists. But the quality of the 'Postscript' is uneven, and scholars are divided in their view of whether it enhances Herbert's reputation. The intensely sad story of its writing does, however, give real insights into the nature of Herbert's intellectual and emotional life, as well as some disturbing glimpses of the costs of exceptional professional success. There is sadness, too, in Dworkin's side of the story. When he read the 'Postscript', he was shocked both to think how long Herbert had been working on it and by what he felt to be its occasionally angry tone: 'It is written as if he had never met me. We could have talked about it.' Dworkin found intensely depressing this evidence of the gulf which had opened up between him and the man whose work had been his original inspiration.

It is tempting to agree with Gavison's interpretation that, by the late 1980s, Herbert simply wasn't feeling 'up to it'. He was, after all, 80 years old, and his health was now very fragile. The 1983 breakdown and subsequent ECT treatment had, inevitably, made him less vigorous: in a car accident in 1987 he suffered broken ribs and a punctured lung—an experience which made it yet more difficult to work, and which prompted him to joke in a letter to Waluchow that he had made a startling metaphysical discovery: the mind-body connection lay in the bones. At the end of the 1980s he was diagnosed as having prostate cancer. But the tragedy of the 'Postscript' has to be set in the context of other, more positive features of both his intellectual and his personal life in the second half of the 1980s. There are several reasons for stating unambiguously that his intellectual capacities remained astonishingly sharp. In 1986, he published in the *New York Review of Books* an acute review of Bernard Williams' *Ethics and the Limits of Philosophy*. Williams himself was struck by Herbert's sure grasp and perceptive critique of his position. (Ironically even this impressive piece of work was fated to cause Herbert worry and disappointment: the editors of the *Review* wanted cuts to be made, and it was only after the intervention of another philosopher that the article was published in its original form.) At this time, Herbert was also enjoying debates with a young Japanese philosopher Yasutomo Morigiwa, with whom he discussed the Williams review and to whom he even agreed to give a set of tutorials. In 1987, he gave a written interview to the Spanish journal *Doxa*, responding to questions about the development of his ideas and his views on contemporary British politics; the interview was translated into Spanish and published the following year. It is of significance mainly for the crisp statement which Herbert managed to formulate of his final, modified position on the nature of legal obligation and its relationship to moral obligation, and for its first published delineation of his 'separate projects' reply to Dworkin:

Even in the case of a simple regime of custom-type rules what is necessary to constitute them obligation-imposing rules is not merely that they should in fact be supported by general demand for conformity and social pressure but that it should be generally accepted that these are *legitimate* responses to deviations in the sense that they are permitted if not required by the system. So such demands and pressure will not be merely predictable consequences of deviations, but normative consequences because they are legitimate in this sense. I now think that this idea of a legitimate response to deviation in the form of demands and pressure for conformity is the central component of obligation.... But I doubt if the new account presented here will satisfy [my critics]. For though it is a new account it is still compatible with the views which I have always held and which most of my critics reject that the concept of legal obligation is morally neutral, and that legal and moral obligations are conceptually distinct....The point of a theory of legal obligation (and indeed of descriptive jurisprudence in general) is to provide an illuminating form of description of a specific type of social institution which will bring out clearly certain salient features of the institution.... A morally neutral conception of legal obligation serves to mark off the points at which the law itself restricts or permits the restriction of individual freedom. Whether laws are morally good or evil, just or unjust, these are focal points demanding attention as of supreme importance to human beings constituted as they are. So it is not the case as my critics claim that a theory of obligation can only make sense if there is some moral ground for the supposed obligation. Of course those who, like Professor Dworkin, regard jurisprudence or legal theory as a branch of moral theory concerned to state why and under what conditions the enforcement of legal standards is justified, will necessarily reject the morally neutral concept I have sought to elucidate here. But I see no good reason for holding that jurisprudence and legal theory must take this morally justificatory form.

As this passage shows, despite poor health and increasing immobility, Herbert's mind remained more than alert in his last years: so concerned was he at the first signs of a weakened memory that he set himself the task of memorizing vast passages of Dante—a practice which he both enjoyed and regarded as an extremely effective form of mental exercise. The year before he died, he published a review of intellectual biographies of two leading Victorian lawyers, Henry Maine and James Fitzjames Stephen. And until his last months, when illness drew him once again into depression, he remained a wide-ranging and avid reader, and a sparkling conversationalist. The old favourites—James, Austen, Eliot, Yeats, Hardy, Shelley—were interspersed with contemporary writers like Nadine Gordimer and Richard Holmes. Even his most widely read friends scarcely ever recommended a book to Herbert without finding that he had already read it. This love of literature provided the basis on which Herbert had some of his most intimate interactions: as Marianne Fillenz observed, his enjoyment of talking about novels constituted an indirect form of personal exchange, allowing him to explore relationships and manifest the real warmth of feeling which tended to remain, as another friend put it, 'at one remove'.

In his last years, Herbert also became more political. This was not just a matter of continuing his support for Greenpeace and Amnesty International, and his involvement with the local campaigns against racism organized by Ann and Michael Dummett. It was also that he was finally becoming less worried about how others—and particularly the 'Oxford establishment'—regarded his views. Herbert had always been willing to uphold liberal principles, however unpopular this made him. A striking instance of this robust attitude was his decision in 1978 to put up money to guarantee the bail of Joanna's friend, Astrid Proll, who had been charged with criminal offences relating to her membership of the German Red Army Faction. Outraged by the fact that she had spent over three years in jail in Germany before being brought to trial, and convinced that she no longer posed any kind of threat, having changed her views during the three years she had spent on the run in England, Herbert's support had a significant impact on her case. He took the disapproval of several of his Oxford colleagues calmly. But when it was a matter of risking more personal offence, he had tended to be cautious.

In his last years, this began to change. A commonplace example is an incident involving his old friend John Sparrow. Sparrow, the man of whom Isaiah Berlin had once joked that 'his head is apt to run away with his heart', but now with a head alcoholically and intellectually muddied in intemperate old age, was a firm opponent of opening up Oxford Fellowships to women. Each summer vacation, University College and All Souls had a reciprocal dining arrangement, and during the period in which All Souls Fellows were dining at University College, Sparrow had made his misogynist views objectionably apparent in the hearing of one of the College's two women Fellows. Outraged by Sparrow's behaviour, a small group of University College Fellows decided to mount a quiet protest by dining in All Souls the following week accompanied in each case by a female guest. Jenifer had always had a taste for this kind of gesture: at one Oxford dinner, she had famously refused to withdraw with 'the ladies' while 'the gentlemen' took their port and cigars. But Herbert had always been reluctant to take part in such protests. Somewhat to his colleagues' surprise, he now agreed that he and Jenifer would join the group. At All Souls, this gathering lined up on one side of the table, confronting the entirely male All Souls team on the opposite side (the College had not a single female Fellow at the time). One place, however, remained empty. To Herbert's embarrassed amusement, 20 minutes into the dinner, this place was filled by a staggeringly (literally and metaphorically) drunken Sparrow, who proceeded to behave like the petulant child which, sadly, he had become. During such conversation as was possible, it was Herbert who took him to task for his views on women at Oxford.

But Herbert's increasing political decisiveness was not born merely of his diminishing fear of offending other people. It was also prompted by his distaste for the Conservative administration which governed Britain from 1979 until after his death. The Thatcher Government offended his liberal instincts and his egalitarianism. Its style also offended his sense of decency and balance in the conduct of political life: its support for unrestricted markets and its celebration of the selfish pursuit of wealth appalled him, while he found its lack of concern for the poor and otherwise underprivileged uncivilized. His reaction to Thatcherite social policies, particularly in the areas of education and sexual morality, reached the level of outrage. The enactment of 'clause 28', which prohibited local government from 'promoting' or using funds to 'support' propagation of the message that homosexual relationships were of equal moral value to heterosexual ones, drew his particular wrath: 'I loathe it: it's all part of the Thatcher world', he told David Sugarman, who interviewed him in 1988. The threat to liberalization of attitudes to homosexuality upset him at a number of different levels: because of its contradiction of the liberal policies to which he had contributed so much; because of his uncomfortable sense that the reformist arguments which he had advanced had not gone far enough; and, perhaps, because of his own homoerotic sensibility. In educational matters, he was an active and public opponent of the award of an Honorary Degree by Oxford to Mrs Thatcher in 1987, and wrote an eloquent article for the *New York Review of Books* defending the University Congregation's overwhelming vote to reject its Council's proposal that the degree be awarded. And later, he was an opponent of the Gulf War. A sense of just how much he disliked the Thatcher regime is given by some remarks to Bob Summers, who visited him in Oxford in 1988. Summers found Herbert 'not very interested in ideas now...Not *nearly* so quick...But still sharp: He said "The Church, the Monarchy and the House of Lords are the institutions now upholding liberalism especially concern for the poor".' He described Margaret Thatcher, memorably, as 'the worst head of Government since Richard III'. (In view of Herbert's overall assessment of the Prime Minister, it is not clear that this was entirely fair to her royal predecessor.) Summers also found him, intriguingly, preoccupied with Wittgentsein, Bryan McGuinness' biography of whom he had just read. As Summers recorded, he:

felt W 'a person absolutely preoccupied with his own soul', a 'most unattractive person—constantly turning life into *work*, yet interested in life...true life as only reading the great philosophers that interest you and getting on with philosophy—Incredible', says H.

Did Herbert's revulsion at Wittgenstein contain a grain of self-disgust, as he looked back over the course of his own work-centred and often self-preoccupied life? Though he regarded with satisfaction the diminished deference felt by legal academics for the legal profession—a change which had been accelerated by the intellectually autonomous and vigorous style of legal scholarship of which he had been the leading exponent—his assessment of his legacy remained tentative. He was able to embrace the inevitable incompleteness of his work in a way which is at once impressive and poignant, as well as being unusually free of the intellectual impulse to dominate his field. Asked by Sugarman to sum up his contribution to legal philosophy, he answered:

I can't. I don't know what to say.... I hope it has enabled people both to take a wider view of the nature of law and problems that arise in the running of the legal system and it has given them a kind of sensitivity to accuracy, clarity of expression, and detail. I don't know. It may be an illusion.

Though the Tanner Trust's institution of an annual Hart lecture in his honour—the first eight of which he was able to attend—gave him pleasure, he continued to doubt the worth of his contributions.

In these final years, Herbert's fading intellectual life was in counterpoint to a richer personal life. He was making deeper emotional connections—particularly with his children—than he had found possible during the days of his more intense professional involvement. He still enjoyed his old friendships, and he was still making new ones, including an especially warm attachment to—almost amounting to a teenage 'crush' on—an attractive young South African scientist at University College. He frequently spent weekends with the Jays at their home in Minster Lovell, insisting on taking Mary to the pub each evening for a pre-dinner drink. He also struggled with moving courage to keep going with the sorts of physical activities he had always loved. In 1989, though extremely lame, he enjoyed a trip to Siena with Margaret Paul and with Charlie and his wife; at Lamledra, he still insisted on his daily walk. Setting himself further targets each day, he ventured precariously but decisively forth, bent at an alarming angle over his stick, attired in seemingly endless layers of increasingly dishevelled clothing, and tolerating occasional tumbles in the mud with good humour. His consideration for others was undimmed: on one occasion, when a guest at Lamledra was taken ill and had to spend some time in hospital 30 miles away, Herbert asked his wife if he might come with her on her daily visit. When they reached the hospital, he made no move to leave the car. When she opened the door for him, he said, 'No, no, he will want to see you on your own: but I knew you wouldn't have allowed me to come if I had admitted that I thought you needed some company on the journey'. Similarly, his sense of personal duty remained acute: despite his own frailty, he visited his sister, Sybil, every fortnight until her death in 1988, and spoke movingly at her funeral about her work and her contribution to the family, as well as in frank terms about her struggle with depression.

What of his relationship with Jenifer? The fascination which he had always felt for her, as well as his fundamental respect for her unique spirit, her intelligence, and her integrity, had survived, to a striking degree, the decades of intermittent distance. On a holiday with Jean Floud in Arezzo in 1983, Herbert saw a wide-brimmed leghorn hat in a shop window. 'I must get it for Jenifer', he said, 'she would look so wonderful in it.' Unfortunately his clumsiness interposed itself between the thought and the deed: stepping into the shop, he tripped and sprained his ankle. The hat remained in the window, just as Herbert's image of Jenifer as a beautiful, quixotic young woman remained in his mind's eye. Though the emotional ground which lay between them was never really made up, Jenifer worked valiantly to adapt to the changed circumstances brought about by Herbert's need for physical care in the last two years of his life and to overcome her impatience at his increasing preoccupation with the state of his health. Within the structure which she provided, his greatest moments of happiness came from talks with friends, from music and books, and from conversations with his family and the young graduate students who took him out for wheelchair-bound walks during the last months of his life. On these outings, his companions remember him 'sucking life dry', drinking in the beauties of nature which had always given him so much joy and which, notwithstanding his illness, he seemed reluctant to surrender. But, as his immobility increased, his mood became increasingly gloomy, and he spent long hours enveloped in the dark, melancholy beauty of Schubert and of Beethoven's plangent late string quartets.

In the last months of 1992, Herbert's health deteriorated rapidly. He was frequently in pain, and his spirits were depressed. On 19 December, he died in his sleep. Immediately, the family came together to construct a funeral which would honour Herbert's life and respect his wishes and commitments. A vivid image of the occasion, which took place in the beautiful winter bleakness of Wolvercote Cemetery, is given in Carolyn Tanner Irish's letter to the other Tanner Trustees:

The day was bitterly cold and a white sun hung starkly in the winter sky. The landscape—also white with a heavy frost—was utterly still as perhaps seventy five mourners walked out across the cemetery to the open grave. We followed Jenifer and the children and grandchildren . . . one of whom carried a tape deck playing Schubert. There were no other sounds. It felt like being in another world or perhaps in this world but in an earlier era.

Herbert's sons and daughter spoke simply and tenderly of their father, and read from Hardy, Shelley, Yeats, J. S. Mill, Brecht, and Shakespeare, so many of whose works Herbert knew by heart. The plain wooden coffin was then lowered, and the strains of Schubert again accompanied our walk away.

Herbert was a truly and fully civilized man. His brilliance and generosity are remarked by everyone, but as I stood near his grave, I recalled also a child-like quality surprising to find in one so distinguished. It showed in his vulnerability, his delight, his wonderment. My own life is immensely richer for knowing him.

This tribute to Herbert echoed the sentiments of the hundreds of letters, filled with sadness, gratitude, and love, which were already flooding into Manor Place from all over the world and from every group of people whom Herbert had encountered in his long life: friends, colleagues, students, fellow committee members, helpers at Manor Place and Lamledra. These letters amounted to nothing less than a collective paean not only to his intellectual achievements but also to his kindness, honesty, wisdom, humanity, modesty, and goodness. Many of them were eloquent in evoking the writers' sense of loss, and the distinctive personality which they had valued: Herbert's love of people and places, of poetry, literature, and music, the warmth he conveyed through 'a few words, a smile, a look in the eyes', and his 'fierce liberal spirit':

My 50 years of friendship [with him] were a great and unforgettable thing in my life [Francis Graham-Harrison, family friend]

The Concept of Law is the most important book about law to have been written this century [Guenter Treitel, Vinerian Professor at Oxford]

... the most important of the group of philosophers to which he belonged: not only because of his work, but because of his personality. [Stuart Hampshire, friend and colleague]

... a man who compelled immediate admiration [Lord Donaldson, former Master of the Rolls]

Of all the distinguished people I came in touch with as a result of the War, Herbert was the one I admired and prized the most [Dick White, MI5 colleague and later head of MI5]

In my mind he and Isaiah had become twin peaks [Lord Jenkins, Chancellor of Oxford University]

I will miss him greatly as a father-figure, as a bridge between the generations in the fight for human values... as the foster-parent of my English adolescence [Felix de Mendelsohn, a friend of Adam's]

He belonged to Oxford, to be sure, but he also had a kinship with those who saw the world in simpler, less clever terms, from places where the lawns were less well tended. The games which many of us played did not interest him, I think. I am tempted to say that the theories with which we were so pleased did not interest him much either, except as a bridge to social realities [Peter Herbst, an Australian graduate student in Oxford and later colleague]

[I remember] his seemingly inexhaustible memory and radiant face as he recited reams of Dante and Thomas Hardy on a long walk in the Cornish countryside .... He had a gift for friendship, not of the ordinary sort, but through intellectual affinities and communing solitudes. [Nicola Jordan, former graduate student helper at Manor Place]

The only Oxford figure for whom I had a totally unqualified admiration. [Sir William Hayter, former Warden of New College and Ambassador to Moscow]

Perhaps most moving of all was the letter from one of Herbert's oldest friends, Richard Wilberforce, which arrived a fortnight after his death:

Dear Jenifer

You may have wondered why I did not write before. But the fact is that in some strange way I thought it almost unnecessary. My love and admiration for Herbert was so great, so unqualified, and to you so well known that there seemed to be nothing more to say, no need to find well chosen words to describe what I thought of him. I did indeed have so much joy in his life and friendship (I could never quite understand why, after some early hesitation, *he* did seem to like *me* with all my conventional and Wykehamical qualities) that these feelings, as of a marvellous friend, are those that are with me, even more than grief.

Thank heaven that he had you for a wife. Thank you so very much for keeping me informed.

Yours ever, Richard

More public tributes were swift to follow. Obituaries appeared in all the main broadsheet newspapers in England and in the press of several other countries. In February, Isaiah Berlin, Ronald Dworkin, Jean Floud, Douglas Jay, Joseph Raz, and Alan Ryan spoke at a memorial meeting packed with family, friends, colleagues, and students eager to show their respect for the man whom many of them believed to have raised the Lazarus of English-speaking legal and political philosophy from the pallet on which it had languished for the best part of a century. The memorial service speeches were reproduced, along with a memoir by Richard Wilberforce, in a widely circulated pamphlet; Tony Honoré wrote a long memoir for the British Academy; and many other scholars wrote memoirs for a wide range of journals all over the world. The tributes to Herbert's outstanding intellectual achievements came not only from those who shared his commitment to legal theory as a branch of philosophy: even those who regretted that such a 'luminous mind' restricted itself to what was in this respect a 'narrow agenda' celebrated his achievements in generous terms. As one of them, Zenon Bankowski, wrote in an obituary which looked back over the last half century of legal theory:

Then, there was only him. Now, a hundred flowers bloom. This is his lasting contribution.

Once the public statements and commemorative events were over, and as her own numbness and exhaustion subsided, Jenifer was left to begin the complicated and sometimes painful process of re-assessing the 55 years of hers and Herbert's relationship. Having completed with characteristic determination and scholarly commitment her post-retirement book on proportional representation, she turned to the project of writing an autobiography—a task which must have had something to do with her need to reflect on the course of her marriage. Working through Herbert's papers and diaries, she revisited the intensity of their early, passionate relationship, and discovered for the first time the full extent of his bouts of angst and depression.

Jenifer's relative lack of awareness of Herbert's complex emotional life, though striking, was not unique. In almost none of the hundreds of tributes, public and private, had there been any whiff of consciousness of the inner turmoil—George Eliot's 'roar on the other side of silence'—which had dogged him not only at the time of his breakdown but, intermittently, throughout his life. Psychologically, Herbert was—as was once said of his favourite author, Henry James, and as perhaps explains Herbert's fascination with James' work—'a man who chews more than he has bitten off'. As Jenifer struggled to understand something of this complicated and largely hidden side to the man with whom she had lived for over half a century, she must have felt a need to ponder the significance of Herbert's contribution to her life. Her retrospective sense of its value—a value which she had never doubted, yet which she felt that her actions had not always shown—is reflected in her decision to include the speeches delivered at his memorial service as an appendix to her own book, published in 1998. The one exception was the speech by Jean Floud; the only person to make any criticism of Herbert (she had affectionately questioned what she saw as his excessive rationalism) and, perhaps, as a woman who had regarded Herbert with virtually unqualified admiration, the speaker whose assessment was most likely to touch the tender spot of Jenifer's feelings of regret.

In the light of the evidence of Herbert's intermittently acute regrets about the state of his and Jenifer's marriage, Richard Wilberforce's assessment of the relationship as a fortunate one may strike an odd note. And yet there can be no doubt that, just as Jenifer and Herbert were brought together by a complex set of complementary needs and desires, a dense web of mutual regard, shared values, and interdependence continued to bind them throughout their life together. A fundamental, albeit shifting, equilibrium survived the pressures of what was, by any standards, both a psychologically and a practically taxing 50 years. Close friends, to whom Jenifer occasionally complained about the state of the relationship, would ask her why they did not separate. She was always horrified by the suggestion. Her reaction was far from being determined by social convention; nor was it primarily to do with factors such as anxiety about the effects on their children. Rather, it was that no one else, Jenifer believed, could possibly match up to Herbert as a life-partner either in terms of stimulation or in terms of shared intellectual interests and world-view. Despite their differences, and despite the inevitable hurt which his sexual ambivalence had caused her, Herbert continued to represent—just as he had in 1937— her ideal of a rational, liberal aristocracy of the intellect; while his professional and institutional status confirmed her in the belief that she had made a wise choice.

In Herbert's case, the explanation of the surviving bond with Jenifer is less apparent, but it is no less compelling. On the rare occasions on which he discussed the state of his marriage with friends, he claimed—ever the rationalist—that he had stayed with Jenifer for utilitarian reasons. This, surely, was disingenuous. Jenifer still held out to Herbert many of the qualities which had attracted him in the 1930s: her acute intelligence, independence of mind, energy, class certainties, and extraordinarily vivid personality drew him and fascinated him for the rest of his life. It is likely that Herbert's underlying predisposition to depressive introspection would have been far more damaging—perhaps even paralysing to his intellectual work—had he not been sustained by the stable structure of family routines. He railed against the demands of family life, worried about his family obligations, castigated himself for his inability to break through his emotional reserve, and regretted his and Jenifer's emotional withdrawal from each other. But the question arises whether, in the light of his psychological makeup, he could have managed a more intimate relationship, or a relationship with a woman less intellectually autonomous and personally independent. In his occasional protestations that one had to be mad to marry and even madder to have children, Herbert was both protesting too much and doing Jenifer an injustice. For her energy and decisiveness, though they presented him with problems, were the primary force in shaping a family structure which gave Herbert a significant part of such sense of belonging and security as he did achieve, and which enabled him to manage his extraordinarily successful professional life.

It was appropriate that the public tributes to Herbert's life focussed on his colossal achievements, his large contribution to the infusion of legal policy with liberal values, his awesomely cultured persona, and his distinctively humane personal qualities. This public story of Herbert Hart's life was, of course, true; its validity in no way compromised by the equally true story of his struggle to overcome depression, his incompletely resolved attitude to both his sexuality and his Jewish and class origins, his volatile shifts between intellectual confidence and insecurity, his unconquerable emotional reserve, and his long-standing sense of not really being what he actually was: an influential and respected insider in the social and professional worlds in which he moved. Rather, in the light of these complexities, his intellectual, institutional, and personal achievements appear all the greater. It is a fitting testimony to his ultimate capacity to reach others, even through the veil of his emotional indirection, that his children understood at least something of the hidden texture of his life. Whether consciously or intuitively, this, perhaps, underpinned their choice of the readings at his funeral: Thomas Hardy's 'Afterwards', Yeats' 'The Man and the Echo', Brecht's 'Pleasures', and Shelley's 'Ode to the West Wind'. The poetry conjured up Herbert's joy in life, his love of literature, and his passionate feeling for the beauties of nature; but it also spoke to the 'Wild Spirit' with which Herbert had so often contended. His own sense of this interior struggle echoes through the lines in which he had wished his beloved sister a last farewell: the words of Emily Brontë's narrator as he gazes at the stones placed in memory of Catherine and Heathcliff on the Yorkshire moors. They are words which evoke a shared Yorkshire childhood and love of the moors, but also a shared experience of the darker side of life:

I lingered round them under that benign sky, watched the moths fluttering among the heath and the harebells, listened to the soft wind breathing through the grass, and wondered how anyone could ever imagine unquiet slumbers for the sleepers in that quiet earth.

Notes

To avoid cluttering the text with endnote numbers, the notes are identified by phrases from the text and page number. Where a full citation is not given in the notes, it will be found in the Bibliography. The notes can also be downloaded from http://www.oup.co.uk/isbn/0-19-927497-5.

INTRODUCTION

2. **'the nearest thing to a manifesto':** interview with Peter Campbell.
5. **quoting J. L. Austin, he sought to use 'a sharpened awareness of words . . .':** J. L. Austin, *Philosophical Papers* p. 130, as quoted in the Preface to *The Concept of Law*.
7. **'A town-planning scheme' for the 'intellectual slum of English jurisprudence';** letter from R. V. Heuston to Herbert Hart on Hart's election to the Chair of Jurisprudence at Oxford, 1952.

CHAPTER 1

The main sources for my description of Herbert Hart's childhood were interviews with his family; two books by his cousin, Teddy Isaacs: *All in a Lifetime* and *Episodes*; Rosalyn Livshin's *The History of the Harrogate Jewish Community*; Leonie Star's biography of Hart's contemporary, *Julius Stone: An Intellectual Life*; and Herbert Hart's own reminiscences in his 1988 interview with Michael Brock and Brian Harrison, in a fragmentary memoir found in his papers, and in a holiday diary written in 1926.

13. **Adelaide and Albert Hart:** Albert Hart came from Schubin, East Prussia, although the family can be traced back to Colmar in the mid-eighteenth century. The family name was originally 'Zadek'—meaning 'righteous man' in Hebrew: the origins of the change to Hart are unclear, but certainly predated Albert's arrival in England at the age of 27 in 1851. Initially he lived with his brother and sister-in-law at 149 Houndsditch in the East End of London. In due course he became a successful cap manufacturer and was made a Freeman of the City of London in 1858. With the expansion of his business made possible by this status, and perhaps as a result of his wife's moderate wealth, he was able to move from Houndsditch to a spacious house in the elegant north London suburb of Canonbury some time after his marriage in 1856. He died in 1889 at the relatively early age of 58.

Sim's mother Adelaide had been born Adelaide Barnett in 1834. She was a great-granddaughter of Phineas and Esther Phillips. Phineas Phillips was a prosperous merchant from Krotoschin in the Grand Duchy of Posen, who travelled widely and finally settled in London in the late eighteenth century. Esther was a descendant of the Katzenellenbogens, who produced three Chief Rabbis of Padua in the sixteenth century, one of whom—Rabbi Saul Wahl, 1545–1617—had at one time been elected temporary King of Poland. Phineas's and Esther's daughter Rebecca, born in 1744, married Rabbi Issachar Baier (known in England as Barnett) who was head of the Beth Din (rabbinical court) in Krotoschin, but who returned to England in 1835. Their son Aryeh Leb—Adelaide's father—born in 1798, was also a rabbi, and on his return to London in 1837 became Dayan, and ultimately the chief judge, of the Beth Din of the Great Synagogue in London—located, as it happens, very near to Albert Hart's Houndsditch home. Aryeh Barnett was thus at the centre of London's orthodox Jewish affairs when some of the main legal disabilities imposed on Jews were being challenged and removed. When he died in 1878, the Jewish Chronicle of 15 February described him as 'a rabbi of the old orthodox stamp: the Talmud and its commentaries formed his constant study'; a man who had borne five years of blindness 'with pious resignation'. In 1841 he had signed the excommunication pronounced jointly by the Sephardim and Ashkenazim on the Liberals and Reformers. His other main claim to fame was his taste for picking onions out of the ground and eating them raw. By a quirk of history, his patron was Lord Rothschild—ancestor of Victor Rothschild, destined to be a close friend of Herbert's. Each time Rabbi Barnett and his wife Charlotte had a daughter (they had seven, as well as three sons) she was given a 'dowry' of £150 by Lord Rothschild.

15. **A Jewish Harrogate contemporary recalled**: My information about the Hart family in Harrogate is drawn from telephone interviews with Richard Camrass and Henry Myers.

   A history of Harrogate: *Exclusively Harrogate* by Malcom G. Neesam.

16. **'An anglicised, orthodox congregation'; 'a community, participating in English cultural activities'**: These and the next two quotations are from Rosalyn Livshin's *History of the Harrogate Jewish Community*, pp. 12, 20, and 17.

17. **'a very, very English—almost military—public school'**: This and the following quotations are drawn from the Brock/Harrison interview.

CHAPTER 2

My main sources for this chapter were Herbert Hart's interviews with Brock/Harrison and Sugarman and his letters to Christopher Cox; Douglas Jay's autobiography, *Change of Fortune*; Leonie Star's *Julius Stone: An Intellectual Life*; Jenifer Hart's *Ask Me No More*; H. A. L. Fisher's *Unfinished Autobiography*; memoirs of Fisher, H. W. B. Joseph, A. H. Smith, and Cox by Smith (Joseph), John Sparrow (Fisher and Smith), and Hart (Cox); and Herbert Hart's travel diaries of the late 1920s.

22. **all-male environment:** Women had won the right to take degrees at Oxford only in 1920. The year of Herbert's arrival marked the transition of Somerville, Lady Margaret Hall, St. Hugh's, and St Hilda's from their second class status as 'permanent private halls' to full college status: St. Anne's followed only in 1952. Across the university, then, there was a large majority of male students. Statistics on student numbers compiled for the University Grants Committee from 1923 record 3,533 male and 820 female full time students in 1926. I am grateful to Caroline Dalton for tracing this information.
    snobbishness: The implicit picture of Oxford as the pinnacle of the universe realized itself in habits such as referring to all other universities apart from Cambridge as 'provincial'; a practice which led one Fellow, newly arrived from University College London, to remark when asked whether he had come from a provincial university, 'No: I come from a metropolitan university: *this* is a provincial university': story recounted to me by Geoffrey de St Croix.

23. **'I think it would suit you very well':** Professor A. (Tony) Andrews to Robin Lane Fox.

24. **'awesomely destructive horseplay':** This and the next two quotations are taken from the Brock/Harrison interview.
    Wykehamist scholars: New College and Winchester share a founder in William of Wykeham, and have maintained a close relationship with one another. In the 1920s, the majority of scholarships to Oxford and Cambridge were 'closed' in the sense of being restricted to candidates from particular (mostly 'public') schools. In 1926 New College had six closed scholarships for boys from Winchester and four open scholarships: my thanks to Caroline Dalton for tracing this information.

25. **a strong Yorkshire accent:** from Douglas Jay's tribute at Herbert Hart's memorial service.
    Bill infected the 'rather orthodox' Herbert: interview with Bill Wentworth.

26. **'When later I took him a paper on logic';** from A. H. Smith's memoir, p. 3.
    He 'worshipped Plato': from the Brock/Harrison interview.
    'also very clever and exuberantly pugnacious': A. H. Smith on Cook Wilson, from the former's memoir of Joseph for the British Academy, p. 21.

27. **'. . . philosophy absolutely wrong':** interview with Stuart Hampshire.
    'almost quixotic desire to . . .': from the memoir of Joseph by A. H. Smith, pp. 3–4.

29. **'some idea of what it felt like to be Caesar or Cicero':** Brock/Harrison interview; see also Herbert Hart's piece in the *New College Record* (1982) p. 10.
    'life-enhancing . . . tonic gaiety': This and other quoted descriptions of Cox are from Hart's speech delivered at his memorial service in New College Chapel on 16 October 1982, later published in the *New College Record* along with other memoirs, on which I have also drawn.

30. **'After being pulverized by the remorseless logic of Joseph':** These descriptions of Smith are drawn from the obituary by Sir Roy Harrod published

in the *Oxford Magazine* on 6 November 1958 and reproduced in the collection of tributes by Sparrow and others produced by New College, pp. 24–9 at p. 27.

31. **Warden of New College:** i.e. the head of the College. Oxford colleges vary in the name they give to this position: other varieties we shall encounter include President, Principal, and Master.
    'No one should teach philosophy . . .'; quoted in H. A. L. Fisher's autobiography at p. 57.

32–3. **'Warden Fisher came to us from higher circles':** John Sparrow, from a speech delivered at the New College Gaudy on 4 July 1958 (5 days before Smith's death) and reproduced in the collection of tributes by Sparrow and others published by New College, pp. 5–10 at pp. 5–6.

33. **'an innocent person':** Both the quotation and my account of the incident are drawn from the Brock/Harrison interview.

34. **scout:** the Oxford term for staff employed to clean students' and fellows' rooms: in the 1920s they also served food and took on a number of other tasks.

38. **'life for me at any rate would be a howling wilderness':** Herbert Hart used this phrase in his speech as returning Lionel Cohen lecturer at Lincoln's Inn in 1964: it is also quoted in Tony Honoré's memoir for the British Academy.

CHAPTER 3

In this chapter I draw mainly on Herbert Hart's correspondence with Christopher Cox and Jenifer Williams; and on Richard Wilberforce's diaries for the late 1930s.

40. **'a South African who believed in apartheid':** Sugarman interview.

41. **All Souls Prize Fellowship:** The Fellowships were offered in law and history and 'in such subjects connected with the studies of the University as the Warden and Fellows may from time to time determine'. Candidates in history could take, besides a general history paper, papers in philosophy, economics, or political theory. I am inferring from Herbert's letter to Cox that he entered in 1929 as a history candidate. My thanks to Jenifer Hart and Tony Honoré for information on this point.
    testimonials: These and the other testimonials quoted in this chapter were among Herbert Hart's papers.

42. **Years later, Herbert described to a colleague:** interview with James Griffin. A strikingly similar incident is described by Richard Wilberforce (*Reflections on my Life* p. 20); Herbert's recollections were not always reliable, and it is possible that Wilberforce's story had become a symbol for his own intensely stressful experience.

43. **'any job Radcliffe might have to offer':** Cyril Radcliffe, a New College graduate, Fellow of All Souls from 1922 to 1937, and at this time a rising junior at the Chancery Bar.

44. 'I shall never learn [not] to be mildly jealous': I have inserted the 'not' for ease of reading. But I suspect that Herbert—typically—meant what he wrote: i.e. that he would never learn only to be *mildly* jealous of John Sparrow.

45. '2 guineas by writing an opinion': letter to Cox.
    As Wilberforce recalled: 'He would arrive at chambers at 9 a.m. . . .': Richard Orme Wilberforce, *Reflections on my Life* pp. 25–6: Herbert's recollection of midnight working sessions at Hunt's home was recounted to Lennie Hoffmann.
    junior barrister: In the jargon of the English legal profession, this term denotes any barrister who is not a Queen's Counsel: Herbert's pupil master was not therefore 'junior' in the sense of being young or inexperienced.

46. 'by far the most talented man . . .': interview with Stuart Hampshire.

47. 'loving the intellectual demands . . .': interview with Richard Wilberforce.
    'one of our most prosperous friends': Isaiah Berlin to Mary Fisher, December 1936 (Berlin, *Flourishing: Letters 1928–1946* p. 221).
    Wilberforce remembered Herbert as 'getting work, making money . . .': Richard Orme Wilberforce, *Reflections on my Life* p. 30.

48. not entirely comfortable with his chosen career: Douglas Jay, speech at Herbert Hart's memorial service (p. 9 of the printed pamphlet).
    legal loopholes which allowed tax evasion: MacCormick, *H. L. A. Hart* p. 12.
    Wilberforce recalled with affection Herbert's 'ability to extract amusement of high value, from low situations', and remembered that 'His great quality . . .': these recollections are drawn from Richard Orme Wilberforce, *Reflections on my Life* at pp. 105 and 30.

49. Balzac's 'mad pages': letter to Jenifer Williams.

50. 'a rich-ish, smart-ish sort of man': interview with Richard Wilberforce.

52. 'felt that everything including Smith was beautiful and faintly alive . . .': This and the following quotations are from a letter to Cox.

54. Oxford and Cambridge Club: Despite the fact that women have been awarded degrees by Oxford University since 1920, it was not until 1996 that the Club admitted women graduates to full membership. In the 1930s, it was exclusively a men's club: women were granted second-class 'associate membership' only in 1952. My thanks to Caroline Dalton for this point.
    'we did not feel so strongly about anti-Jews before the Holocaust': annotation to Richard Wilberforce's diary.
    'I have never forgiven myself for not resigning . . .': letter from Patrick Reilly to Jenifer Hart in response to her inquiry about the story when working on her autobiography.

56. In 1937 he published his first book: cited in Jay's *Change and Fortune* p. 62, from which my quotations are taken.

57. helping Jewish refugees: MacCormick, *H. L. A. Hart* p. 12. The information was given to Neil MacCormick by Herbert Hart: unfortunately I have been unable to trace any details.

looked at each other 'with tears in our eyes . . .': from Richard Wilberforce's memoir published in a pamphlet with other tributes delivered at Herbert Hart's memorial service.

CHAPTER 4

The principal source for this chapter is the correspondence between Jenifer Williams and Herbert Hart between 1936 and 1938: all unattributed quotations are drawn from these letters.

63. 'fell into conversation with another member of the party': Jenifer Hart, *Ask Me No More* p. 101.

64–5. 'When we travelled . . .': *Ask Me No More* p. 68.

65. 'for why should some be rich and others suffer . . .': *Ask Me No More* p. 69.
'I found the whole experience deeply . . .': *Ask Me No More* p. 61.
'pooh-poohing comfort . . .': *Ask Me No More* p. 63.

66. 'I think he supposed . . .': *Ask Me No More* p. 63.

67. 'Hitler's march into Austria . . .': *Ask Me No More* p. 74: see generally pp. 61–75.
It seems likely that this was 'Otto': see Carter, *Anthony Blunt: His Lives* p. 460.

68. The Soviets failed to make contact . . . : see *Anthony Blunt: His Lives* p. 252.

74. Richard Wilberforce recalled: interview with Richard Wilberforce.

CHAPTER 5

My account of Herbert Hart's years at MI5 draws primarily on material held at the Public Record Office, notably memoranda reporting on his work which he wrote for official purposes at the end of the war (KV 4/22), and the diaries of Guy Liddell. Unfortunately the file relating to Hart's work on the top secret ISOS material is missing, and my account of that has been compiled from interviews and on the basis of inferences from other published literature. Useful background information on MI5 and on life among Military Intelligence circles came from Hinsley and Simkins, *British Intelligence in the Second World War* Vol. 4; John Curry, *The Security Service 1908–1945*; J. C. Masterman, *The Double Cross System in the war of 1939 to 1945*; Miranda Carter's *Anthony Blunt: His Lives*; Tom Bower's biography of Dick White, *The Perfect English Spy*; and John Banville's remarkable novel, *The Untouchable*. Specific references are cited in the notes.

84. charged 'dangerously round the streets . . .': Jenifer Hart, *Ask Me No More* p. 108.

85. 'liked Herbert and thought him very able' this and the next quotation, *Ask Me No More* p. 104: the account of Jenifer Hart's further conversation with Brigadier Harker is drawn from an interview with her.

86. As an MI5 officer he was later able to locate his own security file: Carter, *Anthony Blunt: His Lives* p. 245.

Blunt assumed that further information casting doubt on his loyalty: see West and Tsarev, *The Crown Jewels* p. 138: on Blunt's recruitment to MI5, see pp. 129, 131.

Soviet Intelligence had more British graduates working for it: John Curry, *The Security Service 1908–1945*.

87. 'in a little water-tight compartment carrying on his work in a rather pompous and eye-washing way . . .': from Guy Liddell's diary, KV 4/187 (November 1940–June 1941) p. 905. The following two quotations are drawn from KV 4/ 192 (July–November 1943) p. 328 and KV 4/194 (May–September 1944) p. 278 respectively. Liddell's diaries, typed up by his secretary each evening, were in the nature of a 'shadow diary' which would be of use should someone else suddenly have to step into his position: they include relatively little personal material, but a wealth of detail about the activities of B Division, its relationship with MI6, and Liddell's view of its strategic problems and the competence of its staff.

an intake which included a large number of lawyers: see A. W. B. Simpson, *In the Highest Degree Odious* p. 38 n. 29.

88. This allowed counter-intelligence to be used as a positive . . .: J. C. Masterman, *The Double Cross System*.

89. White 'always took Herbert's advice': interview with Stuart Hampshire.

'Hart took the situation in hand': Liddell's diary KV 4/190 (May–November 1942) p. 825.

'Everybody in the world of intelligence adored Herbert': interview with Stuart Hampshire.

90. 'clearly has nobody to give him a general appreciation of this information': KV 4/190 (May–November 1942) p. 938.

91. 'you could always tell when Herbert had had a file': interview with Stuart Hampshire.

'It is hard to imagine Herbert being physically organized . . .': interview with George Cawkwell.

Blunt, with whom Herbert occasionally shared an office: Blunt consulted Herbert about ULTRA information. Though he knew of Blunt's left-wing politics, Herbert was not aware that he was still an active communist. He was outraged and shocked to the point of distress when Blunt's spying was revealed decades later: as compared with Burgess, with whom he had had some social contact but never trusted, he must have felt a personal sense of betrayal by Blunt.

92. 'MI6 owned ULTRA . . .': interview with Stuart Hampshire.

'Dick has had a dream . . .': Liddell's diary, KV 4/189 (December 1941–May 1942) p. 324. On the problem of confidentiality, see also KV 4/188 (July–November 1941) p. 176. On the bargaining between B Division and MI6 about exchange of information, see West and Tsarev, *The Crown Jewels* pp. 139–40.

Liddell's and White's confidence in him led them not only to consult him regularly: for example, Herbert gave Liddell advice on which parts of the ISOS information should be the focus of analysis once its volume became such as to make analysing all of it impossible: see KV 4/190 (May–November 1942) pp. 802, 821.

The Radio Security Intelligence Committee: as reported to Moscow by Philby: see West and Tsarev, *The Crown Jewels* pp. 324–5.

'100% persona grata with Philby': KV 4/193 (December 1943–May 1944) p. 319.

93. **'a natural cryptographer':** interview with Stuart Hampshire.

Liddell's reference to Herbert's identifying security problems with the codes used for sending messages to troops: KV 4/193 (December 1943–May 1944) p. 293.

94. **In October 1942 he presented a memo to Liddell:** KV 4/190 pp. 825–7.

98. **'. . . the appearance on great numbers of the telegraph poles in this country . . .':** KV 4/22.

98–9. **Though in later life he spoke seldom of his intelligence work:** interview with Graham Richards and written communication with Tony Honoré. From a later correspondence with Herbert Hart, Brian Simpson, too, had the impression that his sensitivity about some of the methods used in war time influenced his later vehemence on capital punishment (written communication with Brian Simpson). The case described here bears some resemblance to the case of Duncan A. C. Scott-Ford, a young merchant seaman who had supplied information about convoy sailings to the Germans for money. He was detained in August 1942 under Defence Regulation 18B and was ultimately charged under the Treachery Act: he pleaded not guilty, but was tried in camera and sentenced to death by Birkett J. in October of that year. His detention was in fact requested by Helenus ('Buster') P. J. Milmo of MI5 (later to become a High Court judge). Herbert may well have been involved in the case, his role and other details becoming distorted in my interview accounts by the vagaries of retelling and memory. For an account of the case, see A. W. B. Simpson, *In the Highest Degree Odious* p. 383.

99. **contemplation (as a last resort) of deliberately ramming the ship:** KV 4/190 (May–November 1942) p. 751; The following quotation is taken from KV 4/191 (December 1942–June 1943) p. 271.

100. **his work often concerned activities outside Britain:** Investigations referred to in the Liddell diaries as involving Herbert related to espionage in Norway, Switzerland, Egypt, Portugal, Gibraltar, and Bermuda. An account of the minefield investigation referred to earlier in this paragraph can be found in Liddell's diary at KV 4/188 pp. 964, 983, 990. At KV 4/189 p. 223 Liddell also referred to him as 'the best man [to act as special investigator into a suspected leak of information about British warships from a Spanish source in Gibraltar] as he has had previous experience in Admiralty enquiries and has carried them out most efficiently'.

a long debate between Berlin and Madrid 'as to whether Chester was a port': Liddell's diary, KV 4/193 (December 1943–May 1944) p. 67; see also KV 4/192 p. 125 and KV 4/194 p. 82.

enormously valued by his colleagues: After his death, Herbert's contribution was described to Jenifer by his wartime employers in the following terms:

'Many former members of B1A and B1B have paid tribute to the vital role Herbert played in building up this intelligence base, then in drawing on it in such a way as to maximize the effectiveness of the Double Cross agents. His clarity of mind and his ability to absorb and distil vast quantities of information, allied with his considerable powers of expression, are clearly to be seen in the war-time files he dealt with, now in the PRO. . . . Exceptionally, for someone with so few years' seniority in the Service, he took over B1 section as an Assistant Director in 1944.'

One colleague even felt: interview with Stuart Hampshire.

101. 'The Hungarian economist Thomas Balogh . . .': Jenifer Hart, *Ask Me No More* p. 106. 'Greats' refers to the degree in classics, ancient history, and philosophy.

103. 'worshipping the mother-wife': the terms were taken from a book by Norman Haire.
'deep almost neurotic antipathy towards babies . . .': *Ask Me No More* p. 163.
'wise, compassionate and competent': *Ask Me No More* p. 115.

106. (described by Liddell as 'violently anti-Zionist, as far as I know Hart is too'): KV 4/190 (May–November 1942) p. 792.

108. 'Christopher radiated not only zest . . .': from Hart's memoir in the *New College Record* at p. 16.

CHAPTER 6

This chapter draws mainly on Hart's 1944–6 diaries, on his correspondence with Jenifer Hart and Isaiah Berlin, and on letters of congratulation from friends and colleagues on his election to the Chair of Jurisprudence at Oxford. My sketch of Oxford's philosophical world is informed by Peter Hacker's *Wittgenstein's Place in Twentieth Century Analytic Philosophy*, Jonathan Rée's essay 'English Philosophy in the Fifties', Michael Ignatieff's *A Life of Isaiah Berlin*, and Ben Rogers' life of *A. J. Ayer* as well as by a number of interviews and more specific sources mentioned in the notes.

114. 'an honorary institutionally correct person': interview with Stuart Hampshire.

116. 'not an intellectual in his habits': interview with Stuart Hampshire.

116–17. 'How can you hesitate? . . .': This letter was written in early October 1944: see Berlin, *Flourishing: Letters 1928–1946* pp. 498–9.

117. 'When you say that Ewing's is the voice . . .': from the same letter: Berlin, *Flourishing*, p. 498.

117–18. 'I have known Herbert Hart for the last twelve years . . .': letter from Berlin to Henry Price, 18 December 1944: *Flourishing* pp. 509–10, with the page break coming between the sentences beginning 'He realizes . . .' and 'Nevertheless . . .'.

118. 'the virtues outweigh the defects' and that Hart would 'provide the best obtainable tutor in philosophy': *Flourishing* pp. 511 and 510 respectively. 'I was more than once tempted . . .': *Flourishing* p. 513.

119. 'I cannot wait before letting you know . . .' and 'I understand her feelings . . .': letter from Berlin to Herbert Hart, 23 February 1945: *Flourishing* pp. 533–4.

121. 'Ich biete . . . Ich suche': I am offering, I am looking for. 'But the English don't behave like that': interview with Harry Judge.

123. only five of which were for women: According to the statistics compiled by the University for the UGC (see notes for p. 22), the preponderance of men over women had diminished somewhat since Herbert Hart's student days, with 3,447 men and 1,074 women now in residence. 'frowsty', the fellowship largely composed of a 'backlog of ghastly old boys': interview with Stuart Hampshire. the sweets of dictatorship . . . were not altogether uncongenial to him' and, on the next page, 'he loved a battle': from the New College memoir (Harrod) pp. 25–6; see also p. 32 ('boyishly unassuming') and p. 36 ('a high-minded crook . . . a renegade bureaucrat').

125. 'early risers would be greeted in the rather dank outer kitchen': from the memoir of Cox by Warren Allen, published in the *New College Record* pp. 17–19 at p. 17.

126. 'an intimidating atmosphere': interview with Peter Campbell. 'One had been at school and formed a loyalty to that, and then one had been let loose in the Services . . .': from the New College memoir by Sparrow and others: this was written by J. L. E. Smith, a former student and Steward (i.e. President) of the Junior Common Room in 1947, pp. 35–7 at p. 35.

127. discussions in which, like A. J. Ayer: see Ben Rogers' biography of Ayer. 'Browne plainly thinks . . .' and 'He distrusts and despises my whole approach to the subject': from Herbert Hart's diary, also quoted in Jenifer Hart *Ask Me No More* p. 112.

128. Geoffrey Warnock, later a famous philosopher . . .': Warnock told the story to Colin Tapper, who recounted it to me.

129. 'I must stop this Jewish wailing': *Ask me No More* p. 112.

130. 'I must do something about my growing isolation from Jen . . .': quotation from Herbert's diary. At least one colleague realized: interview with Stuart Hampshire. talked of his utter amazement: interview with Peter Campbell.

131. **apart from some significant annotations in 1949 and 1952:** see pp. 151 and 350.

132. **In 1952, the 50 philosophers in Oxford:** I am drawing here on Jonathan Rée's 'English Philosophy in the Fifties'.
     the small number of women philosophers: Iris Murdoch, Elizabeth Anscombe (later a translator of Wittgenstein's *Philosophical Investigations*), and, later, Philippa Foot all worked in Oxford in the heyday of linguistic philosophy.

133. **'Assumptions are like halitosis':** this and the next story of Ryle are drawn from my interview with James Griffin.
     'I would fish out Major Austin . . .': letter from Berlin to Herbert Hart, 23 February 1945, Berlin, *Flourishing* p. 534.
     'sour, dour schoolmaster-type': interview with Stuart Hampshire.
     'bird of prey': quoted in Rée, 'English Philosophy in the Fifties', p. 8.
     'a sort of parody of a dessicated don . . .': Ved Mehta, *Fly and the Fly-Bottle* p. 151.

134. **Years later, Herbert remarked to a colleague:** remark to Robert Summers, as recounted in Peter Hacker's *Wittgenstein's Place in Twentieth Century Analytic Philosophy* p. 308. As Hacker remarks, 'This, to be sure, was a case of knowledge by description rather than by acquaintance'!
     'If we are to continue to use [the] expression [doing an action] in sober philosophy': J. L. Austin, 'A Plea for Excuses', in his *Philosophical Papers* p. 175, at p. 178.

134–5. **'Time was spent analyzing dispositional concepts . . .':** This and the next quotation are from Hacker, at pp. 151 and 172.

135. **Austin's manner is frequently described:** These and the descriptions of Austin and Oxford philosophy over the next page are drawn from my interviews with John Lucas, James Griffin, and Richard Mulgan.
     'aegrotat': an unclassified degree awarded to a candidate who has been unable to sit the exams, for example because of illness.
     the gradual ascendancy of Peter Strawson: see Hacker p. 155.
     'uncoiled himself, snake-like, from his chair': interview with James Griffin.

136. **'born of an odd feeling of being so clever':** interview with John Lucas.

137. **a ' "Philosophy-Without-Tears" School' . . . :** quoted in Rée's 'English Philosophy in the Fifties' p. 10.
     'The most influential school of philosophy in Britain . . .': Bertrand Russell, *Portraits from Memory and Other Essays* p. 154.
     Ernest Gellner, in *Words and Things*, his famous 1959 critique of the philosophical culture . . . : For an entertaining account of the public row about Ryle's refusal to review the book in *Mind*, see Ved Mehta, *Fly and the Fly-Bottle*: see also Hacker pp. 230–231.

138. **'the strange love-child of Wittgenstein's messianism and Oxonian complacency':** Gellner p. 281.

philosophical iconoclasts: See for example Judith Butler, *Excitable Speech*.

139. 'Some people like Witters but Moore is *my* man.': Both Strawson and Grice have recorded the remark: see Hacker, *Wittgenstein's Place in Twentieth Century Analytic Philosophy* p. 314 note 106.

'although they were in a state of almost constant collision': Isaiah Berlin, 'Austin and the Early Beginnings of Oxford Philosophy' p. 16.

In 1947, Wittgenstein visited Oxford . . . : This account is drawn from my interview with Peter Hacker.

140. 'It was as if the scales fell . . .': to Peter Hacker: Hacker, *Wittgenstein's Place in Twentieth Century Analytic Philosophy* p. 163; the reference to the *Investigations* as 'our bible' was to Bob Summers (see Summers 1995 p. 593 fn. 18). Mary Warnock's story of Herbert's conversation with Geoffrey Warnock is drawn from her interview with *The Guardian* on 19 July 2003, at p. 18.

'an explosion of genius in the middle of the discipline': interview with Stuart Hampshire.

'I felt that I was, for the first time, seeing thought *naked* . . .': Hacker p. 162.

mediated by Waismann's work: Hacker pp. 165, 312.

141. he asserted that logical positivism had contributed to the rise of fascism: recounted in Rée, 'English Philosophy in the Fifties', p. 9.

'The man is a hunchback': interview with Peter Strawson.

142. 'they had won the war, got rid of the evil people': interview with John Lucas.

and the seminar, audience-less, went ahead: story recounted to me by Brian Simpson.

143. He also came to regard the illuminating power of linguistic philosophy: See the Preface to his *Essays in Jurisprudence and Philosophy*.

in a correspondence which he had with Ernest Gellner in 1960: My quotations are taken from letters written on 1 and 20 February 1960, now in the Gellner archive at the London School of Economics. They were kindly drawn to my attention by Gellner's biographer Professor John Hall. Interestingly, the second letter also refers to Herbert's having 'completely lost your temper' and 'employed the word *insanity* in referring to one of your co-symposiasts' in a presentation of his paper on 'Knowledge by Acquaintance' (see pp. 146–7.). 'That really was abusiveness', Gellner suggested; 'Did Ryle ever chide you for it I wonder?' (see the account of Ryle's reaction to Gellner's book at p. 138).

144. 'His understanding and subtle analysis of language absolutely excited me . . .': Sugarman interview.

Defeasibility: The concept was also employed philosophically by Waismann.

145. one of the 'two or three things' he would still advise a student . . . : interview with James Griffin.

146. 'The Ascription of Responsibility and Rights': Notwithstanding Geach's critique of ascriptivism, several of Herbert's colleagues, including Tony Honoré, felt that he was too quick to abandon the arguments of this paper: John Lucas went on to write an (unpublished) paper in its defence, and

Gordon Baker's contribution to Hart's 1977 Festschrift, 'Defeasibility and Meaning' (in Hacker and Raz (ed.) *Law, Morality and Society*) amounted to an attempt to make its arguments more rigorous so as to rescue them.

'little flies making small points in a fashionable way': interview with John Lucas.

Geach's frontal assault on ascriptivism: Peter Geach, *Logic Matters* Chapter 8.

147. **In Gellner's second letter in 1960:** See reference for p. 143 above. It is not entirely clear that it is Findlay to whom Gellner was referring, but the letter certainly attests to the strength of Herbert's reaction.

Herbert was extremely upset: interview with Stuart Hampshire.

In a letter to Noel Annan: written by Berlin on 27 January 1950.

149. **'It had no broad principle, no broad faith, it confronted no large question . . . :** Sugarman interview.

150. **'spiritually anglicised':** interview with Jean Floud.

151. **also heard to remark that Herbert was far too untidy:** interview with Tony Honoré.

CHAPTER 7

This chapter is based primarily on Herbert Hart's working notebooks and published work, and on interviews.

156. **The lecture was inspired by the lengthy discussions of different varieties of rule:** as described by Hart in the Sugarman interview.

156–7. **its failure to come to terms with Austin's distinction between the meaning and the force of statements:** See the Introduction to Hart's *Essays in Jurisprudence and Philosophy*.

157. **C. K. Allen once remarked to Tony Honoré:** letter from Tony Honoré.

casenotes in the *Law Quarterly Review* were famously deferential: I am grateful to Neil Duxbury for alerting me to this point. Frederick Pollock, elected to a Chair of Jurisprudence at Oxford in 1883, noticed the same habit of deference to the legal profession, and disliked it just as much as his mid-twentieth-century successor: see Duxbury, *Frederick Pollock and the English Juristic Tradition* Chapter 2.

158. **'I felt I knew all that from conveyancing':** Sugarman interview.

'the philosophical side of the street I was trying to walk on': Sugarman interview.

Henry Maine, Frederick Pollock, and Paul Vinogradoff: As Neil Duxbury's *Frederick Pollock and the English Juristic Tradition* (Chapter 3) shows, Pollock in fact had a significant interest in analytical jurisprudence notwithstanding his 'vituperative condemnations' of the work of the early positivist John Austin. For further detail on the history of the Chair, see F. H. Lawson, *The Oxford Law School 1850–1965*.

'Oxford philosophy is old hat to lawyers': to Bob Summers: interview with Bob Summers; Summers' diary 1964–5.

159. 'the stuff of his thinking was clarity and distinctions': This and the following quotations are drawn from my telephone interview and subsequent correspondence with Herbert Morris.

160. 'things written by people in ex-colonies and at provincial universities . . . were with some honourable exceptions not worth reading.': This and the following quotations are taken from my correspondence from Vinit Haksar.

'my intellectual hero': interview with Brian Barry: the term was also used in a letter from the Master of University College, John Albery, to Jenifer Hart after Herbert Hart's death.

'taught me how to think': interview with Vernon Bogdanor.

'his very own curiosity and excitement . . .': This and the later quotation are taken from an email from Ruth Gavison.

161. 'Herbert was very distant . . .': This and the later quotation are from my interview with Joseph Raz.

'He rode me on a long rein': interview with John Lucas. Lucas studied under Herbert's supervision for a time but was not one of his doctoral students.

discussing with John Finnis a Jesuit critique of empiricism: interview with John Finnis.

162. the 'Oxford disease' of 'an excessive distrust' of sociology: Sugarman interview.

'A marvellously efficient administrator of his intellectual resources and his energies': These and the following quotations are from Herbert Hart's memoir of Rupert Cross, written for the British Academy, at pp. 433–4.

164. Herbert 'could destroy people': interview with Vernon Bogdanor.

Colin Tapper remembers waiting nervously: interview with Colin Tapper.

'as usual, on the back of an envelope': My account is drawn from interviews and correspondence with Tony Honoré, from his memoir of Herbert Hart for the British Academy, and from his entry on Hart in the *Oxford Dictionary of National Biography* (2004).

166. Each week, the students were given questions to ponder: My account of Herbert Hart's lectures is based on the notes which William Twining took as a student in 1954.

167. 'go and find out what this new professor of jurisprudence is up to': interview with William Twining.

sweep into the room, lean against the lectern, and 'talk thoughtfully to himself for an hour': email from Paul Collins, who attended Hart's lectures in 1963.

one of the two experiences of genuine intellectual excitement in his student career: interview with Lennie Hoffmann.

168. 'The lectures were crowded and were heard with rapt attention': from Tony Honoré's entry for the *Oxford Dictionary of National Biography* (2004).

169. 'Prolegomenon to the Principles of Punishment' (1959), reprinted as Chapter 1 of *Punishment and Responsibility*.

170. 'I remember Herbert's gentle belief, against the evidence, in the rationality of the golf blue': letter from Barry Nicholas to Jenifer Hart after Herbert Hart's death.

'I couldn't say I adored him but I came pretty close to it.': interview with George Cawkwell.

he is reported as having turned up on several occasions to dinner wearing either no tie or, more often, two ties: These lapses were not confined to University College. In his speech at Herbert's memorial service, Ronald Dworkin recalled collecting Herbert for a lecture at Yale: Herbert left his room with two ties but no paper. Since he had also locked himself out of the room, the paper had to be retrieved by climbing in through the window.

171. On one occasion, when Goodhart had successfully opposed: interview with Peter Strawson.

In Harvard in 1956: recorded in his Harvard diary.

'The philosophers thought I was a marvellous lawyer': Sugarman interview.

174. 'run the gauntlet of the fellows': These quotations are taken from Jenifer Hart, *Ask Me No More* p. 132.

176. 'How can you be sitting there talking about responsibility . . .': interview with George Fletcher: the unfortunate dénouement was described to me by Jean Floud.

177. Stuart Hampshire recalled her extreme distress: interview with Stuart Hampshire.

'It's not possible' and 'Isaiah keeps going mad. He says *again* he's in love with you': Michael Ignatieff, *Isaiah Berlin* p. 211; the following story about Aline Berlin's contemplation of buying the house next door was related to me by Jenifer Hart.

178. 'closest friend among his philosophical colleagues': MacCormick, *H. L. A. Hart* p. 11.

CHAPTER 8

My account of Herbert Hart's year in America is drawn primarily from his diaries, his letters to Jenifer Hart and others, and his publications. Unattributed quotations for which the source is neither clear from the text nor provided in the notes are from the diaries. I have also drawn on the Harvard Law School archive and in particular its collection of Lon Fuller's papers.

180. 'The ranges of goods in the shops, the cars, the speed, the enormous factories': letter to Jenifer Hart.

'vast buildings, august traditions, very much the ante-room of the U.S. Supreme Court': letter to Jenifer Hart.

'conducting a *battle*—so uncongenial to the local graduates is my as our mode of philosophising': letter to Jenifer Hart.

181. 'available for consultation with interested students': as advertised in the *Harvard Law Record*.

'a nice New Englander . . .': In fact, Fuller was born in Texas. He moved with his family to a frontier town in California at the age of six, and studied at Berkeley and Stanford. But Herbert's initial impression was not as socially wide of the mark as it was geographically, for Fuller had developed a distinctly East Coast persona.

"You know he's a positivist, but he's quite a nice man": Sugarman interview. It is amusing to contrast the Harvard association of positivism with a kind of conservatism with Hayek's very different view that, in the hands of theorists like Kelsen, it amounted to the legal 'ideology of socialism' because it rejected any justice-based or other 'limitations on the power of the legislator' by defining law as anything which emanates from the state (Hayek, *Law, Legislation and Liberty* II pp. 53, 52). See further notes for p. 199.

183. 'madly egocentric': letter to Jenifer Hart.

184. 'combined the best qualities of Hitler and Goering': letter to Jenifer Hart.
'a mixture of June 4th at Eton and Derby Day at Epsom': letter to Jenifer Hart.
'Mr Fuller's course will be based . . . :' *Harvard Law Record* (1956) Vol. 22 No. 11, 12 April 1956 p. 1.
In an interview for the *Record* . . . : (1957) Vol. 24 no. 9, p. 2.

186. 'gay ugly charming': letter to Jenifer Hart.
'argued badly', though he thought him a 'kind of saint': letter to Jenifer Hart.
'Herbert likes you very much indeed . . .': Berlin to White, 19 July 1957.

187. 'The Law School started today . . .': letter to Jenifer Hart.
'attractive goodhearted v. clever tough Republican . . . with tremendous vitality': letter to Jenifer Hart.
'that chattering monkey Frankfurter's vices': letter to Jenifer Hart.
'interesting though rather gloomy character . . .': letter to Jenifer Hart.

189. Mimi and Gerry Berlin: The couple, who did not at first realize that Herbert was Jewish, were moved if somewhat bemused to be named as the last Hart child's 'godparents'; they describe Herbert as 'one of the great loves of our life'.
'she's insane about Jewish family life which I said we didn't have': This and the following quotations are from a letter to Jenifer Hart.

190. 'relaxed one's neuroses', 'Ideas started pullulating at a rather alarming rate.': Brock/Harrison interview.

192. he earned enough through occasional lectures: letter to Jenifer Hart.

193. 'real talk' with John Rawls: letter to Jenifer Hart.
entertainments included, to his surprised amusement, a game of charades: letter to Jenifer Hart. In this as in several other instances (e.g. the description of Princeton) Herbert's diary descriptions were used again in letters home.

194. 'strange this enormous burden': letter to Jenifer Hart.
'I've been invited by both a Rabbi and a Catholic priest . . .': letter to Jenifer Hart.

'**evil slums and broken down ill-lit houses and pubs**': This and other quoted descriptions of Chicago are from a letter to Jenifer Hart.

195. '**from the fact that their husbands do nothing but work all day and most nights**': letter to Jenifer Hart.

197. '**back and forth at the back of the lecture hall . . .**': letter from Joel Feinberg to Herbert Hart, July 1991.

199. **The positivist position, he argued, was linked to the unquestioningly compliant 'might is right' . . .**: For the reasons canvassed in the notes for p. 181, Hayek, too, took the view that it was 'the prevalence of positivism which made the guardians of the law defenceless against the new advance of arbitrary government' (p. 55). Hayek, however, regarded Herbert Hart's work as 'in most regards . . . one of the most effective criticisms of legal positivism', and saw him as a positivist only in the precise sense that 'it is in no sense a necessary truth that laws reproduce or satisfy certain demands of morality' (p. 56). I am grateful to Tony Honoré for alerting me to this passage.

200. **felt that they had 'learned much from each other'**: letter from Lon Fuller to Frank S. Bayley, 3 March 1958.
'**Meanwhile a spot of trouble!**': letter to Lon Fuller, 13 December 1957.
'**Dear Herbert: After receiving your letter . . .**': letter from Fuller, 17 December 1957.

201. '**I was delighted to see so sharp a joinder . . .** ': letter from Fuller, 3 February 1965.
'**new tack**': '**vague and self-contradictory laws . . .** ': letter from Fuller, 18 October 1965.

202. '**gusts of homesickness**': letter to Jenifer Hart.
'**found his children bores . . .** ': letter to Jenifer Hart.

203. **he initially regarded the prospect of sending Adam to a public school**: letter to Jenifer Hart.

206. '**People like the Harts . . .** ': letter written by Berlin on 19 July 1957.

207. '**Poor Richard W sounds plangent**': letter to Jenifer.

CHAPTER 9

The main sources for this chapter are Herbert Hart's letters, diaries, and working notebooks, and interviews and correspondence with Tony Honoré. All unattributed quotations for which the source is not clear from the text are taken from Hart's diaries or notebooks.

209. **worries about what to lecture on in the autumn term**: In fact, Herbert's teaching followed the familiar pattern, with lectures on 'The Definition of Law and Related Concepts' in the Michaelmas Term and 'Rights and Duties: Ownership and Possession' in the Hilary Term, while in the Trinity Term he taught a seminar with Geoffrey Marshall on 'Varieties of Legal Theory'. From the following year on, the Michaelmas lectures were

re-titled 'The Concept of Law'. Herbert also returned to criminal law theory, with lectures on 'Why Punish?' in 1959 and a seminar on 'Mind and Deed in the Law' in that and the following year. In 1960, he gave a lecture series on 'Legal Theory in Blackstone and Bentham'.

210. *'naturrechtlich'*: i.e. inspired by a natural law approach. There is some tension between Herbert Hart's and Tony Honoré's assumption that there is a 'core notion of causation' and their idea that the context in which causal concepts are used makes all the difference to the meaning of causal terms. This perhaps reflects their different approaches. Another key difference would have been Honoré's argument for 'outcome responsibility'—the idea that we are truly responsible for the outcomes of our actions even when they are 'accidental' in the sense that we could not have done otherwise than we did. Honoré's argument is that the results of our actions become a part of our sense of identity, of who we are ('Responsibility and Luck' 1988). This would have been anathema to Herbert, who defended that view that we are responsible only for the things that we choose to do, in the sense that we had a fair opportunity to do otherwise. Despite its obvious relevance to legal causation, it is therefore not surprising that the idea of outcome responsibility does not appear in *Causation*.

211. **'we mulled over one another's drafts . . .'**: Tony Honoré, 'Herbert Lionel Adolphus Hart', British Academy memoir p. 303.

213. **general, common sense understandings of causation:** This connection with 'common sense', typical of the Austinian school of linguistic philosophy, also spoke in a legal context to the receptiveness of juries who in criminal cases in England, and in both criminal and civil cases in the US, would often be the final arbiter of legal attributions of causation. I am grateful to Jane Stapleton for alerting me to this point.

P. Nowell-Smith, who described the book as 'brilliant': from a review published in *Mind* (1961) p. 553: the review by Newark quoted below is from 76 *LQR* (1960) 592.

214. **it was widely read and came to be cited by judges both in the UK and beyond:** See Jane Stapleton's 'Unpacking Causation' p. 160 and Lord Hoffmann, 'Common Sense and Causing Loss' (1999).

the self-styled 'junior partner' 'felt the need to move away from . . .': letter from Tony Honoré. In 1958 Honoré had in any case become Rhodes Reader in Roman-Dutch Law, and was mainly occupied with South African and Sri Lankan students.

reacting negatively when other scholars suggested: interview with Herbert Morris.

215. **the foundations laid in their joint work:** and which Honoré regards his later work, in particular *Responsibility and Fault*, as continuing.

'a sharpened awareness of words to sharpen our perception of, though not as the final arbiter of, the phenomena': J. L. Austin, *Philosophical Papers* p. 130.

217. **a political activist might attribute a drought:** This and the example about fire in a factory are drawn from p. 35 of *Causation in the Law.*

218. **the approach which might be drawn from Wittgenstein's . . . :** See for example *Philosophical Investigations* paragraphs 197–202. My comparison between Wittgensteinian and Austinian approaches to linguistic philosophy should not be taken to imply that Wittgenstein himself was any more attentive to social context than Austin or than Hart and Honoré. Despite his injunctions about the limits of philosophy, Wittgenstein was, after all, a philosopher, and his method was analytic rather than empirical. Rather, my point is that a more socially contextualized approach is implied by Wittgenstein's work. In making this point, I do not mean to imply that Wittgenstein's ideas had no impact on the argument of *Causation*: for example, as Tony Honoré has pointed out to me in correspondence, the book's approach is significantly more systematic than that which Austin himself might have been expected to take.

219. **as Wittgenstein himself saw:** Again, this is not to say that Wittgenstein's philosophy necessarily followed through on the insight. Indeed, it is not clear how philosophy as a stand-alone discipline could do so. The implication, rather, is for the relationship between philosophy and other disciplines.

221. **'the nearest thing which we had to a manifesto':** interview with Peter Campbell.

222. **'designed to enable 3rd class men [sic] to get 2nds':** as recounted by Barry Nicholas in a letter to Jenifer Hart after Herbert's death.

223. **Herbert Morris in the *Harvard Law Review*:** vol. 75 p. 1452 (1962): my quotations are taken from pp. 1452 and 1461. The other reviews from which I have quoted are as follows: Alf Ross, 71 *Yale Law Journal* 1162 (1962); Marcus Singer, LX *Journal of Philosophy* 197 (1963); O. Hood Phillips, 78 *LQR* 574 (1962).

226. **he omitted Austin's qualifier: 'though not as the final arbiter':** See note for p. 215.

229. **from the direction of the social sciences:** Examples of criticisms of *The Concept of Law* from this direction would be Roger Cotterrell's *The Politics of Jurisprudence* and Peter Fitzpatrick's *The Mythology of Modern Law.* As Joseph Raz's essay 'On the Functions of Law' (in *the Authority of Law* 1979) shows, on occasion philosophical and sociological critics picked up on similar issues.

    that 'Professor Hart's great talents for linguistic analysis': B. E. King, 'The Basic Concept of Professor Hart's Jurisprudence: The Norm out of the Bottle': my quotations are from pp. 277 and 300.

230. **the content of a legal system is entirely contingent:** I am grateful to Daniel Weinstock for drawing my attention to this important point of contrast between the two books.

    The volume which Finnis saw: Hamish Ross, in *Law as a Social Institution* (Chapters 3 and 4), has argued persuasively, at greater length, for Weber's

having had an influence on Hart (though at the time of writing Ross did not
have direct evidence that Hart had indeed read Weber). My account here is
based on interviews and correspondence with John Finnis.

'Conduct . . . can be oriented on the part of actors toward their *idea*
(vorstellung) **of the existence of a** *legitimate order*': This and the next quotation are taken from p. 3 and p. 7 of the Weber volume. The italics are in the
original while the words in capitals were underlined by Herbert. It is, of
course, impossible for me to be sure when Herbert Hart read the book, but
the publication date (1954) and handwriting are consistent with his reading having coincided with his work on early drafts of *The Concept of Law*.

231. **Herbert Morris's review:** See note for p. 221: these quotations are from
pp. 1457 and 1460.

Later on, John Finnis argued that . . . : See *Natural Law and Natural Rights*,
Chapter 1. Finnis's point is that if, as Herbert Hart conceded, a legal system has the minimum social function of promoting peaceful human co-
existence, a theoretical priority should be attached to those who adopt an
internal attitude for moral reasons, since their commitment to the system is
more stable and wholehearted than that of, for example, the person who
adopts an internal attitude for pragmatic reasons.

judges simply use their discretion: This criticism of Herbert's position was
originally voiced by Ronald Dworkin in his article 'Is Law a System of Rules',
reproduced as 'The Model of Rules I' in *Taking Rights Seriously* (1977).

232. **'vague and parasitical little book':** essay by Colin Campbell, 'The Career
of The Concept' in P. Leith and P. Ingram (eds.) *The Jurisprudence of
Orthodoxy* p. 25.

'as an outstanding contribution to legal theory': See reference at note for
p. 229: this quotation is from p. 303.

233. **'except that wretched book':** interview with William Twining.

235. **His legendary absent-mindedness:** related to Joseph Raz by Robin
Marsack: interview with Joseph Raz.

'very thought' of which Jenifer found 'cruel': Jenifer Hart's diary, October
1955, quoted in *Ask Me No More* p. 169.

236. **Adam, the most questioning of the three:** My account of family life on this
page is drawn from Jenifer Hart's *Ask Me No More* and from discussions
with her, Joanna Ryan, Adam Hart, and Charlie Hart.

237. **'I tell H. news at Agrigento . . .':** extract from Jenifer Hart's diary, spring
1959.

240. **'Autism has been described as 'a feeling of being in permanent jeopardy' ':**
Ask Me No More p. 182.

241. **Jacob's conversion to Catholicism:** A moving account of this episode
in Jacob's life is given in Karen Armstrong's *The Spiral Staircase* Chapter 3.
Jacob's difficulties, and his feeling for language, are evoked in the following
passage on p. 118 of Armstrong's book: 'He turned his face away, as he always
did when asked a direct question. He simply could not bear any attempt,

however well-intentioned, to penetrate his inner life. Chin pressed down hard on his chest, he muttered quietly to himself in the first person: "Karen wanted to know what was wrong but Jacob absolutely refused to answer. The question was impossible."'
Herbert told Tony Honoré: letter from Tony Honoré.

CHAPTER 10

The main sources for this chapter are Herbert Hart's letters and diaries for 1961–2 and his Israel diary of 1964: unattributed quotations are from the diaries.

249. **An Austrian Jew whose career had been marked by political adversity**: These facts about Kelsen's life are drawn from the Biographical Outline provided at the end of Bonnie Litschewski Paulson's and Stanley Paulson's translation of the *Pure Theory of Law* ('An Introduction to the Problems of Legal Theory'), with some further details kindly supplied by Stanley Paulson in correspondence.

250. **'If a constitution specifying the various sources of law is a living reality . . .'**: *The Concept of Law* p. 293.
The Southern Rhodesian courts: in *Madzimbamuto v. Lardner-Burke*.
Kelsen endorsed the view that Herbert defended in his debate with Fuller: and did so explicitly in his exchange with Carl Schmitt during the demise of the Weimar Republic in 1931 (see Schmitt *Der Hüter der Verfassung*, Kelsen, 'Wer soll der Hüter der Verfassung sein?'). I am grateful to Stanley Paulson for alerting me to this point, as well as for the record of Hart's remark about Kelsen's comment on Austin and Wittgenstein on the next page.

252. **he liked to say that everything which was right in *The Concept of Law***: interview with Izhak EngIand: Kelsen's remark was made to John Fleming, who related it to England.

253. **Two things are striking about the later paper**: Stanley Paulson has also pointed out to me that Herbert's argument in this paper stands alone among academic commentaries in fully grasping the purport of Kelsen's monistic theory of international law.

256. **His positivist view asserted that law could have any content whatsoever**: I am grateful to Brendan Edgeworth for prompting me to think about the links between Herbert's positivism and the position which he defended in *Law, Liberty and Morality*.

259. **In the *Law Quarterly Review*, J. A. Coutts**: 80 *LQR* p. 279, quotation from p. 280: the Harvey review is from 27 *MLR* p. 865, quotation from p. 866. For a more serious assessment, see David Raphael's review in *Mind* (1966) p. 607.

260. **'one of my better articles'**: Sugarman interview.
throwing himself into lectures on 'Law and Morals', on Kelsen and Hohfeld: The lecture list records 'Patterns . . .' and later 'Problems in

Kelsen's General Theory'. There is no specific mention of Hohfeld in the lecture list until a seminar on Bentham and Hohfeld on legal rights in 1968: Herbert's work on Hohfeld and Kelsen was never published, and no manuscript appears to survive, though the lectures are mentioned in his notebook. Herbert also gave lectures and classes on Bentham in 1962 and 1963. The lectures on 'Law and Morals' tracked closely the arguments of *Law, Liberty and Morality*; I am gateful to Jeffrey Hackney for giving me his notes taken in 1961–2.

regarding *The Concept of Law* **as a 'drink of pure water'**: interview with Jean Floud.

a book on *Law in Society:* the book, by Geoffrey Sawer, was published in 1964.

262. **'Well I liked him** *tremendously'*: interview with Peter Strawson.

this occasionally produced startling errors of judgment . . . : The most famous of these was Herbert's pressing for the appointment to the Readership in English Law at All Souls of a man generally thought to be poorly qualified for the post.

Summers recalls finding himself in Austin's study: This account of Summers' visit to Oxford is drawn from interviews with Bob and Dorothy Summers and from Bob Summers' diary, from which the quotations are taken.

264. **his willingness to talk Berlin's achievements down:** It should certainly not be inferred from this remark that Herbert was without admiration for Berlin's work: indeed, he encouraged Summers to attend Berlin's seminars.

265. **Robert Gorman, a young Fulbright scholar:** This account, including the quotation, is drawn from my correspondence with Robert Gorman.

something 'broken' about Herbert: interview with Stuart Hampshire. One wonders whether Berlin had in mind Sartre's fascinating and sympathetic analysis of the 'inauthentic Jew': *Anti-Semite and Jew* Chapter III.

266. **although somewhat taken aback that she was unable to attend one of his lectures because no women were to be there:** Jenifer Hart's diary.

'The criminal law is a clumsy instrument and we wield it largely in the dark': Each returning Lionel Cohen lecturer is invited to speak on his or her lectures and experiences of Israel: this quotation is taken from p. 3 of Hart's transcript of his speech to an audience at Lincoln's Inn Hall. The transcript is not dated but the context makes it clear that the occasion took place relatively shortly after his return from Israel.

267–8. **Joseph Raz, a young scholar at the Hebrew University at the time:** interview with Joseph Raz.

268. **In conversation, Izhak England, then a young torts scholar:** interview with Izhak England.

270. **In an interview given to an Israeli magazine:** *Between Citizen and State:* interview conducted by Yael Tamir-Rafaeli, published in 1987.
     'Herbert Hart's reactions were *very* similar to L. Woolf's: letter from Isaiah Berlin to Noel Annan, 27 March 1979.
271. **In Santa Monica in 1961, Herbert had remarked to Herbert Morris:** telephone interview with Herbert Morris.
     In 1967, the young Joseph Raz told Herbert at the end of a supervision: interview with Joseph Raz.
     in a striking comment which Herbert made to Ronald Dworkin: interviews with Ronald Dworkin, Aharon Barak, George Fletcher, and Joseph Raz.

CHAPTER 11

The main sources for this chapter are Herbert Hart's letters and 1968 diary; Tony Honoré's memoir for the British Academy; Herbert Hart's collection of letters relating to his appointment to the Monopolies Commission; the Brock/Harrison and Sugarman interviews; versions of Abraham Harari's 'Open Letter' provided by Brian Simpson and John Morison; and the Report of the Committee of Inquiry into Student Discipline (the 'Hart Report').

273. **Herbert formed a particularly close intellectual connection with Joseph Raz:** My account in this paragraph draws on my interview with Joseph Raz.
     a deluge of Honorary Degrees: Stockholm 1960; Glasgow and Chicago 1966; Kent 1969; Cambridge 1978; Hull and National Autonomous University of Mexico 1979; Harvard, Bradford, and Edinburgh 1980; Georgetown 1982; Tel Aviv 1983; Hebrew University, Jerusalem 1985; Commonwealth Prestige Fellow, Government of New Zealand 1971.
275. **He wrote Herbert a series of increasingly accusing . . . :** My account of Herbert's reaction to the Harari episode is based on discussions with Brian Simpson and Joseph Raz.
276. **He accused Herbert—'our Oxonian oracle' . . . :** My quotations from the 'Open Letter' are taken from pp. 1, 2, 3, 12, 14, 20, 85, and 88 of the copy sent to me by Brian Simpson.
278. **On the evening following the marriage:** interview with Adrian Zuckerman.
     The collapse of Douglas and Peggy Jay's marriage in 1971: My account is based on an interview with Mary Jay.
279. **John Rawls' idea of a 'reflective equilibrium':** *A Theory of Justice* pp. 20 ff., 48–51.
282. **His theory, however, gives us no conceptual resources . . . :** As Tony Honoré has pointed out to me, there is a similarity here with the underdevelopment of the paternalism argument of *Law, Liberty and Morality*.
284. **'I loved [it]; it was fascinating . . .':** Sugarman interview.

'I was all that Crossman hated . . .': Brock/Harrison interview.

285. He was therefore 'astonished' to be asked to chair the inquiry: All quotations in this paragraph are from the Brock/Harrison interview.

287. His proposal was to enact a minimal basic offence: proscribing conduct likely to disrupt teaching or study or research or university administration or obstructing a university officer in execution of their duties, or of damaging or defacing the property of any college or of the university, or occupying such property. Disciplinary offences would be divided into major and minor categories, with the Proctors retaining management only of the minor offences: the major offences would go initially to the Proctors but their decision would be subject to appeal to a disciplinary committee. The Report provided that information about the operation of this system would be published each year. The two further chapters of the Report recommended the institution of a system of academic consultation with junior members which nonetheless fell short of full student participation on academic governance. The aim was to foster transparency and critical debate, while recognizing the role of distinct professional interests and academic expertise in the governance of the university.

'almost everything I could get my hands on about student revolts everywhere': Brock/Harrison interview.

Their object, he pointed out, was not the universities as such: But educational institutions, he argued, held a special place in shaping the hierarchical social order to which the radicals objected.

288. with traditionalists like Herbert's former student: interview with John Lucas.

289. Brian Simpson . . . described the Report as 'a dog's dinner': Sugarman interview. Simpson, who was away on leave at the time of the Report's appearance, has no recollection of using this expression.

Interviewed about the history of the University: Brock/Harrison interview.

291. *Must get this ridiculous Kelsen paper under control*: Herbert in fact never published the substantial work he was doing on Kelsen, and no manuscript survives.

292. The informal approach was followed a little later by an official inquiry from the University: My account of Dworkin's recruitment is based on Herbert Hart's diaries and on an interview with Ronald Dworkin.

He even went so far as to ring at least one of the electors: R. V. Heuston: my information on this comes from correspondence with Brian Simpson.

CHAPTER 12

The main sources for this chapter are Herbert Hart's correspondence and his 1970 and 1971 diaries; his interviews with Brock/Harrison and with Sugarman; the papers in Manor Place collected by Jenifer Hart relating to the Macmillan/Hertford story; and interviews with his Brasenose colleagues.

297. As Sydney Smith had observed nearly 150 years earlier: 'Bentham's Book of Fallacies', quoted in Herbert Hart's *Essays on Bentham* p. 1.

298. Bentham's 'extraordinary combination of a fly's eye for detail . . .': *Essays on Bentham* p. 4.

'Nature has placed mankind under the governance of two sovereign masters . . .': Jeremy Bentham, *Introduction to the Principles of Morals and Legislation* ed. Burns and Hart (1982) pp. 11–13.

'Beds stuffed with straw: one side covered with the cheapest linen . . .': Jeremy Bentham, *Outline of Pauper Management Improved*, quoted in Herbert Hart's *Essays on Bentham* p. 5.

299. 'the arch philistine . . . that insipid, pedantic, leather-tongued oracle of the ordinary bourgeois intelligence . . .': Karl Marx, *Capital* 609–10, quoted in *Essays on Bentham* p. 2.

'the son of an impoverished Anglican clergyman . . .': *Essays on Bentham* pp. 54–5.

300. an 'auto-icon'—sits in a glass case: The history of the auto-icon is described in detail in C. F. A. Marmoy's 'The Auto-Icon of Jeremy Bentham at University College, London'. The quoted words are taken from a paper attached to Bentham's will.

312. he offered to resign from the Committee, and even talked to one colleague of suicide: interview with Willam Twining. My account of this episode is also based on correspondence with James Burns and Philip Schofield.

'[S]eemed satisfied, but I made it plain that I wouldn't live in college': This and the following quotations are taken from the Brock / Harrison interview.

313. There was, however, a complex history to the decision not to change the statutes: In writing this account, I have drawn on materials compiled by Jean Floud, Jenifer Hart, and Tony Honoré in their earlier attempts to get to the bottom of the story.

314. Barry Nicholas was taken aback: interview with Barry Nicholas.

'I want to thank you for remaining our candidate . . .': letter from Peter Ganz, October 1971.

'a characteristically generous and urbane reply': letter to Jean Floud from John Torrance, February 1993.

315. 'My whole transition to Brasenose was really rather astonishing . . .': Brock / Harrison interview.

'So glad to hear you've joined the hearties at long last': letter from John Albery.

'Though it has its fair share of individual and corporate myths . . .': letter from Eric Collier.

'the Lit. Hum. conspiracy theory of Oxford social history is correct': This and the next quotation are taken, respectively, from letters from a colleague at Christ Church (whose name is illegible) and Peter Strawson.

316. **a note from another college head:** the Warden of St. Anthony's. My account of Herbert's resignation from the Club is drawn from my interview with Peter Strawson.

317. **the throne once warmed by Last and Sonners:** 'Sonners' was the same person as former Principal Stallybrass, Sonners being a contraction of his original name, Sonnenschein, which he had changed as a consequence of the First World War. I am grateful to Brian Simpson for alerting me to this point: see A. W. B. Simpson, *Biographical Dictionary of the Common Law* p. 483.
    'When I got there there was trouble . . .': Brock/Harrison interview.
    Herbert's modernizing project at Brasenose: My account is drawn from interviews with Vernon Bogdanor, Hugh Collins, Harry Judge, Barry Nicholas, and Graham Richards.

318. **'Herbert had no sense of original sin in people':** interview with Barry Nicholas.
    The Hulme Trust originated: I have drawn here on a taped interview with Leslie Styler about the history of Brasenose, kindly lent to me by the interviewer, Harry Judge.

320. **One colleague remembers this episode as a striking exception . . . :** interview with Graham Richards.

321. **friends remember their alarm at his wobbly ascent:** interview with Marrianne Fillenz.

322. **after an initial reluctance overcome by vigorous discussions:** interview with Jean Floud.

323. **'mild punctuating remarks':** interview with Colin Tapper.
    to find out if he might be interested in being a candidate for the Mastership: This story was recounted to me by David Soskice.

324. **'The Bentham': 'Marvellous,' said Herbert:** interview with George Cawkwell. The account of one of the dinners is my own.

325. **Yet, as one reviewer noticed:** Philip Milton in the *Modern Law Review:* the following quotations are taken, respectively, from Jeremy Waldron in *Mind* at p. 281 and from Milton at p. 759.
    participants in the seminar to which the original version: interview with Brian Barry.

326. **In his later work, Rawls attested:** In *Political Liberalism* (1993) p. 5 fn. 3; Essay VIII of the book is an extended attempt to deal with Herbert's critique of his account of the basic liberties and their priority.

CHAPTER 13

This chapter is based on two main sources. The first is the collection of notebooks and diaries which Herbert Hart kept, irregularly, during the last 12 years of his life, along with some surviving correspondence: unattributed quotations are drawn from these. The second is interviews: with Ronald Dworkin (on his relationship with Herbert Hart and experience of Oxford); with Marianne Fillenz, Charlie Hart, Joanna Ryan, Adam Hart, Jenifer Hart, Jean Floud, Mary Jay, Joseph Raz, and Adrian Zuckerman (on Herbert Hart's reaction to the 'spy scandal' and subsequent breakdown); and with John Finnis, Ruth Gavison, Gerald Postema, and Joseph Raz (on the Jerusalem conference).

328. **'But isn't that just your opinion?':** I witnessed one of these occasions at lectures Dworkin gave during my time as a graduate student.

329. **Douglas Millen, the redoubtable long-serving Head Porter:** As a graduate student at University College, I was one of many people who heard Douglas Millen uttering this opinion.

331. **He suggested that, far from being bound only by rules:** in 'Is Law a System of Rules' and 'Social Rules and Legal Theory', reproduced as 'The Model of Rules I and II' in Chapters 2 and 3 of *Taking Rights Seriously*, and in 'Hard Cases', reproduced as Chapter 4 of the same book.

333. **'one right answer':** See Dworkin, 'No Right Answer?'
'agrees that in such systems no set of principles . . .': This and the following two quotations are taken from the *Essays on Bentham* at pp. 150, 151, 152.

334. **Herbert's complicated attitude to Dworkin also surfaced in his relationship with his final doctoral student, Wil Waluchow:** My account, and the quotations, are drawn from correspondence with Wil Waluchow. A revised version of Waluchow's thesis was later published as *Inclusive Legal Positivism*.

335–6. **As his natural law colleague John Finnis described the dilemma:** interview with John Finnis.

337. **But Herbert still saw Dworkin as, essentially, a legal positivist:** Amid the dozens of works which Herbert was exploring, no reference was made to an article by his old favourite Carrio, who in 1971 had published a paper written in Oxford during 1968–9. The paper deployed classic Hartian techniques—close reading, the drawing of distinctions—to zone in on what he saw as crucial ambiguities in Dworkin's account and to defend the capacity of Herbert's theory to accommodate principles in the limited sense necessary to preserve its plausibility as a concept of law. As Dworkin's theory developed to lay ever greater emphasis on the evaluative or moral dimension of legal reasoning, such classic positivist defences became less and less applicable.
Stephen Guest, who was present at a seminar: as recounted in his letter to Jenifer Hart after Herbert's death.

338. **In 1962 and again in 1966:** See Jenifer Hart's *Ask Me No More* pp. 75–9.

341. **Herbert's Boston friend, Gerry Rubin:** letter from Mimi Berlin, January 2003.

342. **Bishop Wilberforce, who had earned the nickname 'Soapy Sam':** *Ask Me No More* p. 79
'Everyone will think I was a spy: you don't think it do you?': interview with Mary Jay.

'blow everything up and lead to Israel being destroyed': interview with Adrian Zuckerman.

345. **to one of whom he remarked that he had been 'living with madmen'**: interview with John Finnis.

346. **signatory to at least one public letter of protest**: The letter arguing for an end to the occupation was signed by 'A. J. Ayer, Graham Greene, H. L. A. Hart, John Le Carré, John Mortimer, and (Sir) P. F. Strawson', and appeared in the *New York Times*, Friday 8 July 1988.

347. **thought for a long time 'about the fact of that chapter'**: interview with John Finnis.

pages the importance of which Honoré acknowledges: interview with Tony Honoré. The pages in question acknowledge that elements of legal policy enter into causal arguments in the law but argue that these are distinguishable from genuinely causal judgments.

348. **A relatively full reply to Postema**: it was never finished for publication.

349. **In Dworkin's revised view, only these systems counted**: His new theory was, therefore, in its own way as universal as Herbert's: it claimed to cover all genuine instances of 'legal systems', but implied that there were fewer of them in the world than would be identified by positivist criteria.

352. **As Ronald Dworkin would later put it**: in his review of Jules Coleman's *The Practice of Principle* in the *Harvard Law Review* (2002) at p. 1656. In Dworkin's case, the complaint of limited scope is however about morality and not about social facts.

353. **a volume of 12 essays devoted exclusively to its analysis**: Jules Coleman (ed.) *Hart's Postscript* (2001).

353–4. **Williams himself was struck by Herbert's sure grasp**: conversation with Bernard Williams: Williams also expressed this view in a letter to Jenifer Hart written after Herbert Hart's death.

354. **'Even in the case of a simple regime of custom-type rules . . .'**: The quotation is drawn from the English transcript of the *Doxa* interview.

355. **as another friend put it, 'at one remove'**: interview with Adrian Zuckerman.

his decision in 1978 to put up money to guarantee the bail: interview with Joanna Ryan.

an incident involving his old friend John Sparrow: I was sitting near Herbert at the dinner.

'his head is apt to run away with his heart': as noted in Herbert Hart's notebook of jokes.

357. **'not very interested in ideas now . . . Not *nearly* so quick . . . But still sharp . . .'**: This and the following quotations are extracts from Summers' diary.

Though the Tanner Trust's institution of an annual Hart lecture . . .: in 1985. The list of Hart lecturers whom Herbert was able to hear is testimony to the range and depth of his reputation: Richard Wollheim, John Rawls,

Bernard Williams, Quentin Skinner, Justice William Brennan, Thomas Scanlon, Joel Feinberg, and Tony Honoré. Since his death, the distinguished series has continued, with Neil MacCormick, Philippa Foot, Morton Horwitz, Thomas Nagel, Antony Duff, Justice Stephen Breyer, Lucian Violante, Lord Steyn, Ronald Dworkin, Lord Justice Laws, and Richard Epstein.

358. **insisting on taking Mary to the pub:** interview with Mary Jay.
Setting himself further targets each day, he ventured precariously: This paragraph is based on my own memories of Herbert Hart at Lamledra.
his companions remember him 'sucking life dry': interview with Marianne Fillenz: similar expressions arose in several interviews, including those with Adam and Charlie Hart and Joanna Ryan.

359. **'a few words, a smile, a look in the eyes':** letter from John Clarke, family friend and university colleague, to Jenifer Hart.

361. **'luminous mind' restricted itself:** interview with William Twining.
'a man who chews more than he has bitten off': as recorded in Herbert Hart's notebook of jokes.

363. **In his occasional protestations that one had to be mad:** interview with Adrian Zuckerman. Another of Herbert's favourite family allusions was to quote Philip Larkin: 'They fuck you up, your Mum and Dad . . .'
'Wild Spirit': from Shelley's 'Ode to the West Wind'.

364. **'I lingered round them under that benign sky . . .':** the closing passage of Emily Brontë's *Wuthering Heights* (1847).

Bibliography

H. L. A. HART

'Berlin—September 1945', *The Economist* (29 September 1945) p. 446

'A Week in Belgium' 1947 (typescript among Hart's papers)

Editor of volume and author of Preface, H. W. B. Joseph, *Knowledge and the Good in Plato's Republic* (London: Oxford University Press 1948)

'The Ascription of Responsibility and Rights', *Proceedings of the Aristotelian Society* 49 (1948–9) 171

'Is There Knowledge by Acquaintance?', *The Aristotelian Society Supplementary Volume* 23 (1949) 69

'A Logician's Fairy Tale', *Philosophical Review* 60 (1951) 198

'Philosophy of Law and Jurisprudence in Britain 1945–52', *American Journal of Comparative Law* (1953) 355

'Definition and Theory in Jurisprudence', 70 *Law Quarterly Review* (1954) 37

Introduction to *John Austin, The Province of Jurisprudence Determined etc.*, (London: Weidenfeld & Nicolson 1954) vii–xxi; editor of volume

'Are There Any Natural Rights?' *Philosophical Review* 64 (1955) 175

'Theory and Definition in Jurisprudence', *The Aristotelian Society, Supplementary Volume* 29 (1955) 239

'Blackstone's Use of the Law of Nature', *Butterworths South African Law Review* 3 (1956) 169

'Should the Death Penalty Be Abolished?', *The Listener* (19 January 1956) p. 87

'Murder and the Principles of Punishment: England and the United States', *Northwestern University Law Review* 52 (1957) 433

'Analytic Jurisprudence in Mid-twentieth Century: A Reply to Professor Bodenheimer', *University of Pennsylvania Law Review* (1957) 105

'Legal and Moral Obligation', *Essays in Moral Philosophy*, ed. A. I. Melden (Seattle: University of Washington Press 1958) p. 82

'Positivism and the Separation of Law and Morals', *Harvard Law Review* 71 (1957–8) 593

'Legal Responsibility and Excuses', *Determinism and Freedom*, Proceedings of the First Annual New York Institute of Philosophy, ed. S. Hook, New York (1958)

'A View of America', *The Listener* (1958) p. 89

with S. Hampshire, 'Decision, Intention and Certainty', *Mind* 67 (1958) 1

Causation in the Law (with A. M. Honoré) (Oxford: Clarendon Press 1959)

'Immorality and Treason', *The Listener* (30 July 1959) p. 162

'Prolegomenon to the Principles of Punishment' (1959) *Proceedings of the Aristotelian Society* 60 (1959–60) 1

'J. L. Austin', *Dictionary of National Biography* (Oxford: Oxford University Press 1960)

The Concept of Law (Oxford: Clarendon Press 1961, second edition 1994)

'Negligence, *Mens Rea* and Criminal Responsibility', *Oxford Essays in Jurisprudence*, ed. A. Guest (Oxford: Clarendon Press 1961) p. 29

'The Use and Abuse of the Criminal Law', *The Oxford Lawyer* vol. 4 no. 1 p. 7 (Hilary 1961)

'Bentham', *Proceedings of the British Academy* (1962) 48, 297

'Punishment and the Elimination of Responsibility', Hobhouse Memorial Trust Lecture (London: Athlone Press 1962) p. 32

Law, Liberty and Morality (London: Oxford University Press 1963)

'Kelsen Visited', *UCLA Law Review* 10 (1963) 709

'Holmes's Common Law', *The New York Review of Books* vol. 1 no. 4 (17 October 1963) p. 15

'Acts of Will and Legal Responsibility', *Freedom of the Will*, ed. D. F. Pears, (London: Macmillan 1963) p. 387

The Morality of the Criminal Law, two lectures (Lionel Cohen Lectures, 1964), Magnes Press, Hebrew University, Jerusalem; London: Oxford University Press (1965) 54 (a. Changing Conceptions of Responsibility; b. The Enforcement of Morality)

'Self-Referring Laws', *Festskrift tillägnad Professor, Juris Doktor Karl Olivecrona* ed. Fritjof Lejman et al. (Stockholm: P. A. Norstedt & Soner 1964) p. 307

Book review of Lon L. Fuller's *The Morality of Law* in *Harvard Law Review* 78 (1965) 1281

'Beccaria and Bentham', *Atti del Convegno internazionale su Cesare Beccaria*, Memorie dell'Accademia delle Scienze di Torino, Series 4a, no. 9 (Turin: Accademia delle Scienze 1966)

'Rettssystemers bestanddeler' [The Elements of the Legal System] in *Tre Rettsfilosofiske Avhandlinger* [Three Essays in Legal Philosophy] (Oslo: Universitets-forlaget 1966) p. 1

'Social Solidarity and the Enforcement of Morality', *University of Chicago Law Review* 35 (1967–8) 1

'Bentham on Sovereignty', *The Irish Jurist* N.S. 2 (1967) 327

'Intention and Punishment', *Oxford Review* 4 (1967) 5

'Varieties of Responsibility', *Law Quarterly Review* 83 (1967) 364

'Kelsen's Doctrine of the Unity of Law', *Ethics and Social Justice*, ed. M. K. Munitz and H. E. Kiefer, 171, vol. 4 of *Contemporary Philosophic Thought*: The International Philosophy Year Conferences at Brockport (Albany: State University of New York Press 1968–70)

Hart Report: University of Oxford, *Report of the Committee on Relations with Junior Members*, Supplement to the *University Gazette* vol. xcix (Oxford: Oxford University Press May 1969)

Punishment and Responsibility (Oxford: Clarendon Press 1968)

Introduction, critical notes and index to Jeremy Bentham: *Of Laws in General*, ed. H. L. A. Hart (London: Athlone Press 1970) (Collected Works of Jeremy Bentham)

with J. H. Burns (eds.), Introduction, critical notes and index to Jeremy Bentham: *An Introduction to the Principles of Morals and Legislation* (London: Athlone Press 1970) (2nd edition, Oxford: Clarendon Press 1996)

Editor of Jeremy Bentham's *Of Laws in General* (London: Athlone Press 1970) and author of its introduction (pp. xxxi–xlii)

'Jhering's Heaven of Concepts and Modern Analytic Jurisprudence', *Jhering's Erbe; Gottinger Symposium zur 150 Wiederkehr des Geburtstags von Rudolph von Jhering* 68; hrsg. *Von F. Wieaker und Chr. Wollschläger* (Göttingen: Vandenhoeck & Ruprecht 1970)

'Bentham's *Of Laws in General*', *Rechstheorie* 2 (1971) 55

'Abortion Law Reform: The English Experience', *Melbourne University Law Review* 8 (1971–72) 388

'Bentham on Legal Powers', *Yale Law Journal* 81 (1971–2) 799

with David Soskice, 'After the Act', *The Guardian* (3 May 1972)

'Bentham on Legal Rights', *Oxford Essays in Jurisprudence* (2nd series), ed. A. W. B. Simpson (Oxford: Clarendon Press 1973) 171

'Bentham and the Demystification of the Law', *Modern Law Review* 36 (1973) 2

'Rawls on Liberty and Its Priority', *University of Chicago Law Review* 40 (1973) 543

'Law in the Perspective of Philosophy: 1776–1976', *New York University Law Review* 51 (1976) 538

'Bentham and the United States of America', *Journal of Law and Economics* 19 (1976) 547

'American Jurisprudence through English Eyes: The Nightmare and the Noble Dream', *Georgia Law Review* 11 (1977) 969

with E. H. Burns (eds.), 'Jeremy Bentham, *A Comment on the Commentaries and a Fragment on Government*' (London: Athlone Press 1977)

'Utilitarianism and Natural Rights', *Proceedings of the Academy of Athens* 52 (1977) 162

'Morality and Reality', *The New York Review of Books* vol. 25 no. 3 (9 March 1977) 8 p. 35 (Review of Gilbert Harman, *The Nature of Morality* (1977) and J. L. Mackie, *Ethics* (1977))

'Between Utility and Rights', *Columbia Law Review* 79 (1979) 828

'Death and Utility' 8 *New York Review of Books* xxvii (1980) (Review of Peter Singer's *Practical Ethics* (1980): reworked as 'Natural Rights: Bentham and John Stuart Mill' for *Essays on Bentham*)

'The House of Lords on Attempting the Impossible' in Colin Tapper (ed.) *Crime, Proof and Punishment: Essays in Honour of Sir Rupert Cross, Oxford Journal of Legal Studies I* (1981) 149

Essays on Bentham: Studies in Jurisprudence and Political Theory (Oxford: Clarendon Press 1982)

Introduction to paperback edition of Jeremy Bentham: *An Introduction to the Principles of Morals and Legislation*, ed. J. H. Burns and H. L. A. Hart (xxiii–lxx) (London and New York: Methuen 1982)

'Sir Christopher Cox', Address at Cox's memorial service, New College Chapel, 16 October 1982, published in the *New College Record* (1982) p. 10

Essays in Jurisprudence and Philosophy (Oxford: Clarendon Press 1983)

'Arthur Rupert Neale Cross, 1912–1980', *Proceedings of the British Academy*, London, vol. lxx (1984) 705

'Oxford and Mrs. Thatcher', 32 *The New York Review of Books* no. 5 (28 March 1985) p. 7

with A. M. Honoré, *Causation in the Law* (Oxford: Oxford University Press 1959, 2nd edition 1986)

'Who Can Tell Right from Wrong?', 33 *The New York Review of Books* no. 12 (17 July 1986) p. 49: (Review of Bernard Williams, *Ethics and the Limits of Philosophy* (1985))

'Comment', in Gavison (ed.) *Issues in Contemporary Legal Philosophy* (1987) p. 35

Review of *Sir Henry Maine: A Study in Victorian Jurisprudence* by R. C. J. Cocks; *James Fitzjames Stephen: Portrait of a Victorian Rationalist* by K. J. M. Smith, 105, *The English Historical Review* (1990) 700

The Concept of Law (2nd edition Oxford: Clarendon Press 1994) with new 'Postscript' by H. L. A. Hart, pp. 238–76; ed. Penelope A. Bulloch and Joseph Raz

Interviews

Interview with Yael Tamir-Rafaeli, 'Between Citizen and State', *Israeli Democracy* 1 (1987), 27–9

Interview with David Sugarman 1988 (unpublished)

Interview with Juan Ramón de Páramo, translated as 'Entrevista a H. L. A. Hart', *Doxa* 5 (1988) 339–361: reprinted in German translation, 'Hart's "Concept of Law" nach dreissig Jahren' 22 *Rechtstheorie* (1991) 393–414

Interview with Michael Brock and Brian Harrison for the History of Oxford University 1988

OTHER AUTHORS

Karen Armstrong, *The Spiral Staircase* (London: HarperCollins 2004)

J. L. Austin, *Philosophical Papers*, ed. J. O. Urmson and G. J. Warnock (Oxford: Oxford University Press 1961, 3rd edition 1979)

J. L. Austin, *How to Do Things with Words*, ed. J. O. Urmson and M. Sbisa (Oxford: Oxford University Press 1980, 2nd edition 1980)

Michael D. Bayles, *Hart's Legal Philosophy* (Dordrecht: Kluwer Academic Publisher 1992)

Kurt Baier, *The Moral Point of View* (Ithica: Cornell University Press 1958)

John Banville, *The Untouchable* (London: Picador 1997)

Isaiah Berlin, 'Austin and the Early Beginnings of Oxford Philosophy' in *Essays on J. L. Austin* ed. Berlin et al. (Oxford: Clarendon Press 1973)

Isaiah Berlin, *Flourishing: Letters 1928–1946*, ed. Henry Hardy (London: Chatto and Windus 2004)

E. Bodenheimer, 'Modern Analytical Jurisprudence and the Limits of its Usefulness', *University of Pennsylvania Law Review* 104 (1956) 1080

Tom Bower, *The Perfect English Spy: Sir Dick White and the secret war, 1935–90* (London: Heinemann 1995)

Emily Brontë, *Wuthering Heights* (J. Cautley Newby of London 1847)

Judith Butler, *Excitable Speech: a politics of the performative* (New York: Routledge 1997)

Tom Campbell, *The Legal Theory of Ethical Positivism* (Dartmouth: Boorkfied Vt. 1996)

G. Carrio, 'Legal Principles and Legal Positivism', transl. María Isabel O'Connell (Buenos Aires 1971)

Miranda Carter, *Anthony Blunt: His Lives* (London: Macmillan 2001)

Jules Coleman (ed.) *Hart's Postscript* (Oxford: Oxford University Press 2001)

Jules Coleman, *The Practice of Principle* (Oxford: Oxford University Press 2001)

Roger Cotterrell, *The Politics of Jurisprudence* (London: Butterworths 1989)

J. A. Coutts, 80 *LQR* 279 Review of *Law, Liberty and Morality*

John Curry, *The Security Service 1908–1945* (1946)

Patrick Devlin, *The Enforcement of Morals* (Oxford: Oxford University Press 1960)

Patrick Devlin, *The Enforcement of Morals*, Maccabean Lecture in Jurisprudence of the British Academy (London: Oxford University Press 1959)

Costas Douzinas, Ronnie Warrington and Sean McVeigh, *Postmodern Jurisprudence* (London: Routledge 1991)

Ronald Dworkin, 'Is Law a System of Rules?' 35 *University of Chicago Law Review* (1967) 14

Ronald Dworkin, 'Social Rules and Legal Theory' 81 *Yale Law Journal* (1972) 855

Ronald Dworkin, 'Hard Cases', 88 *Harvard Law Review* (1975) 1057

Ronald Dworkin, 'No Right Answer?', in Hacker and Raz (eds.) (1977) p. 58

Ronald Dworkin, *Taking Rights Seriously* (London: Duckworth 1977)

Ronald Dworkin, *A Matter of Principle* (Cambridge: Harvard University Press 1985)

Ronald Dworkin, *Law's Empire* (London: Fontana 1986)

Ronald Dworkin, *Sovereign Virtue: the theory and practice of equality* (Cambridge: Harvard University Press 2000)

Ronald Dworkin, Book Review of Jules Coleman's *The Practice of Principle* 115 *Harvard Law Review* (2002) 165

Neil Duxbury, *Frederick Pollock and the English Juristic Tradition* (Oxford: Oxford University Press 2004)

Brendan Edgeworth, 'H. L. A. Hart, Legal Positivism and Post-War British Labourism' [1989] 19 *Western Australian Law Review* 275

Joanna Field (Marion Milner), *A Life of One's Own* (London: Virago 1986: first published 1934)

J. M. Finnis, *Natural Law and Natural Rights* (Oxford: Clarendon Press 1980)

H. A. L. Fisher, *An Unfinished Autobiography* (London: Oxford University Press 1940)

Peter Fitzpatrick, *The Mythology of Modern Law* (London: Routledge 1992)

Jerome Frank, *Law and the Modern Mind* (London: Stevens 1949)

Lon Fuller, *The Morality of Law* (New Haven and London: Yale University Press 1964)

Lon Fuller, 'Positivism and Fidelity to Law—A Reply to Professor Hart' 71 *Harvard Law Review* (1958) 630

Peter Geach, *Logic Matters* (Oxford: Blackwell 1972)

Ernest Gellner, *Words and Things* (London: Gollancz 1959)

Ruth Gavison (ed.), *Issues in Contemporary Legal Philosophy: Essays for H. L. A. Hart* (New York: Oxford University Press 1987)

P. M. S. Hacker and J. Raz, *Law, Morality and Society: Essays in Honour of H. L. A. Hart* (Oxford: Oxford University Press 1977)

P. M. S. Hacker, *Wittgenstein's Place in Twentieth-Century Analytic Philosophy* (Oxford: Blackwell 1996)

P. M. S. Hacker, 'Sanction Theories of Duty' in A. W. B. Simpson (ed.) *Oxford Essays in Jurisprudence* (Second Series, Oxford: Clarendon Press 1973)

Abraham Harari, *The Place of Negligence in the Law of Torts* (Sydney: Law Book Company of Australasia 1962)

R. M. Hare, *The Language of Morals* (Oxford: Clarendon Press 1952)

Jenifer (J. M.) Hart, *The British Police* (Oxford and New York: Oxford University Press 1951)

Jenifer Hart, *Proportional Representation: critics of the British Electoral System* (London: George Allen and Unwin 1992)

Jenifer Hart, *Ask Me No More* (London: Peter Halban 1998)

W. J. Harvey, 27 *MLR* 865 Review of *Law, Liberty and Morality*

F. A. von Hayek, *Law, legislation and liberty: a new statement of the liberal principles of justice and political economy* (London: Routledge 1973)

F. H. Hinsley and C. A. G. Simkins, *British Intelligence in the Second World War* vol. 4 (London: HMSO 1990)

Lord Hoffmann, 'Common Sense and Causing Loss', lecture delivered to the Chancery Bar Association, 15 June 1999

O. Hood Phillips, 78 *LQR 574* (1962) Review of *The Concept of Law*

Tony Honoré, *Making Law Bind: Essays Legal and Philosophical* (Oxford: Clarendon Press 1987)

Tony Honoré, 'Herbert Lionel Adolphus Hart 1907–1992' *Proceedings of the British Academy* (1994) 295

Tony Honoré, 'Memoir of HLA Hart', *Oxford Dictionary of National Biography* 2004

Tony Honoré, 'Responsibility and Luck: The Moral Basis of Strict Liability', 104 *Law Quarterly Review* (1988) 530, reprinted in *Responsibility and Fault* p. 14

Tony Honoré, *Responsibility and Fault* (Oxford: Hart Publishing 1999)

Michael Ignatieff, *A Life of Isaiah Berlin* (London: Chatto and Windus 1998)

Edwards Isaacs, *All in a Lifetime* (Maidstone: Whitehall Press 1985)

Edwards Isaacs, *Episodes* (Sheffield: Walker and Carson 1997)

Douglas Jay, *Change and Fortune: a political record* (London: Hutchinson 1980)

Hans Kelsen, 'Wer soll der Hüter der Verfassung sein?' *Die Justiz* 6 (1931) 576

Hans Kelsen, *An Introduction to the Problems of Legal Theory* (translation of the *Reine Rechtslehre—Pure Theory of Law*) Bonnie Litschewski Paulson and Stanley L. Paulson (transl., ed.), with an introduction by Stanley Paulson (Oxford: Oxford University Press 1992)

Duncan Kennedy, 'Form and Substance in Private Law Adjudication' (1976) 89 *Harvard Law Review* 1685

Valerie Kerruish, *Jurisprudence as Ideology* (London: Routledge 1991)

B. E. King, 'The Basic Concept of Professor Hart's Jurisprudence: the Norm out of the Bottle' (1963) *Cambridge Law Journal* 270

Matthew Kramer, *In Defense of Legal Positivism* (Oxford: Clarendon Press 1999)

F. H. Lawson, *The Oxford Law School 1850–1965* (Oxford: Clarendon Press 1968)

P. Leith and P. Ingram (ed.) *The Jurisprudence of Orthodoxy* (London: Routledge 1988)

Hermione Lee, *Virginia Woolf* (London: Chatto and Windus 1996)

Rosalyn Livshin, *The History of the Harrogate Jewish Community* (Leeds: Leeds University Press 1995)

Karl Llewellyn, *Jurisprudence: realism in theory and practice* (Chicago: University of Chicago Press 1962)

Neil MacCormick, *H.L.A. Hart* (London: Edward Arnold 1981)

Neil MacCormick, *Legal Reasoning and Legal Theory* (Oxford: Clarendon Press 1979)

John Mackie, 'The Third Theory of Law', in Marshall Cohen (ed.) *Ronald Dworkin and Contemporary Jurisprudence* (London: Duckworth 1984)

Janet Malcolm, *The Silent Woman* (New York: A. A. Knopf, distributed by Random House 1995)

C. F. A. Marmoy, 'The Auto-Icon of Jeremy Bentham at University College, London', *Medical History* vol II no. 2 April 1958 77

Michael Martin, *The Legal Philosophy of HLA Hart: A Critical Appraisal* (Philadelphia: Temple University Press 1987)

Karl Marx, *Capital* vol. 1 (transl. Moore and Aveling) (Harmondsworth: Penguin 1976, *New Left Review*, 1976)

J. C. Masterman, *The Double Cross System in the War of 1939 to 1945* (New Haven: Yale University Press 1972)

Ved Mehta, *Fly and the Fly Bottle: Encounters with British Intellectuals* (London: Weidenfeld and Nicolson 1961)

J. S. Mill, *On Liberty* (New York: Legal Classic Library 1992, first published 1859)

Philip Milton, 'H. L. A. Hart's Jurisprudence and Linguistic Philosophy', Review article on Hart's *Essays in Jurisprudence and Philosophy* and Neil MacCormick's *H. L. A. Hart* (1984) 47 *Modern Law Review* 751

Ray Monk, *Ludwig Wittgenstein: The Duty of Genius* (London: Cape 1990)

Herbert Morris, in the *Harvard Law Review* vol. 75 (1962) 1452 Review of *The Concept of Law*

Malcom G. Neesam, *Harrogate in Old Picture Postcards* (European Library 1983)

Malcom G. Neesam, *Exclusively Harrogate* (Dalesman Publishing Co. Ltd. 1994)

F. H. Newark, 76 *LQR* (1960) 592, Review of *Causation in the Law*

Stanley Paulson, Bibliography of H. L. A. Hart, 8 *Ratio Juris* (1995) 397

P. Nowell-Smith, *Mind* (1961) 553, Review of *Causation in the Law*

Bikhu Parekh (ed.), *Bentham's Political Thought* (London: Croom Helm 1973)

Adam Phillips, *Darwin's Worms* (London: Faber 1999)

Chapman Pincher, *Their Trade is Treachery* (London: Sidgwick & Jackson 1981)

Roscoe Pound, *An Introduction of the Philosophy of Law* (New Haven: Yale University Press 1954)

David Raphael, *Mind* (1966) 607, Review of *Law, Liberty and Morality*

John Rawls, *A Theory of Justice* (Cambridge: Harvard University Press 1971; Oxford: Oxford University Press 1972)

John Rawls, 'Two Concepts of Rules', *Philosophical Review* (1955) 4

John Rawls, 'Justice as Fairness', *Philosophical Review* 67 (1958) 164

John Rawls, *Political Liberalism* (New York: Columbia University Press 1993)

Joseph Raz, *The Concept of a Legal System* (Oxford: Clarendon Press 1970)

Joseph Raz, *Practical Reason and Norms* (London: Oxford University Press 1975)

Joseph Raz, *The Authority of Law: essays on law and morality* (Oxford: Clarendon Press 1979)

Joseph Raz, *The Morality of Freedom* (Oxford: Clarendon Press 1986)

Joseph Raz, *Ethics in the Public Domain* (Oxford: Clarendon Press 1994)

Jonathan Rée, 'English Philosophy in the Fifties' 65 *Radical Philosophy* (1995) 3

Ben Rogers, *A. J. Ayer: a life* (London: Chatto & Windus 1999)

Alf Ross, 71 *Yale Law Journal* 1162 (1962) Review of *The Concept of Law*

Hamish Ross, *Law as a Social Institution* (Oxford: Hart Publishing 2001)

Bertrand Russell, *Portraits from Memory and Other Essays* (London: Allen and Unwin 1956)

Gilbert Ryle, *The Concept of Mind* (London: Hutchinson's University Library 1949)

Jean-Paul Sartre, *Réflexions sur la Question Juive* (1946), translated as *Anti-Semite and Jew: An exploration of the etiology of hate* (transl. George J. Becker: New York: Schocken Books 1948)

Geoffrey Sawer, *Law in Society* (Oxford: Clarendon Press 1965)

Carl Schmitt, *Der Hüter der Verfassung*, ed. J. C. M. Mohr (Tübingen 1931)

A. W. B. Simpson, 'The Common Law and Legal Theory', in Simpson (ed.) *Oxford Essays in Jurisprudence* (Second Series, Oxford: Clarendon Press 1973)

A. W. B. Simpson (ed.), *Biographical Dictionary of the Common Law* (London: Butterworths 1984)

A. W. B. Simpson, *In the Highest Degree Odious: detention without trial in wartime Britain* (Oxford: Clarendon Press 1992)

Marcus Singer, LX *Journal of Philosophy* (1963) 197, Review of *The Concept of Law*

A. H. Smith, 'Horace William Brindley Joseph 1867–1943' xxxi *Proceedings of the British Academy* (1945)

A. H. Smith, 'H. W. B. Joseph 1867–1943', memorial address delivered in New College chapel and published by Oxford University Press

Sydney Smith, 'Bentham's Book of Fallacies' *Edinburgh Review* xlii (84) (1825) 367

John Sparrow and other authors, 'Alic Halford Smith 1883–1958', collection of tributes published by New College, Oxford

Jane Stapleton, 'Unpacking "causation" ', in P. Cane and J. Gardner (eds), *Relating to Responsibility: Essays for Tony Honoré on his Eightieth Birthday* (Oxford: Hart Publishing 2001) p. 145

Leonie Star, *Julius Stone: An Intellectual Life* (Oxford: Oxford University Press 1992)

Julius Stone, *The Province and Function of Law* (Sydney: Associated General Publications 1946)

Peter Strawson, *Individuals: an essay in descriptive metaphysics* (London: Methuen 1959)

Robert S. Summers, 'H. L. A. Hart's *The Concept of Law*: Estimations, Reflections, and a Personal Memorial' 45 *Journal of Legal Education* (1995) 587

Roberto Mangabeira Unger, 'The Critical Legal Studies Movement in America' *Harvard Law Review* 96 (1983) 561

Jeremy Waldron, *The Dignity of Legislation* (Oxford: Clarendon Press 1999)

Jeremy Waldon, *Law and Disagreement* (Oxford: Clarendon Press 1999)

Jeremy Waldron, Review of Hart's *Essays in Jurisprudence and Philosophy* (1985) *Mind* 281

Wil Waluchow, *Inclusive Legal Positivism* (Oxford: Clarendon Press 1994)

Allen Warren, 'C.W.M.C. as Patron', *New College Record* (1982) p. 17

Max Weber *On Law in Economy and Society* ed. Max Rheinstein (Cambridge: Harvard University Press 1954)

Nigel West, *MI5, British security service operations, 1909–1945* (London: Bodley Head 1981)

Nigel West and Oleg Tsarev, *The Crown Jewels* (London: HarperCollins 1998)

Richard Orme Wilberforce, *Reflections on My Life* (Durham: Roundtuit Publishing 2003)

Peter Winch, *The Idea of a Social Science and its Relation to Philosophy* (London: Routledge 1990, first published 1958)

Ludwig Wittgenstein, *Philosophical Investigations* (Oxford: Blackwell 1953)

Patricia White, 'H. L. A. Hart on Legal and Moral Obligations' (1974) 73 *Michigan Law Review* 443

CASES

Madzimbamuto v Lardner-Burke 1 AC 645; [1968] 2 SA 284; [1968] 3 All ER 561; [1968] 3 WLR 1229

INTERVIEWS

Professor Brian Barry (September 2001); Aharon Barak President of the Israeli Supreme Court (June 2000); Professor Vernon Bogdanor (September 2000); Professor Peter Campbell (November 2000); George Cawkwell (October 2000); Professor Hugh Collins (October 2000); Barbara Dupee (September 2003); Professor Ronald Dworkin (March 2001); Professor Yehuda Elkana (July 2000); Justice Itzaak Englard (June 2000); Professor Marianne Fillenz (September 2000); Professor John Finnis (December 2000); Professor George Fletcher (March 2000); Mrs. Jean Floud (September 2000); Professor Ruth Gavison (July 2000); Professor James Griffin (March 2001); Professor Peter Hacker (October 2003); Sir Stuart Hampshire (September 2000, October 2001); John Hart (2000); The Honourable Justice Dyson Heydon (March 2003); Justice David Hodgson (March 2003); Lennie Hoffmann (November 2002); Professor Tony Honoré (March 2000, September 2000); Professor Donald Horwitz (2001); Mary Jay (December 2000); Professor Harry Judge (March 2001); Professor Nan Keohane (September 2002); Justice Michael Kirby (March 2003); John Lucas (September 2000); Professor Herbert Morris (February 2002); Professor Richard Mulgan (April 2001); the late Professor Barry Nicholas (September 2000); Professor Gerald Postema (September 2002); Professor Joseph Raz (March 2000, November 2000); Professor Jonathan Rée (March 2001); Professor Graham Richards (September 2000); Professor Alan Ryan (2001); Professor Sir Peter Strawson (September 2000); Professor David Sugarman (January 2001); Professor Bob Summers and Dorothy Summers (2001, 2002); Professor Colin Tapper (December 2003); Dr. John Tasioulas (November 2000); Professor William Twining (October 2000, March 2001); Professor Jeremy Waldron (September 2001); Bill Wentworth (March 2003); Professor Bernard Williams (March 2000); the late Lord Wilberforce (June 2002); Adrian Zuckerman (December 2000).

Biographical Details of Figures Appearing in the Book

Elizabeth Anscombe

Elizabeth Anscombe, 1919–2001, was Professor of Philosophy at Cambridge from 1970 to 1986 and before that a Fellow of Somerville College, Oxford from 1946 to 1970. Anscombe worked in several fields of philosophy, notably moral philosophy and philosophy of mind. A student and friend of Ludwig Wittgenstein and one of three scholars nominated as his literary executor, she produced a translation of his *Philosophical Investigations* as well as a large corpus of her own work.

A. J. Ayer

Alfred ('Freddie') Ayer, 1910–1989, held a Lectureship and then a Research Studentship (i.e. Fellowship) in philosophy at Christ Church, Oxford, from 1932 to 1944, and a Fellowship at Wadham College from 1944 to 1945. In 1946, he took up the Grote Chair of Mind and Logic at University College London. In 1959 he moved back to Oxford to take up the Wykeham Professorship of Logic at New College, a post which he held until 1978. Ayer was established as a leading representative of logical positivism with the publication of *Language, Truth and Logic* in 1936.

Kurt Baier

Kurt Baier, 1917–Present, was Professor of Philosophy at the University of Pittsburgh, previously having taught at University of Melbourne, Australian National University, University of Illinois, and at Cornell. He wrote *The Moral Point of View* (1958) and contributed to works on ethics and social philosophy.

Thomas Balogh

Thomas Balogh, 1905–1985, worked at the League of Nations in 1931 prior to his work in the City as an economist from 1931 to 1939 for O. T. Falk. He went on to work at the National Institute of Economic Research in 1939 until 1942 and then at the University of Oxford's Institute of Statistics until 1955.

MAURICE BOWRA

Maurice Bowra, 1898–1971, described as 'scholar and wit' by his College, was appointed Warden of Wadham College, Oxford in 1938. Bowra remained Warden until 1970. Bowra was Professor of Poetry from 1946 to 1951, Vice Chancellor from 1951 to 1954, and was knighted in 1951.

CHARLIE BROAD

Charlie Broad, 1887–1971, was a Cambridge contemporary of Russell, Moore, and Wittgenstein. Broad wrote on a wide range of topics including causation, perception, philosophy of space and time, ethics, and the history of philosophy. Broad is widely recognized for his meticulous analysis. His works include *Examination of McTaggart's Philosophy* (1933, 1938) and *Ethics and the History of Philosophy* (1979).

PHILIPPA FOOT

Philippa Foot, 1920–Present, held a Lectureship and then a Fellowship in Philosophy at Somerville College, Oxford, from 1947 to 1969, becoming Senior Resident Fellow from 1970–1988. She is Emeritus Professor of Philosophy at the University of California at Los Angeles, and was Griffin Professor of Philosophy from 1988 to 1991. Her publications include *Theories of Ethics* (1967), *Virtues and Vices* (1978), *Natural Goodness* (2001) and *Moral Dilemmas* (2002). In 1963 Foot published a review of H. L. A. Hart and A. M. Honoré's *Causation in the Law* in the *Philosophical Review*.

PETER GEACH

Peter Geach, 1916–Present, was Professor of Logic at the University of Leeds from 1966 to 1981. He undertook philosophical research at the University of Cambridge from 1945 to 1951, and married Elizabeth Anscombe in 1941. His publications include: *God and Soul* (1969), *Logic Matters* (1972), and *Providence and Evil* (1977).

ERNEST GELLNER

Ernest Gellner, 1925–1995, made significant contributions to linguistic philosophy, anthropological theory, and the sociology of industrial sciences. William Wyn Professor of Social Anthropology at the University of Cambridge from 1984 to 1993 and previously Lecturer and then Professor of Philosophy, Logic and Scientific Method at the London School of Economics from 1949 to 1984, Gellner achieved fame and notoriety among philosophers, notably through his attack on Oxford philosophy in *Words and Things* (1959). Gellner published extensively on the Soviet Union and the satellite states and was noted for bringing work published in Russian to the attention of English- and French-speaking anthropologists.

STUART HAMPSHIRE

Stuart Hampshire, 1914–2004, was a Fellow of All Souls College, Oxford and, from 1936, Fellow and Tutor in Philosophy at New College. During the war, he worked in MI6 before returning to academic life, holding a range of posts including a Chair of Philosophy at Princeton, the Grote Chair of Mind and Logic at University College London from 1960 to 1963, and then a post at Stanford University. Hampshire became Warden of Wadham College, Oxford in 1970 and was knighted in 1979. Hampshire's work included contributions in epistemology, metaphysics, philosophy of mind, ethics, and aesthetics.

RICHARD HARE

Richard Hare, 1919–2002, Fellow of Balliol College from 1947 to 1966 and White's Professor of Philosophy at Corpus Christi College, Oxford from 1966 to 1981, worked to refute emotivism (propounded by, among others, A. J. Ayer). Hare's theory of prescriptivism, first expounded in *The Language of Morals* (1952) and refined in *Freedom And Reason* (1963), was an important contribution to moral philosophy and sparked debate throughout the 1950s and 1960s.

GEORGE MOORE

George Moore, 1873–1958, was Lecturer in Moral Sciences from 1911 to 1925 and Professor of Mental Philosophy and Logic at Cambridge from 1925 to 1939. Moore studied with Bradley and McTaggart and was a friend and colleague of Russell, Ramsey, and Wittgenstein. Moore's best known work was *Principia Ethica* (1903); his later writing went on to consider the nature of the external world and our knowledge of it.

IRIS MURDOCH

Irish Murdoch, 1919–1999, was a moral philosopher and novelist who as a postgraduate studied under Wittgenstein. She married writer and fellow academic John Bayley in 1956. Murdoch worked as a civil servant with the Treasury from 1942 to 1944 and with the United Nations Relief and Rehabilitation Administration in London, Belgium, and Austria from 1944 to 1946. Murdoch returned to Oxford as a lecturer in Philosophy at St. Anne's College from 1948 to 1963 and was later Gifford Lecturer at the Royal College of Art, London from 1963 to 1967. Murdoch received the Whitbread Literary Award in 1974 and the Booker Prize in 1978.

HENRY PRICE

Henry Price, 1899–1984, was Fellow in Philosophy at Magdalen College, Oxford from 1922 to 1924 and at Trinity College from 1924 to 1935. In 1935, he became Wykeham Professor of Logic at New College, a post which he held until 1959. Price's interests were rooted in traditional issues of perception, knowledge, truth, and belief. His works include *Perception* (1932), a detailed analysis and construction of sense-datum theory, *Thinking and Experience* (1969), and *Hume's Theory of the External World* (1981).

HAROLD PRICHARD

Harold Prichard, 1871–1947, was White's Professor of Philosophy at Oxford from 1928 to 1937. Prichard's work combined epistemological realism and moral intuitionism. His classes at Oxford—as well as his 'philosophers' teas'—were attended by Austin, Ryle, Hart, and Berlin.

FRANK RAMSEY

Frank Ramsey, 1903–1930, is considered a pioneer in economics and mathematics as well as logic and philosophy, despite his tragically short life. Elected as a fellow of King's College, Cambridge in 1924, Ramsay went on to become a lecturer in Mathematics in 1926. Although lecturing in Mathematics, his work covered a wide range of areas, including a definitive version of Bertrand Russell's attempted reduction of mathematics to logic and the first quantitative theory of decision making.

W. D. (DAVID) ROSS

W. D. (David) Ross, 1877–1971, worked on ancient and moral philosophy, producing valuable translations of the philosophical works of Aristotle. Ross is better known for his moral philosophy, represented by *The Right and the Good* (1930), in which he criticized the ethical theory of Moore.

JOHN SPARROW

John Sparrow, 1906–1992, was elected to a Prize Fellowship at All Souls College after graduating from New College, Oxford in 1929. He became Warden of All Souls in 1952, and held the position until 1977. Sparrow was called to the Bar by the Middle Temple in 1931 and practised at the Chancery Bar from 1931 to 1939. He was enlisted in 1939 and was later commissioned into the Coldstream Guards, returning to his practice at the Bar from 1946 to 1951.

PETER STRAWSON

Peter Strawson, 1919–Present, was fellow of University College, Oxford from 1948 to 1968, before taking up the Waynflete Professorship of Metaphysical Philosophy at Magdalen College, a post which he held from 1968 to 1987. Strawson's early work dealt with the links between logic and language (*Introduction to Logical Theory* (1952)), and he went on to study the metaphysical structure of human thought about the world (*The Bounds of Sense* (1966)). His other publications include: *Individuals: An Essay in Descriptive Metaphysics* (1959) (a book which was shaped in part by his engagement with Oxford linguistic philosophy), *Logico-Linguistic Papers* (1971), and *Scepticism and Naturalism* (1985).

JIM URMSON

Jim Urmson, 1915–Present, held posts at Madgalen College and Christ Church, Oxford before taking up a Chair in Philosophy at the University of Dundee in 1955. He was Fellow and Tutor in Philosophy at Corpus Christi College, Oxford from 1959 to 1978 and Stuart Professor of Philosophy at Stanford University from 1975 to 1980. His published works include *Philosophical Analysis* (1956), *The Emotive Theory of Ethics* (1968), and *Aristotle's Ethics* (1988).

GEOFFREY WARNOCK

Geoffrey Warnock, 1923–1995, was Fellow by examination and then Fellow in Philosophy at Magdalen College, Oxford from 1949 to 1971. Married from 1949 to the well-known ethicist Mary Warnock (later Baroness Warnock of Weeke), Warnock became Principal of Hertford College, Oxford in 1971 and later Vice-Chancellor of Oxford University, retiring in 1988.

MORTON WHITE

Morton White, 1917–Present, was Professor of Philosophy at Harvard from 1948 to 1970, before moving to Princeton, where he is now Emeritus Professor at the Institute for Advanced Study. A philosopher and historian, White published extensively: his works include *Social Thought in America* (1948), *Foundations of Historical Knowledge* (1965), *Science and Sentiment in America* (1972), and *The Question of Free Will* (1993).

RICHARD WILBERFORCE

Richard (Lord) Wilberforce, 1907–2003, was elected a Fellow of All Souls College in 1932. He had a distinguished career at the Chancery Bar, as head of the British Legal Section of the four power Commission for the administration of Germany from 1944–6, and as Under Secretary at the Control Office Germany and Austria in 1946–7. A Bencher of the Middle Temple from 1961, he held a range of judicial appointments before being made a Lord of Appeal in Ordinary (member of the Judicial Committee of the House of Lords) in 1964, a position which he held until 1982.

JOHN WISDOM

John Wisdom, 1904–1993, was Lecturer in Moral Sciences and then Professor of Philosophy at Trinity College, Cambridge from 1952 to 1968. He went on to the University of Oregon as Professor of Philosophy from 1968 to 1972. Wisdom's works, *Other Minds* (1952) and *Philosophy and Psychoanalysis* (1953), applied the analytic methods of Moore and the later Wittgenstein to significant issues in the philosophy of mind.

The information for these biographical notes was drawn from the following sources: Robert Audi, *The Cambridge Dictionary of Philosophy* (Cambridge: Cambridge University Press 1995); Simon Blackburn, *The Oxford Dictionary of Philosophy* (Oxford: Oxford University Press 1994); Robert Benewick and Philip Green, *The Routledge Dictionary of Twentieth Century Political Thinkers* (London and New York: Routledge 1997); *Concise Routledge Encyclopedia of Philosophy* (London and New York: Routledge, 2000); *Oxford University Gazette* 9 November 1995; Roland Turner, *Thinkers of the Twentieth Century* (2nd edition, Chicago and London: St. James 1987); *Who's Who 2003* (A & C Black, 155th edition, 2003); Geoffrey Wheatcroft, 'The Warden: A Portrait of John Sparrow', *New Statesman*, 25 September 1998; and the website of Wadham College, Oxford (www.wadham.ox.ac.uk/public/overview).

Index

Herbert and Jenifer Hart are abbreviated to H and J throughout